American Fire Engines

Since 1900

Walter P. McCall

Motorbooks International
Publishers & Wholesalers ®

This edition first published in 1993 in the Crestline Series by Motorbooks International Publishers & Wholesalers, PO Box 2, 729 Prospect Avenue, Osceola, WI 54020 USA

© Walter P. McCall, 1976, 1993

Originally published by Crestline Publishing Co., 1976 Editor/Designer: George H. Dammann

Motorbooks International books are also available at discounts in bulk quantity for industrial or sales-promotional use. For details write to Special Sales Manager at the Publisher's address

Library of Congress Cataloging-in-Publication Data
McCall, Walter M. P. (Walter Miller Pearce).
    American fire engines since 1900 / by Walter P. McCall.
       p. cm.—(Motorbooks International crestline series)
    Reprint. Originally published: Glen Ellyn, Ill. : Crestline Pub., 1976.
    Includes index.
    ISBN 0-87938-829-3
    1. Fire engines—United States—History.
I. Title. II. Series: Crestline series.
TH9371.M32 1993
629.225—dc20   93-13160

Printed and bound in United States of America

Many Thanks

Any undertaking of this magnitude would be impossible without a great deal of assistance and cooperation. The author would therefore like to extend his sincere gratitude to the following, who unhesitatingly shared not only their extensive collections of fire apparatus photographs and literature, but also their own specialized knowledge of this fascinating subject.

Special thanks must go to: my good friend Dan G. Martin, who has probably forgotten more about this subject than is contained in this entire book; John F. Sytsma, America's No. 1 Ahrens-Fox fire engine buff and an established author in this hobby in his own right; Harold S. Walker, who provided invaluable assistance in researching the early motor years; John J. Robrecht for the use of some of his superb photos, and to other such well-known and respected fire apparatus photographers as Richard M. Adelman, Shaun P. Ryan, Charles E. Beckwith, Jack Calderone, Jim Burner Jr., Larry Phillips, Walt Schryver, Bill Schwartz, Willard Sorensen, Curt Hudson, R. J. Cook, Norm Gladding and the late Robert J. Barber.

I would be remiss in not also extending my appreciation to: Mrs. Arlene Shingler, Public Relations Dept., American LaFrance; James F. Casey, Editor of *"Fire Engineering"*; A. J. "Al" Burch, Owner and Publisher of *"The Visiting Fireman"*; Alex Matches, author of *"It Began With A Ronald"*; Marvin H. Cohen, President of Monhagen Hose Co. No. 1, Middletown, N. Y., Richard A. Horstmann, one of the prime-movers behind the Society For the Preservation and Appreciation of Antique Motor Fire Apparatus in America, Inc.; Charles Madderom, and Joel Woods.

Also deserving of my special thanks are Eric A. Sprenger, Alan M. Craig, Ted Hanifan, Dave Stewardson, John L. Holden, Richard Story, Robert M. Beals, Elliot Kahn, Al Judge, Dick Garard, Greg Northrop, Bill Durrett, Rodger Birchfield, Dan Ranges, Richard Henrich, Leonard W. Williams, Clarence C. Woodard, Jim Jackson, Steven B. Loftin, Roger Bjorge and Paul Guilbert, Jr.

My valued friends George H. Dammann and Thomas A. McPherson are also in my debt for making this book possible.

Last but by no means least, heartfelt thanks are reserved for my dear wife Denise, who put up with all of the late nights, the lost weekends, and endless typing.

FOREWORD

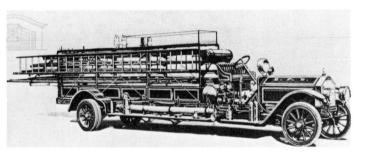

From the outset, this book has presented a formidible challenge. So broad is the subject in scope, and so infinite the variations and exceptions, that to completely chronicle the development of motor fire apparatus in this country would take at least ten volumes of this size.

As the fire apparatus hobby has mushroomed in recent years, a number of excellent books covering specific apparatus makes and the equipment used over the years by various U. S. and Canadian cities, have been published to the delight of fire apparatus buffs. But there has been a crying need for a single, comprehensive volume that would contain, under a single set of covers, a detailed, chronological history of fire apparatus manufacture in the United States. This book was published to fulfill that need.

The photos and material selected were carefully chosen to depict the most significant and interesting models produced over the years by principal fire equipment builders. This book was conceived to provide an overview of the types and makes of fire engines used in America during the first three quarters of this century. Because of the large fleets of firefighting equipment purchased by major cities like New York and Chicago, it was necessary to include numerous photos of rigs used in these areas.

Inevitably, mistakes will occur when handling this amount of information. It is hoped that corrections and additions can be made in a future printing. Every effort has been made to authenticate dates and data, but in most cases we had to rely on information furnished with the photo. The fact that some apparatus remained unchanged basically for a decade or more, and the time lag between order, delivery in commissioning into service also increase the possibility of errors.

This was never intended to be a glamorous coffee-table book. It is a complete working text which, we believe, will be the standard reference work for serious students of the fire engine builder's unique art for many years to come.

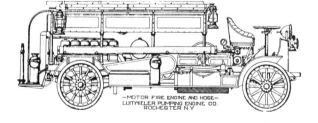

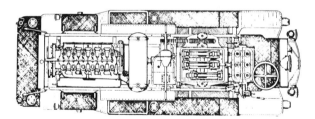

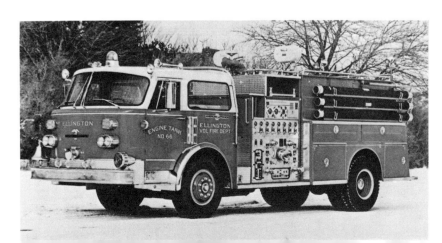

The Seagrave Co. of Columbus, Ohio introduced a spring-raised aerial ladder in 1902, which, it claimed, took the muscle work out of raising the main ladder. A powerful spring lifted the bed ladder to the near-vertical, while the fly ladder was extended by handwheel. This is typical of the type of aerial truck in use in the early years of this century. Two or three horses pulled these aerials, which were usually of 65, 75 or 85-foot length.

One of American LaFrance's predecessor companies, the American Fire Engine Co., offered this unique combination steam pumper and hose wagon in 1900. This two-way combination was known as the Columbian. The hose was carried in a box between the driver's seat and the pump. Playout rollers were provided to facilitate the stretching of hose lines. The Columbian combination was designed to eliminate the need for a hose wagon, which normally accompanied the steamer on every alarm.

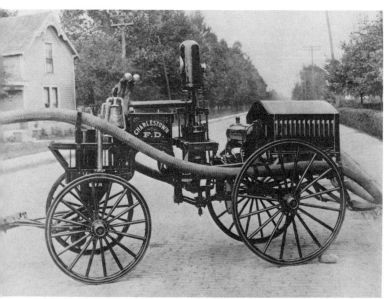

Fire fighting apparatus, in one form or another, has been around almost as long as civilization. The first contrivance that appears to have been built primarily for fire suppression was used in Egypt in about 200 B.C. Named the "Spiritalia Heron" after its inventor, this was a portable engine that consisted primarily of a pair of brass force pumps connected to a single discharge tube. This same basic mechanical principle was embodied in fire engine construction for more than 2,000 years, at least up to the time of the American Civil War.

The Roman Empire was protected by organized fire brigades. Giant syringes and other devices were used during the Middle Ages to defend life and property from man's oldest enemy and friend—fire. The first hose used for fire fighting consisted of oxen entrails, but by 1670, leather hose was being used in Holland to transport water from its source directly onto the fire.

The first fire engines used in the United States arrived in New Amsterdam (now New York) aboard a ship from England in December, 1731. They were Newsham hand engines, built by the famed London fire engine maker. Prior to the arrival of engines from England, the colonies were protected by volunteer bucket brigades, or not at all. Following the American Revolution, American manufacturers made and developed their own hand engines.

Over the next 80 years, hand engine development was rapid. American fire departments were manned by volunteers, and membership in a fire company was considered a high social honor.

Rivalry between fire companies was intense, and more than a few buildings burned to the ground while members of rival fire companies battled it out over a hydrant, or for the privilage of getting first water on the fire.

The next major development in fire fighting was the replacement of muscle power by steam—a transition that was violently opposed by the volunteers. The first practical steam fire engine had been built in England in 1829 by a man named George Braithewaite. The first successful steam pumper built in the United States was constructed by Paul Rapsey Hodge in New York in 1840. In tests the following year, Hodge's engine turned in an impressive performance, but the volunteers would have nothing to do with it, and the engine finished out its days as a stationary powerplant.

In 1852, Moses Latta of Cincinnati designed and built a monstrous steam fire engine called the "Joe Ross". This ponderous self-propeller weighed 10 tons, but was so slow that it was pulled by four horses ridden artillery style. It could throw a stream of water 225 feet through a 1½-inch nozzle. Cincinnati formed the first paid, professional fire department in the U.S. in 1853, and the days of the volunteer were numbered despite their vigorous opposition to the introduction of steampowered fire engines.

The Howe Fire Apparatus Co. of Anderson, Ind. sold many of these gasoline-powered horse-drawn pumpers to smaller communities. Howe used both piston and rotary-type pumps, and four and six-cylinder engines in these units. Notice the long suction hose and automobile-type engine hood used on this model. It was built for the Charlestown Fire Department.

The steam era was undoubtedly the most colorful in American fire service history. To those who can remember, the sight of some modern lime-green monster threading its way through city traffic, electronic siren whooping, can never compare with the thrilling spectacle of a straining, three-horse hitch thundering over the cobblestone with a belching, polished steamer in tow.

The leather-lunged fire fighters of the steam age developed strong sentimental attachment to their fire horses, and the affection they lavished on their beloved and noble animals could never be bestowed on any cold, impersonal machine.

During the horse-drawn era, which lasted from the 1860s into the third decade of this century, the principal types of fire apparatus used included, besides the colorful steamer: the hose wagon, or reel, that accompanied the steamer on all alarms; the long hook and ladder truck with its rear steering wheel, or tiller; the aerial ladder truck with its turntable-mounted main extension ladder; the water tower, a portable standpipe system used to lob streams into the upper floors of burning buildings; the chemical wagon, with its gleaming copper tanks, and later the combination hose and chemical wagon.

Specialized equipment included the chief's buggy, the coal supply wagon, the high pressure turret wagon and even ambulances for the fire hoses. Principal builders of steamers included proud old names like Amoskeag, Silsby, Clapp & Jones, Ahrens and LaFrance. In 1867, Amoskeag introduced a self-propelled steamer, and over the next 39 years this firm delivered no less than 22 of these. American LaFrance and its predecessor company, the International Fire Engine Co., sold several steam-powered hose wagons between 1903 and 1907. As early as 1901, the Chief of the San Francisco Fire Dept. had been transported to fires in an electric car. Some of the first motorized vehicles used by U. S. fire departments were fire chief's runabouts.

Steam fire engines remained in production up to the First World War years, and hand engines continued to protect small towns and villages for some years after the internal combustion engine displaced the horse.

A number of gasoline-powered pumpers, drawn by horses or by hand, were on the market at the turn of the century. In Europe, several fire brigades were already using steam, electric or gasoline-propelled fire engines. As 1906 dawned, even the most visionary fire chief doubted that the day would ever come when these odorous, noisy and temperamental "horseless carriages" of dubious reliability could ever replace horse-drawn equipment.

American LaFrance introduced its own spring-assisted aerial ladder truck design in 1904. This company's spring hoist consisted of a set of large coil springs, a stationary toothed gear segment, a gear train operated by cranks and an automatic hydraulic cylinder which permitted the ladder to be fixed at any angle by closing a valve. Tulsa, Okla. used this American LaFrance 75-foot spring-raised aerial with its handsome three-horse hitch.

American LaFrance and its corporate predecessor, the International Fire Engine Co. produced a few steam-powered combination hose and chemical cars in the dawn of the motor age, and before the Elmira, N. Y. plant began to experiment with gasoline engines. This steam-powered combination was delivered to the Niagara Fire Co. No. 1 of the New London, Conn. Fire Dept. in 1904. The short smokestack can be seen just forward of the chemical hose basket. The chemical tanks were mounted on each side of the apparatus so a full load of hose could be carried in the main bed.

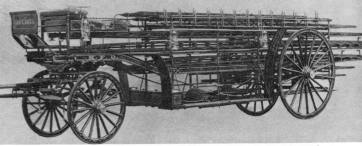

Peter Pirsch & Sons Co. of Kenosha, Wis. built this 55-foot horse-drawn hook and ladder truck in the late 1890's. The 55-foot designation referred to the length of the longest ladder carried. Note the gong mounted on the toe board and the pompier ladders atop this handsome rig.

It is not positively known who placed the very first motor-propelled vehicle into fire department service in the U. S., but records indicate that a considerable amount of experimentation with this fascinating new mode of transportation went on in the very early years of this century. It is believed the first use of automobiles by fire departments was for chief's cars, to transport the Chief Engineer to the fire and on his rounds. The salvage corps auto shown here was tried out in about 1904. It is believed that the location was Cincinnati. The make is unknown. Note the goggles on the driver and the derbys—instead of helmets—on the crew.

The motor fire apparatus age in the United States dawned in 1906. It was in this historic year that the Radnor Fire Co. of Wayne, Pa. placed into service the first automobile fire fighting apparatus in the U. S. This milestone piece of equipment was a dual-engined motor pumping engine designed and built by the Waterous Engine Works, of St. Paul, Minn. A well established builder of steam fire engines at that time, Waterous remains in business today as a major supplier of fire apparatus pumps.

The pioneering pumper built for the Radnor Fire Co. was equipped with two gasoline engines, one for propelling the apparatus and the other for driving the rear-mounted pump. The wagon-like 1906 Waterous could deliver 300 gallons of water per minute. In its later years, this pumper was modified by the addition of a hose box over the rear body.

In the same eventful year, the Knox Automobile Co. of Springfield, Mass. delivered a motor squad car to the Springfield Fire Dept. This apparatus had a squad body built by the Combination Ladder Co. of Providence, R. I., and was mounted on a 4-cylinder, 40-horsepower Knox automobile chassis. Designated "Auxiliary Squad A" by the Springfield Fire Dept., the Knox was used to transport extra manpower to fires.

Toward the end of the year, Knox offered fire departments a comprehensive range of motorized fire equipment, including chemical cars, squad cars, motor hose tenders and chief's autos. The Combination Ladder Co. advertised its Knox-chassised fire apparatus as "The Fire Automobile".

Knox at various auto shows displayed a two-tank chemical car which was equipped with two 35-gallon soda and acid chemical tanks, a chemical hose basket and boasted a top speed of 40 miles an hour.

Also in 1906, the Chicago Fire Insurance Patrol experimented with an electric supervisor's auto built by the Woods Electric Co. The battery-powered runabout was a brief trial and was replaced with a motor car.

That same year, the Seagrave Co. of Columbus, Ohio, introduced a new design of spring-raised water tower.

Frederick S. Seagrave had started his ladder-making business in Detroit in 1881, but moved to Columbus in 1891. His company became a major builder of hand and horse-drawn hook and ladder trucks and chemical and hose wagons, and in 1902 the company marketed a spring-raised aerial ladder truck. Seagrave in 1906 began to study the feasibility of manufacturing motor-driven apparatus, but this project would not bear fruit for another year.

In 1903, the American LaFrance Fire Engine Co. was organized out of the former International Fire Engine Co., a conglomerate of some nine fire equipment companies, including the American Fire Engine Co. of Seneca Falls, N. Y. and the LaFrance Fire Engine Co. of Elmira, N.Y. The new firm moved its head office from New York City to Elmira. Among its most popular products was the "Metropolitan" steam pumper, which had been in production since 1897. The International Fire Engine Co. built one or two steam-powered hose wagons in 1903 and 1904, and offered a complete range of horse-drawn fire apparatus including steamers, aerial and hook and ladder trucks, water towers, hose wagons, chemical wagons and combinations. The company had developed its own spring-raised aerial in 1903.

Another popular steamer was the "Continental" produced by the Ahrens Manufacturing Co. of Cincinnati. In addition to its steam fire engines, Waterous offered a horse-drawn gasoline pumper called the "New Century".

The Knox Automobile Company of Springfield, Mass. exhibited this 40-horsepower Knox Waterless chemical car at several automobile shows in 1906. This apparatus carried two 35-gallon soda and acid chemical tanks in the motor fire apparatus field, building chief's cars, squad cars, hose wagons and pumpers. More than a few Knox passenger cars were converted to fire apparatus.

The Radnor Fire Company of Wayne, Penn. is generally credited with placing the first self-propelled, gasoline powered motor pumping engine in the United States into service in 1906. The 300 gallon-per-minute motor pumper was built by the Waterous Engine Works of St. Paul, Minn. It had two separate power plants, one for propelling the apparatus and the other for driving the pump. A straight pumping car, this apparatus was always accompanied by a hose wagon. It is unlikely that the members of this fire company realized the significance of their bold, pioneering purchase at the time.

Several significant motor fire apparatus deliveries were made this year. The Waterous Engine Works of St. Paul, Minn., which had delivered the first motor-driven pumping engine in the U.S. to the Wayne, Pa., fire company the previous year, built another in 1907. This one was delivered to Alameda, Calif. Where the Wayne truck had two engines, the Alameda job utilized a single engine for both propulsion and for driving the 600 GPM pump.

The Seagrave Co. built and tested its first piece of motor fire apparatus this year. The company had been working on a motorized fire engine design for at least two years. On June 27, 1907, the prototype Seagrave motor combination hose and chemical car made a historic 55-mile run to Chillicothe from Columbus. Seagrave had engaged the Frayer-Miller Co. of Columbus to help it develop a fire apparatus engine, but this apparently did not work out, and Seagrave developed its own line of 4 and 6-cylinder air and watercooled engines, which it built in its own plant. The Oscar Lear Automobile Co. of Columbus also worked with Seagrave in the development of the company's first motor equipment. The experimental model was powered by a 24.25 horsepower, 4-cylinder aircooled engine. The first three motorized Seagraves were all delivered late in 1907 to a Canadian fire department. Vancouver, B. C. received two 1907 Seagrave Model AC-53 hose wagons, Ser. Nos. 2382 and 2383, and a straight chemical car, Ser. No. 2384. All were placed in service early in 1908.

It is not generally known, but American LaFrance delivered its first gasoline-driven fire engine this year, too. It was a combination chemical car that bore the letters B.F.D. on its radiator core. It was said to be capable of doing 35 miles an hour. Later the same year the Elmira company delivered a steam-powered hose wagon to South Africa. American LaFrance did not formally enter the motor fire apparatus field for another three years, although the company delivered at least two Simplex-chassised combination cars in 1909. The 1907 American LaFrance chemical car was used in company advertising, but no indication as to where it was delivered was given.

Another new name appeared on the horizon this year. Al C. Webb of Joplin, Mo. built a straight chemical car for the Joplin Fire Dept. Placed in service in June of that year, it was built on a Buick chassis and carried a 60-gallon chemical tank. This chemical car was eventually nicknamed "The Goat" and saw many years of service. Mr. Webb went on to found one of the largest and most prosperous of all early motor fire apparatus manufacturing concerns.

The Howe Fire Apparatus Co., still in business today in Anderson, Ind., delivered its first motor pumper in December, 1907 to the Charley Rouss Fire Co. of Winchester, Va. It was rated at 400 gallons per minute.

The Combination Ladder Co., of Providence, R. I., continued to build fire engine bodies for the highly regarded Knox Automobile Co. fire apparatus chassis. Knox displayed its new "Empire Model" Chemical Car at the New York Automobile Show in Madison Square Garden, and later at the Chicago Automobile Show where it drew much interest.

Horse-drawn apparatus, however, remained the mainstay of the fire apparatus industry. The steamer had reached the pinnacle of its development, and the encroachment of gasoline power on the domain of the horse was viewed as little more than a passing fad by skeptical fire service officials everywhere. But the automobile had already acquired both respectability and a measure of durability.

New York City took delivery of one of the new style Seagrave water towers, which had its mast nozzle at the rear instead of out front over the horses.

One of the first firms to successfully market motor-driven fire apparatus was the Webb Motor Fire Apparatus Co., which was located from time to time in Vincennes, Ind.; Allentown, Pa., and St. Louis, Mo. Webb delivered this motor pumping engine to the Tulsa, Okla. Fire Department. It was mounted on the highly-regarded Thomas Touring Car chassis, and was equipped with a Mine pump. The hard suction hose is wrapped around the front of the apparatus. The large dome behind the driver is the pump air chamber.

Waterous, which had built its first gasoline-powered motor pumping engine the previous year, delivered a 600-gallon-per-minute motor pumper to the Alameda, Calif. Fire Dept. in 1907. Where the 1906 model had two engines, one for propulsion and the other for pumping, the Alameda apparatus utilized a single four-cylinder motor that performed both functions. Notice the squirrel-tail preconnected hard suction hose attached to the rear-mounted pump. Because it carried no hose, this single-purpose machine always had to be accompanied by a hose wagon when it responded to an alarm.

The Chicago Fire Department tested a 1907 Seagrave AC-30 Combination Hose and Chemical Car in 1908. It is seen here in front of the quarters of Engine Company No. 104. The experiment was not a success, and the rig was returned to the company.

The Seagrave Company of Columbus, Ohio built and tested its first motor-propelled fire engine in 1907. This is the prototype Model AC-30 Combination Chemical and Hose Car that made a 55-mile test run from Columbus to Chillicothe, Ohio on June 27, 1907. Powered by an air-cooled four-cylinder engine, this prototype was shown around the country at various fire chief's conferences. The crank at the forward end of the hose box was used to tip the soda-acid chemical tank to begin the chemical reaction that, hopefully, extinguished the fire. By the end of the year, Seagrave would deliver its first motor-powered apparatus to a fire department.

Although it is certainly earlier than a 1907 model, this Grabowsky motor truck chassis has been converted to a hose wagon. It is not known where this very rare rig saw service. Grabowsky was the forerunner of the Rapid and GMC truck. The company built its first commercial truck in 1902.

This was the first piece of motor-propelled fire apparatus built by American LaFrance. A straight chemical car, it was built on a 30 horsepower Packard automobile chassis and was delivered to the Boston Fire Dept. After several months of use it was returned to Elmira, when for some reason the B.F.D. could not pay for the unit. This apparatus appeared in several ALF ads in "Fire and Water Engineering" in 1907 with "B.F.D." painted on its radiator core. Photographed with members of the Boston department, it appears here in full regalia. This same engine, but in gray primer, appears on page four of this book, as it looked when first emerging from the Elmira plant. American LaFrance did not enter the motor fire apparatus market formally for another four years, although the company delivered at least two chemical-hose combinations built on special Simplex chassis in 1909.

According to factory records, Seagrave delivered its first motor fire apparatus to the Canadian city of Vancouver, B.C. in the latter part of 1907. This Model AC-53 Chemical Car bore registration number 2384. It was one of three Seagrave motor fire engines in the Vancouver order. The other two were straight hose wagons. All three were placed in service in January, 1908.

A rear view of the 1907 Seagrave AC-53 Chemical Car delivered to Vancouver. It was powered by a 53-horsepower four-cylinder Type "C" air-cooled engine mounted under the driver's seat, and was painted white with gold lettering and trim. Seagrave at this time was still a major builder of horse-drawn aerial and hood and ladder trucks.

This year was to see a noticeable advance in the acceptance of motorized fire apparatus by American fire departments.

On December 17, 1908 the Lansing, Mich. Fire Department placed a big combination motor pumping engine and hose car into service. It was built by the newly formed Webb Motor Fire Apparatus Co. of Vincennes, Ind. on an Oldsmobile chassis. Purchased at a cost of $6,500, Lansing's new auto fire engine even boasted pneumatic tires.

On October 15, 1908, the Detroit Fire Department had put an auto-equipped "Flying Squadron" into service as Engine Co. No. 30. This elite manpower squad was equipped with what was described as an "09 Model Packard Squad Car", powered by a 4-cylinder "UB" engine. Engine 30's rig cost $4,700.

This year was to see the formation of what would become one of the most renowned names in the American fire apparatus industry. Charles H. Fox left the Cincinnati Fire Dept. to join John P. Ahrens in forming a new firm to be called the Ahrens-Fox Fire Engine Co. The firm was located on Colerain Ave. in Cincinnati, and its principal product was the highly regarded "Continental" steam fire engine.

Another newcomer was the Robinson Fire Apparatus Manufacturing Co. of St. Louis, which was already advertising its line of "Auto Fire Apparatus". Along with Webb, Robinson was destined to become a major builder of early motor fire equipment.

By now, Springfield, Mass. had no less than six Knox-chassised fire engines in service in its high-speed "Auxiliary Squadron". The Combination Ladder Co. continued to equip the Knox chassis with fire apparatus bodies. Hartford, Conn. also placed a 40-horsepower Knox combination car into service this year.

Also entering the motor fire apparatus field was the Anderson Coupling and Fire Supply Co. of Kansas City, Kansas. Well-known for its sturdy horse-drawn wagons and other equipment, Anderson delivered a combination auto fire engine in 1908 to Hutchinson, Kans.

One of the most famous builders of expensive luxury cars—Locomobile—also got into the fire engine business. Locomobile delivered a 40-horsepower "Fire Car" with 50-gallon chemical tank to the Bridgeport, Conn. Fire Dept.

The Westinghouse Co. built a 600 gallon-per-minute horse-drawn gasoline pumper for Schenectady, N. Y. This apparatus was later mounted on a Mack Model AB truck chassis.

Other firms that delivered motor fire apparatus at this time included the Auto Car Fire Co. of Ardmore, Pa., and another company with the unlikely name of the Tea Tray Co., of Newark, N. J.

The Amoskeag Division of the Manchester Locomotive Works, Manchester, N. H., produced its last self-propelled steam fire engine this year. It is interesting to note that this 1,200 gallon-per-minute monster was built for and delivered to Vancouver, B. C. one year after this Canadian city had placed three motorized Seagrave fire engines into service. Amoskeag had sold its first self-propelled steamer in 1867 and delivered 22 of these in all. Vancouver's big Amoskeag weighed 16,000 pounds and had a top speed of only 12 miles an hour. It was retired from service in the early 1940s and was cut up for scrap in 1953.

Howe Fire Apparatus, which had been formed in 1872 and which had sold its first motor fire engine the previous year, delivered a motor pumper to Lutherville, Md. in 1908.

Seagrave's prototype motor combination hose and chemical car was taken to Chicago, where it was tried out briefly by that city's Engine Co. No. 103. The apparatus was not purchased by the city.

Webb built this automobile pumping engine for the fire department of Lansing, Mich. in 1908. Built on an Oldsmobile chassis, it was delivered to the Lansing Fire Dept. on December 17, 1908 at a cost of $6,500. Lansing was and still is, Oldsmobile's home town. The pride and joy of the L. F. D. rode on pneumatic tires.

Although the automobile was rapidly encroaching on the domain of the horse and steam, builders of steam fire engines were still doing a brisk business. Not all fire chiefs were convinced about the reliability of the newfangled motor fire engines. The Amoskeag Division of the Manchester Locomotive Works located in Manchester, N. H., had delivered a number of self-propelled steamers to fire departments over the years. The last of these juggernauts was delivered to the Vancouver, B. C. Fire Dept. in 1908—the year after Vancouver began motorizing its fire department. Rated at 1,200 Imperial gallons per minute, this huge apparatus cost $12,480 and weighed 16,000 pounds. It was retired in the early 1940's and was scrapped in 1953.

A pioneer builder of motor fire apparatus, Knox was now routinely delivering a wide variety of types of apparatus to American fire departments, most of them in the East. However, this Knox Combination Hose and Chemical Car was delivered to Stockton, Calif. It is lettered "S.F.D. No. 2." Notice the chemical tank mounted under the running board and the turret pipe permanently mounted on the side of the hose box.

With its dashing horses, flying sparks and polished bright-work, the steamer was undoubtedly the most romantic of all fire engines. Steam fire engines first appeared in the United States in the early 1850's and led to the demise of the colorful volunteer era and the creation of the first paid professional fire departments. The last steam fire engines were built in the late 'teens. Ahrens-Fox of Cincinnati built this "Continental" steamer for Engine Co. No. 13 of Detroit in 1908. This steamer was recently completely refurbished by the Box 42 Associates, one of Detroit's three fire buff clubs.

Exactly where this buggy-like Fire Insurance Patrol wagon saw service is not known for sure. But it is an early model Plymouth truck. This Plymouth is not to be confused with the vehicles produced later by Chrysler Corp. The first Plymouths were trucks, built by the Plymouth Motor Truck Co. of Plymouth, Ohio. This company produced its first friction-drive trucks in 1906 and remained in business until about 1914. The company also built at least one passenger car.

Knox delivered this big chain-driven motor hose wagon to the fire department of Chicopee, Mass. in 1908. This new style Knox Waterless had the driver sitting over the air-cooled engine. This apparatus went into service with Chicopee's Engine Co. No. 5.

1909

Motor fire apparatus development was advancing by leaps and bounds, much to the surprise of the skeptics.

The American LaFrance Fire Engine Co. of Elmira, N.Y. delivered two motor combination hose and chemical cars this year, even though the first motorized LaFrance to carry a manufacturer's register number was not delivered until the following year. The 1909 American LaFrance motor combinations were built on the 4-cylinder Simplex automobile chassis and were delivered to Morristown, N. J. and Revere, Mass. The Morristown rig had two chemical tanks mounted under the driver's seat and was equipped with crew seats along each side of its hose bed. Both rode on pneumatic tires.

Monhagen Hose Co. of Middletown, N. Y. is generally credited with placing the first triple combination pumper, hose and chemical truck into service late in 1909. This historic apparatus was mounted on an American Mors auto chassis, and was built by the Tea Tray Co. of Newark, N. J. The Monhagen's truck was equipped with a 400 gallon-per-minute Gould pump, and carried a 50-gallon chemical tank. Four years later the body of this truck was remounted on a 1913 Stearns chassis.

The International Motor Co. of New York, the predecessor of today's Mack truck firm, sold a ladder truck tractor to Allentown, Pa., in 1909. It is believed that this was the first motor-propelled ladder truck used in the U.S.

The Seagrave Co. built its first complete tractor-drawn aerial ladder truck in 1909 and delivered it to Vancouver, B. C. The 75-foot aerial was drawn by a gargantuan Model AC-90 tractor with a 4-cylinder aircooled engine. Vancouver also took delivery of two more Seagrave Model AC-53 hose wagons and an AC-40 chemical car this year.

Seagrave also built aircooled chemical cars for New Orleans and Pasadena, Calif.

New York City placed its first motor fire engine into service this year. The apparatus was a Knox high pressure hose car which was placed in service at the quarters of Engine Co. No. 72.

Webb delivered pumping engines to Birmingham, Ala,; Youngstown, Ohio, and Springfield, Ohio. A fleet of three Webb motor fire engines were also delivered to the "Motor Brigade" of the Akron, Ohio Fire Dept.

The Pope Manufacturing Co. of Hartford, Conn. had also entered the fire apparatus field. Brockton, Mass. ordered a Pope-Hartford combination car, and similar models were delivered to Fall River and Westfield, Mass.

Robinson offered a 700 gallon-per-minute pumper equipped with a piston pump and powered by a 120-horsepower engine. One of the fastest rigs on the road, the big Robinson was said to be capable of doing 60 miles an hour. Alliance, Ohio took delivery of a Robinson this year.

L. W. Luitwieler, of Rochester, N. Y. advertised a new type of automobile fire engine. The Luitwieler featured a full-length hose basket mounted above an open pump compartment. It is believed that only one of these was ever built by the Luitwieler Pump Engineering Co.

Waterous offered its "Pioneer" Model auto fire engines, powered by a 90 horsepower engine, in 600 and 800 gallon-per-minute sizes.

The New York City Fire Department took delivery of this massive Webb high pressure hose wagon in 1909. At this time, New York City fire apparatus was painted white and maroon. This motor wagon had a large hose box and a fixed turret pipe. It went into service with Engine Co. No. 72. There appeared to be no shortage of manpower in New York firehouses in those days.

Seagrave sold its first factory-built motor-driven aerial ladder truck to the city of Vancouver, B. C., which had purchased Seagrave's first motor apparatus two years earlier. Drawn by a four-wheel Model AC-90 tractor powered by a four-cylinder Type "E" air-cooled engine, it went into service in September, 1909. It had a 75-foot spring-raised wood aerial ladder. This huge ladder truck is seen outside Vancouver's headquarters fire station shortly after it went into service.

The Monhagen Fire Company of Middletown, N. Y. claims to have placed the first triple combination motor fire apparatus in the U. S. into service on December 1, 1909. This apparatus was built on an American Mors automobile chassis, built in St. Louis, and was equipped with a 400 gallon-per-minute rotary gear pump. The apparatus was assembled by a Newark, N. J. firm with the unlikely name of the Tea Tray Mfg. Co. In 1913, the body of this apparatus was transferred to a new Stearns chassis. A triple combination carries a pump, hose and chemical or booster equipment.

Another pioneer American automobile manufacturer, the Pope Manufacturing Co. of Hartford, Conn., also dabbled briefly in the motor fire apparatus field. The Bristol, Conn. Fire Dept. purchased this Pope-Hartford combination chemical and hose car. The small crank in the center of the chemical tank was used to release a small bottle of acid into the water tank, creating a chemical reaction that forced water through the chemical hose onto the fire.

Springfield, Ohio received this standard model Webb combination pumping engine and hose car in 1909. The Webb Motor Fire Apparatus Co, then located in Vincennes, Ind., boasted in a 1909 advertisement: "At the Grand Rapids Convention of Fire Engineers, the Webb was the sensation of the hour and demonstrated beyond a question of doubt that the day of the horse in fire departments has passed. . . .it was an 'Automobile Convention' and our machines were accredited with every honor and proclaimed a success."

The Auto Car Co., which had commenced operations the previous year, supplied this big 2-tank chemical engine to the E. H. Stokes Fire Co. of Ocean Grove, N. J., in 1909. The chemical equipment was manufactured by Holloway, an old established name in the chemical fire engine field. This rare photo was turned up by Bill Schwartz of Ocean Grove.

The Pasadena, Cal. Fire Dept. took delivery of this Seagrave Model AC-40 two-tank chemical car in 1909. Rather than the usual basket, the chemical hose on this apparatus was carried on a reel behind the driver's seat. Notice the overhead ladder rack. This white-painted apparatus is lettered "Chemical Engine No. 5".

The New York City Fire Department experimented with this truly gigantic Waterous Combination Motor Pumping Engine and Hose Car in 1909, but did not place it in service. Another two years would pass before the first motorized pumper would go into service on the F.D.N.Y. Notice the exceptionally long hood and the air chamber atop the rear-mounted pump.

American LaFrance

The first motor-propelled American LaFrance fire apparatus was built on a special four-cylinder Simplex automobile chassis. Although the Elmira factory registry shows Lenox, Mass. as having received Register No. 1 in 1910, at least two Simplex-chassised American LaFrance combination cars were delivered in 1909. These units were purchased by Morristown, N. J., and Revere, Mass.

AMERICAN LAFRANCE

Morristown, N. J. received one of the two Simplex-chassised American LaFrance combination hose and chemical cars known to have been delivered by the Elmira plant in 1909. The other went to Revere, Mass. Rather than meet increasing demand for motor fire apparatus with an untried, assembled chassis, American LaFrance chose to utilize the proven and respected (and expensive) 4-cylinder Simplex. Note the goggles worn by the driver of this 1909 American LaFrance-Simplex.

The tires of Morristown, N. J.'s 1909 American LaFrance-Simplex combination hose and chemical car have been changed in this rear view, taken some years after it entered service. A hand-cranked siren has also been mounted above the bell on the dash. Note the two crew benches in the rear body. Curiously, American LaFrance did not begin to register its motor apparatus until the following year: Register No. 1 was an identical Simplex delivered to Lenox, Mass. in 1910 and still owned by this department.

The Seagrave Model AC "buckboard" began to gain wide popularity with fire departments across the country. It is believed that this 1910 Chemical and Hose Combination was delivered to Lewiston, Idaho. The crew appears justifiably proud of its new apparatus.

The Seagrave Co. built this 75-foot, tractor-drawn Model AC aerial ladder truck for the Tacoma, Wash. Fire Dept. Seen pulling out of Tacoma's No. 1 Fire House, this rig is similar to the one built for Vancouver, B. C., the previous year. Note the company number painted on the radiator, and the large opening for the engine crank. This truck is also equipped with a bumper.

American LaFrance Fire Engine Co. announced its formal entry into the motor fire apparatus field in the March 10, 1910 edition of *Fire and Water Engineering.* The company promised its first deliveries by the end of the month. Register No. 1 was delivered on schedule to Lenox, Mass., and this historic old American LaFrance and is still owned by this department and is in perfect operating condition. The second motor combination off the line was delivered to Fort Worth, Tex. Initially, American LaFrance built only motor combination hose and chemical cars. These were four-cylinder chassis powered by an engine of 5½-inch bore and 6-inch stroke. Wheelbase was 130 inches. By October the Elmira plant had delivered 23 more fire engines. One of these combinations was demonstrated at the International Assn. of Fire Engineers Convention in Syracuse, N. Y. that year and topped 50 miles an hour in a test at the local fairgrounds.

The Couple Gear Freight Wheel Co. had developed an electric drive system that would be used by numerous fire apparatus manufacturers in future years. This system featured an electric drive motor mounted inside each wheel hub, giving the unit 4-wheel drive. Battery-powered rigs were notoriously slow, and all too often ran out of juice before they could make it back to the firehouse. But many were actually delivered. Springfield, Mass., in 1910 took delivery of an 85-foot Seagrave aerial ladder truck and a combination hose and chemical rig that utilized the Couple Gear electric drive chassis.

One by one, American cities were installing motor-propelled pumpers in their fire houses, replacing steamers. In June, 1910, the Detroit Fire Dept. placed a Webb pumper into service at Engine Co. No. 3. Webb had outgrown its Vincennes, Ind. plant and this year moved into a new plant in St. Louis.

In a prominent ad carried in fire service trade journals, Knox warned fire chiefs: "Don't Buy Any More Horse Drawn Fire Apparatus!" Knox this year introduced a new 60-horsepower Model M-4 combination.

Ahrens-Fox, still very big in the steam fire engine business despite a waning market, displayed a "Continental" fire chief's auto. This versatile machine was battery powered and carried chemical equipment.

Grand Rapids, Mich. motorized with an Oldsmobile combination built in the department's own repair shops.

A Mack city service hook and ladder truck was placed in service in Morristown, N. J., which only the previous year had placed an American LaFrance motor combination into service. It is believed that this was the first motor city service ladder truck built in the U. S.

Builders of steam fire engines were becoming alarmed at the sudden drop in orders for steam fire engines, and the resulting high inventories of useless parts.

The fire department of Napa, Cal. purchased this 1910 Seagrave Model AC-40 Combination Hose and Chemical Car. On this model, however, the two copper chemical tanks are mounted transversely, and two ground ladders are carried in an overhead rack. White was a popular apparatus color in the early motor era.

Still noted for its big over-the-road truck tractors, the Brockway Motor Truck Co. of Cortland, N. Y. has supplied fire apparatus chassis off and on for many years. Brockway built this hose and chemical truck on its 40-horsepower Model U chassis. With a capacity of 1,000 feet of fire hose, this model was priced at $2,750 complete. The 2-tone red-and-cream paint job was fairly common at this time.

Members of the Haverhill, Mass. Fire Dept. pose proudly on their 1910 Knox Combination Hose and Chemical Car. The bell on this apparatus is mounted in a frame over the chemical hose basket at the front of the hose box. Knox, a successful motor car manufacturer, built its own specialized fire apparatus chassis.

James Boyd and Brother, Inc., of Philadelphia, was one of the first major suppliers of motor-driven fire apparatus to American fire departments. Boyd built this combination chemical and hose car for the Pioneer Fire Co. No. 1, of Jenkintown, Pa., in 1910. This model is equipped with two chemical tanks.

White Plains, N. Y. purchased this racy-looking combination hose and chemical car for its Independent Engine Co. No. 2. The hose and chemical body is mounted on an expensive Locomobile chassis. For obvious reasons of dependability and durability, fire apparatus builders preferred to mount their equipment on heavy luxury car chassis. The single chemical tank on this model is mounted under the seat.

The American Locomotive Co., of Providence, R. I., got into the motor truck business for a short time, and even built a few fire engine chassis. These were marketed under the Alco nameplate. East Providence, R. I. ran this 1910 Alco hose wagon for several years. Albany, N. Y. also had several Alcos on its fire department.

The Webb Motor Fire Apparatus Co. built its early motor-propelled fire engines on the highly-regarded Thomas chassis, one of the more expensive automobiles in its day. Webb delivered a sizeable quantity of pumping engines and motor hose wagons based on the Thomas chassis. This one, a triple combination pumper with suction hoses carried over the front fenders, went to Barberton, Ohio. Webb built this style until about 1913.

Introduced two years earlier, in 1908, Henry Ford's rugged little Model "T" Ford found immediate acceptance by the fire service everywhere. The T's low initial cost, proven reliability and unique adaptability to any purpose appealed to fire departments of every size. Hundreds of Model T's were used as Chief's buggies, and many more were equipped as hose wagons, chemical cars, combinations and small pumping engines. Complete with bell and small equipment box, this Model T Ford was outfitted as a chief's runabout.

American LaFrance in 1910 commenced the manufacture of its first complete motor fire apparatus. The first American LaFrance motor fire engine to carry a factory registration number was this historic Type 5 Combination Chemical and Hose Car delivered to Lenox, Mass. on Aug. 27, 1910. Remarkably enough, old Register No. 1 is still owned by Lenox and is in excellent running condition today, more than 65 years after it entered service. It has a four-cylinder engine.

The Grand Rapids, Mich. Fire Department Motor Shops built up this straight chemical car on a 1910 Oldsmobile chassis. The two chemical tanks are located in the forward end of the body just behind the driver's seat. The crew seems quite proud of its new rig, which saw service with Engine Co. No. 3. The big Olds also carried a set of ground ladders on its right-hand side.

1911

Under mounting pressure from competitors, the Ahrens-Fox Fire Engine Co. had started development of its own gasoline-powered motor fire apparatus.

Always an innovator, Ahrens-Fox decided to go its own way when it finally made the momentous decision to manufacture a line of motor equipment. Instead of mounting the pump amidships or at the rear as other manufacturers had done, Ahrens-Fox came up with a front-mounted pumper design. The piston-type pump was powered directly off the front of the engine crankshaft. The front-mounted configuration also permitted the driver to more easily "spot" his apparatus at the hydrant or in front of the fire. The first Ahrens-Fox piston pumper was a 450 gallon-per-minute Model A Continental, with a small onion-shaped air chamber atop the front-mounted pump. In tests at the Milwaukee International Assn. of Fire Engineers Convention, its performance proved disappointing and a completely new type of pump with a double dome air chamber was later fitted. This pumper was delivered to Rockford, Ill. early in 1912.

The Seagrave Corp. introduced two new styles of engine-ahead-of-cab fire engines this year, while continuing production of its familiar aircooled "buckboards". At Milwaukee, Seagrave showed its very first pumper, a massive 1,000 GPM job equipped with a Gorham centrifugal pump mounted in a compartment at the rear. This huge pumper was powered by a giant 6-cylinder engine with a bore of 7¾ inches and a 9-inch stroke. Seagrave's new G Model apparatus had a barrel-shaped hood and radiator shell. Seagrave boasted that its new apparatus had real "passenger car style". A refined form of the G Model with a more conventional gabled hood came along at about the same time.

JAMES BOYD & BRO., Inc.   Philadelphia

The Montgomery Fire Co. in Norristown, Pa. purchased a combination hose and chemical car from James Boyd and Bro. of Philadelphia in 1911. It was a Model C Boyd combination, with flared Springfield style hose body, which permitted the crew to ride in the rear above the hose load. Note the turret pipe attached to the side of the driver's seat. The wagon pipe was fed by two hose lines.

American LaFrance in 1911 began production of a line of rotary gear pumping engines. The first of these was delivered to San Antonio, Tex., on June 10, 1911, and was a 500 GPM model. American LaFrance had abandoned the Simplex chassis and was now building its own motor fire apparatus from the chassis up, including engines. The Type 10 pumper was built on a 140-inch wheelbase and was rated at 500 GPM. The Type 12, on a 150-inch wheelbase, was a 700 GPM model. By April of 1911, American LaFrance had 38 motorized fire engines in service.

At the IAFE conference in Milwaukee, the Nott Fire Engine Co. of Minneapolis displayed a motor pumper. The Thomas B. Jeffrey Co. of Kenosha, Wis. delivered a Rambler combination car to its home city. Peter Pirsch & Sons Co., also of Kenosha, built three motor combinations for Chicago and an aerial for Winnipeg, Manitoba.

Seagrave came out with a straight-frame aerial ladder truck on which the driver rode "sidesaddle" on the right-hand side of the apparatus. This company also delivered a Model G tractor to Passaic, N. J., which used it to motorize a former horse-drawn city service hook and ladder truck.

New York City, now seriously considering the purchase of motor-driven pumping engines, ran a series of tests on six different types. These included a 700 GPM Waterous pumper, and motor-propelled Nott steamer. The Nott was placed into service at Engine Co. No. 58 on W. 115th St. in March, 1911. The FDNY also attached a Couple Gear electric drive 4-wheel tractor to one of its water towers, replacing a 3-horse hitch.

In another important development, a Mack motor pumping engine with a Gould rotary gear pump was delivered to Bala Cynwyd, Pa. This marked Mack's formal entry into the fire engine manufacturing field.

Perhaps the most interesting development this year was the construction of the prototype of the first Christie front-drive tractor. John Walter Christie, who had acquired quite a reputation in auto racing, designed a 2-wheel auto tractor which could be used to replace the horses on horse-drawn fire equipment. On the prototype, Christie's 4-cylinder engine was mounted on the left-hand side of the chassis parallel to the frame. On the production model, the engine was mounted transversely in the frame. The first deliveries out of Christie's Front Drive Auto Co. plant in Hoboken, N. J. commenced in 1912. An estimated 600 Christie front drive tractors were built in the next eight or so years. These powerful, yet simple tractors bridged the transitional gap between animal and gasoline motive power in nearly every major American city, and preserved the cities' investment in horse-drawn equipment for many more years.

Also in 1911, the Robinson Fire Apparatus Co. started building a "Jumbo" model auto pumping engine with a 700 GPM triple cylinder piston pump. The "Jumbo" was powered by a 110-horsepower engine.

Knox had developed several new products, including a 3-wheeled auto tractor and a buckboard-style pumper that employed an Amoskeag type piston pump. The 3-wheeled tractor was built jointly by Knox and the Martin Carriage Works, of York, Pa.

Another prosperous builder of motor fire engines was the old firm of James Boyd and Bro. of Philadelphia. Boyd apparatus could be found in fire stations in many communities in the U. S. northeast.

Calgary, Alberta, received this Webb-Couple Gear 85-foot aerial ladder truck in 1911. The 2-section aerial ladder was raised by an electric hoist with spring assist. This hybrid was powered by a gasoline engine which generated electric power which was then distributed to a drive unit in each wheel. This motive system was built by the Couple Gear Freight Wheel Co. of Grand Rapids, Mich. Webb, a pioneer builder of motor fire apparatus, was in St. Louis.

Slowly but surely, motor-driven fire apparatus began to replace the horses on larger fire departments. This photograph was taken as a new 1911 Webb High Pressure Hose Wagon was readied for service. It has a large turret pipe at the front of the hose box and the set of nozzle tips at the rear. The inlets for the turret pipe can be seen just below the running board.

A major builder of steam fire engines, the W. S. Nott Co. of Minneapolis was unsuccessful in making the big transition from steam to motor fire apparatus. Nott's standard model was the huge Nott Universal combination pumping and hose engine. Nott Universals were built in two sizes: in 4 and 6-cylinder variations with 600 to 1,000 gallon-per-minute pumps. The juggernaut shown was built for the City of Minneapolis.

The first motor-powered pumping engine to be accepted for service on the New York Fire Dept. was this Nott steamer which went into service at Engine Co. No. 58 on March 20, 1911. The 700 gallon-per-minute pumper had a guaranteed top speed of 30 miles an hour. It cost $9,722. The Nott Fire Engine Co. of Minneapolis boasted that on an alarm 15 blocks from Engine 58's quarters on West 115th St., the gasoline-propelled Nott beat the horse-drawn company to the scene, even though the horse-drawn company was located only four blocks from the fire.

The Couple Gear Freight Wheel Company of Grand Rapids, Mich. built this electric drive four wheel auto tractor for the New York City Fire Dept. The Couple Gear tractor was used to motorize the former horse-drawn water tower shown here. The Couple Gear tractor had an electric motor mounted in each wheel.

The Pueblo Colo. Fire Dept. placed this American La-France motor pumper in service on June 12, 1911. It bore Registration No. 39. Some 15 years later the Pueblo Fire Dept. wrote to American LaFrance to tell the factory that the old pumper was still going strong. By that time, American LaFrance had delivered more than 5,500 motor fire engines to American Fire departments.

AMERICAN LA·FRANCE FIRE ENGINE CO. Elmira, N.Y.

Oroville, California's first motor fire apparatus was this 1911 American LaFrance Type 10 Chemical and Hose Combination. Although modified somewhat over the years, it still closely resembles the original rig and is still in fully operable condition.

Johnstown, Pa. purchased this American LaFrance Combination Hose and Chemical Car in 1911. By mid-1911, some 32 motor-propelled fire engines had been ordered from the Elmira, N. Y. firm. Of these, eight, including this Type 5 Combination, were already in service.

The first Mack fire engine was delivered in 1911 to the Union Fire Association of Lower Merion, Pa., now Bala Cynwyd, a Philadelphia suburb. Resplendent in its bright red paint and brass accessories, this big pumper was equipped with a Gould pump. Mack is still a major fire apparatus builder today.

Fire apparatus historian Bob Barber found this fully operable 1911 Seagrave Model AC Combination Hose and Chemical Car in the firehouse at Columbus, Neb. in 1972. Nicknamed "Old Smokie", the old Seagrave is still the pride of the department. Despite its age, this venerable old rig still appears almost original.

The fire department of Tacoma, Wash. was the owner of this Seagrave Model AC-80 straight hose wagon. This photo appears to have been taken sometime after this machine was delivered, as the carbide headlights have been replaced with electric lights. Other equipment includes overhead ladders and four hand lanterns. Note the front wheel chains and the wire equipment basket behind the front seat.

The Peter Pirsch & Sons Co. of Kenosha, Wis. was another principal fire engine builder. Pirsch specialized in hose and hook and ladder trucks. This company equipped this 1911 Rambler chassis with chemical and hose apparatus for the Aurora, Ill. Fire Dept. Note the hood ornament and the spare tire lashed to the running board.

The Harder Storage and Van Company of Chicago, Ill. built this 1911 Harder hose wagon for the Chicago Fire Department. This heavy wagon was powered by a Waukesha engine. Notice the large equipment basket mounted over the hose bed.

Among the lesser known early motor fire engine builders was the Dixon Cascade Pump Co. of Newark, N. J. This company's home town-boosting advertising slogan was "Newark Knows How". The apparatus shown is a dual combination motor pumping engine and hose car. Note the enclosed rear drive chains and the cagelike bell mounting.

By now, the automobile had replaced the chief's horse and buggy on many fire departments. In Chicago, the Assistant Fire Marshall sped to blazes in this 1911 Halladay touring car.

Another real pioneer in the motor fire apparatus field was the Knox Automobile Co. of Springfield, Mass. Many eastern U. S. fire departments purchased Knox equipment. The combination hose and chemical car shown here was built by Knox for the fire department of Gloucester, Mass. This model carries two chemical tanks and a full set of wood ground ladders.

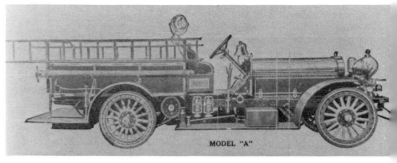

The Ahrens-Fox Fire Engine Co. of Cincinnati started building motor fire apparatus in 1911. This is the first of a long line of front-mounted Ahrens-Fox piston pumpers. It was assembled in 1911 for the Rockford, Ill. Fire Dept., but proved a bit of a disappointment in its first tests. Consequently the pump was torn down and redesigned. The single onion-shaped air chamber was replaced with two larger domes placed side by side. The rebuilt piston pumper was not delivered to Rockford until early in 1912.

The International Assn. of Fire Engineers Conference, held in Denver this year, was a real "automobile convention". A fascinating variety of makes and models were exhibited and demonstrated for the fire chiefs at the Denver convention.

Ahrens-Fox displayed one of its new double-dome Continental Model A piston pumpers. The Cincinnati firm also demonstrated a unique hybrid, a Couple Gear battery-powered Continental steamer. American LaFrance used the occasion to preview its new Type 16 straight frame gasoline/electric aerial ladder truck, and its new high capacity Type 15 pumper which delivered 898 gallons per minute at 130 pounds pressure. The Seagrave Co. demonstrated one of its big 1,000 GPM Gorham-Seagrave Turbine centrifugal pumping engines, and Webb showed the IAFC delegates its powerful new combination motor pumper and hose car.

The American LaFrance Type 16 aerial used a gasoline engine mounted at the front of the chassis between the seats, which was coupled to a General Electric Co. "standard railway type" electric drive unit, that delivered current to electric motors mounted in each wheel hub. These gas-electric aerials were built in 65, 75 and 85-foot sizes, and early deliveries went to Elizabeth, N. J.; Flint, Mich.; Yonkers, N. Y.; Pittsfield, Mass., and Manila in the Phillipine Islands. The Elmira plant's standard tractor-type aerial was known as the Type 17.

Ahrens-Fox delivered its first piston pumper to Rockford, Ill. on January 9, 1912. This was the rebuilt machine that had been shown at Milwaukee the previous year. It originally carried the serial number 500, but after rebuilding with the new double-dome style pump it was redesignated No. 501. The pump was still rated at 450 GPM, and the only 1911 model Ahrens-Fox piston pumper delivered was named the William W. Bennett. Rockford received a second pumper of this type, a 700 GPM model, No. 509, later the same year.

John Walter Christie's newly-formed Front Drive Motor Co., of Hoboken, N. J. found a large and ready market for its 2-wheel conversion tractors. The New York City Fire Dept. ordered 28 Christie tractors, the first of an eventual fleet of more than 300 of these transverse-engined workhorses that would be acquired by the FDNY.

The Webb Motor Fire Apparatus Co. built this Combination Hose and Chemical truck for the fire department of Oakland, Cal. Note the resemblance to Seagrave and some Knox apparatus of this period. Oakland at this time also had a Seagrave Gorham Turbine pumping engine.

New York in 1912 also received four Webb-Couple Gear electric drive aerial ladder trucks. Webb had again moved its manufacturing operations, this time from St. Louis to Allentown, Pa.

Seagrave in 1912 introduced a new series of conventional type centrifugal pumping engines of 600 to 1,000 GPM capacity. Seagrave's new pumper boasted a completely enclosed pump, and later the same year the company introduced the industry's first automatic pressure regulator, which maintained a constant engine speed during pumping. The big Seagrave-Gorham turbine pumpers also continued in production, along with the aircooled "buckboard" hose and chemical cars. Birmingham, Ala. placed an order for 18 Seagrave Model AC combinations this year.

A huge Waterous gasoline motor pumper was placed into service with New York City's Engine Co. No. 39 this year, and the FDNY contracted with American LaFrance for 25 motor tractors.

Also demonstrated at the Denver IAFE convention was Robinson's new "Monarch" 1,000 GPM First-Size Motor Pumper. American cities continued to motorize, and Chicago placed a 900 GPM "Nott Universal" automobile steam pumper into service at Engine Co. No. 94. This same year, a gentleman named C. J. Cross became the New York agent for the new Christie front-drive auto tractor. Within a few years, Mr. Cross left Christie and set up his own firm which built and sold a similar type of conversion tractor.

The Robinson Fire Apparatus Manufacturing Co. of St. Louis delivered this big piston pumper to Chelsea, Mass. Robinson's two principal models were the Monarch and the Jumbo. At the 1912 International Assn. of Fire Engineers' convention in Denver, a Robinson pumper delivered 918 gallons per minute at 125 pounds pressure, and 600 GPM at 205 pounds in a demonstration, at an altitude of one mile.

Morristown, N. J. was an early user of motorized fire apparatus. This city service hook and ladder was built on a 1912 Mack motor chassis, and was one of the first Macks used for this purpose. The company is the Resolute Hook and Ladder Co. No. 1. Morristown purchased one of the first American LaFrance motor fire engines in 1909.

The City of Rockford, Ill. put the first Ahrens-Fox "Continental Model A" Piston Pumper into service on January 9, 1912. This is what the pumper looked like after the pump was redesigned and rebuilt. The hood of the prototype Ahrens-Fox piston pumper was also lower in its original form. Rated at 700 gallons per minute, the first Ahrens-Fox motor pumper was named the William W. Bennett. It served Rockford for many years.

This is yet another Continental "A" Model 700 gallon-per-minute Ahrens-Fox piston pumper delivered in 1912. This pumper served Edgewater, N. J. for many years before going into reserve. Note the preconnected hard suction hose.

Ahrens-Fox built relatively few of its Continental Model "B" piston pumpers. The "B" model differed from the "A" in that it was a straight pumping engine and carried no hose. Crew benches were installed in place of the conventional hose bed. This 700 gallon-per-minute pumper served Engine Co. No. 24 of Washington, D. C. Note the wider, set-back front fenders used on this model.

In addition to four Ahrens-Fox piston pumpers, the Detroit Fire Dept. in 1912 purchased this Ahrens-Fox Model "C" Combination Hose and Chemical Car. This apparatus was later converted into a high pressure hose car. It sports a Pirsch chemical tank and a Van Duesen bell.

Lynn, Mass. purchased a speedy Pope-Hartford chemical car for its fire department. This model carries two 60-gallon chemical tanks, which are enclosed in the two compartments at the front of the rear body. The crew rode on two benches in the rear of the apparatus. Fire apparatus historian Harold S. Walker found this photo in his extensive collection.

Ahrens-Fox at this time offered fire chiefs all three types of fire-fighting power: motor-driven pumpers, horse-drawn steam fire engines, and steamers powered by either gasoline, or electricity. Ahrens-Fox built a very few motor tractors for steamers. The Cincinnati firm demonstrated this Continental steam-electric pumper at the International Assn. of Fire Engineers convention in 1912. Ahrens-Fox used the electric drive system made by the Couple Gear Freight Wheel Co. of Grand Rapids, Mich. The electric-steam and gas-electric hybrids were never very successful.

American LaFrance built this speedy-looking Standard Type 10 Combination Squad and Chemical Car. Powered by a 75-horsepower, four-cylinder engine, it had two benches in the rear for its crew. The chemical hose was carried in a rear compartment. The apparatus was painted white.

The resort community of Ocean Grove, N. J. purchased this 1912 American LaFrance Type 14 City Service Hook and Ladder Truck. These tillerless, straight-frame ladder trucks required considerable musclepower and plenty of room in which to maneuver. This model was powered by an American LaFrance four-cylinder engine.

San Francisco placed this American LaFrance two-tank straight chemical car into service in 1912. During the transition from horse-drawn to automotive equipment, the S.F.F.D. purchased a number of these chemical cars. San Francisco fire apparatus for many years was painted a very dark maroon rather than the traditional fire department red.

Straight chemical cars were still an important part of the average fire department's equipment. This is a 1912 American LaFrance Type 10 two-tank chemical car. It had two 60-gallon soda and acid chemical tanks, and carried two three-gallon Babcock fire extinguishers. It was rated at 75 horsepower and could top 60 miles an hour.

This is a straight Standard Type 10 Hose Car by American LaFrance. The full length hose box could carry 1,220 feet of 2½ inch fire hose. This apparatus was powered by a 75-horsepower four-cylinder motor, and boasted a top speed of 50 miles per hour. Hand-cranked sirens were now beginning to become popular, but locomotive-type bells were still standard equipment on most fire engines.

The Harder Auto Truck Co. of Chicago, which sold fire apparatus under the name of the Harder Storage and Van Co. delivered this chemical and hose truck to the Chicago Fire Department in 1912. Fitted with a windshield, it was assigned to Engine Co. No. 121.

Seagrave began the production of motor pumping engines in 1911. This very large Model WC-144 three-stage centrifugal 1000 gallon-per-minute pumper was equipped with a rear-mounted Gorham Turbine pump. It was delivered to Los Angeles and remained in service with the L.A.F.D. until after the Second World War. This was a straight pumping car and carried no hose.

Tacoma, Wash. also purchased a Seagrave-Gorham 1000 gallon-per-minute centrifugal pumping engine in 1912. The rear-mounted pump was covered with a sloping hood which gave the apparatus the appearance of an early racing car. Notice the two-section hood and hard-suction hose slung above the running board.

Selma, Ala. purchased this Seagrave Model AC Combination, with overhead ladder rack, two chemical tanks and electric lighting. All of these units featured chain drive. This model also boasted a spring-mounted front bumper.

While the company's new centrifugal pumping engines were rapidly gaining favor, Seagrave continued to find strong demand for its air-cooled "buckboards". This is a 1912 Combination Hose and Chemical Wagon that was assigned to Combination "A" on the Stoneham, Mass. Fire Dept. It featured two transverse-mounted chemical tanks and carbide lighting.

Seagrave introduced this new style of apparatus with a conventional hood in 1911. This combination chemical and hose truck, with an overhead ladder rack, was delivered to Engine Co. No. 12 of the Los Angeles Fire Dept. Los Angeles was a good Seagrave customer for many years.

Berkely, Cal. is still the owner of this 1912 Seagrave Model AC-80 Combination Hose and Chemical Car, with the new forward-mounted engine. The chemical tank is mounted under the driver's seat. This engine has an unusually high hose box. The transverse-mounted hose reel and steel wheels were added later in this rig's service life.

1912

James Boyd & Bro., Inc. of Philadelphia was the builder of this two-tank Model "A" Chemical Engine and Hose Car. This apparatus bore a striking resemblance to the Seagrave Model AC series of this era. It is not known where this Boyd was delivered.

James Boyd & Brother, Inc., of Philadelphia was another pioneer motor fire apparatus builder. This 1912 Boyd Combination Hose and Chemical Car, with flared hose body, squad benches and side-mounted turret pipe was built for New Brighton, Pa. This type of flared body was known as the Springfield type, as it originated in Springfield, Mass.

One of the first Christie front-drive motor tractors placed into fire service was delivered to the New York City Fire Dept. This early prototype Christie tractor has a 4-cylinder engine mounted parallel with the chassis frame, rather than transversely as in all later Christies. The Christie tractor, attached to a LaFrance steamer, was capable of pulling 12 tons.

The versatile Christie front-drive tractor fulfilled a real need by large, metropolitan fire departments for a means of converting former horse-drawn fire apparatus to motor power. The department could thus preserve its investment in fairly new horse-drawn apparatus, and at the same time have the speed and reduced maintenance afforded by the motor truck. New York City converted numerous steamers and ladder trucks with Christie tractors. This early-1900's Seagrave 85-foot spring-raised aerial has been converted to motor power.

The W. S. Nott Co. of Minneapolis built this big triple combination motor pumper for the City of Springfield, Mass. It was rated at 500 gallons per minute. New York City purchased two similar style Nott motor pumpers in 1913.

"They're off, and the 'all out' is merely a matter of seconds", boasted this Knox Automobile Co. ad of 1912. Shown here on the fly is a Knox triple combination pumper, chemical and hose car. Knox had been building motor fire engines for six years now and had many in service.

Certainly far ahead of its time in styling was the Nott Universal, a large, streamlined apparatus with a V-type radiator shell. Nott Universals were sold to Minneapolis, Dubuque, Iowa, and Ottawa and Victoria, B. C. in Canada. The engine shown here was built for Battle Creek, Mich., but was not accepted and was resold to another fire department. The sleek Nott Universal featured worm drive.

The Christie Front-Drive Auto Tractor, like the one shown here, temporarily bridged the technological gap between the steam and motor ages. Hundreds of these were built by the Front Drive Motor Co. of Hoboken, N. J. between 1912 and about 1916, and were used to convert former horse-drawn steamers, aerial ladder trucks, hook and ladder trucks and water towers to gasoline power. The Christie tractor used a four-cylinder engine mounted crosswise on the front of the chassis. It can honestly be said that the Christie Front Drive Tractor was the backbone of America's fire defenses in the pre-World War I era. Several other builders, including American LaFrance and Seagrave, developed their own bolt-on two wheel tractor conversions, but none enjoyed the success of the Christie.

In general configuration, this 1913 Knox Piston Pumper resembles a Seagrave "buckboard" or a Webb. The Knox is undergoing a pumping test in Springfield, Mass., where the Knox automobile plant was located. The pump is of the Amoskeag type. The rearmost hose line is supplying a fixed turret pipe.

For more than 30 years, fire departments large and small had relied on chemical apparatus to extinguish small fires. Soda-and-acid chemical tanks were still standard equipment on hose wagons, and even on some pumpers. In 1913, Ahrens-Fox introduced the "booster" system, which eventually replaced the chemical tank and was adopted by all fire engine builders. Developed by Charles Fox himself, the Ahrens-Fox Model "D" Scout Booster Car was built on a light-duty Republic truck chassis, and had a small centrifugal pump mounted in front of the radiator. This pump was connected to a water tank behind the driver's seat. Ahrens-Fox demonstrated one of these booster cars at the IAFE Convention held in New York, and 10 were delivered to the Cincinnati Fire Dept.

Eleven makes of motor pumpers were put through a 12-hour test at the IAFE Conference on Sept. 13. These included models built by American LaFrance (700 and 1,000 GPM rotary gear types); Seagrave's 1,000 GPM centrifugal; a 600 GPM Luitweiler piston pumper; a 600 GPM Knox piston; 600 and 800 GPM Nott rotaries; an Ahrens-Fox Model A piston pumper; 750 and 900 GPM Robinson piston pumpers, and a 700 GPM Waterous rotary gear engine. In this test the LaFrance Type 15 churned out an impressive 1,402 gallons per minute.

Gas-electric apparatus was becoming increasingly popular. New York City ordered 25 American LaFrance Type 16 gas-electric aerials, and the American & British Mfg. Co. of Providence, R. I., had commenced deliveries of 2-wheel conversion tractors that featured the Hoadley drive system. The Commercial Truck Co. of America of Philadelphia had also begun deliveries of battery-powered fire engines, more than 30 of which were eventually sold to fire departments in the Eastern U. S.

Another very old name in the motor fire apparatus field is the U. S. Fire Apparatus Co. of Wilmington, Del. The U. S. Fire Apparatus Co. built this combination hose and 2-tank chemical car for Wilmington's Water Witch Fire Co. No. 5. In the ad in which this cut appeared, the company offered motor-driven, horse-drawn or hand-pulled fire equipment. The hose body is of ventilated metal mesh construction.

Four years after it was placed into service, the Monhagen Hose Company of Middletown, N. Y. removed the body of its triple combination pumper and remounted it on a new Stearns chassis. This body, which the Monhagens claimed was the first motor-driven triple combination pumper placed in service in the United States, was originally mounted on a 1909 American Mors chassis. Note the bulb horn below the driver's seat.

New Orleans ordered an American LaFrance Type 30 gas-electric bevel gear drive 65-foot water tower, which was equipped with a 105-horsepower, 6-cylinder engine. American LaFrance now offered its own front-drive motor tractor for the conversion of formerly horse-drawn steamers, aerial trucks and water towers. Designated the Type 31, this model would remain in production for another 16 years, and even complete factory-built units were identified as Type 31s. The Elmira, N. Y. firm was also building commercial trucks which featured a hydraulic transmission.

Interesting 1913 deliveries included an Ahrens-Fox steam-electric pumper for Baltimore; a Nott motor pumper for Petaluma, Calif.; a KisselKar City service hook and ladder truck built for Hartford, Wisc.; and Waterous motor pumpers placed in service in Cleveland and St. Paul. The American Locomotive Works of Schenectady, N. Y., delivered a 4-wheel motor tractor which was used to convert a former Albany, N. Y. horse-drawn aerial. It was marketed as the Alco. The Harder Storage & Van Co. of Chicago built 20 combination hose trucks for the Chicago Fire Dept., and the Rochester Motor Fire Pump Co. of Rochester, N. Y., advertised its "Hydramobile" 700 GPM rear-mounted motor pumper. Other makes delivered included the Dixon Cascade and the Martin by the Martin Carriage Works.

A gentleman named George C. Hale built a combination car for Tulsa, Okla. Hale's plant was in Kansas City, Kans. The Hale name is still pre-eminent today in the fire pump industry. The International Motor Co. offered fire equipment mounted on the Mack, Saurer and Hewitt chassis and delivered 35 units to New York this year.

Up to now, the familiar fire bell cleared the way for fire apparatus. But a hand-cranked "Sterling Siren Fire Horn" was introduced as the last word in emergency warning devices. Electric sirens appeared a short time later.

Many fire departments with limited funds, but who had members or friends with a mechanical bent, were able to build their own motor fire engines using new or used passenger car or commercial vehicle chassis. The firemen of Chatham, N. J. built this combination on a 1913 Locomobile auto chassis.

Oakland, Cal. was the owner of this immense Seagrave Gorham Turbine Pumping Engine. The front wheels on this engine, for some reason, are set back further than on most models of this type. Power for the centrifugal pump was provided by a gargantuan six-cylinder engine mounted under the two-section hood. Later Seagrave-Gorhams had hose boxes mounted over the rear-mounted pump.

Washington, D. C. was a big user of early Ahrens-Fox piston pumpers. This is a Continental Model "B" straight pumping engine which was assigned to Engine Co. No. 16 in 1913. The 700 gallon-per-minute pumper carried no hose. The crew rode in the short bench-equipped body. This engine and a similar unit at D. C. Eng. Co. No. 24 always responded to alarms with a hose wagon.

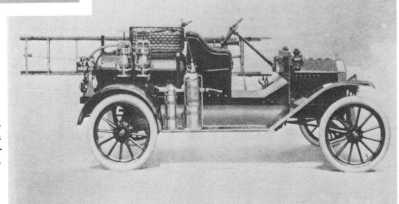

The builder of this 1913 Model "T" Ford two-tank chemical car is not known. This type of apparatus replaced hand-drawn pumpers and hose reels in many smaller communities and made motor-driven fire equipment available to communities that previously could not afford to motorize.

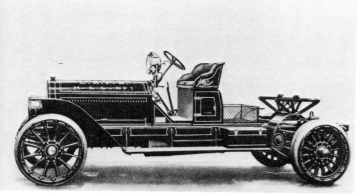

Major fire apparatus builders built many four-wheeled type motor tractors which were used to convert former horse-drawn apparatus. American LaFrance designated this type of tractor the type 17. This particular six-cylinder tractor, rated at 105 horsepower, pulled the Little Rock, Ark. department's aerial assigned to Hook and Ladder Co. No. 1.

This four-cylinder American LaFrance Type 10 Combination Hose and Chemical Car was delivered to Yuma, Ariz. in 1913. It was powered by a four-cylinder engine and had the painted, rather than plated, radiator shell.

Second only in size to the American LaFrance Type 19 was the Type 15 motor pumping engine. This 1913 Type 15 had a one-piece hood. Later models were equipped with two and three-section engine compartment covers. The Type 15 was never noted for its speed—35 miles an hour tops—but it could deliver a steady 1,000 gallons of water per minute and seldom had to travel very far anyway. Purchased only by larger departments, the Type 15 and 19 were generally stationed downtown in the high value areas.

Incredible as it may seem nearly 70 years later, the Wildwood, N. J. Fire Department still owns this 1913 American LaFrance Type 17 aerial. The 65-foot, spring-raised aerial is in almost original condition and is frequently rolled out for parades. The only noticeable change is the substitution of electric lights in place of the carbide lights that were on the truck when it was delivered.

American LaFrance offered this Type 20 two-tank combination chemical engine and hose car. Standard equipment included two 35-gallon chemical tanks, one 20 and one 12-foot ladder, a hand-cranked siren and capacity for 1,000 feet of hose. Carbide lights by now had given way to electric head and spotlights.

This 1913 American LaFrance Combination Hose and Chemical Car was delivered to the City of San Francisco. Note the unusual hose body design and the transverse-mounted chemical hose reel. This speedy apparatus was powered by the new American LaFrance six-cylinder engine. At this time, American LaFrance delivered many rigs with painted radiator shells.

1913

One of American LaFrance's more popular models was the long Type 20-14 City Service Hook and Ladder Truck. This model was powered by a 65-horsepower six-cylinder engine. This ladder truck carries a chemical tank. The chemical hose is carried in the front portion of the wire equipment basket atop the single bank ladder bed.

AMERICAN - LAFRANCE

This 1913 American LaFrance Triple Combination Pumping, Chemical and Hose Engine is owned by Paul Wichman of Sandusky, Ohio. This six-cylinder pumper still has the flat-topped front fenders which were phased out this year. Suction hoses were usually carried in this manner over the rear fenders.

This is the rugged chassis of the American LaFrance Type 20 motor fire apparatus. The 55 horsepower six-cylinder engine and rear drive chains are visible, as are the mounts for the rear step.

Fire apparatus historian Harold S. Walker found this photo of an interesting combination built for the fire department of Lynn, Mass. The chassis is a 1913 Federal truck. The hose wagon body was built and mounted by the O. F. Kress and Sons Co., of Lawrence, Mass. The State of Massachusetts had an inordinate number of small, local fire apparatus builders.

Many larger fire departments continued to use specialized salvage corps, which attempted to minimize losses due to water damage while firefighting operations were being conducted. American LaFrance offered this standard Type 10 Salvage Car, which had a top speed of 60 miles an hour. The crew sat on benches at the rear. Principal equipment carried was tarpaulins and salvage covers which were utilized as quickly as the corpsmen could spread them.

American LaFrance Fire Engine Co. built its last steam pumper this year, but continued to deliver and to take orders for hand engines for another six years. The Elmira, N. Y. fire apparatus manufacturer's Type 12 6-cylinder 800 gallon-per-minute pumper developed 100 horsepower and weighed 8,450 pounds. Boston's Engine Co. No. 10 this year was equipped with an ALF 4-cylinder motor tractor which was attached to the company's steamer.

Seagrave came out with a new 6-cylinder motor pumping engine powered by a T-head engine. The new centrifugal was available in 750 and 1,000 GPM versions. One of the first pumpers of this type was delivered to Saginaw, Mich.

The Cincinnati plant of the Ahrens-Fox Fire Engine Co. was busily turning out the popular Model A Continental piston pumper (the Model B Continental was identical, but carried no hose) and was still assembling steamers for municipalities that continued to order this type of equipment. Up to now, all Ahrens-Fox piston pumpers had been powered by 6-cylinder Herschell-Spillman gasoline engines of 5.75-inch bore and 6.5-inch stroke. Ahrens-Fox by this time had developed its own 6-cylinder engine of T-head design, and in 1914 began installing these in its apparatus.

During the same year, Ahrens-Fox announced an all-new series of piston pumpers designated the Model K. This series sported a completely new hood and body sheet-metal, but its most distinctive feature was a single, spherical-shaped air chamber dome atop the front-mounted pump. This dome was to become an American fire engine legend. This series was powered by a new 4-cylinder engine. The Model K-1 was a straight pumping engine, the Model K-2 a combination pump and hose car and the Model K-3 a triple combination pumper, hose and chemical engine.

The dependable Christie Front-Drive Tractor was used to prolong the service lives of hundreds of former horse-drawn steamers from coast to coast. Chicago's Engine Co. No. 122 used this 1914 Christie attached to a 1912 Ahrens-Fox 700 gallon-per-minute steamer.

This close-up shows the left hand side of a Christie front-drive tractor, a product of the Front Drive Motor Co., of Hoboken, N. J. The 4-cylinder tractor seen here was attached to the former horse-drawn, spring-raised Seagrave aerial ladder truck of Truck 2, in Paterson, N. J. For some reason, this rig carries only one headlight. Engine gauges were considered unnecessary on the utilitarian Christie, as was any kind of protection from the weather.

The Maxim Motor Company of Middleboro, Mass., which is still in business today, built this 1914 chemical and hose combination car on an E. R. Thomas automobile chassis for the Ansonia, Conn. Fire Dept. Notice the bucket seats, chemical tank mounted under the seats and the tool compartment slung below the running board. This Model "F" was one of this company's first motorized fire engines.

Maxim built this handsome combination chemical and hose car for its home town of Middleboro, Mass. This combination uses Maxim's own motor chassis, rather than the Thomas Flyer chassis Maxim started out with when it entered the motor fire apparatus field.

A new name emerged on the scene this year, that of the Maxim Motor Co. Carlton W. Maxim, of Middleboro, Mass., headed a firm which had been in business since 1888. Unimpressed with the apparatus of the day, Mr. Maxim designed and built a hose car for the local fire department. Designated a Model N, it was mounted on an E. R. Thomas "Flyer" passenger car chassis, and delivered faithful service for many years. Maxim's first fire engine cost the community $2,500. This company, of course, is still in business today in Middleboro.

C. J. Cross had established his own company, the C. J. Cross Front-Drive Tractor Co. in Newark, N. J., and was competing with his former employer, the Front Drive Motor Co. of Hoboken. John Walter Christie's firm had a sizable jump on Cross' venture, but both companies did a brisk business in converting former horse-drawn fire equipment to motor power.

The Hale Motor Pump Co. of Wayne, Pa. delivered a pumping engine to the local fire department this year. Built on a Simplex chassis, it was equipped with a 500 GPM rotary gear pump. This apparatus rendered yeoman service at the Wayne Opera House fire in December of this year.

The W. S. Nott Co. of Minneapolis, introduced a radically streamlined new style of pumper this year. Carrying the familiar "Nott Universal" name, it featured worm drive and was rated at 1,000 GPM. Only a few were sold. Among the first were deliveries to Victoria, B. C., Canada and Battle Creek, Mich.

New firms coming on the scene included the South Bend Motor Car Works of South Bend, Ind. and the E. R. Thomas Co., a well-established motor car maker that offered a special fire apparatus chassis to various builders. The Davis Sewing Machine Co. of Dayton, O., announced the "Dayton Tricar" motorcycle chemical car, which was designed to handle minor fires in congested areas or in rural areas.

American LaFrance introduced a new Type 25 aerial ladder truck, which used a new deep-section radiator and conventional style hood between the driver's and officer's seats. The Type 25, in 65 to 85-foot lengths, was a pure gasoline-powered design, unlike the earlier Type 16 gasoline/electric hybrid. This was a forerunner to the popular Type 31 front-drive aerial.

The American and British Manufacturing Co., of Providence, R. I., delivered many front-wheel-drive tractor conversions to fire departments in the eastern U. S. The A & B tractor was similar in appearance to the Type 31 front-drive tractor sold by American LaFrance, but the A & B was a hybrid: the gasoline engine supplied power for independent electric drive motors mounted in each front wheel. The A & B tractor shown here responded as Engine 5 in Lynn, Mass., and is attached to a 900 gallon-per-minute Metropolitan steamer.

One of the oddest contrivances ever to find its way into actual fire department service was the 3-wheeled Knox-Martin tractor, which was designed for converting former horse-drawn equipment to motor power. The 1914 Knox-Martin tractor shown here was purchased by Beverly, Mass., and is drawing a 1903 O. F. Kress Co. hook and ladder truck. The steering gear of the Knox-Martin extended out over the hood to a gearbox above the single front wheel.

Besides American LaFrance, one of Christie's other competitors was the O. J. Cross Front Drive Tractor Co. of Newark, N. J. Cross built this 1914 motor tractor for the New York City Fire Department. Where Christie used a transverse-mounted engine, the engine in the Cross tractor was mounted in the conventional manner.

The Anderson Coupling and Fire Supply Co. of Kansas City, Kan. Built some motor fire apparatus. One of the units produced by this lesser-known firm was the combination hose and chemical car shown here. This single-tank model rides on pneumatic tires at a time when most fire departments specified hard-riding—but puncture-proof—solid tires.

The water tower was a specialized piece of equipment designed to put heavy streams of water into the upper floors of burning buildings. Every large metropolitan fire department had at least one of these towers. This 1914 American LaFrance Type 30 Water Tower, delivered to the New Orleans Fire Dept., was powered by a 105-horsepower six-cylinder engine and was of the two-wheel, bevel-gear drive type. It had a 65-foot telescopic mast. Standard equipment on most water towers included a stationary turret nozzle mounted on the truck's deck, in addition to the powerful tower nozzle.

The largest and most powerful motor pumper in the American LaFrance line was the Type 15, which was rated at a whopping 1,400 gallons per minute. Under that triple-segmented hood lay a 200-horsepower, six-cylinder engine. The Type 15 had a 172-inch wheelbase. Although this model is equipped with a piston-type pump, American LaFrance offered all three principal pump designs—piston, rotary gear and centrifugal. The massive Type 15 had a top speed of only 35 miles an hour. Relatively few were built. The slightly smaller Type 15 could deliver 1,000 gallons per minute and had a two-section hood.

Although American LaFrance offered its new Type 31 Front-Drive Tractor for conversion of former horse-drawn apparatus, fire departments could still buy new steamers powered by gasoline-powered motor tractors. This Type 31 Front-Drive Tractor, powered by a 75-horsepower four-cylinder engine, is attached to an American LaFrance Second Size Steam Fire Engine. This apparatus, which had a top speed of only 25 miles per hour, was delivered to Pittsburgh, Pa. American LaFrance, however, built its last steamers this year.

The Fire Insurance Patrol of the Memphis, Tenn. Fire Department operated this 1914 American LaFrance Type 40 Salvage Car. The four-cylinder apparatus carries a short attic ladder in addition to its full complement of salvage covers. American LaFrance motor fire apparatus of this period bore the ALF badge at the top of the painted radiator shell.

Conneaut, Ohio's 1914 American LaFrance 600 gallon-per-minute pumper, just in from the Elmira, N. Y. factory, is seen here undergoing its acceptance test. Even today it is standard practice for the pump operator to open the hood for additional cooling while the engine is pumping. This is a six-cylinder pumper.

1914

The first straight-frame aerial ladder truck offered by American LaFrance was this gasoline-electric model. A four-cylinder, 75-horsepower gasoline engine generated electric power which was delivered to the wheels. This 85-footer is finished in white and has a tiller to help get its great length around city corners. American LaFrance also offered water towers in this dual-mode configuration.

This was the second American LaFrance Type 31 motor tractor to be used for the conversion of a former horse-drawn steamer. It went into service at Boston's Engine Co. No. 10 in August, 1914. A few weeks earlier, the first of this type of tractor was used to convert Engine 37's steam pumper in the Roxbury district. Notice how high the driver sat above the ground.

This 1914 American LaFrance 750 gallon-per-minute Type 12 pumping engine was on the equipment roster of the Lindsey, Cal. Fire Dept. Notice the solid rubber tires and the squirrel-tail hard suction hose draped around the front end. This practice saved considerable time when hooking the pumper up to its water supply.

The Fresno, Cal. Fire Dept. was the original purchaser of this 1914 American LaFrance 85-foot Type 18 aerial ladder truck, which was later sold to the Salinas, Cal. Fire Dept. The driver's and officer's seats straddled the engine compartment. The aerial ladder was spring-raised, ground ladders were carried in a single bank, and the life net was carried on the running board.

This juggernaut is a 1914 American LaFrance Type 21 six-cylinder motor tractor attached to an American LaFrance "Second Size" Metropolitan Steamer. This large capacity pumper was on the San Francisco Fire Dept. for many years. Note the two varying lengths of hard suction hose.

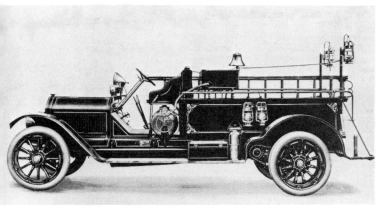

This was the standard American LaFrance Type 10 Combination Chemical and Hose Car. A direct holdover from the horse-drawn era, the Chemical-Hose combination accompanied the pumper to the fire. But the Triple Combination Pumper, which carried on one chassis the pump, hose and chemical or booster system, was gaining in popularity as it could replace three specialized pieces of apparatus.

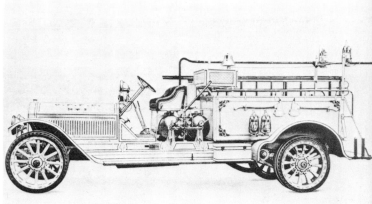

American LaFrance offered this special Combination Chemical Engine and Hose Car, which was powered by the company's 105-horsepower six-cylinder engine. This white-painted rig is equipped with two 35-gallon chemical tanks, has a 1,500-foot capacity hosebed, and has a pompier, or scaling ladder, mounted overhead.

The Hale Motor Co. of Wayne, Pa., predecessor of the Hale Fire Pump Co. of Conshohocken, Pa., a current major fire apparatus pump manufacturer, built this 500 gallon-per-minute pumper on a 1914 Simplex chassis for Wayne, Pa. It was used at the Opera House fire in Wayne on Dec. 14 of that year and delivered a heroic performance. Hale later concentrated on building pumps only.

The Martin Cartage Works of York, Pa. built this straight hose wagon for the Vigilant Fire Company No. 1 in its own home town. It was designated a "Standard Type A Hose Wagon."

The Victoria, B. C. Fire Department placed this strikingly streamlined Nott Universal into service in 1914. The prominent V-shaped radiator shell has a hint of Mercedes in it. Contrast the sleek appearance of this apparatus with the jumbled, utilitarian look of other fire apparatus being built at this time.

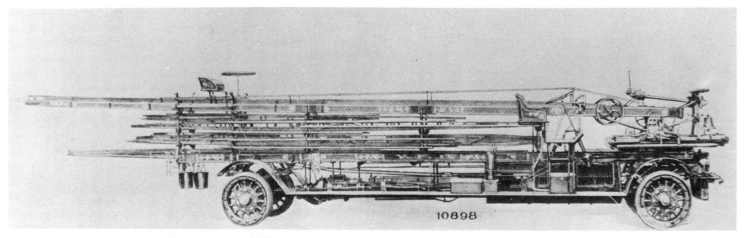

Seagrave also marketed a straight-frame aerial ladder truck in addition to its conventional tractor-drawn types. This 1914 Seagrave 85-foot aerial was built for Youngstown, Ohio. Instead of sitting up front, the driver sat sidesaddle well back on the right-hand side of the rig. How he ever saw where he was going is anybody's guess.

Seagrave's big Gorham Turbine pumper was still in production, but combination pumping and hose engines were outselling the single-purpose straight pumping engine design. This 1914 model is equipped with a front bumper and rear handrail.

The Chicago Fire Department was another big Seagrave customer. This 1914 Seagrave 1,000 gallon-per-minute motor pumping engine was assigned to Engine Co. No. 53. Chicago was one of the first American cities to equip its fire apparatus with windshields. The front-mounted bell tower was to become a Chicago Fire. Dept. trademark.

The Seagrave Company in 1900 established a Canadian subsidiary, the W. E. Seagrave Fire Apparatus Co. in Walkerville, Ontario, in what is now part of Windsor. The first motor pumping engine purchased by the Windsor Fire Dept. was this big 750 gallon 1914 W. E. Seagrave Model WC-144 Gorham Turbine, with a large hose box mounted over the pump. Nicknamed "Old Mike", this pumper saw many years of front line and reserve service before it was scrapped in 1947.

Grand Rapids, Mich. placed this Seagrave-Couple Gear 85-foot electric aerial ladder truck into service in 1914. The electric drive system, built by the Couple Gear Freight Wheel Co. of Grand Rapids, utilized electric motors in each wheel hub. Electrical power was generated through a gasoline engine mounted amidships. These electric-drive units were notoriously slow, however, and it was not uncommon for boys on bicycles to beat them to fires. Notice how far forward the driver sat. This truck was junked in 1937.

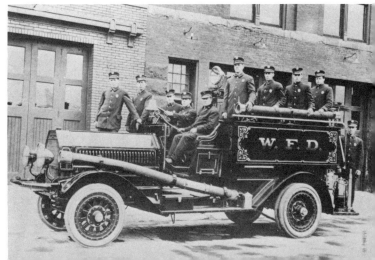

1915

This was to be the last year that Ahrens-Fox would build its double-domed Continental piston pumper series. One of the last of this model was this 750 gallon-per-minute pumper which was delivered to Winchester, Mass. The full-sized hose box would indicate that this was a Continental Model A Combination Pump and Hose Car.

This was the "new look" of the Ahrens-Fox. A single spherical-shaped air chamber replaced the two domes previously used. These were to be a distinctive feature of all Ahrens-Fox piston pumpers built, until this great series went out of production some 37 years later in 1952. Notice the single suction intake at the front of the pump. Later models sported two intakes combined into a "Y" design.

The Ahrens-Fox Fire Engine Co. of Cincinnati introduced its small K Series combination cars in 1915. This Model K-11 Combination Booster and Hose Car was built for Chicago Heights, Ill. Ahrens-Fox had invented the booster system, which consisted of a small pump and self-contained water supply a few years earlier. Later copied by all other manufacturers, the booster system would soon make the soda-acid chemical system obsolete.

Ahrens-Fox phased out its Continental twin-dome piston pumpers this year, ending a production run that saw 46 engines of this type come off the assembly floor in the Colerain Ave. plant in Cincinnati. Oddly enough, the last of this series—Ser. No. 555—wasn't a fire engine at all; it was a stationary pumping plant supplied to the Delco Co. in Dayton, Ohio. Ahrens-Fox introduced several new types of apparatus this year. One of these was the big Model L, which had a 6-piston, 1,200 GPM pump. The company's most prolific model in this era was the Model K, which first appeared the previous year. This series, and the L, featured a single, ball-shaped air chamber atop a front-mounted pump. Ahrens-Fox's multiple piston pump chalked up its third consecutive perfect score at the IAFE Convention that year in New York.

Despite the popularity of its motor pumpers, Ahrens-Fox continued to build steamers for communities that had a preference for this type of fire engine. The company in 1915 delivered a Continental Steamer to the Detroit suburb of Hamtramck, Mich. This pumper was built on a Peerless auto chassis, rode on Sewell Solid Cushion Tires, and weighed 12,556 pounds. Ahrens-Fox also delivered some small combination hose and chemical cars with 4-cylinder engines that bore K-11 and GN-10-4 type numbers. Ahrens-Fox delivered six Model MK-2 piston pumpers of 750 GPM capacity to New York this year, and two more of this type the following year. The popular K Model piston pumper had a 750 GPM pump and a 4-cylinder engine.

The Maxim Motor Co. delivered its first motor pumping engine to the Hamden, Conn. Fire Dept. Like the combination car this company sold the previous year, the Hamden job was built on a Thomas Flyer chassis and had a 500 GPM rotary gear pump.

American LaFrance introduced a new, smaller series of rotary gear pumper known as the Type 40. Also advertised as the Junior pumper, it was sold in 250 and 350 gallon-per-minute variants. It was powered by the American LaFrance 4-cylinder engine.

The Couple Gear Freight Wheel Co. of Grand Rapids, Mich., was supplying electric drive chassis components to

Some fire engines underwent some dramatic transformations during their long service lives. Consider this 1915 Ahrens-Fox, which began life as a Continental Model A twin-dome piston pumper, the first motorized pumper used in Milwaukee. Register No. 546 was converted to a special utility unit in 1938. The device on the running board is a water-powered smoke ejector.

1915

many fire engine builders, including Seagrave and Ahrens-Fox. Seagrave offered a Couple Gear battery-powered aerial ladder truck, and one of these had been built for Grand Rapids the previous year. Grand Rapids also motorized several steamers and city service ladder trucks with Couple Gear electric drives.

New York City commissioned its first combination motor pumper and hose wagon this year, with an apparatus built by the W. S. Nott Co. Accelerating its massive motorization program, New York ordered 50 pieces of motor fire apparatus this year at a cost of $173,800. By the end of the year, the conversion program had reached the halfway point.

Mack Trucks began production of its famed Model AC Bulldog truck this year, a pugnacious commercial vehicle face that would soon become familiar to firefighters everywhere. This was one of the first trucks to feature left-hand drive.

Other firms that built fire apparatus this year included the Dart Motor Truck Co. of Waterloo, Ia., and the Service Motor Truck Co. of Wabash, Ind. The Victor Motor Car Co. of Buffalo, N. Y. also supplied a number of fire apparatus chassis. The Duplex Truck Co. of Lansing, Mich. was another truck builder that sold a few chassis to fire engine builders. Yet another all but forgotten fire engine maker was the little known Thomas Automatic Fire Engine Co. of Columbus, Ohio, which offered a 750 GPM pumper.

The innovative Seagrave Co. this year announced the industry's first self-contained auxiliary cooling system. The Seagrave auxiliary cooler permitted the engine to run cool at a constant temperature, even during long pumping stints.

The Waterous Engine Works of St. Paul, Minn. continued to build some motor fire apparatus. This auto pumping engine, with hard suctions carried over the front fenders, was sold to Southampton, Pa. in 1915. Waterous later specialized in pump manufacture and is a principal supplier of high-quality fire apparatus pumps today.

Seagrave by now was building a highly-popular line of motor pumpers. The AC "buckboard" series by now had been succeeded by this more conventional model. This is a six-cylinder, 750 gallon-per-minute combination pumping engine and hose truck. Note the soft "steamer" suction hose rolled up on the running board. This pumper carried Seagrave Serial No. 12841.

Fortunately for antique fire apparatus buffs, some real old-timers have eluded the cutter's torch and the scrap heap, and appear today much as they did when new. This 1915 Seagrave 1,000 gallon per minute pumper, owned by Bill Foster of Groesbeck, Ohio, is a good example. Bearing Columbus Serial No. 14441, this triple combination was originally owned by Champaign, Ill.

Seagrave's counterpart to the American LaFrance Type 31 aerial was the Model K, which employed basically the same front-drive layout. Where the American LaFrance four or six-cylinder engine was under the tractor floorboards, on the Seagrave K Model the six-cylinder engine was mounted between the seats. The aerial shown here is an 85-foot model. The K was also available in 65 and 75-foot sizes, and with a four-cylinder engine.

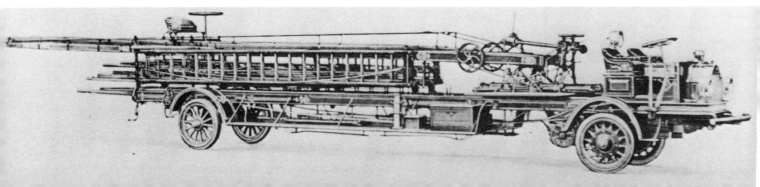

The Los Angeles Fire Department converted its 1906 horse-drawn 65-foot Gorter Water Tower to gasoline power with the addition of a six-cylinder Type 31 American LaFrance tractor in 1915. This monster is still on the L. A. Fire Dept. roster today, although it is used only for parade and demonstration purposes. The tower is water-raised, and there is a second Gorter turret mounted on the truck's deck.

American LaFrance met the needs of smaller communities by mounting its apparatus on various commercial chassis, rather than its own custom-built chassis. Most of these were on the Model T Ford, but this combination hose and chemical car, delivered to Colusa, Calif. was built on a 1915 Brockway chassis. In later years the American LaFrance-Brockway was to become a popular medium-duty firefighting combination.

American LaFrance by this time was building a complete line of piston, centrifugal and rotary gear pumpers in double and triple combinations. This is a 1915 American LaFrance Type 75 double combination pumping engine and hose car of 750 gallon-per-minute capacity. It was powered by the proven ALF six-cylinder, 105-horsepower fire apparatus engine. The corrugated hard suctions are draped over the rear fender.

This is a six-cylinder American LaFrance 1915 Type 31 tractor attached to a 1906 Nott Steamer. This fully-operable firefighting veteran is presently owned by the Exempts of Freeport, Long Island, N. Y. and is a parade favorite in the area.

The powerful American LaFrance Type 31 front-drive tractor was the salvation of metropolitan fire departments caught in the revolutionary transition from horse to motor power. The Pittsburgh Bureau of Fire purchased this 6-cylinder Type 31 tractor and attached it to the former "Second Size" American LaFrance steamer of Engine Co. No. 47. The maltese-cross ALF emblem visible at the top of the radiator shell was used on apparatus built by Elmira in 1915 and 1916.

With large investments in still-serviceable horse-drawn fire equipment, many municipalities continued to prolong the service life of these units by replacing the horses with two and four-wheel motor tractors. It was quickly discovered that despite the higher initial investment, the upkeep of a motor truck in the long run was cheaper than keeping horses. This 1915 White motor tractor was placed under the former horse-drawn hook and ladder truck of Hook & Ladder Co. No. 28 in Chicago.

Exactly 10 years had passed since the first motor-driven piece of fire apparatus had been placed in service in the United States. By 1916, even though hundreds of them were still in use by fire departments across the nation, the steam fire engine had come to the end of the line. Steamers could still be ordered from a handful of manufacturers, but these were invariably mounted on motor truck chassis. As a favor to good customers, some fire apparatus builders even rebuilt and modernized steam equipment.

The Front Drive Motor Co., of Hoboken, N. J., and the C. J. Cross Front Drive Tractor Co. in Newark were doing a brisk business converting former horse-drawn steamers and ladder trucks to gasoline power. Christie and Cross front-drive tractors could be found in most of the larger cities across the country. The Christie, with its transverse engine and breadbox-shaped hood, was by far the most popular. American LaFrance offered its own front-drive tractor. The company's Type 31 tractor was powered by a 75-horsepower, 4-cylinder engine and boasted a "rocking trunnion", to prevent twisting of the frame as the heavy steamer rumbled over unevenly-paved streets. The Seagrave Corp. also built a heavy 2-wheel-drive conversion tractor designed to convert steamers, aerials and ladder trucks from horse draft to gasoline power. Seagrave's massive Model K tractor had a forward-projecting 6-cylinder engine mounted between the driver's and officer's seats.

Some five years after the introduction of its first motor piston pumper, the Ahrens-Fox Fire Engine Co. in 1916 delivered an Ahrens-Fox 1,300 GPM Continental steamer mounted on a White Motor Co. truck chassis to the American Fire Company of Lansford, Pa. This engine is still owned by the company today, cost $8,700 new and bears Serial No. 205. Ahrens-Fox built at least one front-drive steamer tractor conversion, and a small number of Couple Gear steam-electrics.

Also in 1916, Ahrens-Fox built its first aerial ladder truck on a special order basis for Chief E. F. Dahill, of New Bedford, Mass. Chief Dahill was a good friend of Charles H. Fox, and had designed an aerial ladder hoist operated by compressed air. A small compressor ran off the transmission to lift the main ladder off the bed. The fly ladder was extended by hand. The special Ahrens-Fox aerial was a straight frame model built on the Couple Gear electric drive chassis. It had an 85-foot wood aerial ladder built by Pirsch. Ahrens-Fox did not begin to build aerials until 1923, but employed the Dahill Air Hoist.

American LaFrance added a centrifugal pumper to its line, and demonstrated it at the IAFE Convention held this year in Providence, R. I. The first of these was delivered to Troy, N. Y. on December 6, 1916. The Elmira plant had also started building piston pumpers and thus became the only manufacturer to offer fire chiefs a choice between all three principal types of pumps. Rotary gear models far outsold the others.

The Seagrave Corp. took aim at its biggest competitor, and accused the Elmira company of finally admitting the superiority of the centrifugal pump, which Seagrave had used exclusively since 1912.

Peter Pirsch & Sons Co., of Kenosha, Wis. delivered its first pumper in 1916 to Creston, Iowa. Mounted on a White Motor Co. chassis, it had a 500 gallon-per-minute Rumsey pump.

The Maxim Motor Company, of Middleboro, Mass., built its first motor pumper on its own chassis this year. It also had a Rumsey pump. The milestone Maxim featured worm drive, pneumatic tires and a 6-cylinder engine with triple ignition.

Pirsch, which was supplying ladders and chemical equipment to other fire apparatus builders, including Ahrens-Fox, delivered a Couple Gear Electric aerial ladder truck to Decatur, Ill.

Other manufacturers continuing to advertise in fire service trade journals included Hale, South Bend, Boyd, Luverne, Brockway, the Duplex Power Car Co. of Charlotte, Mich., and the Commercial Truck Co. of America.

Some more resourceful fire departments saved their taxpayers money by designing and building their own fire apparatus, utilizing parts available from automotive components manufacturers. The Grand Rapids, Mich. Motor Shops built this sturdy-looking hose wagon from scratch. It was powered by a Wisconsin four-cylinder engine and went into service as Engine No. 4's hose wagon.

Another very popular fire apparatus chassis was manufactured by the well-established White Motor Co. of Cleveland, Ohio. White marketed its own motor fire apparatus for a time, and many builders mounted fire equipment on the White chassis with its distinctive radiator shape which had persisted since the days of the White Steamer. This 1916 White Squad Car was used by Squad Co. No. 3 in Chicago.

This rather unique fire engine responded as Engine No. 9 on the Schenectady, N. Y. Fire Dept. It consisted of a 1909 Westinghouse gasoline motor pump mounted on a 1916 Mack AB truck chassis. A number of these gasoline-powered pumps were used in the early years of this century, but they relied on Old Dobbin for their motive power.

This businesslike snout was soon to become very familiar to firemen all over the United States. The rugged Mack Model AC was also giving a good account of itself overseas as the Great War of 1914-1918 raged on. This combination hose and chemical rig was delivered to Lakewood, N. J. Note the "Baltimore basket" over the hose body.

Chicago over the years purchased very few American La France pumpers, relying instead on a large fleet of Seagraves, Ahrens-Foxes, and Macks. This is one of two 1916 Type 12 pumpers, rated at 750 gallons-per-minute, delivered to the city.

The rugged Mack truck had already acquired an enviable reputation for durability, and was ideal for fire department service. James Boyd and Bro., Inc. of Philadelphia mounted this hose wagon body on a 1916 Mack AB chassis for the Chicago Fire Dept. This hose wagon, with windshield and front-mounted bell, was assigned to Engine Co. No. 122.

The Buffalo, N. Y. Fire Dept. Repair Shops did a credible job of "streamlining" their old Water Tower in later years. The tower was a 65-foot Hale which went into service in 1889. The American LaFrance Type 31 six-cylinder tractor replaced the horses in 1916, but the modern fenders and skirt were added sometime in the 1930's. Notice the siren mounted atop the bell on the rig's cowl.

Milwaukee, Wis. purchased only a few American LaFrance fire engines over the years. In 1916, the Milwaukee Fire Dept. placed three 750 gallon-per-minute American LaFrance rotary gear pumpers in service. The one shown here was assigned to Engine Co. No. 26. Note the old style carriage lamps mounted on the dash.

The Type 14 City Service Hook and Ladder Truck was one of the more popular standard models built by American La France. This Type 14, with chemical equipment and a gong in place of the usual locomotive bell, was delivered to Tacoma, Wash.

Bay City, Mich. ordered this huge American LaFrance Type 19 pumper in 1916. A triple combination carrying a 1,000 gallon-per-minute pump, a soda-acid chemical tank and a full load of hose, it was equipped with a dome-topped piston pump, rode on solid tires and had the two-piece hood.

The American LaFrance Type 31 Front Drive Aerial Ladder Truck could be found in almost every major city in the United States by this time. This 75-footer was delivered to Jersey City, N. J. and ran as Hook & Ladder Co. No. 7. Jersey City used white apparatus with red wheels. This spring-raised aerial was powered by a 105-horsepower, six-cylinder engine. Bumpers and full fenders were not yet considered necessary.

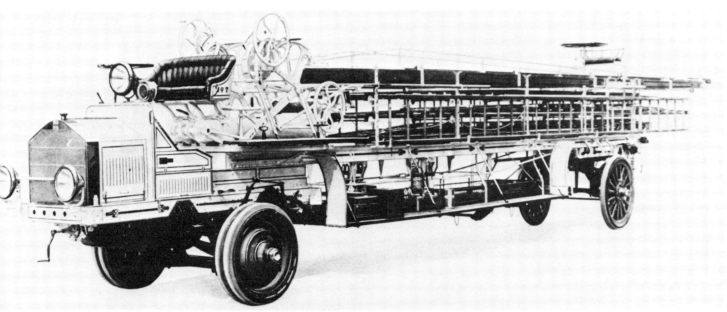

Seagrave's standard city service ladder truck was of this style. This is a 1916 Model "E" Hook & Ladder Truck with factory-installed windshield, built for St. Paul, Minn. It carried no chemical equipment.

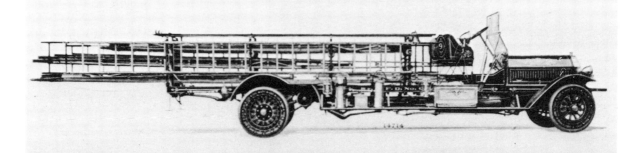

For larger fire departments, the Seagrave Co. offered a larger city service ladder truck equipped with a rear tiller. This 1916 Model "J" City Service Hook and Ladder Truck with rear steer was delivered to Chicago.

Seagrave's mainstay was now the motor pumper. This is a 1916 Seagrave 1,000 gallon-per-minute motor pump and hose car, Ser. No. 15622, which was believed to have been built for the city of Davenport, Iowa. Seagrave usually mounted suction hoses one to a side, with ground ladders above.

The Seagrave Co. also marketed a two-wheel, front-drive motor tractor, but this type was not nearly as popular as the Christie or the American LaFrance Type 31. The Seagrave tractor was sold as the Model "K" and was used to convert former horse-drawn steamers, aerial ladder trucks and water towers to gas power. This "K" tractor appears to be attached to an Ahrens or American LaFrance steamer.

Not all Seagrave pumping engines were monsters. This attractive little four-cylinder combination pumping engine and hose car was the forerunner to the small Suburbanite series the Columbus, Ohio manufacturer was to introduce in the mid-1920's. These small pumpers could be ordered with pumping capacities ranging between 300 and 375 gallons per minute. This 300 GPM job was built for Cheraw, S. C.

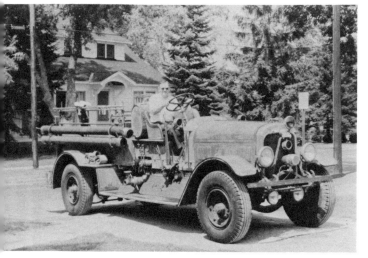

As a result of an accident or some other mishap, fire engine manufacturers were sometimes called upon to rebuild or modernize older apparatus. A good example is this 1916 Seagrave 750 gallon pumper. This rig was rebuilt in 1931, and although it is fitted with the later style radiator, hood and cowl, it retains the older style fuel tank behind the driver's seat, and the chain-drive rear fenders. It was owned by Geneva, N. Y.

Seagrave was a familiar nameplate on the Chicago Fire Dept. This is a 1916 Seagrave 750 gallon-per-minute motor pumping engine that responded as Engine Co. No. 6. Note the Sewell Solid Cushion tires.

The extended shift from horses to motor-driven fire apparatus resulted in some interesting combinations. This is a 1916 James Boyd & Bro. auto tractor which has been bolted to a former horse-drawn 1906 American LaFrance aerial ladder truck. This rig ran as Truck No. 13 on the Pittsburgh, Pa. Bureau of Fire.

Peter Pirsch & Sons Co., of Kenosha, Wis. built its first triple combination motor pumper in 1916. Shown here, it was constructed on the sturdy White truck chassis and fitted with a Rumsey 500 gallon-per-minute pump. It was sold to Creston, Iowa. Pirsch, of course, had built many combination hose and chemical cars and supplied components like chemical apparatus, ladders and other items to other fire engine builders.

New Bedford, Mass. had one of the most innovative fire departments to be found anywhere. This hybrid aerial ladder was built to exacting New Bedford specifications. It is a 1916 Pirsch-Couple Gear battery-powered model, with a Pirsch 75-foot aerial ladder which was raised by a Dahill air hoist. The Dahill hoist was invented by a Chief Engineer of the New Bedford Fire Dept., and was widely used. Battery-powered rigs like these sometimes had to be towed back to the station where their batteries ran down on a long run.

The driver sat well back on this heavy combination hose and chemical car, which was built by Peter Pirsch & Sons. The chassis builder is not known for sure, but the wheel configuration could be by Couple Gear. A gasoline engine is mounted under the hood that protrudes through the cab.

This big Robinson two-wheel, front-drive motor tractor was fitted to the 85-foot American LaFrance wood aerial, a former horse-drawn unit, of Ladder Co. No. 14 in Boston. The Boston Fire Dept. was now engaged in a continuing program of replacement of all horse-drawn apparatus.

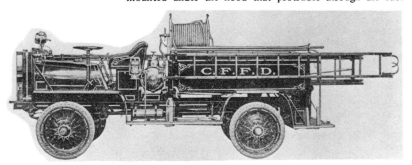

This was one of three 750 gallon-per-minute Ahrens-Fox Model M-2 piston pumpers delivered to the Chicago Fire Department in 1916. Note the louvreless hood, equipment basket mounted over the hose bed and chain drive. This unit ran as Engine Co. No. 45.

Edgewater, N. J. received this Ahrens-Fox Model "K" piston pumper, of 750 gallon-per-minute pumping capacity, in 1916. After many years of front-line service it went into the reserves, filling in for front-line equipment when the newer rigs were in for repair or maintenance. The preconnected hard suction hose saved precious minutes when the engine was being hooked up at fire.

Springfield, Ohio received this Ahrens-Fox Model MK-2 in May, 1916. Notice the single suction intake at the front of the pump. The windshield on this white-painted pumper appears to have been made up locally. The MK series was rated at 750 gallons-per-minute.

Among the largest piston pumpers built by Ahrens-Fox was the 1,200 gallon-per-minute Model "L", the first of which had been built in 1915. This big Model L-2 was originally built for Bryn Mawr, Pa. and was later acquired by Moonachie, N. J. The series was built through 1918.

Not too much is known about this combination hose and chemical car, which saw service in Valley Falls, R. I. It was built on a 1916 Chase chassis.

International Harvester Co. of Chicago was beginning to carve a niche for itself in the booming motor truck market, and it was inevitable that some of these would find their way into the fire service. The builder is uncertain, but this 1916 International two-tank chemical and hose car was delivered to the California, Pa. Fire Dept. The sloping hood of this early International was similar to the style used on the Stewart, Kelly-Springfield, and European Renault.

The First World War was raging in Europe, and several fire apparatus builders were awarded United States Government contracts for fire equipment for the protection of military bases at home and abroad. Howe Fire Apparatus built 110 combinations on the Model T Ford chassis, and Peter Pirsch & Sons delivered 32 chemical cars mounted on the Dodge Bros. chassis.

The Seagrave Corp. in 1917 delivered its first motor water tower. This was a 65-footer built for St. Paul, Minn. The 6-cylinder, telescopic water tower was built on a straight frame chassis powered by Seagrave's big standard engine, and had a rear mounted mast with the nozzle projecting out of the hood when at rest. This water tower had a single deck turret and separate windshields for the driver and officer. This truck was not disposed of until the early 1970s.

The Four Wheel Drive Auto Co. of Clintonville, Wis., delivered its first motor pumping engine this year to Minneapolis. It utilized a Northern pump. A similar pumper was also delivered to Mountain Iron, Minn. A gifted mehcanic and inventor, Otto Zachow perfected his own 4-wheel drive system and had been building 4-wheel drive vehicles since 1910. The FWD Corp., which eventually purchased The Seagrave Corp., is still in business in Clintonville today. The pug-nosed FWD fire engines quickly acquired a reputation for being able to traverse almost any kind of ground.

Mack Trucks, in 1915, started building its tenacious-looking Model AC chassis. This powerful and exceptionally sturdy 4-cylinder model was already familiar to U.S. servicemen overseas, and many were purchased by the U. S. Army. It was only natural that the bull-nosed AC prove ideal for fire service. City service ladder trucks of this type were delivered to Dover, N. J., and Chicopee, Mass. Mack also offered a special "fire department wrecker" built on the rugged AC chassis. This was the truck that gave rise to the popular expression—"Built Like a Mack".

In other developments, the Hale Pump Co. moved to Conshohocken, Pa., where the company still builds fire pumps today, and the Robinson Fire Apparatus Manufacturing Co. of St. Louis, builders of the Robinson Monarch and Jumbo piston pumpers, came out with a new high capacity model. The new Robinson was marketed as the Robinson Greyhound and had an 1,000 GPM Twin Triplex V-type piston pump.

Henry Ford's ubiquitous Model T, which had been in production since 1908, was beginning to find popularity as a rugged, reliable and inexpensive fire engine chassis. Several companies offered standard chemical, hose and combination bodies which could be purchased as units and locally mounted on a Model T chassis, or delivered as a complete unit from the factory.

The Northern Pump Co. of Minneapolis offered motor pumpers and combination apparatus on a wide range of chassis, including Packard, Ford, and FWD. Other builders inlcuded the H. J. Koehler Motors Corp. of Newark, N. J., and the O. J. Childs Co. of Utica, N. Y.

The Front Drive Auto Co. had reached its zenith, with New York City alone operating a fleet of 153 Christie front-drive tractors. More than 600 Christie conversion tractors were eventually sold before the company closed its doors sometime after the First World War.

In one of the more spectacular tests of the year, an Ahrens-Fox piston pumper threw a respectable hose stream 796 feet above street level from the top of the Woolworth Tower in New York on July 1. The New York Fire Dept. also placed in service 10 pieces of apparatus built by the South Bend Motor Car Works of South Bend, Ind. These included seven hose wagons and three South Bend "Scout" chemical-hose combinations.

Peter Pirsch & Sons built this interesting little hose and chemical combination on a 1917 Nash truck chassis. This well-preserved old rig is brought out on special occasions in Glendale, Ariz.

Peter Pirsch & Sons Co. of Kenosha, Wis. built this big hook and ladder truck on a Duplex truck chassis for the Holland, Mich. Fire Dept. This single-bank ladder truck has a tiller for getting it around tight corners and in and out of the firehouse.

Atlantic City, N. J. ran 2-piece engine companies for many years. For some time, this 4-cylinder 1917 American La-France combination hose and chemical car ran as Engine Co. 6's hose wagon. The single chemical tank is mounted under the seat.

Probably the least-known water tower in the U.S. is this unusual combination, which was "discovered" in 1975 by fire apparatus buff Larry Phillips and water tower historian Bill Hass. It started out as a 65-foot horse-drawn aerial delivered to Fargo, N. D. in 1909. An American LaFrance Type 17 tractor, Reg. No. 2857, replaced the horses in 1917. While fighting a fire in May, 1948, the aerial ladder broke, killing a Fargo firefighter. Three years later the ladder was removed and replaced with a custom-made water tower mast. The only water tower in the state, it was replaced by a new elevating platform in 1964 and is now privately owned.

To meet the needs of smaller communities, American La France also offered a line of smaller triple combination pumpers. This 300 gallon-per-minute Type 40 triple combination had a rotary gear pump, full chemical equipment, a set of wood ground ladders and a four-cylinder engine. It is believed that this pumper was sold to the fire department of Boyne City, Mich. It is seen in its maiden portrait outside the American LaFrance factory in Elmira, N. Y.

The old Hale Water Tower of Memphis, Tenn. underwent several major rebuildings during its long service life. This tower started out as a horse-drawn 1894 Hale 65-footer. In 1917, it was motorized by the addition of an American LaFrance Type 31 front-drive tractor. A "crow's nest" containing a second turret nozzle was added to the top of the main mast. This rig was rebuilt again in the mid-1950s by Peter Pirsch & Sons., and the tractor-drawn apparatus was taken out of service only a couple of years ago. Note the Double Giant solid front tires mounted on cast steel disc wheels.

In addition to supplying Type 31 front-drive tractors for converting former horse-drawn aerials to motor power. American LaFrance by now was building many complete Type 31 spring-raised aerials. These ranged in ladder height from 65 to 85 feet. This four-cylinder, 75-footer was built for the Richmond, Ind. Fire Dept.

Compared with American LaFrance, the Seagrave Corporation did not build many water towers. Seagrave's first motor-driven water tower, in fact, was this 65-footer built for St. Paul, Minnesota in 1917. The big chain-driven tower, with twin windshields and a large deck pipe, was around until the early 1970's.

Seagrave did not build very many of the "sidesaddle" straight-frame aerial ladder trucks. This 75-foot model, with tiller and front-mounted bell, was photographed in Poughkeepsie, N. Y. Oakland, Cal. also had one of these rather odd-looking aerials.

This series of photos shows Derby, Connecticut's 1917 Seagrave 375 gallon-per-minute pumper of the "Storm Engine Company" as it was rebuilt by the manufacturer. The original wood artillery-type wheels with solid tires have been replaced with pneumatics.

American fire apparatus builders exported apparatus to many overseas destinations. This Ahrens-Fox Model K-2, a 750 gallon-per-minute piston pumper with four-cylinder engine, went to far-off Soeraboya in the Dutch East Indies in 1917. It served with distinction there and once pumped for 18 hours continuously at a sugar warehouse fire 12 miles out of the city.

Jon Hartz of Detroit is the proud owner of this 1917 Seagrave 750 gallon-per-minute pumper, which served Manistique for many years. In excellent mechanical condition throughout, it is seen here being readied for a 1974 fire prevention week parade. The author can attest to the muscle power required to steer one of these rigs, and to bring it to a stop.

This is a top view of the Ahrens-Fox piston pumper chassis. The four-cylinder piston pump is mounted at the front of the chassis and takes its power off the front of the four-cylinder engine. The driver sits amidships. To the left of the steering wheel can be seen the transfer case which transmits power via short jackshafts to the drive chains. Ahrens-Fox successfully marketed this design for 40 years.

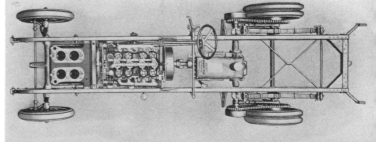

Introduced in 1915, the soon to become famous Mack Model AC "Bulldog" was ideally suited to fire department work. Many U. S. Army-surplus AC's were bought at government auctions following the First World War and had long lives as fire apparatus. This big AC has been equipped with a former horse-drawn Holloway city service hook and ladder body by the Baltimore Fire Dept. Shops. Baltimore apparatus for many years was painted a distinctive white and red with rich striping and trim.

Tulsa, Okla. ran this interesting unit as a rescue squad truck. The chassis appears to be a Nash or Jeffery "quad", many of which were sold as Army surplus following World War I. In fire department red or khaki, this rig looks like it has been around but is ready for more hard work.

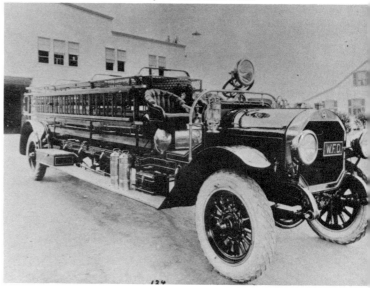

The fire department of Fort Lee, N. J. owned this 1917 Waterous motor pumper, which had a turret nozzle mounted behind its front seat. The wheels were evidently changed from solid to pneumatics later in this vehicle's life.

Not all steamer conversion tractors were of two-wheel, front-drive type. Some departments used four-wheel tractors, or another piece of apparatus to haul still-serviceable steam pumpers to fires. The Grand Rapids, Mich. Fire Dept. motor shops cobbled up this home-built tractor to replace the horses under Steamer No. 4. The front wheels of the steamer have been removed to permit the adaption of a fifth wheel.

The Maxim Motor Company of Middlesboro, Mass. was now building its own fire apparatus chassis. This is a 1917 Maxim single-bank city service hook and ladder truck built for the fire department of Winthrop, Mass. Note the W.F.D. license plate.

Another supplier of conversion motor tractors of the two-wheel, front-drive type was the American and British Manufacturing Co. of Providence, R. I. Here is an A & B auto tractor as retrofitted to someone's former horse-drawn steamer. Although the steamer was still very much in evidence, the motor-driven pumper had already sealed its doom.

One of the most intriguing contraptions ever designed for fire service use went into service with the St. Louis Fire Department in 1918. Ordered the previous year, it was the Iron Mule tractor designed and built by the Coach Wheel Co. of St. Louis. The St. Louis Fire Dept. originally ordered 40 of these one-wheel auto tractors at a cost of $4,500 each, but the other 35 were quickly cancelled when serious problems began to show up with the first five placed in service.

The Iron Mule was powered by a 4-cylinder engine mounted parallel to the frame to the right of the driver. The one-wheel tractor replaced the horses and front wheels of former horse-drawn steamers. But the Coach Wheel Co. tractors showed a disturbing tendency to become locked into street car tracks, and were highly unstable when cornering. Their performance was even worse on snow and ice. The Iron Mules saw only a few years of service before being retired. The company sold these tractors through the "One Wheel Truck Co.", but the Coach Wheel Co. was the name most commonly associated with this automotive oddity. The only other type of one-wheel-steered tractor commonly used was the 3-wheeled Knox-Martin tractor which had been marketed earlier.

The New Orleans Fire Department placed a huge order with the White Motor Co. of Cleveland and for no less than 22 motor pumping engines, at a cost of $7,700 each. This order, which almost motorized the New Orleans Fire Dept. overnight, also included three White city service hook and ladder trucks and two White motor hose wagons. White, a well-established name in the passenger car and motor truck business, now marketed a full line of fire apparatus including pumpers, squad cars, hose wagons and combinations.

In one of the most remarkable fire apparatus production programs ever undertaken by any fire engine manufacturer, the Ahrens-Fox Fire Engine Co. this year delivered 15 Model K-4 combination pumping engines and hose cars with booster equipment to the U. S. Government. Finished in military olive drab, the 750 GPM piston pumpers, powered by 4-cylinder engines, were to be delivered within 45 days after receipt of the order. But the Cincinnati plant went that tall order one better and handed over the last unit in a mere 30 days after production began! The contract called for delivery of the pumpers to the U. S. Army Fort of Embarcation at Hoboken, N. J.

Ahrens-Fox did most of its advertising in imaginatively-worded bulletins mailed to fire chiefs everywhere. Charles Fox himself did much of the writing. An ad featuring the government jobs, Ahrens-Fox Bulletin 120 issued Nov. 1, 1918 boasted . . . "Ahrens-Fox in Khaki—Our Battles With Fire Will Be Won".

American LaFrance had introduced a new type of rear-mounted, straight-frame water tower. This was the highly popular Type 31 with 6-cylinder front-drive tractor and a tiller at the rear. The first two of these were delivered to New York City, and another went to Norfolk, Va.

The Maxim Motor Company was incorporated in 1918, with C. W. Maxim as president. The Middleboro, Mass. firm now offered a complete range of motor pumpers, combinations and hook and ladder trucks mounted on its own chassis.

The Davison, Mich. Fire Department still owns this 1918 American LaFrance pumper, which carries Elmira factory registration number 2017. The straight suction hose arrangement is unusual for this vintage and is not likely original. Also added is the Buckeye Roto-Ray warning light. The headlights have been converted to sealed beams and the bell relocated to a position between the headlights.

Bert Jackson of Birmingham, Mich. is the owner of this four-cylinder 1918 American LaFrance pumper. This apparatus has the later style Vesta headlights and an oversize extension ladder on its right-hand side. This pumper carries ALF Register No. 2349.

The Obenchain-Boyer Company of Logansport, Ind. became a major fire equipment builder. Obenchain-Boyer would mount its fire engine bodies on any chassis supplied or ordered by the purchaser. This is a 1918 Model "TT" Ford equipped with a 150 GPM Barton front-mount pump and two tanks. It was sold to Eloise, Mich.

Ahrens-Fox's home city of Cincinnati was a big user of Ahrens-Fox fire apparatus. Here, Engine Co. No. 43's big piston pumper wheels out of the firehouse. At this time, Cincinnati had close to 50 Ahrens-Fox fire engines. The last Ahrens-Foxes were delivered to this city in the late 1940's.

Baltimore was another user of Ahrens-Fox fire apparatus. This Model K-2 piston pumper saw many years of front-line fire fighting action before it became a second line, or reserve, unit. Baltimore modified this pumper to install dual rear tires.

One of the most unique of all Ahrens-Fox piston pumpers built was this one-off Couple Gear gas-electric built to specifications for Gloucester, Mass. It was designated an M-2 Special. The unit was shipped to Grand Rapids, Mich. where the Couple Gear Freight Wheel Co. added the electric drive system. This unusual pumper ultimately proved too slow for service, however, and it was eventually converted to conventional shaft-drive.

Ahrens-Fox sold its apparatus in several basic forms. Customers could buy relatively "stock" apparatus, or could have a unit built to order. Here are two popular Ahrens-Fox piston pumper models of the late 'teens. Above is a straight pump and hose car. Below is a similar unit equipped with Ahrens-Foxe's booster pump system. The booster tank is located over the forward end of the hose box, and the hose reel is visible under the rear step.

This rather ungainly looking rig is a 1918 Duplex chassis equipped with a Pirsch hose and chemical combination body. It was sold to South Haven, Mich. Duplex was located in Lansing and is still in business today as a division of Warner/Swasey.

This is a real Kelly-Springfield, or maybe that should be Springfield-Kelly. The above is a one-ton Kelly truck chassis equipped with a combination hose and chemical body for the fire department of Springfield, Ohio. The apparatus builder was Peter Pirsch.

St. Paul, Minn. was another good Seagrave customer. This is a 1918 Seagrave four-wheel tractor which has been placed under a 1911 Seagrave 85-foot spring-raised aerial ladder trailer, a former horse-drawn rig. This tractor-drawn aerial lasted well into the 1960's.

There was no other information on the above photo, except for the notation that it is a Locomobile combination hose and chemical engine. The lettering on the hood says F.F.F.E., and it is believed that this engine was built for, and photographed in, Fort Fairfield, Maine.

Albany, N. Y. had several Whites in its fire-fighting fleet. This is a 1918 White TDC chassis, equipped with a Northern 600 gallon-per-minute pump and a 1915 Boyd hose wagon body. Note the plated radiator shell.

Denver is another city that has long favored white fire apparatus rather than the traditional red. This 1,000 gallon-per-minute triple combination pumper has six-inch-diameter hard suctions and pneumatic tires. It's a chain-driver.

Another good example of a complete factory rebuild is this modernization of a 1917 Seagrave 750 gallon-per-minute pumper originally built for Tonawanda, N. Y. Above is this pumper as it was delivered. Below, this is how it appeared when it was rebuilt at the Columbus plant in the mid-1920's. Seagrave often provided this service to good customers.

Model "T" Ford fire engines were not limited to villages and small towns. Ford-chassised apparatus could be found in the fire station of some of the larger cities. Proof of this is this Peter Pirsch-equipped hose wagon on a Ford "TT" chassis that ran with Engine Co. No. 82 of the Chicago Fire Dept.

The Ahrens-Fox piston pumper had been accorded wide acceptance. Some fire chiefs would have nothing else in their stations. This 1919 Ahrens-Fox 750 gallon-per-minute Model MK-4 pumper was shipped to the Goodwill Fire Co. No. 1 of Newcastle, Del. on February 25 of that year. Notice the one piece air chamber ball over the pump and Y-type suction inlet.

Ahrens-Fox

Chicago continued to place substantial orders with Ahrens-Fox. This is a 1919 Model IM-2 which was assigned to Engine Co. No. 46. This pumper carried no booster or chemical equipment. Chicago also began buying Mack pumpers this year.

Two important new fire engines were introduced to the American fire service this year. Mack Trucks offered a pumping engine for the first time and the legendary Harry C. Stutz decided to enter the fire apparatus field.

Harry C. Stutz' new company was the Stutz Fire Engine Co., which had its modern plant in Indianapolis. The new company premiered its handsome Stutz Heavy Duty Pumping Car at the 47th Annual Convention of the International Assn. of Fire Engineers held this year in Kansas City, Kans. In an impressive debut, the prototype Stutz pumper passed its 12-hour pumping test at the convention with a perfect score. The Stutz was immediately accepted by the nation's fire chiefs, and the Stutz Fire Engine Co. became a major fire apparatus builder for most of the next decade. Stutz, of course, had established its corporate identity years earlier with the Stutz Bearcat sportster, and would continue to build premium quality automobiles into the 1930s.

Mack had delivered its first pumper, an assembled job equipped with a Gould pump, to Bala Cynwyd, Pa. in 1911. This company, better known as the International Motor Co., in 1919 demonstrated its first production pumping engine. It was built on the rugged Mack Model AC Bulldog chassis, and had a Northern rotary-gear pump. Mack showed its prototype pumper at several chief's conventions this year. Following the "Great War", many Mack AC chassis became available as military surplus, and some were purchased by fire departments. Baltimore acquired a large number of these and equipped them as pumpers, high pressure hose wagons, city service ladder trucks and aerial truck tractors. Some of these saw service into the 1960s.

American LaFrance delivered four rigs to Belize in the British Honduras. These included two Type 10 pumpers, a tractor-drawn city service hook and ladder truck and a chemical engine. The Elmira firm built two basic types of aerial ladder trucks, the straight-frame Type 31 and the tractor-drawn Type 17. Both series were available in 55

Ahrens-Fox gave its fire apparatus a new look this year, with a classically-styled gabled hood which was used through the 1931 model year. This well-known Cincinnati fire apparatus manufacturer also started to offer its piston pumpers with shaft-drive instead of the usual chain-drive. This is an 800 gallon-per-minute Model JM-3 piston pumper. The highly polished chemical tank mounted under the driver's seat makes it a triple combination.

Compare the size of this four-cylinder Ahrens-Fox Model IK-2 with the IM-2. This is a 750 gallon-per-minute four-cylinder job equipped with pneumatic tires rather than solid tires. The driver could literally aim in on the hydrant as he rolled up to the fire, and using the preconnected hard suction hose, be in business in a minute or two. This was one of the advantages of the front-mounted pump.

through 85-foot sizes, powered by 4 or 6-cylinder engines. The company's highly popular straight frame city service ladder truck was the Type 14.

Ahrens-Fox built one of its most unique products this year. It was an electric-powered piston pumper which had been ordered the previous year by Gloucester, Mass. The Ahrens-Fox Fire Engine Co. shipped a Model M-2 chassis to the Couple Gear Freight Wheel Co. of Grand Rapids, Mich., for installation of the electric drive components. This resulted in a very high appearance to accommodate the Couple Gear drive system. The completed apparatus carried factory Serial No. 862, but did not live up to expectations. The pumper proved too slow and heavy for fire department service, and it was converted to conventional gasoline drive.

The Ahrens-Fox Fire Engine Co. in 1919 introduced its handsomely-styled Model J, a 750 GPM model that would remain in production for the next 11 years. The J-Model Fox was powered by the smaller Ahrens-Fox 6-cylinder engine of 4.75-inch bore and 6.5-inch stroke. The first one was delivered to Detroit. The new Model J had a gabled hood and shaft drive.

The Four Wheel Drive Auto Co. displayed a pumper with a Northern pump at the Chicago Automobile Show, and Robinson introduced a new pumper called the Supreme.

This year also saw the end of electric power for fire apparatus. In addition to the gas-electric piston pumper delivered to Gloucester, Mass., the company delivered an 85-foot Couple Gear aerial to Grand Rapids, Mich., and a 75-foot aerial to Taunton, Mass.

The White Motor Company of Cleveland began marketing fire engines on its own this year, rather than just supply chassis to other manufacturers. This is a 1919 White Triple Combination of pump, chemical, and hose. Hundreds of White fire engines were already in service across the United States and Canada.

The White Motor Co. was aggressively marketing its own fire apparatus, but other manufacturers continued to use the rugged White chassis too. This is a small 500 gallon-per-minute pumper assigned to one of Chicago's suburban fire houses. It has a Pirsch-built body mounted on a 1919 White TDC chassis. Note the large gong just below the driver's seat. This suburban pumper was used by Engine Co. No. 117.

Mack Trucks entered the motor pumping engine market this year, even though it had supplied many tractors and fire engine chassis over the previous decade. Mack's first commercially-marketed pumper was this demonstrator, built on a 1919 Mack AC chassis, and equipped with a Northern 500 gallon-per-minute pump. Note the familiar Mack script on the hood and the split bucket seats. Mack quickly became a real contender in a highly competitive field.

The Independent Fire Co. of Long Branch, N. J. once responded to alarms with this sturdy yet handsome-looking 1919 Mack Model AC city service hook and ladder truck. A windshield has been added, and it would appear that the original solid rubber tires have been replaced with pneumatics. This rig carries a single bank of wood ground ladders.

New Orleans placed its second motor-propelled water tower into service in 1919. It was a 65-foot former horse-drawn 1893 Hale which was converted by the addition of a six-cylinder American LaFrance front-drive tractor. This tower was sold to a private collector and has been seen at apparatus musters in the Eastern United States in recent years. The tractor is a Type 31.

Highstown, N. J. operated this 1919 American LaFrance Type 14 City Service Ladder Truck, which was originally owned by the fire department of Red Bank, N. J. It appears original here, except for the large spotlight mounted at the front of the equipment basket.

American LaFrance had not built a steamer in five years, but the Elmira, N. Y. factory continued to overhaul and repair them for its customers, and continued to convert a dwindling number of these "tea kettles" to motor power. This Type 31 six-cylinder front-drive tractor attached to a crane-neck steamer has two real luxuries—a windshield, and full front fenders. The hood is lettered "Whispering Dunes, Pumper No. 1".

Flint, Mich. was the owner of this 1919 American LaFrance Type 12 1,000 gallon-per-minute pumper. The small bell mounted ahead of the radiator is not original equipment.

Providence, R. I. once ran this interesting hybrid. The tractor is a 1919 American LaFrance Type 17, but the trailer is an earlier vintage Seagrave. This was probably once a horse-drawn aerial. A quarter-fold life net is carried on the tractor's running board.

This is what a standard American LaFrance motor pumping engine of the era looked like. Noteworthy features include the oval gasoline tank behind the driver's seat, the hard suction hoses carried over the rear fender and lashed to the running board, and Gray & Davis-style bullet headlights. The rounded rear fenders gave way to flat-topped fenders with step plates in the early 1920's, although these are to be found on modernized or repaired apparatus. This is a 750 GPM pumper, a Type 75.

American LaFrance built hundreds of these little chemical cars on the ubiquitous Model T Ford chassis. This 1919 two-tank model belongs to the Crescent Beach, N. Y. Fire Dept.

A little thing like the mere loss of an aerial ladder didn't keep this old war horse out of action. A 1919 American LaFrance 4-cylinder Type 31 aerial ladder truck, this rig continued to serve as a city service hook and ladder truck after its aerial ladder had been removed. The location is Engine Co. 9's quarters in Atlantic City, N. J. Note the bell mounted forward of the dash.

This small 1919 American LaFrance pumper is still owned by the fire department of Montrose, Mich. A triple combination, it still has its chemical tank, but a bumper has been added. This photo was taken at a regional firemen's meet at Adrian, Mich. in 1973.

The Pittsburgh, Pa. Bureau of Fire had a large fleet of American LaFrance fire apparatus. Engine Co. No. 58 was assigned this 1919 American LaFrance Type 75 pumper, which has had its original headlights replaced. A set of various sized nozzle tips is carried on the small shelf just behind the rear fender.

WATEROUS

Germantown, Ill. used this 1919 Model T Ford fire engine up until 1958, when it was purchased by George Getz, a wealthy antique fire apparatus collector who founded the "Hall of Flame" museum in the mid-1960's. The lengthened Model T appears to be a Howe.

The Waterous Engine Works continued to build motor pumpers in small numbers. This triple combination has one of the new electric siren horns mounted on its dash in place of the usual warning bell.

Another newcomer to the fire engine business this year was none other than the famous Harry C. Stutz. The newly-organized Stutz Fire Engine Co. of Indianapolis showed a promising triple combination pumper at the 1919 convention of the International Assn. of Fire Engineers in Kansas City. Many Stutz pumpers, combinations, and city service ladder trucks were sold over the next seven years.

This was the type of city service ladder equipment that the Maxim Motor Co. was delivering at this time. Maxim fire equipment was popular throughout the New England states and would eventually be sold across the country. All hook and ladder trucks of this era were of the single-bank design, with ladders stacked one atop the other in a single bed.

Mack's present home town, Allentown, Pa. was protected by this 1919 Seagrave 750 GPM pumper powered by a Seagrave six-cylinder engine. The original headlights have been replaced with later sealed-beam units, but this apparatus is otherwise fairly intact. A bell and spotlight were usually mounted on the dash.

Altoona, Pa. owned this single-bank 1919 Seagrave City Service Hook and Ladder Truck. This model carried no chemical equipment and had no tiller. It is a six-cylinder rig. The longest ladder carried is a 55-footer with tormentor poles. Seagrave ladders can be identified by their distinctive deep truss design.

For many years, fire apparatus in Roanoke, Va. was painted a distinctive battleship gray. This 1919 Seagrave 65-foot chain-drive water tower was no exception. The water tower was taken out of service in 1963 and at last report was on exhibition at a park in the city.

1920

The new Stutz Fire Engine Co. got off to a flying start when it received a huge order for 35 pieces of motor fire apparatus from its home city of Indianapolis. This order included seven 750 gallon-per-minute Stutz pumpers, 18 pumpers of 600 GPM capacity and 10 city service hook and ladder trucks. Deliveries of these units extended into the following year, and the Stutz fleet delivered yeoman service for many years. Some of the pumpers were later rebuilt by the Indianapolis Fire Dept. shops and modernized, and saw many more years of faithful service. Other 1920 Stutz deliveries included three trucks for Wichita Falls, Tex., and a 750 GPM pumper delivered to Frankfort, Indiana.

The O. J. Childs Co. of Utica, N. Y., offered a complete range of fire apparatus mounted on any chassis preferred by the purchaser. The company's most popular models were combination hose and chemical cars, but the Childs product line also included small hook and ladder trucks. Popular truck chassis on which Childs mounted its equipment included Reo, Locomobile, Federal, International Harvester, Selden, Master, Mack, Acme, Day-Elder, Ford, Republic, Packard and Oldsmobile.

The Buffalo Fire Extinguishing Mfg. Co. of Buffalo, N. Y. also began to build fire engine bodies for mounting on popular commercial chassis. This company would soon become a major fire apparatus builder, and would remain in business until the late 1940s.

Northern Fire Apparatus Co. of Minneapolis exhibited a 600 gallon-per-minute pumper on a used 1914 Pierce-Arrow "66" chassis. This company delivered a Northern-Packard Triple Combination Pumper to Bridgeport, Conn., and a Nash Quad 375 GPM pumper to Columbia Heights, Minn.

The Ahrens-Fox Fire Engine Co. had adopted the slogan: "Nothing is too good for the fire service, and nothing but the best will do." Although the company was delivering its new J Series pumpers with the new gable hood design and shaft drive, the earlier style piston pumper with a rounded hood and cowl, and chain drive, would remain in production for several more years. Ahrens-Fox delivered four Model J combination hose and pumping cars and one Model M pumper to St. Paul, Minn. In an impressive demonstration which it used widely in its advertising, Ahrens-Fox managed to get 12 fire streams from a single piston pump.

The Kissel Motor Car Co. of Hartford, Wis. began to market fire apparatus built on the KisselKar truck chassis.

Peter Pirsch & Sons delivered a 75-foot straight-frame aerial ladder truck to Virginia, Minn. This apparatus was mounted on a Winther truck chassis, and had a "sidesaddle" tillerman's seat on its right-hand side.

The Seagrave Corp. delivered a 65-foot 4-wheel water tower to Birmingham, Ala. Seagrave ladder trucks included 4-wheel city service types, and tractor-drawn aerials in 75 and 85-foot lengths. The Columbus, Ohio builder still offered its front-drive K Series aerials in 65, 75 and 85-foot sizes, but found relatively few customers. Most departments preferred the tractor-drawn types.

The 1920 International Assn. of Fire Engineers Convention was held in Toronto, Ontario, Canada.

The dominant fire service publication was "Fire and Water Engineering" published in New York. This twice-monthly publication served both the fire service and municipal waterworks fields.

The City of Indianapolis purchased a sizeable fleet of locally-built Stutz fire apparatus in the early 1920's. This 1920 Stutz pumper of 600 gallons-per-minute capacity ended its service life as a hose tender for Engine Co. No. 23. It was photographed at the Indianapolis Fire Dept. apparatus shops. The I.F.D. has saved several of its old Stutz fire engines.

The Kissel Motor Car Company of Hartford, Wis. marketed its own motor fire apparatus in the early 1920's. This 1920 Kissel City Service Hook and Ladder Truck served the Hartford Fire Dept. for many years before it was acquired and restored by George Getz. It is now in Mr. Getz' Hall of Flame fire equipment museum in Phoenix, Ariz.

The White Motor Co. of Cleveland was now aggressively marketing its own line of motor fire apparatus. This is a 1920 White Combination Hose and Chemical Car with dual chemical tanks. Most metropolitan fire departments still ran two-piece engine companies consisting of a pumper and hose and chemical combination, although the triple combination pumper was rapidly gaining favor.

Cadillac fire engines are relatively rare, but some were built. This is a 1920 Cadillac Combination Hose and Chemical Car built by the Northern Pump Co. of Minneapolis. It is lettered for Redwood Falls. Cadillac at this time built a full line of commercial chassis which were used for light duty trucks, buses, police patrol wagons and hearses.

This American LaFrance Type 31 Aerial is in almost perfect original condition. A 75-foot, spring-raised model powered by a six-cylinder engine, it was purchased new by the Casper, Wyo. Fire Dept., but was later sold to Rawlins, Wyo. The driver's seat on this and earlier Type 31 aerials was attached to the front of the aerial ladder turntable and rotated with the ladder. Later models had a fixed-position seat. That's the fuel tank under the seat.

A four-cylinder American LaFrance Type 10 Triple Combination, this 600 gallon-per-minute pumper is seen here being lined up for a parade in Kayser, W. Va. It has a single discharge gate on the right hand side, above the suction inlet.

AMERICAN-LaFRANCE

Positioned in front of an American LaFrance branch office, this is a spanking-new 1920 American LaFrance Straight Chemical Car built on the prolific Model T Ford chassis. This single-tank model also carries a 24-foot extension ladder.

Another Model T Ford, this is a combination hose and chemical car. Notice the hand-cranked siren on the dash and the small carbon tetrachloride extinguisher mounted just below the driver's seat. The location and builder are not known, but this job looks similar to this type built by American LaFrance.

The Carthage, N. Y. Fire Department still owns this 1920 American LaFrance Type 12 Triple Combination. The 1,000 gallon-per-minute pumper is equipped with oversized tires that give it a low, racy appearance.

Baltimore, Md. has always boasted a very resourceful repair shop crew. The Baltimore City Fire Dept. shop has built up many rigs over the years, prolonging the useful lives of many pieces of apparatus. This is a Mack Model AC Bulldog chassis which has been equipped as a pumper. Note the catch-all "Baltimore basket" over the hose bed and the wide rear fenders required to accommodate the dual rear tires. This rig is shown as "Second Line Engine No. 54."

1920

This city service hook and ladder truck was built up by mounting the body of an old Seagrave city service ladder truck on a new Mack Model AB chassis. It is not known who did the work.

This 65-foot Seagrave Water Tower served the Birmingham, Ala. Fire Dept. for 39 years, before being taken out of service in 1959. The spring-raised mast has a telescopic extension. The tower nozzle was controlled by hand lines from the turntable. At last report, this water tower was rusting away at the local fairgrounds.

Chicago purchased no less than 39 of these Seagrave 750 gallon-per-minute pumpers between 1920 and 1923. This is one of the first five delivered. Photographed on the shipping platform at Seagrave's Columbus, Ohio plant, this 1920 model sports a Chicago style factory windshield, a length of soft steamer suction hose on the right front running board and a bell tower in front of its radiator. A Model F-76, it carries Seagrave Serial No. 30166.

Milwaukee purchased a number of Seagrave pumpers.

This is a 1920 Ahrens-Fox Model JK-4 Piston Pumper, delivered to the Detroit Fire Dept. Detroit purchased only one of these shaft-drive, 750 gallon-per-minute pumpers, but received three Model JM-3C Ahrens-Fox piston pumpers the same year. The chemical tank is mounted below the driver's seat.

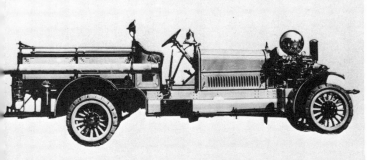

Although most Ahrens-Fox piston pumpers now had the new gabled hood, this style with the rounded hood remained in production. This is a big combination pump and hose car with piston pump and chain drive. The builder's photo does not give the model type or capacity, or the city it was built for.

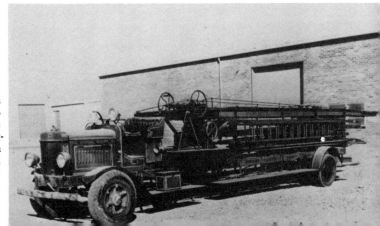

This 65-foot aerial ladder was built by Peter Pirsch & Sons Co. for the Virginia, Minn. Fire Dept., but was later sold to Northfield, Minn. It is now in the famed Harrah Automobile Collection in Reno, Nev. Originally equipped with a tillerman's seat mounted on the right-hand side, it is built on a Winther chassis. The Pirsch aerial ladder was raised by a Dahill Air Hoist. This rig originally rode on solid rubber tires mounted on steel disc wheels.

This is the business end of one of four Ahrens-Fox Model JK-4 750 gallon-per-minute piston pumpers delivered to the Detroit Fire Dept. This one was retired in the mid-1950's and was stored for years in Pontiac, Mich. Three years ago it was purchased by the 5-11 Fire Buff Club of Chicago and now it shares quarters with Chicago Engine Co. No. 22. It was fitted with a leather and celluloid windbreaker in the 1930's, and like all Detroit rigs carried a set of Buckeye Roto-Rays.

This is how Cincinnati's 1921 Ahrens-Fox Model JM-4 piston pumper looked the day it tolled out of the factory. This was the only J-series Ahrens-Fox ever sold to the C. F. D. The round booster tank is located behind the gasoline tank, and the booster hose reel can be seen mounted under the rear step. This pumper carried Registration No. 990.

As the third decade of this century began, the dashing fire horse had all but disappeared from the scene. Most cities had all but completed their fire apparatus motorization programs, and about the only place where horse-drawn equipment could still be found was in the quiet suburbs. More than a few departments, however, kept steamers in reserve for use at major fires. These were often towed to the fire behind a piece of motor equipment. The motor truck had acquired irrefutable reliability, and even the smallest towns and villages were replacing hand and horse-drawn equipment with small motorized fire engines. The Model T Ford took a prominent role in this transition.

Always an innovator, the Ahrens-Fox Fire Engine Co. had developed a small piston pumper for smaller fire departments. Rated at 500 gallons per minute, it had a 5-cylinder front-mounted piston pump, but the new T Model Fox did not have the large, spherical air chamber prominent on all other Ahrens-Fox piston pumpers. The first engine in this series, a Model T-2, Reg. No. 1001, went to a watery grave on its delivery to Soeraboya in the Dutch East Indies in 1920. The only other one built, a 1921 Model T-3, was delivered to Batesville, Ind. and is still in original condition there. The company's J Model, shaft-drive piston pumpers were selling well and in two years had become the Cincinnati plant's most popular model.

A few years earlier, Ahrens-Fox had developed an ingenious patented hydrant-thawing device that attached to the piston pumper's engine. It was essentially a miniature steam generator, and it could be attached to the motor at the beginning of the winter season and taken off in the spring. In its Bulletin No. 124, issued in May, 1921, the company noted that the first piston pumper it had delivered—a 1912 Model A Continental, was still going strong in Rockford, Ill.

The small town of Clyde, Ohio purchased this 1921 triple combination built by Obenchain-Boyer on a Clydesdale truck chassis. The locally-built Clydesdale was certainly appropriately named: this sturdy-looking engine is equipped with two chemical tanks.

Another Ahrens-Fox oddity was this five-cylinder Model T-3 pumper built for the Batesville, Ind. Fire Dept. and still owned by that city. This one-off pumper carries Reg. No. 1002. It does not have the usual plated ball on top of its pump.

The Maxim Motor Co. introduced new M Series of motor fire apparatus that would remain this company's mainstay for the next six years. Maxim's sturdy M type pumpers were offered in 500, 600 and 750 gallon-per-minute versions, and were powered by 6-cylinder engines.

C. J. Cross was still delivering a small number of front-drive auto tractors, but the nearly total completion of motorization programs had already driven the Front Drive Auto Co.'s familiar Christie out of the market. Approximately 600 Christie tractors had been built, and many were still in front-line service. However, the market for new conversion tractors had all but dried up.

The Parrett Tractor Co. of Chicago Heights, Ill. had taken over the former South Bend Motor Car Works' fire apparatus business. Although it remained in this business for only a short time, Parrett offered municipalities "super built fire apparatus" in four sizes including pumpers, ladder trucks, motor tractors, hose wagons, and squad rigs.

An old name in the fire equipment supplies business, the Obenchain-Boyer Co. of Logansport, Ind. was mounting popular fire apparatus bodies on various commercial truck chassis, including the Model T Ford chassis. The Ford-based combination hose and chemical car had become a very familiar piece of equipment, not only in smaller towns but on the fringes of the big cities.

Small departments often fashioned their own motor fire equipment by converting a used auto into a combination hose and chemical rig, or using it as a tractor to pull a former hand or horse-drawn hook and ladder truck.

About the only evident styling change this year was the American LaFrance Fire Engine Co.'s switch to a new two-level step-top type of rear fender on many of its models. Ladder trucks continued to use the older style round-surfaced fenders for a time.

The Seagrave Corp. came out with new styling for its apparatus, in the form of a rounded hood and radiator, and a recessed instrument panel built into a new cowl. Seagrave also began delivering shaft-drive apparatus. This 750 gallon-per-minute pumper has solid tires, chain drive and the cylindrical type of booster hose basket that was unique to Seagrave apparatus. Power was provided by a Seagrave 6-cylinder engine.

Milwaukee motorized its 1891 Hale 55-foot water tower by replacing the horses with a 1921 Seagrave Model K front-drive tractor. Thirty years later it was modernized again, and the Seagrave tractor was replaced by a four-wheel tractor built in the Milwaukee Fire Dept. shops. It was retired from service several years ago and is now owned by a private collector.

The Seagrave Corp. gave its products a new look—even though the older style gable hood remained in production for another five years on certain models. The new appearance included a rounded hood and radiator, and a cast metal cowl which protected the dashboard instruments and controls from the weather. Windshields were still a decade away. This 750 GPM pumper, with steel disc wheels and solid tires, was built for the Billingsport Volunteer Firemen's Assn. The wheels were painted a lighter shade than the rest of the apparatus. Seagrave apparatus of this era was elaborately striped and ornamented.

Chicago continued to place orders with Seagrave. This 750 GPM pumper was one of 16 Model F-76 Seagraves delivered in 1921. Although the Columbus plant had started production of a new style of apparatus, this older style was still being built as late as 1926. Standard equipment on Chicago rigs included a windshield and front-mounted bell.

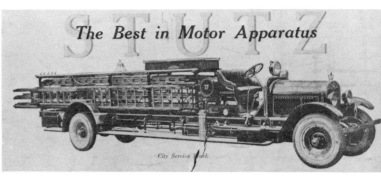

The Best in Motor Apparatus

This is how the Stutz city service ladder truck looked when it was delivered to the Indianapolis Fire Dept. Later additions included new rear fenders, a windshield and steel-spoked wheels. This rig went into service at Hook & Ladder Co. No. 27.

The Stutz Fire Engine Co. built this city service hook and ladder truck for the Indianapolis Fire Department. It was still around in the late 1960's. Seen here, outside the I.F.D. Motor Shops, it is lettered for Hook & Ladder Co. No. 32.

Peter Pirsch & Sons Co. of Kenosha, Wis. also built a lot of small-town fire equipment on the Model T Ford 1-ton chassis. This heavily-laden triple combination carries a small pump, complete chemical equipment, a 24-foot ladder and roomy hose box. It is lettered   Z.F.D. No. 2.

This Model T Ford hook and ladder truck consists of little more than a Model T front end, a much-lengthened frame and two-tank chemical equipment bolted on top. A hand-cranked siren cleared the way. A 45-foot extension ladder was slung beneath the rear frame rails. It is not known where this primitive, yet functional, piece of equipment served.

Thanks to the low cost of the Model T Ford, even small towns could now afford a triple combination motor pumper. This triple was built by Howe Fire Apparatus, and featured a piston pump, chain drive and 24-foot extension ladder. A Lambert extension and Ford roadster body were used for this conversion. It carried preconnected hard suction hose and the small bell. This was a lot of firefighting power in a small package.

This magnificently-restored 1921 American LaFrance pumper is owned by an antique fire apparatus buff in Camden, N. J. American LaFrance began to use step-top rear fenders on its pumpers, aerials and combinations. A hallmark of American LaFrance apparatus which continues to this day is a replica of a spread-winged American Eagle atop the bell.

New York City ordered 20 American LaFrance 750 gallon-per-minute pumpers this year as part of an extensive apparatus modernizations program. These pumpers were equipped with large turret pipes permanently mounted at the front of the hose box and fed by four 2½-inch hose lines. This fully-restored 1921 American LaFrance, authentically lettered for the F. D. N. Y., is being backed off the trailer at an antique fire apparatus meet in New York.

Hard at work is one of 20 American LaFrance 700 gallon-per-minute rotary gear pumping engines delivered to New York City in 1921. Encrusted with ice, the pumper is serving at an extra-alarm fire. The bell has been relocated to the left front fender, and the F.D.N.Y. shops have added a kitchen door-style windshield. This pumper was likely being used as a spare. The big turret nozzle and pompier ladders carried above the hose box are characteristic of New York rigs.

American LaFrance modernized and rebuilt this 1921, 750 gallon-per-minute pumper for Albany, N. Y. The stream-lining included installation of new fenders, a double-bar front bumper and new pump panel. Reg. No. 3675 was one of six American LaFrance 750 GPM pumpers delivered to Albany that year. The author took this photo at a SPAAMFAA muster in Syracuse, N. Y. in 1968.

This type of apparatus is referred to as a Quadruple Combination, or Quad. A Quad carries a pump, hose, chemical or booster equipment and a full complement of ground ladders. This is a 1921 American LaFrance Type 14 Quad equipped with a 600 GPM rotary gear pump. The hose tray is mounted directly under the single bank of wood ground ladders. The hard suction hoses are carried on the running boards.

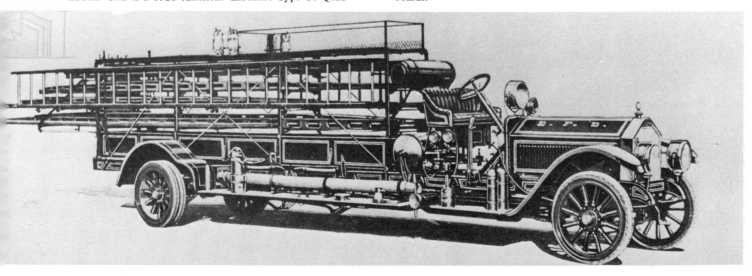

One of the most successful heavy trucks ever designed, the big Mack Model AC Bulldog proved ideal for fire service. Mechanicsburg, Pa. purchased this Model AC city service hook and ladder truck with chemical equipment.

The Chicago Fire Dept. purchased many Mack AC Bulldogs during the 1920's. After many years of service as a ladder truck tractor, this AC was converted into a combination turret and hose wagon by the C.F.D. Shops. This tough-looking rig went to High Pressure Co. No. 6.

A Model T Ford scurries to get out of the way and the crew puts on a real performance for the photographer in this posed shot of a big Mack Type AC triple combination as it thunders down the street on its way to an alarm. Note the precariously-balanced fellow tugging on his boot on the running board, and the citizens enjoying the show from the porch in the background. This engine was owned by Great Neck, Long Island, N. Y.

Similar scenes had already been enacted in many American cities. Detroit's turn came on the afternoon of April 10, 1922. More than 50,000 people lined both sides of Woodward Ave. to watch the last horses on the Detroit Fire Dept. make their last run.

On signal, Pete, Jim and Tom dashed from their stalls in Engine 37's quarters and took their places in front of the big steamer. Babe and Rusty dashed into their harnesses in front of the hose wagon. With nostrils flaring and hoofs flying, the gallant steeds galloped out of the firehouse and into history. Ironically, there was no fire at that last alarm, only waiting dignitaries and the fire department band. There were a few speeches, and more than a few moist eyes in the crowd. Before that commemorative run was over, a pair of shiny new motor fire engines had taken the place of the horses in Engine 37's quarters. Progress, yes. But something had been lost.

New York's turn came on December 20 of the same year. The horse-drawn era in American fire fighting had come to an end.

There was no question that auto fire engines were faster than the horses had been. A motor-driven pumper did not need oats and hay, nor the services of a veterinarian. They did not have to be exercised, and few firemen really missed stable duty. The motor fire engine had proved itself more efficient, and in the long run cheaper to operate.

By 1922, the U. S. fire apparatus industry was dominated by American LaFrance, Seagrave and Ahrens-Fox. Mack, Maxim, Stutz and Pirsch were doing a brisk business too, as were dozens of smaller manufacturers like Buffalo, Obenchain-Boyer, O. J. Childs and the Prospect Fire Engine Co.

The Seagrave Corp. added a shaft-drive pumper to its line. This new series of pumping engines had been handsomely restyled, with a graceful rounded hood, radiator and cast cowl. Customers could choose between the standard wood-spoked artillery-type wheels, or clean-looking solid disc wheels. While the older chain-drive style Seagrave with the Mercedes-type gabled radiator and hood would remain in production on certain models for another six years, the new style would see Seagrave into the next decade.

American LaFrance had complemented its popular Type 14 city service hook and ladder truck with a straight-frame variation with either a 4 or 6-cylinder engine mounted ahead of the front wheels. Called the Type 33,

Hook, Ladder and Hose Co. No. 1 of the Farmingdale, Long Island, Fire Dept. used this 1922 Mack Type AB city service ladder truck for many years. Two ladder safety belts dangle from the handrail just below the chemical hose reel.

1922

this model also came equipped with a rear-steer tiller. Relatively few Type 33's were sold compared with the conventional type Type 14. American LaFrance motor apparatus now sported drum-style Vesta headlights, instead of the older style Gray & Davis headlights that had been on Elmira-built apparatus for about 10 years. Washington, D. C. added a big 65-foot American LaFrance Type 31 Water Tower to its firefighting arsenal this year.

Among American LaFrance's most popular models was the standard Type 75 pumper, of 750 GPM capacity. Most of these were delivered as triple combinations, with a rotary gear pump, a chemical tank and a regular hose box. More and more, the triple combination was replacing former two-piece engine companies that usually had a pumper which was accompanied by a combination hose and chemical truck.

Many communities still preferred solid rubber tires to pneumatics, but in areas with plenty of paved roads, pneumatic or "balloon" tires were the last word in riding comfort.

The Moorestown, N. J. Fire Dept. still owns this almost original 1922 Ahrens-Fox Model RK-4 piston pumper. A 750 gallon-per-minute pumper powered by the Ahrens-Fox 4-cylinder engine, it is still rolling on solid tires. Here, the Moorestown Fox pleases the crowd at a parade.

Detroit placed two of these custom-built Ahrens-Fox Model J-13 high pressure hose cars into service in 1922. Each carried two huge Morse turret pipes and a large load of 3-inch high pressure hose. They were Ahrens-Fox Serial Nos. 1204 and 1205 and served the Motor City for exactly half a century. After years of reserve service as fireboat tenders, they were stripped and sold in 1972.

Elizabethtown, Pennsylvania's Friendship Fire Co. No. 1 ordered this 1922 Ahrens-Fox. The Model IK-4 had a 750 gallon-per-minute piston pump and was a full triple combination. It is seen here in a factory photograph just before shipment to Elizabethtown. This pumper still has the older series rounded hood rather than the gabled design.

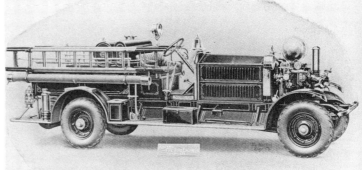

The Ahrens-Fox piston pumper, with its handsome proportions and distinctive front-mounted pump surmounted by a ball-shaped air chamber, is an American classic. These pumpers are avidly sought by antique fire apparatus buffs, and are already the Rolls-Royces of the antique fire engine hobby. Ahrens-Fox used this advertising cut for several years during the mid-1920's. It is of a standard 750 GPM triple combination pump, hose and booster car.

After many years of service as High Pressures 1 and 2, Detroit's two 1922 Ahrens-Fox J-13's were redesignated as fireboat tenders and responded to all alarms answered by Engine 16, the fireboat "John Kendall." This is Boat Tender 3, which ran out of Engine 8's quarters on Bagley St. Boat Tender 2 was quartered with Engine 11. In 1932 the leather windbreaker was added and the bell moved from the dash to the front. Pneumatic tires were also added. These big hose wagons were at nearly every major fire in Detroit for nearly 50 years.

This is a good general arrangement view of an American LaFrance triple combination of this era. The suctions are still mounted over the rear fender, and the chemical hose and basket is mounted over the hose bed. Windshields were still uncommon, but bumpers were standard. This is a 4-cylinder, 600 gallon-per-minute pumper.

This heavily loaded American LaFrance Type 14 city service hook and ladder truck served the Maplewood Township, N.J. Fire Dept. It is of the single-bank type, and carries chemical equipment. The original wood-spoked artillery wheels have been replaced with pneumatics and steel wheels.

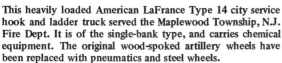

Water Tower No. 2 of the Washington, D. C. Fire Dept. was this 1922 American LaFrance 75-foot spring-raised tower. A Type 31 powered by a 6-cylinder, 105-horsepower engine, it served the capitol for more than 30 years. The tower was an American Automatic. Notice the tillerman's perch immediately behind the base of the mast.

This light combination hose and chemical car was built especially for the North Carolina State Firemen's Assn. The chemical tank is enclosed under the front seat, and a 24-foot extension ladder is carried on the right-hand side.

The Boston Fire Department operated this heavily-laden American LaFrance pumper. Notable features include a huge deck turret with six inlets mounted over the hose box, a shop-built windshield and a Whiting warning light behind the driver's seat. The 4-lens Whiting light was similar in principle to the Buckeye Roto-Ray which came later, but the Whiting lights were fixed and flashed alternately.

The Empire Hook and Ladder Co. of the Carlisle, Pa. Fire Dept. was the proud owner of this 4-cylinder American La France Type 31 aerial ladder truck. Note how the driver's seat is attached to the front of the turntable by the curved frame, seat and tank swung away with the ladder. Standard equipment included a full-length equipment basket under the main frame, and a set of fire buckets which were hung from the rear of the truck.

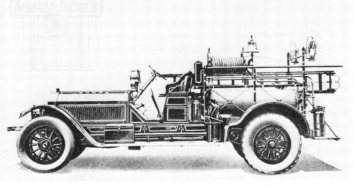

With the increasing popularity of the triple combination pumper, demand for straight chemical cars began to drop off. Some fire departments, however, still preferred this type of apparatus. The Tulsa, Okla. Fire Dept. purchased this American LaFrance Type 75 2-tank chemical car. Each tank carried 80 gallons of chemical. The Type 75 was powered by a 105-horsepower 6-cylinder ALF engine with 5½-inch bore and 6-inch stroke. Wheelbase was 156 inches.

American LaFrance offered two types of city service hook and ladder trucks. Besides the conventional style Type 14, the company built the Type 33, which had its engine mounted ahead of the front wheels. This very nicely preserved 1922 American LaFrance Type 33 front-drive hook and ladder truck was owned by the Oyster Bay Fire Co. No. 1 of Long Island, N. Y. The Type 33 had a tiller where most Type 14s did not.

One of the most important innovations in fire apparatus design—at least for smaller towns and villages—was the introduction of the first Barton front-mount pump. The first of these small units, which took their power off the front of the crankshaft, was installed on a Model T Ford fire engine by the American Steam Pump Co. of Battle Creek, Mich. This company evolved into American Marsh, and finally in the American Fire Apparatus Co. of today. Here is the first Barton, on the Thunderbolt Model T.

Peter Pirsch & Sons Co., of Kenosha, Wis. now offered a complete range of fire apparatus mounted on any chassis specified by the customer. Pirsch's home town received this locally-built triple combination motor pumping engine. The Pirsch apparatus was mounted on a Winther truck chassis built by the Winther Motor Co. of Kenosha. Several years were to pass before Pirsch marketed a line of fire apparatus built entirely in its own plant.

The Hale Fire Pump Co., which had built its first pumper in 1914, still produced some motor pumpers, such as this 300 gallon-per-minute Hale pumper on a Reo Speedwagon chassis. It went to Forked River, N. J. in 1922.

The resourceful Grand Rapids, Mich. Fire Dept. Motor Shops built this combination chemical and hose wagon on a 1922 United truck chassis. A 3-way deck nozzle is attached to the rear of the hose bed.

Port Clinton, Ohio, still owns this nicely preserved 350 gallon-per-minute Stutz pumper, which was photographed at a volunteer firemen's convention at Ada, Ohio, in the summer of 1974. A windshield has been added and the bell moved, but the little pumper is original otherwise.

STUTZ

Baltimore placed its second order for Stutz motor fire apparatus this year. This 6-cylinder, 750 gallon-per-minute Stutz triple was the third of this type placed in service in this city. This engine company sure has plenty of manpower!

Small fire engines were big news in 1923. Two manufacturers, Seagrave and Stutz, introduced scaled-down pumping engines designed to appeal to budget-conscious communities that nonetheless insisted on custom-built fire apparatus.

The Seagrave Corp. introduced its smart little Suburbanite pumper at the 1923 IAFE Convention, held in Richmond, Va. Powered by a 6-cylinder Continental engine, the Suburbanite had a 350 GPM centrifugal pump. It was identical in appearance to the larger series Seagraves. The Suburbanite was an immediate success and was purchased by major cities as well as smaller towns. Seagrave now built three different sizes of pumpers: in addition to the diminutive Suburbanite and its Standard model 750 and 1,000 GPM pumpers, the Columbus, Ohio, manufacturer introduced a huge 1,300 GPM model called the Metropolite. One of the first of these was delivered to Council Bluffs, Ia. It had chain drive and rode on a set of solid "Kelly Kats" tires.

The new small Stutz was also a 350 GPM job. It was identified as the K Model, but was better known as the Baby Stutz. The baby of the Stutz fire engine family was powered by a 4-cylinder engine. Stutz now offered a full line of pumpers ranging in capacity from 350 up to 1,000 GPM. Stutz fire engines were powered by Wisconsin engines. They could be found in fire houses from coast to coast.

American LaFrance also offered small pumpers. Elmira's answer to the Seagrave Suburbanite and Baby Stutz was the Type 40, a 350 GPM rotary gear pumper powered by a 75-horsepower, 4-cylinder engine.

At about this time, American LaFrance also introduced a new series of light-duty fire apparatus built on a special Brockway truck chassis. These were marketed as the American LaFrance Cosmopolitan and bore both the Brockway and ALF names.

The Ahrens-Fox Fire Engine Co. got into the ladder truck business in a big way this year. The Cincinnati manufacturer began production of its first aerial ladder trucks. Over the next 17 years, the company sold 73

This is a standard Stutz 4-cylinder city service hook and ladder truck. The city of Indianapolis, where the Stutz Fire Engine Co. was located, had a sizeable fleet of Stutz apparatus including several ladder trucks of this type.

aerials, all but one of them of the tractor-drawn type. Ahrens-Fox aerials were powered by 6-cylinder engines, were offered in 75 and 85-foot sizes, and all had the Dahill Air Hoist as standard equipment. The first of these was delivered to Nashua, N. H. At the same time the company started building city service hook and ladder trucks in both the straight-frame and tractor-trailer types. At the Richmond convention, the company introduced a new concept in ladder truck design. Up to now ground ladders were carried in a single stack, or bank. But Ahrens-Fox had developed a side-by-side double-bank configuration that not only lowered the height of the truck, but increased ladder carrying capacity. The first of these was delivered to Braintree, Mass. after the convention.

The Prospect Mfg. Co. of Prospect, Ohio offered a popular line of rotary gear pumpers of from 250 to 500 GPM capacity. The Prospect Deluge pump was available on either the Ford or Reo chassis, although some were delivered on other truck makes. Among the more common fire apparatus chassis of the day were Nash, Federal, Packard, GMC, White, International and the Pierce-Arrow truck. Waterous and Hale continued to deliver a small number of custom-built fire engines, and Northern offered a line of fire apparatus bodies that could be locally mounted on almost any chassis.

The previous year, the Foamite Firefoam Co. and O. J. Childs Co. had merged to form the Foamite-Childs Corp. Foamite was a major maker of fire extinguishers as well as its famed fire-smothering foam compound. The new Foamite-Childs Corp. of Utica, N. Y. began building pumpers and combination cars on various commercial chassis. In 1923, this company delivered a racy 4-tank chemical car on a Pierce-Arrow "66" auto chassis to Glyndon, Md.

Council Bluffs, Iowa purchased this 1,300 gallon-per-minute Seagrave Metropolite, which was the Columbus plant's answer to the American LaFrance Type 15. Note the solid tires, chain drive and large diameter hard suction hose. These monsters must have been a handfull to drive.

Considerably smaller than the Metropolite was Seagrave's Standard Series 750 gallon-per-minute pumping engine. This artistically-decorated model went to West Bend, Wis. The chain-drive rear end indicates that this pumper may have been a factory rebuild.

Los Angeles was another good Seagrave customer. This 1923 Seagrave 85-foot tractor-drawn aerial ladder truck ran as the L.A.F.D.'s Truck Co. No. 28. Note the dual spotlights on the cowl and the windshield for the tillerman.

Syracuse, N. Y. ran this 1923 Seagrave 85-foot springhoist tractor drawn aerial ladder truck. After many years of faithful service, it went to the Syracuse-based Society for the Preservation and Appreciation of Antique Motor Fire Apparatus in America, Inc. The tillered rig is always a favorite at SPAAMFAA's annual muster.

American LaFrance rebuilt Pittsburgh's former horse-drawn high pressure hose and turret wagon with a Type 31 motor tractor. This heavy battery wagon had a hand-raised 32-foot mast, and two big deck monitors. The only other one like it was in Atlantic City, N. J.

New York City purchased 26 of these American LaFrance 700 gallon-per-minute pumpers in 1923. Note the big wagon pipe in front of the fuel tank, the siren mounted over the bell, and the reinforcement rods at each side of the radiator. The headlights are of a later type.

The Baltimore Fire Department ordered three of these American LaFrance Type 12 pumpers, equipped with 900 gallon-per-minute piston pumps. This type of pump, surmounted by a large air chamber, was located between the seat and hose box rather than under the seat where gear pumps were installed. Baltimore used red and white-painted apparatus.

Perth Amboy, N. J. owned this American LaFrance 750 GPM Type 75 pumper. The drum-type headlight and step-top rear fenders had become standard equipment on American LaFrance apparatus. Note the siren mounted on the frame over the front of the hose bed.

The Monhagen Fire Company of Middletown, N. Y. owned this red-and-white 1923 American LaFrance Type 38, which was equipped with a Type 39 pump of 600 GPM capacity. The Monhagen's LaFrance is a familiar participant in New York State antique apparatus musters.

In addition to its equipment for mounting on the inexpensive Model T Ford chassis, American LaFrance offered an even cheaper solution to the fire protection problems of small villages. It was the "Village Queen" which consisted of a Model T Ford engine and hood mounted on a light frame and driving a 250 gallon-per-minute pump. This equipment could be pulled to the fire scene by hand, or towed behind an automobile. The box over the pump carried small-diameter hose. The gasoline tank is located just behind the hood.

Providence, R. I. got this 1924 American LaFrance tractor-drawn- 65-foot American Automatic water tower, which was pulled by a 4-wheel Type 17 tractor. In addition to its powerful mast nozzle, this tower had two deck turrets. It was spring-raised and went out of service during the Second World War.

This is a standard American LaFrance Type 75 pumper, of the Manasquan, N. J. Fire Dept. It is a 750 GPM model with an accessory windshield. The company members' helmets are attached to a rail above the small-bore suction hose.

American LaFrance offered a series of light-duty fire apparatus built on the Brockway truck chassis. This 1923 American LaFrance-Brockway, powered by a 4-cylinder engine, is owned by Warren Hardy of Detroit. The windshield was added later.

The American LaFrance Type 31 front-drive water tower could be found in nearly every major city. This 65-footer had a 288-inch wheelbase and was powered by an ALF 6-cylinder, 105-horsepower engine. It was built for Syracuse, N. Y. This tower was rebuilt in 1953. The mast was reversed and the Type 31 tractor replaced with a Seagrave 4-wheel ladder truck tractor. After many years of reserve service, the tower was sold to a collector. It is still a regular participant in SPAAMFAA's national muster at Syracuse each August.

Toronto, Ontario, had several of these American LaFrance Type 33 city service ladder trucks. They were rebuilt in the late 1930's, and the American LaFrance engines were replaced by Ford flathead V-8's. Reg. No. 4319 served H & L 24 for many years before being retired in the late 1950's. The Tillsonburg, Ont. Shrine Club bought it and still uses it in parades today. Here is what the stripped rig looked like when the Shriners got it.

One of Ahrens-Fox's most popular models was the 750 gallon-per-minute piston pumper. This 1923 Model MS-2 ran as Engine No. 70 on the Chicago Fire Dept. This shaft-drive pumper was one of two MS-2's sold to Chicago this year.

Ahrens-Fox commenced the production of city service ladder trucks in 1923. Up to now, the Cincinnati plant had built only pumpers, combinations, squads and ladder truck tractors. This 4-cylinder city service ladder truck went to Braintree, Mass.

Ahrens-Fox

The fire department of Harvey, Ill. responded to fires with this little Ahrens-Fox Model IK-4. The 4-cylinder piston pumper could pump 750 gallons per minute. Ahrens-Fox was now using a 2-piece air chamber instead of the 1-piece ball previously used. These can be identified by the band around the center, which persisted until Ahrens-Fox ceased production of the piston pumper in 1952.

Always an innovator, Ahrens-Fox found a novel way to lower the center of gravity of ladder trucks, and at the same way carry more ladders. Instead of stacking them in a single bank, Ahrens-Fox placed them side by side. This was known as the double-bank style.

The most powerful piston pumper ever built by Ahrens-Fox was the huge Model PS-4, which at 1,300 gallons per minute matched Seagrave's Metropolite. This PS-4, which went to Syracuse, N. Y. was one of only 25 Model P Foxes built. This handsome fire engine was rescued by SPAAMFAA and has been restored to concourse condition.

A striking 2-tone paint job and no less than four lengths of hard suction hose distinguish the 1923 Ahrens-Fox Model MS-4 piston pumper of the Lambertville, N. J. Fire Dept. This model could throw 900 gallons of water per minute.

Another prominent builder of commercial chassis fire engines during the 1920s was the Obenchain-Boyer Company of Logansport, Ind. Boyer's standard model was this small triple combination pump, chemical and hose car. This one was built on a Reo Speedwagon chassis.

Obenchain-Boyer built this 500 gallon-per-minute pumper on a Sanford truck chassis. This triple combination is owned by the Port Byron, N. Y. Fire Dept. and is a regular participant at the annual SPAAMFAA apparatus muster in nearby Syracuse.

This 1923 Obenchain-Boyer combination hose and chemical car is built on an International truck chassis. International Harvester in a few years would begin marketing fire apparatus on its own.

The Buffalo Fire Appliance Corp. of Buffalo, N. Y., became a major fire apparatus builder during the 1920s. Buffalo built this 1923 city service hook and ladder truck on an International truck chassis for Falconer, N. Y. Falconer also had an International pumper of this style.

The Buffalo Fire Appliance Corp. constructed this attractive city service hook and ladder truck on a Larrabee motor truck chassis for the town of Goshen, N. Y. The side-mounted fuel tank is rather unusual.

Howe Fire Apparatus of Anderson, Ind. mounted this 4-tank chemical body on a heavy Nash chassis. Each of the two chemical hose reels faces in an opposite direction. Howe is still in the fire apparatus business today.

The then-new Lincoln motor car provided a dependable, if expensive, chassis for fire fighting service. The Howe Fire Apparatus Co. of Anderson, Ind. built this triple combination pumping engine on a 90-horsepower L Series Lincoln chassis. The engine was a V-8. At least one other Lincoln fire engine was a Northern-Lincoln combination car built in 1924 for Deshler, Neb.

This interesting little job was built by Peter Pirsch & Sons Co. It is a 500 GPM triple combination built on a 1923 Oshkosh, 4 X 4 chassis. It is owned by the Golden Valley, Minn. Fire Dept. Oshkosh is still in business today and builds heavy-duty airport crash trucks and custom fire apparatus chassis.

Peter Pirsch & Sons of Kenosha, Wis. built this small triple combination pumper on a Reo chassis for Whippany, N. J. The front-mounted bell was to become a popular feature of Pirsch-built apparatus in succeeding years.

The Four Wheel Drive Auto Company of Clintonville, Wis. built its first fire apparatus in 1914. The four-wheel-drive configuration was well suited to fire protection districts that had poor roads. This stout-looking FWD, equipped with a Northern pump, was built for the New London, Wis. Fire Dept.

Of all of the fire-fighting experiments tried as the motor age reached maturity, this had to be one of the most interesting. The Foamite-Childs Corp. of Utica, N. Y., makers of a well-known foam fire extinguisher system, teamed up with the Indian Motorcycle Co. of Springfield, Mass. The result was the Indian Fire Patrol which carried in a sidecar a 25-gallon chemical tank, a chemical hose basket and four fire extinguishers. Complete cost of this unit was $785. The Richmond, Va. Fire Dept. had a squad of five of these three-wheeled fire fighters, which could reach small fires in places no conventional fire truck could go. Another model had a seat for a second fireman.

Waterous, which had delivered America's first motor-driven pumping engine back in 1906, was still offering its customers motor fire apparatus bearing the respected Waterous name. This Waterous triple combination pumper was featured in a 1923 ad in Fire & Water Engineering, the leading fire service trade journal.

This 1923 Hale 350 gallon-per-minute pumper was built for Mays Landing, N. J. It is on a GMC truck chassis. Hale apparatus of this era can be identified by the squared rear fenders.

The Maxim Motor Co. came out with a new look in the early 1920s. This gabled hood and massive radiator design was used well into the 1930s. This is a triple combination Maxim pumper with its 750 gallon-per-minute pump mounted between the seat and hose body.

This 1923 Mack Model AC started its fire service career as a rescue squad truck on the New York City Fire Dept. It was later converted to the Foam Powder Supply Unit seen here. New York rigs of this period often carried a spare tire.

Hartford, Wis. was the home of the Kissel Motor Car Co., which produced a small number of fire engines. Hartford had taken delivery of a Kissel city service ladder truck in 1920. In 1923, Pirsch equipped this Kissel chassis with a 500 gallon-per-minute triple combination pumper body. This nicely refurbished rig is still the pride of the department.

In Canada, Bickle Fire Engine Ltd. of Woodstock, Ontario, had signed an agreement with Ahrens-Fox, under which the Canadian firm could build Ahrens-Fox apparatus under license and use some Fox engines and other parts in its own custom apparatus. This Bickle Triple Combination, delivered to Pembroke, Ontario, used an Ahrens-Fox radiator and hood.

Bristling with no less than three turret pipes, the Baltimore City, Md. Fire Dept. assigned this pugnacious-looking Mack Model AC hose wagon to High Pressure Service Co. No. 5. An unmistakeable feature of Baltimore rigs was the "Baltimore basket" equipment tray over the hose bed. This type of apparatus remained in service in Baltimore well into the 1960s.

Dover, N. J. had this Mack AC pumper. Mack pumpers were equipped with pumps built by the Northern Pump Co. of Minneapolis. These two made a formidable fire-fighting combination.

One of the features of this year's International Assn. of Fire Engineers Conference, held in Buffalo, N. Y. was a demonstration of a unique type of aerial ladder truck which had been imported from abroad. The exceptionally compact rear-mounted aerial was exhibited by the American Magirus Fire Appliance Co. of New York, which was formed to import and market in the U. S. the products of the well-known German fire engine builder, Magirus of Ulm, Germany. The Magirus aerial was only one-third the length of a conventional American tractor-trailer type and could be positioned in very tight places. The Magirus was powered by a 4-cylinder engine. Only about half a dozen of these aerials were sold over the next seven years. It is interesting to note that half a century later, the "continental prototype" rear-mount aerial had caught on in a big way with U. S. fire departments.

Another interesting development this year was the appearance of motorcycle fire apparatus. Built by Foamite-Childs in conjunction with the Indian Motorcycle Co., the "Fire Patrol" motorcycle carried two men, a small chemical tank, chemical hose and several extinguishers. The "Patrol" was designed to take care of small fires, saving wear and tear on heavier equipment. The idea was tried out in several cities but this interesting innovation proved to be short-lived as traffic congestion and distances grew.

In yet another milestone development, the American Steam Pump Co. of Battle Creek, Mich. announced a new device called the "Barton Portable Pump". Developed by the Barton Products Co. of Jackson, Mich. this was a small centrifugal pump which could easily be mounted to the front of the crankshaft of almost any standard passenger car. It weighed only 20 pounds, but could put out a steady 200 to 250 gallons of water per minute. This inexpensive yet efficient device found eager acceptance from small towns and villages, and it marked the beginning of the American Fire Apparatus Co. which is still in business in Battle Creek today.

The Foamite-Childs Corp. of Utica, N. Y. in 1923 had demonstrated a Foamite Pumper designed to extinguish major fuel oil fires. The 1923 model was built on a 7½-ton Mack AC chassis. This smaller model, on a 3½-ton chassis, followed. Baltimore tested one of these Foamite Pumpers, which generated several thousand gallons of fire-smothering foam, but this type of apparatus did not meet with popular acceptance.

The fire department of Berlin, Md., maintains this Mack Model AB triple combination pumper in remarkably original condition, right down to the well-worn solid rubber tires. The two separate bucket seats, rear fenders incorporating the chain drive enclosure and Northern pump with gooseneck suction port are worthy of note. Even the Mack emblem has been preserved on the ends of the fuel tank above the front of the hose box.

1924

The previous year, the Foamite-Childs Corp. had demonstrated a special Foamite Fire Engine, designed for extinguishing large fires involving paints, oils, greases, etc. Mounted on a 7½-ton Mack Model AC chassis, it was basically a tanker with foam-producing equipment. Although the company promoted its 1,400-gallon foam pumper, very few were sold.

The Prospect Fire Engine Co. of Prospect, Ohio entered into an agreement with the Biederman Motor Corp. of Cincinnati under which Biederman provided Prospect with special fire apparatus chassis. The medium-sized Prospect-Biederman, which was sold as the Deluge Master Fire Fighter, became the backbone of a large number of fire departments throughout the Midwest. The Prospect-Biederman was a heavy, solid-looking piece of fire-fighting machinery, and it remained in production until the Depression years. This series had a deep cowl, and many sported a bell on a frame above the distinctive cast radiator shell.

Probably the classiest fire engine to go into service this year was a combination hose and chemical car delivered to Deshler, Neb. by the Northern Fire Apparatus Co. This sleek-looking job was mounted on a Lincoln chassis.

American LaFrance delivered a special Type 17 tractor-drawn aerial ladder truck with a shortened trailer to Havana, Cuba. One of the Elmira, N. Y. firm's most popular products was the Ford-LaFrance combination chemical and hose car, built on the Model T chassis. The Ford-LaFrance was the only fire protection to be found in many smaller communities.

Among the chassis used by fire apparatus builders this year were the Bessemer, Winther, Stoughton, Republic, Larrabee, Day-Elder and even the Mason Road King.

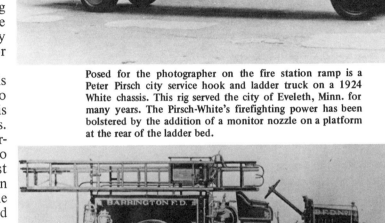

Posed for the photographer on the fire station ramp is a Peter Pirsch city service hook and ladder truck on a 1924 White chassis. This rig served the city of Eveleth, Minn. for many years. The Pirsch-White's firefighting power has been bolstered by the addition of a monitor nozzle on a platform at the rear of the ladder bed.

Peter Pirsch and Sons built this chemical-hose combination car on the Ford Model T 1-ton truck chassis. This particular example was built for Barrington, Ill.

Everything for the Fire Department

PETER PIRSCH & SONS CO.

The Republic was another chassis used by a few fire equipment builders. This Pirsch-Republic triple combination was delivered to Noank, Conn. The Republic Motor Truck Co. of Alma, Mich. appears to have built some fire apparatus.

It is believed that very few fire engines were built on the Day-Elder motor truck chassis. The Day-Elder Motor Co. did business in Newark and Irvington, N.J. This Day-Elder city service hook and ladder was purchased by Belleville, N.J. Peter Pirsch built at least one ladder truck on a Day-Elder chassis.

The Ford Motor Company's sprawling plant complex in the Detroit area was protected by one of the largest industrial fire departments in the country. This American LaFrance two-tank straight chemical car on a Ford T chassis carries the familiar Ford script on the panel below the driver's seat.

1924

This was the standard Ford-LaFrance chemical-hose combination. Hundreds of these were built by American La France for smaller fire departments and industrial fire brigades. A surprising number of them survive. The Henry Ford Museum in Dearborn has an excellent example.

The Canadian American LaFrance plant in Toronto was building a complete line of apparatus, ranging from small combination like this chemical-hose combination on a Chevrolet truck chassis, to 85-foot aerials. This job was photographed in the snow at the West Toronto railway station near the Canadian plant in Toronto's West end.

This 1924 American LaFrance Type 40 hose wagon responded to alarms with Pittsburgh's Engine Co. No. 47. This is a straight hose car, powered by the ALF 4-cylinder engine. A fixed turret pipe is mounted above the hose box. This apparatus carries no chemical equipment.

The bodywork on this attractive little 2-tank chemical car appears to be by American LaFrance, although the bell mounted above the seat is not from Elmira. The chassis is a Chevrolet. The chemical hose reel is mounted transversely above the wire equipment basket between the seat and the chemical tanks. This apparatus is lettered for Colonial Park, Pa.

Fairview Park, Ohio owns this 1924 American LaFrance Standard Type 40 triple combination. It is equipped with a "Junior" 350 gallon-per-minute rotary gear pumper and is in concourse condition.

1924

Shown here is a new American LaFrance Type 40 straight chemical car. Built for Irvington, N. J., it has two 60-gallon soda and acid tanks and compartments under the driver's seat. It is a 4-cylinder model.

There was still sufficient demand for custom-chassis combination hose and chemical cars to keep this type in production. American LaFrance delivered this 2-tank Type 75 combination to Burlington, N. J. The underslung tool compartment is a local addition.

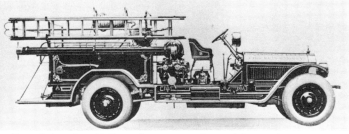

One of American LaFrance's most popular models was the 1,000 gallon-per-minute Type 12. The Type 12 could be ordered with either the conventional chain drive or with worm drive. This Standard Type 12 triple combination pumping, chemical and hose car was delivered to Walla Walla, Wash.

Drawn up on the ramp of the main fire house in Westbury, N. Y. is a 1924 American LaFrance 750 GPM pumper. This model has earlier style headlights, an oval fuel tank, and suction hoses carried in straight troughs rather than over the rear fenders. The metal-framed windshield was also added later.

The New York City Fire Dept. ordered 26 additional American LaFrance 700 gallon-per-minute rotary gear pumpers in 1924. This one was assigned to busy Engine Co. No. 17. All F.D.N.Y. pumpers were equipped with turret pipes.

The American LaFrance Fire Engine Co. always did a fair bit of export business. This special 85-foot Type 17 tractor-drawn aerial ladder truck was built for Havana, Cuba. It differed from the conventional model in that the trailer was shortened so it could negotiate some of the narrow downtown streets in Havana.

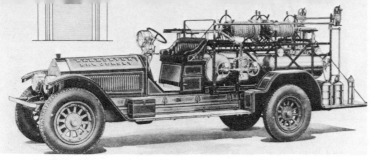

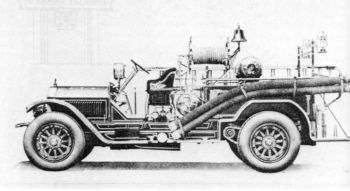

American LaFrance built this Standard Type 75 straight chemical car for the Hammonton, N. J. Fire Dept. This large chemical car has four 60-gallon chemical tanks and two reels each carrying 400 feet of 1-inch chemical hose. The Type 75 chemical car was built on a 156-inch wheelbase and was powered by the ALF 105-horsepower 6-cylinder engine with 5½-inch bore and 6-inch stroke.

1924

Auburn, Maine ordered this American LaFrance Type 39 Standard triple, which was equipped with a 600 gallon-per-minute rotary gear pump. Note the suction intake located under the chassis frame. The running board was cut around this port.

This is a standard American LaFrance Type 14 city service ladder truck. The rig shown above is a Philadelphia truck of the single-bank style. In addition to the usual complement of ground ladders, it carries three portable spotlights.

Another standard model in the American LaFrance product line was the Type 75, which could be ordered as either a pumper or a combination car. This Type 75 combination chemical and hose car was built for Huntington, N. Y. Note the bell mounting on the chemical hose reel frame.

Yet another major builder of motor fire apparatus in mid-America was the Prospect Fire Engine Co. located in Prospect, Ohio. Prospect called its standard equipment package the "Deluge." This Prospect Deluge combination hose and chemical car was mounted on the Pierce-Arrow 2-ton truck chassis. It was delivered to North Greece, and was of the 2-tank style.

The Prospect Fire Engine Company built this heavy-duty 4-tank straight chemical car. This businesslike rig has two hose reels and a bell carried in a frame attached to the rugged front bumper.

Prospect's standard production pumper was called the Deluge Master Fire Fighter. This is a front view of one of these assembled custom pumpers. Many were sold throughout the midwestern United States.

1924

The big news from Seagrave this year was the introduction of a complete line of small fire apparatus called the Suburbanite line. The Suburbanite was a scaled-down replica of the standard Seagrave, and was built in pumper and city service ladder truck variants, as well as hose cars, combinations, etc.

This Seagrave 1,300 gallon-per-minute Metropolite is actually a completely factory-rebuilt 1917 model. Note the box ahead of the rear fender to accommodate the drive chains. This high capacity pumper was originally owned by Lansing, Mich., but was later sold to Ithica, Mich.

Detroit received this Seagrave Model 6-L-F 65-foot spring-raised water tower in 1924. This tower replaced an 1893 Champion tower with a Christie tractor that was sold to Toledo, Ohio. This is how the Detroit tower looked after modernization in 1941. A steel windbreaker was added, the wheels were changed and the driver's seat was lowered. The old tower was junked in 1953. Note the large deck pipe and the tower hose draped over the turntable.

This 1924 Seagrave 750 gallon-per-minute pumper was built for Oak Park, Ill. but was later sold to the Broadview, Ill. Fire Dept. Seagrave was now using drum-style headlights. This pumper appears to be in near-mint condition.

This was the 350 gallon-per-minute Seagrave Suburbanite pumping engine demonstrator that was shown at all major fire chief's conferences this year. The little Suburbanite proved to be a popular model, not only with smaller deaprtments but in the suburbs and fringes of many larger cities.

"Not 'Power To Burn' But Power To Put Out Any Blaze," read the ad copy for this Seagrave 1000 GPM pumper. This engine is equipped with steel disc wheels and solid tires.

This was the Standard model Seagrave 750 gallon-per-minute pumper. It was powered by a 6-cylinder Seagrave-built engine, and could be found in fire houses from coast to coast. The cylindrical booster hose basket was a unique Seagrave feature.

This is another factory rebuild done by Seagrave. The 1924 Seagrave 1000 GPM pumper of the Grosse Pointe Shores, Mich. Fire Dept. went back to Columbus, Ohio in 1938 where it got a Morrow metal windbreaker, new crowned fenders and a complete overhaul. Minus the windshield, this richly striped and decorated pumper is now in the Henry Ford Museum collection.

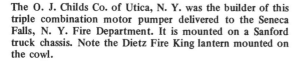

The O. J. Childs Co. of Utica, N. Y. was the builder of this triple combination motor pumper delivered to the Seneca Falls, N. Y. Fire Department. It is mounted on a Sanford truck chassis. Note the Dietz Fire King lantern mounted on the cowl.

The versatile Model T Ford continued to meet the fire protection requirements of smaller towns across the United States and Canada. The builder of this nifty little chemical car, sold to North Syracuse, N. Y. is not known. Dozens of manufacturers offer fire apparatus conversions of the famed "Tin Lizzie".

This medium-duty combination hose and chemical car was built by Obenchain-Boyer on a 1924 Dodge Brothers chassis. It is equipped with two chemical tanks, a roomy hose box, a cowl-mounted spotlight and an electric siren.

The Reo and Dodge Bros. chassis seemed to have been preferred by Obenchain-Boyer, or maybe it was just customer demand. Here is a fully-equipped triple combination pumper built by O-B on a Dodge chassis.

Some fire engines are unrecognizeable after only a few years of heavy urban service. Others wear half a century of service with no noticeable effects. Such is true of this incredibly well-preserved Howe-Reo piston pumper owned by Whitehouse, Ohio. It is seen here at a parade in 1974. With the exception of the locally-fabricated windshield, this rig looks almost as it must have the day it was delivered 50 years earlier.

Ahrens-Fox began building aerial ladder trucks in 1923. Most of these were of the 6-wheel tractor-drawn type. The last was built in 1940. This is a 1924 Ahrens-Fox 75-foot aerial purchased by the city of Kokomo, Ind. Ahrens-Fox aerials used the Dahill Air Hoist that had been developed by Chief Dahill of the New Bedford, Mass. Fire Dept. in 1916.

The Springvale Fire Co. of Sanford, Maine, was the original owner of this 1924 Ahrens-Fox Model JS-44 city service ladder truck, which was later sold to Newbury, Mass. The canvas windshield afforded the driver at least some protection from the wind, rain and snow. This truck carries chemical equipment.

Ahrens-Fox delivered this 4-cylinder Model RK-4 piston pumper to Midland, Park, N. J. It carried Registration No. 1149 and was a 750 GPM unit. The windshield is not original.

Ahrens-Fox delivered one of these special tractor-drawn 4-cylinder city service ladder trucks to Manchester, N. H. in 1923. The department liked it so much that it ordered another one in 1924. The short over-all length and tiller made these ladder trucks highly maneuverable.

This was the "fighting face" of the Ahrens-Fox piston pumper, which appeared in Ahrens-Fox advertising for several years. With its big spherical air chamber, two suction intakes and complex plumbing, the Ahrens-Fox presented a formidable frontal appearance.

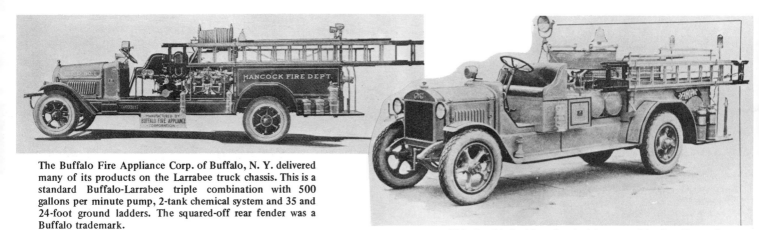

The Buffalo Fire Appliance Corp. of Buffalo, N. Y. delivered many of its products on the Larrabee truck chassis. This is a standard Buffalo-Larrabee triple combination with 500 gallons per minute pump, 2-tank chemical system and 35 and 24-foot ground ladders. The squared-off rear fender was a Buffalo trademark.

This durable-looking chemical hose combination fire engine was built by the Buffalo Fire Appliance Corp. on a GMC truck chassis for Mahopac, N. Y.

Two and 4-tank chemical cars, and even single-tank units, were common. But a 3-tanker was something of a rarity. Buffalo built this rather compact-looking 3-tank straight chemical car for Darien, New York. Ground ladders were sometimes carried on chemical trucks.

Here is another Buffalo-GMC that was supplied to the Mahopac, N. Y. Fire Dept. This is a small triple combination. Note the distinctive manner in which this community's name was painted on the side of the hose box.

General Motors at this time began to promote the use of the GMC truck chassis for fire equipment. It is uncertain who actually built this GMC combination hook and ladder and chemical truck. The leather windshield would indicate that it served in a northern clime, however.

1924

International Harvester successfully promoted fire apparatus built on its truck chassis, and is still a major builder of specialized fire equipment chassis today. This 1924 Model 43 chemical and hose wagon was built for American Fork, Utah.

One of the most interesting fire apparatus builders in the eastern U.S. is the proud old Hahn Motor Co., of Hamburg, Pa. The word Hahn is German for "rooster". Hahn started building fire engines as early as 1915. Audubon Park, Pa., is the owner of this nicely maintained 1924 Hahn Custom 500 gallon-per-minute pumper. The large, rectangular water tank and the set of floodlights were added later.

Exactly who built this triple combination pumper for Valley Falls, R. I. isn't known, but the apparatus is mounted on a heavy Federal truck chassis. The pump could churn out 750 gallons a minute. This rig is certainly loaded down.

STUTZ

The Stutz Fire Engine Co. reached its zenith at about this time. The Indianapolis factory was filling orders from departments of every size all over the country. This is the Stutz Standard Model C 750 gallon-per-minute triple combination.

The "big" Stutz was the 1,000 gallon-per-minute pumper. Stutz was proud of the fact that it built its own engines. The standard Stutz powerplant was a 175-horsepower, overhead camshaft type which Stutz claimed was specially designed for fire department service.

Stutz got into the "small" fire engine market too. The company claimed that its new Model K 350 GPM triple combination was "the biggest little piece of fire apparatus ever built." This model was advertised as the Baby Stutz and gave Seagrave's new Suburbanite a good run for the money.

The Stutz Fire Engine Co. built a complete range of motor pumping engines, ranging in capacity from 350 to 1,200 gallons-per-minute. Kansas City, Kan. purchased this 1,000 gallon-per-minute Stutz, which was powered by a Wisconsin engine. This triple combination carries full chemical equipment.

The American LaFrance Fire Engine Co. virtually dominated the U. S. fire apparatus industry. The Elmira, N. Y. firm could trace its ancestry back to 1834, when Lysander Button began building handtubs on the banks of the King's Canal at Waterford, N. Y. Although it had delivered its first motor fire engine in 1907, American LaFrance did not formally enter the motor fire apparatus field until 1910. Motor fire apparatus development advanced tremendously in only 15 years, with ALF contributing much. By 1925 the company was building a staggering variety of types and models. Principal types included:

The Type 12 triple combination pumper powered by the company's 120-horsepower 6-cylinder engine of 55-inch bore and 6-inch stroke. The Type 12 was available as a 1,000 GPM rotary gear pumper with either shaft or worm drive; as an 850 GPM centrifugal pumper, or with a 900 GPM piston pump. Next came the Type 75, powered by the 105-horsepower Six of similar bore and stroke. The Type 75 had a 750 GPM gear pump, could be ordered with either shaft or worm drive, and was available with a 400 GPM "Junior" pump. The Type 75 series also included a combination chemical and hose car, and a straight chemical car.

The Type 10 was a 600 GPM rotary gear pumper powered by a 4-cylinder, 75 HP engine of 5.5-inch bore and 6-inch stroke. Next came the Type 39, also a 600 GPM gear pumper with 75 HP Four of 5.5-inch bore and 6-inch stroke. The Type 38 had a 75 HP 6-cylinder engine of 4.5-inch bore and 6-inch stroke. The little Type 40 was a 350 GPM rotary gear job powered by the 75 HP Four of 5.5-inch bore and 6-inch stroke. A Type 40 combination chemical and hose car was also available.

In ladder trucks, ALF offered its popular Type 14 city service hook and ladder truck, powered by the 105-horsepower Six. The Type 14 could also be supplied as a quadruple combination with a hose bed and a 600 GPM gear pump coupled to the 75-horsepower Six. The snub-nosed Type 33 service ladder truck was powered by the 105-HP Six. The Type 31 front-drive aerial was built in 55, 65, 75 and 85-foot sizes, powered by the 105-HP Six. The Type 31 front-drive water tower was built in 55 and 65-foot sizes and was powered by the same engine. The

Stutz Fire Engine Co. exported several pumpers to far-off Tokyo, Japan. This 500 gallon-per-minute Baby Stutz, Model K-3, went to the Morishitacho, Tokyo Fire Brigade.

The Tulsa, Okla. Fire Dept. once used this smoke ejector apparatus. The chassis builder is identified as a GMC, but may be some other make. The most unusual feature of this truck is the complete front end—including engine—from a 1924 Buick, on top of the rig. This second powerplant provided the power for sucking the smoke out of buildings. This was done through the oversized tubes carried on each side.

Crookston, Minn. bought this white-painted 1925 Stutz quadruple combination. This department also had a Stutz pumper. The bell is carried well back on the ladder body.

The GMC Model K-41 chassis shown above was delivered to Rockford, Ill. General Motors boasted that this fine rig had "beauty as well as utility."

ractor-drawn Type 17 aerial, also powered by the 105-
orse Six, was built in four sizes ranging from 55 to 85
eet. The company also built a 4-wheel, 6-cylinder Type
7 tractor for modernizing ladder trucks and water towers,
nd a Type 31 tractor with 75-HP 4-cylinder engine for
onverting former horse-drawn steamers, aerials and water
owers.

In addition to these, American LaFrance also built the
rockway-chassised Cosmopolitan and the Model T Ford
ombinations. The company manufactured almost all of
s own components, from engines and transmissions to
umps and ladders.

To counter intense competition from Elmira, Ahrens-
ox in 1925 developed a line of rotary gear pumpers.
hese were midship models sold under the name of
hrens-Fox Rotarystyle.

Foamite-Childs Corp. started production of its own
ustom-chassised fire engines, using a special heavy-duty
hassis supplied by Kearns-Duhie Vau. These were called
Childs Thoroughbreds", and the same basic chassis was
sed briefly by the Buffalo Fire Appliance Corp.

The Stutz Fire Engine Co. built its only aerial ladder
ruck this year. It was a 6-cylinder, 85-foot tractor-drawn
nit designated a Model C-6A which was delivered to
ansas City, Mo. During the same year, Stutz shipped
hree pumpers to far-off Japan. The Tokyo jobs included
wo 350 GPM Baby Stutz pumpers, and a Model C 750
PM pumper.

This nicely preserved old pumper presents something of an
identification problem: the apparatus is definitely a Maxim,
but the radiator, although it bears the Maxim insignia,
appears to be a replacement. The sculptured hood is very
definitely a Middleboro, Mass. product, as are the front
fenders and the rest of the rig. This pumper saw service as
Engine 5 in Hingham, Mass. Note the canvas windscreen,
The Maxim is all decked out for a parade.

The Ahrens-Fox Fire Engine Co.
"Builders of Quality Fire Apparatus"
Cincinnati

Not even the massive Ahrens-Fox piston pumper could stand
up to a trolley car in a collision. Two firemen were
seriously hurt in this 1934 accident involving a 1925 Model
JS-4 in Newcastle, Ind.

This was a peak period for delivery of Ahrens-Fox aerial
ladder trucks. The 75-foot tractor-drawn Ahrens-Fox aerial
shown here was built for the Moyamensing Hook and
Ladder Co., of Chester, Pa. Like most Ahrens-Fox aerials,
this one had a Dahill air hoist. The spotlight mounted
behind the driver's seat was a characteristic of Ahrens-Fox
aerial ladder trucks.

Newark, N. J. ran this 1925 Ahrens-Fox 75-foot tractor-
drawn aerial ladder truck. For many years, Newark apparatus
was painted white. Notice the low windshield, hood-mounted
bell and Dahill Air Hoist.

Fire apparatus photographer Dan Martin got the Kalispell, Mont. Fire Dept. to roll its 1925 American LaFrance pumper out onto the ramp for this photo. The rig is a 1000 GPM Type 12 with worm drive rear axle. Note the steel disc wheels. Standard equipment on other models was wood-spoked artillery-type wheels. Kalispell has added the equipment box over the rear fender.

This 800 Imperial gallon Type 45 triple combination was built by the Canadian American LaFrance plant on Weston Rd. in Toronto. Reg. No. 5170, it went into service with the Windsor, Ont. Fire Dept. as Engine No. 4 in August, 1925. Retired as a spare in 1958, it was sold to the Windsor Branch of the Historic Vehicle Society of Ontario for $1 the following year and is now in the custody of the author. The W.F.D. shops added the windshield in 1938.

Grand Rapids, Mich. purchased a lot of American LaFrance fire apparatus over the years. This 1925 Special 750 GPM pumper has conversion wheels and a shop-built windshield.

The San Francisco Fire Dept. purchased this special Type 75 pumper. It was equipped with a 750 GPM pump and had worm drive. Note the Sewell Cushion tires and the hard suctions carried in straight troughs.

This is Engine Co. No. 9 of the Rochester, N. Y. Fire Dept. Engine 9's crew poses with the rig on their return from helping fight a serious fire in neighboring Newark, N. Y. The big American LaFrance made the 45-mile run through heavy traffic in a respectable 70 minutes.

Chain Drive Construction

The rugged American LaFrance Type 75 chassis had its transmission case cast in a single piece. The jackshafts and sprockets for the roller-type drive chains can also be seen. The 750 GPM rotary gear pump is mounted near the center of the chassis.

Rescue Hook & Ladder Co. No. 1 of the Haverstraw, N. Y. Fire Dept. responded to fires with this 1925 American La-France Type 33 city service ladder truck. The 6-cylinder 105 horsepower rig is in nearly factory-new condition here. The tillerman sat in a basket-type seat. The front-drive ladder truck has Single Giant solid tires on steel discs up front, and wooden artillery wheels on the rear.

The hood of this 1925 American LaFrance triple combination is lettered for "Riverside", likely Riverside, Calif. This 750 GPM pumper has a booster hose system and 6-cylinder engine.

A favorite with apparatus buffs at SPAAMFAA's National Muster in Syracuse for years has been Bob Potter's nearly original 1925 American LaFrance 65-foot Type 31 aerial. Powered by a 6-cylinder engine, it ran as Truck 2 on the West New York, N. J. Fire Dept. It still rolls on solid tires. Bob, of Cicero, N. Y., has several vintage rigs.

American LaFrance Type 14 Quad, carrying a 750 gallon-per-minute rotary gear pump and booster equipment, was used by the fire department of Pompton, Lakes, N. J. The original headlights have been replaced with sealed beams.

The American LaFrance factory in Elmira, N. Y. delivered a sizeable number of these quadruple combination fire engines. These were designated Type 14, the same as the company's straight-frame city service hook and ladder trucks. This Type 14 quad with 600 gallon-per-minute pump was sold to Morristown, Tenn. and is still in close to original condition except for paint. The hose was carried in the large tray under the ladder bank.

The Boston Fire Dept. ran this big American LaFrance high pressure hose wagon. It is equipped with two big turret pipes, dual solid tires on the rear and has a Whiting warning light on its right side. Boston rigs were equipped with the type of leather windbreaker seen here.

Seagrave, compared to its competitor in Elmira, built relatively few straight chemical cars. This is a little 2-tank model on the new Suburbanite chassis.

The Seagrave Corp. furnished this quadruple combination to the Seymour, Conn. Fire Dept. Note the two suction hoses and "steamer" soft suction hose on the running board. This apparatus is furnished with a full-length equipment basket over the ladder bed. Chemical hose is carried in the basket behind the chemical tank.

A 1925 Seagrave Standard 85-foot tractor-drawn aerial ladder truck, with factory windshield, went to Linwood, N.J. The handwheels are for extending the aerial ladder fly. Compressed springs hoisted the main ladder off the bed.

This Seagrave 350 gallon-per-minute Suburbanite is still owned by the Elk Grove Fire Dept. of Elk Grove, Cal.

Chicago purchased three of these Seagrave 65-foot chain-drive water towers, in 1923, 1925 and 1928. This is Water Tower No. 2, which was later equipped with a "crow's nest" and a second tower nozzle at the top of the main mast. These towers were familiar sights at multiple alarm fires in Chicago for many years.

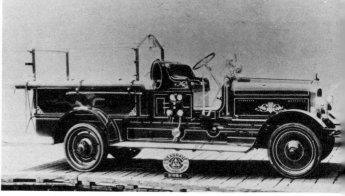

Fresh out of the paint and art shop in the Seagrave Corp.'s plant in Columbus, Ohio, is this Seagrave combination pump and hose car. The high rear rail and frame behind the oval-shaped fuel tank indicate that this apparatus may have been built for a West Coast community. This pumper carries no ground ladders, but ladder holders are visible on the upper framework. The bell is carried at the top of the front hose box frame.

West Palm Beach, Fla. boasted this little 2-tank Model T Ford chemical car. These were useful little fire engines in the suburbs, and often responded with heavier apparatus.

Model T Fords provided some important support service to firefighting fleets. The Pittsburgh, Pa. Bureau of Fire used this Ford fuel tender to keep the pumpers pumping at major fires.

The Foamite-Childs Corp. of Utica, N. Y. began to market its own custom fire apparatus. These were built on an assembled Kearns-Duhie Vau chassis, powered by Wisconsin engines. This is a 600 gallon-per-minute Childs Standard triple combination delivered to Rayne, La. These models were later known as Childs Thoroughbreds.

The Barton Products Co. of Jackson, Mich. found a ready market for its Barton Portable Pumper, which could be adapted to the front of the Model T Ford engine. Barton pumps were manufactured by the American Steam Pump Co. of Battle Creek and could put out 200-250 gallons per minute. Of centrifugal design, this mighty mite could lift water 26 feet and deliver it through hose lines at 20 pounds pressure.

Among the lesser known commercial truck chassis used for fire engines was the Moreland, built on the West Coast. This Moreland chemical and hose wagon ran with Los Angeles Eng. Co. No. 29. Other rare chassis converted for fire department work included the Bessemer and Stoughton.

Obenchain-Boyer mounted this versatile triple combination fire engine body on a Graham Bros. truck chassis. The distinctive "O-B" insignia decorates the radiator.

This one's just for fun. The late Bob Barber of Kalamazoo, one of the most knowledgeable apparatus buffs in the country, poses behind the wheel of a 1925 Pirsch-Reo 350 GPM triple combination. This little rig was part of the Bloomingdale, Ill. Fire Dept. before a local VFW post got it for a parade unit.

Ahrens-Fox built this NS-4 piston pumper, Reg. No. 1656, for Haverhill, Mass. where it responded as Engine 3. A canvas windshield was fabricated around the cowl-mounted bell, and a turret pipe has been installed in the hose bed.

A smaller Ahrens-Fox piston pumper model was the 4-cylinder KS-4. This 750 gallon-per-minute model was built for Berwyn, Ill. The windshield was added later. Note the bell behind the glass.

Orange, Mass. had this 1926 Ahrens-Fox city service hook and ladder truck. Ahrens-Fox was also using drum-style headlights. This is a 6-cylinder model that saw many years of service.

For the first time in more than a decade, American LaFrance in 1926 redesigned and restyled most of its apparatus. Design changes included a new, much higher radiator and hood and a cast, recessed type cowl. The new line was known as the 100 Series, and a 1,000 GPM rotary gear pumper that had previously been identified as a Type 12 became the Type 112. Similarly, the Type 17 aerial with the new style tractor became the Type 117. For the first year, the new 100 Series apparatus carried the same drum-style Vesta headlights that had been used since 1922, but a new bowl-type headlight appeared by 1927. Probably the most popular model in the new line was the 6-cylinder Type 145 Metropolitan, a 1,000 GPM rotary gear triple combination pumper.

The company carried forward its front-drive Type 31 aerial ladder truck without changes, but Type 114 city service ladder truck, however, had the new front end. For the past year or two, Type 31's were delivered with a more streamlined, enclosed lower front end with integral full fenders and front step plates. The rear wheels of straight-frame and tractor-type aerials now were covered by step-top fenders. American LaFrance assembled some of the pre-100 Series type pumpers as late as 1929. These included a sizeable fleet of Type 75 pumpers delivered to Pittsburgh, Pa. Some of these latter-day models were literally assembled from the parts bin.

At the end of 1926, American LaFrance boasted that since 1910 the company had sold and placed in service no fewer than 4,006 rotary gear pumpers, 41 piston pumpers and five centrifugal pumpers. This demonstrated the marked preference for the gear-type fire pump, at least from American LaFrance. The low-volume piston pumper was discontinued four years later.

The Seagrave Co. introduced an important new model this year, too. Sized between its hot-selling little 350 GPM Suburbanite and its Standard 750 GPM model was the all-new Seagrave Special, a 600 gallon-per-minute 6-cylinder pumping engine. Like the Suburbanite, the Special could also be ordered as a light city service hook and ladder

Only four of these Bickle-Ahrens Fox piston pumpers were sold in Canada by Bickle Fire Engines Ltd. of Woodstock, Ontario. One went to Kingston, Ont. in 1924, and the other three were delivered to Hamilton, Ont. in 1926, 1928 and 1930. The author remembers this 1926 Ahrens-Fox Model NS-4 running out of the singlebay John St. fire station in 1956. It was rated at 800 Imperial gallons per minute.

1926

truck, or with a special body for chemical and hose work, a squad truck or a straight chemical or a straight hose car. A Special 600 combination pumper and ladder truck was also made available later. Seagrave continued to place its money solely on the merits of the centrifugal type pump.

In other developments this year, Peter Pirsch & Sons Co. of Kenosha, Wisc., began assembling its own custom fire apparatus chassis, using Waukesha power. Peter Pirsch & Sons was established in 1857, and the company's products included pumpers of from 150 to 750 GPM capacity, combination chemical and hose trucks, and city service ladder trucks.

The Stutz Fire Engine Co., which had previously powered its apparatus with Wisconsin engines, in 1926 commenced production of its own 175-horsepower engine. The new Stutz Six featured overhead camshaft design, and permitted the Indianapolis manufacturer to offer its clientele pumpers of up to 1,200 GPM pumping capacity.

The Sanford Motor Truck Co. of East Syracuse, N. Y., had formed a fire apparatus division and was turning out pumpers and combination on its own chassis. This company still turns out a few custom fire engines annually. The old W. S. Nott Co. of Minneapolis had introduced a new line of motor pumpers which revived the Nott Universal name.

Under the direction of its resourceful master mechanic William F. Striebel, the Milwaukee Fire Dept. in 1926 began to build its own pumpers and city service ladder trucks, rather than order factory-built jobs. The Milwaukee shops turned out three 750 GPM pumpers and a service ladder truck in 1926, using Waukesha 6-cylinder engines and Waterous rotary gear pumps. The Milwaukee Fire Dept. shop crew assembled 11 more pumpers and five more ladder trucks over the next five years. The 1926 models were designated "MFD-TIM", because of their Timken axles. These remarkable, very professional looking shop-built engines were designed and built in the MFD shops right from the ground up. Later models were equipped with Four Wheel Drive Auto Co. axles and bore "MFD-FWD" nameplates.

Merchantville, N. J. fought its fires with this rugged Mack Model AC Bulldog pumper, which was assigned to the Niagara Fire Co. of that city. A separate front bumper was unnecessary on the massive front end of this series. The windshield was probably added later.

Willimantic, Conn. accepted delivery of this big Mack triple combination pumper. Built on the AC "Bulldog" chassis, it had a Northern pump and chain drive. It is now owned by the Trolley Museum Fire Dept. at Warehouse Point, Conn.

Rye, N. Y. was a good Mack customer. This department had four Macks in service by 1926, including this Model AC triple combination pumper which was used by the Milton Point Hose Co. It has a booster system instead of chemical hose.

The Model T Ford, now nearing the end of its long production life, was still in demand by fire departments everywhere. Here is a Howe triple combination piston pumper that went to the Opp, Ala. Fire Dept.

The smaller Mack Model AB was still in demand as a fire truck chassis. Here is a medium-duty triple combination that was delivered to East Rockaway, N. Y.

Engine Co. No. 24 of the Los Angeles Fire Dept. was assigned this 1926 Seagrave combination booster and turret hose wagon. Note the four 2½-inch hose inlets for the fireboat-sized deck turret. Los Angeles ran this type of unit as manifold wagons for its famed Duplex pumpers in later years.

This was the standard Seagrave pumping engine of this period. The rig shown is a 1,000 gallon-per-minute, 6-cylinder model with booster equipment which was delivered to El Monte, Calif. Many departments still specified hard rubber tires and artillery wheels.

New Haven, Conn. was another city that once had white fire equipment. The New Haven motor shops converted this 1926 Seagrave Suburbanite into a pneumatic power unit by replacing the hose body with a big Schramm compressor. This rig supplied power for air hammers and other heavy rescue equipment.

The tillerman on this 1926 Seagrave Standard Series 65-foot tractor-drawn aerial had the luxury of a windshield. This spring-raised aerial- ran as Ladder 4 on the Garfield, N. J. Fire Dept.

Hamtramck, Mich. enclosed this 1926 Seagrave pumper with a big, locally-built cab sometime in the 1930s. Only the rounded hood and radiator is recognizeable as Seagrave on this pumper. The pump panel was located behind the rear doors.

Pride of Centralia, Ohio Fire Dept. was this newly-delivered 1926 Seagrave pumping engine which rode on Firestone Cord balloon tires. This pumper carries two sizes of hard suction hose, and a length of soft suction for hydrant hookups.

American LaFrance introduced a new Metropolitan series 1,000 gallon-per-minute pumper in the latter part of 1926. The new look included a higher radiator and a new hood with double rows of louvres, and a recessed cowl. This 1926 Metropolitan ran on the Highland Park, Mich. Fire Dept. for many years before it was acquired and restored by the Detroit Fire Buffs Assn. in 1962. Named "X-100", this pumper has replacement wheels, Roto-Rays and a Morrow metal windbreaker.

 Apparatus buff Dan. G. Martin of Naperville, Ill. realized a lifelong dream in 1972, when he acquired this 1926 American LaFrance 1000 GPM Type 12 triple combination pumper. This engine, which was built for Grand Rapids, Mich. now occupies a place of honor in the Martin garage. Note the white rubber hard suctions and steel wheels, which were added later in this rig's service life.

American-LaFrance Metropolitan 1000 Gallon Triple

American LaFrance late in the year came out with its all-new Series 100 fire apparatus. The standard model in this series was the 1,000 GPM Metropolitan. The restyled series featured a new double-louvred hood, cast metal cowl with recessed instrument panel and a completely new radiator. The Vesta drum-style headlights were used for the remainder of this model year.

American-LaFrance Fire Engine Company, Inc.

This was to be the last year that this familiar style of fire apparatus was built. Production at Elmira gradually shifted over to the new restyled Series 100. This 1000 GPM Type 12 pumper, with solid tires, was built for the Metropolitan Okura, Japan, Fire Board.

The Winnetka, Ill. Fire Dept. once owned this well-equipped 1926 American LaFrance Type 14 Quad. The rotary gear pump was rated at 750 gallons-per-minute. A rectangular booster tank and a windshield have been added.

The Combination Ladder Co. of Providence, R. I. built some of these junior-series city service hook and ladder trucks for the New York City Fire Dept. In remarkably good shape for an F.D.N.Y. rig is this one, built on a Pierce-Arrow truck chassis.

The Indian Fire Patrol, a three-wheeled motorcycle fire apparatus built jointly by the Indian Motorcycle Co. of Springfield, Mass. and the Foamite-Childs Corp. of Utica, N. Y. was a moderate success. This model could carry two firemen, and was equipped with a small chemical tank, chemical hose and other portable equipment. These Indians were equipped with Rajah spark plugs.

Charging out the fire house to an alarm is a Foamite-Childs Thoroughbred triple combination. This rugged-looking rig was designed for heavy-duty service.

Snow posed no problem for the speedy Childs Thoroughbred, at least as long as the tire chains were in place. This is a 2-tank triple combination on its way to a fire out in the countryside. The crew appears to consider turnout gear as unnecessary.

Foamite-Childs was the builder of this small 4-tank straight chemical car which was supplied to East Greenbush, N. Y. The dash-mounted spotlight was a standard feature of windshieldless apparatus being built at this time.

In Canada, the Bickle Fire Engines Ltd. company in Woodstock, Ont. sold a very successful line of fire engines on the Gotfredson truck chassis. The Gotfredson was built in Walkerville, Ont., now part of Windsor. This Gotfredson-Bickle triple combination pumper was built for the Toronto suburb of Scarborough.

Opelousas, La. ordered two Childs Thoroughbreds this year. Both were triple combinations with cast-steel wheels and solid tires. One was named "Irene" and the other "Sing". Both were used by the Hope Hook & Ladder Co. No. 1.

This is one of the M.F.D. city service hook and ladder trucks built by the Milwaukee Fire Dept. apparatus shops, under the direction of Master Mechanic William Striebel. Note the solid disc wheels, hard tires and chemical equipment.

Milwaukee had one of the most resourceful motor shops anywhere. In 1926, the Milwaukee Fire Dept. shops actually built several complete fire engines. These were known as M.F.D.s and included both pumping engines and city service ladder trucks. This pumper was powered by a 6-cylinder "Ricardo Head" Waukesha engine, and the pump was a 750 GPM Waterous rotary. It is believed the six of these pumpers were eventually built.

International Harvester, an established manufacturer of trucks, buses and tractors, was now promoting its own motor fire apparatus. This is a chemical-hose combination of 1926. The headlights on this series of International truck were mounted on the cowl instead of up front.

Ogdensburg, N. Y. had this International motor hose wagon. This truck was used on occasion to tow Ogdensburg's old steamer to big fires.

In 1926, this International chemical and hose combination car was delivered to Bower Hill, Penn. Chemical hose, lanterns and other small equipment has yet to be installed.

Although steamers were no longer being built, many of these dependable pumpers remained in service with large and small departments. Louisville, Ky. motorized four former horse-drawn steamers by placing International four-wheel tractors under them. This was Engine Co. No. 8's rig.

BUFFALO

The Sanford Fire Apparatus Corp. of East Syracuse, N. Y. marketed a line of pumpers and combinations. This 1926 Sanford triple combination was built for Weedsport, N. Y. It is a regular participant at the SPAAMFAA National Muster held at nearby Syracuse each August.

Buffalo Fire Appliance Corp. built many fire engines on the Larrabee motor truck chassis. This well-equipped triple combination pumper, hose and chemical car went to Wallkill, N.Y.

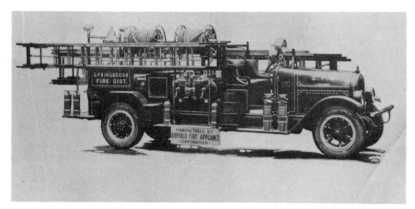

Buffalo - Built

Here is another Buffalo-Larrabee. This is a 4-tank chemical car ordered by the Springbrook, N. Y. Fire Dept. Note the 45-foot extension ladder carried on the left-hand side of this truck.

The Buffalo Fire Appliance Corp. stretched the wheelbase of a Reo Speedwagon chassis to make this small triple combination for Kenilworth, N. J. The small tank on top of the dash is the fuel tank.

This rig started life as a hose and chemical car on the Potsdam, N. Y. Fire Dept. But the 4-cylinder Brockway was rebuilt by Buffalo into a high-banked hook and ladder truck. The converted truck arrived back in Potsdam on Thanksgiving Day.

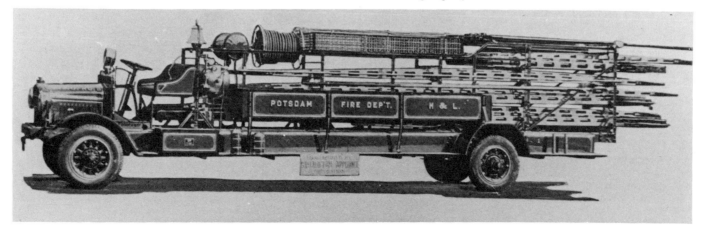

The American LaFrance Fire Engine Co. late in 1927 acquired the Foamite-Childs Corp., and the Elmira firm was renamed the American LaFrance and Foamite Corp. Also in this hear, the new American LaFrance Metropolitan 1,000 GPM pumper was awarded a gold medal at the Philadelphia Sesquicentennial Exposition. American LaFrance this year came out with a new line of small fire apparatus, under the designation of Type 91. This series was quite similar in styling to the larger Series 100 apparatus, and included initially 350 to 500 GPM pumpers and combination hose and chemical cars. The Type 91 had a 2-piece cast radiator shell and full-crowned fenders.

The Ahrens-Fox Fire Engine Co. also had something new in the works. The Cincinnati plant in 1927 started building quadruple combination apparatus. The first of these was a midship-mounted rotary gear quad delivered to Bristol, Pa. Over the next 21 years this company would deliver 12 more of this type, which hardly qualified the J-Series as a high-volume product. Ahrens-Fox quads were eventually built with all three types of pumps—the standard Ahrens-Fox front-mounted piston, the Rotary-style and later, a few were delivered with centrifugal pumps. Capacities ranged from 500 to 1,000 gallons-per-minute. Only 28 Ahrens-Fox Quads of all types were ever built.

Mack Trucks, Inc., which still used the International Motor Co. name on its letterhead, delivered its last Model AC Bulldog fire apparatus this year. The rugged dope-nosed AC was phased out to make room for an entirely new series of pumpers and ladder trucks still on the drawing boards. Mack in 1927 claimed the distinction of introducing the industry's first 4-wheel brakes and power brakes for fire apparatus, as well as the first parallel-series pressure-volume fire pump.

Although the distinctive Model AC with its big, circled "M" on its blunt front seemed to get all the attention, Mack's smaller, more conventional Model AB chassis was also well known to the fire service. Mack had been building smaller series pumpers, city service ladder trucks and combinations on this chassis with its prominent, horizontally-louvred radiator for several years. The Model AB had, in fact, been around since 1914—the year before the AC had made its appearance.

In other developments, Peter Pirsch & Sons delivered its first 750 GPM pumper, mounted on its own chassis, to

Franklin Park, Ill. The Maxim Motor Co. in 1927 introduced its new "B" Model apparatus. Principal models included the B-75, a 750 GPM pumper, and the B-10, of 1,000 GPM capacity. The 6-cylinder Maxim B Models retained the tapered, sculptured hood that had been used earlier.

A new firm, D. E. McCann's Sons Co. of Portland, Me. began production of custom-chassised pumpers and combinations. One of the older, established names in the fire engine business, the Combination Ladder Co. of Providence, R. I. was still going strong. The Combination Co. was still mounting its high-quality fire equipment on various makes of commercial chassis. Out on the coast, the San Francisco Fire Dept. purchased a Kleiber tractor to repower its old Gorter water tower. Another Kleiber chassis was purchased later for use as a searchlight wagon.

One year earlier, the leading fire service trade journal, *Fire and Water Engineering,* had been separated into two separate publications. *Fire Engineering* marked its 50th anniversary in 1927, and is still the dominant publication of the American fire service today. It began as the *Fireman's Journal* in New York City on Nov. 17, 1877.

During 1927, New York City placed a new Ahrens-Fox Model HP piston pumper into service at Engine Co. No. 65. Equipped with a 6-piston pump, the new high pressure model was designed to get water onto the upper floors of skyscrapers some 800 feet above street level. The big HP was powered by the Ahrens-Fox 6-cylinder engine.

With its crew standing proudly by, this is a 1927 American LaFrance Type 114 city service hook and ladder truck that was built for the Mishawaka, Ind. Fire Dept.

The American LaFrance factory at Elmira, N. Y. still did the odd rebuild or modernization of older equipment. This is a 1923 Type 12 pumper of 1,000-gallon capacity that was rebuilt for Milford, Del. The front end forward of the dash is new. In most cases the registration number was not altered, but on extensive rebuilds this was sometimes changed.

Some fire chiefs still preferred chain or worm drive instead of the direct shaft drive some manufacturers were offering. American LaFrance chose to stick with chain drive, but did offer a worm drive setup as an option. This 750 gallon Series 100 pumper with worm drive was shipped to Brewton, Ala.

During 1927, American LaFrance began using a new bowl-shaped headlight design on its 100 Series fire engines. These are shown to advantage on this Type 145 Metropolitan triple combination built for Marlboro, N. J.

Indianapolis used this 1927 American LaFrance 65-foot tractor-drawn water tower for many years. Drawn by a Type 117 6-cylinder tractor, it featured a hydraulic hoist that was activated by water pressure, and had a 3-section, hand-raised main mast. After being stored for years in the I.F.D. shops, it was donated to local fire buffs and moved to a museum.

Sporting a set of Whiting warning lights and a windshield, this is a 1929 Type 117 tractor-drawn American LaFrance aerial ladder truck. American LaFrance still built only the single bank style of ladder truck. It is not certain where this truck served, but it could be a Boston or Philadelphia rig.

The largest apparatus built by American LaFrance was still the 85-foot tractor-drawn aerial. This one was built for Rutland, Vt. Note the step-top pumper fenders used on the trailer, and the lofty perch the tillerman had, without benefit of protection from the weather.

American LaFrance built this special 100 Series rescue squad car with chemical equipment for the Pittsburgh, Pa. Fire Dept. The crew rode in the rear of this speedy rig, which was powered by the standard American LaFrance 6-cylinder engine. Bodies from these hard-used squads were often transferred from one chassis to another.

This is one of those "mystery rigs" that makes this hobby so interesting. This is listed as a 1927 American LaFrance turret and hose car built for Philadelphia. The styling is clearly of the pre-1926 type, and the rear body is not stock either.

American LaFrance built a limited number of special high pressure pumpers. This is a 1927 Type 119 High Pressure Pumping Engine built for New York City. It could pump 1,000 gallons-per-minute at 160 pounds per square inch pressure. This type succeeded the earlier Type 19.

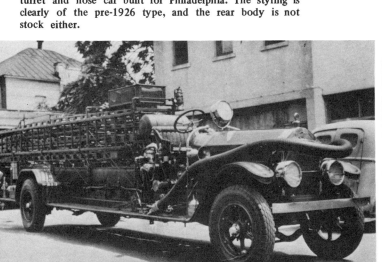

A conventional American LaFrance 100 Series quadruple combination, this well-loaded 750 GPM quad was delivered to Dyersburg, Tenn. Many southern departments liked the convenience of the preconnected hard suction hose.

Pittsburgh's Engine Co. No. 5 once rolled with a 1927 American LaFrance Type 145 triple combination pumping engine, seen here in its later years. The original headlights have been replaced, and the wooden artillery wheels originally used up front have been replaced with a set of steel discs. Note how the booster hose piping from the pump to the rear platform is also used as a hose bed side rail. This 1,000 GPM pumper bore ALF Reg. No. 5877.

General Motors and American LaFrance teamed up to market a completely new series of small fire trucks, aimed primarily at the small town and rural fire districts. This is a 4-tank American LaFrance-GMC chemical car. This special GMC chassis was powered by a Buick 6-cylinder engine. The 199 Series pumper had a 500 GPM American LaFrance rotary gear pump.

Although this older style American LaFrance had been succeeded by the new 100 Series apparatus the previous year, the Elmira plant continued to deliver some of the earlier style models to several communities. The Pittsburgh, Pa. Bureau of Fire's Engine Co. 7 was assigned this 1927 American LaFrance Type 75 pumper, Reg. No. 5860, of 750 GPM capacity.

Six 1927 Ahrens-Fox Model JS-2 piston pumpers were delivered to the Detroit Fire Dept. This 750 GPM pumper was refurbished by the D.F.D. shops in 1962 for Fire Chief Commissioner Paxton Mendelssohn. Comm. Mendelssohn later presented this rig to George Getz' "Hall of Flame", where it is now on display in Phoenix, Ariz.

Pumping all-out, this Ahrens-Fox piston pumper is supplying no less than eight streams. The large diameter hose feeding into the "Y" intake is a steamer, or soft-suction, hose which is hooked up to the water supply.

Ahrens-Fox modestly called this Model PS-2 piston pumper built for New York City "the world's most powerful fire engine." The PS-2, also known as an HP, had a powerful A-F 6-cylinder engine which drove a Twin-Triple, 6-cylinder pump. This pumper was assigned to busy Engine Co. No. 65 in Manhattan, and a few days before entering service gave a convincing demonstration of its firefighting power by throwing two streams from the top of the Woolworth Building, some 800 feet above street level. This model was Ahrens-Fox's answer to Seagrave's Metropolite and the American LaFrance Type 115.

In addition to the popular piston pump, Ahrens-Fox now offered a rotary gear pump. This was named the Rotary-style. This 1927 Ahrens-Fox 600 GPM Quad equipped with a midship-mounted Rotarystyle pump was built for Bristol, Pa. which at one time had a large fleet of Ahrens-Foxes.

The Dahill Pneumatic Hoist was used on all Ahrens-Fox aerial ladder trucks. The two lifting cylinders were kept charged by a small compressor run off the transmission. This air hoist smoothly lifted the ladder off the truck bed. Musclepower extended the fly section.

This 1927 Ahrens-Fox Model MS-4 pumper was delivered to Fort Wayne, Ind. Note the large rectangular booster tank that has been added behind the gasoline tank. This was a 750 GPM model.

Wilmington, Delaware's Engine Co. No. 10 was assigned this 1927 Ahrens-Fox Rotarystyle midship-mounted quadruple combination. This apparatus carried all of the equipment of both an engine and a city service hook and ladder truck, and was equipped with a 750 GPM Ahrens-Fox rotary gear pump. The hose was carried in the hose box above the ladder beds.

Ahrens-Fox introduced a new style of hood and radiator for its midship-mounted rotary gear pumpers and combination cars. This 2-tank chemical car went to Bristol, Pa.

These two fire engines are each built on a different series of International Harvester truck chassis. The combination on the left is built on an IHC bus chassis, with shock absorbers mounted behind the bumper.

Farmingdale, Long Island, N. Y. purchased this sleek 1927 International combination chemical and hose wagon. An electric siren horn is mounted on the cowl.

Paxsonville, N. J. got this 1927 Hale 750 GPM triple combination pumper. The headlights are not original, apparently. This model bore a strong resemblance to earlier series American LaFrance apparatus.

The Hale Fire Pump Company of Conshohocken, Pa. continued to build some custom motor fire apparatus, such as this 1927 Hale 600 GPM pumper supplied to Pine Hill, N. J. Note the whitewall tires and the white suction hoses.

Seagrave could deliver an off-the-shelf fire engine within a very few months. This is a 1,000-gallon Standard that was on the firing line of Evanston, Ill. These pumpers were powered by Seagrave's own 6-cylinder engine.

In direct competition with American LaFrance's new Metropolitan was Seagrave's Standard 1,000 gallon-per-minute pumping engine. Springfield, Ohio had this one, which has been equipped with a wood windshield and a set of Buckeye Roto-Rays.

This Seagrave Special 600 GPM pumper has a factory accessory windshield. It served the Hazelcrest, Ill. Fire Dept.

Seagrave's little Suburbanite proved to be a very popular model. Now small towns and villages could afford to buy a complete, custom-built fire engine. This 500-gallon Suburbanite went to Arlington Heights, Ill.

Manasquan, N. J. protected itself with this 1927 Seagrave 500-gallon Quad. This combination has a high, homebuilt windshield and carries side-mounted ground ladders in addition to those in the main bank.

Sized between the 1,000-gallon Standard and the small Suburbanite was the Seagrave Special, a 600 gallon-per-minute triple combination pumper, This model was ideal for medium-sized communities and was available in a full line of pumpers, city service ladder trucks, squad rigs and quads.

1927

The big Mack Bulldog Model AC continued in production. Here is a 1,000 gallon-per-minute Mack pumper that was assigned to Engine Co. No. 47 of San Francisco.

Hagerstown, Md. called this 1927 Mack Model AB high pressure hose wagon out to major fires. It is equipped with an extra-long hose box and two deck turrets.

East Rockaway, N. Y. bought this 1927 Mack Model AB city service hook and ladder truck, which had full chemical equipment and a plated radiator shell.

Among the most unusual Mack Model AC fire engines built was this compact water tower, one of two identical rigs built for San Francisco. The 35-foot masts, of Gorter design, were fabricated by the Union Machine Co. These ponderous little towers are still on the S.F.F.D. The author found both of them stored in the same firehouse in 1972.

With eye-catching red-and-white paint jobs, Baltimore's fire apparatus was among the most distinctive in the U.S. The Baltimore City Fire Dept. Salvage Corps. was once equipped with this handsome Mack Model AC salvage wagon, which carried enough water repellent covers to protect the contents of a good-sized building. The pattern above the rear fender would indicate that this body was transferred to a new chassis from an older truck.

This 1927 Studebaker originally ran as a salvage car on the Los Angeles City Fire Dept., but it was later converted into a carbon dioxide chemical car. The CO_2 bottles can be seen in the former squad body. The special service unit was designated "CO-2 Co. No. 1."

The Four Wheel Drive Auto Co. of Clintonville, Wis. built this large motor tractor for the New York City Fire Dept. One of many of this type used to modernize aerial ladder trucks and water towers, this FWD tractor is pulling F.D.N.Y.'s Water Tower No. 1, an 1898 Hale 65-footer originally built by Fire Extinguisher Mfg. Co.

Peter Pirsch & Sons Co. had also been selling fire equipment built on the company's own custom chassis. This 500 gallon-per-minute Pirsch Model 19 Special was built for Roselle, Ill. Note the deck nozzle mounted on a platform over the large booster tank.

The Buffalo Fire Appliance Corp. began selling Buffalo fire apparatus on its own assembled custom chassis. This is a small triple combination built for the South Wales Fire Co. It carries quite a few ladders for a rig of this size.

As a memorial to his mother, Detroit Fire Commissioner Paxton Mendelssohn presented this 1927 Packard combination ambulance and commissary to the Detroit Fire Dept. as a gift. He replaced it with a V-16 Cadillac ambulance in 1937, at which time the former canteen unit was converted into a searchlight wagon. It is seen here standing by at a fire in 1948.

Here is a Prospect Deluge Master Fire Fighter with windshield, two chemical tanks and hose reels and a spotlight mounted on the cowl ahead of the windshield. These were also advertised as Biederman-Prospects, and were built by the Prospect Fire Engine Co. of Prospect, Ohio. It is lettered for "Lisbon."

This 1927 Diamond T pumper, with Boyer equipment, is still owned by the Hamler, Ohio Fire Dept. which uses it extensively on the parade circuit. It is painted white. Note the rear-mounted spare tire.

American LaFrance introduced yet another new series of medium-duty fire apparatus this year. The Elmira, N. Y. firm teamed up with General Motors to develop a special pumper designed for rural and suburban fringe duty. The new model was marketed under the trade name of American LaFrance–GMC, and was designated the Type 199.

The chassis for the new series was a special General Motors Truck that was powered by a 6-cylinder Buick engine. The standard triple combination Type 199 pumper was equipped with a 500 GPM rotary gear pump, but Elmira also offered a 4-tank straight chemical car, a hose wagon, and a chemical hose combination car on the same chassis. The Type 199 met immediate favor from smaller towns, and a sizeable number were sold. An improved model called the Type 299 came along a few years later. General Motors in the early to mid-1920s had aggressively promoted its fire apparatus chassis under its own name.

American LaFrance had started to use full-crowned fenders on its apparatus, and the shift away from chain drive to shaft-drive power trains had also begun. One of this company's more interesting deliveries this year was a Series 100 tractor-drawn 65-foot water tower for Utica, N. Y., which used a water-raised main mast. A similar type of apparatus, drawn by the earlier Type 17 tractor, had been delivered to Albany, N. Y. two years earlier.

One of the major advances in fire engine design was made in 1928 by Peter Pirsch & Sons Co. The Kenosha Wis. firm delivered a 600 gallon-per-minute pumper to Monroe, Wis. What made this pumper unusual was that it had a completely enclosed custom-built cab—the first fully closed-in piece of fire apparatus to go into service in the U. S. from a major manufacturer. Remember, most apparatus built at this time did not even have a windshield for the protection of the crew. Monroe's milestone Pirsch is still around, and in excellent condition.

San Francisco placed two interesting rigs into service this year. The SFFD purchased two "small" water towers. These were built on solid-tired Mack Model AC chassis with steel-spoked wheels, and were equipped with 35-foot Gorter masts built by the Union Machine Co. For the next 40 years, these stubby towers were familiar sights at all extra-alarm fires in 'Frisco. The SFFD also operated a 65-foot Gorter tower drawn by a Kleiber tractor. During a 1972 visit, the author was delighted to find both of the Mack-Gorter towers stored at the same fire station, along with a converted 400 Series ALF hose wagon.

Ahrens-Fox restyled its midship-mounted Rotarystyle pumpers this year with new full-crowned fenders, and a pleasingly designed rounded hood and radiator. Crowned fenders also began to appear on the company's big piston pumpers, which retained their classic gabled hoods for another two years. One of the most interesting features on 'Foxes in this era was the use of extremely thin Ryan headlights. The Ahrens-Fox Fire Engine Co. in 1928 exported seven Model NS-2 piston pumpers to Rotterdam, Holland.

In a noteworthy finale to the Foamite-Childs story, American LaFrance after the takeover of this firm delivered no less than 51 Childs Thoroughbreds before it closed the Utica, N. Y. plant and transferred all operations to Elmira.

Other noteworthy 1928 deliveries included a 600 GPM pumper built by the Southern Apparatus Co. of Dallas, to Wharton, Tex.; a Seagrave Special long-wheelbase special squad car for Cleveland, and a 100-foot Magirus aerial for Milwaukee. The American Magirus Fire Appliance Co. now had its offices in Indianapolis. Sidney, Ohio and Aberdeen, S. D. also purchased Magirus rearmount aerials.

Mack Trucks was about to make a major commitment in its fire engine business. Mack had already an impressive new line of fire engines, ranging from small pumpers to 1,000 GPM jobs, and including a totally new tractor-drawn aerial that featured an engine-driven hoist. The stunning new Macks had classic lines, with bold new radiator shells, and rakishly-angled hood louvres. A surprising number of these beauties are still on the road today. The new Macks did not get into volume production until 1929.

American LaFrance came out with a new, smaller series of apparatus called the Type 92. This series had a 2-piece cast aluminum radiator shell and a new hood with a single set of louvres to each side. This Type 92 pumper of 600 gallon capacity was delivered to the Tarrytown, N. Y. Fire Dept. Note crowned fenders, warning light atop the lower section of the radiator, and the same type of bumper and headlights used on the larger Metropolitan Series.

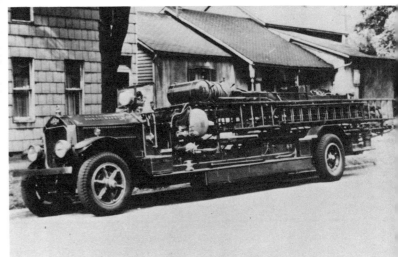

This 1928 American LaFrance Type 114 combination was built for the Department of Public Safety of the City of Grand Rapids, Mich. Although it mounts a 750 gallon-per-minute rotary gear pump, it does not qualify as a quadruple combination, or "quad", because it has no hose bed. The G.R.F.D. added the long tool box under the running board, and the canvas windshield.

This well-preserved American LaFrance pumper is still on the roster of the Muskegon Heights, Mich. Fire Dept. The shop-built windshield is barely visible from this angle. Note the full-crowned fenders that were starting to appear on ALF apparatus.

Ocean Grove, N. J. ran this American LaFrance Type 117 aerial ladder truck. This slightly smaller tractor had a 2-piece cast radiator rather than the plated shell. This is a 75-footer. The use of pneumatic tires fore and aft, and solid tires on the rear of the tractor, was common practice.

This is the mate to the deluge and turret wagon rebuilt by American LaFrance for Pittsburgh, Pa. in 1923. Also built by the old Fire Extinguisher Mfg. Co. as a horse-drawn unit, this one was rebuilt with a Type 31 6-cylinder tractor by American LaFrance in 1928 for the Atlantic City, N. J. Fire Dept. Generally identical to the Pittsburgh rig, it also features a 32-foot water tower mast, side-mounted turret pipes and artillery tires in the rear. Note the bowl-type headlights and enclosed front fenders.

This is a big American LaFrance 100 Series quadruple combination. The 750 gallon quad was built for Santa Rosa, Cal. Note the large booster tank behind the seat and the crowned fenders. This model was classified as a Type 114.

This Type 31 American LaFrance aerial is something of a mystery. It has the earlier Gray & Davis styled headlights, but the type of front and rear fenders and tractor running gear enclosure not seen until after 1926. It ran as Truck 1 in West New York, N. J. and may be an updated 1920 model. The two-tone rig had a 75-foot aerial.

Minneapolis, Minn. ordered this 1928 American LaFrance Type 119 high pressure pumper, with factory windshield. It could pump 1,200 gallons per minute. Type 119s were also delivered to New York City and Philadelphia. This model used wider front-end sheet metal than the standard line. Note the disc wheels and 4-section hood louvres.

1928

The Seagrave Corp. was still selling many of its little Suburbanite pumpers, combinations and ladder trucks. This 500 gallon-per-minute 1928 Seagrave Suburbanite, of the Germantown, Wis. Fire Dept. has a front suction intake, visible just below the front bumper, a tall booster hose basket, and basic pump panel.

The Syracuse, N. Y. Fire Dept. was the original owner of this 1928 Seagrave Standard Series 1,000 gallon-per-minute, 6-cylinder pumper. This was one of the first rigs acquired by SPAAMFAA when that group was being organized. White in color, it is seen on the field at one of SPAAMFAA's annual musters in Syracuse. Note the dual spotlights on the cowl.

Seagrave's standard big-city pumper, of course, was still the Standard series. This 1928 Seagrave 1,000 gallon-per-minute Standard pumping engine was built for Rome, N. Y. It is one of a dozen antique rigs owned by collector Andy Henderson of Weedsport, N. Y. It retains its rich original striping and trim.

A 400 gallon-per-minute Seagrave Suburbanite served the Ocean Gate, N. J. Fire Dept. This rig sports four lengths of hard suction hose, has a rakishly-angled windshield, and a suction strainer attached to the front end of the bottom length of hard suction.

Bearing more than a little resemblance to a Seagrave of this era is this 1928 Southern combination pump and hose car delivered to Wharton, Texas by the Southern Fire Apparatus Co. of Dallas. This is a 600 gallon-per-minute pumper. It underwent a 12-hour Board of Fire Underwriters test before being placed in service.

The Chicago Fire Dept. shops built this tractor-drawn city service hook and ladder truck, using a Seagrave 6-cylinder tractor and a trailer built in the C.F.D. shops. Note the tiller windshield.

The Ahrens-Fox piston pumper with its distinctive front-mounted pump and big ball-shaped air chamber could be found in fire houses across the nation. This is a 1928 Model NS-3, built for Lynn, Mass. A 1,000 GPM model, it has a small turret pipe atop its hose box. It responded as Lynn Engine No. 5.

1928

At work is a 1928 Ahrens-Fox Model NS-4, of the Paterson, N. J. Fire Dept. With the front-mounted pump, spotting the pumper on the street was a breeze: the driver simply zeroed in on the hydrant closest to the fire, hooked up the preconnected soft suction hose and went to work. This is a 1,000 GPM model.

The Ahrens-Fox piston pumper was for many years a real workhorse on the Chicago Fire Department. Chicago placed many repeat orders for Ahrens-Fox piston pumpers. This 1,000 gallon Model NS-2 is one of seven ordered in 1928. It went to Eng. Co. No. 128.

Ahrens-Fox exported a number of its piston pumpers over the years. The largest export order went to Rotterdam, Holland, where seven 1,000 GPM Model NS-2s were shipped in 1928. The author was astonished to stumble across these pleasant reminders of buffing at home, on a trip to Europe in 1963. The Rotterdamsche Brandweer, or Fire Dept. still had four of these pumpers in service, two with this style of home-made enclosed cab and two with open cabs. Other Foxes were exported to Java, Japan, and New South Wales, Australia.

Although the piston pumper reigned supreme, Ahrens-Fox was selling a few of its new Rotarystyle pumpers. The Rotarystyle featured a midship-mounted rotary gear pump instead of the front-mounted piston type. This 1928 Ahrens-Fox 750 GPM Rotarystyle was delivered to the movie community of Beverly Hills, Cal. The windshield was added later.

The big Ahrens-Fox 6-cylinder engine was a lot of motor to keep cool during the summer months, and many fire departments that operated Fox piston pumpers ran them steadily with the hood wide open. This 1928 Model MS-4 is still on the roster in Reading, Ohio, a Cincinnati suburb. Note the two 2½-inch hard suctions preconnected to the "Y" intake.

1928

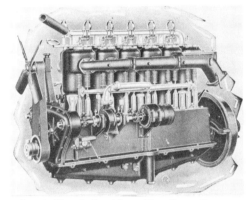

This is the right-hand side of an Ahrens-Fox Rotarystyle rotary-gear pumper. Ahrens-Fox was probably at its zenith at this time, and the company's slogan was "Nothing is too good for fire service, and nothing but the best will do."

This 1928 Ahrens-Fox Rotarystyle midship-mounted pumper sports the new rounded-style radiator and hood. The 600 gallon-per-minute pumper was delivered to Holden, Mass.

The exhaust side of the Ahrens-Fox Super Power motor, which was standard equipment in the Ahrens-Fox piston pumper, was completely built in the company's Cincinnati plant.

This 1928 Buffalo Type 75 pumper, of 750 GPM capacity, was built for the U.S. Veterans' Hospital at Northport, Long Island. It is built on the same type of assembled chassis previously used by the Foamite-Childs Corp., which by now had been absorbed by American LaFrance.

Well ahead of its time in low, streamlined styling was this series of Mack fire apparatus built on that company's rugged bus chassis. This 1928 Mack city service hook and ladder truck was built for Humane Fire Co. No. 1 of Royersford, Pa. Relatively few fire apparatus deliveries were made using this chassis series.

This combination chemical and hose car, built by the Buffalo Fire Appliance Corp. is on a Larrabee motor truck chassis. In service with the Oceanside, N. Y. Fire Dept., it features two hose reels and a factory-built windshield.

The Albany, N.Y. Fire Department built up this "Illuminating Car" for use at night fires and at fires where heavy smoke complicated firefighting operations. The 1928 Mack Model AB chassis was a former rescue squad truck. The body of this unit was remounted on a new American LaFrance Series 200 chassis, and saw many more years of service. The Albany Fire Dept. workshops converted the older Mack chassis into this versatile searchlight unit. Note the power cables carried on the reels above the running board.

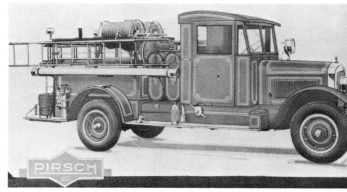

Another chassis that was becoming popular with fire apparatus builders was the Studebaker. American LaFrance built this handsome squad car for Greenwich, Conn. on a Studebaker Big Six bus chassis. The Studebaker had an enviable reputation for both quality and durability.

One of the very first closed-cab fire engines built in the U.S. was this closed-cab pumper, built by the Peter Pirsch & Sons Co. of Kenosha, Wis. and sold to the Monroe, Wis. Fire Dept. The cab was probably specified by the purchaser. The pumper was a 750 gallon-per-minute model: most of the pump panel was enclosed by the cab doors. This enclosed unit was at least seven years ahead of its time. Note the two elliptical booster tanks, and the twin booster hose reels.

Peter Pirsch and Sons Co. of Kenosha, Wis. outfitted this 1928 Studebaker Big Six bus chassis as a 500 gallon-per-minute triple combination pumper. The rig was built for Richfield, Wis. The white rubber hard suctions were a Pirsch trademark at this time.

Howe Fire Apparatus of Anderson, Ind. built this rather large triple combination pumper on a Studebaker chassis for the Martin County Co-Operative Fire Protective Assn. of Fairmont, Minn. This big Stude pumper packs no less than six lengths of hard suction hose for those long, rural hookups. It has a 350-gallon pump.

The Four-Wheel-Drive Auto Co. of Clintonville, Wis. delivered 18 of these tough-looking combination hose and turret wagons to the New York City Fire Dept. Riding on solid tires, they sported large deck pipes. The overhead rack carried two scaling ladders. Note the "subway strap" hangers on the rear rail for the F.D.N.Y. crew.

The Obenchain-Boyer Co. also delivered some fire engines built on the Studebaker commercial chassis. This one started out as a 500 gallon-per-minute pumper, but the St. Joseph, Mich. Fire Dept. eventually converted it into a combination turret and hose wagon.

The biggest announcement of this year came from American LaFrance. At the 57th Annual Conference of the International Assn. of Fire Chiefs, American LaFrance took the wraps off its completely new Master Series apparatus. Introduced at the company's big exhibit at the Birmingham, Ala. convention, the new Master Series apparatus was billed as the most important achievement in motor fire apparatus design ever announced to the fire chiefs of America.

Among the features of the new Master Series apparatus was left-hand drive, 4-wheel safety brakes, which had been under development for four years; a fully-automatic cooling system, and completely new deep-section "fish belly" chassis frames. The new Master Series aerials boasted extra wide running boards and one-man operation, and all of the new models, whether equipped with solid rubber tires or pneumatics, rolled on hollow spoke, cast steel wheels. Officially designated the ALF Type 200 Series, the new Master Series models included the Metropolitan 1,000 GPM rotary gear pumper, a 750 GPM pumper, the Type 217 tractor-drawn aerial in 75 and 85-foot sizes, and the Type 214 straight frame city service ladder truck. American LaFrance used a big 140 horsepower T-head 6-cylinder engine for the new series. The new Series 200 fire engines had a massive, handsome appearance, and it is interesting to note that windshields were still considered unnecessary., Deliveries of the first Master Series pumpers and aerials began late in the year.

The Fire Engine Division of Mack Trucks also had something new to show at Birmingham. A feature exhibit at the IAFC Convention was Mack's new Type 19 tractor-drawn aerial ladder truck. Power by a 150-horsepower engine, the new Mack aerial employed a power takeoff from the engine to raise the big stick. One of the first of these new aerials was delivered to Ardmore, Pa.

Also included in the beautifully restyled Mack fire apparatus line was the Mack Type 19 triple combination pumper, built in 750 and 1,000 GPM sizes and powered by a 150-horsepower 6-cylinder engine. The smaller Mack Type 90 was powered by a 120-horsepower six, and included a 750 GPM pumper, a city service ladder truck and special hose and combination cars.

Mack and American LaFrance, however, did not have a corner on innovation this year. Ahrens-Fox Fire Engine Co. introduced its lithe little Ahrens-Fox Skirmisher quadruple combination. Designed as a 4-way combination for smaller communities, the 6-cylinder Skirmisher had a midship-mounted 600 or 750 GPM rotary gear pump, carried a full complement of wood ground ladders, a full

The Arundel Engine Co. of Keenebunkport, Maine, ran this 1929 Mack Type 19 pumper, with three hard suctions. Note how the suction port is mounted below the frame. The bell was still standard equipment on most fire apparatus, although the coaster siren had moved in in a big way.

Mack introduced its first aerial ladder truck. This aerial had an engine-driven hoist, with engine power used to lower as well as raise the 65-foot ladder. A 75-foot model was also available. The Type 90 Tractor-Drawn Aerial was powered by a Mack 120-horsepower, 6-cylinder engine and featured truss bracing on both the fly and bed ladders.

The Detroit Fire Dept. broke away from Seagrave and Ahrens-Fox in 1929 and placed three of these Mack Type 19s into service. All were 750 gallon-per-minute models. This one saw many years of service at Engine Co. No. 10. After retirement in 1952, it was loaned to Royal Oak, Mich. to protect the Detroit Zoo. In 1963 it was acquired by the Franklin, Mich. Volunteer Fire Dept. which restored it as seen here. The big Mack still wears its leather windbreaker.

The AC Bulldog series Mack by now had vanished from the firefighting scene. It had been replaced by the powerful Type 19 shown here. This 750 GPM Mack Type 19 triple combination pumper was delivered to Salt Lake City.

1929

New York City took delivery of this Seagrave Duplex water tower. The 65-foot tower, assigned to Water Tower No. 3, had two mast nozzles and two large turrets mounted on its trailer deck. The water-raised hoist was replaced with an FWD spring hoist in 1938. This tower was one of the most powerful ever built. The F.D.N.Y. still rolled on hard-rubber tires.

New York City this year placed one of the largest single orders ever with the Seagrave Corp. This order called for 50 1929 Seagrave Suburbanite combination hose and turret wagons. These small Seagraves were familiar sights on New York streets for years. This one was assigned to Engine Co. No. 1's hose wagon.

Wellesley, Mass. was the original owner of this 1929 Seagrave 75-foot tractor-drawn aerial ladder truck. Note the separate lockers for the turnout gear of each member of the company. This handsome aerial was later sold to the Hamden, Conn. Fire Dept. Note the canvas and celluloid windshield.

Some fire engines are proudly passed from department to department. A good example is this 1929 Seagrave 750 GPM Standard series pumping engine that served Grosse Point, Mich. for many years. It is now owned by Metamora, Mich. and is gradually being restored by this volunteer department. Note the Roto-Ray flashers.

load of hose which could be played out of a V-ended bed above the ladders, and booster equipment. The Skirmisher employed a Waukesha engine and Timken axle.

Peter Pirsch & Sons came out with two significant new fire engines this year. One was the company's first 1,000 GPM pumper, which was powered by the new Waukesha 6-RB 6-cylinder Ricardo Head fire apparatus engine rated at 130 horsepower. The other was a Pirsch Special 90-horsepower pumper built for smaller departments. The Pirsch Special had a 500 GPM pump and carried an over-sized booster tank as well as hose, ladders and other equipment.

Seagrave had introduced a new, improved Standard model centrifugal 1,000 GPM pumper with 4-wheel brakes. The company's small Suburbanite was still going strong in its seventh year, and could be ordered as a city service ladder truck as well as in pumper and combination models. The Boyer Fire Apparatus Co. of Logansport, Ind. had succeeded the old Obenchain-Boyer Co., and American LaFrance quietly ended production of commercial trucks, Sidney, Ohio placed an 85-foot Magirus rearmount aerial into service, and W. S. Nott marked its 50th anniversary in the fire engine business.

Henry Ford's new Model A, like its Model T predecessor, quickly found its way into wide fire service use. Many manufacturers offered fire apparatus adaptations designed for the Model AA Ford commercial chassis. Sanford offered pumpers in 500, 600 and 750 GPM sizes as well as various types of combinations and ladder trucks, and one of Buffalo's best-selling models was its 500 GPM Type 50.

Then, at the height of this new wave of prosperity, came the Stock Market Crash.

Chicago purchased two of these 1929 Seagrave 750 gallon-per-minute quadruple combinations in 1929. Another Seagrave Quad of this type was delivered in 1930. Equipped with an 80-gallon booster tank, this 6-cylinder model, with side-mounted spare tire, was assigned to Engine Co. No. 97.

1929

The standard production Pirsch custom fire engine of this period used Waukesha engines. This is a triple combination pumper equipped with two chemical tanks and a 500-gallon rotary gear pump. Note the front-mounted bell.

Peter Pirsch & Sons was also prospering. This is a 1929 Pirsch 500 gallon-per-minute pumper with triple hard suctions and a chemical system. Pneumatic tires were now favored on fire apparatus.

PIRSCH

Pirsch had swung away from commercial truck chassis and was now mounting its fire apparatus on its own assembled custom motor chassis. This is a junior series 350 gallon-per-minute pumper. The booster hose on this model was carried in a well on the rear step. Windshields were still not considered necessary.

Peter Pirsch & Sons built its first patented trussed-type fire department ladders before the turn of the century. Hook and ladder trucks were among this company's first products. This is a 1929 Peter Pirsch city service hook and ladder truck with chemical equipment. The ground ladders are of carefully selected Douglas Fir.

This 1929 Seagrave Standard Series 85-foot aerial ladder truck was used by the fire department of Rye, N. Y. The same basic type of spring-raised aerial hoist introduced by this company in 1902 was used until the introduction of the hydraulically-raised metal aerial ladder in the mid-1930s. Photographed at a SPAAMFAA muster at Valhalla, N. Y., this aerial has windshields fore and aft—a real luxury at the time.

In excellent original condition is this 1929 Seagrave Suburbanite pumper delivered to Rockledge, N. J. Note the accessory windshield and the suction intake mounted below the front bumper. The popular Suburbanite was powered by a 6-cylinder Lycoming engine.

Seen rolling out of the fire house in Fond Du Lac, Wis. is a Peter Pirsch & Sons 1,000 gallon-per-minute Model 16 triple combination pumper. In an underwriter's test, this pumper delivered 1,008 gallons of water per minute at 138 pounds net pressure through two hose lines. Pirsch fire apparatus used Waukesha 6-cylinder engines for many years.

The biggest news of the year was the introduction of the completely new Master Series apparatus by American La-France. This totally new series of pumpers, ladder trucks and aerials featured left-hand drive, 4-wheel brakes, new steel wheels and an improved cooling system. This is the new Master Series Metropolitan 1,000 GPM pumper.

1929

Demand was falling compared to a decade earlier, but there was still a place for the combination hose and chemical car on many fire departments. This one went to Reading, Pa. It is an American LaFrance. The water booster system was rapidly moving in on the old chemical tank system.

John D. Rockefeller Jr. provided much of the money used to restore Williamsburg, Va. to its pre-revolutionary grandeur. American LaFrance built this small Type 91 triple combination pumper for Williamsburg. The 40-gallon chemical tank is mounted at the front of the hose box. The hand-wheel and piping for the chemical system can be seen just ahead of the community's name.

New York City took delivery of seven of these American LaFrance 700 gallon-per-minute pumpers. It has steel wheels, turret nozzle mounted ahead of the fuel tank, and the over-head rack for carrying pompier, or scaling, ladders.

American LaFrance built this medium-sized Type 94 city service hook and ladder truck for Owego, N. Y. This ladder truck utilized the same front-end sheet metal used on the Type 91 pumper. The 50-foot extension ladder, the longest carried, extends under the driver's seat.

The Series 100 continued to be built by American LaFrance right up to the introduction late in the year of the all-new Master Series apparatus. This 1,000 gallon-per-minute Metropolitan was delivered to Chatham, N. J. The above photo clearly illustrates the fully-crowned fenders, enclosed chain drive, and double-bar front bumper.

The all-new Master Series was also known as the Type 200. This is one of the first Type 214 city service hook and ladder trucks built by American LaFrance. The single-bank style was still available, but Elmira now also offered double-bank ladder trucks as well.

Henry Ford's new Model A, which had been introduced the previous year, proved to be as popular as its predecessor, the Model T, as a fire apparatus chassis. American LaFrance built this attractive 3-tank straight chemical car with two hose reels on a Model A chassis for Maple Springs, N. Y.

1929

At one time, American LaFrance was a competitor in the prolific commercial truck market, even though the company's principal product remained fire apparatus. Very few American LaFrance commercials, however, were sold for fire service. But Wilkes-Barre, Pa. had two. One of these was the 1929 combination chemical and hose truck shown here. This very rare apparatus bore ALF Ser. No. F-1055. Jack Robrecht photographed it in the early 1950s. The ALF commercials bore a strong resemblance to the factory's smaller series custom fire engines.

Another new Ahrens-Fox model was the Satellite pump and hose car. This 750 gallon-per-minute midship pumper used Ahrens-Fox's Rotary-style rotary gear pump and a booster system. Relatively few were sold compared with the popular Ahrens-Fox piston-type pumper.

Ahrens-Fox came out with a new, small quadruple combination aimed at the smaller fire department. Called the Skirmisher, it had a midship-mounted rotary gear pump, booster system, full complement of ground ladders and a full-length hose bed over the ladder bank. This 1929 Ahrens-Fox Skirmisher was sold to Glendale, Ohio. It was powered by a 6-cylinder engine.

The Maxim Motor Co. was still doing a good business in the northeastern states. This is the 1929 Maxim 750 GPM pumper. Twin bucket seats were used, and the pump was mounted on the frame behind the seat instead of under it. Note the massive radiator shell and big drum-type headlights. The bell is carried in an A-frame at the front of the hose bed.

The American Magirus Fire Appliance Co. had been formed in Indianapolis to market the famous German-made Magirus aerial ladder in this country. A number of these European-style, rear-mounted aerial ladders were, in fact, sold in the United States. It is interesting to note that this rearmount style, with its short over-all length, has become very popular with American fire departments in recent years. This 85-foot Magirus aerial, mounted on a Magirus motor chassis, was delivered to Sidney, Ohio.

Loaded for bear is this 1929 Model A Ford triple combination motor pumping engine with small capacity pump built by the Howe Fire Apparatus Co. This well-equipped apparatus has a booster tank and two hose reels, in addition to a standard hose box. It was sold to Mount Bethel, Penn.

This unusual little pumper is built on a 1929 FWD chassis and is equipped with a Waterous pump. It was used by Lead, S.D. The Four Wheel Drive Auto Co. of Clintonville, Wis. had been building fire engines, although in small numbers, since 1914.

Bickle Fire Engines Ltd., of Woodstock, Ontario, Canada was now building its own custom-chassis apparatus. This is a 1929 Bickle Chieftain triple combination pumper. Larger models were designated the Canadian and Dominion. The Bickle Custom was designed by Vernon B. King, who still heads King-Seagrave Ltd., this firm's successor. The Bickle had a classic gabled radiator shell and hood with horizontal louvres.

The simple Barton front-mount pump was proving to be something of a Godsend to budget-conscious small town and village fire departments. This is a Model U-34 Barton front-mount pump on a Chevrolet 6-cylinder fire truck. Because it took up no space on the truck body, extra equipment could be carried. This Barton-Chevrolet was used by the Sacred Heart Fire Dept.

The straight chemical car was still holding its own. This is a heavy-duty 4-tank chemical car with two hose baskets, built by the Boyer Fire Apparatus Co. of Logansport, Ind.— successor to the old Obenchain-Boyer Co. The chassis builder is unknown.

Edward J. Kenny, Honorary Deputy Chief of the New York City Fire Dept. presented the F.D.N.Y. with two special searchlight cars as a memorial to his father, a Battalion Chief. They were mounted on Packard 8-cylinder touring car chassis and cost $7,500 each. Each car carried two Koehler electric power plants of 500 kilowatt capacity and seven large searchlights mounted on the tonneau. They were assigned to fire houses in Manhattan and Brooklyn.

In addition to its custom units, Bickle still built apparatus on all popular commercial chassis. The Model A Ford and its rival, the Chevrolet, were the most popular commercial models. This is a 1929 Bickle-Chevrolet 350 Imperial gallon-per-minute triple combination pumper built on the 1½-ton 131-inch wheelbase chassis.

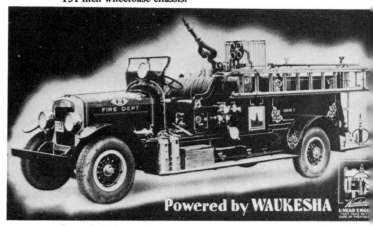

One of the lesser-known makes was the McCann, which was built by D. E. McCann's Sons of Portland, Maine. This 1,000 gallon-per-minute McCann pumper responded as Engine 2 of the Portland Fire Dept. It was powered by a Waukesha engine. Note the windshield, Whiting light and painting on the side of the booster tank.

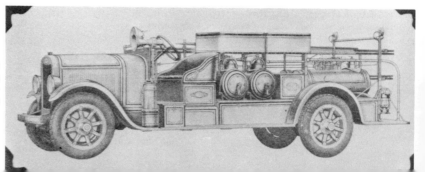

The stock market crash and resulting depression dealt a severe blow to all American industry, including the fire apparatus business. But the worst was yet to come. American LaFrance's new Master Series apparatus was well received, and Reg. No. 7004, a 1,000 GPM pumper, was delivered to Chattanooga, Tenn. In 1930 the Elmira, N. Y. manufacturer complemented the tractor-drawn Type 217 Master Series aerial introduced at the Birmingham IAFC convention with an all-new, improved Type 231 front-drive aerial. This new straight-frame aerial was built in 75 and 85-foot sizes, and like the articulated Type 217, could be ordered with either single or double ladder banks. The big ALF 140-horsepower Six was the standard powerplant. The Type 231 had a massive, towering front end. It did not sell well, however, as fire departments showed a marked preference for the more maneuverable tractor-trailer type aerial.

Special Master Series models delivered by American LaFrance this year included a huge 65-foot tractor-drawn water tower with rear turntable, and a rescue squad car, both finished in white and built for Jersey City, N. J.

Ahrens-Fox Fire Engine's bread-and-butter was still the highly-regarded front mounted piston pumper, But in 1930, this company came out with a new small fire engine series designated the Ahrens-Fox Model V. The extremely low Model V line was built on a special light-duty chassis supplied by the Schacht Motor Truck Co. of Cincinnati, with which Ahrens-Fox would soon form a long corporate alliance. The pleasingly styled Model V could be ordered as a 500 GPM rotary gear pumper, or in special hose car and combination models or even as a squad car or junior hook and ladder truck. One of the first of these delivered went to the Borough of Saddle River, N. J.

Late in 1929, Ahrens-Fox had announced its new Tower Aerial ladder trucks. A new, improved variation of the company's standard tractor-drawn aerial ladder truck, this series used the new rounded style hood and radiator and featured a double-reinforced tubular main ladder truss rods on both the bed ladder and the fly section. This design made for a very strong unit that permitted its safe use as a water tower. The company's midship-mounted rotary gear pumpers, the Skirmisher quad and city service ladder trucks also used the new rounded hood and radiator, while the familiar gabled hood and radiator was retained on the familiar Ahrens-Fox piston pumper.

New York City had taken delivery of what was billed as the world's most powerful water tower. The 65-foot tractor-drawn tower was built by American LaFrance. Its main mast was equipped with a second turret nozzle, making it a Duplex Tower. With its two powerful deck turrets also in use, this tower could throw an incredible 8,500 gallons of water per minute. Also in 1930, Seagrave had delivered a special short-wheelbase tractor-drawn city service ladder truck to the Empire Hook & Ladder Co. of Upper Nyack, N. Y.

Mack Trucks delivered its first Type 70 pumper of 600 GPM capacity to Revere, Mass. This job was equipped with a factory windshield. The Buffalo Fire Appliance Corp. came out with its own new custom chassis. The 1930 IAFC Convention was held in Winnipeg, Manitoba, Canada.

Traffic congestion had become a real problem in the cities. To help clear the way, progressive fire chiefs ordered new apparatus equipped with a set of whirling Buckeye Roto-Rays, consisting of three flashing lights mounted on a post. A somewhat similar type of light, with four fixed red lights mounted in a circular panel, was known as the Whiting light. Electric sirens were almost universal now, but no new fire engine could be considered complete without a gleaming locomotive-type bell.

Among the very last Model AC Mack fire engines built were seven of these 700 gallon-per-minute Type 20 pumpers, built for New York City. The AC's served the F.D.N.Y. until well after the Second World War. Like all New York engines and hose wagons, this one carried a turret pipe and pompier ladders.

Mack

Mack's medium-duty pumper was the sturdy Type 70, which was rated at 600 gallons per minute. The Type 70 was powered by a Mack 100 horsepower, 6-cylinder engine and was aimed at the large apparatus market between 500 and 750 gallons-per-minute. Many were sold.

Mack's most popular high capacity pumper was the Type 19. This 1,000 gallon-per-minute pumper, with centrifugal pump, saw many years of faithful service in Oak Park, Ill. It is parked next to a Seagrave of similar vintage.

Jersey City, N. J. was a big user of American LaFrance fire apparatus through the 1920s and 30s. This 1930 American LaFrance started out as a Jersey City rescue squad truck, but was converted later into a searchlight wagon. Jersey City operated white apparatus for many years.

The new American LaFrance Master Series apparatus was immediately successful. Powered by a big 6-cylinder engine, the Series 200 pumpers, city service ladder trucks and aerials were soon being delivered to large and small fire departments. This is a 1,000 GPM American LaFrance Series 200 Metropolitan. Pneumatic tires were standard on many models in this new series.

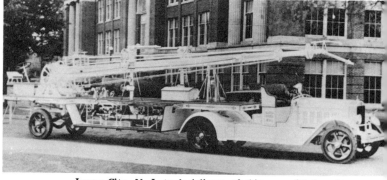

Another Jersey City rig is this 1930 American LaFrance Type 217 85-foot tractor-drawn aerial ladder truck. Most Master Series aerials had pneumatic tires on the tractor front wheels and trailer wheels, but the rear of the tractor was usually fitted with solid tires because of the weights carried. This aerial has solid tires all around. Note the windshield and the double-bank ladder bed.

Jersey City, N. J. took delivery of this powerful American LaFrance 65-foot American Automatic tractor-drawn water tower. Finished in white, this big tower saw many years of service before it was taken out of service in the 1960s. It was drawn by a 6-cylinder Type 651 tractor, rode on solid tires, had two deck turrets and a tiller.

Although lettered "Ladder One," this 1930 American LaFrance is actually a Type 214 quadruple combination. The double-banked truck has had a canvas windshield added but is otherwise original in appearance. This apparatus saw service in Old Orchard, Maine.

The Chicago suburb of Hinsdale received this American LaFrance combination hose and chemical car, built on a Chevrolet 6-cylinder auto chassis. The small box over the front of the hose box is a foam system. The foam nozzle on the reel is fed by two hose lines. Note the two copper chemical tanks.

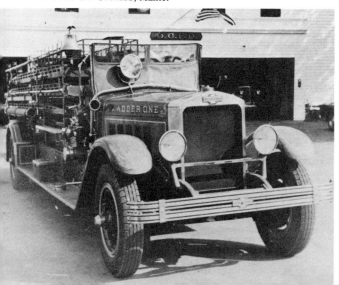

1930

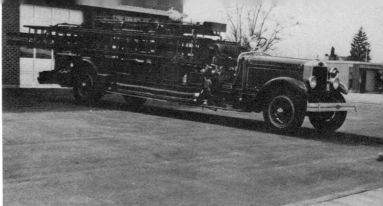

This is a straight Type 214 city service ladder truck by American LaFrance on the new Master Series chassis. Customers could still choose either a single or double bank of ladders. This 200 Series ladder truck, sold to Spring Lake, N. J. is of the double bank style and is equipped with a chemical tank.

American LaFrance for some reason did not build many Series 200 quads. This one, equipped with a 1,000 gallon-per-minute rotary gear pump, was built for Nampa, Ida. The hose bed is mounted in the long tray below the ladder bed.

The American LaFrance Type 31 aerial had given way to the all-new Type 231 front-drive aerial. The straight-frame aerial had given way to the more maneuverable tractor-drawn type, however, and very few Type 231s were ever built. This is a 75-foot model. An 85-footer was also offered. The 6-cylinder ALF engine was mounted directly below the cab.

A 1930 American LaFrance Type 94 city service ladder truck, owned by Owings Mills, Md. though not a quad, is equipped with a full-length hose bed. This smaller series rig has a single bank of ground ladders.

New York City continued to prolong the useful life of many of its older, former horse-drawn aerial ladder trucks and water towers by repowering them with new tractors. This is a 1930 Walter motor tractor which is drawing a modernized American LaFrance springhoist 65-foot aerial. Note the huge artillery wheels on the ladder trailer.

With a strong resemblance to a Stutz, this triple combination pumper was built by the Trenton, N. J. Fire Dept. shops. The rear fenders look like they might have come off an American LaFrance. Note the brooms slung beneath the running board, and the canvas and celluloid windbreaker. The Trenton shops built several of these 1,000 gallon-per-minute pumping engines.

The Buffalo, N. Y. airport was once protected by this gleaming 4-tank foamite car. The special purpose apparatus was built by American LaFrance on a 1930 GMC truck chassis. This early airport crash truck carries three hose reels. The Elmira plant built many medium-sized fire engines on a special GMC chassis supplied by General Motors.

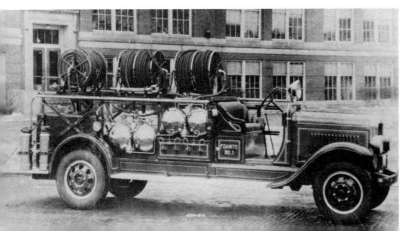

This unusual 1930 Seagrave tractor-drawn city service hook and ladder truck was originally owned by the Empire Hook & Ladder Co. of Upper Nyack, N. Y. It was later purchased by the Cooperstown, N. Y. Fire Dept. but is owned today by apparatus collector Andy Henderson of Weedsport, N.Y. The trailer is shorter than that of an aerial ladder truck. This rig is exquisitely striped and decorated.

Dyersburg, Tenn. was the owner of this 1930 Seagrave Special 600 gallon-per-minute pumper equipped with a 4-stage pump, squirrel-tail hard suction hose, and turret pipe mounted on a platform over the hose bed. This engine has probably been converted for use as a hose wagon.

New York City took delivery of five of these 1930 Seagrave 75-foot spring-raised, tractor-drawn aerial ladder trucks. The tiller wheel has been removed and the seat swung aside to prepare for raising the main ladder.

This exceptionally well-preserved 1930 Seagrave 750 GPM pumper was used by the fire department of Sound Beach, Conn. Members of this company carry their boots and helmets in a rack mounted over the hard suction hoses.

At last report, the Riverside, Ill. Fire Dept. still owned this 1930 Seagrave Suburbanite city service hook and ladder truck. This rig carries a booster system. The large rectangular tank is probably a replacement for the original.

Seagrave came out with an Improved Suburbanite in the early 1930s. Some of these were equipped with dual rear tires. This Improved Suburbanite 400 gallon-per-minute pumper is equipped with cast-steel wheels.

Los Angeles was another good Seagrave customer. This 1930 Seagrave combination hose and booster wagon has been equipped with a Gorter turret pipe. It was assigned to Engine Co. No. 14.

Macedonia, Ohio is the owner of this 1930 Seagrave Suburbanite 500 gallon-per-minute pumper. This little engine appears to be in highly original condition, except for the whip antenna and later-model siren. Seagrave apparatus used the oval-shaped gasoline tank through the late 1930s.

Kalamazoo, Mich. purchased a lot of Seagrave motor fire apparatus over the years. This 1930 Seagrave 750 GPM pumper is equipped with a Morrow windbreaker. Note the booster hose basket behind the driver's seat and the wood ground ladders.

Anyone who served in the armed forces in the Second World War will likely recognize this make. The U.S. Army Ordnance works at Camp Holabird, Md. built many of these U.S.A. fire engines from about the mid-1920s through the Second World War. These should not be confused with the rigs built by U.S. Fire Apparatus Co. of Wilmington, Del. The 750 gallon-per-minute U.S.A. shown here was eventually acquired by Croydon, Pa.

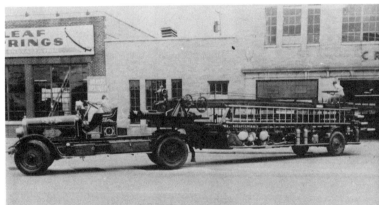

Two members of SPAAMFAA's home chapter carefully back the group's 1930 Seagrave 85-foot tractor-drawn aerial ladder truck into her storage quarters. The big spring-raised "stick" served the Syracuse Fire Dept. for many years before being rescued from the cutter's torch by SPAAMFAA.

The White Motor Co. was still building a reputable medium-duty truck chassis, which, with its rival the Reo, was enjoying continued popularity with the fire service. This 1930 White chassis once responded as a Chicago Fire Dept. rescue squad car, but was later outfitted as a chemical car. Note the large gas cylinders carried just behind the driver's seat.

The big Ahrens-Fox piston pumper kept right on chalking up sales. A 1930 Model HP-4 of 1.000 gallon-per-minute capacity, originally owned by Paterson, N. J., this Ahrens-Fox was subsequently purchased and completely restored by the Mountain Lakes, N. J. Fire Dept. Note the new style crowned fenders.

This 1930 Ahrens-Fox Model V 500 gallon-per-minute pumper was delivered to the Borough of Saddle River Township, N. J. Note how low the Model V sits. This series was competition for Seagrave's small Suburbanite and was moderately successful.

Ahrens-Fox

Ahrens-Fox this year came out with yet another new model, again aimed at the smaller fire department. Built on a special Schacht truck chassis, it was called the Model V. This 1930 Model V 500 gallon-per-minute pumper was originally sold to Delphi, Ind. but later went to Medarville, Ind.

Ahrens-Fox called this model a "Four-Way Combination" rather than a quad. It is a 1930 Rotarystyle midship-mounted job with a 600 GPM pump. This apparatus, delivered to Island Heights, N. J. is externally similar to the Skirmisher model introduced the previous year.

The Cincinnati Salvage Corps. responded to fire alarms with this 1930 Ahrens-Fox salvage car. An exceptionally small rig, it is equipped with two squad benches in the rear, a folding attic ladder, and the three Dietz lanterns. Most large cities still had Insurance Patrols which attempted to minimize water damage at fires, holding down insurance losses.

The Ahrens-Fox Model V was offered in a full range of models, including this city service hook and ladder truck. This small ladder wagon was delivered to Tisbury, Mass. Model V pumpers were usually equipped with rotary gear pumps.

The Buffalo Fire Appliance Corp. still offered a full range of fire apparatus built on the customer's favorite commercial chassis. The new Model A Ford, of course, was especially adaptable for fire apparatus use. This 1930 Buffalo-Ford 350 GPM triple combination pumper was delivered to the fire department of Hohenwald, Tenn.

Buffalo 1930

Elwood, N. J. is the owner of this little Buffalo 350 GPM pumper built on a Model A Ford truck chassis. The dual rear tires give it a husky look. Like its predecessor, the TT, the Ford AA chassis proved suitable to a large number of fire-fighting tasks.

The Buffalo Fire Appliance Corp. of Buffalo, N. Y. was now building its own fire apparatus chassis. This is a 1930 Buffalo 500 gallon-per-minute triple combination motor pumping engine. Note the hand-crank siren mounted on the right side of the cowl on the handrail.

Buffalo built a full line of apparatus on its new custom chassis. This 1930 Buffalo 500 gallon-per-minute quadruple combination was supplied to Wanaque, N. J. Note the high ladder bank, the factory windshield, and the booster reel.

The Hahn Motor Company of Hamburg, Pa. built its first fire engine in 1915. The company is still in business today. This is a 1930 Hahn 750 gallon-per-minute triple combination pumper. Hahn offered a full line of pumpers, combinations, hose wagons, city service ladder trucks and squad cars built on its own assembled chassis.

The Midlothian, Ill. Fire Dept. received this unusual pumper from the Prospect Fire Engine Co. of Prospect, Ohio. It is built on the Mars chassis, marketed by Prospect and powered by an 8-cylinder Lycoming engine. The classic-looking pumper was rated at 500 gallons per minute.

To a firefighter who has been slugging it out at a multiple-alarm fire on a cold winter night, the most beautiful sight in the world is the coffee wagon. Canteen service is provided in larger centers by local fire buff clubs or the Salvation Army. The Second Alarmers Assn. of Philadelphia dispensed thousands of cups of coffee, broth, and soft drinks from this coffee wagon, believed to be a Brockway. The canteen, manned by a volunteer crew, usually responds to all extra-alarm fires.

Despite the worsening depression, one of the most important advances in motor fire apparatus history was made this year. In a surprise announcement at the annual conference of the New England Fire Chiefs Assn., held in Boston in June, the American LaFrance Fire Engine Co. introduced its first V-12 engine. The big 12-cylinder engine had been secretly under development in the ALF laboratory in Elmira for five years, and it quickly set a new standard in fire apparatus powerplants.

The new American LaFrance V-12 was actually a dual-six motor, and consisted basically of two 6-cylinder engines sharing a common crankshaft. The banks were banked at an unusually shallow 30 degrees. This engine put out an impressive 240 horsepower. Later in the same month, the new V-12—mounted in a 1931 American LaFrance 1,000 GPM Metropolitan triple combination pumper—set out on a demonstration tour. This grand tour took the pumper into 102 cities in 24 states, and ended in San Francisco some four months later. A total of 81 pumping demonstrations were held along the way. The new V-12 drew great interest among fire chiefs all along. Deliveries of Master Series pumpers and aerials powered by the V-12 began later in the year.

American LaFrance had also developed a 325-horsepower V-16 engine, but the smaller V-12 proved more than adequate for fire service use. The V-12 was later used in buses, heavy trucks, boats, an experimental army tank, and even in the Budd Streamliner passenger locomotive. The V-12 would be this company's standard engine for the next three decades.

The Seagrave Corp. wasn't standing still, either. In 1931 this company introduced its greatly improved Sentry fire apparatus series. The new Seagrave Sentry was powered by the new G-6 6-cylinder engine, and sported a redesigned radiator and hood, full crowned fenders and a double-beam front bumper.

Another important development this year was the entry by Peter Pirsch & Sons Co. of Kenosha, Wisc., into the aerial ladder field. Pirsch made a major contribution to aerial ladder design with its patented hydro-mechanical aerial ladder hoist. This revolutionary new type of aerial could be easily operated by one man. The main ladder was smoothly raised into position by a pair

The Goodwill Fire Co. of Chester, Penn. operated this 1931 Mack 500 gallon-per-minute pumper. What makes this apparatus unusual is the large hose reel mounted at the rear of the hose bed. This allowed for rapid playout of hose, but did cut down the capacity that could be carried. It appeared to be a throwback to the days of the hand or horse-drawn hose reel. Interestingly enough, reels like this are being used again today to carry large-diameter hose.

One of Mack's smallest fire engines was the Type 50. This was a 500 gallon-per-minute pumper which could be ordered as a full triple combination. It was delivered to Collegeville, Pa.

Mack Trucks built some truly handsome aerial ladder trucks in the early 1930s. The 75-foot tractor-drawn aerial shown here was built for the Moyamensing Hook and Ladder Co. of Chester, Pa. This aerial has double ladder banks and the aerial ladder hoist is driven directly by the rig's 6-cylinder engine.

Shown here is the racy-looking Mack Type 70 city service hook and ladder truck. This low-slung model presented an unusually low, clean appearance. This was made possible by the low frame used for this series, which kept the center of gravity down for better handling at higher speeds.

1931

f hydraulic lifting cylinders. The turntable and fly
xtension were mechanically operated. One of the first
ydro-mechanical aerials delivered was an 85-footer built
or Spokane, Wash. which was drawn by a White tractor.
    The Maxim Motor Co. introduced a handsomely-styled
ew series of pumpers and city service ladder trucks. The
ew series was powered by the Hercules 6-cylinder engine,
nd used a Hale pump. The new look included a new
ounded hood and radiator shell, full crowned fenders and
oors instead of the usual louvres in the engine hood.
    After 12 years, Ahrens-Fox restyled its big piston
umpers, replacing the old style gabled hood and radiator
ith the rounded type introduced earlier on most of its
ther models.
    Montreal, Que. placed two 100-foot Magirus rearmount
erial ladder trucks into service this year.
    American LaFrance continued to build its small Series
0 apparatus and the GMC-based Type 299. The Type 94
as a small quadruple combination with a 600 GPM
otary gear pump and full ladder equipment.

The Ahrens-Fox Model V found many customers in these
Depression days. This 1931 Model V city service hook and
ladder was delivered to South Meriden, Conn. Notice the
large round booster tank, and the small rescue boat carried on
top of the ladder bed.

AHRENS-FOX

Ahrens-Fox had been building aerial ladder trucks since the
early 1920s. In 1929 the company introduced a new type of
reinforced aerial which it called the Tower Aerial. This is a
1931 Ahrens-Fox 85-foot Tower Aerial originally delivered
to Harrison, N. J. The Ahrens-Fox aerials still used the
Dahill Air Hoist.

The Ahrens-Fox Fire Engine Co. was now using this new,
rounded hood and radiator on all of its standard-size fire
apparatus. This 750 GPM pumper, with Ahrens-Fox Rotarystyle midship-mounted rotary gear pump is a Model GN,
Reg. No. 5062, and saw service in Rutherford, N. J. The
full-crowned fenders first appeared in 1930.

Ahrens-Fox also built a comprehensive line of city service
type hook and ladder trucks, of both single and double-bank
design. This 1931 Model PS-44 city service ladder truck was
delivered to San Angelo, Tex. It was powered by Ahrens-
Fox's 6-cylinder engine with 5-7/8 x 7 inch bore and stroke.

Montreal, Quebec, took delivery of two Magirus 100-foot
combination aerial ladder and water tower trucks. These
four-section wooden aerials saw more than a quarter century
of service before they were remounted from the German-
built Magirus chassis to other chassis in about 1950. This
100-foot rearmount aerial was assigned to Montreal's busy
Ladder Co. No. 25. The wood aerials were around through
the 1960s.

American LaFrance continued to find sales for its smaller models. This is a 1931 American LaFrance Type 94 quadruple combination delivered to Stillwater, Minn. This single-bank quad was equipped with a 600 gallon-per-minute pump. The large, round protuberance is the filler for the rig's booster tank. A life net is carried on the running board.

1931

The American LaFrance Type 91 and 92 also remained in production, even though the larger Type 200 models were accounting for most of Elmira's sales now. This 1931 American LaFrance hose wagon with windshield was used by the fire department of Oceanside, Long Island, N. Y.

American LaFrance had introduced its new V-12 engine this year. This is a 1931 American LaFrance Type 217 tractor-drawn 75-foot aerial ladder truck powered by this revolutionary new type of fire service engine. This aerial was delivered to Glen Cove, Long Island, N. Y.

Toronto, Ontario received the only American LaFrance Type 233 city service ladder truck ever built. This truck was built by LaFrance Fire Engine & Foamite Ltd., Elmira's Canadian subsidiary. The 6-cylinder truck had no windshields when originally delivered. Reg. No. 7351, this unusual specimen has been completely restored by the Toronto Fire Dept. shops and is taken out only for special occasions.

Not all of the apparatus being turned out by American LaFrance was designed for metropolitan service. This little pumper is a real oddball. It is described as a LaFrance-Republic booster and hose car. This 100 gallon-per-minute pumper is equipped with Pirsch apparatus. It was used by Preble, Wis.

Although this series used an earlier style radiator, hood and body sheet metal, American LaFrance continued to offer its limited-production Type 119 high pressure pumping engine. These were the largest pumpers built by American LaFrance and examples were sold to New York City, Philadelphia, and Minneapolis. Notice the different type pump panel used on this model, and the large gasoline tank mounted over the front of the hose box.

The Washington, D. C. Fire Dept. responded to rescue calls with this 1931 American LaFrance rescue squad car. This rig started out as a booster and hose truck, but it was rebuilt using the squad body from a 1929 American LaFrance, and a closed cab added by the D.C.F.D. shops in 1946.

The New York City Fire Dept. in 1931 received 21 of these American LaFrance Type 200 pumpers. Built to F.D.N.Y. specifications, they were equipped with turret pipes, 700 gallon-per-minute rotary gear pumps and an overhead rack for carrying scaling ladders. Note the spare tire mounted on the rear step.

One of New York's 1931 American LaFrance 700 GPM pumpers is seen in action at a fire. The hood has been raised for pumping, and the pompier ladders have been removed from their overhead racks.

New York City attached this 1931 FWD tractor to a rebuilt American LaFrance 65-foot water tower. The tower trailer is a holdover from the horse-drawn era. These tractors saw more than 30 years of hard service before they were finally consigned to the scrap heap.

Albany, N. Y. has been a big user of American LaFrance pumpers, aerials and specialized fire apparatus for many, many years. The Albany Fire Dept. purchased a number of these Series 200 pumpers during the early 1930s. The 1931 American LaFrance 1,000 gallon-per-minute pumper shown here, on the ramp in front of Engine Co. No. 8's quarters, carries Reg. No. 7317 and originally saw service as Engine 6. Note the red flasher mounted above the company number plate.

Even with its front end obscured by a squirrel-tail length of hard suction hose, this 1931 American LaFrance/GMC triple combination pumper presents a clean, solid appearance. Note the simple, straightforward striping and the deep equipment compartments on each side of the hose bed.

In addition to the 21 pumpers, the F.D.N.Y. also received 10 American LaFrance Type 217 tractor-drawn aerial ladder trucks in 1931. These were 75-foot, spring-raised models. They were powered by 6-cylinder ALF engines. Even the F.D.N.Y. was starting to equip its apparatus with windshields.

1931

Some fire companies adopted some unusual color schemes for their apparatus. Take Kulpmont, Pa. for example. This community's West End Fire Assn. once used this all-black 1931 Buffalo 600 gallon-per-minute pumper. Springfield, Mass. also used black-painted fire engines for many years.

Buffalo

This beauty was once the pride of the Liberty Fire Co. No. 5, in Reading, Pa. This rig is a 1931 Buffalo 1,000 gallon-per-minute triple combination pumper. A windshield has been added. Note the fancy radiator ornament. This one must have been a parade favorite wherever it went.

This is a small Howe triple combination pumping, booster and hose engine built on a Graham Bros. truck chassis. It was delivered to the Willshire, Cal. Community Fire Dept. Note the wraparound suction hose and the single chemical tank.

Howe Fire Apparatus built this little 2-tank straight chemical car on a Ford Model A chassis. Note the steel disc wheels and the single hose reel. This apparatus was built for the Oak Hill Fire Dept.

This 1931 Reo chassis with Boyer equipment was used by the Howell, Mich. Fire Dept. until about 1965. The old Reo has been completely restored and is one of three vintage rigs refurbished by Father Quinn's Sacred Heart Rehabilitation Center in Detroit. The Reo is seen here in a 1974 parade.

Montreal, Quebec, used this Reo Speedwagon hose truck. It ran out of Montreal's busy Fire Station No. 31. The Reo Speedwagon was a popular fire equipment chassis in both Canada and the U.S. It is not known who built the body for this unit, but it was likely a local body builder.

The Pirsch-Ringer smoke ejector truck played a heroic role at the Chicago Tunner Disaster in April, 1931. The Pirsch factory in Kenosha received an emergency call for this new type of equipment. The truck, however, was still being built. But a crew of men went to work on it and had it ready for the road within three hours. Despite the fact that the engine had never been turned over before, the 60-mile trip to Chicago was made under police escort in 88 minutes. The unit was put to work and 16 lives were saved. This unit was conceived by Fire Chief Charles Ringer of Minneapolis and was developed by Peter Pirsch and Sons. The smoke ejector truck was eventually delivered to the Hyattsville, Md. Fire Dept.

"PIRSCH"

This 1931 International B-4 truck chassis has been converted into a small turret wagon. The turrets are Pirsch equipment. This unit was used in Peoria, Ill.

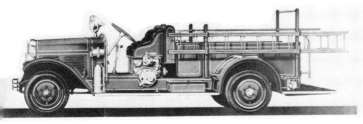

The old Stutz Fire Engine Co. folded with the rest of Harry Stutz' automotive empire in the late 1920s. But the fire apparatus branch was revived in the early 1930s and was renamed the "New Stutz Fire Engine Co.", operating out of Hartford, City, Ind. This is a 1931 New Stutz triple combination pumping engine.

Peter Pirsch & Sons Co. of Kenosha, Wis. in 1931 came out with a hydro-mechanical aerial ladder hoist that took all of the muscle work out of raising the aerial ladder. This was America's first all-powered aerial ladder hoist. The Pirsch patented device raised, lowered, extended and even rotated the aerial ladder. The tractor was powered by a 130-horsepower 6-cylinder engine.

The Seagrave Corp. introduced a new series called the Seagrave Sentry this year. It was powered by Seagrave's G-6 engine, a big 6-cylinder. The radiator was restyled, and the new hood had two sets of louvres set at different heights. This 750 GPM Seagrave Sentry with single-stage centrifugal pump was delivered to Hackettstown, N. J. Note the side-mounted spare tire and the siren mounted between the headlights.

Detroit ordered and received two Seagrave Model 6-GF 85-foot tractor-drawn aerial ladder trucks in 1931. These aerials were delivered with factory windshields and Roto-Ray warning lights. They also carried a single chemical tank and chemical hose reel on their trailer frames just behind the goose-neck. These aerials remained in service as reserve pieces well into the 1960s.

1932

The Seagrave Corp. of Columbus, Ohio quickly countered the new competition from American LaFrance by introducing its own V-12 fire apparatus engine. This company's big 240 HP 45-degree V-12 was later joined by a smaller V-12 engine that was based on the Pierce-Arrow V-12 engine design. American LaFrance also later came out with a small V-12, based on the Auburn V-12 engine design.

Seagrave's recently introduced Sentry Series apparatus was being well received. In 1932, The Seagrave Corp.'s standard models included the small Suburbanite line of 350 and 500 GPM pumpers, service ladders trucks and combinations; the Junior series 600 GPM pumpers and quadruple combinations; the Standard series 750 and 1,000 GPM pumpers, service ladder trucks and 75-foot and 85-foot tractor-drawn aerials, and the new Sentry series pumpers and quads. Windshields were standard equipment now on Seagrave's larger models. The Suburbanite and medium-sized Special series apparatus was powered by Continental 6-cylinder engines.

During 1932, Seagrave delivered its last water tower. This was a magnificently-decorated 65-foot straight-frame tower with special heavy duty radiator built for Washington, D. C. The last Seagrave tower had a huge, single deck turret, solid tires mounted on disc wheels and no windshield. Other one-off models delivered by Seagrave this year included an Electric Lighting and Squad Car on Suburbanite chassis, finished in white, for Somerville, Mass., and a unique Suburbanite Wreck and Towing Car in red for the same department. All Seagrave pumpers continued to use centrifugal pumps.

Peter Pirsch & Sons Co. introduced its new Series 15 pumpers, powered by Waukesha 6-cylinder engines and with centrifugal pumps of 500, 600 and 750 GPM capacities. The Series 15 was an unusually handsome looking rig, with its Lincolnesque front end, complete with Greyhound radiator ornament. Pirsch this year also introduced a simple, low-cost aerial ladder hoist that enabled the smallest volunteer fire departments to acquire the versatility of an aerial ladder for the first time. This hoist

could be fitted to the butt end of the department's longest ladder—usually a 45 or 55-footer—and was designed for mounting on any standard type of city service ladder truck frame regardless of make. It was mechanically operated. Pirsch also offered its first full quadruple combinations, which it marketed as the Pirsch Four-Way Pumper.

In other 1932 developments, the General Manufacturing Corp. of St. Louis began production of its own assembled custom-series pumpers. A distinctive feature of the General-St. Louis pumpers was a large, red-lensed spotlight mounted on the spacer bar between the headlights.

American LaFrance was now using Buda 6-cylinder engines in its smaller Type 92 apparatus. Elmira still offered a special high pressure pumping engine of 1,000 GPM capacity. This very low volume series used the same sheetmetal and styling of the old Series 100 apparatus, which had been discontinued three years earlier. Examples of this type were delivered to Minneapolis, New York City, and Pittsburgh.

The Ward LaFrance Truck Corp. of Elmira Heights, N. Y. (not to be confused with American LaFrance of the same city) had started to build 500 and 750 GPM pumpers on its own chassis. One of the first of these was delivered to Factoryville, Pa., and is owned by Ward LaFrance today for promotional purposes. It has been painted the company's controversial lime-green.

American LaFrance built this 500 gallon-per-minute pumper on a 1932 GMC Model T-30-CF truck chassis for Lexington, Tenn. Pumpers on this chassis were usually designated Type 199. Note the transverse-mounted hose reel and shop-built windshield.

This 1,000 gallon-per-minute 1932 American LaFrance quadruple combination was assigned to Chicago "Combination Co. No. 81". Chicago had several of these American LaFrance quads. One was stationed at O'Hare Field for several years.

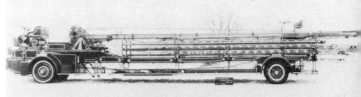

American LaFrance delivered two Type 231 aerial ladder trucks to Canadian fire departments. This 6-cylinder, 75-footer was sold to Verdun, Quebec. The other went to Shawinigan Falls, Quebec. Rapid City, S. D. also had one of these late-model front-drive aerials.

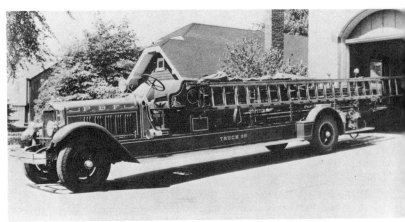

Pittsburgh's Truck Co. 36 was assigned this standard model 1932 American LaFrance Type 214 city service hook and ladder truck. This rig had a single bank of ladders. The ground ladders carried on the side were canted upward slightly to facilitate removal.

Denison, Tex. took delivery of this 1932 American La-France Type 92 pumper. The 600 gallon-per-minute rotary gear pumper had no windshield. The pump is located between the seat and the hose box, and the gasoline tank is mounted over the front of the hose box.

The Valley Stream, N. Y. Fire Department operated this American LaFrance squad and searchlight apparatus. It was built on the small Type 92 6-cylinder chassis. This specialized type of equipment was uncommon on smaller fire departments.

The cast aluminum radiator shell formerly used on American LaFrance Series 200 apparatus since the Master Series was introduced in 1929, had now given way to a conventional plated-type metal radiator shell. This 1932 American La-France Type 214 city service ladder truck has been authentically restored by the Taylor, Mich. Fire Department. The side ladders are mounted at an angle on this series.

The new Maxim triple combination pumper had twin bucket seats and a set of Whiting warning lights. Most Maxims were powered by 6-cylinder engines. Pump capacities ranged from 500 to 1,000 gallons per minute.

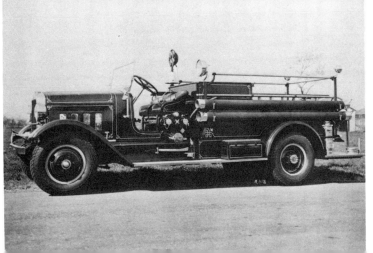

The Maxim Co. of Middleboro, Mass. restyled its custom fire apparatus chassis. The new appearance included this rounded-off radiator shell and hood doors instead of the usual louvres. Windshields had also become standard on most new Maxims. This is a 750 gallon-per-minute pumper.

1932

The City of Los Angeles for many years ran 2-piece engine companies, consisting of a pumper and a combination booster and hose truck. This 1932 Seagrave booster and hose wagon ran with L.A.F.D. Engine Co. No. 2 Los Angeles is still a good Seagrave customer.

New York City continued to place substantial orders with the Seagrave Corp. In 1932, the F.D.N.Y. took delivery of nine 700 gallon-per-minute Seagrave motor pumping engines with the new style radiator and hood. Seagraves were still powered by large Seagrave-built 6-cylinder engines.

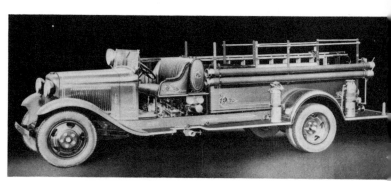

Among the most unusual of all custom-chassised apparatus turned out of the Columbus, Ohio plant of The Seagrave Corp. was this special Wreck and Towing Car on a Seagrave Suburbanite chassis for Somerville, Mass. This unique apparatus was used for towing disabled rigs, and for heavy rescue work.

Unlike most other major manufacturers, Seagrave had built very few fire engines on anything but its own motor chassis. However, the deepening depression forced Columbus to develop a line of low-cost apparatus for financially-strapped municipalities. The Seagrave Volunteer was built on the new Ford V-8 truck chassis. The 75-horsepower V-8 engine drove a Seagrave centrifugal pump.

Honolulu, Hawaii also bought a lot of Seagrave fire apparatus, including this 1932 Seagrave Standard 750 gallon-per-minute triple combination pumping engine. Note the elaborate striping and hand-painting that ornaments this rig. Windshields were now being installed on a high percentage of the apparatus being delivered.

In 1932 and 1933, the City of Somerville, Mass. placed a large order for new fire apparatus with Seagrave. One of the units delivered was this sporty-looking little Suburbanite combination squad and electric lighting car. The dual-faced whitewall tires are worthy of note, as are the Whiting flashers mounted behind the driver's seat.

Shown here is a 1932 Mack Type 75 triple combination pumper. This model was powered by a 140-horsepower Mack CT 6-cylinder engine of 4¼-inch bore and 5½-inch stroke. The 750 gallon-per-minute Type 75 could be ordered with either a rotary gear pump or a centrifugal multi-stage pump. Standard equipment also included 4-wheel brakes and a 4-speed transmission.

MACK

The Aerial Division of the fire department of Stroudsburg, Pa. was once the proud owner of this 1932 Mack 75-foot tractor-drawn aerial ladder truck. Mack aerials of this period boasted engine-driven ladder hoists that did not rely on springs or hydraulic pressure. This double-banker is painted a gleaming white.

Mack's larger series Type 95 pumper was built in 750 or 1,000 gallon-per-minute versions. The Type 95 was powered by a Mack 130-horsepower 6-cylinder engine, and buyers could choose between a centrifugal or rotary-type apparatus pump.

A new name was added to the custom fire apparatus field when the Ward LaFrance Truck Corp., of Elmira Heights, N. Y., began marketing fire apparatus on its own truck chassis. This is a 1932 Ward LaFrance 500 gallon-per-minute pumper delivered to Ocean Gate, N. J.

Take a good look at this combination. It consists of a 1932 Ahrens-Fox Model P 6-cylinder tractor attached to an older model American LaFrance 75-foot aerial ladder trailer. Such hybrids were not uncommon as older-model tractors were out. This aerial saw service in East Orange, N. J.

Elkins Park, Pa. was another community that stayed away from the traditional fire department red. Elkins Park's 1932 Ahrens-Fox Model H-44 city service hook and ladder truck was painted a color called Tampa Beige. This ladder truck carried Ahrens-Fox factory number 6007.

Peter Pirsch & Sons Co. built this 85-foot hydro-mechanical aerial ladder truck for Spokane, Wash. Instead of the usual Pirsch 6-cylinder tractor, it was drawn by a White Motor Co. 4-wheel tractor. Note the W emblem in the center of the double-beam front bumper.

Through a series of corporate reorganizations, Ahrens-Fox became closely linked with the Schacht truck nameplate during the 1930s. But a few other builders mounted fire engine bodies on the Schacht chassis, too. Peter Pirsch and Sons Co. supplied this 500 gallon-per-minute Pirsch-Schacht triple combination pumper to Matawan Township, N. J.

The Howe Fire Apparatus Co. of Anderson, Ind. by now had come out with its own custom fire apparatus line. These were known as Howe Defenders, a name used up to this day. This 750 gallon-per-minute Howe Defender was built for use in the U. S. Canal Zone. Howe used the Defiance truck chassis for a number of years.

Ford's huge Rouge manufacturing complex outside of Detroit was protected by its own company fire department. Over the years, the Rouge used a real variety of motor fire apparatus — mounted, of course, only on Ford truck chassis. This is a 1932 Ford hose wagon. It is equipped with a Morrow metal windbreaker and has an American LaFrance bell mounted on its right front fender.

New York's Fire Chief certainly rode to blazes in style during the classic car era. This 1932 Chrysler Imperial limousine is equipped with a front-mounted bell, F.D.N.Y. number plate and a roof flasher. The car is a direct descendant of the one-horse "Chief's Buggy" that preceded the roadsters and runabouts that became popular chief's runabouts later.

The Ford Motor Co. continued to supply a lot of fire engine chassis. This is a 1932 Ford booster and chemical car. Note the large water tank behind the small chemical tank. This would be classified as a booster truck. It could handle quite a bit of fire if the operator was careful how he used his water supply.

1933

The Great Depression had reached its depths. Everywhere, plants were closed and thousands of men were out of work. Fortunes had been wiped out and bank failures were many. Municipalities, without funds to even pay their employees, could not afford to buy new fire apparatus. Orders for new fire equipment had shrivelled to a mere trickle. In some plants there was barely enough work to keep the place open. The work force and sales staffs had been cut to the bone.

Despite all this gloom, most of the major fire apparatus builders managed to struggle through. There were even some new developments.

The Ahrens-Fox Fire Engine Co. had developed several new types of high-capacity piston pumping engines. One of these was the Model CT-4, advertised as the Ahrens-Fox Big Six. Examples of this sturdy-looking piston pumper were delivered to Passaic, N. J. and York, Pa. New York City received two big Model AHP piston pumpers of 1,000 GPM capacity. The AHP's rolled on cast-steel spoked wheels and had solid tires and left-hand drive.

American LaFrance in 1933 built two special high pressure pumping engines for New York City. Specifications for these pumpers called for them to be capable of delivering 250 GPM to the top of the Empire State Building. They had 4-stage pumps and discharge pressure of a fantastic 600 pounds per square inch. But, according to Elmira, "Politics" intervened and the pumpers were never delivered to New York. The following year they were sold to Ithaca, N. Y., and Youngstown, Ohio. Also in 1933, American LaFrance redesigned its aerial ladder to incorporate new tubular steel handrails which greatly increased the strength of the bed ladder.

American LaFrance had introduced a new 300 Series which employed a new style of hood, radiator shell and front bumper. The line of small 500 GPM pumpers in this series was powered by an in-line, 8-cylinder engine purchased from Lycoming. The full-sized ALF pumpers sported a plated radiator shell instead of the assembled, cast-aluminum one used through 1930, and some 12-cylinder models bore a V-12 emblem on the radiators.

The Stutz Fire Engine Co., which had started building fire engines in Indianapolis in 1919, had ceased fire apparatus production in about 1928. In the early 1930s an effort was made to revive the proud Stutz name. The New Stutz Fire Engine Co. was organized by new owners, and set up operations in Hartford City, Ind. The new firm delivered a relatively small number of pumpers through 1940. Some New Stutz fire apparatus was built on the Defiance truck chassis, and others were assembled using various components.

In 1932, Henry Ford had announced his famed V-8 engine. This powerful, yet economical powerplant was immediately picked up by a number of fire apparatus builders. Even the Seagrave Corp. came out with a new low-cost pumper mounted on the Ford V-8 truck chassis. This was called the Seagrave Volunteer. The Columbus, Ohio manufacturer also offered its economical pumper body on a Reo truck chassis.

In 1933, American LaFrance redesigned and strengthened its 75 and 85-foot wood aerials by replacing the former small-diameter handrails with steel pipe attached to the Douglas Fire side rails at no less than eight points. This type of main ladder was supplied up to the 1950s. Asbury Park's 1933 American LaFrance Type 217 seventy-five foot spring-raised aerial is seen here parked on the street. This rig has been repainted.

Ridgefield, N. J. responded to rescue calls with this American LaFrance rescue squad car. The open rear compartment has been outfitted with a canopy to protect the crew from the elements.

American LaFrance had come out with a new 300 Series, which used a new, thinner radiator shell and a new, more rounded hood. This is a 1933 American LaFrance 500 gallon-per-minute pumper delivered to Fredonia, N. Y. It succeeded the Type 92 as Elmira's small custom-built pumper.

This parade view shows the new frontal appearance of Seagrave to good advantage. For the next several years, the siren was mounted on a frame between the headlights. This is a 500 gallon-per-minute pumper of the Montvale, N. J. Fire Dept. Note the spotlights carried on the platform above the hose box.

Shown here is one of Somerville, Massachusett's Seagraves, part of a large single order. This is a 1933 Seagrave Standard Series 1,000 gallon-per-minute pumper. The windshield on this model could be folded down. Note the suction inlet port just ahead of the rear wheel. This pumper responded as Somerville Engine No. 6.

Seagrave's little Suburbanite also got the full restyling treatment. This is a 500 gallon-per-minute Suburbanite pumping engine. Its 6-cylinder engine had a seven-main-bearing crankshaft. This model had two discharge gates on its centrifugal pump. Seagrave fire apparatus now had left-hand drive.

The big Somerville, Mass. order also included a Seagrave 75-foot tractor-drawn aerial ladder truck. This is a standard spring-raised model. The tiller has been equipped with a canvas windshield. These aerials had a set of manual jacks mounted at the front of the trailer frame, to stabilize the truck when the ladder was raised.

A companion piece to the pumper, this is a 1933 Seagrave hose and booster car of the Somerville, Mass. Fire Dept. The hose wagon responded with the engine on fire calls. A small monitor nozzle is mounted at the rear of the hose box.

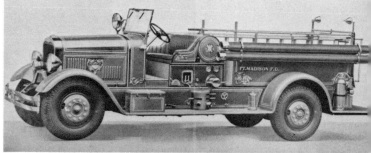

The restyled Seagrave Special 750 gallon-per-minute pumping engine was a middleweight fire engine, powered by a 129-horsepower Seagrave 6-cylinder engine. It was sized between the small Suburbanite and the larger Standard series pumper.

The Bakersfield, Cal. Fire Dept. owned this streamlined Seagrave squad car. Note the enclosed compartments, and the power cable carried on the reel at the rear. This is also one of the earlier Seagraves to be equipped with the cab doors. This rig carried Seagrave Reg. No. 77880.

In addition to the large Seagrave pumpers delivered this year, New York bought six of these medium-sized Seagrave hose and turret wagons. These wagons ran as hose tenders with the pumping engines. Standard F.D.N.Y. armament included a large-capacity turret pipe, the inlets for which can be seen just above the running board.

The New York City Fire Dept. continued to place orders with Seagrave. The F.D.N.Y. placed eight of these big 1933 Seagrave 1,000 gallon-per-minute pumpers into service. An indication of the size of this pumper can be gained from the men riding the running boards—these were big machines. Note the large equipment box over the hose bed.

In addition to the small Volunteer on Ford V-8 chassis, Seagrave also built the Firemaster on a Reo chassis. This small-town pumper was powered by a 73-horsepower, 6-cylinder engine and had a 400 gallon-per-minute pump. The hose box could carry 1,000 feet of 2½-inch fire hose. This rig carries twin booster reels.

AHRENS-FOX

After years of buying large numbers of American LaFrance and Seagrave motor pumping engines, the New York City Fire Dept. in 1933 returned to Ahrens-Fox. Two of these big Model AHP 1,000 gallon-per-minute piston pumpers were placed in service this year. They featured left-hand drive and were powered by 6-cylinder valve-in-head Ahrens-Fox engines. They had solid tires mounted on steel spoked wheels.

The Walter Motor Co. of New York delivered five of these 75-foot tractor-drawn aerial ladder trucks to the New York City Fire Dept. The engines in these powerful tractors were mounted completely forward of the front axle. They also rode on solid tires.

A Pirsch fire engine could be built on other than the Pirsch custom fire apparatus chassis. This is a 1933 Sterling truck chassis with Pirsch pumping equipment. The 500 gallon-per-minute unit was delivered to Mequon, Wis.

Inspired perhaps by such stylish ornaments used on the radiator of the Lincoln and to a lesser extent on well-appointed Fords, Peter Pirsch and Sons offered a greyhound hood ornament on its fire apparatus. This 1933 Pirsch 500 gallon-per-minute centrifugal pumper was sold to Lake Villa, Ill.

The City of Baltimore, Md. purchased two of these 1933 Mack Model BQ tractors which it used to modernize two of its ancient water towers. This is Water Tower No. 1, an 1898 Hale tower. The other BQ pulled Tower 2's 1891 Hale. Formally retired in 1970, this intriguing apparatus is now a popular exhibit at the Fire Museum of Maryland.

The Barton front-mount pump continued to win friends on rural fire departments across the country. This is a Barton pump of 200 gallon-per-minute capacity mounted on the front of a Reo Speedwagon pumper built for the Bangor, Maine Fire Dept. The Barton pump was marketed by the American Steam Pump Co. of Battle Creek, Mich.

This is a Maxim triple combination pumper. Instead of the conventional metal factory windshield, this pumper is equipped with a canvas windbreaker. Note the small electric siren mounted just over the front bumper.

A 1933 Maxim 750 gallon-per-minute pumper was delivered to Lewiston, Maine. It sports disc wheels and carries a monitor nozzle atop the large equipment box over the front of the hose bed. Maxims were still built with individual bucket seats.

The ruinous effects of the depression wore on. New orders were few and far between, but the worst was over.

In an editorial carried in its August, 1934 issue, *Fire Engineering* pointed out the merits of enclosed fire apparatus. Only a handful of fire engines with closed cabs were in service across the U. S. Manufacturers were encouraged to consider the advantages of enclosed equipment, which would provide greater safety and protection from extremes in weather to the crew.

The Ahrens-Fox Fire Engine Co. received a substantial boost in activity from a large order for new apparatus from Hoboken, N. J. During 1934, Ahrens-Fox delivered five 1,000 GPM Model CT-4 piston pumpers and three special Model 6-VLB combination hose and booster cars to the New Jersey city. New York City in 1934 took delivery of four 1,000 GPM Model NT-2 piston pumpers from Ahrens-Fox. These were equipped with pneumatic tires and had right-hand drive.

New models were introduced by the Buffalo Fire Appliance Corp. of Buffalo, N. Y., and General-St. Louis. Buffalo's new look included streamlined fenders and a new hood with louvred doors. The high-styled new General Monarch pumper had a windsplit V-type grille and streamlined, fully faired front fenders. General's new model was built on the company's own assembled chassis and even boasted a V-type windshield.

Among the victims of the depression was the Prospect Fire Engine Co. of Prospect, Ohio, which had been forced to close its doors. Prospect had been a major fire apparatus builder through the 1920s.

American LaFrance had introduced its V-12 engine in 1931, and sold many pumpers and aerials powered by this special firefighting unit. Many of the units delivered carried special V-12 identification on the radiators. This is a 1934 American LaFrance 1,000 gallon-per-minute V-12 pumper delivered to Englewood, N. J. The front bumper is not original.

Historically, Detroit has used relatively little American LaFrance fire apparatus, relying instead on a large fleet of Seagraves and Ahrens-Foxes. In 1934, however, the Motor City purchased this special American LaFrance Series 300 rescue squad car, powered by a V-12 engine. A V-12 American LaFrance tractor was also delivered to Detroit this year. Note the unusual half-doors on the cab and the louvreless hood.

Elizabeth, N. J. took delivery of this American LaFrance 75-foot tractor drawn aerial ladder truck on Nov. 5, 1934. Powered by a 140-horsepower 6-cylinder engine, it featured cast steel wheels and 6-wheel brakes. Officially, a type 317, it carried 377 feet of wood ground ladders in its double bank ladder bed. This type of American LaFrance aerial was also available in an 85-foot versions.

Under a 1933 contract, American LaFrance built two special high pressure pumpers for New York City. These pumpers had 4-stage pumps and were designed to deliver 250 gallons-per-minute to the top of the Empire State Building. However, Gotham "politics" intervened, and these two pumpers were never accepted by the F.D.N.Y. One of these special 1250 GPM pumpers eventually was delivered to Ithica, N. Y. The other was sold to Youngstown, Ohio.

The 1934 Seagrave 600 gallon-per-minute pumper was powered by a Seagrave 6-cylinder engine rated at 100 brake horsepower. It had a 4-stage Seagrave centrifugal pump. Standard equipment included full crowned fenders, a floating rear axle and automatic pressure regulator.

Sometimes local garages were called upon to modernize older apparatus in smaller cities and towns. A local shop enclosed the cab of this 1934 Seagrave 600 gallon-per-minute pumper of the Hasbrouck Heights, N. J. Fire Dept. The cab was similar in style to the canopy style introduced a few years later by Seagrave.

This big Seagrave 1,000 gallon-per-minute triple combination pumper served Tiffin, Ohio, until late in 1972. The 6-cylinder pumper, in virtually original condition, was purchased by bid by Dave and Barb Rex of Northville, Mich. This pumper is a familiar sight at Greenfield Village International Antique Fire Apparatus Assn. musters in the Detroit area.

The District of Columbia Fire Dept. also ran 2-piece engine companies. This 1934 Seagrave booster and hose car was assigned to Washington, D.C. Engine Co. No. 16. It has been repainted. Note the assortment of small nozzle tips on the front tool box.

Bickle Fire Engines Ltd. of Woodstock, Ontario, delivered this 800 Imperial gallon-per-minute quadruple combination to Brockville, Ontario. This quad was retired only a few years ago and is now owned by a collector. This large series Bickle was usually powered by an Ahrens-Fox 6-cylinder engine, although Waukesha engines were also used. The original wooden ground ladders have been replaced with metal ladders.

The Chino Rural Fire Department of Chino, Calif. boasted this well-equipped Seagrave 500 gallon-per-minute pumper. This model was equipped with two booster hose reels and a single-stage pump. Seagrave did a good business in California.

This is Engine Co. No. 294 of the New York City Fire Dept. The pumper is a 1,000 gallon-per-minute Ahrens-Fox Model AHP. Note the spare tire carried on the running board and the electric siren horn mounted on top of the front-mounted pump.

Ahrens-Fox delivered this 1,000 gallon-per-minute Model NT-2 piston pumper to New York City. It had left-hand drive, and was powered by an Ahrens-Fox 6-cylinder T-head engine. This one was assigned to F.D.N.Y. Engine Co. No. 294. Note the plated doors on the hood.

Hoboken, N. J. ordered several Ahrens-Foxes this year. One of these was this 1,000 gallon-per-minute Model CT-4 piston pumper. Even Ahrens-Fox was now delivering most of its apparatus with factory-installed windshields. This Ahrens-Fox was assigned to Engine Co. No. 6.

The Hoboken, N. J. order included this 1934 Ahrens-Fox Hose Car with booster equipment. Note the large flasher mounted between the headlights. This small hose wagon was placed in service with Hoboken Engine Co. No. 3.

Yet another part of the big Hoboken delivery was this Ahrens-Fox Rotarystyle pumper with foam proportioning equipment. The Depression had severely reduced municipal fire apparatus orders, and this order for several units for a single city was a Godsend to the Cincinnati factory. Some cities were unable to order new equipment for years.

This old pumper had quite a history. It started out as a Martin motor pumper—actually a small booster and hose wagon—and when the original chassis wore out the apparatus was simply transferred to a new International Harvester chassis. The rig was used in Womelsdorf, Pa.

Springfield, Mass. originated the flared-type hose body, which incorporated crew benches over the hose bed. This style was delivered by numerous manufacturers and was known as a Springfield body. The Springfield, Mass. Fire Dept. ordered this 1934 Mack Type 75 combination booster and high pressure hose wagon with overhead ladder rack and fixed turret pipe.

Mack
FIRE APPARATUS

This is a 600 gallon-per-minute 1934 Mack pumper in service with the Lynnfield, Mass. Fire Dept. Note the factory windshield. The overhead rack for the 45-foot metal ladder was added later. The Mack Bulldog mascot can be seen on the radiator cap.

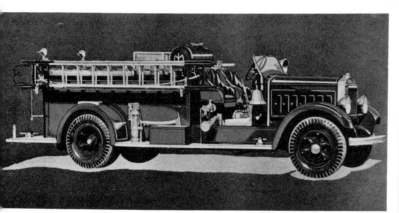

This was the "junior series" Mack. The Type 55 pumper had a pumping capacity of 600 gallons per minute and was powered by a 100-horsepower Mack 6-cylinder engine. Standard equipment also included 4-wheel brakes and a 4-speed transmission.

San Francisco prolonged the useful lives of several of its old former horse-drawn hook and ladder trucks by rebuilding them and adding new motor tractors. The SFFD bought a number of Mack tractors for this purpose. Some of these old ladder trucks had four or five different tractors over the years. All of these trailer type ladder trucks were eventually replaced with aerials.

By all rights, this photo should be filed under the year 1956, because that was when Peter Pirsch & Sons Co. completely rebuilt the Memphis Fire Department's old 1895 Hale water tower. But the modernization was centered around one of Memphis' very nicely preserved 1934 Pirsch ladder truck tractors. A new radiator shell was fitted, complete with Pirsch nameplate, and a canvas roof was provided for the cab. The former horse-drawn water tower had been motorized with an American LaFrance Type 31 tractor. This rig was only recently retired from service.

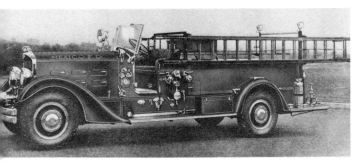

The General Fire Truck Corp. of St. Louis built an assembled unit called the General Monarch. This 750 gallon-per-minute pumper was delivered to Mexico City. The pump controls are mounted on the cowl.

Screaming down the street in response to an alarm is a General Monarch triple combination pumper. This 750-gallon job was powered by a 200-horsepower engine. The preconnected hard suction hose wrapped around the front of this rig could be hooked up quickly, saving precious moments. Note the spotlight between the headlights.

The W. S. Darley Co. of Chicago was now competing with Barton in the low-cost, basic fire engine market. A small town could purchase a complete Darley-Ford fire engine for under $2,000. This 500 gallon-per-minute, front-mount Ford pumper sold for an incredible—by today's standards—$1,495 complete, including the Ford V-8 chassis. All equipment except hose was provided. The pump was guaranteed to pump 500 gallons a minute from suction and 650 GPM from a hydrant.

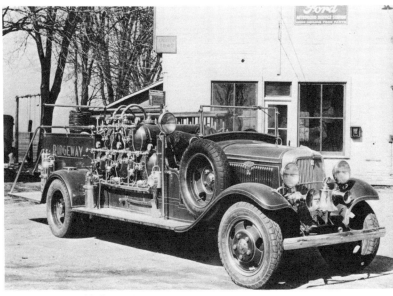

This is a rather heavy 5-tank chemical and hose car mounted on a Ford V-8 chassis by an unknown builder. The American LaFrance bell indicates that it may have come from Elmira. It was built for a Ridgeway Fire Dept. The radiator shell is plated, and a spare tire is carried on the right-hand side.

Howe Fire Apparatus Co. built this little triple combination pumper for the Grand Coulee Dam Fire Department. The 400 gallon-per-minute unit is built on a windshieldless Chevrolet truck chassis. The suction hose is carried side by side instead of one above the other.

The builder of this small Ford front-mount pumper, shown on the right, is not known, but this photo appears to have been posed in front of the Dearborn, Mich. fire station. Dearborn, of course, is home to the World Headquarters of Ford Motor Co. The chassis is a Ford V-8 and the pump is of about 400-gallon capacity. This could be a Barton model. Note the electric siren on the roof.

The Buffalo Fire Appliance Corp. built this small pumper on a 1934 Ford V-8 truck chassis for Belo Horizonte, Brazil. The closed-cab apparatus had a 400 gallon-per-minute midship pump and carried 300 gallons of water. Note the spare tire mount.

This 1934 Buffalo 500 gallon-per-minute pumper was used by the Middleton, Mass. Fire Dept. The headlights have been changed, and the company's gear is carried in a rack over the hard suctions. Note the post-mounted beacon ray warning light, a modern-day addition.

The Hahn Motor Co. of Hamburg, Pa. built this small 350 gallon-per-minute triple combination pumper. It was used by the Portland, Pa. Fire Dept. Hahn assembled its own motor chassis and is still in the fire apparatus business today.

The Maxim Motor Co. of Middleboro, Mass. built this sturdy-looking 750 gallon-per-minute triple combination pumper. In addition to the two standard lengths of large-diameter hard suction hose, this pumper carries three 2½-inch lengths. The booster hose is carried in the wire basket above the hose bed. The boxlike affair on the running board is a suction strainer.

The New York City Fire Dept. placed eight of these big Walter 75-foot tractor-drawn aerial ladder trucks in service in 1934. These Walters had tractor windshields. The hoists used on this series were different from those delivered earlier. This truck has just answered an alarm and awaits its crew on a busy street.

Several important developments occurred in the fire apparatus industry this year.

Peter Pirsch & Sons Co. of Kenosha, Wis. in 1935 delivered the country's first domestically produced 100-foot, all-powered aerial ladder truck to Melrose, Mass. This impressive aerial had a 3-section main ladder made entirely of metal. The ladder, which had handrails on all three sections, was entirely hydraulically operated. This historic unit was replaced by another Pirsch aerial in 1971. Pirsch was now using a new V-type radiator on all of its custom apparatus. Also in 1935, this company built a special 500 GPM pumper for the big U. S. Navy base at Oahu, Hawaii. Designed for operation on conventional roads, it could also be driven on railway tracks.

The Seagrave Corp. restyled its standard series apparatus this year. The new appearance included a stylish, new radiator grille that was slightly 'Vee'd and raked, and consisted of a series of bright vertical bars. A series of horizontal streamers used on the ventilation louvres of the new hood gave an impression of length. Seagrave continued to assemble its flat radiator, earlier style apparatus on smaller models into the next year. To Seagrave this year also went the credit for the introduction of America's first 65-foot junior metal aerial. Mounted on a city service ladder truck chassis, the new 3-section ladder was of all metal construction, had siderails on each section and was completely hydraulically operated. This innovation greatly increased the usefulness of smaller ladder trucks. Seagrave's new small-block V-12 engine also appeared this year.

Fire Chief Hendrix Palmer of Charlotte, N. C. had read with interest the *Fire Engineering* editorial concerning enclosed fire apparatus that had appeared the previous year, and was so taken with the idea that he ordered the first sedan-cab pumper built in the U. S. The 750 GPM pumper was built by Mack, and was called the Mack Fire Sedan. It was placed in service in July, 1935, and had a completely enclosed van-type body. Also in 1935, Mack demonstrated a unique one-truck fire department. The tractor-drawn rig carried a 1,000-gallon water tank, a full supply of ground ladders, hose and other equipment. This apparatus was designed for use by communities without a water system.

Ahrens-Fox, which had made its formidable reputation with its front-mounted piston pumpers, introduced a line of handsome, new pumpers with midship-mounted centrifugal pumps this year. Development of the centrifugals had been very expensive, and coupled with the low level of depression-era business, had brought Ahrens-Fox close to the brink. The new centrifugal pumps were mounted in a pleasingly styled new chassis and body, which was purchased through Schacht. The apparatus was built, however, in the Ahrens-Fox plant, and the company continued to deliver piston pumpers for many more years. The centrifugals were available with pumps ranging in capacity from 500 to 1,250 GPM.

American LaFrance introduced one of its most beautiful models ever this year. This pleasing new design featured an exceptionally long hood, to house the pump which was located immediately behind the engine in the cowl. This new style was known as the 400 Series and employed the big ALF V-12 engine. It was available in 750, 1,000, 1,250 and 1,500 GPM versions. The new style had oversized wheels and a low windshield. Chain-drive was a

thing of the past: the new model featured shaft drive. Most apparatus of this type was delivered from 1935 through 1937, but a few were assembled as late as 1939. Most had the bells mounted in front of the radiator just above the bumper, and the bell was topped by a V-12 emblem set on a Maltese Cross background.

Low-cost fire engines did not have to be homely, as attested by this W. S. Darley triple combination pumper mounted on a Ford V-8 chassis. This pumper has a 500 gallon-per-minute front-mount pump. This type of equipment was the backbone of small-town America's fire defense well into the middle of this century. There is no question that the highly efficient equipment represented real value for the money.

Here is a nicely preserved example of the budget-priced "kit" type fire equipment designed to appeal to Depression ridden smaller towns and villages. The old Luverne Automobile Co. of Luverne, Minn., which had dabbled in the fire equipment field from time to time, offered the Luverne Fire Car, which consisted of a 250 GPM rear-mounted rotary gear pump mounted on a Ford V-8 truck chassis. Red Wing, Minn., still owns its Fire Car, which sold for $1,400 complete.

This American LaFrance pumper appears to be a "transitional" model. It has the new style skirted front fenders, like those used on the new 400 Series, and the new style plated front bumper. This example was owned by the Goffstown, N. H. Fire Dept. Note the factory windshield which is an integral part of the cowl assembly.

After many years of service as a small pumper, the fire department of Somerville, Tenn. converted its 500 gallon-per-minute American LaFrance Ford to a hose and turret wagon, even though the pump was retained. A platform has been constructed over the cab on which is mounted a portable turret gun. When photographed by Dick Adelman, this truck had only 1,200 miles on its odometer!

The American LaFrance Series 400 pumper had an angled suction port and two discharge gates. This is one of these pumpers delivered to San Francisco. Note the streamlined hood and large windshield. This series was most commonly supplied in 1,250 and 1,000 gallon-per-minute versions. San Francisco fire apparatus was still being painted a very dark maroon.

North Manchester, Ind. owns this 1935 American LaFrance Model 460 pumper. The 600 gallon-per-minute rotary gear pump is located between the seat and the hose body. This pumper appears to carry no hard suction hose. The lettering on the hood is original and is a good example of the style American LaFrance was using at this time. Striping also tended to be simple and straightforward.

American LaFrance in 1935 introduced a new, radically different-looking series of high capacity pumping engines called the Series 400. This stylish new model featured a very long hood and cowl, with integral windshield. Pumps were mounted in the deep cowl, immediately behind the engine. Most 400's were V-12 powered. This model was built in volume for only three years, although a few were assembled as late as 1939. The Township of Maplewood, N. J. owned this 1935 1,000 gallon-per-minute Series 400 pumper.

San Francisco used this American LaFrance Series 400 high pressure battery wagon. The bodies of these trucks were frequently transferred to new chassis as the older ones wore out from heavy use. This battery wagon has a high-capacity Gorter turret nozzle mounted in front of the unusually high hose bed. The hose beds on these models were baffled into four separate compartments.

The Liberty, Mo. Fire Dept. owned this 1935 American LaFrance 750 gallon-per-minute pumper. This model had a centrifugal pump, however, and a shaft-drive rear axle. Otherwise it is very similar in appearance to the Master Series pumper introduced six years earlier. Windshields were now being installed on most American LaFrance apparatus.

American LaFrance aerial ladder trucks now used a much heavier, tubular type of truss rod on the main ladder. This 1935 American LaFrance Series 300 tractor-drawn aerial ladder truck was used by Red Bank, N. J. The 75-foot aerial was powered by a V-12 engine.

This 1935 American LaFrance 500 gallon-per-minute quadruple combination shows the new radiator and hood used on medium-duty American LaFrance apparatus. Hose is carried in the full-length tray atop the double-bank ladder bed, and a Y-shaped trough permits two hose lines to be stretched simultaneously. This quad was used by the Pascoag, R. I. Fire Dept.

The Hahn Motor Co. built this custom-chassised triple combination pumper for the Linwood Fire Co. of N. J. For many years, this company's slogan was "The Dependable Hahn". Note the cast radiator and the bell which has been relocated to the running board. Hahn still builds custom-chassis fire apparatus today.

With the chief himself behind the wheel, this 1935 Seagrave-Ford Volunteer triple combination pumper is ready to respond at the sound of the alarm bell. The 500 gallon-per-minute pumper is mounted on a Ford V-8 truck chassis. This low-cost apparatus had all but replaced the Seagrave Suburbanite.

Although Seagrave began marketing its first metal aerials this year, the old reliable spring-raised wood aerial was still being sold. The Detroit Fire Dept. in 1935 purchased two Seagrave 85-foot tractor-drawn aerials powered by the new V-12 tractor, and two additional tractors. These were the last wood aerials purchased by this city. These aerials had chemical equipment, and were of the single ladder bank style.

The first Seagrave metal aerial ladder built was this 65-footer which was delivered to Lancaster, Ohio in 1935. The 65-foot service aerial quickly became one of Seagrave's most popular models. Early models sported this style of hood and radiator. The ladder has three sections. Delivery of 85 and 100-foot tractor-drawn metal aerials began the following year.

Seagrave was still building a light-duty line of triple combinations on commercial truck chassis. This is a 1935 Seagrave-Reo. It has a 500 gallon-per-minute pump, and was used by the Peotone, Ill. Fire Department. Note the standard oval-shaped Seagrave fuel tank.

The year 1935 was one of major change for Seagrave. The Columbus, Ohio manufacturer came out with its first V-12 engine and its first hydraulically-raised metal aerial ladder in 1935. Seagrave's standard models also got a handsome new V-shaped grille with vertical bars, and a new hood with horizontal louvres highlighted by four chrome streamers. This is the prototype of the new Seagrave 1,000 gallon-per-minute pumper which was powered by Seagrave's new 240 horsepower V-12.

This is the new Seagrave V-12 fire service engine. Rated at 240 horsepower, it was a direct competitor to the American LaFrance V-12. This engine was based on a Pierce-Arrow design, and remained in production, with improvements, for nearly 30 years.

1935

This 1935 Mack 1,000 gallon-per-minute pumper protected the Village of Bedford, N. Y. The pumper is equipped with a windshield, and carried a 40-foot extension ladder that blocked access to the seat from the left-hand side. In this photo, the old Mack is ready to roll. This is a Type 19.

1935

This huge combination pumper-tanker was originally delivered to the town of Lake, Wis. but through annexation, wound up on the Milwaukee Fire Dept. This 3-axle model has a 750 gallon-per-minute pump and carries 2,500 gallons of water—enough to extinguish a good-sized fire if used carefully. At last report, Tank No. 4 was still going strong on the M.F.D.

Mack had the distinction of delivering the first completely enclosed, sedan-style pumper built for an American fire department. This 750 gallon-per-minute Mack went into service with the Charlotte, N. C. Fire Dept. in July, 1935. It was built to specifications laid down by Fire Chief Hendrix Palmer. The men rode inside this pumper, protected from both traffic and the weather. Note the "command post" observation platform on the roof.

The Bradford, Pa. Fire Dept. used this 1935 Mack 75-foot tractor-drawn aerial ladder truck for many years. It is a Type 95, equipped with the Mack engine-driven aerial ladder hoist. This aerial was subsequently purchased by Andrew Henderson of Weedsport, N. Y., who has more than a dozen operable vintage rigs in his collection. It is in exceptionally good original condition.

This 1935 Ward LaFrance 600 gallon-per-minute triple combination pumper was delivered to Woodridge, N. Y. Ward LaFrance went on to become one of the biggest names in the fire apparatus business, and is still a major manufacturer today. Ward LaFrance had built heavy trucks for years before it entered the fire engine field in the early 1930s.

The Ward LaFrance Truck Corp. of Elmira Heights, N. Y. acquired this early-vintage Ward LaFrance in the early 1970s. Ward LaFrance was the first fire apparatus manufacturer in the U.S. to aggressively promote lime-green equipment over the traditional red. As a result, when the company restored this pumper the rig was painted in this controversial hue. This pumper is a familiar sight at antique fire apparatus meets in the East.

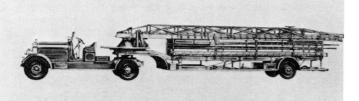

Ahrens-Fox introduced an attractive new line of streamlined fire engines. This is a 1935 Ahrens-Fox Model IRU quadruple combination, equipped with a Hale 1,000 gallon-per-minute pump. It bore Ahrens-Fox Register No. 5019, and was built for Louisville, Ky. Note the squirrel-tail hard suction and the three transverse crew seats on top of the ladder bed. This was a uniquely Louisville style. The unit shown here responded as Quad No. 8.

The Ahrens-Fox Fire Engine Co. still found a good market for its smaller models. A good example is this 1935 Model VR pumper built for Fair Lawn, N. J. This was a 500 gallon-per-minute pumper, which is seen here at work at a fire. The piston pump still reigned supreme at Ahrens-Fox, however, even though the company had been forced into marketing both rotary gear and centrifugal pumpers in order to remain competitive.

One of the most significant developments of the year was the delivery by Peter Pirsch & Sons Co. of the first 100-foot hydro-mechanical, metal aerial ladder truck built in the U.S. This historic piece of apparatus was delivered to Melrose, Mass. and is still owned by this department. The three-section metal aerial remained in service until 1971 when it was replaced by another Pirsch. This aerial featured safety siderails on all three aerial ladder sections, and carried all metal ground ladders. The tillerman sat in a bucket seat that flipped over the side of the main ladder when the aerial was to be raised. The Pirsch aerial immediately earned a reputation for strength.

Although the new aluminum-alloy metal aerial would eventually replace it, the Pirsch wood aerial was still preferred by many fire departments. This 85-foot tractor-drawn, hydro-mechanical aerial was delivered by Peter Pirsch & Sons to Ladder Co. No. 1 in Cambridge, Mass. The Pirsch hydro-mechanical hoisting mechanism resulted in a clean, uncluttered aerial ladder turntable. The tractor on this truck has a windshield, but the poor tillerman still has to contend with the elements.

In 1935, Pirsch introduced a new V-type radiator and restyled hood on its fire engines. Pirsch offered its customers either rotary gear or centrifugal pumps of from 500 to 1,250 gallons-per-minute capacity. This is the new Pirsch 1,000 Gallon Pumping Engine, Model 16.

This is the Pirsch Model 21, a 500 gallon-per-minute pumper. Pirsch models at this time also included the 750 gallon-per-minute Model 25; the Model 20 in 500, 600 and 750 GPM variants; the Model 15 in 500, 600 and 750 GPM versions; and the Model 19 in 500 and 600-gallon models. Largest in the Pirsch line was the Model 14, rated at 1,250 gallons-per-minute.

Shown at left is the Chatham, N. J. Fire Department's locally-built Ford city service hook and ladder. The company used this rig for quite a few years. Note the big deck nozzle mounted on top of the booster tank.

The fire service showed strong interest in enclosed-body fire apparatus, and a number of pumpers of completely enclosed design were placed in service this year.

The Detroit Fire Department in 1936 placed four streamlined Seagrave Safety Sedans into service. Designated Model JW-440Ts, they were 1,000 GPM pumpers powered by Seagrave's big 240 horsepower V-12 engine. The Seagrave sedan pumpers were stunningly streamlined compared with conventional pumpers of their day. Even the hard suction hose and ground ladders were carried out of sight inside. The pumpers had front suction intakes and a length of preconnected soft suction hose was carried over the right front fender. The integrity of this design was not long in proving itself. One month after it entered service, Engine Co. No. 1's new Seagrave sedan was involved in a broadside collision with High Pressure Hose Co. 1. Both rigs were badly damaged, but the pumper crew escaped without injury. Four men were seriously hurt on the older, open rig. Detroit purchased 1,000 GPM sedan pumpers regularly over the next 29 years.

American LaFrance delivered several van-type pumpers to American fire departments. Hampstead, Md. received a white-painted Protector with a 600 GPM centrifugal pump and the new small V-12 engine. Brookline, Mass. took delivery of the first of two huge, enclosed 1,500 GPM pumpers built on the big 400 Metropolitan chassis, and Topeka, Kans. received a smaller LaFrance enclosed-style pumping engine. Also in 1936, American LaFrance built a huge 400 Series tractor-drawn water tower with a 65-foot rearmounted mast and duplex tower nozzles, for Newark, N. J. The glistening white Newark tower sported two big deck turrets in addition to its tower artillery.

Ahrens-Fox came out with yet another new line of light-duty pumpers. The new SC series fealtured a 500 gallon-per-minute centrifugal pump, and was mounted on the Schacht commercial truck chassis. The company's mainstay, despite the new centrifugal series introduced a year earlier, was the big piston pumper. Ahrens-Fox had commenced deliveries of the 1,250 GPM Model BT the previous year, and a whole new series using a 1,000 GPM piston pump was on the drawing board.

Seagrave redesigned its smaller series pumpers this year. The most distinguishing feature of the new Seagrave line was a new, rounded grille and hood design. Within a few years this new front end would become standard on all Seagrave apparatus. Early pumper models in this series retained the familiar oval Seagrave gasoline tank just behind the seat.

The Maxim Motor Co. in 1936 began to use a new grille, with a mild V and a vertical center bar, on its apparatus.

Peter Pirsch & Sons of Kenosha, Wis. delivered this 1,000 gallon-per-minute pumper equipped with an enclosed two-man cab to Racine, Wis. in 1936. The frame mounted in front of the radiator carries the bell, siren and a Mars warning light. This pumper has a black-painted roof. Pirsch had actually delivered its first closed-cab pumper some six years earlier.

The PIRSCH

Here is another closed-cab Pirsch pumper. This 500 gallon-per-minute model, equipped with a 500 gallon booster tank, was built on a 1936 International chassis with factory-built closed cab. It served the Oak Creek, Wis. Fire Department.

Champaign, Ill. used this 1936 Peter Pirsch & Sons quint for many years. When the original wood aerial ladder wore out, the department replaced it with a new 75-foot Pirsch aluminum alloy aerial. This rig still has its original paint and lettering. Note the double bumper bars.

The fire service was beginning to appreciate the added safety factor afforded by the completely enclosed body. Here is another American LaFrance van-type pumper. This one, finished in white, was delivered to Hampstead, Md. It was a Protector Model, powered by the 150-horsepower American LaFrance V-12 engine, and equipped with a 600 gallon-per-minute, single stage centrifugal pump. This pumper was converted into a rescue squad car in its later days.

American LaFrance delivered this one-off, van-bodied pumper to the Topeka, Kan. Fire Dept. It was equipped with a midship-mounted 750 gallon-per-minute pump. Note the unusual type of hood louvres utilized on this model. The headlights have been converted to sealed beams. The front fenders are the same type used on the 400 Series.

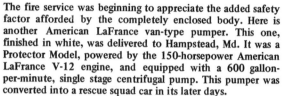

Green Bay, Wis. owned this handsome 1936 American La-France 500 gallon-per-minute quadruple combination with a rotary gear pump. This quad has a turret pipe mounted above the pump. Note the full-length hose box above the ladder bed. The rollers for the booster hose basket can be seen just behind the booster tank, which is lettered "Truck No. 3."

LaFrance Fire Engine & Foamite Ltd., American LaFrance's subsidiary in Toronto, delivered this Type 92-TA Automatic 85-foot tractor-drawn aerial ladder truck to Windsor, Ontario. Powered by the American LaFrance V-12 engine, and with a double-bank trailer, this was the largest apparatus built by the company at this time. Bearing Register No. L-747, this aerial cost $17,900 and was in service for 31 years, being retired in November, 1967. The two-section, spring-raised aerial ladder was of the finest selected Douglas Fir. The author had the honor of tillering this aerial out of service.

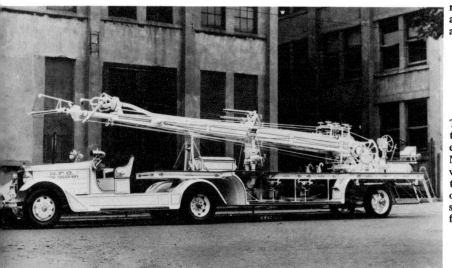

This 1936 American LaFrance 65-foot tractor-drawn water tower is said to have been the most powerful water tower ever built. An American Automatic, it was built for Newark, N. J. It was painted white, with gold striping and trim, and was drawn by a Series 400 tractor. This huge tower had two tower nozzles and two big deck turrets. The tower is seen outside the Elmira, N. Y. plant prior to delivery. Note the solid rear tires on the trailer, and the steps with handrails for the tillerman.

The cradle-mounted bell on the front of this 1936 American LaFrance 500 gallon-per-minute quadruple combination does not appear to be original, although front-mounted bells were common on American LaFrance equipment at this time. American LaFrance and most other fire apparatus builders used fixed-mount bells with a movable clapper: with the cradle type, the bell tilts striking the clapper. This quad was used by Verona, N. J.

American LaFrance was still delivering apparatus built to order on the customer's preferred commercial chassis. This is a 1936 American LaFrance-Dodge pumper. It has a 500 gallon-per-minute Hale pump mounted on the frame behind the driver's seat. It was photographed at a SPAAMFAA muster at Syracuse, N. Y.

At about this time, American LaFrance began to identify some of its models by name instead of using simply colorless series numbers. This American LaFrance Invader Model, 750 gallon-per-minute pumper was delivered to Jefferson City, Mo. A trim-looking job, it was powered by a 170-horsepower American LaFrance V-12 engine. Note the modern bullet-shaped electric coaster siren with flashing red light lens.

This 1936 American LaFrance Type 475 pumper was used by the Hawthorne Fire Co. No. 1, of Hawthorne, N. J. This is a 12-cylinder, 750 gallon-per-minute pumper equipped with a rotary gear pump. The Chief's white helmet is the first of the 10 carried on the rack above the hard suction hoses. Note the old-style playpipe and the siamese fitted with two nozzles, mounted on the rear step.

The larger series pumpers being delivered by American LaFrance were in the new 400 Series. Shown here is a 1,000 gallon-per-minute 1936 American LaFrance 400 equipped with a rotary gear pump. This rig was built for Clarksdale, Miss. It has dual 2½-inch hard suction hoses carried in squirrel-tail fashion, attached to a swivel-mounted "Y" intake for quick hookup at the fire. Note the standard front-mounted bell topped by the American LaFrance V-12 emblem.

Shown below is a standard model American LaFrance double-bank city service hook and ladder truck. This one was delivered to Bristol, Va. The factory listed this rig as a Type 948. It was powered by an 8-cylinder engine. Note the scaling ladder mounted over the front of the ladder bed. The longest ladders carried on this type of truck were usually 55-footers in three sections with tormentor poles.

While the old style wood, spring-raised aerial was still available, the new Seagrave all-metal, hydraulically-powered aerial ladder was enjoying considerable success. This 1936 Seagrave tractor-drawn 75-foot three-section metal aerial, finished in white, was used by the Suffern, N. Y. Fire Dept.

This big Seagrave V-12 pumper was delivered to Jackson, Miss. It sports dual booster hose reels, packs a portable three-way turret pipe on the running board, and has a Mars oscillating warning signal light mounted on the post beside the cowl. Open-cab Seagrave apparatus still came with a fold-down windshield.

The Seagrave Corp. also got into the enclosed fire apparatus business in 1936. The Columbus, Ohio plant delivered four of these Model JW-440-T safety sedan pumpers to the Detroit Fire Dept. These streamlined pumpers, powered by V-12 engines and of 1,000 GPM capacity, carried all equipment inside—including the crew, ground ladders and hard suctions. Note the front suction intake, Buckeye Roto-Rays, and the black roof and black paint band above the beltline. This enclosed style pumper became standard equipment on the D.F.D. for the next 31 years.

Seagrave's earlier style radiator and hood was still being used on a small number of rigs still being delivered. Seymour, Conn. received this 1936 Seagrave 500 gallon-per-minute pumper, equipped with a single stage centrifugal pump. This pumper was used by Seymour's Citizen's Engine Co. No. 2.

Seagrave continued to build quite a few small pumpers on commercially-available truck chassis. This is a 1936 Seagrave-Reo pumper of 500 gallons-per-minute capacity, built for Neffsville, Pa. Seagrave also delivered many small pumpers of this style on the Ford V-8 chassis.

This earlier style Seagrave was built in 1936 for Swampscott, Mass. The 600 gallon-per-minute triple combination pumping engine was equipped with a 4-stage centrifugal pump. This was the last year this style of apparatus was built in the Columbus, Ohio plant.

Seagrave came out with this new, streamlined front-end styling during 1936. With various modifications, this same style of front end was used on Seagrave fire apparatus until 1951. This striking yellow-and-red 1936 Seagrave 750 GPM pumper was originally owned by Mount Holly, N. Y., then saw service on Michigan's Mackinac Island. Note the continued use of the oval-shaped fuel tank behind the driver's seat.

Kalamazoo, Mich. purchased many Seagrave fire engines over the years, including this 1936 Seagrave straight city service hook and ladder truck with booster equipment. The windshield is folded forward at a rakish angle. Note the letter "S" built into the center of the double-beam front bumper.

The familiar piston pumper continued to be the mainstay of the Ahrens-Fox Fire Engine Co. of Cincinnati, Ohio, but an increasing number of these medium-sized, centrifugal pumpers were rolling off of the Ahrens-Fox assembly floor. This is a Model YC 800 gallon-per-minute pumper delivered to Bryan, Ohio in 1936.

Unlike other fire apparatus manufacturers, Ahrens-Fox built relatively few fire engines on commercial chassis. This 1936 Ahrens-Fox Ford was built on the Ford V-8 chassis, and was equipped with a midship-mounted Hale 500 gallon-per-minute pump. Ahrens-Fox, of course, used the Cincinnati-built Schacht chassis for some of its lighter models over the years.

Old aerial trucks never die, it seems; they just get re-tractored and go on answering the alarm bell. This is a 1936 Ford V-8 replacement tractor is drawing an older model American LaFrance 75-foot aerial, which could be a former Type 31 front-drive job. It is believed this photo was taken in Highland Park, Mich. The bell mounted in front of the radiator probably came off the same LaFrance aerial when this rebuilding was done.

Ahrens-Fox only built one of these big Model BR 1,250 gallon-per-minute rotary-gear pumpers. It was delivered to the Pittsburgh, Pa. Bureau of Fire in May, 1936. This pumper was assigned to Engine Co. No. 3. It is seen here shortly after it entered service. The crew seems to be proud of its big mount.

The Buffalo Fire Appliance Corp. of Buffalo, N. Y. delivered many fire engines built on its own custom fire apparatus chassis. This is a 750 gallon-per-minute triple combination pumper delivered to the city of Lynn, Mass. where it responded as Engine 13. Buffalo and Maxim fire apparatus of this era looked startlingly similar. Note the bumper-mounted bell and siren.

This is one of the most unusual fire engines ever built in the United States. The chassis is a classic Dodge Airflow—one of the very few Airflow trucks produced by Chrysler Corp. This unit began life in all probability as a Socony-Vacuum (Mobil predecessor) fuel tank truck. It was converted in the late 1940s into this squad and booster apparatus for the Teaneck, N. J. Fire Dept. It is not known who did the conversion, but it is certainly a professional job.

The Chelsea, Mass. Fire Department still owns this very nicely preserved 1936 Maxim 750 gallon-per-minute pumper. Maxims were still being built with twin bucket seats. Note the mesh-type radiator grille. This pumper was displayed for buffs attending the 1974 International Fire Buff Associates Convention in Boston, which included a side trip to the site of the Chelsea Conflagration of 1973.

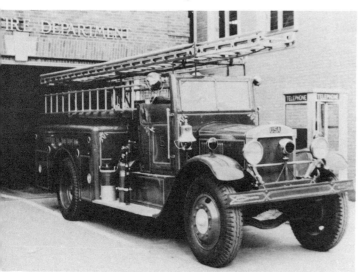

One of the lesser-known fire apparatus builders for many years was the United States Army. The U.S.A. was built at the big Ordnance Depot at Camp Holabird, Md. Lockport, Ill. purchased this 1936 USA from Army Surplus. It has a 750 gallon-per-minute Northern pump, and modernized bodywork by the Farrell Manufacturing Co. of Lockport, Ill.

The Walter Motor Co. delivered six of these big combi-nation hose and turret wagons to the New York City Fire Dept. in 1936. Walter also supplied a large number of aerial ladder and water tower tractors, and some complete aerial ladder trucks, to the F.D.N.Y. This hose wagon was assigned to Engine Co. No. 268. Note the nozzles and tips carried on the shelf just behind the rear fender.

Mack's new streamlined E Series trucks provided the basis for a very attractive series of Mack fire engines. In appearance, this 1936 Mack Model EH Quadruple Combination was definitely ahead of its time when compared with the angular, functional models then being built by other fire apparatus builders. Notice the streamlined fuel tank above and behind the seat on this 500 GPM quad. The truck served Norwood, Pa.

New York City placed many large repeat orders with Mack Trucks, and is still the world's largest user of Mack fire apparatus today, In 1936, the F.D.N.Y. took delivery of these open-cab Mack Type 21 pumpers of 1,000 gallons-per-minute capacity. The following year, the F.D.N.Y. began buying apparatus with enclosed cabs.

The rugged little triple combination pumper at the right was built by the Howe Fire Apparatus Company of Anderson, Ind. on an International Harvester truck chassis. It is equipped with a 400 gallon-per-minute pump. It was built for the Fire Department of Plain, Wis. International listed this chassis in its C-40 Series.

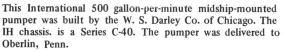

For many years, this big International floodlighting unit was a familiar sight at night fires in Memphis, Tenn. It was built on the International Harvester C Series truck chassis. Like much Memphis apparatus, it carries the name of a former Memphis fire official—the "Clifford Davis".

This International 500 gallon-per-minute midship-mounted pumper was built by the W. S. Darley Co. of Chicago. The IH chassis. is a Series C-40. The pumper was delivered to Oberlin, Penn.

Two of the most unusual pumping engines ever to see service in the U. S. were delivered to Los Angeles this year. They were a pair of 2,000 gallon-per-minute Duplex pumpers built by American LaFrance to the specifications of L. A. Fire Chief Ralph J. Scott. These fascinating pumpers were actually two pumping engines built on a single chassis. Each of the two Duplex pumpers had two American LaFrance V-12 engines and two 1,000 GPM pumps. The front engine drove the apparatus and the pump mounted in the cowl. The rear engine powered a second pump mounted just behind the driver's seat. The Duplex jobs carried no hose, and were designed for use with manifold wagons at large fires. The idea behind this remarkable concept was to reduce the number of pumpers on the street at the scene of a big fire. The engines used in the big Duplex jobs were ALF 240-horsepower V-12s.

According to Ahrens-Fox historian John Sytsma, the Cincinnati plant built only eight piston pump quadruple combinations. This one, a Model CTU with a 750 gallon-per-minute pump, was the last. It was delivered to Ho-Ho-Kus, N. J. and was retired from service only a few years ago. Note the painted front bumper and contoured windshields.

Ahrens-Fox also gave its piston pumpers a smart, new look, consisting of a new, rounded hood, chrome streamers over the ventilation louvres, and long, sweeping new front fenders. This is a 1937 Ahrens-Fox Model BT 1,250 gallon-per-minute piston pumper delivered to Rockville Centre, Long Island, N. Y.

Two more Duplex pumpers of 3,000 GPM capacity were delivered to Los Angeles the following year, along with an American LaFrance Manifold Wagon and two Seagrave manifolds.

American LaFrance in 1937 delivered four special Metropolitan pumping engines to the Los Angeles Fire Dept., in addition to the two Duplex jobs. The pumpers had 4-door sedan cabs which permitted the entire crew to ride inside. Because of their great size, these pumpers were known as Lulubelles by the L. A. firemen. American LaFrance also delivered a few pumpers of this style to other departments.

It was in this year that Ahrens-Fox began building what was probably its greatest model. The first Ahrens-Fox Model HT piston pumper was delivered to South St. Paul, Minn. The 1,000 GPM Model HT was powered by the Hercules HXE 6-cylinder engine, and 67 were delivered over the next 15 years. The last HT went to Tarrytown, N. Y. in 1952 and was the last piston pumper the company ever built. The powerful Hercules engine had a 5.75-inch bore and 6-inch stroke.

The Seagrave Corp. this year introduced a new enclosed cab pumper configuration that would remain in production for nearly 30 years. Called a canopy-cab style, it featured an extended roofline open at the rear. A catwalk between two separate hose beds led to a full-width crew seat facing to the rear. This would become Seagrave's standard closed-cab model within a few years. The steel tubular frame construction used was the same employed in building the Detroit Safety Sedan pumpers. Seagrave delivered four more 1,000 GPM sedans to Detroit this year, along with a 100-foot tractor-drawn aerial with a sedan-type 4-door cab. The company's 65-foot metal service aerial was selling well, and the company had introduced tractor-drawn 75, 85 and 100-foot aerials.

Fully-enclosed pumpers continued to gain in popularity. Among the new sedans delivered this year were a special 500 GPM Ahrens-Fox centrifugal painted black with contrasting red wheels for the West End Hose Co. of Pottsville, Pa.; a Buffalo sedan pumper built for Canandaigua, N. Y., and a 500 GPM FWD sedan for Hartford, Wis. The General Fire Truck Corp. of Detroit,

The Friendship Fire Co. of Sunbury, Penn. used this 1937 Ahrens-Fox piston pumper for 35 years. A Model BT, it was rated at 1,250 gallons per minute. The big Fox was retired in 1971 and was purchased by a private collector. The heavy block-style lettering used on the hood was unusual.

1937

was also developing a streamlined, limousine-style pumper. Ahrens-Fox delivered a pumper with a closed, 3-man cab to Salt Lake City, and Peter Pirsch and Sons supplied a city service ladder truck with a closed cab to Mishawaka, Ind., and a closed-cab pumping engine to Racine, Wis.

New York City placed 33 new pieces of apparatus in service in 1937. Demonstrated at a spectacular public exhibition in Battery Park, they included 19 new Mack Type 21 pumpers of 1,000 GPM capacity with closed cabs, and 10 Seagrave 85-foot wood aerials. The other five units in the order were closed-cab hose wagons built by the Ward LaFrance Truck Corp.

The new hydraulically-raised metal aerials sold by Pirsch and Seagrave were beginning to seriously rival the old spring-raised, wooden aerials that had been around almost since the turn of the century.

The Ahrens-Fox Fire Engine Co. of Cincinnati now offered its customers a line of smaller pumpers built on the well-known Schacht truck chassis. These were known as the Model SC, for Schacht Centrifugal. New Albany, Ind. received this Ahrens-Fox/Schacht 500 gallon-per-minute pumper, Reg. No. 9040. A 2½-inch preconnected hard suction hose is slung around the front of the rig.

In order to be fully competitive, and at great cost to the company, Ahrens-Fox could supply any type of pump the customer wanted—rotary gear, centrifugal, or the famed Ahrens-Fox piston type pump. Here is a 1937 Ahrens-Fox Model ERU quadruple combination, equipped with a Hale Rotary pump. This apparatus was delivered to the St. Paul Boulevard Fire District of Irondequoit, N. Y.

The San Francisco Fire Department prolonged the service lives of many of its former horse-drawn aerial ladder trucks, water towers and city service hook and ladder trucks by years by modernizing them and placing new motor tractors under them. In 1937, the S.F.F.D. purchased this Ahrens-Fox Model H-6 tractor, which is seen here drawing a 1903 American LaFrance 75-foot spring-hoist aerial. Some of these conversion units remained in reserve service into the 1960s.

Ahrens-Fox was also turning out closed-cab jobs. This 1937 Ahrens-Fox Model YC with 2-man cab was supplied to Darien, Conn. It had a 600 gallon-per-minute centrifugal pump, plated radiator shell, and the clothing racks mounted over the hose bed.

The Everett, Wash. Fire Department ordered this 1937 Ahrens-Fox Model ICU quadruple combination. The Everett quad had a 750 GPM pump and an almost fully enclosed ladder bed. Note how the three lengths of hard suction hose are carried, and the short attic ladder riding on top.

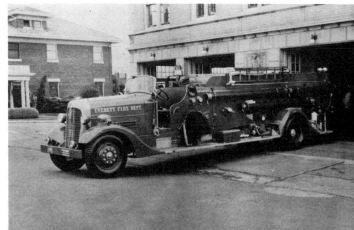

Cicero, Ill. bought this 1937 American LaFrance 400 Series V-12 tractor to replace the worn-out tractor of an older-model aerial. In 1952, the Cicero Fire Dept. purchased a new 85-foot metal aerial ladder trailer from American LaFrance and hooked it up to the 400 tractor. Four years later, a new American LaFrance 700 series tractor replaced the 400 model. Here, the 1937 tractor is seen drawing the 1952 ALF trailer.

1937

The Department of Public Safety of the City of Grand Rapids, Mich. placed this American LaFrance 85-foot tractor-drawn aerial ladder truck into service in 1937. This imposing piece of equipment, with its cowcatcher grille and tiller windshield, remained in service until the mid-1960s as a spare. At last report it was still under wraps in the Grand Rapids F.D. shops, and was in excellent original condition. This was a V-12, spring-raised wood aerial. The post-mounted beacon ray warning light on the turntable was added during the 1950s. The trailer is of the double-bank type.

Another one-of-a-kind American LaFrance is this tractor-drawn city service hook and ladder truck for Rockford, Ill. This was a double-bank model, which looked like it could have been easily retrofitted with an aerial ladder. This was never done, however. A rubber-covered platform was fixed over the area usually used for the turntable.

A companion unit to Hempstead, N. Y.'s Engine No. 3 was this American LaFrance city service hook and ladder truck. The ladder truck is also equipped with half-doors on its cab. The drop-center style of bumper on this truck was used on American LaFrance apparatus for several years. This rig was used by Hempstead Hook and Ladder No. 2.

This is a 1937 American LaFrance Type 945 quadruple combination. It used a 125-horsepower, 8-cylinder engine, which was coupled to a 500 gallon-per-minute rotary gear pump. American LaFrance used a Lycoming 8-cylinder engine as an option in its apparatus, beginning in the mid-1930s. This quad was delivered to the Berwyn, Ill. Fire Co. No. 1.

Omaha, Neb. took delivery of this 1937 American LaFrance straight city service hook and ladder truck. This double-bank ladder truck was designated a Veteran model, a name reserved for this series for many years. This apparatus was equipped with a 100 gallon-per-minute booster pump, the control panel for which can be seen on the cowl. The booster line was carried in a shallow box at the front of the ladder bed. The rollers are visible just behind the driver's seat.

Among the most interesting special-order jobs ever built by American LaFrance were the four dual-engined "Duplex" pumpers delivered to Los Angeles. Two were built in 1937 and two more were delivered the following year. Each of these unique high-capacity pumpers had two V-12 engines. The front engine propelled the apparatus and powered the forward pump. The rear engine powered a second pump. The two Duplex pumpers delivered in 1937 were equipped with two 1,000 gallon-per-minute pumps. The 1938 models each had two 1,500-gallon pumps. This is the first of the American LaFrance Duplex pumpers delivered.

1937

Los Angeles places substantial orders with American La-France in 1937 and 1938. The Los Angeles City Fire Department purchased four of these custom-built 1937 American LaFrance 1,250 gallon-per-minute pumpers with 4-door sedan cabs. The rear crew seats faced outward, and no equipment was carried on the sides, presenting an unusually tidy appearance. These Series 400 pumpers had the new "cowcatcher" grille bars and were powered by V-12 engines.

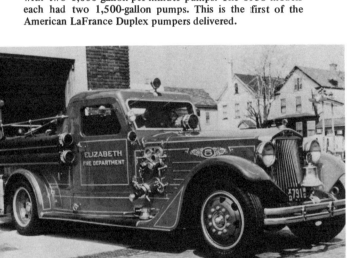

American LaFrance did not build too many rigs with 3-man cabs. This Series 400 pumper with 3-man cab was used on the Elizabeth, N. J. Fire Dept. The gates and intakes of the cowl-mounted pump were angled downward for easier hose hookup. The pump was mounted directly behind the V-12 engine.

Here is one of Los Angeles' unique Duplex pumpers at work during a training session. Both pumps are hooked up. The Duplexes were conceived by L. A. Fire Chief Ralph J. Scott as a means of reducing the number of pumpers needed at major fires. Each Duplex took the place of three conventional engine companies, reducing congestion on the street. The Duplexes responded with special Manifold engines, which took the water provided by the Duplex engines and distributed it as needed on the fireground.

LaCrosse, Wis. also had a 1937 American LaFrance 400 Series pumper with a closed, 3-man cab. It was powered by the ALF V-12 engine. Note the V-12 Maltese Cross emblem on top of the bell, a standard American LaFrance feature. This 400 does not have the angled grille bars used on the Elizabeth, N. J. job. The pumper shown here was assigned Engine No. 3.

Another unusual American LaFrance delivery during 1937 was this special Series 400 van-style pumper built for Brookline, Mass. This apparatus had a very high roofline, and was equipped with a 1,250 GPM pump. The Brookline Fire Dept. ordered two more of these slope-roofed vans from American LaFrance in later years. It had a cradle-type bell carried up front and the three nozzles on the rear running board. This pumper used the American LaFrance V-12 engine.

This small pumper was designated the Scout by American LaFrance, which delivered it to the fire department of Monahans, Tex. The 500 gallon-per-minute pumper, a triple combination, was powered by a 125-horsepower Lycoming 8-cylinder engine.

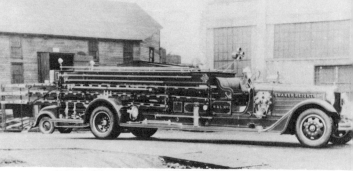

The Cleveland, Ohio suburb of Shaker Heights ordered this beautiful American LaFrance 400 Series quadruple combination. This quad was powered by a 250-horsepower ALF V-12 engine, and carried a set of Buckeye Roto-Rays. The spanking new rig was photographed in the yard at the American LaFrance plant at Elmira, N. Y. before leaving on its delivery trip. Note the cowl-mounted pump and the triple tiers of ground ladders carried in two banks.

Engine No. 3 of the Hempstead, L. I., N. Y., Fire Dept. was equipped with this 1937 American LaFrance 750 GPM pumper. This model has half-doors, and has the new, sloping mesh-type grille.

This 1937 American LaFrance 600 gallon-per-minute centrifugal pumper was used by the fire departments of Gladstone and Peapack, N. J. Note the American Eagle atop the bell, and the angled suction intake which made the hookup to the water supply easier.

Another custom model which American LaFrance built to the specifications of the purchaser, was this completely enclosed city service ladder truck, with 4-door sedan cab, built for Waterloo, Iowa. It had booster equipment, and carried a load of hose above the double bank ladder bed. The playout trough is visible at the upper rear. This was a real streamliner in its day.

The versatile San Francisco Fire Dept. motor shops became very adept at remounting the bodies from older rigs on new chassis. This is a 1937 American LaFrance 400 Series chassis, which has been fitted with a high pressure battery wagon body. The ship's type handwheel behind the seat controls the main inlet for the big Gorter turret nozzle, which has four inlets. These heavy artillery units could literally knock down brick walls with their high pressure streams. The battery wagon also carried a large supply of large-diameter hose.

Wildwood, N. J., which still owns a 1913 American LaFrance Type 17 aerial, also owns this 1937 American LaFrance Series 400 pumper. It is powered by a V-12 engine, and has a 1,250 gallon-per-minute centrifugal pump. Note the cowl-mounted pump and the wide rear fenders to accommodate the dual tires.

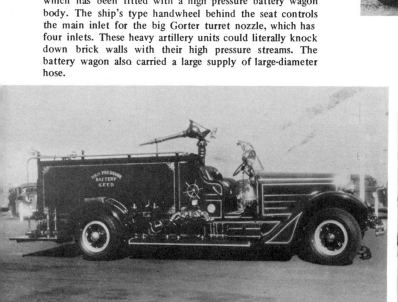

1937

The 1937 Peter Pirsch and Sons Co. pumper shown here was the pride of the Liberty Fire Co. No. 5, of Reading, Pa. Besides being capable of providing yeoman service at a fire, Liberty's attractively 2-toned rig put up a fine appearance in a parade. The booster hose on this 500 GPM model is carried in a basket behind the seat.

Some fire engine builders saved costly tooling bills by adapting commercially available body components to their own custom fire apparatus chassis. Pirsch, for instance, used the GMC 2 or 3-man cab for years. These were purchased directly from General Motors. This is the first one delivered. It was a 500 gallon-per-minute pumper built for Lemont, Ill.

Pirsch's standard model pumper in 1937 was this style. This is a 500 gallon-per-minute Model 20 triple combination. This type of pumping engine was popular with small town fire departments throughout the U.S. Midwest, and could be found in many other parts of the country.

PIRSCH

Peter Pirsch & Sons Co. Ltd. built this 500 gallon-per-minute quadruple combination on a Diamond T truck chassis, for Barrington, N. J. A portable generator and three search-lights are carried on top of the ladder bed. Note the long hose tray carried under the ladders. West Belmar, N. J. bought a similar rig from Pirsch, also on a Diamond T, two years later.

This 1937 Pirsch 750 gallon-per-minute aerial quad was originally built for Niles Center, Ill., which later became Skokie, This small quad, with a manually-raised Pirsch 55-foot Junior aerial ladder, finally wound up on the West-chester, Ill. Fire Dept. Note the pre-connected 1½-inch hose attached to the pump.

Here is a 1937 Pirsch Quintuple combination. A quint carries a pump, hose, booster equipment, ground ladders and an aerial ladder. This rig has a Pirsch 55-foot Junior aerial ladder, which was raised, rotated and extended by hand. This unit was originally sold to Waukegan, Ill., but was sold second-hand to the Geneva, Ill. Fire Dept. Pirsch sold many of its Junior aerial ladders as separate units for mounting on other apparatus.

In 1936, The Seagrave Corp. came out with a totally restyled series of smaller fire engines, which utilized an attractive new grille, hood and front fenders. Initially, this was called the Sentry series. A new canopy-style cab was also introduced this year. The pumper is a 600 gallon-per-minute triple combination that has been equipped with a locally-built cab. It was originally owned by Hasbrouck Heights, N. J., but was later purchased by Lebanon Township, N. J.

This front-end design first appeared on Seagraves built in 1936. The first apparatus of this style, however, retained the oval-shaped fuel tank and separate seat used on the earlier series. By 1937, the rear body design had been revised and most of the Sentry models delivered had half-doors on the cab. This 500 gallon per minute Seagrave pumper was sold to Paramus, N. J. It is believed the later style front bumper was added some years after this engine went into service.

The Independent Hose Co. of Frederick, Md. owned this 1937 Seagrave Sentry model enclosed sedan pumper. The 500 GPM pumper was painted white and green, and is now owned by a private collector. The body of this engine is similar to the sedan pumpers Seagrave was then supplying to Detroit. The name on the door reads Carroll Manor Volunteer Fire Co.

Oberlin, Ohio's 1937 Seagrave quadruple combination, although somewhat faded, is still in almost original condition today. A post-mounted beacon flasher has been added, however, for extra safety in modern traffic. This Seagrave quad carries two large booster hose reels and a set of portable floodlights.

The most popular aerial built by Seagrave was now the all-metal, 65-foot service model, with hydraulic control. This one was delivered to Glen Ridge, N. J. Note the elaborate gold trim decoration on the base of the ladder. Seagrave probably used the most ornate striping and artistic embellishment of any fire apparatus builder.

Seagrave's larger apparatus retained the styling that had been introduced in 1935. This is a 750 gallon-per-minute canopy-cab pumper built for Evanston, Ill., which was powered by the Seagrave Model G 6-cylinder engine. The canopy cab design featured a catwalk up the middle of the body between tho hose beds, and a 3 or 4-man rearward-facing seat. Seagrave built this body style for 34 years and discontinued it only because of a fire service preference for the cab-forward canopy cab.

Arlington, Mass. ordered this 1937 Seagrave 85-foot tractor-drawn aerial ladder truck, with a closed 3-man cab. Note the short over-all length of this serial. Coupled with a tiller, its crew could take it almost anywhere. The Seagrave tiller seat was a self-contained bucket which swung to the left over the side of the ladder when the aerial was to be raised.

New York City in 1937 took delivery of 10 of these Seagrave 85-foot wood, spring-raised aerial ladder trucks. These aerials featured the earlier style radiator and hood. New York did not purchase its first metal aerial ladders until after the Second World War. A good crew could spot one of these "sticks" at an upper floor window in one or two minutes. The trailer is of the single ladder bank style.

The General Fire Truck Corp. of Detroit built this interesting pumper for Reistertown, Md. General used its own assembled chassis. This 600 gallon-per-minute pumper was powered by a Packard 8-cylinder engine. The cab should be familiar to Ford fans: it is a complete coupe body that has been adapted to the General chassis. The double-faced whitewall tires give this unique engine a really spiffy appearance.

Many commercial-chassis fire engines were built by the General Fire Truck Corp. This small pumper is a General-Dodge, with a plated radiator shell. This pumper was photographed at an antique fire engine muster held at Lapeer, Mich. in 1974 and is in authentic original condition.

Reo continued to use the respected Speed Wagon name on its trucks. This is a small triple combination built by the General Fire Truck Corp. on a Reo chassis. The pump appears to be of about 500 GPM capacity. The author photographed this white-apinted rig at an antique fire apparatus muster held at Lapeer, Mich.

General-Detroit built this big quadruple combination on a 1937 Federal cab-over-engine, long-wheelbase chassis for Arlington Heights, Ill. This apparatus had a 500 gallon-per-minute pump and carried a full complement of wood ground ladders.

New York City began purchasing closed-cab fire apparatus this year. This is one of 19 Type 21, 1,000 gallon-per-minute Mack pumpers delivered to the F.D.N.Y. in 1937. The doors were cut out around the pump panel. Note the high rear rail with subway-strap hangers for the crew, the deck turret and the round gasoline tank. These pumpers were similar in design to the open-cab models delivered the previous year. This one ran as Engine Co. No. 36.

Ward LaFrance had come out with this new style of chassis for its custom fire apparatus. This is a specially-built 1937 Ward LaFrance searchlight wagon built for the New York City Fire Dept. It was assigned to Searchlight No. 1. These powerful searchlight wagons could literally turn night into day, and were called out on all night multiple alarms.

Another enclosed van-type pumper built by the Buffalo Fire Appliance Corp., this one is quite different in appearance from the one delivered the same year to Canandaigua, N. Y. The engine was delivered to Winona, Minn., and had a completely enclosed 750 gallon-per-minute pump.

Hartford, Conn. bought this 1937 Mack tractor, and used it to pull the department's 1911 American Automatic 75-foot wood aerial by American LaFrance. In June, 1972, the retired truck was bought by Jack Jansen, of Hartford's Truck Co. No. 4, who takes it to parades and antique fire apparatus musters in the area.

The Ward LaFrance Truck Corp. delivered five of these hose and turret wagons to the New York City Fire Dept. in 1937. All had enclosed cabs. Spare tires were carried on many F.D.N.Y. rigs through the Second World War. Note the deck turret, and the pompier ladder carried on the side of this hose wagon, which ran with Engine Co. No. 40.

Buffalo was getting into the van-type fire apparatus market, too, This streamlined pumper with fully-enclosed body was built for Canandaigua, N. Y. Note the rear wheel fender skirts, and the spotlight mounted above the V-style windshield. The General Fire Truck Corp. of Detroit built a model very similar in appearance to this rig.

1937

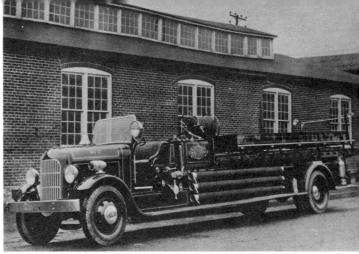

The low-slung triple hard suction hoses give this 1937 Hahn quadruple combination apparatus an unusually low, long look. This quad was built for Hahn's home town of Hamburg, Pa. Hahn assembled its own custom chassis. This same radiator style was used for about 15 years, with modifications.

Van-type pumpers were really in vogue in 1937. This one was built by the Four Wheel Drive Auto Co. of Clintonville, Wis. for the Hartford, Wis. Fire Dept. The 500 gallon-per-minute van had Howe apparatus, and the bodywork was done by the Jackson Body Co. of Jackson, Wis. After years of service in Hartford, the FWD was sold to Neosho, Wis.

This little Howe-Ford, delivered to Hibbing, Minn. is a little unusual. The body sides have been extended upward into a sort of half-cab, and the top has been fitted with what looks like a canvas roof. This is a 500 GPM triple combination on a 1937 Ford V-8 chassis.

The builder of this rural-type, front-mount pumper on a 1937 Ford chassis is not known, but it could be a Darley. The pump is of about 350 gallon capacity. Note the rear fender skirts which have been ornamented with a Ford V-8 emblem and extra chrome trim.

The Louisville, Ky. Salvage Corps responded to alarms with this 1937 Ford squad car with bodywork by Proctor-Keefe of Detroit. This sedan-style apparatus had no rear doors. Note the bell and warning light mounted in front of the grille. Salvage squads were common in the larger cities well into the 1950s. Their function was to minimize water damage at fires, thereby keeping insurance losses down.

The mainstay of many smaller fire departments was this type of light-duty pumper built on a commercial chassis which could be serviced locally, and for which parts were readily available. The Howe Fire Apparatus Co. built this 500 gallon pumper on a Chevrolet chassis for Natrona County, Wyo. Note the black paint trim used on the hood, beltline, and fender edges.

Mack also came out with a new, streamlined look in 1938. The new Type 80 fire apparatus had a mesh-patterned grille topped the the famed Mack Bulldog. This is a 1938 Mack 750 gallon-per-minute Type 80 pumper delivered to Mahwah, N. J. The Type 80 was powered by Mack's 168-horsepower Thermodyne engine.

Mack's smaller series pumper was the Type 55. This 600 gallon-per-minute triple combination was delivered to the Community Fire Co. of Leonardo, N. J. A large equipment box has been added behind the closed 2-man cab. The beacon ray light on the roof was added much later.

This is a 1938 Mack Type 50 straight city service hook and ladder truck built for the fire department of Yeadon, Penn. Twin bucket seats and wood ground ladders were carried on this long-wheelbase truck.

This was to be a year of major developments for American LaFrance. In June, 1938, the Elmira, N. Y. manufacturer announced its radically new 500 Series. The new 500 Series pumpers were of exceptionally clean design with a wide, horizontal-bar grille, a full width that all but eliminated the running boards, and a startlingly streamlined overall appearance. The standard 500 Series pumper had a roomy 3-man cab. Hard suctions were carried inside the hose body, with only the couplings visible, and ground ladders were stowed in a streamlined, enclosed overhead trough that was faired into the cab roof. The new 500 was available also in an open-cab version. The two-stage centrifugal pump, coupled to the ALF V-12 engine, was mounted in the cowl, but the suction ports were flush mounted in the center of the body just behind the front doors. The new series marked a radical departure in design, even for American LaFrance.

During the same eventful year, American LaFrance had introduced its first hydraulically-operated metal aerial ladders. The first one delivered was a 4-section 100-foot aerial, drawn by a 400 Series tractor, built for Annapolis, Md. Later the same year the company delivered its first Series 500 tractor-drawn aerial using the new style of tractor to Newark, N. J. The American LaFrance metal aerials differed from all others in that they had four instead of three sections. This permitted the use of a fixed tillerman's seat and wheel at the rear, which did not have to be disconnected or removed to raise the main ladder. American LaFrance continued to supply spring-raised wood aerial ladders for another 12 years.

American LaFrance delivered two more Duplex pumpers to Los Angeles this year. The 1938 models were equipped with two 1,500 GPM pumps. In the same order, Los Angeles also received the last American LaFrance water tower built, and a tractor-drawn American LaFrance city service ladder truck. Both the tower and the ladder truck had 4-door sedan cabs.

The last of the ALF water towers was a unique combination hook and ladder truck and water tower. It had a 65-foot mast, but carried a full complement of wood ground ladders. This combination did not work out, however, and in 1949 the LAFD shops converted it to a straight water tower. Two big deck turrets were added at this time.

Ahrens-Fox delivered 20 Model HT-1000 piston pumpers with closed 2-man cabs to the New York City F. D. This contract was awarded to Ahrens-Fox in a bidding contest that saw Mack Trucks beat out by a mere $5 on each rig. This order was placed on January 7, 1938, and the last one was delivered on May 21. New York also purchased three small Ahrens-Fox Model SC-3 Schacht-chassised 500 GPM pumpers. These were originally assigned for fire protection at the New York World's Fair, but were later used by the FDNY as hose wagons. The most unusual Ahrens-Fox placed in service this year was a special Model XCT piston pumper with an enclosed van-type body delivered to Pawtucket, R. I.

The General Fire Truck Corp. of Detroit delivered one of its first streamlined sedan pumpers, on a GMC truck chassis, to Petoskey, Mich.

The previous year, Peter Pirsch & Sons delivered the first 100-foot aluminum-alloy aerial ladder of the closed lattice design that was to make this company's product

1938

...stantly recognizable anywhere. This same very sound ...esign is still being produced at Kenosha today.

Ahrens-Fox delivered three special closed-cab pumpers ...o the Cincinnati Fire Dept. this year. What made these ...odel HCs especially interesting was the fact that they ...ere equipped with Seagrave centrifugal pumps.

Most manufacturers were now using half-doors on their ...pen cab apparatus.

Mack Trucks, Inc. in 1938 came out with its all-new ...ype 80 fire apparatus. This series used a nicely styled, ...reamlined grille and front end. The new Macks were ...owered by a 168-horsepower Mack Thermodyne engine.

Peter Pirsch & Sons Co. now concealed the radiator ...ehind a new, mildly-raked grille with bright horizontal ...rille bars. This style was used until 1940, when a slightly ...ifferent, more vertical style replaced it. Pirsch delivered ... 1,000 GPM pumper with 4-door sedan cab to Chicago ...his year. Mack Trucks delivered five Type 21 pumpers of ...imilar design to the C.F.D. With the transition from open ...o closed-cab apparatus this year, Chicago painted the ...abs of its rigs above the belt line a contrasting black. This ...as done to match the chief's buggies used in Chicago at ...he time, and all Chicago fire apparatus retains this ...istinctive black-over-red livery to this day.

The Bureau of Fire of Wilmington, Del. received this big 1938 Mack Type 21 pumping engine, equipped with a 1,500 gallon-per-minute pump. This was the most powerful pumper built by this company. Note the sharply raked windshield and the siren mounted on the cowl..

This is a true classic among fire engines. The General Fire Truck Corp. of Detroit actually built and delivered several fire engines on the Packard Motor Car Co. chassis. This 1938 General-Packard, delivered to Santa Barbara, Cal. had a 750 GPM pump. It was powered by a Packard V-12 engine, and was equipped with a 200-gallon booster tank. This beautiful rig—complete with cormorant radiator ornament—has twin booster reels. It served Santa Barbara's Engine Co. No. 5.

The Chicago Fire Department placed five of these 1938 Mack Type 21 pumpers with 4-door sedan cabs into service this year. These sleek rigs were powered by Hercules engines and had Hale 1,000 gallon-per-minute pumps. This one went to Engine Co. No. 22. Chicago also had switched to closed-cab apparatus. The black-painted cab, above the belt line, was to become a Chicago Fire Dept. characteristic and was also adopted by numerous other departments in Chicago suburbs.

The New Brunswick, N. J. Fire Department was the recipient of this new-style Mack 750 gallon-per-minute pumper. A 1938 Type 75, it has the fully-open cab and a front-mounted warning light.

Another General-Packard is this 1938 Model delivered to Grand Ledge, Mich. It was powered by a Packard V-12 engine, and had a 500 GPM pump. Unlike the Santa Barbara job, the Grand Ledge pumper had cab doors. The front bumper appears to be a replacement.

In June, 1938, American LaFrance announced its completely new Series 500 fire apparatus. This exceptionally clean, streamlined design was considered far ahead of its time. To get some idea of how far fire apparatus styling had come in a short time, just look at an American LaFrance pumper of five years earlier. The new 500 Series had a wide, roomy cab. The overhead ladder rack was faired into the roof, and the hard suction hoses were even enclosed in the curved upper body side panels. The pump was still mounted in the front cowl, but the suction ports were flush-mounted amidships. This 1,250 gallon-per-minute Series 500 pumper was delivered to Asbury Park, N. J.

Los Angeles again placed a major order with American LaFrance. This is the specially-designed Manifold wagon which ran with the L.A.F.D. big Duplex pumpers. The Manifold took water from the Duplex engines, and distributed it to where it was needed on the fireground. Note the huge, fireboat-sized deck turret, and the discharge gates above the running board. This Manifold wagon also carried hose in the side compartments, and had a 4-door sedan cab. Seagrave also delivered a Manifold wagon to Los Angeles in 1938.

The Village of Oak Park, Ill. received this big American LaFrance Series 400 pumper with 4-door sedan cab in 1938. It was patterned after the four delivered to Los Angeles the previous year. The Oak Park pumper was rated at 1,250 gallons-per-minute and was powered by the American La-France V-12 engine.

American LaFrance delivered two more Duplex pumpers to Los Angeles during 1938, bringing to four the number of these unique, high-capacity pumping engines built for the L.A.F.D. The 1938 models differed from the 1937 types, however, in that they were equipped with two 1,500 gallon-per-minute pumps driven by two 250-horsepower V-12 engines. These monsters could deliver more than 3,000 gallons of water per minute, replacing three conventional pumpers at major fires. This Duplex was assigned to Engine Co. No. 17.

It is not clear which Springfield—Massachusetts or Illinois—got this specially-built 1938 American LaFrance Series 400 van-style pumper. The pumper was equipped with a 1,250 gallon-per-minute rotary gear pump, and was generally similar to a van-type engine delivered to Brookline, Mass. earlier.

This is a left-hand view of one of the famous Los Angeles Duplex pumpers built by American LaFrance. The rear engine hood had four doors which were opened when the apparatus was pumping. The front V-12 engine propelled the apparatus and drove the front pump which was mounted in the cowl. The rear engine, also a V-12, powered only the rear 1,500 GPM pump. The L.A. Duplex and Manifold engines remained in service in the high value and industrial districts of Los Angeles until the mid-1950s.

American LaFrance certainly offered a diversified product line at this time. At the small end of the scale was the Invader model 750 GPM pumper with a rotary gear pump and a 2-man enclosed coupe-style cab. This one was delivered to Baltimore County, Md. in 1938. This was to be the last year this style of apparatus was built as production at Elmira gradually swung over to the new Series 500 apparatus.

This small American LaFrance pumper, with its overhead ladder rack, looks rather British. It is a 500 gallon-per-minute rotary gear pumper built for Frankfort, Ill. Note the four lengths of hard suction hose, and the coaster siren mounted on top of the bell. It has a 2-man cab.

The year 1938 was one of major product development for American LaFrance. In addition to the radically restyled Series 500 apparatus, the Elmira, N. Y. plant this year built and sold its first hydraulically-operated, all-metal aerial ladder truck. The first of these utilized a Series 400 tractor. The 100-foot, 4-section aerial was delivered to Annapolis, Md. The first Series 500 all-steel American LaFrance aerial was the 100-footer shown above, which was delivered to Newark, N. J. The new metal aerials found immediate acceptance by the fire service, but American LaFrance continued to deliver spring-raised, wood aerials for another 12 years.

Another one-off job built by American LaFrance this year was this van-type pumper, described as a 400 Series. But, it bears no resemblance to other pumpers of this type. Delivered to Virginia, Minn., it had a 500 gallon-per-minute pump and was powered by a Lycoming 8-cylinder engine.

Los Angeles in 1938 also had the distinction of receiving the last water tower ever built. It was an unusual combination water tower and city service ladder truck built by American LaFrance. It was a 65-foot American Automatic with a single mast nozzle. This combination did not prove successful, however, and in 1949 the rig was stripped of its ground ladders and was converted to a straight water tower. Two big turret nozzles were installed on the trailer deck. This is how the L. A. tower looked before it was shipped from Elmira. The L. A. F. D. in 1938 also received a tractor-drawn American LaFrance city service hook and ladder truck with the same type of 4-door sedan tractor shown here.

Hawthorne, N. J. ordered this unusual 1938 American LaFrance Series 500 combination city service hook and ladder truck and hose wagon. This rear view shows the baffled hose bed, with separate playout troughs for each line. This rig was painted white.

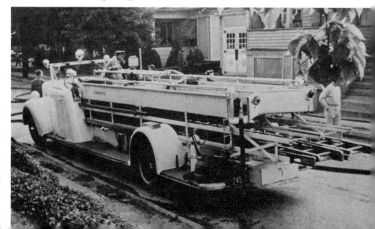

One of the ex-World's Fair Ahrens-Fox piston pumpers wears its F.D.N.Y. livery. New York City purchased 20 of these 1,000 gallon-per-minute piston pumpers in 1938—the largest single order ever won by Ahrens-Fox. This company beat Mack out in the bidding on this contract by a mere $5 on each truck. All 20 of these pumpers were delivered to the F.D.N.Y. apparatus bureau within four months. The contract price was $12,145 each.

Ahrens-Fox built five fire engines for use at the New York World's Fair of 1938-39. The fair site was protected by two 1938 Ahrens-Fox 1,000 GPM Model HT piston pumpers, and three model SC Ahrens-Foxes built on Schacht chassis. When the fair closed, these rigs were absorbed into the New York City Fire Dept. Here is one of the big HT's, lettered for the New York World's Fair, and sporting the fair insignia on its doors.

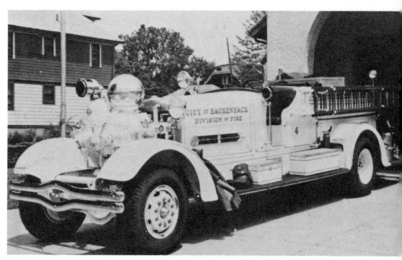

Even Ahrens-Fox built at least one van-type pumper of the piston type. This was a special Model XCT that was delivered to Pawtucket, R. I. This one-off Fox had a 750 gallon-per-minute pump, and bore serial number 4021. Note the later style headlight faired into the front fenders. Ahrens-Fox also delivered a small Model VC 500 GPM van-type pumper to Pittsville, Pa. in 1937.

Still on the Sandusky, Ohio Fire Dept. equipment roster is this 1938 Ahrens-Fox Model HT piston pumper. The HT series utilized a Hercules engine, and had a 6-piston pump. This particular engine had single rear tires rather than duals. It was factory register number 3445.

The Ahrens-Fox Fire Engine Co. introduced its famous HT Series piston pumper in 1937. Designed by Richard "Curt" Nepper, the HT remained in production until the end of the piston pump era at Ahrens-Fox in the early 1950s. The first was delivered to St. Paul, Minn. in 1937 and the last went to Tarrytown, N. Y. in 1952. This is a 1938 Model HT of 1,000 gallon-per-minute capacity built for the City of Hackensack, N. J.

Among the most distinctive-looking Ahrens-Fox piston pumpers was this racy Model BT, a 1,250 gallon-per-minute pumper built for Shelton, Conn. This pumper has a coupe-style cab which tends to enhance the length of the hood. It is still around, and is a regular participant in the many fire department parades and apparatus musters held in the northeast.

1938

The Fame Fire Company of Lewiston, Penn. still owns this magnificent 1938 Ahrens-Fox Model BT piston pumper. The 1,250 GPM pumper is finished in rich cream, with dark blue fenders and running gear. Note the headlights built into the front fenders and the siren mounted on top of the pump. This company's apparatus has always been painted in this eye-catching two-tone color combination.

Ahrens-Fox's medium-sized Model V-R was a pleasingly-styled fire engine that enjoyed considerable success. This 1938 Model VR-8030 is still maintained in excellent original condition by the Mount Healthy, Ohio Fire Dept. This model has a 600 gallon-per-minute rotary gear pump.

The Felton Fire Co. of Chester, Pa. once owned this 1938 Ahrens-Fox Model EC pumper. The C denotes that it is equipped with a centrifugal pump. This Fox has a canopy style cab. Felton's rig is awaiting the signal to move off in a parade.

Truck 1 of Trenton, N. J., a 1937 Peter Pirsch & Sons 100-foot metal aerial, is seen here drawn up on the street near its quarters. The ladder is a 3-section, aluminum alloy type of close lattice construction. Pirsch has used this same type of aerial ladder for more than 35 years, and continues to use it today. This type of construction makes Pirsch aerials the easiest of all to identify.

The Berkely, Cal. Fire Dept. replaced the original metal ladder on this 1938 Pirsch tractor-drawn aerial with a new metal aerial ladder some 30 years after the truck was delivered. The new ladder is a 3-section 100-footer. Note the later style Federal Q siren atop the bell frame, and the post-mounted beacon ray flasher above the windshield.

The radiator on Peter Pirsch & Sons fire engines disappeared behind a new grille that featured a series of thin, horizontal chrome bars. This 1938 Pirsch 65-foot Junior aerial ladder truck was built for Dover, N. J. Pirsch built its first 100-foot aerial in 1935 and introduced its aluminum-alloy, lattice type metal aerial two years later.

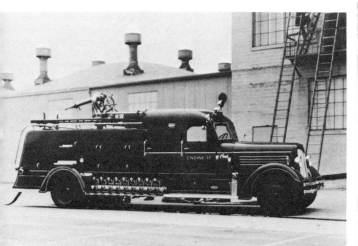

Seagrave built two of these big Manifold Wagons for the Los Angeles Fire Dept. in 1938. American LaFrance had delivered one similar rig. The Seagraves had 4-door sedan cabs, carried booster equipment and had large fireboat turret nozzles mounted on top. The manifold wagons responded with L. A.'s Duplex pumpers. This Seagrave was assigned to Engine Co. No. 17.

The Detroit Fire Department purchased five more 1,000 gallon-per-minute sedan pumpers from Seagrave in 1938, These differed from the eight delivered in 1936 and 1937 in that they had more streamlined bodies and rounded windshield frames. Here is one of these new sedan pumpers at work at a fire. The soft suction hose was carried over the right front fender.

Hayward, Cal. owned this 1938 Seagrave 600 gallon-per-minute pumper. Doors were standard equipment now, but these could be left off if specified. Some departments considered doors unnecessary, and were convinced that turnout time was a few precious seconds faster without them.

Lansing, Mich. used this 1938 Seagrave 100-foot tractor-drawn aerial with open half-cab for nearly three decades. These aerials had 3-section ladders and were built in 75, 85 and 100-foot lengths. The Lansing aerial is seen here parked on the ramp in front of the Lansing Fire Department's Fire Station.

Denver, Col. was another city that preferred white-colored fire apparatus. Fire apparatus buff Shaun Ryan took this fine portrait of a 1938 Seagrave,1,250 GPM pumper, powered by a V-12 engine, which was used as a reserve engine by the Denver Fire Dept. Note the half-cab doors, the warning light on top of the radiator, and the Roto-Ray lights atop the booster tank.

Los Angeles didn't place all of its business with Elmira. The Seagrave Corp. got its share too. In 1938, the Columbus, Ohio plant shipped this 100-foot tractor-drawn aerial ladder truck out to the coast. The all-metal hydraulic aerial was powered by a Seagrave V-12 engine, had a 7-man sedan cab, and a sidemounted spare tire. This aerial was assigned to L.A.F.D. Ladder Co. No. 3 for many years.

The builder of the body on this big emergency squad truck is not known, but the chassis is a Diamond T. This rig was used by the Friendship Fire Co. No. 4 of Reading, Pa. An oversized loud speaker dominates the forward portion of the roof. A catwalk has been provided atop the rear roof for fireground operations.

1938

The builder of this handsome rig is not known. The apparatus, on a 1938 Ford V-8 truck chassis, is a combination hose and chemical engine, with a front-mounted pump. The five chemical tanks mounted in the middle of the chassis supply several hose lines carried in the metal basket over the front of the very short hose box. This photo was found in the Ford Archives. The pumper has a small set of Roto-Rays on its roof and a bell on the right front fender.

The Dearborn, Mich. Fire Department operated this big Rescue Squad rig built on a Ford chassis. The body was built by the Proctor-Keefe Body Co. of Detroit. Proctor-Keefe built many squad and rescue vehicles from the mid-thirties until well into the 1950s. Dearborn is the home of the world headquarters of the Ford Motor Co., and this city has used Ford-chassised fire apparatus and municipal vehicles almost exclusively.

The builder of this front-mount pumper is uncertain. The unit is built on a 1938 Ford truck chassis, and is a triple combination pumper. Note how the grille has been cut away to accommodate the front-mount pump, which appears to be of about 500 GPM capacity. This engine was built for the Farmington Township, Mich. Fire Dept.

The Maxim Motor Co. of Middleboro, Mass. built this special rural model pumper-tanker for Falmouth, Mass. The closed-cab pumper has a 1,000-gallon booster tank and a 500 gallon-per-minute pump. The tandem axles are necessary to support the heavy weight of the truck, which sometimes had to fight fires along secondary roads.

This trim-looking pumper was built by the Maxim Motor Co. of Middleboro, Mass. for the Dighton, Mass. Fire Department. It is a 500 gallon-per-minute triple combination with turret pipe and three small-diameter hard suction hoses. The box-like affair carried on the running board is a suction hose strainer. The Maxim grille was veed slightly.

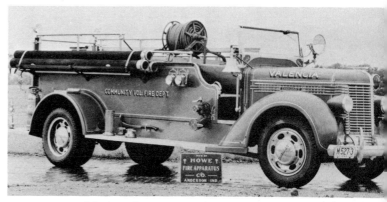

Fort Wayne, Ind. was another fire department with a resourceful motor shop crew capable of building its own fire apparatus. The Fort Wayne Fire Dept. shops built this 1,000 gallon-per-minute pumper on a 1938 International Harvester truck chassis, and turned out a very professional-looking job. Milwaukee and Grand Rapids, Mich. were other cities that at one time built some of their own fire apparatus.

The busy factory of the Howe Fire Apparatus Co. has turned out hundreds of commercial-chassis fire engines over the years. Typical of this old firm's products during the late 1930s was this 200 gallon-per-minute triple combination pumper built on a Diamond T truck chassis. It was built for the Valencia Community Volunteer Fire Dept. Note the Howe name cast into each side of the metal windshield frames.

Water towers tended to lead long, multiple-faceted lives. A case in point is one used for many years by the Omaha, Neb. Fire Dept. This 55-foot Hale water tower was built in 1888. It was motorized in 1918, and 20 years later, in 1938, was modernized once more and remounted on a GMC cab-over truck chassis. At last report the old tower was still going strong after an incredible 87 years on the firing line!

Howe built this stock-model pumper with a 400 gallon-per-minute pump on a 1938 Ford chassis. Notice how the cab door had to be cut around the midship-mounted pump. The hard suction hoses on this job are carried side by side, rather than over-and-under.

One of the smaller and lesser-known West Coast fire apparatus builders was the F.A.B. Manufacturing Co. of Oakland, Cal. This concern built a small number of fire engines under the Fabco name. This is a 1938 Fabco 1,000 gallon-per-minute triple combination pumper with a 300-gallon booster tank that was built for Emeryville, Cal.

New York City placed nine of these 1938 Ward LaFrance combination hose and turret wagons in service. This one was rebuilt with a later style grille in 1949. This wagon is original in appearance from the cowl back. Engine Co. No. 216's wagon has a Mars flight on its roof and adjustable windshield glass.

1939

The American LaFrance Fire Engine Co. made yet another breakthrough in 1939. The Elmira, N. Y. manufacturer took the wraps off the industry's first cab-ahead-of-engine service aerials.

The new American LaFrance 4-wheel aerials were as strikingly different in appearance as the company's new 500 Series apparatus had been the year before. The new aerials were built in two sizes—85 and 100 feet. Both had all-metal, hydraulically-operated aerial ladders as standard equipment. The new 4-wheel, straight frame aerials were powered by the company's 190 horsepower V-12 engine, and had an overall length of only 41 feet, 10 inches. The new cab-forward aerials had an extra wide cab that seated three men. The standard model had open ladder beds, but a deluxe version was available with streamlined rear fenders and fully enclosed ladder racks. This series remained in production for seven years, until it was replaced by the 700 Series.

Oddly enough, one of the most significant events of the year came from one of the smallest manufacturers and was scarcely noticed at the time. The New Stutz Fire Engine Co. of Hartford, Ind. delivered the first diesel-powered fire engine placed in service in America to Columbus, Ind. The 1,000 GPM pumper was powered by a locally-built Cummins Diesel engine. This milestone pumper gave many years of faithful service and is still owned by the Columbus Fire Dept. today. Only in the past decade has diesel power become standard on most fire apparatus built in this country. At the time, Columbus' diesel was considered something of an automotive oddity.

The Ahrens-Fox Fire Engine Co. had fallen on hard times. Undercapitalized and badly weakened during the depression, the company three years earlier had been forced into a merger with the LeBlond-Schacht Truck Co. of Cincinnati. In 1939 the company that had been organized as the Ahrens-Fox Engine Co. in 1905, and renamed the Ahrens-Fox Fire Engine Co. in 1908, was liquidated. But it was not the end of the line. The company was reorganized, and in 1939 delivered quite a few pieces of apparatus. Some of these were worthy of note. One was a Model HT piston pumper with a Cadillac cab and completely enclosed body built for Ocean Grove, N. J. In October, 1939, the Fairview, N. Y. Fire Dept. took delivery of the only quint ever built by Ahrens-Fox. Officially designated a Model BJQ, it had a 1,000 GPM

piston pump and a 70-foot metal Bascule aerial ladder. Fairview's monstrous one-truck fire department also carried 220 feet of ground ladders and 1,200 feet of hose. Somehow, room was even found on the straight-frame chassis for a 100-gallon booster tank. This one-of-a-kind Ahrens-Fox was sold to an individual early in 1975.

The Seagrave Corp. was building a lot of enclosed-cab apparatus now. In 1939, this company delivered a special pumper with a 2,500-gallon booster tank to the Los Angeles County Fire Dept.

The Buffalo Fire Appliance Corp. in mid-1939 introduced an all-new line of fully-enclosed, streamlined pumpers. The very clean-lined Buffalo pumpers bore a resemblance to the American LaFrance 500 Series, but there the similarity ended. The pump on the Buffalo pumpers was completely hidden behind the cabinet doors when not in use.

The General Fire Truck Corp. of Detroit was building a complete range of apparatus now, including ladder trucks and quadruple combinations. This company delivered one of its new custom-chassis Deluxe Sedan pumpers to Decatur, Ill. The 1,000 GPM pumper was built on a 206-inch wheelbase.

A new fire apparatus manufacturer entered the picture at about this time. The Sealand Corporation, located in Southport, Conn., assembled its own custom chassis which looked like a cross between a Studebaker, an International and a Buffalo. This Sealand 500 gallon-per-minute was built for the Highland Park Hose Co. in Lewiston, Pa.

Maxim Motor Co. apparatus was still using the same radiator design introduced some five years earlier, but the Maxim hood had open louvres instead of louvre doors. This is a Maxim 750 gallon-per-minute pumper that was delivered to Lee, Mass. in 1939. The hard suctions are carried side by side on this model.

The Middleboro, Mass. plant of the Maxim Motor Co. built this streamlined sedan-style pumper with a 4-door cab. It is not known where this 750 gallon-per-minute pumper was eventually delivered. This design kept the crew off the running boards and out of the weather and made for a neater appearance.

The next major development from American LaFrance was the 4-wheel, cab-ahead-of-engine service aerial ladder truck, which was introduced in 1939. This new type of aerial combined relatively short over-all length with excellent forward visibility. This was the deluxe model, with completely enclosed ladder bed. The aerial pictured is a 75-foot model delivered to Charleroi, Penn. The V-12 American LaFrance engine was located between the driver's and officer's seats.

At right is the standard model American LaFrance service aerial, with open ladder racks and standard rear fenders instead of the streamlined type used on the deluxe job. These aerials were built in 65, 75, 85 and 100-foot sizes. The 100-footer had a 4-section steel ladder while all the others used 3-section ladders. This rig was built for the Marietta, Ohio Fire Department.

The front end of this American LaFrance quadruple combination is quite different than that of the standard Series 500. For one thing, it is considerably narrower, uses running boards, and has a vertical grille with a mesh-pattern screen instead of the horizontal chrome bars used on the 500. This 750 GPM quad was delivered to the Western Enterprise Fire Co. No. 4 of Hagerstown, Md. American LaFrance built many fire engines of this type in later years, some as Series 600 models. Note the narrow V-type windshield.

Although American LaFrance was concentrating on production of its new Series 500 apparatus, and the even newer cab-forward aerials, the Elmira plant continued to turn out some unusual custom-built models. This is a 500 gallon-per-minute pumper, one of two generally identical models built for Old Town, Maine, These units had centrifugal pumps and featured International Harvester 2-man closed cabs. They also used the old 200 Series-style radiator, and had three chrome streamers on the front of each front fender.

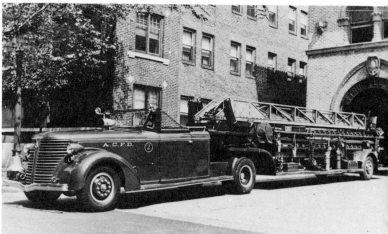

Truck Co. No. 2 of Atlantic City, N. J. once ran with this 1939 American LaFrance Series 500 tractor-drawn aerial ladder truck. Truck 2's rig has an open semi-cab and a 4-section 100-foot metal aerial ladder. The oversized bell mounted in front of the right front fender did not come from the Elmira factory. The small lights below the headlights are red flashers. This roomy cab could seat a crew of seven.

American LaFrance offered its streamlined 500 Series apparatus in a complete range of models, including pumpers, city service ladder trucks, quadruple combinations and tractor-drawn aerial ladder trucks. This is a 1939 Series 500 city service ladder truck with open cab built for the fire department of Rumson Borough, N. J. The square panel just behind the cab door is for the booster pump.

The INVADER, 750 G.P.M.

The new Series 500 apparatus was now in volume production on the assembly line at Elmira. This was the standard closed-cab model. The pumper shown is a 750 gallon-per-minute Invader model with overhead ladder rack, the pump mounted in the cowl immediately behind the engine, and the suction intake port located just behind the cab door. The bell of some American LaFrance 500 models was located behind the grille, which was hinged for access.

This American LaFrance Series 500 pumper is unusual in that it has no cab doors. The type of overhead rack for the aluminum 45-foot extension ladder was probably added later. This pumper ran as Engine No. 12 on the Wheeling, W. Va. Fire Dept. The siren on all Series 500 fire engines was out on the hood in front of the windshield.

The pride of the Highland Park, Mich. Fire Department once was this 1939 American LaFrance 500 Series pumper. The last word in modern firefighting equipment at the time, this engine could deliver 1,250 gallons of water per minute. The entire crew rode to fires out of the weather in the roomy 4-door cab. Following retirement from the H.P.F.D., this pumper was sold to the City of Lapeer, Mich.

Reno, Nev. ordered this 1939 American LaFrance Series 500 pumper. It was powered by the American LaFrance V-12 engine and had a 1,250 gallon-per-minute pump. The Reno pumper combines a 4-door sedan cab with an overhead ladder rack. The 500s were massive fire engines with exceptionally long hood lines, which required good judgement on the part of the driver when moving through traffic.

LaFrance Fire Engine & Foamite Ltd., the Canadian subsidiary of American LaFrance, built this interesting 6-wheeled hose wagon for the fire department of Revelstoke, British Columbia. The tandem rear axles with dual tires were required to take this apparatus over some of the unpaved roads in the area. LaFrance-Foamite's plant in Toronto, Ontario turned out a dual-rear-axle pumper in 1947 for Mont-Joli, Quebec.

This is the very first diesel-powered fire engine to go into service in the United States. It was built by the New Stutz Fire Engine Co. of Hartford City, Ind. for the fire department of Columbus, Ind. The 1,000 gallon-per-minute pumper was powered by a 175-horsepower Cummins 6-cylinder Diesel engine. This milestone pumper went on the reserve roster in 1967, and at last report was still owned by the Columbus Fire Dept.

Perhaps the most unique piece of apparatus ever built by Ahrens-Fox was this one-of-a-kind quintuple combination built for Fairview, N. Y. Officially, it was designated a Model BJQ-70. It has a 1,000 gallon-per-minute piston pump up front, and a 70-foot Ahrens-Fox Bascule aerial ladder. This was the only quint ever built by Ahrens-Fox, and at $20,000 was the most expensive single unit to ever roll out of the Cincinnati plant. The ladder could be extended to its full height in 30 seconds. The rig was powered by a 234-horsepower engine. At the time of writing, this rare rig was up for sale.

Another unusual Ahrens-Fox was this super-streamlined piston pumper built for the E. H. Stokes Fire Company of Ocean Grove, N. J. The 1,000 GPM Model HT had a Cadillac coupe cab, and was completely enclosed. The booster hose reel on this gracefully proportioned rig was carried on the rear step. The pumper went into reserve service in 1970.

San Francisco purchased two of these Ahrens-Fox Model HS-85 tractor-drawn aerial ladder trucks in 1939. They were Serial Nos. 2066 and 2067, and were shipped to Frisco in June, 1939. These big aerials had 2-section Ahrens-Fox Bascule Tower 85-foot aerial ladders. Notice how far back to the rear the tillerman sat on this model.

Some of San Francisco's ladder truck tractors really got around, hauling a variety of ladder truck trailers over the years. This Ahrens-Fox tractor has been attached to the S.F.F.D.'s 1902 Gorter 65-foot water tower. This tillerless tower with water-raised mast was later repowered with a Seagrave tractor of about 1948 vintage. The Gorter tower is similar in design to one still owned by Los Angeles. The L. A. tower has an American LaFrance Type 31 tractor.

The Ahrens-Fox EC Series apparatus had yet another style of grille. This is a 1939 Ahrens-Fox 750 GPM Model EC with canopy cab, built for Orange, Mass. The Model EC utilized a centrifugal pump.

New York City followed up its big Ahrens-Fox order of 1938 with an order for six more Model HT 1,000 gallon-per-minute piston pumpers in 1939, the last of this type purchased. Here is Engine Co. No. 260's rig at work at a multiple-alarm fire. The hard suction hose is hooked up to a hydrant, and it looks as if the turret pipe has been shut down. New York engine companies carried pompier, or scaling, ladders. The rear handrail was equipped with wind wings, a narrow canopy and hand grips for the crew.

Cleveland, Ohio, over the years, used quite a variety of makes of fire apparatus, including Seagrave, American LaFrance and Buffalo. In 1939 the Columbus plant delivered this unique pumper with a big 4-door sedan cab to the Cleveland Fire Dept. Assigned to Engine Co. No. 1, this pumper had a 1,250 gallon-per-minute pump. Ladders and suction hoses were carried inboard. Note the 2-tone paint treatment and the type of lettering used.

The Seagrave Corp. built a few of these smaller series Sentry model pumpers with van-type bodies. This one had a 750 gallon-per-minute pump. It was delivered to Wakefield, Mass. A similar Seagrave sedan pumper was built for Danville, Ill. The crew rode on a bench seat along one side of the rear body. Ladders were carried upright down the center of the body.

Like American LaFrance, Seagrave used some colorful names to designate various models within its product line. This is a Cavalier quadruple combination with 1,000 gallon-per-minute pump. The smaller series Seagraves were still equipped with one-piece, fold down windshields and no side window glass.

It is believed that this was the only open cab, 4-door sedan tractor ever built by Seagrave. It was on a 100-foot metal aerial built for Portland, Ore., Detroit, Cleveland and Los Angeles were among U. S. cities that had Seagrave tractor-drawn aerials with closed, 4-door sedan cabs.

Caught in profile is this Seagrave 600 gallon-per-minute pumper. Doorless models had a curved handrail to keep the crew members in their seats during turns at speed. This white-painted rig was used by the Upper Penn's Neck Township Volumteer Fire Dept. of Carney's Point, N. J.

The San Francisco Fire Dept. for many years ran 2-piece engine companies. Dual-combination pumper and hose trucks responded to fires with booster hose-tank wagons, which were direct descendants of the old chemical cars. This is a 1939 Fabco tank wagon, with twin hose reels and a 410-gallon booster tank. The S.F.F.D. did not start using triple combination pumpers until the early 1960s. Many of the former dial combinations were converted to triples, and the tank wagons were gradually phased out of service.

General-Detroit built this big rescue squad truck for the Cleveland Fire Dept. This heavy rescue unit had double rear doors. The custom chassis used by the General Fire Truck Vorp. of Detroit was similar in appearance to that used on the new streamlined Buffalo apparatus. This unit was assigned to Cleveland's Rescue Squad No. 3.

The General Fire Truck Corporation of Detroit built this big Deluxe Safety Sedan triple combination pumper for Decatur, Ill. This heavy, streamlined engine was equipped with a 1,000 gallon-per-minute pump and was built on a 206-inch wheelbase. It was built on the General-Detroit assembled chassis. Notice the full rear fender skirts and the bullet headlights. This delivery photo was taken on Detroit's Belle Isle.

The Ford Motor Co. had the General Fire Truck Corp. build this combination pumper to protect Ford's huge Rouge Plant complex. The 600 GPM pumper, on a 1939 Ford V-8 chassis, has a small set of Roto-Rays behind the driver's seat. Note the "Ford Motor Company" script on the hood. This short-wheelbase pumper was designed to thread its way down crowded plant aisles and through busy plant yards.

Shown here is another product of the busy Detroit plant of the General Fire Truck Corp. This is an enclosed city service hook and ladder truck with 4-door sedan cab that was built for the fire department of Hamtramck, Mich. This very long straight-frame job is built on the new General custom chassis, which was very similar in appearance to the new streamlined design introduced by the Buffalo Fire Appliance Corp. this same year.

Here is another General-Ford, This 500 GPM triple is built on the new Ford cab-over-engine chassis, which had been introduced late in 1938. The pumper shown was built for the fire department of Wyoming Township, Mich.

The builder of this straight-frame city service hook and ladder truck is not known. This photo of Hook & Ladder No. 2 of the Pawtucket, R. I. Fire Dept. came from the Charles E. Beckwith collection.

With its two-tone red-and-white paint job, this Mack Type 80 pumper presents a rather dashing appearance. The Type 80 was a 750 gallon-per-minute pumper, powered by the Mack Thermodyne engine. Mack in its advertising referred to this job as "the Pocket Battleship of modern fire fighting."

The Los Angeles County Dept. of Forester and Firewarden ordered several of these special 1939 Mack Type 90 pumper-tankers. Designed for use in fighting brush fires in rough, hilly country, these jobs carried 600 gallons of water and 1,600 feet of fire hose. They were specially geared down, but could hit 55 miles an hour with a full load.

Here's a Mack with a somewhat unusual cab. Delivered to Clinton, Mass. the pumper is a Type 80 with a closed 3-man cab with triangular side windows and two rectangular windows in the rear. Clinton's Engine 1 is rated at 750 gallons-per-minute.

Mack Trucks turned out some interesting offbeat models. This pumper is a 300 gallon-per-minute Type 45 on the Mack E chassis. What makes it really unique is the front-mounted pump—a rarity for Mack. The rig was owned by Deer Park, N. J.

This huge rescue squad truck was used by New York's busy Rescue Squad No. 1. It was built by Ward LaFrance and had a 4-door cab. The rear wheels were completely enclosed. Rescue Squad No. 1 has radio aerials on each front fender, and a loud speaker on its roof. These heavy rescue rigs carried everything from small hand tools to heavy jacks and cutting saws.

Ward LaFrance built this long-wheelbase quadruple combination with 750 gallon-per-minute pump. It served Bedford Hills, N. Y. Ward LaFrance apparatus of this era used plated or brushed-metal radiator shells. This quad has an oversized booster hose reel and carries a set of spotlights above its hose bed.

1939

The Howe Fire Apparatus Co. of Anderson, Ind. built this big triple combination pumper on an Autocar truck chassis. The pump, however, is a small one of perhaps 400 gallons per minute. This rugged-looking Howe-Autocar bears Indiana dealer plates for its delivery trip to Duluth, Minn., where it quickly became part of that city's hard-working fire department.

The Ward LaFrance Truck Corp. of Elmira Heights, N. Y. was at this time building relatively few commercial chassis fire engines. The author spotted this interesting 1939 Ward LaFrance pumper on a Dodge chassis at a SPAAMFAA muster at Syracuse, N. Y. Note the full rear fender skirts.

The Buffalo Fire Appliance Corp. in 1939 came out with an all-new, streamlined line of pumpers and ladder trucks. The new front end featured a grille texture of thin horizontal bars. The hoodline was quite long, and the cab exceptionally wide. This is a 1939 Buffalo 750 GPM pumper with 4-door sedan cab that was delivered to St. Paul, Minn.

This is a small triple combination pumper built by the Buffalo Fire Appliance Corp. of Buffalo, N. Y. on a 1939 Dodge truck chassis. The open-cab 500 gallon-per-minute pumper was built for Skaneateles, N. Y.

Oradell, N. J. received this very long Buffalo quadruple combination. The new Buffalo custom-built models were completely enclosed;the pump on this unit is concealed behind the door just to the rear of the cab. Even the ground ladders are fully enclosed.

Buffalo built some big fire engines. This massive quadruple combination with an enclosed 750 GPM pump is a good example. It was built for Chisholm, Minn. The playout rollers for the booster hose are visible at the front of the hose bed above the ladder racks. The pump control panel is behind the door just behind the cab.

1939

This is a 1939 Peter Pirsch Junior quadruple combination fire truck. It has the new style grille, and packs a 500 GPM pump and a 55-foot manually-raised junior aerial ladder. Note how the siren is integrated into the grille. The Pirsch Junior aerial was available in 50 or 55-foot lengths.

The Joplin, Mo. Fire Dept. ordered this 1939 Peter Pirsch 100-foot metal aerial, with 4-wheel tractor. This aerial has the older style radiator instead of the new grille that began to appear the preceding year, and a 3-section aluminum alloy aerial ladder. This type was known as a Pirsch Senior tractor-drawn aerial.

Truck Co. No. 2 of the West Belmar, N. J. Fire Dept. responded to alarms with this 1939 Pirsch 500 gallon-per-minute quadruple combination, built on a Diamond T truck chassis. This low-slung quad carries a set of big spotlights behind the cab. The hose bed is below the ladder racks.

The Four Wheel Drive Auto Co. did not build very many city service ladder trucks or quads. The Clintonville, Wis. manufacturer delivered this big quadruple combination to De Pere, Wis. It was on a long-wheelbase 4 x 4 chassis, and carried a 750 gallon-per-minute pump.

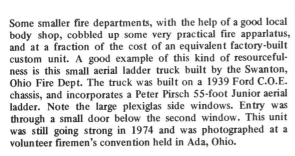

Some smaller fire departments, with the help of a good local body shop, cobbled up some very practical fire apparatus, and at a fraction of the cost of an equivalent factory-built custom unit. A good example of this kind of resourcefulness is this small aerial ladder truck built by the Swanton, Ohio Fire Dept. The truck was built on a 1939 Ford C.O.E. chassis, and incorporates a Peter Pirsch 55-foot Junior aerial ladder. Note the large plexiglas side windows. Entry was through a small door below the second window. This unit was still going strong in 1974 and was photographed at a volunteer firemen's convention held in Ada, Ohio.

The nation had all but recovered from the effects of the depression, but a new crisis was in the offing. The Second World War was raging in Europe, and it was only a matter of time before the United States would be plunged into the war. Plans were already being made for defense production, and more than a few American firms were regularly shipping war materials overseas. The fire apparatus industry found itself pressed to develop special new products for military and civilian duties.

American LaFrance's new Series 500 pumpers, and cab-ahead-of-engine aerials were rolling off the assembly lines at Elmira. The company in 1940 introduced a new two-stage, parallel-series Centraflow pump.

Ahrens-Fox delivered no piston pumpers this year, but the Cincinnati firm did deliver a number of Model EC

centrifugal pumpers, and at least one city service ladder truck. The Ahrens-Fox Fire Engine Co. also delivered its last aerial ladder trucks in 1940. The last Fox aerials built were four 85-foot tractor-drawn trucks for New York City. San Francisco had received two 85-footers in 1939. Ahrens-Fox built only one aerial each in the years 1934, 1935 and 1937. Although the company assembled one piston pumper in 1942 from parts in stock, peacetime production did not resume until 1946.

In other developments, the New Stutz Fire Engine Co. went out of business this year, and the Hale Fire Pump Co. which had built only a very small number of motor fire engines on a special order basis through the 1930s, announced that it would discontinue the manufacture of fire apparatus and instead would concentrate on building pumps only. The Four Wheel Drive Auto Co. of Clintonville, Wis. had come out with a restyled series of Waukesha-powered pumpers with four-wheel-drive, and had greatly increased its fire engine business.

The General Fire Truck Corp. of Detroit delivered this handsome pumper to East Marion, Long Island, N. Y. General used this assembled chassis briefly for its smaller apparatus. This is a 500 gallon-per-minute triple combination with an open seat. The type of striping visible on the front fenders was standard trim on General fire equipment.

 While the company did a big business in commercial chassis and small custom jobs, not all General Fire Trucks were lightweights. General built this big 1,250 GPM pumper with a 4-stage pump for Minneapolis. Some Generals of this type were powered by Packard V-12 engines.

The Buffalo Fire Appliance Corp. had been building enclosed, cab-type apparatus for several years. This is a 1940 Buffalo 500 gallon-per-minute sedan pumper, with an all-steel Buffalo Clear Vision body, delivered to Brooklyn Hose Co. No. 3, of Lewistown, Pa. Note the large driving lamps mounted on the front bumper. The slightly rounded Buffalo grille was finely textured.

Buffalo's new streamlined body style, introduced in mid-1939, provided for the enclosure of all equipment. Even the pump panel, on both left and right-hand sides, was located behind a door. Ladders, suction hose and all other equipment was carried inside the wide rear body. This is a 1940 Buffalo 750 gallon-per-minute pumper with semi-cab.

This is an all-steel canopy type cab which The Seagrave Corp. started building in 1937. By 1940, the cab roof had been extended farther back. This Seagrave centrifugal pumper responded as Engine No. 10 on the Baltimore County, Md. Fire Dept. Note the three lengths of hard suction, and the fog applicators carried above. Seagraves of this period had the type of front bumper visible here. The center bar of the grille was painted white.

Ypsilanti, Mich. ran this 1940 Seagrave 750 gallon-per-minute canopy cab pumper. Note how the soft suction hose is carried on the shelf over the pump. Three or four men could ride on the rearward-facing seat under the canopy.

Here is another open-cab Seagrave. This 1940 model 600 gallon-per-minute pumper was used by the Rockledge, Pa. Fire Dept. Note the fully open doorless cab. The post-mounted spotlight which also supported the bell was a standard Seagrave feature from about 1932 through about 1946.

Many fire departments still preferred the open or half-cab, despite a marked trend toward enclosed bodies on fire apparatus. This is a 750 gallon-per-minute Seagrave with semi-cab. The siren mounting on the cowl just ahead of the windshield is unusual. The barrel is missing from the turret pipe mounted on the platform just behind the cab.

Seagrave delivered the last of this older style apparatus at about this time. This series had been introduced in 1935, along with the company's V-12 engine. In its final years, this type of radiator and hood were used only on Seagrave's larger models. This 75-foot tractor-drawn aerial was delivered to Hoboken, N. J. where it responded as Truck 2.

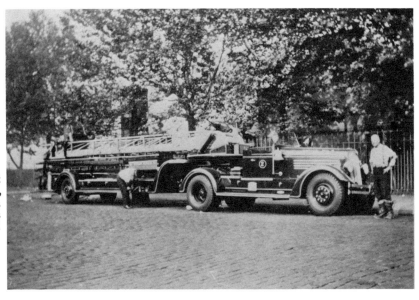

The American LaFrance 500 Series fire apparatus now accounted for a large portion of the Elmira plant's annual production. In 1940, American LaFrance announced its new Centraflow 2-stage, parallel-series centrifugal pump. This American LaFrance 500 GPM Series 500 pumper was delivered to the Washington No. 3 Fire Co. in Salem, N. J. This deluxe model has the full-length enclosed overhead ladder rack which is faired into the cab roof.

The lack of a suction intake and full pump panel would indicate that this American LaFrance Series 500 engine is a combination booster and hose truck. A small portable pump is carried just behind the cab. This apparatus was used by Corning, N. Y.

The new American LaFrance cab-ahead-of-engine aerials were well accepted by the fire service. This is an 85-foot steel aerial with a 3-section ladder. This model was also known as the Model JOX. The 100-foot version was designated the Rescue model.

This style of American LaFrance fire engine began to appear in substantial numbers at about this time. Some were designated Series 600s. This style had a narrow cab and body, a squared-off hood and radiator grille and a vee-type windshield. This 1,000 gallon-per-minute American is in service on the Palmer Township, Pa. Fire Dept.

The Memphis, Tenn. Fire Dept. for many years specified that its new pumpers be equipped with an extra-long hard suction hose connected to a swivel elbow for quick hookup to the water supply. This is a 1940 American LaFrance pumper that was later rebuilt with a Waukesha engine and Hale 1,000 gallon-per-minute pump. The suction hose is carried squirrel-tail style around the front of the rig.

American LaFrance was using some GMC truck cabs on some of its apparatus. The pumper shown here is a 500 gallon-per-minute model with 2-man cab built for Winkler County, Texas. This model had a screened-type grille instead of the chrome horizontal grille bars used on other rigs in this series.

Ahrens-Fox produced its last aerial ladder trucks in 1940. Four 85-foot Ahrens-Fox tractor-drawn aerials with special spring hoists, were delivered to New York City this year. This one, however, has had its original radiator replaced with an older one by the F.D.N.Y. shops.

Ahrens-Fox had merged with the LeBlond-Schacht Truck Co. in 1936, and subsequently built many smaller-model fire engines on the Schacht chassis. This is a Model SR pumper of 500 gallon-per-minute pumping capacity, delivered to Elkins Park, Pa. The "S" indicates that the apparatus is built on a Schacht chassis, while the "R" denotes that the unit is equipped with a rotary gear pump. This Ahrens-Fox was painted white.

The Peter Pirsch & Sons Co. plant in Kenosha, Wis. was turning out some very streamlined fire equipment. This 1940 Pirsch 1,000 gallon-per-minute enclosed pumper with 4-door sedan cab was built for Cambridge, Mass. All equipment was carried inside, giving this engine an unusually clean appearance. Note the grille cutouts to accommodate the siren and bell.

Chicago had switched from open to closed, sedan-style cabs for its pumping engines in 1938. In 1940, Peter Pirsch & Sons delivered two of these 1,000 gallon-per-minute pumpers with 4-door sedan cabs to the Chicago Fire Dept. These pumpers were powered by Hercules engines, and had Hale 4-stage pumps. Dan Martin took this portrait of Engine Co. No. 46's rig. Nine men could be seated in the spacious cab. This pumper has Pirsch's new vertical-style grille.

The Ahrens-Fox Fire Engine Co. built its last pre-war models in 1940. While the company did turn out a very few fire engines between defense jobs during World War II, production did not resume again until 1946. This is a 1940 Ahrens-Fox city service ladder truck with a semi-enclosed ladder bed, which was built for Liberty Fire Co. No. 2, of Salem, N. J.

Pirsch didn't limit its streamlining to closed-cab apparatus. Conventional type open-cab jobs could be cleanly-styled, too, as is evidenced by this 750 gallon-per-minute pumper. Suction hoses, ground ladders and all other equipment is carried inside the plain body. Note how the siren has been fitted into the lower portion of the grille. Even the bell is behind the grille bars.

Kalamazoo, Mich. bought this 1940 Mack Type 80 pumper. The 750 gallon-per-minute pumper has a canopy cab, similar to the type introduced by Seagrave. This pumper responded as Kalamazoo's Engine No. 8 for many years, and was eventually repainted.

The Town of Delafield, Wis. owned this 1940 FWD pumper with a closed 2-man cab. This rig had a 500-gallon pump. The Four Wheel Drive Auto Co. of Clintonville, Wis. was a major builder of 4 X 4 truck chassis used in heavy construction and off-road work. Still in business today, this company has been building fire engines since 1914.

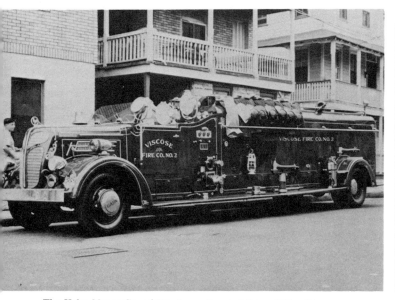

The Hahn Motor Co. of Hamburg, Pa. used this artistic grille design for a number of years. This monstrous quadruple combination was built for the Viscose Fire Co. No. 2, and has a completely enclosed ladder bed. Even the hubcaps bear the Hahn name. Note the full-length handrail and the single piece windshield.

The last fire engine to bear the Stutz name was built in 1940. It was a 750-gallon triple combination pumping engine, delivered to the "Mount Union" Fire Dept. Harry C. Stutz got into the fire engine business in 1919, and when the Indianapolis factory discontinued the manufacture of fire apparatus in the late 1920s, a new firm called the New Stutz Fire Engine Co. went into business in Hartford, City, Ind. in the early thirties. This pumper was one of the last products turned out by New Stutz.

Although it is a thinly-disguised 1939 GMC, this is a 1940 Hanley quadruple combination built for Dover, Ohio by the Hanley Engineering Service of Prospect, Ohio. What made this piece of apparatus really unique was the engine that lay under its hood—a Marmon V-16. The Hanley concern was headed by Keenan Hanley, who had once been chief engineer of the Prospect Fire Engine Company. Hanley Engineering built two more custom fire engines in 1941, also powered by V-16 Marmon engines. Truck expert James K. Wagner took this photo of the 1940 Hanley built for Dover, now owned by a private individual.

By the end of the year, the United States would be at war with Japan and Germany. But for months prior to the Japanese attack on Pearl Harbor, American industry had been on a war footing. The fire apparatus industry was one of the few U. S. industries that went right on producing, while at the same time making other war materials. Fire engines were considered vital to national security for the defense of our cities and defense plants. While American fire apparatus builders developed and produced specialized new types of fire equipment for the military, they also continued to supply a limited number of new fire engines for municipal use. Permission to order new fire equipment had to come directly from various government boards.

But before the complete transition to the war effort began, American fire apparatus builders were still doing a brisk business supplying new rigs to replace machines that had been worn out during the long depression years. More than a few municipalities had been unable to buy any new equipment since the late 1920s.

American LaFrance's 500 Series apparatus could now be found almost everywhere. The Type 500 was available in pumping engine models with open or closed cabs

ranging from 600 to 1,500 gallons per minute. There were tractor-drawn aerials of 85 and 100-foot sizes, with open or closed tractors. The big, wide-bodied 500s could also be delivered as city service ladder trucks or quadruple combinations. Among the special models the Elmira plant turned out in 1941 were a towering 500 Series enclosed sedan pumper with 1,500 GPM pump for Brookline, Mass., and the company's first 125-foot 5-section tractor-drawn aerial. Finished in white and built to order for the Boston Fire Dept., this one-off ladder truck had a short and tragic career. It was exhibited at the IAFC Conference held in Boston that year, but was destroyed by a falling wall at a big fire in East Boston that killed six firefighters in November, 1942.

Seagrave had delivered its last apparatus using the grille style that had been introduced in 1935. All custom-chassis Seagraves now bore the more rounded type of front end that had been introduced on the company's smaller models in 1936. A flat, fold-down windshield was standard on this series, and half-doors were generally used on all open-cab models. The company's canopy cab had become standard on closed cab pumpers. Closed tractor-drawn aerials starting the late 1930s were usually equipped with a canopy-style cab equipped with a rear-facing crew seat.

No history of fire apparatus building in this country would be complete without a reference to the remarkable handful of 16-cylinder jobs turned out by the very versatile Mr. Keenan Hanley. Mr. Hanley had been the chief engineer for the old Prospect Fire Engine Co. When Prospect ceased operations in 1934, Mr. Hanley formed his own engineering service. Over the next few years his small shop turned out a number of small pumpers built on various commercial chassis. In 1940, Mr. Hanley built a special combination pumper and ladder truck on a GMC chassis for Dover, Ohio. This apparatus was powered by a V-16 engine based on the old Marmon Sixteen. Mr. Hanley had acquired the rights to make this engine, but not the Marmon name. In 1941, the Hanley Fire Apparatus Co. of Prospect, Ohio delivered a custom-chassis pumper and a big quadruple combination to Marion, Ohio. These huge rigs resembled postwar Ahrens-Fox centrifugals. Both were powered by the big Marmon-based V-16.

The W. S. Darley Co. of Chicago built this unusual pumper for Winfield, Ill. The 500 gallon-per-minute pumper was built on a 1941 Ford cab-over-engine V-8 chassis with 4X4 conversion by Marmon-Herrington. The 4-door cab is certainly unique, as is the style of hose body with the ground ladders mounted above rather than carried on the sides.

American-Marsh pumps, of Battle Creek, Mich.—builder of the famed Barton front-mount pump—built this 500 gallon-per-minute quadruple combination for Three Rivers, Mich. The ladder racks on this 1941 Chevrolet cab-over job are open, whil the rest of the body is fully enclosed.

American LaFrance did built a few van-bodied Series 500 fire engines. This gleaming white Series 500 sedan, with a 600 gallon-per-minute rotary gear pump, was built for the Harrisburg, Pa. sirport. The fairing on the roof is an enclosed, overhead ladder rack. Watervliet, N. Y., also had an American LaFrance of this type.

Brookline, Mass., which ordered a Series 400 van-style pumper from American LaFrance in 1937, took delivery of this big Series 500 van in 1941. This huge pumper had a 1,500 gallon-per-minute pump. Compare the roofline and body height of this engine with the Harrisburg, Pa. job. It would appear that the crew could almost stand up in the rear of this imposing rig.

Perth Amboy, N. J. assigned this 1941 American LaFrance 600 Series pumper to Engine Co. No. 4. The 1,250 gallon-per-minute unit has the open semi-cab, but carries an enclosed full-length overhead ladder rack. The bell on this pumper is mounted under the forward ladder rack support.

Engine Co. No. 2 in Chelsea, Mass. used this American LaFrance 500 Series pumper, which is seen in this Charles Beckwith photo at work at a fire. This engine differs from most 500s in that the hard suction hose is carried outside, rather than inside, the hose body. The roof-mounted siren is also a departure from conventional practice on this series.

Albany, N. Y. purchased one of the few Series 500 American LaFrance rescue squad cars built. This rig logged many miles in the quarter-century it was in service in the New York state capital. It carried a wide array of heavy rescue gear, as well as a turret nozzle. It was replaced by a new American LaFrance Series 900 squad in 1967.

American LaFrance built very few quintuple combinations on its new cab-ahead-of-engine aerial truck chassis. This, in fact, may be the only one. This 1941 American LaFrance quint with a 600 gallon-per-minute pump and 65-foot metal aerial ladder, was delivered to Sturgis, Mich. The hose bed is under the aerial ladder, and the pump control panel is on the right-hand side of the truck.

The Elmira plant at about this time started building 65-foot service aerial ladder trucks on straight-frame chassis. Previously, the metal aerials were available only on tractor-drawn and cab-forward models. The type of small aerial shown here was built on both the 500 and 600 Series. This 65-footer was delivered to Andover, Mass. The wood ground ladders extend out further behind the truck than the aerial ladder does.

This is another of those fire engines with a colorful, and extended, service life. A 100-foot American LaFrance tractor-drawn Series 500 aerial, it was one of the few non-Ford-chassised rigs purchased by the City of Dearborn, Mich. After more than a quarter century of service, it was retired and sold to the Lakeside, Ohio Volunteer Fire Dept., near Sandusky. On the trip to Lakeside, the V-12 engine blew and the truck had to be towed the rest of the way home. A deal was made with Elmira, and a used 1949 Series 700 open-cab American LaFrance tractor, said to be an ex-Mount Vernon, N. Y. unit, was purchased by the Lakeside department and placed under the refurbished trailer. This aerial was used to fight the fire that destroyed the old Ford Rotunda in Dearborn, in 1962.

Boston received the first—and only—125-foot aerial ladder truck ever built by American LaFrance. This Series 500 tractor-drawn aerial had a 5-section main ladder, and was painted white. The closed-cab aerial was shown at the International Assn. of Fire Chiefs Convention held in Boston that year. It was powered by the American LaFrance 240-horsepower V-12 engine. This big truck had a short but tragic career—it was crushed by a falling wall at a fire in 1942, and several Boston firefighters were killed. American LaFrance boasted that this big ladder truck was a full 10 feet shorter than an 85-foot wood aerial.

As its crew helps battle the multiple-alarm fire raging in the background, this 1941 American LaFrance 85-foot tractor-drawn aerial stands on the street in Philadelphia. The Philadelphia Bureau of Fire took delivery of no less than nine of these spring-raised, wood aerials in 1941. The post-mounted Roto-Rays were a trademark of Philly rigs for many years. This photo was provided by noted apparatus photographer Jack Robrecht of Philadelphia, who has been keeping track of Philadelphia's fire apparatus for years.

Seagrave built a sizeable number of these medium-sized pumpers with 2 or 3-man closed cabs. This is a 750 gallon-per-minute model that was delivered to Ottawa, Ill. The striping and lettering on this 1941 Seagrave is original. Note the carbon-tetrachloride fire extinguisher mounted just below the small triangular cab window.

All of the fire apparatus being built in the Columbus, Ohio plant of The Seagrave Corp., with the exception of commercial chassis models, was now of this style. This 1941 Seagrave 65-foot service aerial was used by the West Patterson, N. J., and Union, N. J., fire departments before being acquired by C. Kennard Robinson of Peekskill, N. Y., a fire buff and member of the Van Cort Volunteer Fire Dept. Note the one-piece windshield.

Among the specials turned out by the Columbus plant was this speedy-looking little squad car, for Whittier, Calif. It carried the Whittier city emblem on its doors, and was Seagrave Serial No. A-6600. Seagrave used the type of siren mounted on the cowl of this rig from the early 1930s until after World War II.

The tractor of this 12-cylinder Seagrave 85-foot aerial ladder truck has a semi-cab that can seat five men. Three crew members face rearward in a seat reached through the space between the tractor and the trailer. This aerial was used by Hook & Ladder Co. No. 1 of the Valley Stream, N. Y. Fire Dept. Some Seagrave tiller buckets had glass down to the level of the top of the ladder rails. Most had a single-piece windshield mounted atop the curved windbreaker. This ladder rig has the fully glazed style.

Seagrave continued to build a small number of commercial chassis jobs for smaller towns and villages. This is a 500 gallon-per-minute triple combination pumping engine built by The Seagrave Corp. on a 1941 Ford V-8 truck chassis. It was sold to Lovelock, Nev. and had an open cab with no doors.

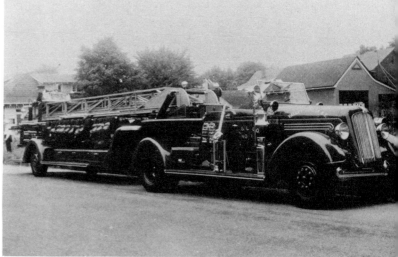

Baltimore over the years has used some of the most distinctively-trimmed fire equipment on this continent, and some of the most interesting. For many years, Baltimore rigs were painted white and red and were ornately striped and lettered. The Baltimore City Fire Cept. once had several old aerials of this type. This is a 1941 Seagrave tractor, which is pulling an 1888 Hayes wood aerial with an oversized Dahill air hoist. The tillerman on Hayes aerials sat under rather than on top of the aerial ladder. This is Second Line Truck No. 17, an 85-footer in reserve service.

Seagrave delivered its last wood aerials prior to the outbreak of World War II, even though the Columbus plant supplied parts and service for wooden "sticks" for many years after. Among the last new ones built were seven 75-foot tractor-drawn wood aerials sold to the New York City Fire Dept. in 1941. These spring-raised aerials had open-cab tractors. The radiator shells of these rigs were left in natural metal instead of being painted. The F.D.N.Y. did not receive its first metal aerials until after the war.

The Philadelphia Bureau of fire purchased 13 of these big Autocar 1,000 gallon-per-minute pumpers with booster equipment. The pumps on these engines were mounted in the open on the truck frame between the driver's seat and the hose body. The cylindrical tank above the pump is the booster tank. This Autocar was assigned to Engine Co. No. 9.

Here is a right-side view of one of Philadelphia's big 1941 Autocar pumpers. The booster hose was carried in the round basket above the front of the hose box. These engines had exceptionally low windshields, and Roto-Ray warning lights mounted on a high post beside the cowl on the left-hand side. This is also Engine 9's rig, one of 13 identical units delivered to the P.F.D. that year.

During the 1950s, one of Philadelphia's 1941 Autocar Pipe Line high pressure wagons was converted into a special Giant Deluge unit. Assigned the special number 99, this apparatus carried a huge, hydraulically-operated Stang Intelli-Giant turret gun, and two portable Eastman-type monitors mounted on a platform behind the seat. This special service battery wagon was called out to major fires and was a real "Big Bertha" when it came to delivering powerful master streams.

Philadelphia's apparatus purchasing program in 1941 also included two Autocar high pressure hose wagons. These were known as "Pipe Line" units. Each was equipped with two large fireboat turret nozzles, and each carried a load of large-diameter fire hose. This one is lettered No. 20.

Cadillac, Mich. ordered this 1941 Mack Type 75 pumper with a 750 gallon-per-minute pump. This handsome rig has a 5-man canopy-type cab. Mack delivered many pumpers of this type. The hose was carried in two separate hose beds in the rear, separated by a catwalk that led to the crew seat.

Neversink Fire Co. No. 3 of Reading, Pa. had this tough-looking 1941 Mack Type 80 pumping engine. The fully open cab model had a 750 GPM pump. Note the fully loaded boot rack above the hard suctions, and the oval Mack emblem on the mesh pattern grille.

MACK

New York City remained among Mack's most loyal customers. A big repeat order resulted in the delivery of 12 of these 1941 Mack Type 21 pumpers to the F.D.N.Y. These big vehicles had 1,000 gallon-per-minute pumps, deck turrets and plated radiator shells. Note the Mars light on the cab roof. The large handwheel on the pump panel is the main valve control for the deck pipe.

After years of service as a pumper, the Grand Rapids, Mich. Fire Dept. ran this 1941 Mack triple combination as a squad company. The squad provided extra manpower at the fire scene, and, of course, the rig could be hooked up to a hydrant if needed. Note the later style Federal Q siren mounted above the front bumper. This engine has a 5-man canopy cab.

Deal, N. J. ordered this exceptionally large Mack quadruple combination with an extended roof, 5-man canopy cab. This quad is a Type 50, and has a 500 gallon-per-minute pump. Note the height of the hose bed above the ladder rack. A pair of red flashers is mounted on the front bumper.

1941

Baltimore was another city with an unusually resourceful apparatus shop crew. Baltimore completely rebuilt many of its rigs over the years. One of the most remarkable conversions done in the BFD shops was this city service ladder truck, the last used on the department. This rig started out as a horse-drawn Holloway hook and ladder truck. In about 1917, the Holloway body was transferred to a Mack AC Bulldog chassis. In 1941, it was modernized and rebuilt with a new Mack front end. After many more years of service, this rig was cut down into a spare aerial ladder truck tractor and at last report was still on the Baltimore equipment roster as a reserve unit.

With an inordinate number of fully-equipped spare rigs compared to other major cities, Baltimore's reserves constituted a veritable second fire department. Second Line Truck Co. 17 at one time was assigned this tractor-drawn aerial, which was built not by Mack, but by the very versatile Baltimore Fire Dept. repair shops. The tractor is a 1941 Mack Type 19. The hoist for the 85-foot wooden aerial ladder is an Ahrens-Fox hoist of the Dahill type.

The year 1941 was a big one for Philadelphia as far as apparatus purchases went. In addition to the 13 Autocar pumpers and two Autocar high pressure hose wagons, the Bureau of Fire also received 15 of these 1941 Ward La-France 1,000 gallon-per-minute pumpers. The 28 new pumping engines replaced a lot of old, outdated apparatus. Like the Autocars, these Wards had low windshields, carried booster equipment and sported a set of post-mounted Roto-Rays on the left-hand side.

The Cleveland, Ohio Fire Dept. in 1941 placed four of these Buffalo 750 gallon-per-minute triple combination pumpers into service. These pumpers had 4-door sedan cabs that could seat seven men, and were of the Buffalo "clear vision" design. All equipment was carried within the streamlined body. The pump control panel was behind the first door behind the rear cab door.

The Hanley Engineering Service of Prospect, Ohio built two of these custom fire engines, a triple combination pumper and a city service ladder truck, for Marion, Ohio. Although based on GMC chassis, they were powered by Marmon V-16 engines, and had custom-built cabs that eliminated all traces of their GMC ancestry. Their designer and builder, Keenan Hanley, had once been chief engineer of the Prospect Fire Engine Co. This was the only view of these very unusual rigs available.

The bell is visible behind the grille cage of this 1941 Peter Pirsch 750 gallon-per-minute quadruple combination. The quad has a 5-man sedan cab with four doors, and a large equipment compartment behind the rear fender. This quad ran as Engine No. 8 in Two Rivers, Wis.

The Town of Niles, Ill. bought Peter Pirsch & Sons Co. fire apparatus for many years. Still in almost original condition is this 1941 Pirsch 500 gallon-per-minute pumper with International 2-man cab. The ground ladders and suction hose are carried inside the rear body, which is faired in with the cab. Note the small windshield on the rear handrail for the men riding the back step.

This is what the restyled Pirsch Junior aerial ladder truck looked like. This 60-footer with semi-open 3-man cab saw service in Bridgeton, N. J. The 2-section aerial ladder was manually operated. The bell has been relocated to a spot just behind the cab door.

Only three Pirsch metal aerial ladder trucks were ever sold in Canada. All three wound up within a 75-mile radius in Southwestern Ontario, in Windsor, Sarnia and Chatham. The City of Chatham received this unique 1941 Pirsch 65-foot aerial on a forward-control International chassis. International Harvester has a large truck plant in Chatham, so this city has always used mainly International-chassis fire equipment. This open-cab aerial was still in reserve in 1975.

Pirsch used this grille design on its apparatus for more than 20 years. This is a 1941 Pirsch 65-foot service aerial with aluminum-alloy ladder and hydraulic hoist which was delivered to Waukesha, Wis. This city is the home of the Waukesha engine, which was used in Pirsch and numerous other makes of fire apparatus for many years.

Among the more unusual pumpers built by Pirsch was this one for the United States Navy. It was designed to run on rails at a Naval Ammunition Depot. The 750-GPM pumper was designated only as a special rail-type pumping engine. Although the United States did not officially declare war until the last month of the year, the war clouds had been gathering, and American industry was already gearing up for war production.

All of America's principal fire apparatus builders continued production through the war years. Civilian apparatus was delivered only on a high priority basis, with appropriate Government approval. But the factories of American LaFrance, Seagrave, Mack, Pirsch, Maxim, Buffalo, and the smaller manufacturers like Howe, Hahn, General, Barton-American and Central between them built hundreds of specialized fire engines for the war effort at home and abroad.

Restrictions on vital materials resulted in some pretty austere-looking wartime rigs. Chrome and bright metalwork disappeared altogether. Parts like bumpers, body trim, bells, pump caps, handrails and even headlight rims were painted either a dull grey or the same color as the rest of the apparatus. The use of sirens was outlawed in major cities; these were reserved for emergency civil defense use only. Many cities used exhaust whistles for the duration.

The wartime production role assumed by American LaFrance was fairly typical of the industry. The Elmira, N. Y. plant built hundreds of special purpose fire trucks, ranging from small commercial-chassis pumpers to giant tractor-drawn aircraft crash and foam tenders. But it also turned out thousands of nose wheel landing gear spindles, forks and gun mounts for the Bell P-39 Airacobra, and bomber tailgun mounts. American LaFrance also worked closely with Bell Aircraft on components for the highly secret P-59, America's first jet fighter aircraft.

But there was still time for new product introduction and development. In 1942 American LaFrance began full production of a new 600 Series. This model resembled the earlier 500 Series, but had a narrow cab and body, a V-type windshield and a vertical, mesh-type grille.

In the latter years of the war, American LaFrance conducted a survey of U. S. fire chiefs to determine what kinds of fire apparatus would be required when peacetime production resumed. The long-term result of this survey was the radically new Series 700 cab-forward apparatus that would go into production in 1947. As early as 1944 American LaFrance had built model mock-ups of its experimental new models. One of these was of a compact, rear-mounted aerial ladder truck that would not go into production for nearly a quarter of a century.

A prototype Series 700 pumper with a closed, canopy cab was built in 1945, and was announced to the company's sales force in late 1945. It was announced to the public in the December, 1945 issue of *Blazes,* the company's own magazine. American LaFrance decided to make a total commitment to this bold, new series and immediately began to tool up for it. A prototype cab-forward aerial was also being built.

Seagrave in 1943 began using a V-type windshield on its open-cab apparatus. By late 1945 the Columbus, Ohio manufacturer was working on a completely new fire apparatus body which would be much wider, and would have a rakishly sloped windshield.

Ahrens-Fox in 1942 had assembled a single HT-1000 piston pumper from its parts bin for Harrison, N. J., which had a vital defense plant in its protection area.

Mack Trucks had introduced a handsome new series of pumpers with a new upright radiator shell and V-type windshield in the early 1940s. The parts and service departments of all fire engine builders were kept busy servicing and keeping older model fire apparatus on the road.

The triangular Civil Defense emblem began to appear on fire apparatus. Strapped for manpower, fire departments formed auxiliaries and took on temporary men. Several manufacturers produced thousands of small, portable trailer pumps which would be towed to fires behind a conventional automobile, and out of World War II came the widespread use of "fog", a high-pressure hose stream that was broken up into millions of fine particles, and which had an effective, cooling effect. A properly applied fog stream could knock down an entire roomful of fire with minimum water damage. One of the principal early suppliers of this type of equipment was the John Bean Division of the Food Machinery Corp., based in Lansing, Mich. John Bean High Pressure Fog Fire Fighters could be mounted on any commercial truck chassis.

All fire apparatus manufacturers were called upon to develop special types of firefighting equipment to meet special military and civil defense requirements. American LaFrance built this huge tractor-drawn Series 500 foam engine for the Air Force. The two foam turrets could lay down a blizzard of fire-killing foam at the scene of an aircraft crash. When not being used, the roof-mounted turret boom rested on the cradle behind the cab.

Although the United States was at war, fire apparatus production continued on a limited basis for the essential protection of cities and vital industry. The Chicago Fire Department placed two of these 100-foot American LaFrance Series 500 tractor-drawn aerials, powered by V-12 engines, into service in 1942. In 1953, this aerial was re-engined with a Cummins Diesel. These aerials had 4-section ladders. The tiller of the American LaFrance 100 and 85-foot tractor-drawn aerials was fixed and did not have to be moved to raise the main ladder.

This Pirsch 750 gallon-per-minute pumper has an unusual 5-man closed cab, and its pump control panel located behind compartment doors. This plain-looking engine was sold to Mattoon, Ill.

This 1942 Pirsch quadruple combination has led a double life. The 1,000 gallon-per-minute quad with 4-door sedan cab and booster equipment served the Memphis, Tenn. Fire Dept. for many years as a regular fire company. It is lettered here for Truck Co. No. 11. This quad wasl ater converted by the Memphis shops into a special battery wagon called the Multi-Master. Memphis rigs have been named after former Memphis chiefs and other department personnel for years.

Here is how the 1942 Pirsch quad looked after conversion to the Multi-Master heavy stream rig. Captain Richard Adelman of the Memphis Fire Dept., himself a well-known fire apparatus photographer, notes that the Multi-Master is equipped with 10 hose inlets in the rear, and 12 discharge gates along the sides. A big- power-operated turret nozzle is mounted on top. This deck pipe can also be fed a wetting agent from a tank on the truck. The rear cab doors have been closed off, and the booster reel relocated to a compartment above the Multi-Master sign. This firefighting battle-wagon has seen action at many major fires in Memphis.

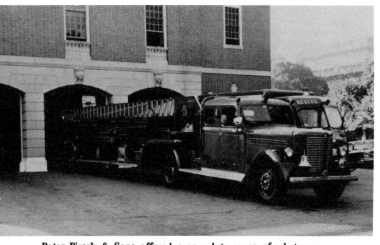

Peter Pirsch & Sons offered a complete range of cab types on its Senior 100-foot metal aerials. The one shown here is a canopy style, with open rear. This aerial was delivered to Cambridge, Mass., a very good customer for Pirsch. This city had its name painted in the white panel at the cab belt line. Pirsch front ends at this time came in two widths; contrast the grille on this aerial with the thinner one on the Mattoon pumper.

Pirsch built some very streamlined apparatus during the early 1940s. This exceptionally clean job is a 600 gallon-per-minute quadruple combination. The bell is visible behind the grillework, and even the ladders are totally enclosed on this model. This style was also built as a straight city service ladder truck with open, closed or sedan-style cab.

This style of Peter Pirsch & Sons Co. apparatus featured a narrower radiator shell than that used on other Pirsch fire engines of this same style. The aerial shown is a 100-foot tractor-drawn Pirsch Senior ladder truck, assigned at the time this photo was taken to Truck Co. 22 in Memphis, Tenn. Dick Adelman caught it at the Memphis Fire Dept. Training Academy.

The Chicago Fire Dept. motor shops rebuilt this 1942 Pirsch-Dodge 500 gallon-per-minute pumper into a small airport crash truck. This engine was quartered in the fire station at Chicago's waterfront Meigs Field. Chicago bought the pumper as U. S. Army surplus. Note the big chemical tank on the running board.

Here is another early wartime Seagrave. Even the headlights on this one were painted, as was the front bumper. This is a 1942 Seagrave 750 GPM pumper with canopy-style cab delivered to Wilmette, Ill. The extension ladder appears to be a 35-footer instead of the usual 24-foot type. Note how the soft suction hose is carried, ready for instant use.

Seagrave delivered this 85-foot tractor-drawn aerial with open semi-cab to Hazelton, Pa. Note the use of a painted rather than a plated bumper. Brightwork would virtually disappear from fire apparatus because of wartime rationing and restrictions. The one-piece windshield on the Hazelton aerial has been folded down.

Deliveries of new fire apparatus, although curtailed by the war effort, continued. The Seagrave Corp. built this 100-foot tractor-drawn aerial with a 4-door, 7-man cab for Norristown, Pa. Dan Martin grabbed this shot while on tour of suburban departments during an International Fire Buffs Association Convention in Philadelphia. Note the roof bar equipped with two beacon lights.

One of the more unusual commercial chassis fire engines built by the Maxim Motor Co. was this tractor-drawn city service hook and ladder truck built for Coventry, R. I. The tractor is a 1942 Ford V-8. This long truck had no tiller, It was Coventry's Ladder No. 1.

This was the only piston pumper built by the Ahrens-Fox Fire Engine Co. during the second World War. It was literally assembled from the parts bin for Harrison, N. J., which was the home of several important defense plants. The 1942 Ahrens-Fox Model HT 1,000 gallon-per-minute pumper was used as the Harrison Fire Dept.'s Engine No. 2. Harrison purchased an identical Ahrens-Fox when production resumed in 1946.

Because of the hazardous nature of fire fighting, ambulances are usually dispatched to all major fires. Larger cities frequently have very elaborate emergency medical units which automatically respond to multiple alarms. The Philadelphia Fire Dept. used this complete Mobile Hospital unit, which was built by the Kalamazoo Coach Co. on a 1942 Ford truck chassis. Department doctors could actually operate on patients en route to the hospital in this type of unit.

Make no mistake about it—this was a big piece of fire apparatus. A straight city service hook and ladder truck, it was built for Darby, Pa. on a 1942 Autocar chassis with extra long wheelbase, by the U. S. Fire Apparatus Co. of Wilmington, Del. This company specialized in mounting fire department bodies on the sturdy Autocar truck chassis, although it did turn out apparatus on other makes as specified by the customer. Note the half-fold life net on the running board.

Milton, Mass. was the owner of this Maxim Motor Co. 750 gallon-per-minute pumper with a full rear entrance canopy style cab. Note the speaker on the front fender and the small siren bolted to the front bumper support. Maxim offered its customers, most of them in the east, a complete range of cab and body styles.

The Howe Fire Apparatus Co. built this triple combination pumper for its home city of Anderson, Ind. Built on a 1942 General Motors Truck (GMC) chassis, it features a canopy style cab and has a midship-mounted 750 gallon-per-minute pump. Note the booster reel behind the cab, and how low the headlights are mounted on this job.

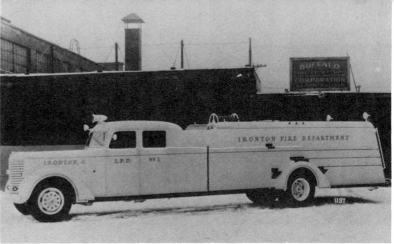

With the outbreak of the Second World War, Alaska became a strategic outpost. The Four Wheel Drive Auto Co. of Clintonville, Wis. shipped this open-cab Model KHS pumper to Anchorage. It was equipped with a 500 gallon-per-minute pump, and carried 300 gallons of water in its booster tank. A foam hopper is carried on the running board just forward of the rear fender. The hard suction hose and 30 and 14-foot ladders were enclosed in this rig's all-steel body.

The Buffalo Fire Appliance Corp. of Buffalo, N. Y. built this very long quadruple combination for Ironton, Ohio. Photographed in front of the Buffalo plant, it was painted white and had a 4-door sedan cab. The pump was of 750 GPM capacity, and the ladders were completely enclosed. The booster hose reel can be seen on top of the ladder body.

Following the Second World War, a number of amphibious Ducks were sold by the Government as surplus. More than a few fire departments purchased these units for use as specialized rescue vehicles. Jamestown, N. D. only retired this 1942 Ford Duck in August, 1975. This unit played an important role in the 1969 Jamestown Flood. A sizable number of Ducks—large and small—remain on the equipment rosters of American fire departments.

The plating department in the Seagrave Corp. plant in Columbus wasn't very busy during the war years. The bumper, grille bars and siren on this 500 gallon-per-minute Seagrave pumper were painted the same color as the rest of the apparatus. Seagrave was using a new V-type windshield on most of its rigs. This pumper was delivered to Comstock, Michigan.

The American-Marsh Pump Co. plant in Battle Creek, Mich. built hundreds of small rural pumpers of this style. This one, on a 1942 Chevrolet chassis, was equipped with a front-mount pump and an overhead ladder rack. It was on the Battle Creek Township Fire Dept. for many years and was eventually sold to Louis Shellenburger of Marshall, Mich. The Marsh-Chevy is seen here at an antique fire apparatus muster held by the Great Lakes Chapter of SPAAMFAA in the Detroit area in 1974.

This Seagrave quadruple combination pumping engine, or quad, has evidently been repainted. The three chrome streamers over the hood louvres have not been replaced, nor has the circular Seagrave emblem used at the front of the hood. The striping and lettering aren't factory, either. This 750 GPM quad was used by the Pennhurst, Pa. Fire Dept. Note the older style ventilated metal booster hose basket on top, and the absence of doors.

1942 - 1945

American LaFrance had introduced its improved 600 Series apparatus in 1942. Outside of mechanical improvements under the hood, about the only way to tell a 500 from a 600 Series American LaFrance is the depth of the fillet between the grille and the front fender. The 600 had a slight extension, where on the 500 the front fenders were almost flush with the grille. This is a 1943 American LaFrance Series 600 pumper of 1,250 GPM capacity delivered to Sioux Falls. S. D. The makeshift cab was added locally.

Although the LaFrance Fire Engine & Foamite Ltd. plant in Toronto, Ontario remained in production throughout the war, this 65-foot Model 4-65 American LaFrance metal aerial ladder truck for the Royal Canadian Navy was built at the parent company's plant in Elmira and was shipped to Canada. Most of the LaFrance apparatus sold in Canada was built in the Toronto plant, but a few units were brought in complete, or nearly completed, from Elmira.

Thousands of small trailer and portable pumps were built during the war for civil defense, and for additional protection in and around large industrial plants. The LaBour Co. of Elkhart, Ind. had been marketing a successful self-contained firefighting trailer for several years before the war. This pump could deliver 150 gallons of water per minute, and it carried 500 feet of hose and a 24-foot length of suction hose. This type of trailer could be hitched to a passenger car or truck and hauled to where it was needed. The complete LaBour Fire Trailer sold for less than $1,000. LaBour was a major manufacturer of stationary pumps.

With war raging, American fire apparatus builders were permitted to build a limited number of new fire engines for the protection of cities and towns. Louisville, Ky. received this 1943 American LaFrance 100-foot metal aerial, with open 3-man cab. Note the gray-painted bumper and brightwork. The Federal "Q" siren and the rotating beacon flasher were later additions. American LaFrance was now using box-type fenders on the trailer, and a squared-off rather than rounded fender on the front of the trailer. This aerial ran as Louisville's Hook & Ladder No. 3.

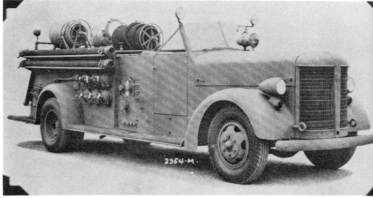

The Elmira, N. Y. plant of American LaFrance built many special fire engines for the protection of military bases and government installations. This is a big combination pumper and chemical engine. It is finished in olive drab or khaki, and has no brightwork whatsoever. The front hose reel is for a CO-2 system, the bottles for which are visible behind the pump. The other reel is for the booster system. These were utilitarian jobs, but they did the job they were designed for.

Peter Pirsch and Sons also continued to build a limited number of custom and commercial chassis fire engines during World War II, while doing defense work at the same time. This 1943 Pirsch 750 gallon-per-minute quad was delivered to Chattanooga, Tenn. The newer style plated bumper was probably added later.

The General Fire Truck Corp. of Detroit also built quite a few fire trucks for the U. S. government during the war. This is a combination hose and turret wagon built on a General Motors truck chassis. This apparatus was built for protection of the U. S. Naval Supply Depot at Bayonne, N. J.

Trenton, N. J. took delivery of this wartime Buffalo. The massive Buffalo customs now had a new style of grille made up of heavy horizontal bars. The 1,000 gallon-per-minute pump is visible.

Memphis was one of Peter Pirsch and Sons Co.'s best customers for many years. Memphis purchased several of Pirsch's biggest aerials—the tractor-trailer 100-foot Senior type with metal ladder and a canopy style cab. Memphis rigs have distinctive dark green painted running boards instead of the usual aluminum.

Now here's something unusual—a 70-foot aerial. But it didn't start out that way. The City of Chicago in 1944 took delivery of three new Peter Pirsch 85-foot tractor-drawn aerial ladder trucks with 2-section, wood spring-raised ladders. Through fire or accident, the "stick" on this one was cut down to the unorthodox new length. The Chicago Fire Dept. had received two 100-foot hydraulically-operated metal aerials in 1942, but continued to use wood, spring-raised aerials into the late 1950s, the last major city to purchase new ones this late.

Cambridge, Mass. bought a lot of Pirsch fire apparatus over the years. Most of the rigs delivered to Cambridge in the early 1940s were of the closed, canopy cab type. But this 1944 Pirsch 750 gallon-per-minute pumper had an open half-cab. Here, Engine 6 is supplying a 2½-inch line at a fire. Pirsch had started mounting its bells on the right-hand side of the front bumper.

The Available Truck Co. of Chicago began to market a special custom fire apparatus chassis, which was used by quite a few fire engine builders. The General Fire Truck Corp. of Detroit built this large city service ladder truck for St. Paul, Minn. using the Available chassis. No matter how the fire equipment builder attempted to disguise it, the sturdy-looking Available chassis was always recognizable.

Mack, faced with the same restrictions concerning the use of chrome and brightwork as the other manufacturers, attempted to spruce up the appearance of its civilian jobs by employing modest striping and the type of gold ornamentation visible on the painted radiator shell of this 750 gallon-per-minute pumper. The canopy-cab pumper was built for North Andover, Mass.

North Chicago, Ill. was the recipient of the new Mack Type 50 pumper, with a 500 gallon-per-minute pressure-volume centrifugal pump. Note the wig-wag warning light on the roof of the 3-man closed cab. Again, the bumper and other usually bright metal plated parts are painted gray or red because of wartime austerity.

Another plain-looking Mack civilian job was this Type 80 triple combination pumper that was delivered to Manchester, N. H. It was equipped with a 750-gallon pump. After the war, some departments eventually plated some of the painted parts that came on wartime units.

This fully enclosed (except for the cab) Mack pumper was photographed by the author in the summer of 1974. What makes it interesting is the fact that its wartime appearance, including the type of scrollwork used on the sides of the radiator shell, has been perfectly perserved. The pumper is owned by the Deshler, Ohio, Village Fire Department, and the whole gang is aboard for this important parade in Ada, Ohio.

Mack

New York City kept right on buying Macks. The FDNY placed 10 of these Type 21 Mack pumpers with 1,000 gallon-per-minute pumps into service in 1944. Note the painted radiator shell and front bumper. Standard equipment on New York engine companies included two scaling ladders and a powerful turret pipe. This 1944 Mack was assigned to Engine Co. No. 28.

Ward LaFrance fire apparatus now sported a new style grille that would be around for nearly 20 years. This is a spanking new triple combination pumper that the Elmira Heights, N. Y. plant delivered to the District of Columbia. Note the austere wartime appearance, lack of hard suction hoses, and the Roto-Ray warning lights on the roof.

Rolling serenely along during a local parade is this Seagrave quadruple combination. The rig has the painted wartime bumper, the new V-style windshield and enough turnout gear on its racks to clothe a good sized fire department. The community that had this quad is not known.

The front bumper of this 1944 Seagrave 65-foot service aerial ladder truck has evidently been replaced, as this style of bumper did not appear on Seagrave fire apparatus until late in 1948. The canopy cab aerial ran as Truck Co. 23 on the Memphis, Tenn. Fire Dept. All Seagrave custom jobs now sported this style of radiator.

The Seagrave Corp. built relatively few of these quintuple combinations. This one had a 65-foot metal aerial ladder and a 750 gallon-per-minute main pump. It was used by the Bryn Mawr Fire Co. of Bryn Mawr, Pa. The 1945 Seagrave has the earlier style one-piece windshield. Note the pump panel and the length of hard suction hose carried over the rear fender.

Summit, Ill. had this 1945 Seagrave quadruple combination, with a 750 gallon-per-minute pump. The Seagrave Corp. built its own trussed wood ladders in its Columbus, Ohio plant. The deep type of truss characteristic of Seagrave ladders can be seen here. Note the Mars light perched atop the radiator shell, and the steel-spoked wheels.

Louisville, Ky. was another city that got three-quarters of a century's service out of its venerable water tower. This 55-foot Hale tower was built as a horse-drawn unit in 1892. A 1936 Mack tractor was placed under it later. The Mack tractor was replaced with this 1944 Chevrolet, and the old water tower remained on the reserve roster until the late 1960s. The trailer portion of this tower was remarkably original, right down to the big deck pipe mounted on the right rear of the trailer platform.

Pittsburgh, Pa. took delivery of this 1945 Seagrave 85-foot tractor-drawn aerial ladder truck. The narrow type of "V" windshield on this truck, would soon be replaced by a lower, wider one designed to fit Seagrave's new, wider postwar cab. The front bumper appears to be a replacement. The ladder has three sections.

A local body shop did a very creditable job of rebuilding this 1945 American LaFrance Series 600 pumper after it was struck by a train in 1951. The cab was probably added at the same time. The 1,000 GPM pumper was delivered to Chico, Cal. A booster reel has been added above the cab.

The Pittsburgh, Pa. Bureau of Fire ordered several of these 1945 American LaFrance 600 Series straight city service hook and ladder trucks, with open semi-cabs. The rig shown was used for a time by Truck Co. No. 17. Sharp eyes are needed to tell an ALF Type 600 from a 500—the deeper fillet between the front fender and the grille indicates that this is a 600.

As headquarters of the Ford Motor Co. empire, the City of Dearborn, Mich. has understandably always used Ford-chassised fire apparatus. But during the 1940s, the city bought several American LaFrances, one of which was this 1944 Series 500 pumper. This pumper had a 750 gallon-per-minute pump, and it featured a canopy-type cab similar in design to the one introduced by Seagrave some seven years earlier. Note the bell behind the grille. One half of the grille was hinged, so the bell could be reached for polishing.

Grand Rapids, Mich. took delivery of three American LaFrance Series 600 pumpers with 1,250 GPM pumps in 1944. These big pumpers had canopy cabs with two doors, and were known locally as "boxcars" because of their massive size. In 1968, one of these pumpers was converted into a spare rescue squad rig by the GRFD shops. With the new canopy-style rear body, this rig looked more formidable than ever. Note the two fire extinguishers carried on the extended front bumper pan.

The trailer of this 85-foot wood aerial appears to be an earlier model, but the Series 600 tractor was built in about 1945. This tractor-drawn aerial ran as Truck No. 6 on the Denver, Col. Fire Dept. Not all cities switched immediately to the new metal aerials. Wood aerials with this style tractor were delivered as complete, new units to departments like Newark, N. J., and Albany, N. Y., but Boston and Chicago continued to buy wood aerials into the 1950s.

The American LaFrance aerial truck shown here was a quarter of a century ahead of its time. Elmira was hard at work on the design of a radically different type of fire apparatus for postwar production, and this model constituted one proposal. It was rejected. The cab-forward 700 Series pumpers and aerials were announced late in 1945, but deliveries did not commence until early in 1947. Some 24 years after this model was built for evaluation, American LaFrance in 1968 announced its "Ladder-Chief" rearmount aerials of precisely this configuration. This remarkable photo turned up in a dusty drawer at Elmira in 1974.

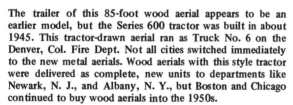

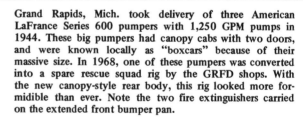

The American LaFrance plant slowly resumed full-scale civilian production following the war. This is a 1945 American LaFrance 500 GPM pumper delivered to Pass Christian, Miss. The siren was still mounted out on the hood on these models. Production of this series continued into 1947.

A peek into the future: it was generally known throughout the industry that American LaFrance was working on a radically different new fire engine design, which would go into production as soon as peacetime production could be resumed. In December, 1945, the Elmira factory revealed its stunningly new cab-forward Series 700. This is the prototype of the closed-cab pumper. By the time production began, however, the rear cab window had been altered in shape. American LaFrance claimed that the V-12 cab-forward model offered 250% better forward vision than pre-war models. The first 700 Series fire engines were not delivered until March, 1947.

American LaFrance formally announced its radically new 700 Series fire apparatus in its company magazine "Blazes", in December, 1945. This is the pilot model of the pumper, a 1,500 GPM job that was to be the precursor of many hundreds yet to come off the assembly floor at Elmira. On the production model, the first of which was not delivered until March, 1947, the rear cab window was changed from the same frame used for the cab door glass, to a rounded style fixed in a rubber bead. The type of handrails at the rear of the cab was used on early production closed cab 700s. This photo was provided by American LaFrance.

With the cessation of hostilities, Philadelphia made a wise move when it picked up six 1945 American LaFrance 750 gallon-per-minute pumpers as U. S. Army surplus. Some of these nearly new engines had cab doors while others didn't. This is Reg. No. L-2092, assigned to Engine 46, hard at work. Note the integral flashers built into the headlight stanchion.

The custom chassised fire engines built by the Howe Fire Apparatus Co. of Anderson, Ind. were known as Howe Defenders. For a time, Howe Defenders were based on the Defiance truck chassis. This is a 1944 Howe Defender with a 500-gallon pump. The grille on this model is very similar to the one used on Pirsch apparatus from 1935 to 1939. Note the "beavertail" rear body sides, and the high clothing racks above the hose box.

With World War II behind them, American fire apparatus manufacturers resumed peacetime production. The manufacturers enjoyed a virtual seller's market, as they plunged into a huge backlog of orders. Many municipalities had been unable to purchase new equipment since the depression, and larger cities sought to replace entire fleets that had seen hard service through the war years.

American LaFrance tooled up to production its daring new 700 Series cab-forward fire apparatus. In addition to a prototype 1,500 GPM pumper, the Elmira plant had built an open-cab 100-foot service aerial using the new 700 sheetmetal. By the end of the year the new series was in production, but the first deliveries would not be made until early in 1947. Meanwhile, American LaFrance continued to build its earlier 600 Series apparatus, which got a new horizontal-bar grille treatment, and the bulbous cab-forward aerials it had been delivering since 1939. Deliveries of these earlier types continued into the early months of 1947. The company had committed its production facilities entirely to the new 700 Series, which was destined to become probably the most famous and most easily recognized fire engine ever built in this country.

Production also resumed at the big Seagrave Corp. plant in Columbus on a large scale. Late in the year, Seagrave began installing its new wider cab on its apparatus. This design included a sharply-raked, wide V windshield. On canopy cab models, including service-type aerials as well as on tractor-drawn types and closed cab quads and city service ladder trucks, a new oval-shaped window was used in the upper rear body panels. This was a styling feature on these models until the mid-1950s, and was carried forward on the new 70th Anniversary models introduced in 1951.

The Ahrens-Fox Fire Engine Co. resumed production at a new location in 1946. The company, which had been reorganized in 1939, abandoned its original Colerain Ave. home and moved into another plant on Beech St. in the Cincinnati suburb of Norwood. Ahrens-Fox's most popular model was its highly regarded Model HT piston pumper. But the centrifugal pump had become a serious competitor from a manufacturing cost point of view, and piston pump orders had fallen off sharply over the previous decade. The 1,000 GPM Model HT front-mount had changed little in appearance in the past 10 years, and continued to be powered by the big Hercules engine. Ahrens-Fox was also building a line of centrifugal pumpers. These used a massive new body.

The Maxim Motor Co. in 1946 launched a whole new line of handsomely restyled pumpers, city service ladder trucks and quadruple combinations. The new Maxims sported a vertically styled grille, had a new wider cab, and a low, full-width V-type windshield. Maxim's new pumpers included 750, 1,000, 1,250, and 1,500 GPM models with open, closed and canopy type cabs.

One of the busier smaller firms was American-Marsh Pumps, based in Battle Creek, Mich. This company, which became the American Fire Apparatus Corp. which is still in business today, was the maker of the famed Barton-American front-mount pump. The small centrifugal pump was made in capacities of up to 600 GPM. Mounted on popular commercial truck chassis including Ford, Dodge, GMC and Internationals, these front-mounts were the backbone of rural and small town fire departments throughout the Midwest. The front-mounted pump permitted the entire rear body to be used for carrying hose and an extra-large booster tank.

All fire apparatus builders found themselves with more than they could handle as they struggled to meet pent-up demand for new apparatus.

Truck Co. No. 2 of Birmingham, Ala. once used this Seagrave 100-foot tractor-drawn metal aerial with 3-man semi-cab. A rescue basket and acetylene cutter are carried on the side of this rig. The elongated front fenders indicate that this truck is powered by Seagrave's big V-12 engine.

The Seagrave Corp. introduced this canopy cab type of service aerial. Two men rode in the cab, and three more crew members could be seated on the bench seat behind. This is a 65-foot Seagrave that once ran as Truck 2 on the Jackson, Miss. Fire Dept., but was later put on the reserve list. Note the handrail that encircles the edge of the side-entrance canopy cab.

With its hood sides open for more efficient operation in hot weather, Missoula, Montana's 1946 Seagrave 85-foot service aerial poses on the station apron for fire apparatus photographer John Sytsma. This aerial has a 4-section main ladder and sports the new wide Seagrave cab and the new style windshield. Note the radio speaker attached to the top of the aerial ladder.

Cambridge, Mass. continued to equip its fire department with Pirsch apparatus. This sleek 1,000 gallon-per-minute pumper with 4-door sedan cab was delivered in 1946. Note the double front bumper bars and the siren mounted on top of the grille. This pumper is lettered for Engine Co. No. 6—the same company that was running a late-model Pirsch open-cab pumper only a couple of years earlier.

1946

Two more Pirsch 85-foot tractor-drawn wood aerials were bought by the Chicago Fire Department in 1946. The order also included two Pirsch sedan-cab pumpers. This truck, with hydraulic hoist, was assigned to Hook & Ladder Co. No. 10. Note the Mars light built into the grille.

Along with two 85-foot tractor-drawn aerials, Peter Pirsch & Sons Co. delivered these two 1,000 gallon-per-minute pumpers to the Chicago Fire Dept. in 1946. These enclosed-body rigs had 7-man, 4-door sedan cabs, and front-mounted bells. Chicago rigs were the traditional red, but had black cabs and roofs.

Tacoma, Wash. commenced a fire apparatus modernization program immediately following the war. Peter Pirsch & Sons delivered four of these 1,000 gallon-per-minute pumpers with 2-man GMC cabs to Tacoma in 1946, and followed these with two 100-foot Senior aerials and a quad. In tests, these pumpers exceeded contract specifications by delivering a very respectable 1,575 gallons per minute at 125 pounds pressure.

Another Pirsch Senior 100-foot aerial ladder truck with a rear-entrance canopy cab was delivered to Ladder 1 in Cambridge, Mass. in 1946. This rig also has a double front bumper. On Pirsch aerials, the tiller seat flipped up and over, and the windshield swung away when the aluminum alloy aerial ladder was to be raised.

The Buffalo Fire Appliance Corp. refined the frontal appearance of its custom-built apparatus after the war by replacing the finely-textured grille bars used earlier with a heavier series of chrome grille bars. This 750 GPM triple combination with 3-man cab was delivered to Terre Haute, Ind. This pumper also had a rear suction intake.

The Fairview Park, Ohio Fire Dept. owns this 1946 American LaFrance Series 600 quadruple combination with open cab. This rig is in near-mint condition. A rotating flasher has been added to the windshield frame, but otherwise this quad looks exactly like it did the day it left the Elmira factory. It is a 750 gallon-per-minute job, with aluminum ground ladders.

Another postwar American LaFrance is this quadruple combination with 500-GPM pump and a 2-man GMC cab. It was built for Euclid, Ohio. A portable monitor nozzle is mounted behind the cab, and the rig carries American LaFrance wood ground ladders.

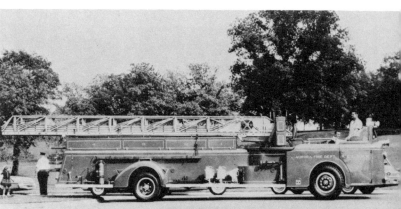

This American LaFrance Series 600 Aerial has undergone quite a transformation. The 65-foot service aerial, with special side-entrance canopy cab, was originally sold to Jamestown, N. Y. In 1972 it was purchased by the Brunswick, Ohio Fire Department and completely refurbished. Changes included a bright yellow paint job and bucket seats out of a Ford Mustang.

Originally used as a salvage truck, this 1946 American LaFrance 600 Series fire engine was later converted to serve as a foam rig. Three foam playpipes and a foam hopper are visible on the running boards of this San Francisco apparatus. This 600 has the narrow body. The suction hose troughs defy explanation.

American LaFrance continued to build its cab-forward metal aerials. This is a 1946 Model 4-100 delivered to Aurora, Ill. The type number indicates that this is a 4-wheel service aerial with 100-foot ladder. The device near the base of the ladder that looks like a Maltese cross is an indicator which tells the operator how many men can be safely carried on the aerial ladder, depending on angle of inclination, length of extension, etc. This Deluxe model had streamlined rear fenders and enclosed ladder beds. This series, introduced in 1939, was replaced by the all-new 700 Series aerials in 1947.

American LaFrance had already made the bold decision to convert its production entirely to the radically new 700 Series fire engines. Retooling and preparation for production continued through 1946, and work on the first production models had started by the end of the year. In the meantime, models developed before the war remained in production. This is the prototype of the 700 Series 4-wheel service aerial ladder truck. The factory photo came from the Bill Durrett collection.

1946

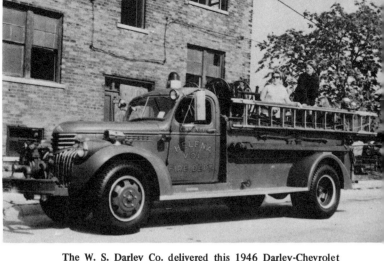

Very few tractors of this style were found under American LaFrance aerials. The semi-cab has a rearward-facing 3-man crew seat behind the driver's seat. This 85-foot tractor-drawn aerial was delivered to Mankato, Minn. in 1946. The aerial ladder has three sections. This truck carries a full complement of wood ground ladders. Notice how far back the tillerman sits—the tiller seat does not have to be moved to riase the main ladder.

The W. S. Darley Co. delivered this 1946 Darley-Chevrolet 750 GPM front-mount pumper to the Helena, Ohio Community Volunteer Fire Dept. In 1973, this low-mileage pumper was sold intact to Allan B. Judge, of Livonia, Mich., who is a Past-President of the Greenfield Village International Antique Fire Apparatus Assn., the Great Lakes Chapter of SPAAMFAA, Inc. This Chevrolet pumper is a reliable source of water supply at Greenfield Village musters.

High pressure fog—a fine spray stream with excellent fire extinguishing characteristics—had been perfected during the war years and was becoming popular with several fire apparatus builders. The Oren Roanoke Corp. built this high pressure fog pumper on a Dodge chassis for Columbia, Pa. It was equipped with a Hardie LCXA high pressure pump, and Hardie trigger-controlled fog nozzles, and had a 400-gallon booster pump.

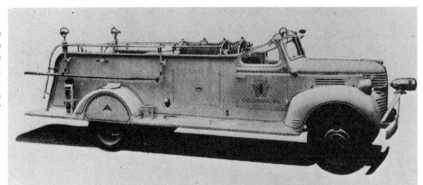

Another product of the Oren Roanoke Corp. was this attractive rescue squad truck with a 7-man canopy cab, built for the Adams Township Fire Dept. on a 1946 Chevrolet chassis. Note the wide cab and the handrail around the front door. Oren Roanoke later moved its manufacturing operations to Vinton, Va. and is still in the fire apparatus business today.

New York City commenced a major fire apparatus modernization and replacement program as soon as the fire equipment makers resumed peacetime production. This is one of 20 Ward LaFrance 750 gallon-per-minute pumpers received in 1946. Unlike later Wards purchased by the F.D.N.Y., this one has a front suction hose intake and a radiator shell left in natural metal color, rather than painted. The rig shown responded as Engine Co. No. 275.

Ward LaFrance also gave its products a new frontal appearance. This 3-section grille with a series of horizontal bars at the sides was used for the next 17 or 18 years. This 1,000 gallon-per-minute Ward LaFrance pumper has the narrow style body, and sports a V-frame windshield. A foam hopper is carried on the running board.

1946

Mack Trucks had resumed full production, and was hard-pressed to keep up with a very strong postwar demand for new fire apparatus which was needed to replace worn-out older equipment. One of Mack's more popular models was the Type 45, a 500 gallon-per-minute pumper. The Type 45 was powered by Mack's reliable 6-cylinder engine. This 1946 Type 45 has an open-style cab.

This big Mack pumping engine presents a pleasing parade appearance with its whitewall tires and two-tone paint job. The lower body is standard fire department red, but the upper section above the belt line is painted black in the Chicago style. This 1946 Mack Type 75 pumper with 5-man, 4-door sedan cab and 750 GPM pump was delivered to Flossmoor, Ill.

Toledo, Ohio received the last city service ladder truck built by Ahrens-Fox. This 1946 Model 4-ED was still in service as late as 1973 as a reserve rig. When this photo was taken, it was running as Ladder 18. The Ahrens-Fox ladder truck has an open half-cab and carries a full complement of wood ground ladders. Ahrens-Fox had been building city service ladder trucks since the early 1920s. The Cincinnati manufacturer continued to build quadruple combinations.

The Maxim Motor Co. came out with a completely restyled line of custom fire apparatus following the war. Maxim would use this pleasing radiator design for the next 15 years. This 500 gallon-per-minute pumper with enclosed pump and 3-man cab was delivered to Strasburg, Ohio. It is painted a light buff color, with brown striping and trim.

The Borough of Chatham, N. J. placed this fully-enclosed pumper into service in 1946. Built on a Ford cab-over-engine chassis, it was constructed by the Trautwein and Sons Co., of Woodbridge, N. J. This firm, which also used the name Trautwein's, Inc., delivered custom built apparatus throughout the New Jersey area under the name of "TASC."

For obvious reasons, Maxim's home town of Middleboro, Mass. has always purchased Maxim fire equipment. The Middleboro Fire Dept. was especially proud of this local product, a 1946 Maxim 750 GPM quadruple combination. Note the streamlined bodywork, the playout troughs at the rear of the hose box, and the portable turret gun on top. This quad's booster hose reel is visible just behind the cab.

1947

American LaFrance early in 1947 began deliveries of its new 700 Series apparatus. The first two 700 pumpers delivered were a pair of 1,250 GPM closed-cab models delivered to Elkhart, Ind. Hundreds of chiefs watched the new trucks go through their paces at underwriter's tests held March 6. The first 700 Series aerial placed in service went to Binghamton, N. Y. It was an 85-foot service aerial with a closed cab. Three of the new pumpers were delivered to Middletown, N. Y. The first big single order for the new type came from New York City, which ordered no less than 20 pumpers with open cabs, 750 GPM pumps and big deck turrets. By June of 1947, the Elmira plant was building only the new 700 types, which were well-received by fire departments everywhere. Nonetheless, American LaFrance had taken quite a gamble committing all of its resources to such an advanced new model. All of the apparatus being delivered by The Seagrave Corp. had the company's sleek, new cab. Seagrave's powerplant was still the big V-12. One of the company's more popular products was its 4-wheel service aerial, which could be delivered with a 65, 75 or 85-foot metal aerial ladder. This type of apparatus was rapidly replacing the old city service hook and ladder truck. Straight city service trucks were already almost special-order models. Mack Trucks also offered a comprehensive postwar product line, with many engineering refinements. Mack's standard models included the Type 45 pumper of 500 GPM capacity; the Type 75 open-cab 750 GPM pumper; the Type 95 pumper of 1,000 GPM capacity; the Type 85 pumper, a 750 GPM model with a canopy style cab or 4-door sedan body, and the Type 19 city service ladder truck. Mack also built a Type 45 squad car. Among the more interesting Macks delivered in 1947 were two 1,000 GPM pumpers for Hammond, Ind. These pumpers were equipped with 750-pound Cardox low-pressure carbon-dioxide systems for fighting chemical fires. Boston later received several Macks that carried similar equipment. The Maxim Motor Co. in 1947 announced its first metal aerials. The Middleboro, Mass. manufacturer offered 65, 75 and 85-foot three-section metal aerial ladders of its own manufacture. Initially, these were offered only on straight-frame service aerial ladder trucks, but within a few years Maxim was building 85-foot 6-wheel tractor-drawn aerials. The Roanoke Welding and Equipment Co. and Oren Fire Apparatus Co. merged in 1947 to form the Oren-Roanoke Corp. This company built custom-chassised and commercial fire apparatus in its Roanoke, Va. plant for many years before moving into a new plant at Vinton, Va. Oren-Roanoke is still a major fire apparatus builder today. The Central Fire Truck Corp. of St. Louis delivered a fleet of 12 new pumpers to its home city. Based on a disguised GMC chassis with a full open cab, these pumpers were equipped with 750 GPM pumps. The General Fire Truck Corp. of Detroit had also become a highly competitive fire engine builder. The company delivered five 750 GPM General-Detroit pumpers to Dallas, Tex., this year, and sold many more to this city over the next few years. The Generals used a special fire engine chassis supplied by the Available Truck Co. of Chicago. Central-St. Louis also delivered some apparatus based on the Available chassis. Ward LaFrance Truck Corp. in 1947 redesigned the model it had been building since the early 1940s. Styling changes included a new, wider cab with a low, full-width

windshield and a large cab door that extended down to the running board.

The Waukesha 6-cylinder gasoline engine was used by several major fire apparatus builders, including Pirsch and Ward LaFrance.

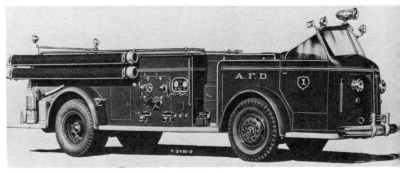

During the closing years of World War II, American LaFrance commenced development of a radically new series of fire engines with cab-ahead-of-engine design. The revolutionary 700 Series was announced late in 1945, but deliveries did not commence until early in 1947. Elmira took a big gamble on the acceptance of this all-new series, by committing all of its production to the new model. This is a 1947 Series 700 pumper of 750 GPM capacity, with the 5-man open semi-cab.

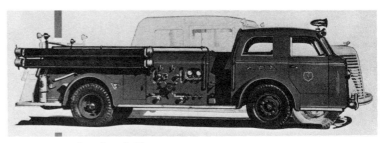

American LaFrance composed this illustration to show how the new Series 700 pumper compared in size with the prewar Series 500. The new 700 was considerably shorter, had a tighter turning radius and vastly improved visibility. The driver of the Series 500 pumper, as the illustration shows, sat back near the middle of the apparatus and looked through a narrow windshield out along a very long hood. The new 700 Series cab seated three in front, while 2 more men rode in seats on each side of the engine compartment. Three more men could ride on the rear step.

The City of New York placed the first large-volume order for Series 700 fire apparatus. American LaFrance delivered 20 of these 750 GPM pumpers to the FDNY in 1947. These pumpers were equipped with fixed turret pipes, and like all New York engine companies carried one length of hard suction hose and one scaling ladder on each side. The inlets for the deck pipe and the handwheel controlling the turret inlet valve can be seen on the pump panel.

This is the classic American LaFrance 700 Series front end as it appeared between mid-1947 and late 1948. The style of front bumper visible here had been replaced by a plain, flat bumper by the time 1949 deliveries started, although a few of this type have been found on some early production 49s. This is a 1,000 GPM pumper delivered to Teaneck, N. J.

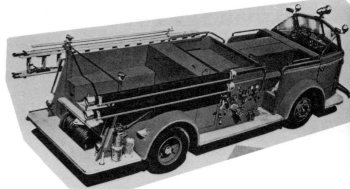

This overhead view shows nicely the general arrangement of the new 700. The engine is mounted behind the front seat and does not intrude into the cab. It is linked directly to the Tripleflow centrifugal pump. A large equipment compartment is provided above the pump. The T-shaped booster tank can be seen in the front of the hose body, and the booster reel is transversely mounted on the rear step. The 700 provided a compact, yet functional configuration and was immediately accorded wide acceptance by the fire service.

Here is an early production American LaFrance 700 Series triple combination pumper with the closed canopy style cab. It is not known if this pumper was delivered to Marion, Ohio or Indiana. The style of rear handrail visible on this pumper was used on only some of the closed-cab models delivered in 1947. A chrome number "1" is mounted on the cab front just below the ALF nameplate.

The new American LaFrance 700 Series fire apparatus line also included 4-wheel and tractor-drawn aerial ladder trucks, with closed or open cabs. This is a 1947 service aerial with 3-section ladder and dual booster hose reels. It carries a full complement of wood ground ladders. The lack of bumper guards indicates that this was an early delivery.

This is a 1947 American LaFrance Series 700 pumper with open semi-cab. The 750 gallon-per-minute pumper was delivered to the City of Wadsworth, Ohio. Note the portable deck monitor and the Mars light mounted on the post at the front of the cab. A rotating flasher has been added to the center of the windshield. The steamer suction hose on this engine is carried in the rear cab entryway.

American LaFrance built the last of its 600 Series apparatus this year, as the Elmira plant was being converted over to full production of the new Series 700. This style had been introduced as the Series 500 nine years earlier. This 500 gallon-per-minute Series 600 pumper is still on the Medina, Ohio Fire Dept.

Some fire departments named their apparatus after former chiefs or other civic or departmental officials. This 1947 Seagrave 1,000-gallon pumper of the Lowell, Mich. Fire Dept. is named the S. S. Lee. It carries three lengths of hard suction hose and has the standard canopy cab.

This 750 gallon-per-minute Seagrave shows the new style windshield as it appeared on Seagrave's open-cab models. This pumper, of the Riverhead, N. Y. Fire Dept., carries a turret nozzle on a frame behind the seat. Note the Mars light on top of the radiator shell, and the alternating red flashers on the outboard windshield posts.

The Seagrave Corp. also made some big changes to its apparatus in 1947. The most significant of these was an attractive new cab design, which was wider than the type formerly used, and which had a sharply-raked V-type windshield. All Seagraves now used this style of hood, grille and front fenders. This is a standard 750 GPM canopy cab pumper.

Westchester, Ill. purchased this 1947 Seagrave 65-foot service aerial, which was originally owned by the St. Louis, Mo. fire department. Seagrave built many aerials of this type. Junior aerials like this replaced city service hook and ladder trucks on many fire departments.

This is the new Seagrave 750 gallon-per-minute quadruple combination. The short canopy cab with the small oval window was introduced this year, and was standard on closed-cab Seagrave aerials and quads until the late 1950s. The booster hose reel is carried under the rear frame on this unit.

Seagrave's Canadian cousin, Bickle-Seagrave Ltd., of Woodstock, Ontario, delivered this straight city service ladder truck to the Toronto suburb of the Township of York in 1947. Bickle-Seagrave built Seagrave fire apparatus under license, importing body panels, engines, pumps and aerial ladders, but building the entire unit in its own plant. This ladder truck was retired from service in 1974.

The standard Seagrave pumping engine of 1947 had a 750-gallon pump, and was powered by the Seagrave V-12 engine that was used in almost all of the custom apparatus being built in the Columbus, Ohio plant. Few models without doors were being built anymore, although a fully-open cab could be specified by the purchaser.

Seen here in its maiden portrait at the Cincinnati factory is a 1947 Ahrens-Fox Model HT-1000 piston pumper delivered to Carlisle, Pa. This beautiful pumper, powered by the big Hercules HXE 6-cylinder engine, was in service until 1970. Upon retirement, it was bought by members of the volunteer company. Reg. No. 3464 is a popular participant at parades and musters all over the state.

The Ahrens-Fox Fire Engine Co. had resumed fire apparatus production in 1946. Despite the growing popularity of the centrifugal pump, some departments continued to favor the piston pump. This 1947 Ahrens-Fox Model HT Twin Triple 1,000 gallon-per-minute piston pumper was built for the Hanley Hose Company of the Chester, Pa. Bureau of Fire. The metal rooster perched atop the air chamber ball is a company relic that dates back to the volunteer era. This mascot is proudly transferred from old to new rigs. This big Fox has a Morse turret pipe built into the body behind the seat.

The Bryn Mawr Fire Company of Bryn Mawr, Pa. also received a new 1,000 gallon-per-minute Ahrens-Fox Model HT piston pumper in 1947. This Twin Triple was the latest in a long line of Ahrens-Fox piston pumpers which had served this fire company since 1916. The soft suction hose is carried in a compartment behind the Ahrens-Fox nameplate.

The City of River Rouge, Mich. placed this Ahrens-Fox pumper with roomy sedan cab into service in 1947. This Model HC with 1,000 gallon-per-minute pump was retired from service in 1974 and is now in the process of being restored.

For those who preferred centrifugal pumps over the positive displacement piston type, Ahrens-Fox built its Model VC apparatus. The VC Series got a new front end with wide hood and boxed-in fenders following the war. This Model VC-500 with 500 gallon-per-minute pump was delivered to Abington, Pa.

The Approved Fire Equipment Co. out of Rockville Center, N. Y., built all kinds of motor fire apparatus, but this company's specialty was heavy rescue truck bodies. This style of body, with many large equipment compartments and a pair of searchlights that retracted into the roof, became one of Approved's most popular products. Approved built this heavy rescue unit on a 1947 Brockway chassis for Rescue Squad No. 1 of the Philadelphia Fire Dept. Note the well-protected grille.

The Approved Fire Equipment Co. of Rockville Center, N. Y. specialized in building heavy-duty rescue truck bodies. But the company also turned out pumpers and ladder trucks, too. This 1947 White-Approved quadruple combination, sold to Franklin Township, N. J. could accurately be described as a "white White".

The Four Wheel Drive Auto Co. was now building quite a bit of fire apparatus, in addition to its heavy off-road truck chassis. The 4 X 4 configuration was ideal for many fire service applications. This is a 1947 FWD with 750 gallon-per-minute pump. All equipment is stowed out of sight in the streamlined rear body.

Port Byron, N. Y. received this Buffalo Pathfinder Model 500 gallon-per-minute triple combination with closed, 3-man cab. This well-equipped pumper carried 400 gallons of water in its booster tank, and 1,000 feet of 2½-inch hose, and 500 feet of 1½-inch line. Portable pumps and a portable generator were carried in special compartments.

The Buffalo Fire Appliance Corp. built this clean-lined 750 gallon-per-minute triple combination pumper for Frankfort, Ind. The pump panel is enclosed, and this engine carries a set of spotlights. Buffalo listed this simply as a Type 750 Triple combination Fire Apparatus.

The Fire Engine Division of the Mack Manufacturing Corp. delivered this Mack Type 85 pumper of 1,000 gallon-per-minute capacity, to the Edge Hill Fire Co. of North Hills, Pa. This triple combination has an open semi-cab, and twin booster reels.

Mack also built a full line of city service trucks and quads. This is a 1947 Mack Type 19 city service hook and ladder truck, with open-style cab, delivered to San Antonio, Tex. This ladder truck has booster equipment and a semi-closed ladder bed.

Mount Clemens, Mich. ordered this big Mack Type 19 pumper which was fitted with auxiliary fog equipment. The 1,000 GPM pumper has a canopy style cab, and a pair of large spotlights at the rear. Hose is carried in two beds separated by the catwalk leading to the rear crew seat.

Marion Fire Co. No. 10 of Reading, Pa. had this 1947 Mack 750 gallon-per-minute pumper, with a full open cab. This model was only slightly changed in appearance after 10 years of production. Note the red flashers atop the forward ends of the clothing rails.

The Ford Motor Co. purchased this pumper to protect its huge Rouge Plant complex near Detroit. The Rouge produced completed automobiles from raw steel, and the sprawling complex was protected by a large and well-equipped plant fire brigade. This pumper was built on a Ford truck chassis by the General Fire Truck Corp. of Detroit.

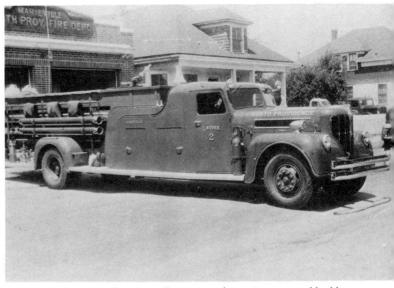

The Maxim Motor Co. would build any style of body specified by its customers. Shenandoah Heights, Pa. received this 1947 Maxim 750 gallon-per-minute pumper built on an extra-long wheelbase, with a 4-door sedan cab and overhead ladder rack. Note the pair of floodlights mounted on the rear cab roof.

The Maxim Motor Co. was turning out some good-looking rigs. This 750 GPM quadruple combination, delivered to North Providence, R. I., is a good example. The high rear body blends in nicely with the 3-man cab, and the enclosed pump panel makes for a very tidy appearance. Note the double-bar front bumper.

The Baltimore City Fire Department placed eight of these Ward LaFrance 750 GPM triple combination pumpers into service in 1947. They were equipped with fixed turret pipes. This one has been modified by the Baltimore shops, with the addition of compartmented rear fenders, and the protective plexiglas shield for the crew riding the rear platform.

The Ward LaFrance Truck Corp. of Elmira Heights, N. Y. began using this style of body on its standard pumping engines. This is a 500 gallon-per-minute job delivered to South Amboy, N. J. The post-mounted siren on the cowl was a standard Ward LaFrance feature, but the rear wheel fender skirts were an extra-cost option. This pumper was used by South Amboy's Progressive Fire Co.

The John Bean Division of the Food Machinery Corp. of Lansing, Mich. developed an effective high pressure fog system that could knock down a surprisingly large fire with relatively little water. Bean marketed a complete high pressure fog fire engine mounted on any make of chassis desired by the customer. This 1947 Bean-International delivered to Ann Arbor, Mich. was typical of hundreds built for fire departments all over the United States. Two-tone paint jobs were common on Beans. Standard equipment on this Fog Fire Fighter included two fog guns—one on each hose reel—and two searchlights. Note the rear windshield. The two built-in equipment boxes forward of the rear wheels made Bean fire apparatus easily recognizable.

The Pirsch aluminum alloy aerial ladder can be easily recognized because of its closely trussed lattice design. This type of Pirsch aerial was first built in 1937, and is still being made today some 38 years later. This is a rear view of a 1947 Pirsch 100-foot Senior tractor-drawn aerial on the Pottstown, Pa. Fire Dept. Pirsch also makes its own metal ground ladders.

The busy Peter Pirsch & Sons plant at Kenosha, Wis. continued to turn out commercial chassis jobs on request. This is a 750 GPM triple combination pumper built on a K-series International chassis. Note the bell and siren mounted on the front bumper pan. The dual hose reels appear to have been added later.

Pirsch at this time was building pumpers of from 500 to 1,500 gallons-per-minute capacity. This is a 1,250 GPM job delivered in 1947 to West Allis, Wis. It has a GMC cab integrated into a canopy roof. Most Pirsch apparatus was powered by the Waukesha 6-cylinder fire service engine.

This is another Pirsch commercial. It is a 500 gallon-per-minute pumper built up on a Chevrolet truck chassis for Homewood, Ala. Pirsch used all types of commercial chassis, ranging from the popular Ford and Chevy, to heavier Internationals and Diamond Ts.

Here is something a little different. Studebaker supplied a popular fire apparatus chassis during the late 1920s, but few appear to have been sold after that. This streamlined little 500 gallon-per-minute pumper with overhead ladder rack was built by the Howe Fire Apparatus Co. on a 1947 Studebaker truck chassis. It is not known where this Howe-Studebaker saw service.

By far the most unique fire engine delivered this year was a product of one of the smaller firms in the business. Designed by D. Herbert Spangler, then president of the Hahn Motor Co. of Hamburg, Pa., the Dual Spangler rural fire fighter was built by Hahn for the Morgantown, Pa. Fire Dept. This truly remarkable apparatus was powered by two Ford V-8 engines. It carried two 500 GPM front-mounted pumps, and two 300-foot booster hose lines. The big Dual Spangler also carried 1,500 gallons of water, and it had dual axles front and rear. Despite its considerable size, it was designed to traverse rough terrain with ease. The Dual Spangler was to be distributed through the D. H. Spangler Engineering and Sales Co. of Hamburg, Pa., and the Leidy Electric Co. of Phillipsburg, N. J. But the Spangler was not a success. No more were built, and the prototype was dismantled after only a few years of service.

New York's fire department made its first break with spring-raised wood aerials this year when it conducted extensive evaluation of three makes of all-metal, hydraulically operated ladder trucks. Tractor-drawn 85-foot models with open cabs were purchased from American LaFrance, Seagrave and Peter Pirsch & Sons Co. New York also took delivery of 20 Ward LaFrance replacement tractors this year.

American LaFrance delivered two unique 700 Series pumpers this year. One was a 750 GPM 4-wheel-drive pumper and airport crash truck constructed for Hartford, Conn. Powered by the 240 HP V-12 engine, it had an open cab. Waterloo, Ia. received a special 4-wheel-drive pumper designed for service in outlying districts of the city. To accommodate a large booster tank and the 4-wheel-drive rear train, the pump in the Waterloo job was mounted just forward of the rear wheels. American LaFrance boasted in 1948 that it had sold more than 800 of its bold, new cab-forward fire engines, including 500 to 1,500 GPM pumpers, service and tractor-drawn aerials, quads and city service ladder trucks, and special models like squad cars and crash trucks.

Mack Trucks, Inc. introduced its first aerial ladder trucks built since the mid-1930s. Mack's new service type aerial ladder trucks were available with 65, 75 and 85-foot metal aerials supplied by Mack by the Maxim Motor Co. Maxim supplied Mack with its aerials for many years. Mack did not offer tractor-drawn aerials again until about 1955. Mack delivered a 75-foot aerial and a 750 GPM pumper, both elaborately striped and decorated and finished in an eye-catching white and black, to Riverdale, Ill.

The Seagrave Corp.'s big plant in Columbus, Ohio was very busy fulfilling a big backlog of orders. During 1948, Seagrave delivered 10 pumpers to the Los Angeles County Fire Dept. Also this year, the company again began to promote its light-cuty, commercial chassis pumpers, most of which were built on standard Ford, Chevrolet and GMC chassis.

A proud old name in the motor fire apparatus field succumbed this year. The Buffalo Fire Appliance Corp., which had been building motor fire engines since about 1920, went out of business in 1948. Although the company delivered quite a few pieces of apparatus in its last year, the last Buffalos did not go into service for another two years. Buffalo ahd sold several chassis to

Indianapolis, and this city's versatile shops equipped them as long-wheelbase city service ladder trucks in 1950.

The Walter Motor Co. of New York built a one-off service aerial ladder truck for Newburgh, N. Y. This company would soon become well-known for its big crash truck chassis, which was used by several manufacturers.

"Fire Engineering" conducted a national survey of the nation's fire departments, and concluded that fully 25% of the apparatus in service was obsolete and badly in need of replacement.

Boyer Fire Apparatus of Logansport, Ind. offered a full line of commercial chassis pumpers ranging from 500 to 1,250 GPM. Boyer apparatus was distributed by H. O. DeBoer Associates, which had its national sales office in Lombard, Ill.

The successor to the old Obenchain-Boyer Co. was the Boyer Fire Apparatus Company of Logansport, Ind. Boyer built this triple combination pumper on a White Motor Co. chassis for Melrose Park, Ill. It is equipped with a 750 GPM pump. Note the preconnected soft suction hose, and the A-frame on the bumper for the bell and Mars light. This Boyer-White has a cut-down 2-man semi-cab.

Boyer built this good-looking straight city service ladder truck for Riverdale, Ill. Built on a Ford F-7 chassis with open cab, it has completely enclosed ladder beds with no rear overhang. Boyer sold a lot of apparatus in Illinois, and the Boyer name can still be found on the list of fire apparatus in business today.

Agawam, Mass. received this Seagrave 750 gallon-per-minute triple combination pumping engine. The booster hose reel on this model was usually located in a well on the rear step, but some were delivered with one or two reels mounted above the front of the hose beds. The pumper shown here has a single hose reel. The booster tank was built into the canopy cab under the rearward facing crew seat, or just behind it.

Another product of the Seagrave Corp. was this quintuple combination. It carried a 3-section, 65-foot metal aerial ladder, a 750 gallon-per-minute pump and hose ladders. These aerials had two hydraulic jacks which extended down to the ground to support the truck when the aerial ladder was in use. The jacks were located under the center of the truck outboard of the frame. This quint was built for the Fairmont Fire Co.

The Los Angeles County Fire Dept. (not to be confused with L. A. City) placed 10 of these Seagrave 1,000 gallon-per-minute pumpers into service in 1948. These county rigs protected large areas of brush and canyon, so were equipped with large booster tanks and two booster reels. The pumper shown here was assigned to Engine Co. No. 45. NOte the older style horn-type siren, and the Mars light perched on top of the grille.

This is one of San Francisco's "double combinations". A 1,000 gallon-per-minute pumper, this 1948 Seagrave carried no water or booster equipment. This was a pump and hose car only. These two-way combinations were accompanied on alarms by another double combination, a tank and booster rig. The S.F.F.D. eventually did away with this type of pumper and started buying triple combinations.

This pumper was shown as a 1947 model, but the type of front bumper it carries did not begin to appear on Seagraves until late in 1948 or in early 1949. This is a 1,000 gallon-per-minute Seagrave with 3-man closed cab. These cabs had two small, rounded rear windows. Built for Cape Girardeau, Mo. this pumper carried one length of hard suction hose and one ladder on each side.

1948

Seagrave had been building this canopy-type cab for 11 years, but during that time the design had been improved continually. The 1948 version bore little resemblance to the first built in 1937. This is a 750 GPM Seagrave triple combination pumping engine that was built for Grand Island, Neb. Note the fender mounting of the siren.

This 4-wheel service aerial with 3-section 65-foot aerial ladder became one of Seagrave's more popular models after the war. This one, with the closed canopy cab, was delivered to North Little Rock, Ark. Four closed compartments are provided above the ladder bed.

San Francisco purchased some new tractors after the war, which it used to modernize some of its old city service hook and ladder trucks. The ladder trailer being pulled by this 1948 Seagrave tractor was originally a horse-drawn piece. With a siklled tillerman in the rear, this combination could thread its way through almost any of Frisco's streets.

Compared with the number of open-cab models produced, Seagrave did not build too many of these 100-foot tractor-drawn aerial ladder trucks with closed, canopy style cabs. This aerial, delivered to Cleveland, Ohio has the canopy cab with small oval side windows. The elongated front fenders were used on rigs equipped with the large version of the Seagrave V-12 engine.

Arlington, Va. owns this 1948 Ward LaFrance 750 gallon-per-minute triple combination pumper. A beacon type flasher has been added above the windshield. Fire apparatus photographer Shaun P. Ryan took this portrait of Arlington's open-cab Engine No. 3.

Posing for the photographer here is one of the Ward La-France 750 GPM pumpers delivered to Boston, Mass. This spanking new rig has been assigned to Engine Co. No. 56. Like all Boston engine companies, it carries a portable turret pipe up behind the cab, and has booster equipment. Boston has used a fascinating assortment of fire apparatus makes over the years.

This 1948 American LaFrance 700 Series pumper, modernized and rebuilt by the Minneapolis Fire Dept. shops, is barely recognizable. The 1,500 gallon-per-minute open-cab pumper has been repainted, and is equipped with a locally-fabricated protective cab. Note the second set of ground ladders mounted above the short attic ladder. This pumper responded as Engine Co. No. 28 on the M.F.D.

Most American LaFrance 700 Series fire engines built were off-the-shelf standard production models. But the Elmira plant did build a small number of salvage and rescue squad trucks on its new cab-forward chassis. San Francisco ordered this 700 Series open cab squad for its Salvage Company. This V-12 apparatus carried booster equipment as well as protective covers and overhaul gear.

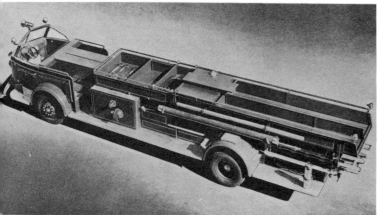

The quadruple combination, a versatile fire engine that carried a pump, ladders, hose and booster equipment, often replaced straight hook and ladder trucks on smaller city and town fire departments. This is a standard American LaFrance 700 Series quad equipped with a 500 gallon-per-minute pump. This top view shows the divided hose bed, the booster hose compartment and two other equipment compartments above the pump.

Fire Chief Ray Tiller of Waterloo, Iowa drew up the specifications for this unique Series 700 American LaFrance pumper with 4-wheel drive. The 750 gallon-per-minute pumper was designed to operate in suburban areas. To accommodate the part-time 4-wheel drive, the pump was moved back on the frame to a location just ahead of the rear wheels. The pumper is equipped with a 500-gallon booster tank, and is powered by a 204-horsepower engine. Note the flotation-type tires for use on soft ground, and the single rear tires. In Canada, LaFrance Fire Engine & Foamite Ltd. of Toronto built a similar FWD pumper for use in British Columbia in 1955.

Franklin, Ohio ordered this American LaFrance quadruple combination. It has the open-style cab, and carries a 750 gallon-per-minute centrifugal pump. This is one of the new Series 700 models, which were now coming off the Elmira assembly floor in a steady stream. The cab-forward 700 was built in all models, including pumpers, 4 and 6-wheel aerials, squad cars, city service ladder trucks and quadruple and quintuple combinations.

Here is another American LaFrance 700 Series quad. This one has a closed cab and a 750 GPM centrifugal pump. Note the extra bracing for the ladder overhang, and the Y-shaped playout troughs for each side of the hose bed. Two hose lines could be laid simultaneously. American LaFrance 700 Series fire apparatus was powered by the company's proven V-12 engine, which was available in several sizes and horsepower ratings.

The Chicago Fire Department continued to show a preference for the closed sedan-type cab on its new pumpers. Mack delivered six of these Type 95 pumpers with sedan cabs to the Windy City in 1948. They were equipped with 1,000 gallon-per-minute Hale pumps and could seat nine men in their roomy cabs. Note the soft suction hose draped over the side, and the frame for the bell and Mars light in front of the grille. Mars also made the new style oscillating light mounted on the roof.

1948

Hudson, Ohio still responds to fire calls with this nicely preserved 1948 Mack 750 gallon-per-minute pumper. This engine has the 2-man closed cab, and is equipped with two booster hose reels. Note the plated radiator shell, and the original Mack striping. The type of chrome-trimmed bumper of this truck was used from approximately 1948 until the new "B" Series Macks came along in 1954.

This is one of the very few fire engines ever used on a postage stamp. The rig is one of two identical 1948 Mack Type 85 triple combination pumpers delivered to the volunteer fire department of Riverdale, Md. The 750 GPM pumpers were painted white with contrasting black lower bodies and fenders and ornate gold trim. The design on the cab doors was hand-painted. Note the turret pipe mounted at the rear. One of these pumpers was featured on a 3-cent stamp issued in 1948 to commemorate the founding of the first fire brigade in the United States 300 years earlier.

Mack built this open-cab Type 85 triple combination pumper to order for the City of Coos Bay, Ore. The pumper has a 750-gallon pump and carries 300 gallons of water in its booster tank. A 3-section, 50-foot extension ladder is carried in the enclosed overhead ladder rack, and the pump has four discharge gates and a rear suction hose inlet. It also packs a centrifugal high pressure fog pump and dual booster hose reels.

Many standard production panel trucks were used in fire service, most commonly as light-duty rescue squads and supply vehicles. The Detroit Fire Dept. purchased five of these 1948 GMC panel trucks for use as foam carriers. Three years later another was purchased and is still in service as a lighting unit. Note the bell mounted on the right front fender. Several of these rigs, which carry a supply of cans of foam powder, were still around in 1974.

This is the standard model FWD. A Model F-75-T, it is powered by a 6-cylinder engine of 554 cubic inch displacement. The pump is a 750 gallon-per-minute 2-stage centrifugal. This model had a 200-gallon booster tank and carried 150 feet of booster hose. Wheelbase is 160 inches. Ready for service, it weighed 13,600 pounds. The FWD included four-wheel-drive as standard equipment, making this type of fire engine popular with suburban and rural departments. This model was also available with an open semi-cab.

One of the most beautifully maintained Ahrens-Foxes left in fire service captivity is this magnificent 1948 Model HT 1,000 GPM piston pumper. A rotating flasher has been added above the windshield,. but otherwise this handsome fire fighter looks about like it did the day it went into service in Abington, Pa.

1948

New Orleans placed one of the last multiple orders for Ahrens-Fox piston pumpers. Four of the 1,000 gallon-per-minute Model HT's with 3-man "Cadillac" cabs were delivered to the N.O.F.D. in 1948. These rigs carried three lengths of hard suction hose, and sported a set of Roto-Rays atop the front-mounted pump. As late as 1973, these pleasingly-proportioned pumpers were still running as reserve units.

After many years as one of America's foremost fire apparatus manufacturers, the proud old Buffalo, N. Y. firm known as the Buffalo Fire Appliance Corp. went out of business in 1948. One of the last Buffalo custom-built fire engines manufactured was this 750 GPM pumper with 4-door sedan cab, which was built for the Felton Fire Co. of Chester, Pa. Buffalo had built motor fire apparatus since the very early 1920s.

After more than three decades of building motor fire apparatus, the Buffalo Fire Appliance Corp. of Buffalo, N. Y. quit in 1948. The well-known firm delivered some fire engines that year, however. One of these was a long-wheelbase chassis sold to Indianapolis, Ind. which was built into this city service hook and ladder truck by the I.F.D. shops. Note the turret nozzle attached to the side of this open-cab ladder truck. While the chassis was built in 1948, this conversion was not completed until about 1950.

Aircraft landing and taking off from Chicago's O'Hare Field was protected by this big crash truck. Built on a heavy Autocar chassis, it was equipped by Cardox, a Chicago firm that built many specialized fire-crash trucks. This Cardox-Autocar carried 4,500 pounds of carbon dioxide, or CO-2, in the large tank at the rear. This chemical was poured on the fire by remote control from the front-mounted boom. Another foam nozzle can be seen below the front bumper. This rig has 4 X 6 drive for off-runway operation. The Chicago Fire Department mans the fire stations at O'Hare and Midway airports.

One of the most remarkable fire engines ever built in the United States was the Spangler Dual, which was marketed by the D. H. Spangler Engineering and Sales Co. of Hamburg, Pa. This very unusual piece of apparatus was manufactured by the well-established Hahn Motors, Inc. of the same city. The Spangler-Dual was powered by two 100-horsepower Ford V-8 engines. It had two 500 gallon-per-minute front-mount pumps, and carried no less than four booster hose reels. Tank capacity was 1,500 gallons. This ungainly looking rig could turn within 48 feet, and carried 5,000 feet of hose. Both rear axles were driven, and the unit sold for $16,800. Unfortunately, the Dual-Spangler was not a success. As far as is known, only one was sold. It went to the Morgantown, Pa. Fire Dept., but was retired from service and scrapped.

Crestline Publishing's offices are protected by this 1948 Peter Pirsch quadruple combination, which is still on the Glen Ellyn, Ill. Fire Dept. This Waukesha-powered quad has a 750 gallon-per-minute pump and a 3-man semi-cab. This truck also carries a full load of hose and metal ground ladders ranging in length from 10 to 50 feet. Note the Indian portable pump tank carried on the running board.

The Boston Fire Dept. in 1947 and 1948 embarked on a major fire apparatus replacement program. Sharing in this business were Pirsch, Mack, Maxim and Ward LaFrance. Peter Pirsch & Sons Co. delivered several of these 750 gallon-per-minute triple combination pumpers with canopy cabs to Boston. This one went to Engine Co. No. 17. Note the roof-mounted Mars light and the double-beam front bumper.

Peter Pirsch & Sons built this small commercial chassis triple combination pumper for St. Johnsbury, Vt. The pumper is built on a 1948 Ford F-8 truck chassis, and the roof has been cut off to make an open semi-cab. This pumper is equipped with a 600 gallon-per-minute pump, and carries two booster hose reels. The Pirsch-Ford ran as Engine 1 on the St. Johnsbury Fire Dept.

Fire apparatus photographer Dan Martin had to stand on the roof of his car to get all of this ladder truck into the camera lens. The eig is a 1948 Peter Pirsch Junior aerial ladder truck delivered to Ottawa, Ill. The 2-section aluminum aerial ladder was manually operated and extended to 55 feet. This low-cost model permitted smaller towns to afford aerial ladder equipment, often for the first time. This little aerial has a GMC cab.

At first glance, this looks like an FWD, but it is actually a Darley-FWD. The W. S. Darley Co. of Chicago built this 750 gallon-per-minute pumper for Chippewa Falls, Wis. on a 1948 Four Wheel Drive Auto Co. 4 X 4 chassis. Note how high the hard suction hoses are mounted. The Darley-FWD has four compartments on this side. An attempt has been made to streamline the cab into the rear body.

The General Fire Truck Corp. built this hose wagon for the Detroit Fire Department. For many years, Hose 1 was quartered with Engine 1, Ladder 1, Squad 1, High Pressure 1 and the Water Tower in the D.F.D. Headquarters Station. Hose Co. 1 rarely responds to fires today, and is quartered with Engine 6 and Ladder 5 in a station which is attached to the Detroit Fire Dept. Apparatus Shops. At one time, Hose Co. No. 1 carried two portable deck pipes just behind the cab. General-Detroit built this rig on a 1948 GMC chassis.

Mack Trucks built a very complete line of fire apparatus, but some Mack chassis were sold to other makers and fitted with special bodies. The General Fire Truck Corp. built this special rescue squad body on a 1948 Mack chassis for Curwensville, Md. Note the high headroom on this unit, which permitted the crew to stand in the rear. This squad also has generous compartment space for stowing heavy rescue gear.

Palatine, Ill. received this 1948 General-Detroit 750 gallon-per-minute pumper in 1948. This rig is built on the Available chassis, and has a 6-man, 2-door cab. The pump and all other equipment is concealed within the completely enclosed body. General built a lot of enclosed-body rigs. The plain exterior was highlighted by a bright metal trim strip that ran the length of the rear body. Palatine ran this big pumper as Engine No. 3.

Not to be confused with General-Detroit was the General-Pacific Corp., which began building custom-chassis fire apparatus at its Alcoa plant in Los Angeles in 1948. This company offered a line of motor pumping engines ranging in capacity from 100 to 2,000 gallons-per-minute. Single or two-stage midship-mounted centrifugal pumps with positive priming were used in the big General-Pacifics. This is a prototype model.

Engine Co. No. 3 in Everett, Mass. had this 1948 Maxim 1,000 gallon-per-minute triple combination pumper. A portable turret pipe is carried on top, and the pumper has twin booster reels. The pump panel is out of sight behind the first compartment door. Note the double bumper bars, a standard Maxim feature at this time. Maxim apparatus is widely used throughout New England.

Maxim's "home territory" has always been the New England states and the northeastern U. S. But the products of this Middleboro, Mass. manufacturer can be found in fire houses in scattered locations right across the country. This 1,250 GPM triple combination pumper, for instance, was shipped out to the West Coast, to Oakland, Cal. Portland, Ore. also had a couple of Maxims at one time. The largest Maxim customer in the midwest was Indianapolis, which had a large fleet of Maxims. A couple were also delivered in Illinois.

Three years after they had resumed peacetime production, American fire apparatus manufacturers were still swamped with orders, as communities large and small sought to bring their fire protection up to date.

The Ward LaFrance Truck Corp. of Elmira Heights, N.Y., had redesigned and restyled its standard model fire apparatus and was doing a brisk business. This company's premier model pumpers were identified as Ward LaFrance Elmira Eagles. These 500 to 750 GPM models were powered by Waukesha engines and were equipped with Waterous pumps. Most were still of the open semi-cab style, but 3-man closed cabs were optionally available. Ward also offered a long-wheelbase quadruple combination. Among the more unusual options available on Ward LaFrance apparatus was a convertible canvas roof for open-cab models, and stylish fender skirts for the rear wheel openings. With these classy appearance items in place, a town's new Ward was as snappy in appearance as the most modern passenger cars of the day.

A new name was added to the roll-call of U. S. fire apparatus builders this year. The Crown Coach Corp. of Los Angeles, a builder of quality motor coaches and specialized transportation equipment, delivered a custom-built 1,250 GPM pumper to West Covina, Calif., in 1949, the company's first venture into this field. Crown Fire-coach remains today a respected West Coast builder, and over the years has delivered hundreds of pumpers to California communities large and small. Crown apparatus utilized the Waterous pump and the standard engine was the Hall-Scott. Crown is still the only custom fire apparatus builder on the West Coast.

The Boston Fire Department was engaged in a major fire apparatus modernization program and had purchased a large fleet of new apparatus from Mack, Pirsch, Ward LaFrance, Maxim and FWD.

The Oren-Roanoke Corp. previewed its new line of custom-chassis Big Job pumpers of 750 and 1,000 GPM capacity. These were powered by 190 and 240 horsepower engines. The company also offered a complete line of smaller pumpers mounted on commercial chassis.

The Young Fire Equipment Corp. of Buffalo, N. Y., had been appointed the official service agent for all apparatus built and sold by the Defunct Buffalo Fire Appliance Co. Young went on to become a very successful local builder, and is still in business today at Lancaster, N. Y.

Barton pumps, best known for their front-mount in-stallations by the American Fire Apparatus Co. of Battle Creek, Mich., were also available in conventional midship-mounted versions.

Not all fire apparatus sales were limited to municipalities. Wealthy individuals with vast holdings to protect were good customers, too. In 1949, Boston millionaire Cy Hyde purchased his third John Bean High Pressure Fog Fire Fighter, to protect his 2,000-acre estate in New Hampshire. Mounted on an International chassis, it had a 600-gallon booster tank and high pressure twin reels capable of putting out 60 GPM at 850 pounds pressure.

The L. B. Smith Co. of Camp Hill, Pa. introduced a unique tractor-trailer combination pumper and tanker designed for rural fire protection districts. Pulled by a Ford F-7 or F-8 tractor, or a White Model WC-20T, it carried 2,000 gallons of water and was equipped with a Hale pump of from 60 to 150 GPM capacity. Standard equipment included portable floodlights and miscellaneous other fire department tools. This reservoir on wheels was marketed as the Smithco Fire Fighter.

The Four Wheel Drive Auto Co. of Clintonville, Wis., had added tractor-drawn wood aerial ladder trucks to its line.

Here is one of Philadelphia's 1949 Ford booster and hose wagons hard at work at a fire. The turret pipe on the left side of the apparatus is being shut down. This was one of 24 identical units built by the Approved Fire Equipment Co. of Rockville Center, N. Y. on Ford F-6 truck chassis. This is Engine 55's wagon pouring it on.

Included in the big Philadelphia Bureau of Fire equipment order were 24 of the combination hose and booster trucks. This order was fulfilled by the Approved Fire Equipment Co. of Rockville Center, N. Y. These rigs were built on medium-duty Ford truck chassis. This one mounts a large deck nozzle on the left rear side, and it has an American LaFrance bell. The rig shown here ran as Wagon 46.

Philadelphia purchased an incredible amount of new fire apparatus in 1949. These include 32 new Autocar pumpers, 24 hose wagons, four 85-foot Pirsch tractor-drawn aerials, and the rescue squad truck shown here. This is a 1949 International chassis with an Approved Fire Equipment Co. heavy rescue squad body, which was assigned to Rescue Squad No. 3.

Watertown, N. Y. got this Seagrave 750 GPM pumper with a standard canopy cab. The Seagrave Corp. was proud of the fact that it built its own pumps, bodies, engines and aerials ladders all in its own Columbus, Ohio plant. The old Seagrave plant was at 2000 South High Street in Columbus and had been built before the turn of the century. It served the company until 1964, when the operation was transferred to Clintonville, Wis., after Seagrave's acquisition by the FWD Corp.

Starting with four in 1936, the Detroit Fire Department purchased only Seagrave Safety Sedan pumping engines until 1960. Seven of these 1,000 gallon-per-minute sedans were delivered to Detroit in 1949, and several are still in service as "X", or spare, rigs. Note the Mars signal light on the roof. These powerful engines had Seagrave V-12s and saw much heavy fire service. This delivery photo shows Ser. No. D-7847 prior to shipment to the Motor City.

Seagrave built a small number of Detroit-type sedan pumpers for other fire departments. Cleveland, Ohio had several. This one was delivered to Coatesville, Pa. A number of fire departments found the Seagrave sedan body ideal for rescue squad use, and at least four were sold as squads. This Coatesville job is all decked out with flags for its appearance in a fire department parade.

Upper Darby, Pa. ordered this 1949 Seagrave 85-foot service aerial. It has a 4-section hydraulic aerial ladder and carries a complement of Seagrave wood ground ladders. This ladder truck is powered by Seagrave's big V-12 engine.

Jackson, Tenn. placed this Seagrave 1000 gallon-per-minute pumper with conventional 3-man open cab into service in 1949. The Seagrave bell was always mounted on the upper cowl on the right-hand side of the rig. A Mars light on top of the radiator shell clears the way through traffic for this pumper, and a large rotary beacon light has been added on a post behind the cab. Ladders carried on this side include a 24-foot extension and a 12-foot roof ladder with folding hooks.

Another chassis not uncommon under fire apparatus was the Federal truck. The General Fire Truck Corp. built this big triple combination on a Federal chassis, and equipped it with a streamlined 4-door sedan cab. This engine, with 500 GPM pump, was delivered to the Detroit suburb of Allen Park, Mich. Note the compartmented rear fenders and the wide metal trim strip along the side of this General-Federal. Like a great many fire trucks in this cold war period, this one carried the Civil Defense emblem.

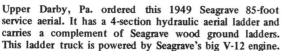

Waterloo, Iowa, which received an unusual American La-France 4-wheel-drive Series 700 pumper in 1948, also purchased this all-wheel-drive pumper from Elmira. The Ford F-7 chassis is equipped with a Marmon-Herrington 4 x 4 drive system, and an American LaFrance 500 GPM pump. This pumper was designed for use in Waterloo's suburbs, and carried a large booster tank. When delivered, it responded as Engine No. 8.

Here is a more conventional Ford-LaFrance. American LaFrance built this 500 gallon-per-minute triple combination pumper for Streator, Ill. It is painted white, and has a 400 gallon booster tank, and is built on a Ford F-5 chassis. American LaFrance delivered a sizeable number of these small commercial jobs, which were available on any chassis. But Fords seemed to outnumber all others.

Most of the 700 Series fire engines built in the U. S. and Canada were fairly stock jobs—pumpers, aerials, quads and quints, plus a few squad and booster cars. Two of the most unique 700 Series models built were designed and built for the Toronto, Ontario Fire Department by LaFrance Fire Engine & Foamite in that Canadian city. They were Model 700-BJC high pressure hose and booster cars built to the specifications of Toronto Chief Peter Herd. Still in service in 1975, they respond to alarms only in the downtown high value district. They can deliver 2,700 GPM, and carry 125-gallon booster tanks. Each also carries a fixed deck turret and a large portable Eastman turret gun. Alan Craig caught High Pressure Monitor No. 2 on the ramp in front of Toronto's No. 5 fire station.

Shown above is an American LaFrance 700 Series quadruple combination. This quad has a 500 gallon-per-minute centrifugal pump, and was delivered to Protection Hook and Ladder Co. No. 1, of Maywood, N. J. American LaFrance apparatus starting in late 1948 was built with the new flat-faced bumper shown here. This style of bumper was used until the early 1960's, on the later Series 800 and even 900 apparatus. Note the fire extinguishers handily mounted on the front running boards.

American LaFrance began production of this type of Series 700 tractor-drawn aerial in 1947. These were normally built only in 85 and 100-foot sizes, but at least one 75-footer was sold. Philadelphia had six of these 85-foot metal aerials. These aerials were equipped with four stabilizer jacks. The front two extended out from the loading edge of the trailer platform. The other two dropped down just behind the front fender of the trailer. They were manually operated. This aerial was assigned to Ladder 12.

Boston, Mass. proceeded with its major equipment replacement program. The Boston Fire Department purchased a number of heavy hose wagons of this type, all built on Mack chassis, in 1947, 1948, and 1949. Some of these hose wagons were equipped with Cardox chemical equipment. All carried two big deck turrets, one at the front of the hose body and the other mounted at the rear. This is Engine Co. No. 10's Mack Hose Wagon not long after it entered service. Several of these battle-scarred veterans are still in front-line service in Boston today.

One of Mack's most popular models was the ubiquitous Type 85 pumper with 750 GPM pump. These handsome fire engines had earned a reputation for quality and dependability and could be found on fire departments from coast to coast. The Type 85 pumper shown here was delivered to the Cos Cob Station in Greenwich, Conn. Note the lunging Mack Bulldog ornament on top of the Radiator shell.

Chicago placed a major order with Mack for no less than 32 of these 1,000 gallon-per-minute pumpers, most of which were delivered and put into service in 1949. These pumpers were powered by Mack 6-cylinder engines and had Hale pumps. They were Type 95 triple combinations. Chicago had begun to shift away from the sedan-cab type of pumper purchased earlier, and specified 2-man closed cabs on these units.

New Orleans was also on a major fire equipment replacement program in 1949. The New Orleans Fire Department followed up its 1948 purchase of four new Ahrens-Fox Model HT piston pumpers with an order for six Macks. The 1949 order included five Type 95 pumpers with 1,000 GPM pumps and one 750 GPM Type 85 pumper. Some of the new Macks are seen lined up here shortly after being placed in service.

Mack's smaller series pumper at this time was the Type 45. This is a 1949 Mack Type 45 with 500 gallon-per-minute pump that was delivered to the town of Harbor Springs, Mich. This pumper has two booster hose reels mounted as a unit on top of the booster tank. Mack had been building this style of apparatus since the late 1930s.

The Mack Truck Manufacturing Corp. had built no aerial ladder trucks since the early 1930s, when it had marketed a successful line of 75 and 85-foot tractor-drawn aerials with engine-driven hoists. But Mack got back into the aerial-ladder field in 1948, when it began to offer its customers a 3-section, hydraulically-operated aerial of 65 and 75-foot height. This 1949 Mack 75-foot service aerial was delivered to Niles, Mich. It was a Type 85 with 2-man semi-cab.

One of the more unusual Macks built in 1949 was this "dual-cowl phaeton" with 4-door cab and two separate windshields, delivered to Los Angeles, Calif. This was a special manifold hose wagon, designed to supplement the single American LaFrance manifold delivered in 1938, and the two Seagrave manifolds delivered the same year. A Type 21, this Mack sported a powerful fireboat turret nozzle and had 10 outlets for 2½-inch hose. The manifold wagons served as water distributors for L. A.'s famed Duplex Engine Companies. This Mack carried 3½-inch hose in its rear hose bed, and a load of 2½-inch line was carried transversely in side compartment in the middle of the body. The Mack was assigned to L.A.F.D. Engine Co. No. 3.

With hood up, Newark, New Jersey's Engine No. 20 is seen here hard at work at a fire. This pumper is a 1949 FWD Model F-100-T equipped with a 2-stage 1,000 gallon-per-minute pump. Engine 20 has a 150-gallon booster tank and is powered by a Waukesha 6-cylinder engine. The Four Wheel Drive Auto Co. of Clintonville, Wisc. was aggressively marketing its 500 to 1,250 GPM pumpers, which came with all-wheel-drive as standard equipment. There weren't many places an FWD could not go.

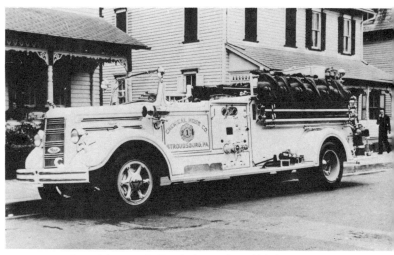

Stroudsburg, Pa.'s Chemical Hose Co., which has traditionally used white-painted apparatus, owned this 1949 Mack Type 45 pumper. Mack soon discontinued this smaller size line, which had been in continuous production since the late 1930s. This pumper carries three lengths of small diameter hard suction hose, probably 2½-inch.

In addition to several Macks, the Boston Fire Dept. also ordered several FWD hose wagons in 1949. The one shown here on the firehouse ramp was assigned to Engine Co. No. 21. These hose wagons ran with pumpers as 2-piece engine companies. Boston hose wagons carried two turret pipes—one large-volume fixed monitor and a smaller one which could be operated off the truck or removed and placed where needed on the fireground.

The Pittsburgh, Pa. fire department repair shops built several of these long wheelbase city service ladder trucks, all on Reo truck chassis. The result was a fleet of practical, good-looking rigs that saw many years of service. The 1949 Reo shown was assigned to Truck Co. No. 45.

1949

Ahrens-Fox continued to find customers for its powerful piston pumpers. This 1,000 gallon-per-minute Model HT Twin Triple was built for the Freeport, Long Island, N. Y. Fire Dept. It has a short canopy-style cab. When it was retired from service a few years ago, this pumper was saved from the scrapyard by some appreciative fire buffs. Consequently, the Freeport Fox is still an active participant in fire department parades and at apparatus musters in the area.

The Akron suburb of Stow, Ohio is the owner of this good-looking 1949 Ahrens-Fox Model VC pumper, equipped with two booster reels, it is a 500 gallon-per-minute model with open 3-man semi-cab. Stow's Ahrens-Fox carries Serial No. 9142.

The John Bean Division of the Lansing, Mich. based Food Machinery Corp. was selling a lot of these high pressure fog fire fighters. This one was used by Bay City, Michigan to augment its Civil Defense program, and is built on a 1949 Reo chassis. These Bean High Pressure Fog trucks carried their own water supply. Standard equipment included two trigger-type fog guns, or nozzles which unleashed their fire-killing spray at 850 pounds pump pressure; by contrast, normal pump pressure is about 160 pounds. Note the standard equipment spotlights and the windshield for the men riding the rear step.

John Bean built a large proportion of its high pressure fog fire fighters on International, Ford, Reo and Dodge truck chassis, but the company would mount its equipment on any chassis specified by the purchaser. This Bean high pressure job, built on a White Motor Co. truck chassis, is unusual in that it also has an open semi-cab. The bulk of Bean fog units had three-man cabs. This one was built for the Leonardo Fire Co. in New Jersey. John Bean also delivered some high pressure fog equipment mounted on city service hook and ladder trucks.

A new name joined the fire apparatus industry this year. The Crown Coach Corp. of Los Angeles entered the fire engine field in 1949. The first apparatus delivered to a fire department by this company was the 1,250 gallon-per-minute pumper shown here, which was sold to West Covina, Calif. Crown is still in business today. Current Crowns look strikingly similar to this Job One. Note the rounded rear cab entrance and the deck turret.

Another firm doing a lot of business was the American Fire Apparatus Division of American-Marsh Pumps, of Battle Creek, Mich. American delivered hundreds of these commercial-chassis fire engines, with midship or front-mounted pumps, to smaller fire departments all over the country. Here is a 500 GPM midship model built on an International K-Series truck chassis. Note the bell on the front bumper, and the roto-ray lights on the cab roof. This unit carried two hose reels, each equipped with Barton Super Fog Gun nozzles.

This is Philadelphia's second "Giant Deluge 99" master stream unit. The 1949 Reo chassis was equipped by the U.S. Fire Apparatus Co. of Wilmington, Delaware as a high pressure pipe line wagon and ran for years as the P.F.D. Pipe Line No. 5. When the original Giant Deluge 99—a converted 1941 Autocar—was taken out of service, its heavy firefighting artillery was transferred to the 1949 Reo. The big gun in 99's arsenal is a power-operated Chiksan Intelli-Giant turret nozzle.

To co-ordinate vital communications on the fireground, the Philadelphia Fire Dept. dispatched this mobile command center to all major fires and disasters. It was used by both the fire department and the police as a command post. The body builder is unknown, but the Civil Defense job was built up on a Chevrolet chassis in 1949. Fireground tactics and strategic moves were plotted in this unit while the fire raged nearby.

Exactly who built the body on this high-bodied rescue squad truck is not known for sure—it resembled the bodywork done by General-Detroit, but it could be a Proctor-Keefe. At any rate, this heavy Ford squad was used by the Harper Woods, Mich. Fire Department up to about 1963. This long-wheelbase rig sports Mars lights on each front fender, and a Federal "Q" siren on its roof. Note the bell in front of the grille.

This is one of the 32 Autocar 750 gallon-per-minute pumpers delivered to the Philadelphia Bureau of Fire in 1949. It is believed that these pumpers were built by the U. S. Fire Apparatus Co. of Wilmington, Del. Note how the pump is mounted out in the open between the cab and the hose body. The booster reel is carried directly above the pump. All Philly rigs of this era were equipped with a set of whirling Buckeye Roto-Rays. This tough-looking Autocar saw service with Engine Co. No. 22.

Atlantic City, N. J. had a few of these small hose and booster wagons, which responded on alarms with regular engine companies. This one is built on a 1949 Ford F-6 truck chassis and carries 125 gallons of water. Note the front-mounted bell and the 3-way turret pipe attached to the side of this rig.

One of the smaller West Coast fire apparatus builders was the L. N. Curtis and Sons operation in Oakland, Calif. Curtis built this 500 gallon-per-minute triple combination pumping engine on a 1949 Diamond T truck chassis for the Roseland Dsitrict in Santa Rosa, Calif. The Curtis-Diamond T has an enclosed pump panel, and a cut-down 3-man open cab.

This Maxim quadruple combination was originally built for Thomaston, Conn., but when replaced by a newer rig was sold to the Terryville, Conn. Fire Dept. Maxim built several quads of this style, with 3-man closed cabs and enclosed pump panels. This one was rated at 750 GPM. Note the Eastman portable deluge gun atop the hose bed. This rig has been retrofitted with small West Coast-type rear view mirrors.

The Hahn Motor Co. of Hamburg, Pa. built custom-chassis fire engines for a number of fire companies in the northeast part of the country. Most were pumpers, but Hahn did turn out some quadruple combinations, and a very few straight city service ladder trucks. This 1949 Hahn city service hook and ladder truck was used by the fire department of Sparkill, N. Y. It uses the assembled Hahn chassis, and has a big 3-man cab. Note the bell mounted far back on the completely enclosed ladder bed. Two pike poles are carried on the side of this truck and there is a wire equipment basket on top.

Long Branch, N. J. took delivery of this 1949 Peter Pirsch 85-foot tractor-drawn aerial ladder truck. Pirsch apparatus was powered by the popular Waukesha 6-cylinder fire apparatus engine. This rig has an open 3-man cab and carries wood ground ladders. The flags have been attached to the front bumper for a parade.

The heavy custom fire apparatus chassis built by the Available Truck Co. of Chicago was used by a number of fire apparatus builders. This Available chassis carries a 750 gallon-per-minute pumper body with 3-man closed cab built by the Oren-Roanoke Corp. It was delivered to Ellicott City, Md. in 1949 and was subsequently purchased by the fire Department of Forest Hill, Tenn. Dick Adelman took the photo of this rig at its second home.

1950

At the mid-point in the 20th Century, the state of the fire engine builder's art had reached a new plateau. Only the old-timers could remember the fire horses, and all but a few steamers left in museums had long been relegated to the junkpile. It was hard to believe that 44 years had passed since the first motor fire engine was placed in service away back in 1906. More and more modern fire engines had enclosed cabs for the comfort and safety of their crews, and in the years following the Second World War 2-way radios made instantaneous communication with the central alarm office possible at all times. Radio communication was probably second only to the internal combustion engine in revolutionizing firefighting operations.

The familiar American LaFrance 700 Series fire engines could be found in fire houses from coast to coast. Standard powerplant in the 700 was one of four American LaFrance V-12 engines. These were as follows: the company's 500 and 600 gallon-per-minute pumpers were powered by what was known as the F Engine, a 170-horsepower Twelve. Next in size was the G Engine, a V-12 rated at 204 brake horsepower. The most prolific was the popular J Engine, certified to deliver 215 horsepower. This engine was standard equipment in American LaFrance 1,000 GPM pumpers, all aerials whether of the service type or tractor-drawn; in quadruple and quintuple combinations, and city service ladder trucks. The largest of Elmira's V-12s was the big E Engine, which was available in pumpers of 1,000, 1,250 and 1,500 GPM capacity. The smaller ALF 12-cylinder engines were based on the aging Auburn-Lycoming design.

The Seagrave Corp. proudly proclaimed that a Seagrave was a Seagrave from the front bumper right back to the rear step. Seagrave in its Columbus, Ohio plant produced its own 12-cylinder, V-type engines, centrifugal pumps, bodies, aerial ladder and aerial ladder hoists.

The Mack International Truck Corp. announced its new Golden Anniversary Model 85 service aerial ladder truck. Built on the improved and modestly restyled Mack fire apparatus chassis, the new Model 85 was a 75-footer with open cab and semi-closed ladder beds. The 3-section, all-powered aerial ladder unit was supplied by Maxim.

In yet another reorganization, Ahrens-Fox was dissolved again and all of its assets were sold to the Cleveland Automatic Machine Co. Harold LeBlond was named president of the new Ahrens-Fox Division of this company. The manufacture of piston and centrifugal type pumpers continued in the Norwood plant which Ahrens-Fox shared with the machine tool company.

The Howe Fire Apparatus Co. built this well-equipped triple combination pumper on a Diamond T truck chassis. It has a 500 GPM midship-mounted pump, and a 4-door sedan cab. Note the three lengths of hard suction hose, and the overhead ladder rack. This engine was delivered to the Smithfield Volunteer Fire Dept., Inc.

In other industry developments this year, American LaFrance delivered its last wood, spring-raised aerial ladder trucks to Boston, Mass. These were 700 Series 85-footers. The Approved Fire Equipment Co. of Rockville Center, N. Y. was building a highly popular line of heavy duty rescue squad trucks, and the Four Wheel Drive Auto Co. was delivering many of its go-anywhere 750 and 1,000 GPM pumpers. The distinctive FWD's were powered by Waukesha engines and were offered in both open and closed cab models.

Bells were still standard equipment on most new fire apparatus, but the latest thing in warning lights was a bubble-shaped dome light called the Beacon Ray Fireball. It was produced by the Federal Sign and Signal Corp.

Buffalo, N. Y. in 1950 received a large fleet of Ward LaFrance pumpers and aerial ladder truck tractors. A new General-Detroit subsidiary, the General-Pacific Corp. of Los Angeles, was now building custom-chassis fire apparatus. Los Angeles County purchased a number of these.

The Boyer Fire Apparatus Co. of Logansport, Ind. built this 600 gallon-per-minute pumper for Glen Ellyn, Ill. This pumper is built on a 1950 Available chassis, and is equipped with a high pressure fog pump. It carries 1000 gallons of water, too. Note the compartmented rear fenders and bumper-mounted siren and bell. This Boyer responds as Engine No. 4 on the Glen Ellyn Volunteer Fire Company.

Another major West Coast fire apparatus builder is the P. E. Van Pelt Co., of Oakdale, Calif. Van Pelt is still in business today. This interesting photo shows a Van Pelt triple combination pumper on a White Motor Co. chassis, with open semi-cab and squirrel-tail suction hookup, parked beside an aircraft owned by Van Pelt. The plane was used to speed parts and service to municipalities using Van Pelt fire trucks.

Truck Co. No. 7 of the Philadelphia Bureau of Fire received one of the four American LaFrance 85-foot tractor-drawn aerial ladder trucks purchased in 1950. These aerials had 3-section metal ladders and fixed-position tiller seats. Four 100-foot aerial trucks of this type were also placed in service in Philadelphia this year. Note the protective cover over the aerial ladder control pedestal on the turntable, and the Roto-Rays mounted on the left front of the 700 Series cab.

1950

American LaFrance in 1950 built its last spring-raised, wooden aerial ladders. At least three of these 85-foot tractor-drawn aerials were shipped from Elmira to the Boston Fire Department. Drawn by Series 700 tractors, they carried booster hose in a basket on the tractor just behind the V-12 engine. This is one of these rare aerials, as used by Boston's Ladder Co. No. 12. The 700 Series tractors were eventually replaced by other makes. As late as 1974, one of these venerable wood "stocks" was still on the Boston reserve roster, drawn by a 1956 Mack B-model tractor. Paul Finn of Boston Ladder Co. No. 20, an apparatus buff, came up with this photo of one of the last of a line that dates back in principle to the turn of the century.

Philadelphia's fire apparatus modernization program continued into 1950 with the delivery of 13 more American LaFrance aerial ladder trucks, eight hose and booster wagons, seven more Autocar pumping engines and several additional special-purpose units. This is one of five 1950 American LaFrance 65-foot "junior" service aerials in this order. Note the lack of any overhang of the 3-section metal aerial ladder at the rear. This spanking-new truck has just been placed into service at Truck Co. No. 17.

American LaFrance delivered this Series 700 quintuple combination to the U. S. Canal Zone. It had a 750 GPM "Twinflow" pump, and a 3-section, 75-foot aerial ladder. The quint carried a pump, aerial, hose, ground ladders and booster system and was a complete fire fighting unit. The Series 700 quint could be equipped with any size pump, a 150 or 200-gallon booster tank, and 65, 75, 85 or 100-foot aerial ladder.

Rescue Co. No. 1 in East Orange, N. J. ordered this big American LaFrance 700 Series Rescue Squad Truck. This heavy rescue unit carries tons of rescue gear in its many side compartments, and the entire crew can ride in the enclosed rear body. There is room in the canopy cab for five more. This was a one-off body. American LaFrance built a standard rescue squad car body on the 700 Series pumper chassis, but this had an open rear body. The length of the frame on this truck indicates that it was probably built on a ladder truck chassis.

The American LaFrance 700 Series fire apparatus kept rolling off the Elmira, N. Y. assembly floor as U. S. fire apparatus manufacturers struggled to meet a huge backlog of orders precipitated in the postwar years. Series 700 pumpers were supplied with 750, 1000, 1250 and 1500 gallon-per-minute centrifugal pumps. The larger series 700 pumpers were powered by the American LaFrance 275-horsepower V-12 engine. This is a 1000 GPM job with closed 5-man cab. Booster reels were optional; the booster hose was often carried in a compartment just above the pump panel. The booster reel could be mounted on top, or on the rear step.

The San Francisco Fire Dept. received this 1950 American LaFrance 700 Series pumper, which eventually became a spare engine. Note the several sizes of hard suction hose carried. The 1,000 GPM pumper has been retrofitted with the Federal Q siren.

The versatile Chicago Fire Department motor shops turned out some real hybrids. This aerial is a good example. The tractor is a 1950 Available, but the trailer was built by the C. F. D. shop crew in 1938, and has an 85-foot American LaFrance wood aerial. Chicago had two rigs like this. The one shown here ran as Hook & Ladder No. 17. Note the cut-out in the grille to accommodate the Mars warning light, and the bell concealed behind the lower grille bars.

Kenworth motor fire apparatus is fairly common in the northwestern states. Kenworth did build some fire engines in its Seattle, Wash. main plant, but a number of chassis were sold to other fire equipment builders. This is a Kenworth-chassis triple combination built by the Howard Corp. of Portland, Oregon. It has a 1250 GPM Hale pump and carries 2,400 feet of hose. It is lettered for the D.C.F.D.

Here is yet another Approved heavy rescue squad truck built for the City of Philadelphia. The hatch visible on the roof of this rig covered a pair of big spotlights which could be raised to illuminate the scene of a night fire. This one is built on an International R Series chassis. Note the small moveable windows at the top of this big squad body. The rig shown here was used by Rescue Squad No. 4.

The Oren-Roanoke Corp. was also building an assembled, custom-chassis job. The big 1000 gallon-per-minute triple combination pumper shown above is an Oren Model 1000/1600, with a 550-gallon booster tank and a "wet water" proportioning system. The semi-cab could seat three. This Oren Custom was built for Ludlow, Mass. Oren-Roanoke offered a choice of 190 and 240-horsepower engines in its apparatus.

Norwood, Ohio received this 1950 Ahrens-Fox Model HT piston pumper of 1000 GPM capacity. Norwood's rig has a rather angular coupe cab. It is doubtful whether the transverse mounted booster hose reel came from the factory installed this way. Ahrens-Fox was building fewer and fewer piston pumpers by this time.

Mount Healthy, Ohio received this big 1950 Ahrens-Fox Model I-C-U quadruple combination. Carrying Serial No. 9153, it has a midship-mounted 750 GPM centrifugal pump. This is one of two Ahrens-Fox fire engines on this department. The other is an equally well-maintained 1938 Model VR-500. Note the 3-man semi-cab and hood mounted siren. The ladder bed is also semi-enclosed.

The "HC" in the model designation of this 1950 Ahrens-Fox Model HC pumper, delivered to Royersford, Pa., indicates that the truck is powered by the Hercules engine and has a centrifugal pump. Note the big 7-man canopy cab and extra-wide enclosed rear body on this rig. The single red flasher tunnelled into the center of the cab roof is also unique.

The Greensburg, Pa. Fire Department ordered this striking 2-toned Seagrave quadruple combination. This apparatus has the short canopy cab with oval side windows, and the elongated front fenders. Note the compact appearance of this truck and lack of ladder overhang. The V-12 Seagrave is equipped with a 1000 GPM pump. There appears to be a catwalk down the center of equipment compartments atop the ladder bed.

Compare this Seagrave quad with the one built for Greensburg, Pa. It has the "standard" front fenders, and an open 3-man cab. The pump is a 750 GPM Seagrave Centrifugal. This is the rig's maiden portrait, before it set out on its delivery trip. It is not known which Newton purchased this apparatus.

This Super Deluxe Mack pumper was the center of attention at the 1950 International Association of Fire Chiefs Convention held out on the West Coast. The 77th Annual Conference of the IAFC was held in San Francisco. Mack exhibited this elaborately trimmed 125 pumper built for Palm Springs, Calif. The white-painted 1250 GPM pumper has hand-painted city emblems on each side of the seat, whitewall tires and air brakes. It carries 400 gallons of water and has two booster hose reels with electric rewinds. Note the preconnected, swivel-mounted length of hard suction hose carried over the rear fender. This permitted hookup to the hydrant or water supply within seconds.

1950

This Mack has had two careers on the Detroit Fire Department. It was purchased in 1950 as an aerial ladder tractor, and replaced a worn-out Seagrave tractor under one of the city's wooden aerials. After several years as a spare and driver-training unit, it was converted to a wrecker by the D. F. D. shops to replace the department's 1920 Standard wrecker. Most large cities have wreckers to tow damaged or disabled rigs, or for rescue work at major disasters. The Mack shown here has just towed Detroit's restored 1908 Ahrens steamer to a parade where the horses were waiting.

Here is another one of San Francisco's shop rebuilds. The body of this High Pressure Battery Wagon was transferred from an older model American LaFrance chassis to this new Mack chassis by the S.F.F.D. motor shops. Note the complex system of valves, and the inlets for the high capacity Gorter turret nozzle mounted between the semi-cab and the high hose body. San Francisco rigs at this time were still painted a very dark maroon instead of the traditional fire department red. The round emblem on the door is the San Francisco city crest.

The Hahn Motor Co. of Hamburg, Pa. built this massive-looking triple combination pumper for Fire Co. No. 1 of Roslyn, Pa. Hahn assembled its own custom fire apparatus chassis and had its own distinctive front-end design, which was unmistakeable for anything else. Another Hahn is parked behind the Roslyn rig in this photo, taken at one of the many fire department parades held annually throughout the northeast.

The City of New Orleans, which had placed a fleet of six new Mack engines into service the previous year, got this custom-built Mack rescue squad truck in 1950. This squad has a full-width compartmented body and 3-man semi-cab. Note the fixed deck monitor at the rear of the body, and the Bresnan distributor cellar nozzle carried on the running board just below the cab door.

St. Paul, Minn. upgraded its fire department in one fell swoop in 1950. In a massive apparatus modernization program, St. Paul Fire Dept. engine companies 1 through 14 each got new Mack Type 95 triple combination pumpers. These 1000 GPM pumpers had single booster reels and open semi-cabs. Note the Federal Q siren mounted on the cowl. The pumper shown here went to St. P. F. D. Engine Co. No. 14.

Mack
FIRE APPARATUS

1950

This Ford-chassised rescue squad truck started its fire service career as a salvage patrol wagon on the Chicago Fire Dept. It was later sold to Midlothian, Ill. This rig was built by the Jacob Press Sons Co. of Chicago on a 1950 Ford F-7 chassis, but it apparently proved too light for heavy-duty fire insurance patrol duty. Fire apparatus photographer Dan Martin caught Midlothian's squad as it wheeled out of quarters on a run. Note the Chicago paint job and the bumper-mounted bell.

This pumper is another fascinating melange of manufacturers. To start with, the chassis is a 1950 Ford F-8. The body was built by the Yankee Body Co. of Los Angeles, and utilized a Seagrave 500 gallon-per-minute centrifugal pump. This hybrid was built for the Ventura County, Calif. Fire Dept., where it responded as Engine Co. No. 51.

Ward LaFrance also built some fire apparatus on commercial truck chassis. This is one of the "Pipe Line" high pressure hose wagons delivered by Ward LaFrance to the Philadelphia Bureau of Fire in 1950. These big hose wagons were built on Ford chassis. Note the height of the hose body and the two huge turret nozzles. Like all Philly rigs, Pipe Line 2 sports a set of revolving roto-ray warning lights.

This high pressure hose truck is still rolling to extra-alarm fires in Detroit, but on a new set of wheels. The General Fire Truck Corp. of Detroit built this big job in 1950 on a GMC chassis. It responded for many years as High Pressure Co. No. 1. When Detroit's high pressure pumping system was closed down, this rig was redesigned as Boat Tender 1. responding to waterfront alarms with Engine 16, the fireboat "John Kendall." In 1972, the rear body of this unit was transferred to a new Chevrolet chassis and the General-Detroit, with its two large turret pipes, became the first lime-green rig on the D.F.D.

The General-Pacific Corporation delivered a number of these custom-chassis fire engines to fire departments on the West Coast. This is one of several 900 gallon-per-minute General-Pacific triple combination pumpers purchased by the Los Angeles County Fire Dept. Note the amount of gear piled on top of the hose bed. L. A. County Engine 54 has two booster reels and a portable deluge nozzle.

The Four Wheel Drive Auto Company of Clintonville, Wisc. started building tractor-drawn wood aerial ladder trucks in 1949. In 1950, FWD delivered this 85-foot, tractor-drawn wood aerial to the fire department of Superior, Wisconsin. Note the siren mounted out on the front of the hood, and the large equipment compartment on the trailer. Many aerials of this type, but with closed 2-man cabs, were built for the Chicago Fire Department between 1949 and 1956.

The Seagrave Corp. observed its 70th anniversary in 1951. It was in 1881 that Frederick S. Seagrave set up shop in Detroit to build ladders for use in the verdant Michigan fruit orchards. His well-built ladders were soon being used by volunteer fire departments, and Mr. Seagrave added 2 and 4-wheel hand-drawn ladder carriages to his line. Before long he was specializing in fire equipment, and in 1891 moved his factory to Columbus, Ohio.

To mark this important anniversary, Seagrave introduced a whole new series of dramatically restyled fire apparatus which it christened the 70th Anniversary Series. The new models began to come off the assembly line in Columbus in the middle of the year. The restyled Seagraves had a wide, sweeping grille design with the siren built right into the nose. Two deep-skirted grille bars spanned the wide front end between new style box fenders with integral headlights. The new design gave Seagrave's pumpers and aerials a massive new look. This engine-ahead-of-cab style Seagrave remained in production for the next 19 years, and hundreds of the 70th Anniversary models are still in service today. The big V-12 powerplant and powerful centrifugal pump were retained. The rear fenders included spacious, built-in equipment compartments as standard equipment.

Ahrens-Fox underwent another agonizing reorganization in 1951. The year previous, the company had been dissolved, then reformed into the Ahrens-Fox Division of the Cleveland Automatic Machine Co. of Norwood, Ohio. On August 7, 1951, this division was sold to General Truck Sales, Inc. of Cincinnati. The announcement was made by Walter Walkenhorst, president of General Truck, which had been the Cincinnati area distributor for General Motors Corp. trucks since 1938. Ahrens-Fox was now building only a few front-mounted Model HT piston pumpers annually, and fewer and fewer of its big centrifugals.

The Kenworth Motor Truck Corp. of Seattle, Wash., a well-known and highly respected builder of heavy-duty highway truck tractors, was building a small number of triple combination motor pumping engines and city service ladder trucks. The Kenworth fire engines were powered by 6-cylinder Waukesha engines rated at 240 horsepower. Kenworth's Model 720 pumper featured a 750 gallon-per-minute centrifugal pump and had a 300-gallon booster tank. The Kenworth fire apparatus was available with open or closed 3-man cabs, and closely resembled the company's famous highway line haulers in appearance.

The General Fire Truck Corp. of Detroit was at its zenith during this period. The company delivered eight 750 GPM General-Detroit pumpers with fully open cabs to Dallas, Tex.

The 1951 International Association of Fire Chiefs Conference was held in Grand Rapids, Mich. this year. Seagrave's new 70th Anniversary models made their formal fire service debut here, and the Grand Rapids Fire Dept. put on an impressive display of its fire-fighting power during the convention.

One of the more unusual fire engines built this year was the Monarch, which was hand-built by the Custom Body Service Co. of Piscataway, N. J. Built on a White truck chassis and incorporating a 750 GPM pump, the Monarch was superstreamlined, had an open cab and carried all of its equipment inside and out of sight. A red warning light was built into the front of the hood, and its appearance was exceptionally sleek. The high-styled Monarch, however, proved too costly to build, and the single demonstrator was sold to the Oldwick, N. J. Fire Dept. which still owns it.

Ward LaFrance pumping engines of this period were generally powered by Waukesha 6-cylinder Fire Fighter engines, and were equipped with Waterous pumps. The businesslike-looking pumper shown here was built for Peabody, Mass. Note the extended playout arms on the single booster reel, and the flashers mounted on the outboard ends of the front bumper.

Ward-LaFrance Truck Corporation, of Elmira Heights, N. Y., not to be confused with American-LaFrance of Elmira proper, built hundreds of pumpers of this type through the 1950s. The good-looking unit shown here is a 750 GPM Model 83-T. Options on this pumper include the Beacon Ray warning light and gated suction intake on the pump panel.

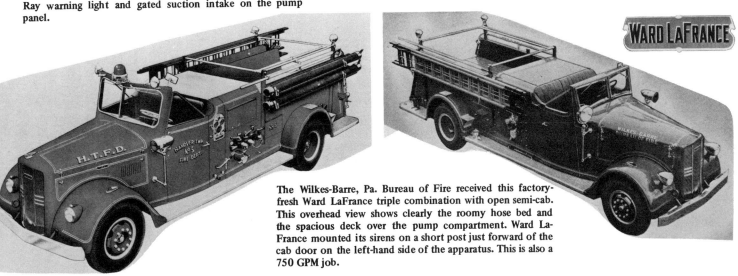

The Wilkes-Barre, Pa. Bureau of Fire received this factory-fresh Ward LaFrance triple combination with open semi-cab. This overhead view shows clearly the roomy hose bed and the spacious deck over the pump compartment. Ward La-France mounted its sirens on a short post just forward of the cab door on the left-hand side of the apparatus. This is also a 750 GPM job.

The Seagrave Corp. marked its 70th year in the fire apparatus business with the introduction of this totally-new front end design. This streamlined model, with the siren built into the nose, was known as the "70th Anniversary Model". This soon became the standard Seagrave front end on all models. Frederick S. Seagrave built his first hand-drawn apparatus in Detroit in 1881, He moved his flourishing business to Columbus, Ohio, about 10 years later. The last Seagrave of this style was built in 1970.

Cleveland, Ohio received a number of pumpers of this style from Seagrave during the 1950s. These were equipped with 1,250 gallon-per-minute pumps, and had 7-man, rear entrance canopy style cabs. This one is of the new 70th Anniversary Series.

One of the first Seagrave 70th Anniversary models delivered went to Lake Forest, Ill. It was a 750 gallon-per-minute pumper with the standard Seagrave canopy cab. The 70th Anniversary model also had an enclosed rear fender design with built-in equipment compartment. The standard engine in this series was still the proven Seagrave V-12.

Seagrave's Canadian cousin, Bickle-Seagrave Ltd. of Woodstock, Ont., also began building the new 70th Anniversary Series apparatus during the latter half of 1951. The Woodstock firm sold a pumper and a city service ladder truck to Vancouver, B. C. It is believed that the 1951 Bickle-Seagrave shown here was the only straight city service ladder truck of this series delivered in Canada. With the decline in population of city service trucks, the Columbus, O. plant also built only a few of these.

The Los Angeles City Fire Dept. used very few quadruple combinations over the years. This Seagrave 1,250 gallon-per-minute quad was ordered in 1951, and went to L.A.F.D. Engine Co. No. 86. It had a front suction intake, and carried a fixed turret pipe. The side-mounted ladders are unusual for this type of apparatus.

This was the last of the older style Seagrave service aerials purchased by the City of Detroit before the first 70th Anniversary models began to come in. Two of these 65-foot service aerials with booster equipment were delivered to Detroit in 1951. This one was eventually assigned to Ladder 16. Detroit had started buying these small aerial ladder trucks in 1945 and purchased 14 of them between then and 1952. Most of these service aerials replaced city service hook and ladder trucks.

The older style of Seagrave, which had been built since late in 1946, remained in production until parts stocks were used up. The 70th Anniversary Model did not appear until mid-year, so many Seagraves of this design were built while the prototype 70th Anniversary job was still being assembled. In 1951, Detroit purchased six more Seagrave 1,000 GPM sedan pumpers, including the first couple of 70th Anniversary models. This sedan was delivered in March, 1951, and was assigned to Detroit's Engine Co. No. 30. It cost $16,245 and weighed 13,100 pounds.

Spring City, Pa. was another city that ordered one of the relatively few Seagrave sedan pumpers not built for Detroit. This is a 1,000 GPM model identical in appearance except for the lighter color to those shipped to Detroit. Note the older style of siren on the cowl. The flags have been attached to the bumper for the rig's appearance in a parade.

This unusual Cadillac ambulance served the Detroit Fire Department for more than 36 years, before being retired as a reserve piece in 1973. It began life as a custom-built 1937 Cadillac V-16 ambulance, a gift of Detroit Fire Commissioner Paxton Mendelssohn. In 1951, the worn-out 1937 chassis was completely rebuilt using new Cadillac front-end sheet metal and rear fenders. Comm. Mendelssohn footed the bill for this costly conversion. This ambulance replaced the original 1927 Packard given to the D.F.D. by Comm. Mendelssohn, and this unit in turn was replaced by a mobile hospital donated by the same man in 1968.

The builder of this stubby Ford cab-over-engine pumper is not known, but the chassis used makes it somewhat unusual. The distinctive F Series chassis with its "fireplace" grille was used on only a small number of fire engines. This 500 GPM pumper was built for Blackwood Terrace, N. J.

American LaFrance delivered this 700 Series pumper to the Cleveland suburb of Brook Park, Ohio. It is a 1,000 GPM triple, and has the same type of black-painted upper cab found on Chicago rigs. Note the preconnected hose lines on the pump panel. The "American LaFrance" script nameplate below the rear cab window appeared on most American LaFrance apparatus built from late 1954 on, but is unusual on a rig of this year. A small-diameter hard suction hose is carried inside the lower suction on the Brook Park Fire Department's Engine No. 2.

Cleveland Heights, Ohio received this fairly stock 1951 American LaFrance 700 Series triple combination pumper, with a 750 gallon-per-minute pump. A beacon-type flasher has been mounted above the windshield. The block lettering on this pumper is typical of the style used at Elmira at this time. A 2½-inch line has been preconnected to the lower intake on the pump panel.

Because of the exceptional all-around visibility afforded by this design, the open half-cab 700 Series American LaFrance was preferred by many fire departments over the closed-cab model. Somerville, Mass. received this 700 open-cab 1,000 GPM triple combination pumper. The booster reel on this series could be mounted in the compartment over the pump, or on the rear step. Somerville's Engine 3 has the standard front-mounted bell, and a rear hose reel.

One of the relatively few 700 Series fire engines built by American LaFrance with special bodywork is this unusual job with a 4-door sedan type cab. It was built to order for the Brooklyn Hose Co. No. 2 of Lewistown, Pa. Other interesting features include a 6-inch front suction intake, a fixed McIntyre turret pipe, and clothing racks on each side of the hose bed. Note the roof vent and the special windows with sliding glass. This was the only 700 Series sedan built by the Elmira plant. It has a 1,000 GPM centrifugal pump.

The versatile quadruple combination provided smaller communities with all of the standard equipment carried on a triple combination pumper, plus the appurtences of a city service ladder truck. The quad commonly accompanies the first-due engine to the fire, and if needed can be hooked up as a second engine. In some areas, the quad runs alone as an engine and ladder company. This is an American LaFrance 700 Series quad with closed cab and a 750 GPM pump. It was built for Mayfield Heights, Ohio.

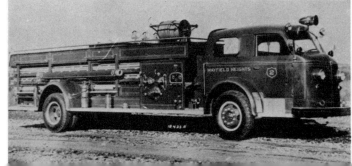

Benton Harbor, Mich. received this American LaFrance 700 Series Type 4-100 service aerial. These aerials are equipped with two manually-operated stabilizer jacks that drop to the ground under the turntable. The aerial ladder has four sections. Note the half-fold life net carried on the rear running board and the special handrail mounted above the engine compartment. Elmira also supplied chrome-plated metal company numbers on order, like the "1" that adorns the front of this open-cab aerial ladder truck.

1951

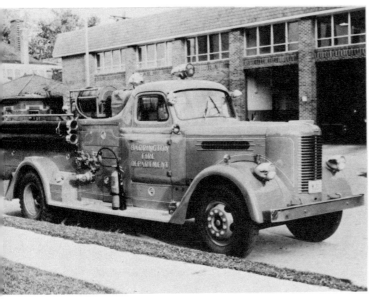

The small box built into the leading edge of the front fender of this 1951 Pirsch pumper houses a road sander designed to improve traction on icy roads. The discharge pipe can be seen below the running board. This 750 GPM Pirsch pumper was built for Barrington, Ill. Note the International Harvester two-man cab and how the cab has been streamlined into the rear body. This triple combination has a 300 gallon booster tank and two booster reels.

Although by now far outnumbered by metal aerials, 2-section wood aerials were still specified by some cities—Chicago and Boston, among others. Minneapolis also purchased some late-model wooden aerials. This 85-foot tractor-drawn model was built by Peter Pirsch & Sons Co. for the M.F.D. in 1951. A decade later the Pirsch tractor was replaced by a cab-forward International. Note the number plate carried just ahead of the windshield.

Salt Lake City ordered this 1951 Peter Pirsch 85-foot tractor-drawn metal aerial. Note the International cab, which has been faired into a rear-entrance canopy cab design by Pirsch. This 85-footer has a three-section aluminum alloy main ladder. The conical aerial ladder control pedestal is visible on the turntable. The large equipment box has been added to the side of the ladder bed.

Long Branch, N. J. took delivery of this 1951 Peter Pirsch and Sons 85-foot tractor-drawn aerial ladder truck. It has the full open cab, and a 3-section main ladder. Pirsch sold its 85 and 100-foot tractor-trailer aerials as Senior models.

One of the smaller fire apparatus builders in the east was the Harwick Manufacturing Co. of West Point, Pa. Harwick built this neatly enclosed rig for the West End Fire Co. No. 2 of Quakertown, Pa., on a 1951 Dodge chassis. The full width rear body provides plenty of compartment space for equipment.

The City of Millins, S. C. took delivery of this 1951 Ahrens-Fox Model SC pumper with 750-gallon centrifugal pump. Ahrens-Fox continued to mount its bells below the seat just behind the cab. Note the new style rear fenders with built-in equipment compartment. Ahrens-Fox centrifugals by now considerably outnumbered piston pupmers on the Ahrens-Fox assembly line.

Although preferred over all other types by some fire departments, the Ahrens-Fox piston pump was nearing the end of the line. Ahrens-Fox was still building a few Model HT piston pumpers, like this one with a 1,000 GPM pump that was delivered to Turtle Creek, Pa. Besides the cab doors—rare on Arehns-Fox piston pumpers,—this job was painted a bright green. The open half-cab and classic front-mount proportions give this fire engine an especially handsome appearance.

The Crown Coach Corp. of Los Angeles was a relative newcomer to the motor fire apparatus field, but a growing number of Crown fire engines were beginning to appear in West Coast fire houses. The 1951 Crown 1,000 GPM pumper shown here was built for Stockton, Cal. It has a large 400-gallon booster tank, rounded rear cab sides, and a preconnected 21-inch hard suction hose carried over the rear fender. This model also has two booster reels.

The rugged FWD was already familiar in the public works departments and road departments of many American municipalities. It was not surprising then, to find FWD fire engines in municipal fleets. Here, a 750 GPM FWD pumper with 3-man closed cab charges over a secondary road on its way to a suburban fire call.

The go-anywhere FWD with its jutting grille and husky appearance was enjoying widespread popularity with fire departments across the U. S. The Four Wheel Drive Auto Co. delivered this 1951 model 750 GPM triple to Nevada City, Cal. Note the absence of hard suction hose and the twin booster reels. FWD's were delivered with heavy block-style lettering visible here.

Mack also exported some of its firefighting apparatus. This 1951 Type 85 triple combination pumping engine was shipped to the Insular Fire Service in Puerto Rico. It has a 750 GPM pump. Note the open-style cab and the turret pipe permanently fixed to the rear of the hose body.

The biggest pumpers built by Mack at this time utilized the roomy 7-man sedan cab with four doors. The pump is mounted amidships, between the two rows of seats. This is a 1,250 gallon-per-minute Mack built for Minneapolis. The company number 15 is painted on the roof above the small center window. The box-type rear fender is a shop replacement.

Chicago's Engine Co. No. 1 responded to loop area fires with this 1951 Mack Type 95 pumper, one of five of this type purchased and placed into service in the Windy City that year. These pumpers had 1000 GPM Hale pumps. Standard Chicago Fire Dept. equipment included the dual-faced Mars light on the roof, black-painted upper cab and front-mounted bell with another white-lens, oscillating warning light on top.

While a fair number of Kenworth fire engines could be found in the Northwestern part of the country, fire apparatus built on the Peterbilt truck chassis was decidedly uncommon. One manufacturer that did build a number of fire engines using the Peterbilt chassis was Coast Apparatus Inc., of Martinez, Cal. Coast delivered this "Pete" 1,250 gallon-per-minute pumper with 400 gallon booster tank to Oakland, Cal. Note the turret pipe and the equipment compartment built into the rear fender.

Dallas, Texas modernized its fire department in the early 1950s with eight 750 GPM pumpers of this style built by General Fire Truck Corp.. of Detroit. These pumpers were powered by Waukesha engines and used the assembled General-Detroit custom chassis. Note the sharply canted windshield, and the plain-almost austere-appearance of this pumper.

Forty years after it had delivered its first, the Ahrens-Fox Fire Engine Co. in 1952 delivered its last piston pumper. The piston pump, and even the rotary gear-type fire pump, had given way to the more practical centrifugal. While no one disputed the efficiency of the front-mounted piston pump, it had simply become prohibitively expensive to manufacture. The last Ahrens-Fox piston pumper delivered was a 1952 Model HT-1000 built for the Hope Hose Co. of Tarrytown, N. Y. This historic Ahrens-Fox was placed in service in May, 1952.

But there was an epilogue. Later the same year the Ahrens-Fox Fire Engine Co. rebuilt a 1948 Model HT-1000 piston pumper that had been badly damaged in an accident. The rebuilt pumper, owned by Phillipstown, N. J. was given a new factory registration number. Where the last Fox piston pumper assembled bore Ser. No. 3488, the rebuilt job went back into service as No. 3489.

Ahrens-Fox marked its 100th year in the fire apparatus field this year. Exactly one century earlier, Moses Latta, founder of the company that ultimately evolved into the Ahrens-Fox Fire Engine Co. in 1908, placed America's first steam-powered fire engine into service in Cincinnati, ending the era of muscle and manpower, and the volunteer era. The International Assn. of Fire Chiefs, meeting in Boston, observed its 75th anniversary in 1952.

In an attempt to diversify its product line, the reorganized Ahrens-Fox Fire Engine Co. began to build a few medium-sized pumpers on General Motors truck chassis supplied by its new corporate parent, General Truck. But not even this could save the proud old firm, and only a few Ahrens-Fox commercials were built over the next few years. These models had 750 GPM centrifugal pumps.

The American LaFrance 700 Series fire apparatus had become almost universal across the United States and Canada. Hundreds had already been delivered, and the Elmira, N. Y. plant continued to fill orders at a furious pace.

Houston, Texas had placed an order with American LaFrance for 18 new pieces of 700 Series apparatus. These included eight Invader model 750 GPM pumpers; four Empire Model 1,000 GPM pumpers; 2 65-foot service aerials, 2 85-foot service aerials and 2 100-foot service aerials. Cleveland in 1952 also took delivery of a fleet of 700 Series American LaFrance fire apparatus, including six 85-foot service aerials, three 1,250 GPM pumpers and one 1,500 GPM pumper.

The Maxim Motor Co. demonstrated a new rear-mounted compact aerial ladder truck. Only slightly longer than a conventional Maxim pumper, the new short-wheelbase model carried a 100-foot Magirus aerial ladder. A 170-foot Magirus aerial was also available on this chassis. Wheelbase was only 203 inches.

International Harvester announced a new special fire apparatus chassis. Called the Model L-306, it had a 167-inch wheelbase, was powered by a 245-horsepower 6-cylinder engine with 266 and 318 HP engine options. International advertised that no less than 17 fire apparatus manufacturers offered equipment on the International chassis.

Waukesha's popular 6-cylinder fire apparatus engine was now standard power in fire engines built by Ward LaFrance Oren, Ahrens-Fox, FWD, Central, Pirsch and General-Detroit.

Despite the number of major builders, there was still room for the custom-craft, local manufacturer. A firm called Ribley and Harbinger, for instance, delivered a handsome pumper on a Federal chassis to Latham, N. Y. There have always been local craftsmen and garages who have turned out a very few one-off fire trucks for their local fire departments.

Cleveland, Ohio placed a large order with American LaFrance as part of a major fire department modernization program. This order included six 85-foot Series 700 service aerial ladder trucks with closed cabs, three 1,250 GPM triple combination pumping engines, and the single 1,500 GPM pumper shown here. Deliveries from Elmira commenced in late 1951 and were completed in the spring of 1952. The pumpers carried three lengths of hard suction hose, and had individual pressure gauges for each discharge gate. With the trend toward beacon-type warning lights, American LaFrance began mounting its sirens on the cab nose just ahead of the windshield.

With the outbreak of the Korean War in 1950, specialized military fire apparatus was again required for the armed forces. American LaFrance was awarded a huge government contract for O-10 and O-11 aircraft crash trucks of this type. The Elmira plant built more than 1,100 of these big crash rigs, which had remote controlled foam turrets on the roof, and swing-out hose reels. Many of these units are still in service today. The one shown here was built for the U. S. Air Force.

American LaFrance also offered a series of lower priced suburban and rural fire engines built on popular commercial truck chassis. These pumpers could be delivered in a fraction of the time required to build a custom-built unit. LaFrance Fire Engine & Foamite Ltd. of Toronto, ALF's Canadian subsidiary, built this small triple combination on a Ford chassis. It has a 625 Imperial gallon-per-minute pump and carries 415 Imp. gallons of water in its booster tank. A 500 IGPM model was also available.

In its largest single order in many years, the Detroit Fire Department in 1952 ordered thirteen new 1,000 gallon-per-minute motor pumping engines and two 65-foot service aerial ladder trucks. This big order went to The Seagrave Corp., of Columbus, Ohio. All 13 pumpers were of the new 70th Anniversary style. Detroit pumpers are all equipped with front suction intakes. The 1952 Seagraves purchased by Detroit were all powered by V-12 engines.

Beginning in 1945, Detroit started to replace all of its city service hook and ladder trucks with Seagrave 65-foot service aerials. The last of these were delivered in 1952. These small aerials, with canopy cabs, were also equipped with booster equipment. Detroit did not begin buying straight-frame aerials again until 1969. This 1952 Seagrave, one of two, was assigned to Ladder Co. No. 8.

The Seagrave Corp. delivered a small number of Detroit-style sedan pumpers to other fire departments around the country. The Mantell Hose Company of Atlantic Highlands, N. J., received this 1952 Seagrave sedan with 750 gallon-per-minute pump in 1952. Unlike the Detroit jobs, this pumper carries three lengths of hard suction hose and has a booster reel mounted transversely on the rear step. The catwalk between the hose beds leading to the crew seat can be seen in this view.

Among Seagrave's more popular models was the standard canopy cab pumping engine. The 1,000 GPM triple combination 70th Anniversary series canopy cab pumper shown here was built for Cicero, Ill. This roomy cab could carry seven firefighters in comfort and out of the weather. Seagrave customers had a choice of either wood or metal ground ladders. This rig carries a 24-foot wood extension ladder and a 12-foot roof ladder with folding hooks.

Like American LaFrance, Seagrave built relatively few special-purpose fire engines on its custom motor chassis. But Belmont, Cal. in 1952 received this Seagrave tanker. The 70th Anniversary model tank wagon is equipped with a 400-gallon booster tank, and also mounts a protable turret pipe. The Seagrave tanker was used by Belmont's Tank Co. 3.

MODEL 900 ENGINE

Waukegan, Ill. ordered this 1952 Seagrave 85-foot tractor-drawn aerial ladder truck with open half-cab. All Seagrave aerials up until the early 1960s had three sections, and were built in 65 foot, 75 foot, 85 and 100-foot lengths. Note the battering ram carried alongside the aerial ladder and the closed compartments above the trailer running boards.

Seagrave's largest pumpers were designated Series 900, and were powered by this 268-horsepower, 12-cylinder engine. Displacing 906 cubic inches, it had a 4½-inch bore and 4¾-inch stroke. The 900 Series was built on a 174-inch wheelbase. Seagrave's Series 400 pumpers were powered by a 202-horsepower V-12, and the Series 500 by a 215 HP Twelve.

The Pennsylvania State Fire School ordered this 100-foot Seagrave tractor-drawn aerial ladder truck for training purposes. The 3-man closed cab is unusual for a Seagrave aerial; most of the aerial ladder trucks of this type were built with open or canopy style cabs. A wraparound handrail encircles the rear roof.

The Fire Department of Memphis, Tenn., for many years purchased pumpers with 7-man sedan cabs. Peter Pirsch & Sons Co. of Kenosha, Wis. delivered this 1,000 GPM triple combination pumping engine with 4-door dab to Memphis in 1952. Note the wrap-around preconnected hard suction hose. Named the Frank T. Tobey, this pumper was assigned to Engine Co. No. 3.

The Four Wheel Drive Auto Co. of Clintonville, Wis. gave this 1952 FWD pumper the deluxe trim treatment, including a chrome-plated radiator shell. The 750 GPM pumper was built for Horsham, Pa., and carried four lengths of hard suction hose, two booster reels and a chrome-plated front bumper.

The Ahrens-Fox Fire Engine Co. produced its last piston pumper in 1952, bringing to an end what was probably the most distinctive fire engine model ever built in the U. S. Ahrens-Fox had been building piston pumps for more than 40 years. The last front-mount built was this Model HT which was delivered to the Hope Hose Co. of Tarrytown, N. Y. This 1,000 GPM pumper carried Ser. No. 3488. However, later in the same year the Ahrens-Fox factory rebuilt Phillipsburg, N. J.'s 1948 Model HT which had been badly damaged in an accident, and assigned it Ser. No. 3489. This, however, was the last of a proud line.

With the demise of the piston pump, Ahrens-Fox concentrated on production of this type of apparatus, equipped with a centrifugal pump. This triple combination was built for Newport, Ky. and featured a full open cab and twin booster hose reels.

Seeking to diversify its product line and to become more competitive with other fire apparatus builders, Ahrens-Fox at this time investigated the possibility of marketing a lower cost line of pumpers on commercial truck chassis. This proved to be prohibitively expensive, however, and very few of these Ahrens-Fox commercials were built in 1952 and 1953. The Model 470 shown here on a GMC chassis, has a 750 GPM pump and a 500 gallon water tank. It was sold to Mount Prospect, Ill. Note the Ahrens-Fox nameplate in the center of the front bumper.

One of the very last Ahrens-Fox piston pumpers delivered was this 1952 Model HT which went to Oceanside, Long Island, N. Y. The Oceanside job features cab doors and compartmented rear fenders. Latter series Ahrens-Fox piston pumpers had the headlights mounted inside the sweeping front fenders. Centrifugal fire pumps, which were much less expensive to manufacture, had finally overtaken the venerable positive displacement piston pump for good.

Certainly no stranger to the fire apparatus field, International Harvester introduced its new R-306 fire engine chassis. Standard engine in this special IH fire apparatus chassis was a Hall-Scott G-1 6-cylinder rated at 266 brake horsepower. The standard R-306 wheelbase was 169 inches. The set-back front axle provided excellent weight distribution and a relatively short turning radius for a truck of this size. The International pumper shown here was built for a West Coast department.

Like their familiar commercial model trucks, Mack fire engines have always imparted a connotation of massiveness and durability. Mack's fire engine production line by 1952 was turning out a complete line of pumpers, aerials and special purpose fire apparatus. But the bread-and-butter of the line was still the triple combination pumping engine, like this big Type 95 pumper of 1,000 GPM capacity.

Some Mack truck chassis were used by other fire apparatus builders. The Brumbaugh Body Co. of Altoona, Pa. built this van-type combination squad rig and pumper on a Mack chassis. Note the small front-mounted pump. Brumbaugh, perhaps better known under the Bruco name, is still in business today.

One of the more unusual products built by the Maxim Motor Co. of Middleboro, Mass. was this big quadruple combination delivered to the Yorkville Hose and Fire Co. of Pottstown, Pa. This 750 GPM quad is built on a Duplex 4 x 4 chassis, but carries the standard Maxim hood, grille and front fenders. Note the Duplex cab and the three bumper face bars. Each front fender is also equipped with a Mars warning light.

In 1952, the Maxim Motor Company of Middleboro, Mass. acquired a North American license to market the well-known German-built Magirus aerial ladder. Maxim mounted a 4-section, 100-foot Magirus aerial on one of its own standard custom chassis. This compact aerial had an over-all length of only 31 feet, or less than half the length of a conventional aerial ladder truck. Although the rear-mount continental style aerial was slow to catch on in this country, this configuration is widely built in the U.S. today. This is Maxim's 1952 prototype. Philadelphia purchased a 100-foot Maxim-Magirus aerial identical to this one in 1954.

A fairly small number of Kenworth fire engines were built to order for fire departments in the Northwestern U. S. Several were even exported to Canada. Vancouver, B. C. received this 1952 Kenworth city service ladder truck in 1952. Victoria, B. C. received two Kenworth pumpers and a city service ladder truck.

1953

Only a few years following the end of the Second World War, the "cold war" began. With the outbreak of hostilities in Korea in 1950, and the fear of massive nuclear bombings of our major cities, the nation's civil defense forces were mobilized again. The fire service was an important part of Civil Defense planning, and much federal and state money went into the modernization of fire departments, the training of auxiliary firemen, and the construction of bomb and fallout shelters. The triangular "CD" emblem was affixed to fire apparatus as departments built up their reserves, and fire apparatus plants which were just beginning to catch up on postwar production were busier than ever.

The American LaFrance Fire Engine Co. of Elmira, N.Y. had won a major U. S. Air Force contract for special crash trucks. From 1950 through 1953, American La-France built more than 1,100 Type 0-11 and 0-11A crash trucks for use at U.S.A.F. installations around the world. Some of these big, boxy V-nosed crash trucks are still in service today. The 0-11 was designed for high-speed travel over unpaved terrain, and could hurl a powerful stream of fire-killing foam while in motion.

The Seagrave Corp. boasted that more than 2,000 communities were now protected by Seagrave V-12-powered fire apparatus. The new 70th Anniversary series was in full volume production, and the line included 750 to 1,250 GPM pumpers, 65 to 100-foot aerial ladder trucks, quadruple and quintuple combinations, city service ladder trucks and specialized units like rescue squad trucks and foam units.

The Maxim Motor Co. had added a big airport crash fire truck to its product line. This heavy-duty crash truck, designed for service at civilian airports, was built on a special off-road chassis supplied by the Walter Motor Co.

Late in 1953, the Ahrens-Fox Fire Engine Co. terminated its fire apparatus manufacturing operations in the Cincinnati suburb of Norwood, and franchised the assembly of its fire equipment to the C. D. Beck Co., a builder of big intercity buses located in Sidney, Ohio. This would be the final chapter in the long and proud history of Ahrens-Fox.

A new fire apparatus builder had started production in a plant at Mount Clemens, Mich. near Detroit. The new Fire Master Corp. offered a complete line of pumpers on commercial chassis, or on its own assembled custom fire apparatus chassis with Waukesha power.

The Howe Fire Apparatus Co. of Anderson, Ind. had introduced a line of new Howe Defenders built on a special Duplex fire apparatus chassis. This sturdy-looking new model had a wide lower grille area between its modern box-type front fenders, and a low profile, V-type windshield. Howe's big Defenders were offered in 750, 1,000 and 1,250 GPM models with closed or open cabs. This series was powered by the 6-cylinder Waukesha 145 Fire Fighter engine.

Another firm that delivered many commercial chassis pumpers, as well as other specialized types, was the W. S. Darley Co. of Chicago. Already an old name in the fire equipment field, Darley manufactured its own pumps. This firm is still in business today in the Chicago suburb of Melrose Park. The company's popular 750 GPM midship-mounted pumper, on a commercial chassis, usually a GMC, was marketed as the Darley Champion. Darley equipment can be found on large and small fire departments throughout the midwestern U. S.

The Oren-Roanoke Corp. in 1953 delivered five custom chassis, open-cab pumpers to Dallas, Tex.

Looking much as it did the day it left the factory is this American LaFrance 700 Series quadruple combination delivered to Wheaton, Ill. The open-cab 1,000 GPM quad carries a complement of wood ground ladders, and has a portable turret pipe mounted on top of its booster tank. Note the unusual mounting of the booster reel under the rear of the ladder bed.

New York City's first major order for metal aerial ladder trucks went to American LaFrance. During 1953, the Elmira, N. Y. plant delivered 21 of these Series 700 tractor-drawn 85-foot aerials to the FDNY. The New York aerials were interesting in that they were built with no cab doors, but had grab handles on the windshield pillar and cab side. These aerials had 3-section ladders. This one went to Hook & Ladder Co. 102.

American LaFrance built more than 1,100 aircraft crash trucks for the U. S. Government. This 2 x 6 Type O-10 has a single foam turret on its roof and was built for the U. S. Air Force. These versatile, hard-hitting crash rigs could go almost anywhere. Speed on off-road responses and agility over rough terrain were prerequisites of this utilitarian but successful design.

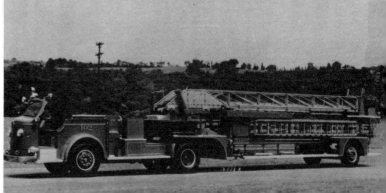

Goodwill Hose Co. No. 1, of Frackville, Pa. in 1953 received its new Seagrave canopy cab pumping engine. The 750 gallon-per-minute pumper is equipped with clothing rails for members of the company. An oscillating warning light is mounted on the cab roof.

1953

The heavily laden quadruple combination shown here was delivered to Jeffersonville, Ind. by The Seagrave Corp. in 1953. The 1,000 GPM apparatus carries an oversized booster reel and a portable Eastman deluge gun. This type of turret could be used mounted on the truck, or could be dismounted for placement closer to the fire. The rig shown here ran as Quad 1 on the Jeffersonville Fire Dept.

The Maxim Motor Co. delivered this 75-foot service aerial ladder truck to Brookline, Pa. Maxim built both 4-wheel and tractor-drawn aerial ladder trucks in 65, 75, 85 and 100-foot sizes. This open-cab aerial has a 3-section metal aerial ladder. The siren is mounted on the left front fender and a Mars light on the right.

Gary, Indiana's Engine Co. No. 1 is hooked up to a hydrant at a fire. The 1,250 gallon-per-minute pump is being supplied through a length of hard suction hose attached to one of the two intakes, in a "V" configuration. The hood is open for maximum cooling during pumping operations. The pumper is a 1953 Maxim with 3-man semi-cab.

The old familiar city service hook and ladder truck was declining in popularity, as more and more communities replaced them with more useful service aerials. Consequently, Seagrave built only a very few straight city service ladder trucks in its new 70th Anniversary series. The city service truck shown here, delivered to Ocean Grove, N. J. is built on a short wheelbase and carries booster equipment. The bell mounted above the hose bed was not standard equipment. Seagrave bells were always carried on the right-hand side of the cowl just below the hood line.

The Maxim Motor Co. built this commercial chassis 750 gallon-per-minute pumper for Jonesboro, Tenn. The chassis is a Ford F-800. This well-equipped pumper carries two booster reels and a portable deluge nozzle.

Mack at this time built only 4-wheel service aerials and no tractor-drawn ladder trucks, although more than a few Mack tractors were used to modernize older aerials in various cities. The Binghamton, N. Y. State Hospital was protected by this Mack Type 85 aerial with 75-foot, 7-section ladder. It was powered by a 225-horsepower Mack 6-cylinder gasoline engine.

New York City bolstered the protection of its high value district in Manhattan below 34th St. with the purchase of 25 of these powerful Mack Type 19 pumpers in 1953 and 1954. All were assigned in numerical sequence to Engine Companies 1 through 25. These pumpers had 4-stage Hale pumps that were rated at 1,000 GPM at 160 pounds pressure. Standard equipment also included fixed turret pipes and subway strap hangers on the rear handrails for the crew.

The Ward LaFrance Truck Corp. built this experimental base fire truck in a bid to win a Government contract for military fire trucks. Powered by a front-mounted 200 horsepower engine, it was equipped with a 500 GPM pump and 4-wheel drive. This agile performer had an approach and departure angle capability of 30 degrees. This type of engine was designed primarily for the protection of military bases and structures, rather than as an airport crash truck.

Schenectady, N. Y. purchased this 1953 Ward LaFrance 1,000 GPM pumper. Note the very busy-looking pump control panel and the fixed deck monitor. This engine also has a chrome-plated radiator shell. On standard production Ward LaFrances, the radiator shell was painted the same color as the rest of the apparatus.

The Ward LaFrance Truck Corp. delivered this 1953 model pumper to the White Horse, N. J. Fire Dept. The color scheme was white all over with a deluxe chrome-plated radiator shell. The 750 GPM pumper has twin booster reels and three-quarter doors.

This white-painted 1953 Ward LaFrance, with a plated radiator shell, was built for Western Springs, Ill. Note the closed, 3-man cab, compartmented rear fenders and the enclosed overhead ladder chute for the 45-foot aluminum extension ladder. This Ward LaFrance also has a gated front suction intake with preconnected steamer suction, which is carried in a basket built into the front bumper extension.

This International R-306 chassis is equipped with a 1,250 gallon-per-minute triple combination with deck turret. Note the divided hose bed, and the two portable Indian tanks on the rear running board. The R-306 was the largest and heaviest of the special chassis—seven in all—supplied to fire apparatus builders by International Harvester.

This is International's new R-306 fire apparatus chassis, with a single-piece flat windshield, equipped as a 1,250 GPM triple combination pumper. The chassis included Hall-Scott power as standard equipment and was offered to fire apparatus builders with either the flat windshield and cowl shown here, a standard curved IH windshield with ¾-doors and side glass, or with the standard closed 2-man cab.

Pirsch's standard Model 54 pumper is powered by a 6-cylinder, 150-horsepower Waukesha engine and has a 600 GPM 2-stage, parallel centrifugal pump. Standard equipment on this model included 150 feet of booster hose, a 100-gallon tank; two 10-foot lengths of hard suction hose, a suction hose strainer, 24-foot extension ladder, 12-foot roof ladder, 8-foot pike pole, two extinguishers, an axe, crowbar and electric siren. Aluminum alloy ground ladders were optional.

Peter Pirsch & Sons also offered commercial chassis fire apparatus in a complete range of body styles. This 1953 Pirsch-GMC with 750 GPM pump was built for the city of Pontiac, Mich. and has a canopy cab. Note the booster reel mounted on the running board, an unorthodox arrangement. Pontiac's Engine No. 9 also carries a portable turret nozzle.

When Philadelphia decided to modernize a number of its older model aerial ladder trucks, it replaced the 1941 American LaFrance tractors with new International R Series tractors with open cabs. Truck Co. No. 1's 85-foot spring-raised aerial is seen here being drawn by one of these Internationals, one of five purchased. Note the oversized bell mounted on the bumper.

Although it is still lettered for its original owner, Monroe, Wis., this 1953 Peter Pirsch & Sons 75-foot service aerial ladder truck is actually in use in Germantown, Tenn., its new home. This aerial is equipped with manual stabilizer jacks.

Engine No. 16 on the Omaha, Neb. Fire Department was assigned this new FWD 1,000 gallon-per-minute triple combination pumper with open semi-cab. The Four Wheel Drive Auto Co. delivered fire apparatus all over the U. S. and had a Canadian subsidiary in Kitchener, Ontario. Waukesha 6-cylinder Fire Fighter engines were standard equipment in FWD fire apparatus.

The Chicago Fire Department, in its largest apparatus replacement program in years, placed an order for 30 FWD pumpers and 12 FWD tractor-drawn aerials in 1953. The Clintonville, Wis. plant of the Four Wheel Drive Auto Co. completed deliveries in this big order the following year. The pumpers were 1,000 gallon-per-minute Model F-1000-Ts equipped with Waterous 2-stage centrifugal pumps and were powered by Waukesha 6-cylinder 240 horsepower engines. These sturdy 4 x 4 pumpers rode on steel spoked wheels. This 1953 FWD went to Engine Co. No. 8.

Tulsa, Okla. ordered several of these General-Detroit custom pumping engines in 1953. These were built on Duplex chassis, and had 1000-gallon pumps, booster equipment and fixed deck turrets. Engine No. 2's new General is seen here undergoing its acceptance tests shortly after it was delivered to the department.

Dearborn, Mich. ordered this custom-built Ford city service hook and ladder truck. The body builder is uncertain, but appears similar to that found on four Howe-Ford pumpers delivered at about the same time. Note the 4-door sedan cab and the equipment compartments atop the ladder bed. This ladder truck has wood ground ladders and a turret pipe.

The American Fire Apparatus Co. of Battle Creek, Mich. built this handsome triple combination pumper on a GMC chassis for the Good Will Fire Co. of Pottsville, Pa. The 750 GPM pumper has an open semi-cab and dual booster reels. Note the ornamental Cormorant on the hood. The white paint job is complemented by gold striping and lettering.

This was to be a big year for new fire apparatus introductions and innovations.

The biggest news of the year came from Mack, which introduced its totally new B Model fire apparatus in the fall of 1954. The new B Series had a pleasingly rounded front end dominated by a massive, plated radiator shell and streamlined front fenders. The new B Models were offered in a complete line which included pumpers of from 500 to 1,250 gallons-per-minute capacity; 4-wheel service and tractor-drawn aerials, and custom squads and combination ladder trucks. Power was delivered by the Mack Thermodyne 6-cylinder engine. Pumper body styles included a 3-man coupe cab, a 3-man open or semi-open cab; 5-man canopy and sedan cabs, and a huge 7-man Deluxe canopy or sedan-style cab. Among the new B Model's features was a fully-adjustable driver's seat. The attractively-styled Model B Macks remained in production for the next 12 or so years, and hundreds are still in front-line fire department service today.

Also new this year was a restyled Fireball Special series of small pumpers by Ward LaFrance. The Ward Fireball retained the appearance of earlier models, and was designed primarily for rural fire serfice. The standard model Fireball was powered by a 183-horsepower Chrysler Fire Power V-8 engine and carried a 500 gallon-per-minute pump. Ward LaFrance in 1954 delivered a fleet of special sedan-cab pumpers to Minneapolis, Minn. With the delivery of 25 new Civil Defense pumpers to New York City Ward LaFrance boasted that it had no less than 24 pieces of apparatus in service with the FDNY.

The Four Wheel Drive Auto Co. received a huge order from Chicago this year. This order included 30 Model F-1000T pumpers and 12 Model FA-85K tractor-drawn aerial ladder trucks. All had 3-man closed cabs, and were powered by Waukesha engines. The pumpers had Waterous pumps.

The Chicago order also included a spare aerial truck tractor. Late in 1954, FWD introduced a restyled series of smaller pumpers known as the FWD Special 500. This model sported a new, flat-front grille, a one-piece curved windshield and flattened front and rear fenders. The Special 500 came equipped with a 500 GPM centrifugal pump and the company's well-known four-wheel-drive system.

The Maxim Motor Co. delivered one of its new rear-mounted 100-foot Maxim-Magirus aerials to Philadelphia. Only slightly longer than a conventional pumper, this aerial had a 3-man semi-cab and went into service at Ladder 1. An identical 100-foot Maxim-Magirus aerial was delivered to the same city in 1955, and another in 1956.

Howe Fire Apparatus in 1954 delivered 22 of its new Howe Defenders to the Atomic Energy Commission. Ten of these were assigned to the AEC at Los Alamos, N. M. The other 12 went to the big AEC installations around Atlanta, Ga. Other Howe Defenders on the Duplex chassis delivered this year included two 750 GPM pumpers for Dallas and a 1,000 GPM canopy cab job for Tampa, Fla. Howe in 1954 built four sedan-cab pumpers on Ford chassis for Ford's world headquarters city of Dearborn, Mich. This city also received a special Ford-chassised, sedan-cab city service ladder truck.

Another company using the Duplex fire apparatus chassis was Zabek Fire Apparatus of Palmer, Mass. Zabek delivered a 750 GPM model to Atlantic City, N. J. this year and another in 1956. The Universal Fire Apparatus Corp. of Logansport, Ind. was building fire trucks for both Boyer and the Midwest Fire and Safety Equipment Co. of Indianapolis. The Approved Fire Equipment Co., which had specialized in custom-built, heavy-duty rescue bodies, now offered its own commercial chassis pumpers in Chieftain and Captain Series. Chieftains had 750 GPM pumps and Captains, 500 and 600 GPM midship-mounted pumps.

Chicago continued its massive apparatus modernization program by ordering no less than 30 of these Mack type 95 combination pumping engines and hose cars. Rated at 1,000 gallons-per-minute, they were powered by Mack 6-cylinder gasoline engines and had Hale pumps. These pumpers carried no booster equipment. Note the massive double-beam front bumper, and the Mars light on the cab roof.

The Bureau of Fire of Chester, Pa. owned this highly efficient 1954 Mack 75-foot service aerial ladder truck. It is equipped with a set of Roto-Rays mounted on a post just forward of the windshield, and has an open semi-cab. The 3-section aerial ladder is by Maxim.

In the autumn of 1954, Mack introduced its totally-new B Model fire apparatus. The new Mack B Models sported attractive new front-end sheet metal and many significant engineering improvements. The standard engine was the Mack Thermodyne overhead valve 6-cylinder gasoline engine. This is the new 1954 Mack Model B-95 triple combination pumper with open semi-cab.

1954

Clean, angular lines characterize the styling of this Ward LaFrance pumper with a closed, 3-man cab. It was built for Port Chester, N. Y. Instead of the usual set of hard suction hoses carried on the pump operator's side, this 750 GPM pumper has four brass Indian portable pump tanks. The shallow hose bed indicates that this pumper has a very large booster tank.

Minneapolis ordered four of these big Ward LaFrance 1250 GPM pumpers with 4-door, 7-man sedan cabs. These pumpers were equipped with Waterous pumps. The unit shown was assigned to Engine Co. No. 14. Note the Federal Q siren mounted in front of the grille, and the company number tag in front of the windshield. Standard power in Ward LaFrance fire apparatus was the Waukesha 6-cylinder Fire Fighter engine.

Late in 1954, Ward LaFrance came out with a new line of special low-cost pumpers designed for suburban and rural fire service. This attractive new model was called the Fireball Special, and included as standard equipment a 500 GPM pump and an oversized 500-gallon booster tank. Standard engine in this new series was a 183-horsepower Chrysler Fire Power V-8. A 750 GPM pump and more powerful Waukesha 6-cylinder engine were optionally available in the new Ward Fireball Specials.

The Seagrave Corp. built this small pumper for the Town of Surfside, Fl. The chassis is a 1954 Ford F-750. Seagrave commercials were now being built with the same compartmented rear fenders used on the company's custom chassis apparatus.

At the time it took delivery of this new Seagrave triple combination pumping engine, the City of Torrington, Conn. was using all-white apparatus. The white color scheme was abandoned in favor of the traditional red, however, within a few years and all of Torrington's fire engines were eventually repainted red. Torrington's new Engine No. 8 was photographed against a scenic backdrop at the Seagrave plant in Columbus prior to delivery. The 750 GPM pumper carries the city seal on its doors.

Kalamazoo, Mich. purchased this very unusual 1954 Seagrave combination rescue squad car and pumping engine. The 750 GPM pumper carries full rescue equipment in the large side compartments. Note the preconnected soft suction hose carried on the front bumper pan. One of the grille bars has been purposely left off to carry the steamer suction in this manner. Kalamazoo's fire apparatus was painted red generally, but Rescue 5 has a red-and-white paint job.

Protection begins at home, it would appear, which is why the City of Kenosha, Wisc. went to a local firm when it shopped for a new aerial ladder truck. The new 1954 Pirsch Senior 100-foot tractor-drawn aerial didn't have to make much of a delivery trip from the Peter Pirsch & Sons Co. plant in Kenosha to the city's main fire station. Pirsch was now using box-type fenders on its aerial trailers. Note the enclosed compartments above the running boards. For obvious reasons, Kenosha has used Pirsch fire engines for more than three-quarters of a century.

Liberty, N. Y. received this well-equipped American La-France 700 Series pumper. The 1000 GPM triple combination has compartmented rear fenders, a feature that later became standard on American LaFrance pumpers. This pumper carries three lengths of hard suction hose, has clothing racks on each side of the hose bed, dual booster reels mounted above the pump compartment, and a portable deluge set. Liberty's 700 also has a front suction intake. The axe mounted over the front fender also became a standard ALF feature within a few years.

Here's a piece of fire apparatus designed with future requirements in mind. It was built as a quadruple combination for the City of East Grand Rapids, Mich., but provision was made for the addition of an aerial ladder later if needed. The heavily-laden American LaFrance 1000 GPM quad carries floodlights, a portable turret pipe, wood ground ladders and booster equipment.

In its literature, American LaFrance described its service aerials as "four-wheel" models, and its tractor-trailer jobs as "six-wheel rescue aerial ladder trucks." This is a standard Model 4-100 of the 700 Series, which was built for the city of Galveston, Tex.

American LaFrance offered its customers a complete line of small to medium-capacity triple combination pumpers built on commercial truck chassis. The 750 GPM pumper shown here, built on a 1954 GMC chassis, was delivered to Lexington, Tenn. It has a 500 gallon booster tank.

1954

With few exceptions, the Ford Motor Co. head office and plants in Dearborn, Mich. have been protected by fire apparatus built on various types of Ford truck chassis. When the Dearborn Fire Dept. went shopping for four new pumpers, Ford chassis were specified. The Howe Apparatus Co., of Anderson, Ind., got the order. The 750 gallon-per-minute triple combinations had 4-door sedan cabs and red warning lights tunnelled into the cab roof. Howe built these pumpers on the Ford F-8000 chassis.

Philadelphia, Pa. placed one of these 100-foot Maxim-Magirus aerial ladder trucks into service at its busy Truck Co. 1 in 1954. Not much longer than a standard pumper, this type of aerial could get into spaces that a conventional aerial could not. Philadelphia's Maxim-Magirus aerial also carried a supply of ground ladders. This aerial was ahead of its time; the American fire service did not start ordering rear-mount aerial ladder trucks in numbers for another 14 years.

The Maxim Motor Co. built three of these big airport crash trucks for the Port of New York Authority. Built on Walter Motor Co. chassis with high flotation tires for use on unpaved ground, each carries two foam turrets which are operated from the platform over the cab roof. The crash rig shown here was delivered to Idlewild Airport (now John F. Kennedy International) while similar units were built for the other two airports serving New York City—LaGuardia and Newark.

1954

Along with 30 new pumpers built by the same company, the City of Chicago ordered 12 of these FWD Model FA-85K tractor-drawn aerial ladder trucks. and one spare tractor. The ladder trucks were powered by Waukesha 240 horsepower 6-cylinder engines, and had 2-section, manually-raised main ladders. Manually-operated stabilizer jacks dropped down from the front of the trailer.

The utilitarian Willys Jeep proved ideally suited to many specialized roles in fire service. Ocean City, N. J. mounted a turret pipe on the front of this Jeep. So equipped, this vehicle could be driven directly into a burning building, or it could be used close-in as a heavy stream platform. Many war surplus Jeeps were converted into versatile brush and grass fire rigs, and a number of companies specialized in building small pumpers on the civilian Jeep chassis.

The Oren-Roanoke Corp. supplied this triple combination pumper to the famed Greenbrier Hotel at White Sulphur Springs, W. Va. This pumper was built on Oren's own assembled custom fire apparatus chassis, and has a 750 GPM pump. It is not uncommon for large private institutions and resorts to have their own fire departments.

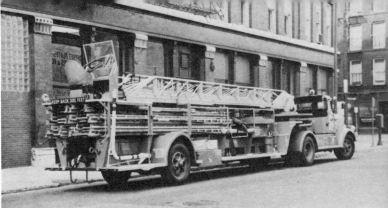

After years of hard fire service, this 1954 FWD tractor-drawn aerial went into the Chicago Fire Dept. shops for major repairs, which included the replacement of the original wooden 85-foot aerial with a new 100-foot Seagrave 4-section aerial and hydraulic hoist. The ground ladders have been also replaced with new metal ladders. Note the fixed position tillerman's seat which does not have to be moved in order to lift the aerial ladder. This truck was used by H & L Co. No. 9.

Burbank, Cal. owns this International R-306 triple combination, with open semi-cab. The 1,000 GPM pumper also carries two preconnected 1½-inch hose lines in transverse beds visible above the main hose bed. It also packs two booster reels. Note the wig-wag warning light on top of the grille.

Engine Co. No. 49 of the Los Angeles County Fire Dept. received this big International triple combination pumper, on the IH R-306 fire apparatus chassis. It is equipped with a 1,000 gallon pump, and carries 500 gallons of water in its booster tank. LA County rigs covered vast areas of frequently flammable brush.

Gloucester City, N. J. had a pair of these Oren-Fords, Engine No. 3 is built on a 1954 Ford F-750 truck chassis, with cutdown semi-cab. A portable Indian tank is carried above the pump compartment. This conversion was done by the Oren-Roanoke Corp., then located in Roanoke, Va.

1954

Philadelphia, Pa., in 1954 placed six of these 750 gallon-per-minute combinations with booster equipment into service. They were built on Federal truck chassis by the General Fire Truck Corp. of Detroit. Note the simple one-piece flat windshield, the post-mounted Roto-Ray warning lights and the open pump compartment. The PFD shop number is stenciled onto the front bumper.

In 1954, the Philadelphia Fire Department purchased four of these 750 gallon-per-minute triple combinations. Built by the John Bean Division of FMC Corp., Lansing, Mich., they were mounted on 1954 GMC chassis and were equipped with high pressure fog pumps, high windshield frame, and compartmented rear fenders. The chambered rear edge has been a John Bean trademark for years.

Oakland, Cal. ordered this 1954 Coast-Peterbilt pumper. It was built by Coast Apparatus, of Martinez, Cal., on a set-back axle Peterbilt truck chassis, and carries a 1250 gallon-per-minute pump. It also carries 250 gallons of water. A beacon-type warning light has been added above the windshield. Note the cast aluminum radiator shell.

A newcomer to the fire apparatus field was the Fire Master Corp. of Mount Clemens, Mich. Fire Master delivered this big 1,000 gallon-per-minute pumper to St. Clair Shores, Mich. Built on an Available chassis, it has two enclosed booster hose reels. A portable turret nozzle is carried on top of the booster hose compartment, behind the 4-door sedan cab. Note the squared-off front fenders, and the pre-connected soft suction hose.

In November, 1953, the C. D. Beck Co. of Sidney, Ohio acquired the Ahrens-Fox Fire Engine Co., and all Ahrens-Fox operations were moved from the company's ancestral home in Cincinnati, to Sidney. The first Sidney-built Ahrens-Fox centrifugals were soon coming off the assembly floor in the big Beck plant, whose principal product was large inter-city buses. This 1954 Ahrens-Fox Model EC 750 gallon-per-minute pumper was delivered to Lester, Pa. Note the new screen-type grille, and the Roto-Rays atop the windshield.

The Chicago Fire Department received eight of these big cab-over-engine Autocar Squad trucks in 1954. Quite streamlined in appearance, they had lofty 4-door cabs and a cat-walk in the rear between two big equipment compartments. Each was also equipped with a 4-way turret pipe mounted just behind the cab. Squad 1's rig, shown here, has been retrofitted with an Aurora Borealis warning light by Mars.

Ten years after its 700 Series fire apparatus was announced, American LaFrance in 1955 introduced the first new models in this series. The new models consisted of a line of low-cost fire apparatus designed for rural and district fire service. Called Ranger, Protector and Crusader, these pumpers were equipped with 500, 750 and 1,000 GPM pumps of a new, improved American LaFrance Twinflow centrifugal design. What made these models truly unique is that they were powered by 6-cylinder Continental in-line engines, instead of the ageing American LaFrance V-12. The 500 GPM Ranger was powered by a 170-horsepower Continental; the 750 GPM Protector with a 200 HP engine, and the 1,000 GPM Crusader by the 200-horse Continental. This series used a ribbed front bumper painted the same color as the body, and the open cab had no side door glass.

In June of 1955, American LaFrance President George R. Hanks announced that the company had merged with the Sterling Precision Instrument Corp., and would henceforth be known as American LaFrance Corp.

The Seagrave Corp. in 1955 came out with a line of new, economy-priced 65-foot metal aerial ladder trucks mounted on standard commercial truck chassis. This truck used a type of aerial ladder totally different from the company's custom-chassis 65 to 100 foot aerials. The most popular chassis employed were the Ford F-Series and Internationals. Virtually all were delivered with semi-open, 3-man cabs. Also in 1935, Seagrave delivered a special tractor-drawn aerial to West Milwaukee, Wis., which featured two tinted windows in the roof to enable the driver to more conveniently spot the truck in front of the fire building. Nashville, Tenn. received a Seagrave aerial with this feature several years later. Seagrave in 1955 announced a new premium model of its big V-12 engine. The new Seagrave 906 engine was rated at 300 horsepower.

The Four Wheel Drive Auto Co. in 1955 received an order for 25 tractor-drawn, 85-foot spring-raised wood aerial ladder trucks from New York City, said to be the largest civilian order for aerial trucks ever placed in the U. S. up to that time. These aerials had fully-open cabs. Like the 85-foot tractor-trailer aerials delivered to Chicago the previous year, the FDNY ladder trucks had manually-raised, 2-section main ladders.

The FWD Corp. followed its Special 500 series apparatus introduced in late 1954 with a new, restyled design of similar appearance for the rest of its pumper line. The new

FWD Deluxe model was previewed at the 1955 International Assn. of Fire Chiefs Convention held in Omaha, Neb., and included 700, 1,000 and 1,200 Models. New features included higher horsepower engines, pumps mounted lower in the chassis for a lower center of gravity, and a new rear body design with fully compartmented rear fenders.

The Memco Aerial Ladder Co. of Oklahoma City, Okla, had developed a low-cost, electrically operated aerial ladder designed for installation of any commercial truck chassis. Available in 55 and 65-foot sizes, this aerial was available to most fire apparatus manufacturers. The Howe Fire Apparatus Co. of Anderson, Ind. mounted one on its new Howe Defender chassis, for Erie, Pa.'s West Lake Fire Dept., making this unit a quadruple combination.

Mack's new B-Models were now rolling off the assembly lines, and a 1955 delivery was an 85-foot tractor-drawn aerial with full open cab for St. Louis, Mo. Mack still sourced its aerial ladders, in 65 to 85-foot lengths, from the Maxim Motor Co.

Oren-Roanoke introduced a new, improved custom pumper line with restyled fenders and general appearance. Available in 750 to 1,500 GPM models, this series used Hale pumps and the proven Waukesha Fire Fighter 6-cylinder engine.

Philadelphia, Pa. took delivery of three new Maxim aerial ladder trucks in 1955. Two were tractor-drawn 85-footers and the third was a 100-foot straight frame model. This is one of the two 6-wheel 85-foot models, with 4-section main ladders. Note the very long overhang of the metal ground ladders. The 85-foot tractor trailer aerials were assigned to Truck Cos. 12 and 16, while the 100-footer went to Truck 1.

Indianapolis is the only midwestern city in the U.S. that operates a large fleet of Maxim fire apparatus. In 1955, Indy received this new Maxim with a high capacity 1,500 gallon-per-minute pump—the largest produced by Maxim. Note the dual "V" suction ports. This big job was assigned to IFD's Engine Co. No. 18.

Photographed against a Massachusetts winter background is this brand-new Maxim 1,000 GPM canopy cab triple combination pumper delivered to Lexington, Mass. Note the absence of hard suction hoses in the carrying troughs. Sometimes these were transferred from an older rig to a new one.

Harry S. Truman's home town of Independence, Mo. received this 70th Anniversary Series Seagrave triple combination pumper with 1,000 gallon-per-minute pump. This pumper differs from standard models in that it carries one length of hard suction hose on each side, enabling it to carry additional ground ladders. Note the fixed Morse turret pipe, the Federal Q siren in the nose, and the oscillating warning light atop the grille.

This 1955 Seagrave 65-foot service aerial ladder truck has the new style compartmented rear fenders, which permit protected storage of small equipment. It carries a full complement of wood ground ladders in its double bank ladder bed. Note the red flashers mounted at the top of the windshield posts. This small aerial carries Seagrave registration number H-6625.

The Seagrave Corp. in mid-1955 came out with an all-new, low-cost metal aerial ladder designed to appeal to smaller towns which could not afford a conventional modern aerial truck. This lightweight, 3-section metal aerial was designed for mounting on standard commercial truck chassis. Seagrave was proud of the fact that this new ladder was manufactured in the same plant that built the standard Seagrave aerial: "This ladder," Seagrave advertised, "is ALL SEAGRAVE." The prototype economy aerial is seen here mounted on a Ford chassis.

Providence, R. I. ordered this Seagrave 85-foot tractor-trailer aerial ladder truck with rear entrance canopy cab. Note the absence of any type of warning light on the cab roof, and the red flasher siren in the nose. The trailer of this aerial appears to be extra short in length, and overhand of the wood ground ladders exceeds that of the tip of the 3-section aerial ladder. A continuous handrail encircles the rear of the cab.

The Milwaukee suburb of West Milwaukee, Wis., ordered a few extras on its new 1955 Seagrave 100-foot tractor drawn aerial ladder truck. The two tinted skylights in the front of the cab roof permit the driver to spot his rig more accurately in front of the fire building. The covered box beside the aerial ladder contains the 3-inch hose for the ladder pipe. The pipe itself is carried beside the tillerman's seat for quick attachment to the aerial ladder tip.

This 75-foot Seagrave tractor-drawn aerial ladder truck was built for the Empire Hook and Ladder Co. of Upper Nyack, N. Y., and replaced a 1930 Seagrave tractor-drawn city-service ladder truck. Note the handpainted company emblem on the cab door, and the post-mounted rotating beacon light. A guardrail has been provided on the turntable for the operator, and the tillerman's "bucket" has full glazing for extra visibility. Road sanders ride ahead of the rear tractor wheels.

For obvious reasons, Columbus, Ohio was protected mainly by Seagrave fire apparatus for many years. Columbus Truck Co. No. 9 received this Seagrave 65-foot metal service aerial in the mid-1950s. It has the standard Seagrave canopy cab with oval side windows, and carries a full complement of Seagrave trussed wood ground ladders, but has the older style trumpet-type siren mounted in the nose.

After years of using specialized combination pumper and hose engines which responded to alarms with a separate tank wagon. San Francisco began to buy triple combination pumpers. This 1955 Seagrave has a 1,000 GPM pump, dual booster hose equipment and a full load of hose. Subsequently, the S.F.F.D. shops began to convert some of its newer dual combinations to triples.

1955

Another type of Seagrave canopy cab has a full width walkway between the tractor-style canopy and the rear body. This heavily-loaded 1955 model was built under license by Bickle-Seagrave Ltd. of Woodstock, Ontario, for Brantford, Ontario. The 1,000 GPM pump is rated at 840 Imperial, or Canadian, gallons. Cleveland had several Seagraves with this type of cab, and Lorain, Ohio had at least one.

Oak Lawn, Ill. has this standard model 1955 Seagrave quadruple combination. It has a 1,000 gallon-per-minute pump, and a side mounted booster hose reel. The sharply-chopped three-man closed cab has two small windows in the rear. Seagrave built some 3-man cabs of this type which were rounded off in the rear. This one ran as Oak Lawn's quad 8.

One of the last fire engines turned out by the General Fire Truck Corp. of Detroit, was this big quadruple combination delivered to the Detroit suburb of Allen Park, Mich. Built on a 1955 Federal truck chassis, this General-Detroit has a 750 GPM midship-mounted pump and a 5-man canopy cab. The ladder racks are completely enclosed. A Civil Defense insignia is on the cab door.

Four of these plain-looking John Bean triple combination pumping engines were delivered to Philadelphia in 1955. Like the ones delivered the previous year, these 750 GPM pumpers carried high pressure fog equipment and were built on GMC truck chassis. The pumps on these jobs, however, were fully enclosed. The pole mounted above the rear of the apparatus was installed in the late 1960s for protection of the crew and equipment; large canvas covers were placed over this pole, enclosing the entire rear of the rig.

The Ahrens-Fox Division of the C. D. Beck Co., of Sidney, Ohio, continued to turn out this style of centrifugal pumper. The 1955 Model EC pumper of 750 GPM capacity shown here was built for Oakhurst, N. J. Ahrens-Fox used the Waukesha 6-cylinder engine in its late-model fire apparatus. Still an innovator, Ahrens-Fox had a whole new series of cab-forward fire engines on the drawing board.

The City of Fresno, Cal. ordered this standard model 700 Series American LaFrance 85-foot service aerial ladder truck. In American LaFrance literature for this year, this model was designated a Type 4-85. The enclosed rear fenders with integral equipment cabinets later became standard equipment on all ALF aerials.

This 1955 American LaFrance 700 Series rig is barely recognizable as an Elmira product. It began as an open-cab tank wagon for the San Francisco Fire Dept., but when the SFFD began to swing away from 2-piece engine companies (combination engine and hose responding with a tank wagon) in favor of triple combination pumpers, this former tanker was converted by the San Francisco shops into a Rescue Squad. Not only that, but a homemade closed cab was installed.

Muskegon Heights, Mich. got this 1955 American LaFrance 700 Series pumper with 5-man canopy cab. The step plates on top of the front fenders were optional, but came in handy for washing the roof. The pumper shown is a 1,000 gallon-per-minute model.

A few minor changes had been made on American LaFrance 700 Series apparatus by the mid-1950s. The windshield glass was now mounted in a continuous rubber molding, and the American LaFrance badge had given way to script-type name-plates which were mounted on the cab front and on the sides just above the chrome belt line. The headlights were also faired into the front sheet-metal, instead of being housed in separate pieces. Upper Darby Township, Pa., owned this 1955 American LaFrance 1250 GPM pumper.

The Rochester, N. Y. Protectives, the city of Rochester's salvage patrol, used this shop-built GMC salvage truck. Rochester apparatus was identified for many years by large, cast company nameplates that were transferred from rig to rig. This truck carries an older style cradle-type bell.

1955

Ward LaFrance Truck Corp. of Elmira Heights, N. Y., delivered this Model 85-T triple combination pumper to the community of Warren, R. I. The new Ward LaFrance model was designed for village, town and suburban fire service. Warren's new Engine 1 has a Waterous 750 GPM pump and carries 250 gallons of water in its booster tank. The single booster reel has 150 feet of one-inch line.

International Harvester, in addition to its big R-306 fire apparatus chassis, built a specialized medium-duty fire engine chassis which was widely used by many manufacturers. This 1955 International Type R-1856 with open semi-cab has a triple combination pumper body with 750 GPM pump. Note the plated upper radiator shell. The builder is unknown, but the bodywork is similar to that done by L. N. Curtis of Oakland, Calif.

The Howe Fire Apparatus Co. of Anderson, Ind. began to market its own custom-chassised fire apparatus, reviving the proud old name of the Howe Defender. Howe, which had earlier used a Defiance chassis for its custom jobs, now used the rugged, angular-lined Duplex as the base for its new custom line. This Howe Defender with 5-man open semi-cab has a 750 GPM Waterous pump and is powered by a Waukesha engine.

For the first time, Ward LaFrance in 1955 began to market its own aerial ladder trucks. These were offered in 65, 75 and 85-foot sizes and in 4-wheel service or tractor-drawn variations. Skokie, Ill. received this 1955 Ward LaFrance 85-foot service aerial. Like Mack, Ward LaFrance purchased complete aerial ladder units from a competitor, the Maxim Motor Co.

The new lower-priced Fireball Specials introduced by Ward LaFrance late in 1954 found immediate acceptance by smaller fire departments. The Ward Fireballs could be delivered in less time than it took to build a custom-built unit, and while it was built on Ward LaFrance's own custom fire apparatus chassis, the Fireball came with basic standard equipment like a 500 GPM pump and 500-gallon booster tank. Many options were available, however. The 1955 Ward LaFrance Fireball Special shown here has a Waukesha 6-cylinder 145 engine, a 750 GPM pump and dual booster reels as well as floodlighting equipment.

A thriving Canadian fire apparatus builder is the firm of Pierre Thibault Ltd., of Pierreville, Quebec. Thibault built its first fire engine on a Model T Ford chassis in 1918. In the early 1950s, this company began production of a custom line of fire apparatus on its own assembled chassis. This 1955 Thibault 1,050 Imperial gallons-per-minute pumper (1,250 U. S.) was delivered to Quebec City, Que., one of the few Canadian cities using white-painted rigs. Most Pierre Thibault custom fire engines are powered by Waukesha engines.

Princeton Junction, N. J. ordered this custom-built 1955 Mack Model B. A very large combination pumper-tanker, it has tandem rear axles and a 3-man closed cab. Designated a Model B-505, it has a 500 gallon-per-minute pump and carries 1,500 gallons of water in its huge booster tank.

This big Mack B Model 750 GPM pumper, has the roomy 5-man canopy cab, which Mack described as a 2-door sedan cab. Two men sit forward, and three ride on the bench seat in the rear. Note the four lengths of hard suction hose. It is a 1955 Model B-85.

Mack's all-new B Model fire apparatus was now rolling off the Mack fire apparatus assembly line. This series remained in production for more than a decade. One of the earlier B Model Macks delivered was this 750 GPM triple combination pumping engine delivered to Wakefield, Mass., in 1955. Note the open semi-cab and the compartments built into the front of the rear fender.

With the start of production of its new Model B, Mack once again began to market 6-wheel, tractor-drawn aerial ladder trucks. One of the first delivered was this 85-foot tractor-trailer that went to St. Louis, Mo. Designated a Model B-85, it has an open cab and 4-section aerial ladder. Mack had discontinued the manufacture of its own aerial ladders and was buying complete aerial ladder assemblies from the Maxim Motor Co. of Middleboro, Mass. This big Mack was assigned to St. Louis' busy Ladder Co. No. 8.

Philadelphia, Pa. ordered six of these Mack Model B-85 triple combination pumping engines. Equipped with 750 gallon-per-minute pumps and high pressure fog equipment, these units have open pump compartments. The large company number on the grille was a standard feature of Philly rigs for many years and made each company easily recognizable on the fireground.

After a nine-year production run, American LaFrance in 1956 replaced its highly successful 700 Series. The venerable 700 was succeeded by a much-improved, re-engineered 800 Series, which closely resembled its predecessor. The new 800 Series had its formal debut at the 1956 IAFC Conference held in Miami.

The new American LaFrance 800 models were built on a new chassis and were offered in two series—a standard Custom line, and a new Deluxe highline series. Buyers could choose from a range of seven engines, including two American LaFrance V-12s, and five Continental 6-cylinder engines. The new 800 sported redesigned rear fenders with built-in equipment compartments, and an improved American LaFrance Twinflow centrifugal pump. The 800 was soon in full production and the line included open and closed-cab pumpers, service and tractor-type aerial ladders and specialized custom-built models like quads and airport crash trucks. Although every bit as successful as the earlier 700 Model, the 800 remained in production at Elmira for only two years.

The other major new product news of the year came from Ahrens-Fox, which two years earlier had shifted its production from Cincinnati to the modern C. D. Beck Co. bus manufacturing plant at Sidney, Ohio. Beck continued production of the conventional Ahrens-Fox centrifugal pumpers, but early in 1956 took the industry by surprise by introducing a handsome series of cab-forward fire engines. A proud old name in the business, Ahrens-Fox had once again preserved its reputation as an innovator. The new Beck-built Ahrens-Fox cab-forward models were available in open and closed-cab models with pumps ranging in capacity from 500 to 1,500 GPM. One of the first was delivered to East Rutherford, N. J. So sound was the Ahrens-Fox cab forward fire engine design that it was eventually taken over by Mack for the company's first line of cab-forward fire apparatus.

One of the more important corporate developments of the year was the acquisition of the Maxim Motor Co. by the Seagrave Corp. Maxim continued, however, to function as a totally independent division of Seagrave, and continued to build all of its own apparatus and major components including bodies and aerial ladders.

Ward LaFrance in late 1956 introduced a new, restyled custom fire apparatus series. Officially designated 1957 models, the new Ward LaFrance design incorporated a smooth, rounded hood and grille design and enclosed rear fenders with integral equipment compartments.

The Four Wheel Drive Auto Co. also came out with

some new models this year. The company had signed an agreement with a prominent Dutch fire apparatus firm—Geesink—for U. S. distribution of the Geesink aerial ladder. The Geesink rear-mounted ladders were built in 65, 75, 85 and 107-foot lengths, and were offered on the FWD fire apparatus chassis. The Clintonville, Wis. builder in 1956 also introduced modestly restyled FWD pumpers built in two series: a standard FWD Special line of 500, 750 and 1,000 GPM pumpers, and the Deluxe in 500, 750, 1,000 and 1,250 GPM variations.

Reo Motors of Lansing, Mich., certainly no stranger to the fire service, introduced a special fire apparatus chassis this year. The heavy-duty Reo fire engine chassis was offered with engines ranging from the Reo Gold Comet Six up to a 235-horsepower V-8.

The Boardman Co. of Oklahoma City was now building custom-chassis pumpers based on the angular Duplex fire apparatus chassis. This heavy-duty chassis was still being used by Howe for its big Howe Defenders, and was also used by Zabek and other manufacturers.

In Canada, Bickle-Seagrave Ltd. had filed for bankruptcy and was succeeded by King-Seagrave Ltd., also in Woodstock, Ontario.

San Francisco was still specifying dual-combination pumpers and single-purpose tank wagon, both of which responded as 2-piece engine companies. Seagrave delivered this 400-gallon tanker in 1956. Note the booster reels mounted one behind the other instead of side-by-side. San Francisco apparatus was still painted a very dark maroon.

Lansing, Mich. was another city which used 2-tone red and white fire apparatus. Lansing was a good Seagrave customer, purchasing quite a few Seagrave pumpers and aerials over the years. In 1956, Lansing put this attractive 1,000 GPM canopy cab pumper in service at Engine No. 5. The West Coast rear view mirrors were added later.

Interestingly enough, the Detroit Fire Dept. purchased no 100-foot aerials between 1938 and 1961. Detroit purchased quite a few 85-foot tractor-drawn aerials and 65-foot service aerials in this period, however. The only new ladder truck placed in service in 1956 by this department was this Seagrave 85-footer, which was assigned to Ladder Co. No. 14. From the 1930's through the early 1960's, Detroit was one of Seagrave's biggest customers.

This is certainly one of the most unusual quadruple combinations ever built. It has no hose bed, as found on conventional quads, but it is a tractor-trailer job and has an 85-foot, 3-section aerial ladder. Seagrave built this unique unit for the metropolitan Detroit area city of Hamtramck, Mich. The tractor is equipped with a 1,000 GPM Seagrave centrifugal pump, and a preconnected soft suction hose is carried in front of the grille. Here, this rare type of quad is seen hooked up to a hydrant at a fire.

This profile photo shows the Seagrave three-man closed cab to advantage. The cab roof is chopped sharply at about the point the side window begins on the canopy cab model. This 1,000 GPM pumper, with overhead ladder rack, was delivered to St. Charles, Ill. by The Seagrave Corp. in 1956. It is equipped with a 350-gallon booster tank.

Stoneham, Mass. received this 1956 Seagrave 750 gallon-per-minute pumper with standard canopy cab. Note the oscillating flasher on the roof, and the extra length of hard suction hose. This photo came from the Charles E. Beckwith collection.

This must have been the most elaborately trimmed Seagrave to roll out of the Columbus, Ohio plant in 1956. The 1,000 gallon-per-minute canopy cab pumper, built for the Pikesville Volunteer Fire Co. in Baltimore County, Md., has a white roof, a plated upper radiator shell and booster hose reels recessed into the rear of the roof. The standard rear side windows have been eliminated, and in their place are playout openings for the booster lines. The pinstriping was probably applied after delivery.

Atlantic City, N. J. purchased two 750 gallon-per-minute pumpers from Zabek Fire Apparatus, of Palmer, Mass. The first was delivered in 1954. Two years later, this 1956 Zabek joined the ACFD. The Zabeks were built on Duplex truck chassis. The 1954 model had a slightly different frontal appearance with horizontal grille bars spanning the area between the front fenders. This pumper has a 285-gallon booster tank.

1956

At first glance, this pumper looks astonishingly similar to a Mack C-85. This resemblance is understandable, because Mack's fire apparatus division adopted the Ahrens-Fox cab-forward design when it acquired C. D. Beck in the fall of 1956. This, however, is a 1956 Ahrens-Fox Model FCB that was delivered to Hempstead, Long Island, N. Y. It has a 1,000 GPM pump. Note the Federal Q siren mounted on the roof, and the white upper cab paint job. This pumper has a fixed turret pipe and dual booster reels.

Ahrens-Fox early in 1956 announced its completely new cab-forward line of fire apparatus. Only one other fire apparatus manufacturer—American LaFrance—offered true cab-forward apparatus at this time. The Ahrens-Fox Fire Engine Division of C. D. Beck built six rigs of this type in the Sidney, Ohio plant before the operation was bought out by Mack Trucks in September of the same year. The first of the new Ahrens-Fox cab-forward models delivered was this 750 GPM triple combination with centrifugal pump, built for East Rutherford, N. J.

International Harvester's new VCO-196 cab-over-engine fire apparatus chassis found immediate favor with fire apparatus builders. The Chicago Fire Dept. purchased a number of these for special-purpose apparatus like this small high pressure hose wagon. Note the plain body, and the fixed turret pipe between the cab and rear body.

Another Ahrens-Fox cab-forward model was delivered to Ho-Ho-Kus, N. J., which at the time still owned a 1937 Ahrens-Fox piston pump quad. This is a 1956 Ahrens-Fox Model ECB with 750 GPM centrifugal pump. Frank X. Greisser, a long-time Ahrens-Fox salesman, was responsible for making most of the company's many sales in the Eastern U. S.

This little fire engine packed quite a fire-killing whallop for its size. It is the "Blitz Buggy". a forerunner to the mini-pumper of today. The Blitz Buggy Co. of Old Forge, N. Y. built up quite a few of these on various commercial chassis. This one is on a 1956 Ford. The Blitz Buggy carried its own water supply, two booster reels and enough line and equipment to handle a moderate sized fire.

American Fire Apparatus Co. of Battle Creek, Mich. had established a Canadian subsidiary in the early 1950s. American Marsh Pumps (Canada) Ltd. built many fire engines on commercial truck chassis for Canadian fire departments between about 1950 and 1964 when the business was dissolved. One of the more unique units built by American Marsh Pumps (Canada) in its plant at Stratford, Ontario, was this completely enclosed city service ladder truck on an International VCO-196 cab-forward chassis. This apparatus has two booster reels, a heated ladder compartment and ten large, closed equipment compartments on top. It is believed that this ladder truck was built for Edmonton, Alberta.

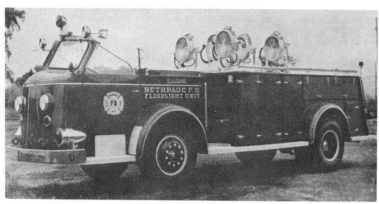

Among the relatively few special 700 Series fire engines built by American LaFrance was this floodlight unit built for Bethpage, Long Island, N. Y. This same basic body was used for rescue squad trucks. The rubber-mounted windshield glass and flat-faced parking light lenses visible on this truck first appeared on early 1955 models.

After a 9-year production run, American LaFrance phased out the Series 700 and replaced it with an improved design designated the Series 800. Among the improvements in the new 800 Series was a redesigned rear body with compartmented rear fenders, and a new type of cab mounting. The sure way to tell an 800 from the earlier 700 is the raised front bumper, mounted above, rather than even with, the front running boards, the deep side running boards with tapered leading edge, and the boxed-in fenders. LaFrance Fire Engine & Foamite Ltd. of Toronto, Ontario, ALF's Canadian subsidiary, delivered this 840 IGPM (1,000 U.S.) Series 800 pumper to Burnaby, British Columbia.

Production of the new 800 Series began at American LaFrance in mid-1956. This series used cutout-type ALF nameplates in front of the cab, and on each side above the chrome belt trim. Marysville, Calif. received this 1956 Series 800 pumper of 1,000 GPM capacity. Note the absence of hard suction hose — unnecessary in an area so far away from a major water supply like a river or lake.

St. Louis, Mo. received a large fleet of American LaFrance 800 Series pumpers and aerial ladder trucks in 1956. Engine Co. No. 20's pumper is one of these. The indentation in the front fender was to accommodate a preconnected length of hard suction hose that extended from the left-hand side pump panel around the front of the truck. For some reason, this has been removed from the LaFrance shown here. These engines carried wood ground ladders.

St. Louis, Mo. placed a huge order for new fire apparatus with American LaFrance. This order included two 100-foot tractor-drawn aerials and four 85-foot tractor-trailer aerials, and a number of 1,000 GPM pumpers. All were the new 800 Series. Note the siren mounted in the front of this 100-foot metal aerial. All of these new rigs were delivered in 1956. The pumpers had preconnected hard suction hoses carried around the front of the cab.

Peter Pirsch & Sons Co. built this 75-foot aerial ladder truck on an FWD chassis. It has an open semi-cab and three-section ladder. The customer is not known for sure, but it could be Union, N. J. Pirsch apparatus buff Roger Bjorge came up with the photo.

1956

Louisville, Ky. is another city that operates two-piece engine companies in its downtown high value area. Conventional triple combination pumpers are accompanied to downtown alarms by turret wagons of this type. The one shown here was built on a 1956 Ford cab-over-engine chassis by Peter Pirsch & Sons. Short in overall length but high, this rig has a 500 GPM pump with squirrel-tail preconnected hard suction hose, booster equipment and a fixed turret pipe. The Louisville Fire Dept. has at least two wagons of this type. The unit pictured is assigned to Engine Co. No. 5.

This is the Mack Model B-85 4-wheel service aerial with open semi-cab. It is equipped with a 3-section Maxim 75-foot metal aerial, and carries booster equipment. This aerial, with enclosed ladder compartment, was delivered to the Berwyn Fire Co. No. 1 of Berwyn, Pa. Note the facing Mack Bulldog emblems on the front bumper.

Boston, Mass. has many 2-piece engine companies. Most of these consist of two pumpers, one of which responds as a conventional triple combination, and the other as the company's hose wagon. This 1956 Mack 1,000 GPM pumper, seen in action at a multiple fire in downtown Boston in July, 1974, runs as Engine 3's wagon. Both units, however, are lettered Eng. 3. Note the deck monitor and the makeshift roof that has been added over the open semi-cab for the protection of the crew.

Wakefield, Mass. still responds to alarms with this 1956 Mack B Model 1,000 GPM pumper. This engine saw front-line service at the Chelsea Conflagration that destroyed a large industrial area of Chelsea, Mass. in October, 1973. Wakefield was one of many Boston area communities that sent men and equipment to this fire, one of the worst in the U. S. in modern history. The Wakefield engine was displayed at a Chelsea portion of the program at the 1974 International Fire Buffs Assn. Convention in 1974.

The historic cities of Lexington and Concord, Mass. both purchased new Mack B Model pumpers with open 3-man cabs. This is Lexington's recently delivered Engine No. 1, shown outside this company's colonial-styled quarters. The pumper is a Model B-95.

The Maxim Motor Co. had been building this style of fire apparatus for 10 years now, but the design had not become dated in appearance and continued for quite a few more years. The 1,000 GPM pumper shown here was delivered to Johnson City, Tenn. This city had purchased a Maxim 75-foot aerial six years earlier.

The latest in a long line of aerial ladder trucks purchased for the Moyamensing Hook and Ladder Co., of Chester, Pa., was this 1956 Maxim 85-foot tractor-trailer rig. The big Maxim carries wood ground ladders. The double-beam front bumper could be found on most Maxim custom apparatus built during the 1950s.

Ward LaFrance delivered this quintuple combination aerial ladder truck to DeKalb, Ill. It mounts a 500 GPM pump and has a 4-section 85-foot Maxim aerial ladder. The booster hose reel is located above the enclosed ladder bed. Note the compartments above the two banks of ground ladders.

The custom-chassis fire engines built by the Oren-Roanoke Corp. of Roanoke, Va. at this time appeared to incorporate some Duplex body components. But the squared-off front and rear fenders were exclusive to Oren. This 1956 Oren with 750 GPM pumper is owned by the Highland Fire Co. of Pennsauken, Pa.

The standard Ward LaFrance pumper had this type of open semi-cab, with a complete range of enclosed cab and body styles optionally available. This is a stock 750 GPM pumper with two booster reels. Ward LaFrances were popular throughout the Eastern seaboard, and could be found in Midwestern communities, but very few were delivered in Western U. S. states. Today, Ward LaFrance sells its products from coast to coast.

Some commercial chassis fire apparatus could be quite elaborate, such as this long-wheelbase Ford photographed by Jim Burner. The bodywork appears to be by Oren-Roanoke Corp. The chassis is a Ford F-800 equipped with a 4-door sedan cab and a 750 GPM pump. The body builder used an extra set of Ford front doors for the cab extension. This pumper was built for the Community Fire Co. No. 1 of Newfoundland and Oak Ridge, N. J.

After more than a half century of prominence, the proud old name of Ahrens-Fox disappeared from the American firefighting scene in 1957. In the latter part of 1956, Mack Trucks had acquired C. D. Beck. This purchase gave Mack a ready-made cab-forward fire apparatus line, and Mack took over the Ahrens-Fox cab-forward design that had gone into production early the previous year. This design became the basis for Mack's very successful C-85 and C-95 cab-forward models which remained in production for another 11 years. Production of the cab-forward model was moved to Allentown, Pa., and the first major order for this style won by Mack was for 44 pumpers for New York City.

The last Ahrens-Fox pumper built was an open cab job sold to Dumont, N. J. But when Dumont heard that Ahrens-Fox was about to go out of business, it cancelled its order. The pumper, a 1956 model, was resold to Northern Hills, N. J. A small number of the Ahrens-Fox Waukesha-powered, centrifugal pumper chassis went to other manufacturers at this time. Approved delivered several. But the final chapter in the Ahrens-Fox story would not be written for several more years—in 1961.

In 1957, the Ford Motor Co. introduced a new tilt-cab medium duty and heavy duty truck line that used a new forward-control cab supplied by Budd. This was destined to become probably the most popular fire apparatus chassis ever built, and the type is still in production today as Ford's famed C-Series Tilt Cab. In its first few years, however, this chassis was used by a few other manufacturers, including Mack. With the outward appearance of Ford, the Mack tilt-cab model was sold as the Mack Model N. A small number of Mack N Model fire engines were built.

The Seagrave Corp. built and delivered several special custom-chassis fire engines this year. One of these was a huge, rear-mounted aerial ladder truck sold to Green Bay, Wis. This monstrous aerial, with a 3-man closed cab, was equipped with a 144-foot Magirus 6-section aerial ladder, and at the time was the tallest aerial ladder in the nation. Grand Rapids, Mich., in 1957 took delivery of a special Seagrave combination 1,000 GPM pumper and rescue squad. The chassis and pump were built at Columbus, but the squad body was fabricated by The Gerstenslager Co. of Wooster, Ohio. Seagrave this year introduced a new version of its big V-12 engine. Designated the Model 531,

it was rated at 251 horsepower.

Peter Pirsch & Sons Co. had announced a new series of aerial ladders for mounting on commercial truck chassis. These were offered in 65, 75 and 85-foot lengths, and most of the early deliveries were on GMC chassis. Pirsch offered its first commercial-chassis aerials away back in 1939.

Ward LaFrance was building a new Fireball Special series of 500 and 750 GPM pumpers on its restyled chassis. These economy model customs were designed for communities with limited budgets.

Rear-mounted aerials were gaining in popularity. Milwaukee in 1957 took delivery of three 100-foot Magirus rearmounts built on Mack Model B fire engine chassis, and Cedarburg, Ia., purchased an 85-foot Geesink rearmount on an FWD chassis.

International had added a new V-Line to its wide range of specialized fire apparatus chassis. The basis of the new V-Series conventional was a 257-horsepower IH V-8 engine. Hall-Scott advertised that Los Angeles City and L. A. County had more than 200 Hall-Scott powered fire engines in service.

The 1957 IAFC Conference was held in New Orleans, La.

Peter Pirsch & Sons Co. had started to make some of its aerial ladders available on heavy commercial truck chassis. This three-section 85-foot Pirsch metal aerial is mounted on a 1957 GMC chassis. It was delivered to Downers Grove, Ill. Note the safety rails around the turntable, and the road sanders just forward of the dual rear tires.

This is how far some fire apparatus manufacturers will go to meet the requirements of a community with definite preferences. Troy, N. Y. was a big user of Ward LaFrance pumpers, but the city's officials liked the Pirsch lattice-girder aluminum alloy aerial. The result was this unusual Pirsch-Ward LaFrance 85-foot tractor-drawn aerial delivered in 1957. The tractor is a Ward, but the unit was completed and delivered by Peter Pirsch & Sons Co. of Kenosha, Wis.

Another Peter Pirsch & Sons Co. commercial chassis delivery was this 750 GPM triple combination pumper built on a 1957 International Harvester R Series chassis. This pumper has a full open cab and a 200 gallon booster tank. It was built for Davenport, Iowa. Pirsch, of course, continued to build a full line of custom-chassis fire apparatus on its own chassis.

During the 1957 model year, The Seagrave Corp. began to use a new style squared-off front fender on its apparatus. The older type of rounded fender remained in use as parts stocks were used up. This 1957 Seagrave 750 GPM pumper has the new style fenders. It was delivered to Evanston, Ill., a long-time purchaser of Seagrave fire apparatus.

1957

The Seagrave Corp. continued to offer its Safety Sedan enclosed pumper, most of which were sold to Detroit. Three of these were delivered to Detroit in 1957. The soft suction hose on these 1,000 GPM sedans, previously carried over the right front fender, was now carried on the pan between the front bumper and the grille. The deep-skirted standard grille bars were replaced by flat chrome strips to accommodate the soft suction. This 1957 Seagrave was assigned to Engine 31.

Belmont, Cal. ordered this 1957 Seagrave 1,250 GPM pumper, which has a 300-gallon booster tank. Note the number of gates above the running board, and the 6-inch diameter hard suction hose. An extra-long length of 2½-inch hard suction is carried above. This engine has the older style rounded front fenders.

One of Seagrave's best sellers was still the standard 65-foot service aerial. This one has the new style squared front fenders and a 3-section hydraulically-operated aerial ladder. It was built for Nahant, Mass. These smaller aerial trucks, commonly referred to as junior aerials, have almost completely replaced the straight-frame city service hook and ladder truck.

One of the most unusual Seagraves ever built is this huge Seagrave-Magirus Aerial Ladder Truck, which was built to order for the progressive Green Bay, Wis. Fire Dept. Equipped with a German-made 146-foot Magirus aerial ladder, it was the tallest aerial in North America at the time. It carries no ground ladders and usually responds with another ladder truck. The main ladder has six sections and is stabilized by four mechanical outrigger jacks. Note the chrome-plated upper radiator shell.

Grand Rapids, Mich. ordered this unusual combination pumping engine and rescue squad. It was built by Seagrave but the rescue squad body was fabricated by the Gerstenslager Co. of Wooster, Ohio. The only white rig on the Grand Rapids Fire Dept., it has a 1,000 gallon-per-minute pump but carries no hose. The front bumper was extended to permit the installation of a heavy-duty winch. This big squad was replaced by a new Ward LaFrance rescue truck in the early 1970s and is now on the reserve list.

1957

Some communities desired equipment built by major fire apparatus manufacturers, but could not afford custom-built units. The solution was a pump, body, and equipment built by a major manufacturer, but mounted on a lower-priced commercial chassis. Seagrave had been building commercial-chassis fire engines for smaller departments since the early 1930s. This is a 750 GPM Seagrave pumper body mounted on an International Model V-190 truck chassis with standard coupe cab. A full range of IH 6 and 8-cylinder engines was available.

The lower-priced 65-foot commercial-chassis aerial which The Seagrave Corp. had introduced the previous year was a moderate success. Most of those built were on Ford or International truck chassis, but some were sold on other maker's chassis. Waukegan, Ill. ordered this 1957 Seagrave-International 65-foot Junior aerial on an IH V-Line chassis with open semi-cab.

Responding to a definite interest in more compact, shorter aerial ladder trucks, the Four Wheel Drive Auto Co. of Clintonville, Wis. signed an agreement with the Dutch firm of Geesink, giving FWD U. S. marketing rights to the Geesink aerial ladder manufactured in Holland. The FWD Co. sold a number of these FWD-Geesink aerials in the U. S. Cedarburg, Iowa, received this 85-footer in 1957. It is built on the FWD chassis with open semi-cab.

The Maxim Motor Co. of Middleboro, Mass. delivered this 1,000 GPM pumper to Memphis in 1957. Like all Memphis pumpers, it has a swivel-mounted, preconnected 20-foot length of hard suction hose and carries a short attic ladder. This Maxim has a 3-man coupe cab. The booster hose reel is visible immediately behind the cab. The bell and siren are mounted on the frame that supports the suction hose above the dual front bumper.

Ward LaFrance late in 1956 came out with a new front end design that featured a rounded hood, squared-off front fenders and a new flat-faced grille. The plated radiator was a dress-up option. This 1957 Ward LaFrance 750 GPM pumper was built for Middleton, Mass.

This is the last fire engine built that carried the Ahrens-Fox name. The open-cab 750 gallon-per-minute pumper was originally ordered from C. D. Beck by the fire department of Dumont, N. J. But when Dumont heard that Ahrens-Fox was going to be sold to another company (it turned out to be Mack) the department felt that they would be stuck with an orphan, and thus cancelled the order. The pumper was then snapped up by the Northern Hills, Ohio Fire Department. Note the deluxe nozzle mounted on the frame over the engine compartment. Northern Hills put its Ahrens-Fox into service in 1958, even though the unit is listed as being of 1957 register.

The new American LaFrance Series 800 fire engines, introduced in mid-1956, incorporated a number of improvements including a new, heavier chassis frame, the new ALF Twinflow centrifugal parallel-series pump, and a pump operator's panel which was switched from the right-hand to the left side of the truck. Also, for the first time, 6-cylinder Continental Red Seal engines were offered in addition to the ALF V-12. This is a 1957 American LaFrance 800 Series 1,000 GPM pumper delivered to Bristol, Va.

Ten years after the first apparatus in this series was delivered, the standard American LaFrance bore only a superficial resemblance to the 1947 product. This is a 1957 American LaFrance 800 Series pumper built for Tullahoma, Tenn. It is a 750 gallon-per-minute model with the open semi- cab. Notice how much higher the rear body is compared with 700 Series pumpers of this type. A preconnected 2½-inch soft suction line is carried atop the compartmented rear fender.

American LaFrance's new 800 Series fire apparatus was built in Custom and Deluxe series. The basic Custom model had a painted front bumper and narrow side running boards, while the highline Deluxe model sported a chromed bumper, the type of dropped running board seen here, and half-glass in the cab doors. This 1957 American LaFrance 800 Series 1,000 GPM pumper was delivered to Reading, Mass.

Elmira continued the use of distinctive model names to identify its various sizes of 800 Series pumpers. The 1,000 gallon-per-minute Class A pumper shown here was called the Sparton. Note the Federal Q siren on the front cab step, and the beacon-type flasher above the windshield. The engine shown here was delivered to Pekin, Ill.

East Detroit, Mich. received this American LaFrance 800 Series quad, which was designed for the later addition of an aerial ladder. Note the fully-enclosed ladder beds and the generous equipment compartments. This quad has a 750 GPM pump and canopy-type 5-man cab. It also carries two booster reels.

Another special purpose unit built for the Chicago Fire Department was this lighting apparatus, mounted on a 1957 International VCO-190 truck chassis. The closed body, built by the Pierce Manufacturing Co. of Appleton, Wis. contains a large power generating plant. Several batteries of powerful Mars searchlights are mounted on top, and can be swung into position for use at night fires or in very heavy smoke.

Mack Trucks, which had bought the C. D. Beck operations in Sidney, Ohio, in the autumn of 1956, continued the production of the Ahrens-Fox cab-forward fire apparatus and adopted this design for its first forward-control fire apparatus. Mack commenced deliveries of its new C-85 and C-95 pumpers and aerials using this design in 1957. The nimble cab-forward design, with excellent visibility, proved ideal for urban fire service. Consequently, Mack received an order for no less than 33 of these new cab-forward pumpers from New York City. This is the prototype for the FDNY jobs, with turret pipe mounted on the cab roof, and the transverse booster hose reel with playout over the rear handrail.

1957

Mack continued production of its highly-regarded B Model fire apparatus alongside the new cab-forward C Series. Boston, Mass., in 1956 and 1957 placed a number of these big 1,250 GPM Macks into service as combination engine-squads. They had special compartmented bodies, ladders carried in a canted position on the right-hand side, and preconnected 1½-inch hose in the transverse bed over the pump panel. This pumper's armament also includes a 3-way turret pipe.

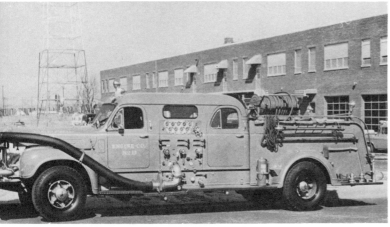

Memphis, Tenn. ordered this extremely long 1957 Mack Model B triple combination pumper. Desginated a Type B-21, it is powered by a Hall-Scott engine and has a 1,500 GPM pump. Seven men can be seated in the 4-door sedan-type cab. Note the preconnected hard suction hose carried around the front of this pumper. The engine seen here is assigned to Memphis' Engine Co. No. 13.

Milwaukee, Wis. placed three of these special Mack-Magirus 100-foot rear mount aerial ladder trucks into service in 1957. The 4-section aerial ladder was imported from Germany. The chassis is of the Mack B Series. Four screw-down stabilizer jacks supported the truck's weight when the ladder was raised. The truck shown was assigned to Ladder Co. No. 20.

This is one of the first Mack C Series fire engines delivered following adoption of the C. D. Beck/Ahrens-Fox cab forward design. Bob Robinson's photo is of Reserve Engine 2, in Providence, R. I. Note the rounded Mack standard rear fenders—very rare on this model. Reserve Eng. 2, running as Providence Engine 10, is seen in action at a fire.

Milwaukee, Wis. purchased four new aerial ladder trucks in 1957, all built by Mack on the Model B chassis. Three of these were 100-foot Mack-Magirus rearmount aerials, and the fourth was this rare Model B tractor-drawn 85-footer with Maxim 4-section aerial. This aerial, with open semi-cab, has a fixed tiller seat and mechanical stabilizer jacks.

Although it was hardly noticed at the time, the most significant event of this year was the addition of a new word — "Snorkel" — to the fireman's vocabulary. The concept of the fire-fighting elevating platform originated in Chicago. As the story goes, Chicago Fire Commissioner Robert Quinn was walking on a downtown street when he stopped to watch a crew cleaning an overhead sign. He was fascinated at how the men could move around in a bucket attached to the end of an articulated boom. Why, he reasoned, couldn't the firefighter have the same kind of aerial mobility? Quinn consulted with the Chicago Fire Dept. apparatus shops, and a 50-foot boom and basket were purchased from the Pitman Mfg. Co. of Grandview, Mo. the CFD shops mounted the unit on a conventional

GMC 354 truck chassis. A 1200 GPM monitor was mounted in the basket, and a length of boat hose was slung to the side of the two-section boom. "Quinn's Snorkel" was placed in service in October, 1958. This historic piece of fire apparatus had cost only $14,000 but it would soon revolutionize firefighting all over the world. Only a few weeks after it went into service, Quinn's Snorkel showed its capabilities at a 4-alarm lumber yard fire, silencing some of the skeptics.

In June, 1958 American LaFrance announced its completely new Series 900 fire apparatus. The all-new 900 Series replaced the 800 Series which had gone into production only two years earlier. The 900 Series would remain in production even longer than the earlier 700 Series, and was still being built in the mid-1970s. Thousands of American LaFrance 900 Series fire engines are still in service all over North America. The new 900 Series pumpers and aerials featured a dramatically restyled cab with a smooth, rounded front end, a wrap-around windshield and dual headlight units. The new cab-forward cab, available in both open and closed canopy cab styles, was 76 inches wide. No less than eight engines were available in the 900 Series, including the American LaFrance V-12, various Continental Sixes and a new 300-horsepower V-8. Elmira began deliveries of the new 900 models almost immediately.

Mack Trucks was now delivering its new cab-forward models in volume. The original Ahrens-Fox design had been modified and improved by Mack's engineers. This new C-Series Mack was featured at the company's big exhibit at the 1958 IAFC Conference in Los Angeles. Mack delivered five of its new cab-forward pumpers to the Los Angeles City Fire Dept. The company continued to build its popular B Model conventional series apparatus in addition to the new cab-forward jobs.

The Valley Fire Truck Co. of Bay City, Mich. had come out with a small 4-wheel-drive pumper built on Willy's new Jeep forward-control chassis. Called the Champion, this nimble little go-anywhere pumper was equipped with a 500 GPM pump and carried 200 gallons of water in its booster tank. It was designed to save wear and tear on larger apparatus by being able to reach grass and brush fires without having to stretch long hose lines. The basic chassis was the Willys Model FC-170.

The Seagrave Corp. was now using a squared-off front fender design on its conventional custom series fire

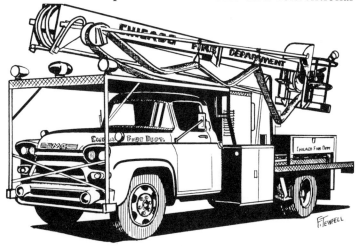

An important new word was added to the firefighter's vocabulary this year—Snorkel. To the Chicago Fire Dept. goes the credit for recognizing the value of the public utilities-type elevating platform as a new kind of firefighting tool. The CFD purchased a 50-foot boom and bucket from the Pitman Manufacturing Co. of Grandview, Mo., and mounted it on a 1958 GMC Model 354 chassis. After a series of extensive tests, Commissioner Robert Quinn's "Quinn's Snorkel" was placed in service in October, 1958. This innovative new type of mobility for the firefighter proved its worth at more than 250 fires in its first year, and in 1959 Chicago ordered two more. The granddaddy of all Snorkels is the crude affair seen in this line drawing by F. Twefell. Note the 3-inch hose slung alongside the two articulating booms. This pioneering new kind of fire engine cost the Chicago Fire Dept. only $14,000.

The Chicago suburb of Harvey, Ill. ordered this FWD-Geesink 85-foot rearmount aerial ladder truck. This compact design combined the short European-type aerial with the added traction of a 4-wheel-drive configuration. The Four Wheel Drive Auto Co. of Clintonville, Wisc. had obtained U. S. distribution rights for the Dutch-made Geesink aerial ladder. Lengths ranged from 65 to 107 feet.

Tacoma, Wash. took delivery of this FWD 1,000 gallon-per-minute triple combination pumper with standard 3-man closed cab. Assigned to the TFD's Engine Co. No. 16, it has a preconnected 2½-inch soft suction hose attached to the pump panel for quick hydrant hookup.

1958

apparatus. Use of this new type of front fender had begun late in 1957.

In other developments, American LaFrance for the first time offered a metal aerial ladder mounted on a conventional commercial truck chassis. The 3-section 65-foot aerial could be mounted on a standard GMC, Chevrolet, Ford or International truck chassis.

Philadelphia took delivery of eight special high pressure volume 1,000 GPM pumpers built by John Bean on an open-cab GMC chassis. Peter Pirsch & Sons also began using box-type front fenders on its pumpers and aerials.

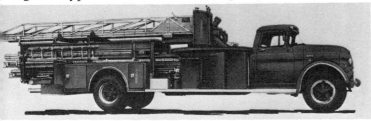

For the first time, American LaFrance in 1958 offered a budget-priced aerial ladder truck for smaller communities, built on commercial truck chassis. The standard 3-section American LaFrance aerial was used. This 1958 American LaFrance Type C-65 aerial is built on a GMC 554 chassis. A 75-foot aerial for commercial chassis was added later.

Shown here is one of the first closed-cab 900 Series pumpers built. Production of the new 900 models began simultaneously in Elmira, N. Y. and in the Canadian subsidiary's plant in Toronto, Ont. This 840 IGPM LaFrance pumper was delivered to Toronto, where it went into service as Pumper No. 1. Note the location of the siren in the lower front end sheetmetal.

Some very early production American LaFrance 900s were equipped with painted headlight bezels, instead of the usual plated ones. This one, built for San Francisco, has the painted bezels. Engine Co. No. 27's pumper started out as an open cab job, but it has been fitted with a "Witten Protectall" fiberglass top. This after-market item, sold through ALF, is designed to fit all American LaFrance 700, 800 and 900 Series models.

In mid-1958, American LaFrance introduced its first completely new model since the 700 Series went into production following World War II. The new 900 Series fire engines were much more than just improved 800 models. The new design featured a totally new, wider cab with unbroken, rounded lines and dual headlight units. This is the 900 Series prototype. Production of 900 models began immediately, even though some 800 models were delivered into the early months of the following year.

Production of 800 Series fire apparatus continued well into 1958, even though the new 900 model was on the way. Miami Beach, Fla. took delivery of this Model 800 pumper of 750 GPM capacity. The front suction intake pipe runs under the cab and up over the front bumper.

One of the last 800 Series aerial ladder trucks built by American LaFrance was this closed cab Model 4-100 delivered to the Detroit suburb of Livonia, Mich. This 100-foot aerial has a 4-section ladder and carries two booster hose reels in addition to full ladder company equipment. The rear fender extension contains two large equipment compartments.

The Los Angeles City Fire Department ordered five of these Mack Model C-125 triple combination pumpers with open semi-cabs. These engines were powered by Hall-Scott 300-horsepower engines and drove 1,250 GPM Hale pumps. Note the older style of rear fender. The open trough above the rear fender is for carrying a length of soft suction hose. Engine 89's rig has a deck turret and a loudspeaker over the pump compartment.

Mack Trucks delivered hundreds of these C Series cab-forward fire engines over the next 10 years. Standard engine in this series was the Mack Thermodyne 6-cylinder gasoline engine available in 464 and 707 cubic-inch versions. The principal pumper models included the C-85 (750 GPM), C-95 (1,000 GPM) and the 1,250 GPM Model C-125. The pump was a two-stage centrifugal. This is a Model C-95 Mack. Note the coaster siren on the roof. Early Model C Macks had standard type rear fenders, but the compartmented type shown here soon became standard.

No, this is not a Ford! It is a Mack Model N. This little-known series utilized the new Budd-built steel tilt cab which Ford also used on its new C Series trucks introduced in 1957. The Model N had quad headlights and carried the familiar Mack Bulldog mascot just below the windshield. This floodlighting truck on a Mack chassis was built for Hicksville, Long Island, N. Y. This well-designed cab was soon to become one of the most popular fire apparatus chassis ever used in the United States.

Mack's proven and popular B Model Conventionals remained in production and continued to sell well even after the new cab-forward C Series made its appearance. This 1958 Mack Type B-95 pumper with 4-man sedan cab and 1,250 GPM midship-mounted pump was built for Minneapolis, Minn. Note the narrow center cab window above the pump compartment. This rig is MFD's Engine Co. No. 7.

The new Mack Model C was also available in this open-cab body style. This 1,000 gallon-per-minute pumper was displayed at the International Assn. of Fire Chiefs Convention in 1958. What made this engine of special interest was that it was equipped with an automatic transmission linked to a 276-horsepower Mack Thermodyne 6-cylinder engine. Mack had announced an automatic transmission option for its fire apparatus the previous year.

The New York City Fire Department in 1958 commenced a major fire apparatus replacement program. This huge contract went to Mack Trucks, Inc. in its entirety. A total of 52 of these Type C-85 triple combinations with 750 GPM Hale pumps and 375-gallon booster tanks were delivered in 1958, along with 12 Type C-95 pumpers with Hale 1,000 GPM pumps. All were powered by Mack 707 Thermodyne engines and had 1,250 GPM portable deluge nozzles mounted on the cab roof.

The Seagrave Corporation for the first time offered its customers a straight frame aerial ladder truck with a 4-section 100-foot ladder. Parma, Ohio owns this 1958 Seagrave series aerial, with 2-tone paint job and a canopy cab. Up until now, the largest ladder available on a Seagrave 4-wheel aerial was an 85-footer.

1958

This was still The Seagrave Corporation's standard closed-cab pumper. The 750 GPM pumper was built for Wilmette, Ill., with the electronic siren mounted in the nose, and the pre-connected soft suction hose carried on the front bumper pan. Some manufacturers began installing dual headlight units on their apparatus this year to meet new Federal lighting standards.

This Seagrave open-cab pumping engine has two windshields. The men riding the rear step thus have about the same protection from the elements enjoyed by the driver and the officer. Note the rear-mounted booster reel. On this style of Seagrave, hose is carried in a full-width shallow bed above a large booster tank. The gate above the rear running board on the right-hand side of the rig is for attachment of a 1½-inch line. This 750 GPM pumper was built for Penn Hills Township, Pa.

Like American LaFrance, Seagrave in 1958 switched to 4-unit headlights to comply with new Federal vehicle lighting standards. Seagrave built this 1,000 gallon-per-minute canopy cab pumper for Brook Park, Ohio. Still in excellent original condition, this pumper went into reserve service in 1975.

Green Bay, Wis. received this 1958 Seagrave quadruple combination. The plated upper radiator shell is a special option. This quad has a single large booster hose reel mounted immediately behind the canopy rear entrance cab. By now, all Seagraves were being delivered with the new squared front fenders.

A number of Canadian fire departments had been using the continental prototype rearmount aerial for many years. Narrow, congseted streets in cities like Montreal and Quebec City made this type of apparatus imperative. Pierre Thibault, Ltd. of Pierreville, Que., delivered this rearmount aerial with an English-made 100-foot Merryweather ladder to the City of Levis, Que. Fire apparatus in Quebec is frequently lettered in French on one side and in English on the other.

Ford's new C Series tilt-cab truck chassis was an immediate hit with fire apparatus manufacturers large and small. This basic style is still produced today, and literally thousands of Fords of this type are in service on fire departments all over North America. This is a small rescue squad truck on a 1958 Ford C Series chassis. A small portable wagon pipe is carried just behind the cab. The body builder is not known.

Peter Pirsch & Sons Co. of Kenosha, Wis. delivered this 750 GPM triple combination pumping engine to Winnetka, Ill. Note the 2-tone paint job and front-mounted pre-connected soft suction hose. Two booster reels are carried immediately behind the canopy cab.

The center-dipped 2-tone paint scheme used on this 1958 Peter Pirsch & Sons Co. pumper is interesting. The canopy cab pumper, with side entrance doors, was delivered to Springfield Township, Ohio. It has a 750 GPM pump and carries 750 gallons of water in its booster tank.

Pirsch custom-chassis fire engines were now being built with box-type front fenders and compartmented fenders in the rear. This is a 750 gallon-per-minute Pirsch pumper with open semi-cab. The booster reel is carried on the rear step. Most Pirsch pumpers now had the siren mounted on the left front fender and the bell atop the right.

Peter Pirsch & Sons Co. built this 500 GPM triple combination pumper on a 1958 Ford conventional chassis. This pumper has a 500-gallon booster tank, and is equipped with two booster reels. Fire engines of this type are still the mainstay of thousands of small-town and rural fire departments throughout America today. Their advantage over custom-chassis apparatus is their much lower initial cost, fairly quick delivery, and local availability of parts and service when maintenance is required.

Coast Apparatus Inc. of Martinez, Cal. built a small number of these cab-forward fire engines. This 1,250 GPM pumper was delivered to Grant's Pass, Ore. The protruding lower grille section containing the headlights and parking lights was a distinguishing feature of Coast apparatus. This cab was similar to the cab-forward design later introduced by Pirsch.

Coast Apparatus built quite a few of its conventional engine-ahead-of-cab custom fire engines for west coast fire departments. This triple combination pumper, which went inland to Salt Lake County, Utah, uses an International 2-man coupe cab which has been extended into a short canopy. It is powered by a Hall-Scott engine. The Coast name appears in the lower section of the grille between the head and parking lights.

Here is another light-duty Ford pumper of the type commonly found on suburban, rural and district fire departments. This pumper has a 500 GPM front-mounted pump protected by a grille cage. The bodywork appears to be that of Towers Fire Apparatus, of Freeburg, Ill.

1958

John Bean also built this compact junior quintuple combination on the new Ford C-Series tilt-cab chassis. It has a 600 GPM midship-mounted pump, and carries a 65-foot Memco aerial ladder. The Memco Aerial Ladder Co. of Oklahoma City, Okla., supplied many of these sturdy, yet inexpensive, aerial ladders to small towns and villages. This company is known as Sponco today.

The John Bean Division of the Food Machinery Corp. of Lansing, Mich. delivered seven of these GMC-Bean triple combination pumpers to Philadelphia in 1958. Similar in design to pumpers supplied to the Philadelphia Bureau of Fire by this company since 1954, these units had 750 GPM pumps and carried high pressure fog equipment. Note the high rear body and open semi-cab. This GMC-Bean went to Engine Co. No. 43.

At first glance, this appears to be a salvage or rescue unit. But it is in reality a compact city service ladder truck. This apparatus was built up by the Knoxville, Tenn. Fire Dept. shops on a new Ford C-600 tilt-cab chassis. This versatile piece of equipment is only slightly lower than a standard pumper.

Maxim performed some admirable nasal surgery here, in order to disguise this 1958 International Type V-190 chassis with a grille patterned after the standard Maxim front end. The squared front fenders are also unique. This 750 GPM pumper was delivered to North Reading, Mass.

The Maxim Motor Co. built this special pumper-squad truck for Fort Wayne, Ind. It is equipped with a 500-gallon per-minute midship-mounted pump and a fully compartmented rear body. It also carries booster equipment. Note how the cab door is cut around the pump panel, and the rear windshield. Fort Wayne's Rescue Unit is seen here rolling on a run.

Pawtucket, R. I. ordered this Maxim 100-foot tractor-drawn adrial ladder truck, with rear-entrance canopy style cab. Up to now, aerials built by Maxim with ladders longer than 85 feet had Magirus aerials, but the Middleboro, Mass. plant began manufacturing its own 4-section, 100-footers. This big trailer aerial has an electronic siren on its left front fender.

Three major fire apparatus manufacturers introduced their first cab-forward fire apparatus this year. American LaFrance, which had introduced its 700 Series in 1947, had a virtual monopoly on this configuration until 1956, when Ahrens-Fox came out with a cab-forward line of pumpers. In mid-1959, The Seagrave Corp. announced its first modern cab-forward apparatus. But the Columbus, Ohio company continued to build its 70th Anniversary style conventional series apparatus for another 11 years, even though the new cab-forward design was soon outselling the conventional model by leaps and bounds.

The Maxim Motor Co. of Middleboro, Mass. in 1959 introduced its own cab-forward design. Designated the Maxim Model F, it featured crisp, clean lines and continues in production almost unchanged today. Like Seagrave, Maxim did not put all of its sales eggs in this one basket; the company continued to make its popular engine-ahead-of-cab models.

The Four Wheel Drive Auto Co., which had built its reputation of all-wheel-drive apparatus, had begun building 2-wheel rear drive apparatus. The company's new Golden Line featured a good-looking cab-forward design.

In only one year, the Snorkel had proved its worth as a firefighting tool. One of its most convincing demonstrations was at an elevated train collision in Chicago, where the city's first elevating platforms rescued 60 passengers, bringing them down to ground level safety in a matter of minutes. So elated was the Chicago Fire Dept. with the versatility of its first Snorkel that it placed two more into service in 1959. They were mounted on Ford truck chassis, and were built by Mobile Aerial Towers of Fort Wayne, Ind. These Snorkels, a 65-footer and a 75-foot model, used Hi-Ranger booms of open lattice construction. Like the experimental prototype, they were nicknamed Quinn's Snorkels after the fire commissioner who had originated the concept.

The adaptation of the elevating platform to fire department service was no longer limited to the Windy City. The Chicago suburb of Bedford Park, Ill. in 1959 purchased a 65-foot Snorkel built on a GMC chassis with tandem rear axles. This Snorkel had a Pitman boom, and featured bodywork by the Pierce Mfg. Co. of Appleton, Wis., which would soon become a principal builder of elevating platform bodies.

At least four other companies now offered elevating platforms to fire departments. These included the Strato-

Tower Division of Young Spring and Wire Corp. of Elkhart, Ind., the J. H. Holan Corp. of Cleveland, Ohio, the Peters Co. of Portland, Ore., which built a telescopic platform, and the Truck Equipment Co. of Denver. But Pitman and Hi-Ranger were to become the big names in the early days of the firefighting Snorkel.

American LaFrance in 1959 observed its 125th Anniversary. The company could tract its origin back to 1834, when Lysander Button had started to manufacture hand-operated fire engines in Waterford, N. Y., not too far from the company's present location at Elmira. The new 900 Series apparatus was now coming off the line in high volume.

Chicago had taken delivery of four 100-foot Mack-Magirus rear-mounted aerial ladder trucks, and would soon receive two 144-foot Mack-Magirus aerials.

One of International's most popular fire apparatus chassis was now the company's new cab-over-engine VCO-196. The tilt-cab International chassis would be ordered with 401, 461 and 549 cubic-inch engines. The short bumper to back of cab design made this chassis ideal for fire apparatus. Almost all American fire apparatus builders were now building apparatus on the Ford C Series tilt-cab chassis.

Chicago's first experimental Snorkel proved so successful in its first year of service that two more were added in 1959. The two additional snorkels—a 65-footer and a 75-footer—were mounted on Ford truck chassis. The booms, of open-lattice design, were supplied by Mobile Aerial Towers, Inc., of Fort Wayne, Ind. and were identified by the trade name of Hi-Ranger. The 75-foot job went to Snorkel No. 2, and the 65-footer to Snorkel 3. Snorkel 1 was the original 50-foot Pitman on a GMC chassis that had been placed in service the previous year. Chicago newsmen dubbed these versatile devices Quinn's Snorkels after Chicago Fire Commissioner Robert Quinn.

International Harvester Co., of Chicago, built a number of VCO-190 chassis with standard 3-man cabs for the Chicago Fire Dept. The Chicago motor shops designed and had fabricated special purpose fire apparatus bodies for them. Several saw service as high pressure hose wagons of this type.

Coast Apparatus, Inc., of Martinez, Calif. built this 1,250 GPM triple combination pumper for the city of Oakland, Calif. Note the unusual front-end treatment and the resemblance to an International. Oakland rigs generally had full-open cabs of this style. A rotating beacon light has been added above the one-piece windshield.

New York City placed 64 of these Mack Type C pumpers into service in 1958, and added 20 more in 1959. The 1959 order included seven of these Model C-85-F's with 750 GPM Waterous pumps, and 13 C-95's with 1,000 GPM pumps. All were powered by Mack 707 Thermodyne engines. The FDNY jobs all had the older style contoured fenders without compartments. Engine Co. No. 79's spanking-new Mack is seen just before it entered service.

Also delivered to the New York City Fire Department during 1959 were eleven of these 1959 Mack Type C-85F tractor-drawn 85-foot aerial ladder trucks. These open-cab aerials had 4-section Maxim ladders and fixed tiller seats. On the same big order were two 1959 Mack C-85F tractor-drawn aerials with Magirus 100-foot aerial ladders, on Maxim hoists. This 85-footer was placed in service with Hook & Ladder Co. No. 13.

New York had—and still has—a distinct preference for Mack firefighting apparatus. In addition to the 20 new Mack pumpers and 13 Mack aerials purchased in 1959, the FDNY also ordered this huge rescue truck for its busy Rescue Company No. 1, quartered in Manhattan. The chassis is a 1959 Mack B Model powered by a Thermodyne engine, but the special-purpose rescue body was built by the Approved Fire Equipment Co. of Rockville Center, N. Y.

Chicago in 1959 purchased four special rear-mount aerial ladder trucks from Mack Trucks. Two of these were equipped with 146-foot Magirus 6-section aerials, and two had 4-section 100-foot Magirus ladders. All four were built on Special B-85 chassis. The 146-foot aerials are considerably shorter in overall length than conventional service or tractor-drawn aerials, but carry no ground ladders. This 146-footer served H & L Co. No. 39.

The Mack cab-forward was becoming a familiar sight in fire houses across the nation. Glen Ellyn, Ill. purchased this 1959 Mack C-95 pumper with a big 1,000-gallon booster tank. The pumper-tanker carries a 750 gallon-per-minute pump. Note the front suction intake,

Small pumpers like this were often built for large corporations that had their own industrial fire brigades. Industrial rigs had to be small to move down narrow plant aisles and through often-crowded plant yards. This Ford C Series pumper has a 350 GPM pump and carries 150 gallons of water in its booster tank. The builder and purchaser are not known.

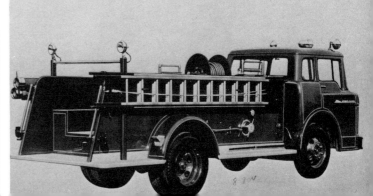

Paris Township ordered this Seagrave 1,000 gallon-per-minute pumping engine with 3-man closed cab. The rear fenders have two large equipment compartments instead of the single one used on earlier Seagrave custom pumpers. This apparatus also carries twin booster reels. Note the speaker on top of the cab; this is provided for the convenience of the pump operator on the fireground, so he does not have to climb back into the cab to receive messages from the central fire alarm office.

1959

Seagrave built this special rescue squad truck for Youngstown, Ohio utilizing the same basic body used for Detroit's well-known sedan pumpers. The Seagrave V-12 engine was later replaced with a Cummins Diesel, and at last report this squad was still in front line service.

The Seagrave Corporation introduced its first cab-forward fire apparatus in 1959. Up to now, only American LaFrance had offered a cab-forward line of pumpers and aerials. The new Seagrave cab-forward series featured a flat-faced cab and seated five men. This 1,000 GPM pumper has a front suction intake and a Federal Q siren. Note the bell mounted on the right-hand side of the cab. This basic style is still being built today, but has a considerable lower overall height.

Among the first cab-forward Seagrave pumpers delivered to a fire department was this 1,000 gallon-per-minute job for Lombard, Ill. It has the older style Seagrave nameplate used on the engine-ahead-of-cab models. Combination turn signals and alternating flashers are mounted just below the windshield, and the siren is integrated into the cab front sheetmetal.

West Chicago, Ill. ordered this 1959 Seagrave quintuple combination on the new cab-forward Seagrave chassis. It has a 4-section, 85-foot metal aerial ladder and a 1,000 GPM centrifugal pump. Seagrave's principal powerplant was still the old, reliable V-12. West Chicago's quint is seen here in a parade appearance.

The 1959 Seagrave 1,000 gallon-per-minute pumper in this photo was delivered to Denver, Colo., where it is now a reserve engine. Like all Denver rigs, it is painted white. The hard suction hoses have been removed to make room for a large breathing apparatus cabinet mounted on top of the rear fender.

The Seagrave Corp. had discontinued the manufacture of its low-cost commercial aerial ladder, and was now mounting its standard metal aerial ladders on commercial truck chassis. This is a 3-section 65-foot service aerial built on a Ford C Series tilt-cab chassis. The result is a compact, highly efficient little aerial truck which also carries a full complement of ground ladders and truck company equipment.

American LaFrance Corp. marked its 125th anniversary during 1959, and the company's production line was committed to full scale production of the new 900 Series fire apparatus. This is a closed cab model 900, with 1,250 GPM pump. The big ALF V-12 was still the standard powerplant, but a full range of Continental engines were also available. This pumper was delivered to Strongsville, Ohio.

American LaFrance built this compact little pumper on the new Ford C Series tilt-cab chassis. The pumper is a full triple combination, with 500 GPM pump, a 250-gallon booster tank, dual booster hose reels and an ample hose bed. Note the siren mounted on the nose. The cab-forward configuration considerably reduced overall length with no sacrifice of carrying capacity.

During the transition from 800 to 900 Series apparatus, American LaFrance turned out a very small number of late 800 Series fire engines that were equipped with the same quad headlight units used on all 900 Series trucks. Several 700s were rebuilt using this same type of headlight unit, and combined flasher/turn signal lights mounted above. LaFrance-Foamite, Ltd. of Toronto delivered this 100-foot Series 800 service aerial to the Toronto Fire Dept. late in 1958. This aerial was placed in service at No. 10 Station early in 1959 and was still running out of Yorkville Hall in 1975. The author knows of five 800s of this style.

American LaFrance during 1959 introduced a small crash truck called the Little Mo. Built on a Dodge Model 205 4-wheel-drive chassis, this hard-hitting, compact fire fighter was designed for airport and thruway service. Powered by a Chrysler-built V-8 engine, it had a 90-GPM roof turret, a 200-gallon water tank and separate tanks for 20 gallons of air-foam liquid and five gallons of wetting agent. It also carried two 150-foot booster reels. The Little Mo was conceived by "Army" Armstrong, who had earlier built a similar type of rig called the Blitz Buggy in his own shop in Old Forge, N. Y.

San Francisco purchased many 100-foot tractor-drawn aerial ladder trucks from American LaFrance in the late 1950s and into the 1960s. Truck Co. No. 4 of the S.F.F.D. was assigned this 1959 American LaFrance 900 Series tractor-trailer aerial with turntable levelling device—a necessity on the city's hilly streets.

The Cincinnati suburb of Evendale, Ohio received this Peter Pirsch & Sons Co. triple combination pumper, finished in striking white-and-red. The 1,000 GPM pumper carries no hard suction hose on its sides, and has a canopy-type cab. Note the small side-entrance door immediately behind the pump panel, and the handrail that encircles the rear of the roof. Two Mars lights on the fenders and another atop the grille clear the way through traffic.

Peter Pirsch & Sons Co., of Kenosha, Wisc. built this unusual commercial-chassis tractor-drawn aerial ladder truck. The tractor is a Ford conventional, and the trailer by Pirsch has a 3-section, 85-foot metal aerial. It is lettered for DeKalb County. Note the single air horn on top of the windshield. Fire departments were beginning to find the raucous air horn an effective means for moving through heavy traffic, in addition to the regular siren and bell.

Here is another unusual commercial-chassis aerial built by Peter Pirsch & Sons. It is a 75-foot 3-section aerial on a 1959 FWD 4 x 4 chassis, which was built for Syosset, Long Island, N. Y. This style of FWD chassis first appeared in 1955, and the aerial shown has a 5-man canopy cab.

Another special-purpose heavy truck chassis occasionally used by fire apparatus builders on request was the big Oshkosh, built by the Oshkosh Truck Corp., of Oshkosh, Wisc. Peter Pirsch & Sons Co. built this monstrous pumper on a 1959 Oshkosh 4 x 4 chassis for Oshkosh's home town. It has a 1,250 gallon-per-minute pump, and is every bit as big as it looks. This Oshkosh-Pirsch has a canopy style 5-man cab.

Peter Pirsch & Sons built this attractive and compact little 500 gallon-per-minute triple combination pumping engine. The Pirsch apparatus is mounted on an International Harvester VCO chassis, with cut-down semi-cab. Note the three lengths of 2½-inch hard suction hose.

Many smaller fire apparatus manufacturers were building pumpers and other types of fire equipment on the Ford C Series tilt-cab chassis. This 750 GPM pumper with standard three-man cab was built by the Oren-Roanoke Corp., of Roanoke, Va. Note the Federal Q siren mounted in the nose and the alternating red flashers on the roof. This practical pumper has two booster reels and a 400 gallon tank.

Fire apparatus in America entered the jet-age in 1960, albeit only for a short time.

The American LaFrance Fire Engine Co. delivered two turbine-powered fire engines to American fire departments in the latter half of 1960. These highly advanced units were both powered by Boeing 325 horsepower gas turbines. The first one delivered was a 900 Series 100-foot tractor-drawn aerial ladder truck with closed, 5-man canopy cab built for Seattle, Wash. This tiller aerial also featured a completely enclosed ladder bed and waterproof side compartments. The second American LaFrance jet-job was a 900 Series 1,000 GPM Class A triple combination pumper with open semi-cab delivered to San Francisco. These models were similar in appearance to conventional 900 Series apparatus, except for the big rear-angled stainless steel exhaust stack jutting out of the top of the engine compartment. American LaFrance also delivered a turbine-powered fire engine to Mount Vernon, Va.

Alas, however, the turbine power experiment proved to be premature. The jet-propelled fire apparatus proved unreliable in service. The turbos were noisy, and they lacked dynamic braking power. Acceleration was sluggish at best. Within a very few years, all of the American LaFrance turbine-powered rigs had been quietly converted back to conventional gasoline power. But the turbine engine continued to hold promise. Twelve years later, American LaFrance and another manufacturer would again experiment with turbine-powered fire fighting apparatus.

Howe Fire Apparatus of Anderson, Ind., in 1960 introduced a new line of Custom Howe Defenders on a new 5-man, cab-forward chassis. Power was by Waukesha.

The cab-forward cab used by Howe, and the one used by FWD for its new Golden Line cab-forward apparatus introduced the previous year, was a special type manufactured by the Truck Cab Manufacturers Inc. of Cincinnati. This style of cab would eventually be used by nearly every fire apparatus manufacturer in the business. Still in production today, the universal Cincinnati Cab is probably the most prolific since the original American LaFrance 700 design.

In October, 1960, the Maxim Motor Co. announced a new, short-wheelbase conventional line of pumpers. Designated the Maxim Model S, this engine-ahead-of-cab model complemented the new F Series cab-forward line the company had come out with in 1959, and boasted an extremely short over-all length and short turning radius. The new Maxim Model S was designed to make fire apparatus handling easier in heavy traffic.

Ward LaFrance in 1960 came out with its first cab-forward apparatus. The new Ward LaFrance Premium model had a flat-faced 5-man forward control cab with a grille located in the lower front sheet metal. This new model was also available in a special Ward LaFrance Fire Brand series, which was externally identical to the Premium model. New York City took delivery of 16 Ward LaFrance 1,000 GPM cab-forward pumpers this year. Ward's new cab-forward jobs were available with open or closed cabs.

In other developments, the American Fire Pump Co. introduced a 750 GPM version of its highly popular Type UA front-mount pump, and the Walter Motor Truck Co. came out with a new line of big, cab-forward airport crash and rescue fire trucks. Chicago had placed its fourth Snorkel into service, an 85-foot Hi-Ranger on a Ford chassis.

Fire fighters in St. Albans, Vermont give their new Peter Pirsch & Sons pumper the spit-and-polish on the ramp in front of their firehouse. The pumper has a front suction intake which has been fitted with a gated wye to take two short lengths of 2½-inch hose for hooking up to a hydrant that does not have a steamer connection.

The Maxim Motor Company of Middleboro, Mass., delivered this unusual fully-enclosed combination pumper and rescue squad truck to the Lafayette Hill, Pa., Barren Hill Fire Co. Built on a 1960 Ford C-600 tilt-cab chassis with standard 3-man cab, it has a 750 GPM pump. Dual headlight units were standard on Ford C models from 1958 through 1960.

One of the largest users of Maxim fire apparatus in the Midwest, Indianapolis placed this Maxim 1,000 GPM triple combination pumper with open semi-cab into service in 1960. Note the dual headlight units. The pumper shown was assigned to Engine Co. No. 2.

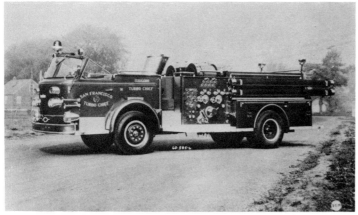

In one of the most revolutionary steps ever taken in fire apparatus design, American LaFrance in 1960 entered the jet-age. A highlight of the exhibits at the International Association of Fire Chiefs Conference, held in Rochester, N. Y., was this American LaFrance 900 Series triple combination pumper powered by a Boeing 325-brake-horsepower turbine engine. The 1,000 GPM Class A pumper was built for the San Francisco Fire Department. Note the stainless steel exhaust stack over the engine compartment.

American LaFrance also delivered a turbine-powered aerial ladder truck in 1960. It was this 100-foot tractor-drawn aerial built for the Seattle, Wash. Fire Department. This aerial featured a completely enclosed ladder bed and extra equipment compartment. Note the pompier, or scaling, ladder carried atop the front of the ladder bed. These jet-jobs were known as the Turbo-Chief Series. A third turbine-powered American LaFrance was delivered to Mount Vernon, Va., but the turbine engine proved disappointing in performance and all were eventually converted to gasoline power. The Elmira plant did not build its next turbine job until 1972.

In 1958, for the first time, American LaFrance began mounting its aerial ladders on medium to heavy-duty commercial truck chassis. At first, only the ALF 65-foot ladder was available, but by 1960 the 3-section 75-foot ladder had been added to the line. The most popular truck chassis used were the Ford tilt-cab shown here, the International VCO cabover, and the conventional series GMC. The 75-foot Ford-LaFrance aerial shown here was built for the Citizens Hose Co. No. 5, of Catskill, N. Y.

The American LaFrance 900 Series Aerial Ladder Truck was built in both open and closed-cab versions, and in the 6-wheel tractor-trailer type. Ladder lengths ranged from 65 to 100 feet on the 4-wheel service type, and were offered only in 85 and 100-foot lengths on the tractor-drawn Rescue Aerial series. This is a standard Model 4-100 Service Aerial on 1960. Note the compartmented rear fenders, and the partially-enclosed ladder bed.

Full custom chassis tankers are exceedingly rare. But American LaFrance delivered this big 900 Series tanker to Pleasantville, N. J. The size of the water tank it carries is not known, but it was obviously big enough to supply the two booster lines for some time. The plain style bumper on this truck was used on some 900 models from 1958 until about 1962.

American LaFrance designed and built some unusual rescue trucks on its new Series 900 chassis. Cheektowaga, N. Y. ordered this unique combination pumper and rescue apparatus. The 750 gallon-per-minute pump is enclosed behind the double doors immediately behind the rear cab entrance. Note the electronic siren–PA system on the front cab step.

Seagrave's new cab-forward models were enjoying considerable success, and more and more of the Columbus, Ohio plant's production was of this type. The 1,000 GPM triple combination Seagrave pumper shown here was delivered to Westchester, Ill., a suburb of Chicago. Note the extra length of hard suction hose carried on the right-hand siee of this pumper.

1960

One of the sportiest-looking fire engines anywhere is this River Edge, N. J. Seagrave in white with complementing gold leaf trim. Everything else appears to have been chromeplated. Note the absence of doors and the air horn built into the left side of the grille. Even the door below the cab entrance has been given the plating treatment.

Oak Lawn, Ill. specified this interesting Seagrave pumper. The prominent bumper extension carries both a winch and a length of soft suction hose. The 3-man closed cab has been nicely rounded off, and the new style squared rear fenders contain a forward compartment as well as a rear one.

Seagrave, which had pioneered the lower-cost, commercial-chassis aerial ladder truck, delivered a fair number of 65 and 75-foot aerials on standard trucks for smaller cities and towns, Corry, Pa., received this 1960 Seagrave-GMC 75-foot aerial, which is mounted on a GMC V-6 chassis with standard 3-man cab.

Quite a few fire departments still preferred the conventional engine-ahead-of-cab design, which The Seagrave Corp. continued to deliver in substantial numbers. This 1960 Seagrave, delivered to Lansing, Mich. is something special. It is an emergency squad truck, not a pumper. The canopy cab rig carries two booster reels and has a high pressure fog pump. It responds as Lansing's Squad 1.

Philadelphia received three of these 1960 Seagrave 100-foot tractor-drawn metal aerial ladder trucks. Up to now, Seagrave's largest aerials—the 85 and 100-foot types—were built only in three sections. The addition of the 4-section ladder shown here made it possible to switch to a fixed tiller seat, which saved precious seconds when the ladder was to be raised. The 100-foot ladder was now also available on a 4-wheel service aerial for the first time. Note the shop-built plywood cab on the tractor and the protective canopy erected over the tillerman's seat.

1960

Chicago in 1960 ordered two Mack Type B-85 aerial ladder truck tractors, which it used to modernize a couple of older wood aerials. These aerials used American LaFrance spring hoists, and were mounted on trailers which had been built in the Chicago Fire Dept. shops in 1937. The ladders were 85-footers in two sections. This is one of the 1960 Macks, which went to Hook & Ladder Co. No. 35.

The Vigilant Hose Co. No. 2, of Freeport, Long Island, N. Y., owns this brute of a Mack pumper. The 2-tone apparatus is a big Model B with a canopy cab and extra long wheelbase. The turret pipe mounted on the roof adds to its businesslike appearance. Federal sirens are mounted on each front fender.

Minneapolis received this big 1960 Howe Defender, based on the sturdy Duplex chassis. Engine 21's rig has a 1,250 gallon-per-minute pump, but carries no booster equipment. The Minneapolis Fire Department preferred this 4-door sedan type cab because of the city's harsh winters.

A major manufacturer of squad and rescue truck bodies, the Gerstenslager Co., of Wooster, Ohio, built this short, but roomy, semi-enclosed rescue squad truck on a 1960 Ford C-700 tilt-cab chassis. The forward-thrusted window design and the full rear wheel fender skirts give this truck a look of speed and action even when it is standing still. The closed portion of the rear body is equipped with doors for the comfort of the crew.

In addition to the many pumpers and aerials the Allentown, Pa. plant was building on the highly-successful C Series cab-forward chassis, Mack Trucks also delivered some special-purpose fire apparatus using this design. Freeport, Long Island, N. Y. ordered this special floodlight truck built on a C-85 Mack chassis. Note the full-width rear body with generous compartmentation.

Chicago added a fourth snorkel to its fire defenses in 1960. Snorkel No. 4 was built on a 1960 Ford chassis and featured more finished bodywork than that used on its predecessors. This 85-foot Hi-Ranger has four flop-down hydraulic stabilizer jacks located at each corner of the rear body. Three men could be carried in the basket, which is also equipped with a turret nozzle.

Ward LaFrance augmented its lower-priced Fireball Special line of smaller conventional-style pumpers with a new economy cab-forward job called the Firebrand. Not too many of these were built. The Firebrand had a clean, extra-wide cab that could seat seven men. The engine compartment was between the driver and officer's seats, and five men occupied the rear-facing, full-width bench seat. This model was also available with a closed cab.

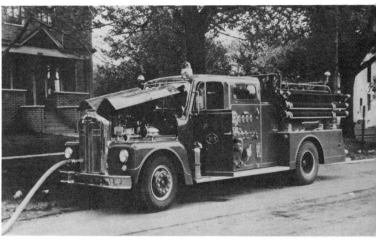

Ward LaFrance's standard model was still this type. Wheaton, Ill. purchased this 1960 Ward LaFrance 750 gallon-per-minute triple combination, with canopy style cab and a 700-gallon booster tank which almost qualifies it as a pumper-tanker. Wheaton's Model 85-T was assigned as Engine 9, and is seen taking water through a 2½-inch soft suction line.

The Four Wheel Drive Auto Co. had introduced its first cab-forward fire apparatus the previous year. The FWD cab-forward models were available in both open and closed 5-man styles, on 4 x 4, 6 x 6 or conventional 2-wheel drive chassis. Wausau, Wisconsin purchased this 1960 FWD cab-forward 750 gallon-per-minute pumper.

On January 1, 1960 every first-line pumper and ladder truck on the Detroit Fire Department was a Seagrave, but this loyalty to the Columbus, Ohio firm was broken later in the year when a 1960 FWD sedan-style pumper was purchased and placed in service at Engine Co. No. 6. The 1,000 GPM van pumper was powered by a Waukesha 6-cylinder engine, and like all Detroit pumpers, has a front suction intake. In 1969 this one-of-a-kind FWD was reassigned to Engine Co. No. 46.

Impressed with Chicago's experience with this new type of firefighting weapon, other fire departments began ordering elevating platforms, or snorkels. The Chicago suburb of Steger, Ill. received this 50-foot Pitman Snorkel, which is mounted on a 1960 FWD cab-forward chassis with Cincinnati cab. The rear bodywork was done by the Pierce Manufacturing Co. of Appleton, Wisc., which began to specialize in building Snorkel bodies, most of them on FWD chassis.

Baltimore, Maryland received two of these 1960 FWD conventional-style pumpers. These triple combinations have open semi-cabs and carry wagon pipes. The pumper shown here, resplendent in its attractive red-and-white paint job, responds as Engine 5.

In less than three years, the elevating platform, or Snorkel, had been accorded a full and enthusiastic acceptance by the fire service. By the middle of 1961 there were 21 in service with fire departments across the country. The Pitman Snorkel, which had started it all, was the most prolific. The Pitman Snorkel was now being manufactured by a separate Snorkel Fire Equipment Co. division at Grandview, Mo.

Among the new types of Snorkels delivered by this company were its first mounted on a commercial (Ford tilt cab) chassis, designed to carry a full complement of ground ladders; its first mounted on a conventional pumper chassis, a 50-footer delivered to Loves Park, Ill.; the first mounted on a commercial chassis (IH VCO-196) with a pump, a 50-footer delivered to Elko, Nev., and an 85-foot Snorkel mounted on a Ford C Series chassis built for Roseburg, Ore. The Chicago suburb of Steger, Ill. had also received a 50-foot Snorkel on a custom cab-forward chassis.

The Seagrave Corp. was the first of the major fire apparatus builders to offer an aerial platform. Seagrave in 1961 announced its Seagrave-Cemco Eagle elevating platform in 65 and 85-foot sizes. The 2-boom Cemco unit was designed for installation on Seagrave's standard custom cab-forward fire apparatus chassis, or on any suitable commercial truck chassis. In 1961, Seagrave delivered what was probably its most elaborate aerial ladder truck to the Excelsior Hook and Ladder Co. of Freeport, N. Y. This dazzling 100-foot, closed canopy cab tractor-drawn aerial was elaborately striped and trimmed. It rode on chrome-plated wheels, and even boasted a completely enclosed tillerman's compartment with sliding doors.

Seagrave had introduced its first 4-section, 100-foot aerial ladder. The company's tractor-drawn aerials using this ladder had a fixed tillerman's seat that did not have to be moved to raise the main ladder. The 3-section 100-foot ladder with swing-over tiller was still available. The 4-section 100-foot aerial was offered in both service and tractor-drawn models on the Seagrave Conventional or cab-forward custom chassis.

American LaFrance in 1961 built its last V-12 engine. The J-Model V-12, based on the old Auburn/Lycoming 12-cylinder engine design, was the last of a proud line of V-12 engines that had been introduced exactly 30 years earlier.

Mack Trucks at this point in time was urging fire chiefs to seriously consider the advantages of Diesel power for fire apparatus. In 1959, the company had installed one of its Thermodyne Diesels in a Mack B Model chassis, and found it highly suitable for fire apparatus service. In 1960, Mack had delivered three Diesel-powered B Model fire engines to Hamilton, Bermuda. Mack had been a real innovator in fire apparatus power. In 1956 it displayed a pumper with a torque converter, and the following year offered an optional automatic transmission. The first Diesel-powered fire engine in America was a New Stutz that had been delivered to Columbus, Ind. in 1939. The Cummins-powered New Stutz was still going strong.

In other news, New York City had ordered 20 American LaFrance tractor-drawn aerials, and Milwaukee had placed in service a 75-foot Geesink rear-mounted aerial on a cab-forward FWD chassis.

Many fire departments were now using electronic sirens.

The Hahn Motor Co., Hamburg, Pa., built this unusual Autocar 750 GPM pumper for Hockessin, Del. With a 3-man open semi-cab, it is powered by a Diesel engine. The big "H" on the front bumper stands for Hockessin, while the nameplate under the bumper face bar identifies the builder.

East St. Louis, Ill. got this triple combination pumper which was built by the Central Fire Truck Corp. on an International VCO-196 tilt-cab chassis. Central apparatus can be easily identified by the shape of the gauge panel on the pump operator's side of the apparatus.

The District of Columbia purchased a few of these Ward LaFrance Fire Brand 750 GPM cab-forward pumpers. These economy jobs were powered by International Harvester engines, and even sported International grilles. A makeshift roof has been added over the cab.

1961

These effective warning devices emitted an attention-grabbing "whoop" instead of the familiar coaster siren sound, and some even incorporated a public address system.

In one of the lesser known transactions of the year, the last remaining vestiges of the old Ahrens-Fox Fire Engine Co. were sold to a former Ahrens-Fox employee, Richard C. Nepper. Mr. Nepper acquired from General Truck not only the rights to the Ahrens-Fox name, but also all of the company's records and remaining parts stocks. Curt Nepper set up his own one-man Ahrens-Fox Co. at 1638 Central Ave. in downtown Cincinnati, and is still in business today. Mr. Nepper is dedicated to keeping all of the Ahrens-Foxes still on the road rolling. The last fire engine to bear the Ahrens-Fox name has yet to be delivered. For the past several years, Mr. Nepper has been hand-crafting a midship-mounted pumper on a Ford C tilt-cab chassis for the fire department of Southern Campbell, Ky.

American LaFrance delivered this Series 900 Rescue Model 100-foot tractor-drawn aerial ladder truck to Baltimore County, Md. This aerial has the closed 5-man cab, a 4-section metal aerial and carries booster hose in the raised compartment immediately behind the engine hood. This aerial is stabilized by four manually-operated jacks. The American LaFrance V-12 engine was beginning to decline in popularity, and Elmira offered a full range of Continental gas engines in its apparatus.

This very busy-looking quintuple combination by American LaFrance is mounted on a 1961 International Harvester VCO-196 chassis. It has a 750 GPM pump under the turntable, and a 3-section 75-foot aerial ladder. The booster hose compartment and tank are above the ladder racks, and the rear portion carries hose. This quint was delivered to Endwell, N. Y.

American LaFrance delivered this factory-fresh 900 Series pumper to Loudonville, N. Y. Note the unusual striping treatment around the edges of the door. This 1,000 GPM closed canopy cab pumper carries two booster reels and has clothing racks on each side of the hose bed.

The 1961 American LaFrance 900 Series pumper shown here was shipped all the way out to Walla Walla, Wash. It is equipped with a single booster reel and a portable deluge nozzle. The playout rail for the booster hose on the right-hand side of the apparatus is higher than the one on the left, to permit it to pass over the ground ladders carried on that side.

The Maxim Motor Company built four of these 100-foot tractor drawn aerial ladder trucks for the Philadelphia Fire Dept. The 1961 models had open semi-cabs and the new, short S Model tractor. Manual stabilizer jacks are visible below the trailer front, and the main ladder is the 4-section type. The rig shown is in service as Ladder Co. No. 13.

This heavy-duty rescue squad has a greatly-extended front bumper pan which carries a large winch. American LaFrance built this unit for St. Mary's. Pa. on a Series 900 chassis. It is used by St. Mary's Crystal Fire Dept., No. 6. Note the full width, completely enclosed rear body.

In less than three years, the versatile snorkel had reached maturity as the most revolutionary piece of firefighting equipment since the invention of the aerial ladder. Fire departments all over the country were now ordering elevating platforms from numerous manufacturers. One of the first platform placed in service on the West Coast was this 65-footer built for Downey, Calif., by the Crown Coach Corp. of Los Angeles. This snorkel also carries a full set of ground ladders. The boom is a Pitman.

Honolulu, Hawaii's first elevating platform was this interesting hybrid built up by the Crown Coach Corp. of Los Angeles. The chassis is a long wheelbase International and the boom is an 85-foot Pitman. The Crown Firecoach emblem can be seen at the top of the A frame support in front of the radiator.

The use of elevating platforms, or snorkels, was by no means limited to large cities. The small city of Wyoming, Mich. received this 65-foot Pitman snorkel mounted on an FWD chassis. The principal suppliers of elevating platforms were the Pitman Manufacturing Co. of Grandview, Mo. and Mobile Aerial Towers of Fort Wayne, Ind., makers of the Hi-Ranger.

The Four Wheel Drive Auto Company of Clintonville, Wis. continued to deliver conventional engine-ahead-of-cab fire engines as well as its new cab-forward units. This 1,000 GPM triple combination was built by FWD for the Village of Plandome, N. Y., in 1961. Note the absence of hard suction hose.

The Four Wheel Drive Auto Co. built only a small number of FWD cab-forward fire engines of this design. The apparatus shown is a big tanker that was built for Salem Township, Pa. The chassis is the go-anywhere FWD Tractioneer. This rural service tanker resembles an airport crash truck.

Milwaukee, Wis., which had purchased three Mack-Magirus rearmount aerial ladder trucks four years earlier, placed another rearmount into service in 1961. The 1961 rig, however, was an FWD cab-forward chassis with a closed cab, which carried a 4-section 85-foot aerial ladder built by Geesink, in Holland. Like the Macks. Ladder Co. No. 12's FWD-Geesink could squeeze into places that were inaccessible to a conventional aerial.

The Chicago Fire Department ordered a series of diminutive, special-purpose fire trucks built on the small Jeep FC-170 chassis. Two of these were special smoke ejector rigs built by John Bean, of Lansing, Mich. The large, round tubes are accordion-folding smoke pipes which attach to the round connection visible on the side of the apparatus. A powerful motor literally sucks the deadly smoke and gases out of the building.

Another one of Chicago's special purpose fire engines was this little high pressure turret wagon. Designated Jeep Pressure No. 1, it could be driven directly into a burning building, its 4-way deck monitor blasting its way through the flames, Jeep Pressure 1 was built on a Jeep FC-170 chassis. The Chicago firehouse that quartered several of the little Jeep rigs was nicknamed Disneyland.

Probably the most ornate piece of fire apparatus delivered to any American fire department in 1961 was this elaborately-appointed tractor-drawn 100-foot aerial ladder truck built by Seagrave for the Excelsior Hook and Ladder Co. No. 1 of Freeport, N. Y. This aerial is richly striped and lettered. It has chromed wheels, but its most interesting feature is the completely enclosed and heated tillerman's compartment at the rear of the apparatus. It is believed that this was the first such enclosed tiller seat in the U.S. Note the extra flashers on the front of the cab, and the wrap-around handrail on the cab rear.

The Howe Fire Apparatus Co. of Anderson, Ind. introduced a new line of custom cab-forward Howe Defenders. This 1961 Howe Defender was built for Fargo, North Dakota. After years of service, it was repainted chrome yellow for improved after-dark visibility. Apparatus photographer Larry Phillips took this photo of the repainted rig, which was originally the traditional fire department red.

Washington, D.C. during the 1960s began to specify a wide, white band around the middle of its red-painted fire apparatus, for improved visibility. Truck Co. No. 4's 1961 Seagrave 100-foot tractor-drawn aerial has also been equipped with a shop-built cab and tiller seat enclosure for the protection of the crew. This Seagrave is unique in that it has three full-width grille bars instead of the two usually used. The aerial is a 3-section one with swing-over tiller seat.

Howe's bread-and-butter was still the small and medium-duty fire apparatus built on commercially-available chassis. Howe delivered this interesting fire engine to Cody, Wyo. It has a cut-down semi-cab, and mounts a 750 GPM pump up front. The chassis is a 1961 GMC.

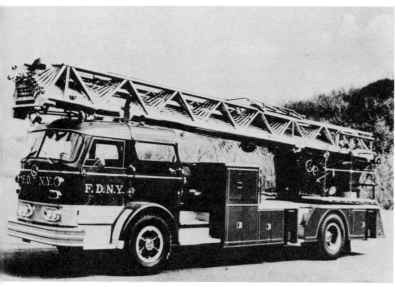

Mack Trucks built this massive B Model pumper for Bryan, Ohio. Bryan's businesslike-looking Mack has a 4-door sedan cab and a 1,000 GPM pump. Note the two narrow profile booster reels immediately behind the cab.

New York City joined the high-ladder club in 1961 with the acquisition of two of these 146-foot Magirus rearmount aerials mounted on Mack C-85F closed cab-forward chassis. The main ladder had six sections. The FDNY's two high ladders were taken out of service and refitted with 100-foot Grove aerial ladders in 1969.

Eagle Hook and Ladder Co. No. 1 of Ocean Grove, N. J., was re-equipped with this big Peter Pirsch & Sons Senior 100-foot tractor-drawn aerial ladder truck in 1961. This aerial truck differed from earlier Pirsch 100-footers, in that it had a 4-section ladder and a fixed tiller seat which did not have to be removed to raise the aerial. The new Pirsch cab-forward model had a flat, plain face.

The Cleveland suburb of Lakewood, Ohio received this new cab-forward Mack 750 gallon-per-minute pumper. This C Series pumper has a 150-gallon booster tank and a narrow-style single booster reel. The bell is mounted just behind the engine compartment. Mack was still building the conventional type B Series fire apparatus.

Pierre Thibault Ltd., a Canadian fire apparatus manufacturer located in Pierreville, Quebec, introduced a new line of cab-forward custom fire engines. These were built on the Thibault custom chassis, and employed some Budd sheet metal for the cab front and doors. These components were the same as used on the Ford C Series tilt-cabs. This 1961 Pierre Thibault Custom 840 Imperial gallon-per-minute pumper (1,000 U. S. gallons) was built for the Town of Dundas, a suburb of Hamilton, Ontario. It sports a LaFrance bell.

The Sutphen Fire Equipment Co. of Amlin, Ohio delivered this 750 gallon-per-minute pumper to Medina, Ohio. It is built on an International chassis, and carries 1,000 gallons of water. The pump gauges are built into the top of the chrome-plated radiator shell.

American LaFrance in 1962 entered the aerial platform field. The Elmira, N. Y. fire apparatus manufacturer unveiled its Aero-Chief elevating platform at the 1962 International Association of Fire Chiefs Conference held in Toronto, Ontario. The prototype American LaFrance Aero-Chief was a 70-foot unit mounted on an open cab 900 Series chassis. The rear body of the first American LaFrance Aero-Chief was completely enclosed. It was powered by a 305-horsepower Continental Red Seal 6-cylinder gasoline engine.

The Aero-Chief's upper boom nested in the U-shaped upper end of the lower boom. The roomy basket could carry three men and was equipped with a fixed monitor nozzle. An optional feature of the American LaFrance elevating platform, which had been under development for several years, was a hydraulically-operated split windshield, which could be opened up. The boom could then be lowered to permit the unit to work its way under obstructions. The prototype Aero-Chief was eventually sold to Berkely, Calif.

Another important new product introduced by American LaFrance this year was the company's line of Airport Chief crash, rescue and airport structural fire engines. Based on the 900 Series design, with 4-wheel drive and high flotation tires, the Airport Chief pumpers and crash trucks featured a wide bank of high visibility paint around the front and sides of the closed canopy cab. A large foam turret was mounted on the roof. Hatches permitted the crew to direct operations from the top of the apparatus.

Peter Pirsch and Sons Co. of Kenosha, Wis. had introduced its own distinctive cab-forward fire apparatus chassis and was now delivering pumpers and aerials of this type, in addition to its conventional series. The Pirsch forward control cab had flat, angular lines, and this same basic style is still built by Peter Pirsch & Sons today.

Elevating platforms continued to gain in popularity. Mobile Aerial Towers of Fort Wayne, Ind., builders of the Hi-Ranger platform, franchised the distribution of its units to Ward LaFrance Truck Corp., Elmira Heights, N.Y., in the east, and on the West Coast to P. E. Van Pelt Inc. of Oakdale, Calif. Ward LaFrance was developing a new cab-forward chassis on which it would mount the open-lattice Hi-Ranger platforms. Among the most popular elevating platforms in the country were the big 85-footers built by Snorkel Fire Equipment and mounted on the FWD cab-forward custom fire apparatus chassis. Most of these FWD-Pitman featured bodywork by Pierce Manufacturing.

Seagrave had introduced a new conventional-chassised combination pumper and foam engine. Called the Seagrave Vigilante, it featured a 1,000 GPM centrifugal pump and had a large foam turret behind the 3-man closed cab. Designed for the protection of oil fields, industrial complexes, etc., the first of these was delivered to Port Everglades, Fla. Hall-Scott engines by Hercules were now available in Seagrave conventional apparatus, and were popular in Seagraves delivered in the Western U. S.

Mack had found increased interest in its Diesel-powered fire apparatus. During 1962, this company delivered a cab-forward Diesel pumping engine to Cresson, Pa.; a B Model Diesel pumper to the Sunset Fire Co. of North Versailles, Pa., and a fleet of three cab-forward Diesel pumpers with open cabs to Cheyanne, Wyo.

Maxim delivered a special combination foam pumper with roof turret to East Providence, R. I. This apparatus was mounted on a Model F cab-forward chassis. A Canadian fire apparatus manufacturer, Pierre Thibault (Canada) Ltd. of Pierreville, Que. began to market its custom and commercial chassis pumpers and aerial ladder trucks in the United States. Yankee-Walker Corp. of Los Angeles, introduced a new series of twin-engined crash trucks designed for use at major airports.

American LaFrance Corp. built this big 1,000 GPM pump for the Liberty Fire Co., of East Berlin, Pa. The oversized tires indicate that this pumper is built on the low-volume Ford C-1100 heavy-duty chassis. The cab has been extended to the full canopy style. Note the plated mounting blocks for the siren and bell on the front of the cab.

American LaFrance got into the elevating platform fire apparatus market in 1962. This company's platform had been under development for some time. It differed from all others in that the upper articulating boom unit nested into the lower boom. American LaFrance named its new aerial platform the Aero-Chief. The first one built, a 70-footer, was shown at the LAFC Conference held in Toronto, Ontario, Canada in September. It is believed that this prototype—the only one produced with completely enclosed rear body—was eventually sold to Berkely, California.

American LaFrance built this commercial-type 75-foot aerial on a Ford C Series tilt-cab chassis. This aerial also carries booster equipment. The ladder is a 3-section, hydraulically-operated unit. American LaFrance aerial ladders were generally painted battleship gray, while Seagrave's were silver in color, and Pirsch's were left in natural aluminum.

Nashville, Tennessee—the home of Country Music—was a good Seagrave customer. This 1962 Seagrave 1,000 GPM canopy-cab pumper built for the Nashville Fire Dept. has a painted rather than plated front bumper, a chrome-plated upper grille housing, and a bell mounted on the front bumper pan rather than on the right-hand side of the cowl. Nashville's Engine Co. 19 also carries a portable deluge set. Note the Fire Department sunburst emblem above the suction port.

1962

Gallup, New Mexico's volunteer fire department ordered this 1962 Seagrave 1,000 gallon-per-minute pumper. The Seagrave Corp. had started to offer its customers the choice of other engines besides its now-ageing V-12. This pumper is powered by a Hall-Scott engine. Seagraves delivered to Western fire departments in warm climates, and with some of these optional engines, had special hoods with extra ventilation slots.

This is the one and only quadruple combination ever to see service in Detroit. It was purchased to meet the special requirements of Engine Co. No. 48, which was often cut off from other responding companies by a drawbridge in its district. The 1962 Seagrave 1,000 GPM Quad carries a full supply of ground ladders as well as hose and 500 gallons of water and two booster reels. Like all Detroit engine companies, it has a preconnected soft suction hose up front. This canopy-cab quad is still in service at Engine 48 at Bayside and Sanders.

Detroit purchased only one Seagrave sedan pumper in 1962. This 1,000 GPM van went into service as Engine Co. 1, but was later assigned to Engine Co. No. 21. In 1961, the Seagrave Corp. had started using the smaller, square nameplate visible in the center of this rig's grille. This photo was taken across the street from D.F.D. Headquarters at Washington Blvd. and Larned St.

The W. S. Darley Co., formerly of Chicago and now located in Melrose Park, Ill., built this heavy-duty rescue squad truck for Bensenville, Ill. The tandem axle rig is on a 1962 International 1700 6 x 6 chassis, that was delivered to Darley as a chassis-cowl. Note the front-mounted winch. This apparatus carries a wide array of emergency and rescue gear in storage compartments inside the roomy, enclosed body.

The Gerstenslager Co. of Wooster, Ohio, builds a complete range of squad and rescue bodies ranging from light-duty utility-type bodies for small chassis on up to huge, enclosed van-type rescue trucks on any custom or commercial chassis preferred by the customer. East Chicago, Ill. ordered this canopy-cab Gerstenslager squad built on a Ford C Series tilt-cab chassis. East Chicago's Emergency Squad No. 1 is seen here in action at a major fire. A turret pipe mounted between two main compartments lobs a master stream into the heart of the fire.

Engine Co. No. 14 of the New Orleans Fire Department got this 1962 Mack Type C-95F triple combination pumper with open semi-cab. This pumper has a 1,000 GPM Hale pump and carries two of the narrow-type booster hose reels. New Orleans was a good Mack customer, having ordered a sizable number of Mack pumping engines in previous years.

1962

The Mack C-Type pumper could be found in fire houses from coast to coast. This is a standard Type C-85F cab-forward demonstrator model with a 750 GPM pump and 300-gallon booster tank. Engine choices in the C Series pumpers included the Mack 6-cylinder ENF-540 Thermodyne engine, rated at 204 horsepower, and the big 276-horsepower ENF-707C. The 707 engine was standard in all Mack aerials. The C Series pumpers were built on standard 160-inch wheelbases. Note the Q siren mounted between the headlights.

Chicago, the city that gave the fire service the elevating platform, also developed this extremely versatile, compact Snorkel-Squad. Mounted on an International VCO-196 chassis, this rescue truck is equipped with a 40-foot snorkel. Snorkel Squad 2's rig has bodywork by Erlinder, and a Strato-Tower platform. These extremely functional squad units quickly proved themselves in service, and snorkel-squads were still on the C.F.D. roster in 1975.

The Central Fire Truck Corp. built this special pumper for the St. Louis, Mo. Fire Dept. It is stationed at Lambert Field, the St. Louis Municipal Airport. Painted safety yellow, it has a 1,000 GPM pump, a fixed deck turret and a Cincinnati cab.

This interesting fire engine has fooled a lot of people. At first glance it appears to be a Maxim on a Ford tilt-cab chassis. Actually, it is a rare Mack Model N Aerial with 75-foot Maxim ladder. This unique aerial was delivered to the Viscose Fire Co. in Marcus Hook, Pa., in 1962.

Paterson, N. J. has riot-proofed Truck Co. No. 1's 1962 Pirsch aerial ladder truck by erecting hideous-looking, but functional, protective roofs over the cab and the tillerman's seat. This aerial has the standard three-section 100-foot aluminum alloy ladder. Civil unrest during the mid to late 1960s forced many cities to provide similar protection for its firefighters.

Ward LaFrance built relatively few of its Firebrand cab-forward models between 1960 and 1962. This Firebrand, with closed cab, was delivered to the Delaview Fire Co. of Pennsauken, N. J. It is equipped with a 750 GPM pump and a 500-gallon booster tank. Note how the bell has been cut into the front of the cab. The flashing beacon light has been mounted below the roofline to permit the apparatus to fit into the limited clearance of the firehouse.

Boston, Mass. received 10 of these Ward LaFrance semi-cab pumpers in 1962. Four were 1,250 GPM pumpers. The other six were 1,000 gallon-per-minute models like this one. The pumper pictured—battered and battle-scarred after years of hard urban service—was assigned as Engine 37's hose wagon. Note the shop-built protective cab and rather basic front fenders. The author caught 37's wagon on a run in July, 1974.

The first elevating platforms to enter the fire service were highly-specialized, single-purpose machines. But the versatile snorkel proved highly adaptable to many different types of fire engines, including pumpers and quadruple combinations. This 65-foot snorkel quint was delivered to Abilene, Kansas in April, 1962. Built on a Ford C Series tilt-cab chassis, it has a 750 GPM pump and 300-gallon booster tank. In addition, it carries more than 200 feet of ground ladders and a full hose load. The chassis is a C-1000 and the platform is a Pitman.

The Maxim Motor Co. built this large commercial chassis pumper on a Ford F-750 truck chassis. The rig is all Maxim back from the cowl. Note the side-by-side placement of the hard suctions, below the ground ladder, and the deck pipe pointed skyward.

Technically, this very well equipped triple combination qualifies as a quad because of the added firefighting punch afforded by the 50-foot Pitman Snorkel carried on it. The chassis is a Ford C-850 powered by Ford's 534-cubic inch V-8 engine. Built by the Crown Coach Corp. of Los Angeles, this compact snorkel-pumper has a 1,000 GPM pump, two booster hose reels, a 350-gallon water tank and carries 1,200 feet of 2½-inch hose and 400 feet of 1½-inch line. This type of equipment proved ideal for smaller communities that did not have aerial equipment, because it combined a specialized piece of equipment with a standard pumper.

Memphis, Tennessee's second aerial platform was this 1962 FWD-Pitman 75-foot snorkel, built on an FWD cab-forward chassis and carrying a full complement of metal ground ladders. Stabilization is provided by two sets of hydraulic A-frame jacks. The Pitman elevating platform was sold by the Snorkel Fire Equipment Co. of Grandview, Mo. Memphis' Snorkel Truck Co. No. 1 is powered by a Waukesha gasoline engine.

1963

This was to be a big year for The Seagrave Corp. On June 28, 1963, the Columbus, Ohio firm announced that it had been sold to the FWD Corp. of Clintonville, Wis. The company said it would gradually close down its old Columbus plant and transfer fire apparatus manufacturing operations to the FWD plant in Clintonville.

In 1963, Seagrave introduced its own design of rear-mounted aerial. Called the Seagrave Rear Admiral, this new aerial had its turntable mounted at the rear, and was designed for the company's custom cab-forward chassis. Production and deliveries of the new type, however, were delayed by the move to Clintonville and none were built or sold for several more years. Also in 1963, Seagrave built its first 90-foot elevating platform. The first 3-boom, 90-foot Eagle platform was delivered to the Kentland Volunteer Fire Co. of Kentland, Md. This same year Seagrave built a small one-off 70-foot Eagle elevating platform for Nashville, Tenn. This one featured a 2-section, tubular boom and was mounted on the company's conventional series custom chassis.

The Los Angeles City Fire Dept. in 1963 replaced its aging Duplex-Manifold pumper system with a pair of huge specially designed fire engines built by the Crown Coach Corp. Assigned to Engine Co. 17, they included a monstrous manifold wagon equipped with a 2,000 GPM pump and 14 outlets for 2½-inch hose, and a 2,000 GPM pumper. The wagon was equipped with a huge, hydraulically-operated Stang turret pipe, complete with tractor-type seat for the operator. The pumper was equipped with a fireboat-sized Greenburg deck monitor. The 1937 and 1938 American LaFrance twin-engined Duplex pumpers, and the 1938 ALF and Seagrave manifold wagons delivered in 1938 had been retired from service.

One of the lesser known smaller manufacturers, the Sutphen Corp. of Columbus, Ohio, in 1963 demonstrated a new type of aerial tower of its own design. The Sutphen elevating platform featured a telescopic, lattice type aluminum boom with a basket on the end. This was the forerunner to the hundreds of Sutphen Aerial Towers in service all over the United States today. That first Sutphen

Tower was a 65-foot model mounted on a Ford C Series tilt-cab truck chassis.

American LaFrance commenced deliveries of its new Aero-Chief elevating platform. The Aero-Chief was available in 70, 80 and 90-foot sizes. One of the first Aero-Chiefs delivered was shipped to Juneau, Alaska. Despite the harsh Alaskan weather, it had an open 900 Series cab.

International Harvester had added yet another model to its range of special fire engine chassis. The new International CO-8190 was a cab-forward model with a 5-man canopy cab. This new chassis proved to be very popular with many fire apparatus builders, and joined the cab-over-engine VCO-196; the new Loadstar conventional; the V-Line conventionals, and the old, reliable R-Series International fire truck chassis which had been in production since the mid-1950s. The new CO-8190 cab closely resembled the standard Cincinnati cab, except for a small transverse grille located between the towing eyes on the International.

The Oren-Roanoke Corp. was also building a line of cab-forward pumpers now, utilizing a special chassis supplied by Duplex. This chassis also bore a Cincinnati cab.

Tulsa, Okla. modernized its fire department with the purchase of 12 Central-Ford C Series 1,000 GPM pumpers and three Boardman elevating platforms. The Boardman Snorkels were on Ford C Series chassis and included one 65-footer and two 75-foot models. All had Pitman booms.

The American LaFrance 900 Series pumper in this photo was delivered to the City of Livonia, Mich. It has a front suction intake with preconnected soft suction hose carried on the extended front bumper, and an extra length of hard suction hose. The handwheel at the lower left of the pump panel opens and closes the front intake. Note the electronic siren-PA system on the roof.

American LaFrance Corp. shipped this new Series 900 aerial ladder truck all the way up to Ketchikan, Alaska. For obvious reasons, this rig has a closed cab. It is a Model 4-85 with 3-section 85-foot aerial ladder. The roomy compartment above the split ladder bed was an extra-cost option.

In 1962, American LaFrance came out with a new specially-designed series of crash, rescue and airport structural fire engines based on the Series 900. These were called Airport Chief models. Their most distinguishing feature was a high-visibility standard paint scheme, consisting of a wide, reflectorized band around the middle of the cab and a similar treatment on the roof and upper cab. The 1963 Airport Chief pumper shown here protects Washington's Dulles International Airport.

A good percentage of the fire apparatus coming off Seagrave's assembly floor in Columbus, Ohio was still of the conventional engine-ahead-of-cab type. West Milwaukee, Wis. ordered this options-laden 1963 Seagrave 1,250 GPM pumper with standard canopy cab. Note the two tinted glass skylights in the front of the cab roof, the permanently-mounted turret pump behind the canopy, and the front suction intake. This well-equipped pumper also has road sanders.

The Seagrave Corp. delivered its first elevating platform this year. Most of the Seagrave snorkels produced during the mid-1960s were of the 3-boom type on Seagrave's cab-forward chassis. Only one of these 70-foot Eagle platforms, mounted on a conventional Seagrave aerial ladder truck chassis, was built. This one-off snorkel was delivered to Nashville, Tenn. It has a 2-piece tubular boom.

By now, Seagrave's standard model was the cab-forward type. The engine-ahead-of-cab conventional was still available, but fewer and fewer customers were specifying it. Westlake, Ohio received this 1,000 GPM Seagrave with sun-reflecting white paint above the cab belt line.

One of the more unusual commercial-chassis jobs turned out by the Seagrave Corp. was this big tractor-trailer pumper-tanker. The tractor is an International VCO-196, equipped with a 500 GPM pump. The trailer is a standard tank truck trailer that carries nearly 3,000 gallons of water. Note the ladders carried atop the tank trailer. The tractor has generous compartment space. This big pumper-tanker was built for Carlisle Township, Mass.

Seagrave built several of these Seagrave Eagle 3-boom aerial platforms. Mounted on the Seagrave cab-forward chassis, they were available in 75 and 85-foot working heights. The aerial platforms used by Seagrave were built by the Daybrook Division of the Young Spring and Wire Co. of Bowling Green, Ohio. This 90-foot Seagrave Eagle 3-boom snorkel was built for the City of Los Angeles, but it never went into service on the LAFD. Note the location of the aerial platform turntable, in the middle of the apparatus.

Detroit purchased only two Seagraves this year—a 1,000 GPM sedan pumper and the 100-foot tractor-drawn aerial ladder truck shown here. Even Detroit was swinging away from V-12 power. These Seagraves were both powered by Waukesha 6-cylinder gasoline engines. This aerial was originally assigned to Ladder Co. No. 1.

The Brumbaugh Body Co. of Altoona, Pa. is well-known for its custom-built rescue squad bodies. But Bruco also built pumpers and other types of fire apparatus. Morningside, Md., ordered this unusual pumper, which was built by Bruco on a cut-down GMC tilt-cab chassis. It mounts a 1,000 GPM pump, and has a windshield for the crew riding the back step. The bell and an electronic siren are mounted atop the protruding red flashers on the front of this tenacious-looking engine.

1963

This type of heavy duty, all-purpose crash truck can be found in the fire stations of most major airports. The Massachusetts Port Authority's Engine 4, based at Boston Logan International Airport, is a 1963 Walter Model CB crash truck that is powered by two large V-8 gasoline engines. This monstrous apparatus carries 2,500 gallons of water and 500 gallons of fire-smothering foam. Moving in on a downed aircraft, it discharges its entire load in minutes through the two large turrets on the roof. This crash rig can respond to any location on the airport property, and is designed for effective operation on unpaved, off-runway terrain.

Detroit, which had purchased Seagrave pumpers almost exclusively for the previous 30 years, placed this Mack Model C-95F into service at Engine Co. 31 in 1963. This was the first Mack pumper purchased by Detroit since 1929. The 1,000 GPM pumper is powered by a Mack Thermodyne 6-cylinder gasoline engine. Note the twin oscillating lights on the cab roof. Unlike most pumpers used in Detroit up to now, the new Mack carried booster equipment. Detroit later purchased three more C Series Mack pumping engines.

Mack Trucks built relatively few 4-wheel service aerial ladder trucks on its C Series chassis, compared with the number of pumpers rolling out of the big Allentown, Pa. plant. Most of the C Series aerials built had open cabs. Massapequa, N. Y. received this 1963 Mack 85-foot service aerial with semi-enclosed ladder bed and a Maxim ladder.

The City of Lapeer, Mich. owns this white-painted 1963 Mack Type C-95 triple combination 1,000 gallon-per-minute pumper. This engine has dual booster reels housed in enclosed, heated compartments. Lapeer is one of the few cities in Michigan that uses white fire apparatus.

Another Detroit suburb, the downriver community of Trenton, Mich. received this Mack C-95 1,000 GPM triple combination in the early fall of 1963. A standard model, it is seen here a few days after it went into service. This C Model has directional signal lights located above the dual headlight units.

Peter Pirsch & Sons Co. had also come out with its own custom cab-forward fire apparatus chassis. Mount Clemens, Mich. received this 1963 Peter Pirsch 85-foot service aerial ladder truck, with fully enclosed and compartmented ladder body. Note the unusual location of the bell, in front of the windshield. This aerial is finished in white.

Pirsch was also delivering commercial-chassis aerial ladder trucks. Macon, Georgia ordered this 85-foot service aerial built by Peter Pirsch & Sons Co. on a Ford tilt-cab chassis. This aerial has hydraulic A-frame outriggers, a type that was rapidly replacing the manual jacks formerly used on aerial trucks.

For understandable reasons—mainly the presence of the General Motors Truck and Coach Division plants in the city—Pontiac, Mich. used mostly GMC-chassised fire apparatus for many years. Most of these Jimmies bore Peter Pirsch equipment. Pontiac's Engine Co. No. 13 received this Pirsch-GMC 1,000 GPM triple combination.

Detroit, one of the first cities in the nation to use "flying manpower squadrons", starting in 1910, also pioneered in the use of fully-enclosed, van-type rescue squad trucks, beginning in 1935. In 1962 the Gerstenslager Corp., of Wooster, Ohio, delivered two rescue squad trucks to Detroit, mounted on GMC chassis. Another was added in 1963, also on a GMC. Nine more Gerstenslager squads of this type, on Dodge and Ford chassis, were added to the D.F.D. over the next seven years. From 1948 through 1957 Detroit purchased 11 Proctor-Keefe squads of this type, all mounted on GMC chassis.

Western States Fire Apparatus, Inc., of Cornelius, Ore. delivered many commercial-chassis fire engines in the U. S. Northwest. This is a 1963 Mid-Western States 1,000 GPM pumper mounted on the ubiquitous Ford C Series tilt-cab chassis. Note the transverse hose bed for the preconnected 1½-inch hose, and the portable deck nozzle. This pumper appears to be on an extended wheelbase.

The Maxim Motor Co. several years earlier had come out with a new short-wheelbase, conventional-type pumper called the Model S. This model boasted an exceptionally short turning radius and overall length. Glenbrook, Conn. received this 1963 Maxim S 1,000 GPM pumper, with fully-open cab. Maxim built very few of these open-seat jobs.

Forest Park, Ill. has the distinction of owning the only Crown Firecoach in service in the midwestern U. S. In fact, this is likely the farthest east any Crown has been delivered. This company's products are almost exclusively limited to the western states. The Forest Park Fire Dept. ordered this massive Crown snorkel quint, which mounts a 1,250 GPM pump and an 85-foot Pitman elevating platform.

1963

Los Angeles replaced its 1938 American LaFrance Manifold wagon with a new custom-built Crown in 1963. Wagon 17 is equipped with a 2,000 gallon-per-minute pump, and has 14 2¼-inch hose outlets for distribution of water supplied by only a few high-capacity pumpers. The Crown Manifold is also equipped with a huge, power-operated turret complete with seat for the operator. Two baffles of 2½-inch hose are carried in the transverse hose beds, while the rear bed is loaded with big 3½-inch line. This rig also carries preconnected 1¼-inch line. It is accompanied on runs by another special 2,000 GPM Crown Triple.

Custom-chassis apparatus built by Coast had an appearance all of its own. These jobs could not be mistaken for anything else. The cab is International Harvester, but all the rest was built in the Coast Apparatus, Inc. plant in Martinez, Calif. This Coast 1,000 GPM pumper was delivered to sunny Sunnyvale, Calif.

The open-lattice Hi-Ranger elevating platform, manufactured by Mobile Aerial Towers of Fort Wayne, Ind., were generally mounted on Ward LaFrance chassis in the east, and on apparatus built by P. E. Van Pelt, Inc., of Oakdale, Calif., in the west. New Orleans purchased this 1963 Ward LaFrance Hi-Ranger 65-foot platform in 1963. Note the very slight cab overhang.

Coast Apparatus of Martinez, Calif. built this hose wagon for the City of Oakland, Calif. It is mounted on a standard Ford C-850 tilt-cab chassis, which has been modified with a cut-down open semi-cab. This hose wagon carries booster equipment, and a fixed turret pipe.

At first glance, this appears to be a long-wheelbase pumper. But it is in fact an enclosed city service ladder truck. This rig is built on International's new CO-8190 cab-forward custom fire apparatus chassis. The apparatus was built for Kokomo, Ind. by Boyer Fire Apparatus, of Logansport, Ind., and has Midwest equipment. Kokomo's Ladder No. 6 has booster equipment.

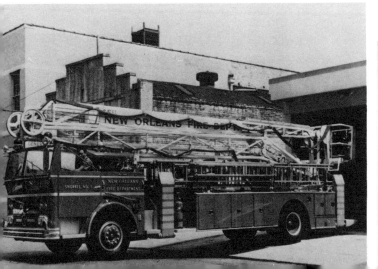

Following several years of development and testing, Mack in 1964 introduced its first elevating platform. The company's newest fire apparatus design was called the Mack Aerialscope, and was mounted on the standard C-Series custom cab-forward fire apparatus chassis. Built only in a 75-foot size, the Mack Aerialscope employed a telescopic boom rather than the articulated type sold by most other manufacturers of aerial platforms. The first Mack Aerialscope was delivered to the New York City Fire Dept., where it was placed into service as Tower Ladder 1. It is interesting to note that the FDNY has purchased no other make of elevating platform, and the largest fire department in the U. S. currently has close to 60 of these Tower Ladder companies in service.

Mack continued to aggressively market its Thermodyne Diesel fire apparatus engine. In July, 1964, the company staged a convincing test of the Diesel's stamina in Detroit, Mich. A standard 1,000 GPM Mack C-95 Diesel pumper pumped water from the Detroit River for seven straight days and nights without a shutdown. When the marathon was over, the Mack Diesel had pumped more than 10 million gallons of water, and had consumed only 1,108 gallons of diesel fuel. The pumper used in the Detroit test was eventually sold to Blue Ash, O. and was later fitted with a 50-foot Snorkel. Also in 1964, Glen Ellyn, Ill. received a 65-foot Pitman Snorkel which was mounted on a Mack C Model cab-forward chassis. The bodywork on this apparatus, however, was done by Pierce Mfg. of Appleton, Wis.

The American LaFrance Division of Sterling Precision Corp. in 1964 came out with a new low-cost line of custom chassis cab-forward pumpers. This new economy series was known as the American LaFrance Pioneer. It had a 5-man canopy cab with a forward-raked windshield, and made a custom-built American LaFrance pumper available to smaller communities at a cost well below that of a 900 Series pumper.

Also in 1964, American LaFrance delivered a 70-foot Aero-Chief elevating platform mounted on a Ford conventional truck chassis to Springvale, N. Y.

The Seagrave Fire Apparatus Division of FWD Corp. during 1964 made the big move from Columbus, Ohio to Clintonville, Wis. This transition played havoc with the company's production schedules, but Seagrave fire apparatus was delivered from both plants this year. Seagrave had called the old Columbus plant complex at 2000 South High St. home since 1891. The company had been founded by Frederick S. Seagrave 10 years earlier in Detroit.

Ward LaFrance had placed its new custom cab-forward fire apparatus chassis into production, and was delivering pumpers and Hi-Ranger elevating platforms with its new look. The new Ward LaFrance design was angular and simple in its lines, with a double-angled windshield that gave the driver excellent forward visibility. This same basic design is still produced by Ward LaFrance today.

Peter Pirsch & Sons delivered an 85-foot elevating platform to its home city of Kenosha, Wis. built on the custom Pirsch cab-forward chassis, it was equipped with an 85-foot Pitman Snorkel. Some interesting hybrid fire apparatus began to come out of the old Pirsch plant this year. The company delivered a 100-foot Senior aerial to Milwaukee this year. What made this truck unusual was that it was drawn by a Mack C-Series canopy cab tractor with rear bodywork by Pirsch. Pirsch was now building a 4-section, 100-foot aerial ladder. Tractor-drawn models using this ladder had a fixed tillerman's seat. Pirsch offered a choice of cab-forward or conventional engine-ahead-of-cab service and tractor-type aerials.

Los Angeles placed its 100th Crown Firecoach into service, and Los Angeles County ordered 16 Crown pumpers and a Crown-Pitman Snorkel. The Lakeside, Ohio volunteer fire department ordered a Sutphen-GMC tilt-cab pumper that had an integral turret nozzle mounted on top of its front-mount pump.

One of the first Mack-chassised aerial platforms to go into service was this special model built for Glen Ellyn, Ill. It consists of a 65-foot Pitman Snorkel mounted on a 1964 Mack Type C-85 cab-forward chassis with bodywork by Pierce Manufacturing of Appleton, Wisc. The completely enclosed rear body gives this Snorkel a clean, compact appearance.

Rolling out of the Florrisant Valley Fire Protection District's quarters is the company's new Mack C Series triple combination pumper with 500-gallon booster tank. Note the ornate style of lettering that adorns the front of this pumper and the Federal Q siren mounted between the headlights.

Mack's hard-working B Model series had now been in production for a full decade, but the conventional-style B Series fire engines kept rolling off the Allentown, Pa. assembly line by popular demand. The Ada-Liberty Township Fire Dept. in northern Ohio uses this spotlessly-maintained Mack B-85 triple combination with extra-large booster tank.

The Hahn Motor Co. of Hamburg, Pa., which had been building custom and commercial chassis fire apparatus for eastern fire companies for many years, could turn out some pretty sophisticated jobs. A good example is this massive combination pumping engine and rescue squad truck built for Collingswood, N. J. This monster is built on a 1964 Hahn custom cab-forward chassis with four doors. Note the 750 GPM pump and the lofty location of the enclosed booster reel.

American LaFrance in 1964 introduced a new series of lower cost custom fire apparatus, designed to bridge the gap between commercial-chassis jobs and full custom fire engines. The new series was knows as the American LaFrance Pioneer. It featured the same American LaFrance rear body and chassis, but had a simpler, more basic cab and less brightwork and trim. The economical Pioneer was offered in a full range of pumper models such as this 750 GPM.

The Three Towns Fire District, serving Moravia, Niles and Sempronius, N. Y., received this Waukesha-powered 1964 Hahn pumper with 750 GPM pump and a 500-gallon booster tank. The front-end sheet metal is similar to that used by Diamond-Reo.

The standard model being turned out by the Elmira, N. Y. plant of American LaFrance was still the familiar 900 Series. Fewer open cabs were being ordered now. Danvers, Mass. ordered this 1964 ALF 1,000 GPM pumper, which has the earlier style plain bumper. Axes on 900 Series apparatus were usually mounted over the front fenders.

This is a good example of the special purpose fire apparatus built by American LaFrance to meet a very special need. It is a custom-designed "Airfoam Engine" delivered to Franklin Township, Ohio, which is charged with the responsibility of protecting an adjacent airport. The special 900 Series foam pumper has an extra large water tank, a 1,000 GPM pump and a big foam turret.

The Pershing County Fire Dept., based in Lovelock, Nevada, ordered this 1964 American LaFrance commercial chassis pumper. The 750 GPM pumper is built on a Ford conventional chassis and has a 1,000-gallon booster tank for rural service. Note the front suction intake below the front bumper.

1964

Engine Co. No. 8, the busiest in Minneapolis, was assigned this 1964 Pirsch 1,250 gallon-per-minute pumper with 4-door sedan cab. Note the company number plate above the bumper. Engine 8's rig is equipped with road sanders and also carries a deck pipe.

Some interesting combinations began to roll out of the Peter Pirsch and Sons Co. plant in Kenosha, Wis. Milwaukee received this 1964 Pirsch 100-foot Senior aerial, which was drawn by a Mack C-Type tractor. More of these Pirsch aerials on Mack chassis were built later. This "McPirsch" is assigned to Milwaukee's Ladder Co. No. 6. Note the fixed tiller.

Dearborn, Mich. in 1964 placed this Pirsch-Ford quintuple combination into service. It has a canopy cab extension on its Ford C Series chassis, and is fitted with a 750 gallon-per-minute pump, a 75-foot Pirsch aerial ladder and carries a booster reel in the forward compartment on its left rear fender. The bell and siren are mounted on each side of the cab front corners.

The Peter Pirsch & Sons Co. factory in Kenosha, Wis. was still delivering enough conventional type fire engines to keep this series in production, despite the popularity among its customers of its cab-forward models. Pleasantville, N. J. ordered this 1964 Pirsch conventional, with open semi-cab.

This is a whole fire department on a single set of wheels. Peter Pirsch & Sons built this compact quintuple combination for Wadsworth, Ohio. It has a 75-foot aerial ladder, a 750 GPM pump, booster equipment, a full complement of ground ladders and carries its own supply of hose.

The Crown Coach Corp. of Los Angeles built this very well-equipped snorkel-pumper demonstrator. It is built on a 1964 Crown Firecoach chassis and carries a 1,000 GPM pump and a 50-foot Pitman Snorkel. While it did cut down on hose-carrying capacity somewhat, the Snorkel unit greatly increased a triple combination pumper's usefulness, especially in smaller cities and towns which could simply not afford highly specialized apparatus.

During 1964, the Seagrave Corp., which had been acquired by the FWD Corp., gradually transferred all of its manufacturing operations from its old home in Columbus, Ohio to FWD's main plant in Clintonville, Wis. Kalamazoo, Mich. ordered this 1964 Seagrave Conventional 100-foot service aerials with open semi-cab, and A-frame hydraulic jacks. Four men can be seated in the rear of the cab.

1964

The Seagrave Corporation built this big quintuple combination for Grosse Point Woods, Mich. On a 1964 Seagrave custom cab-forward chassis, it has a 1,000 GPM pump and a 65-foot Pitman Snorkel boom. Ground ladders are completely enclosed in the long boxes along the sides of this compact, clean-lined rig.

The Maxim Motor Co. built this cab-forward triple combination pumper for Glen Cove, L. I., N. Y. It has a 1,000 GPM pump and the standard Maxim 5-man canopy cab. Note the location of the booster hose reel in the rear fender compartment. A pair of plated air horns are mounted on the cab roof.

Swampscott, Mass. received this 1964 Maxim 85-foot tractor-drawn aerial ladder truck. The tractor is a short-wheelbase Maxim Model S, and the aerial is Maxim's own 4-section metal unit. Ladder 1's handsome new rig carries a full complement of wood ground ladders.

Detroit purchased three more Seagraves in 1964, including this 100-foot tractor-drawn aerial ladder truck, an 85-foot tractor-drawn aerial, and the first cab-forward Seagrave pumper on the D.F.D. The standard model 100-foot aerial shown here was placed in service at Ladder Co. No. 7 and was still there in 1975. Like most Detroit aerials, it carries booster equipment.

Maxim's stubby Model S was designed for maximum maneuverability in congested areas. Lincoln Park, N. J. took delivery of this Maxim triple combination pumper, which is equipped with a front suction intake.

1964

It is believed that this was the only sedan-cab pumper Ward LaFrance ever built on its Mark I cab-forward custom chassis. This special 1,000 GPM pumper was built to order for Detroit, which ran it as Engine Co. No. 1 for five years. It has a preconnected soft suction hose carried in a basket built into the extended front bumper.

The Philadelphia Bureau of Fire in 1964 ordered this special foam pumper. It was built by National Foam Systems, Inc., of West Chester, Pa., on a 1964 International Harvester chassis and has a 1,000 GPM foam system and a 1,000 gallon tank. Note the foam turret at the front of the body, and the various sized foam nozzles carried on the side of this apparatus, which was designated Car 512.

South San Francisco ordered this 1964 Coast Custom cab-forward 1,250 gallon-per-minute pumper. Note the front cab extension housing the headlights, a Coast Apparatus trademark. This pumper, South San Francisco's Engine 7, carries no hard suction but has five large compartments built into the left rear fender.

This is an example of the large, commercial-chassis pumper-tankers built by Western States Fire Apparatus Inc., of Cornelius, Ore. It is built on a Ford T-850 chassis powered by a 534 cubic-inch Ford V-8 engine. The front-mounted pump is a 750 GPM American UA-75. It has two booster hose reels that are supplied by a 1,500-gallon water tank mounted under the hose bed. Dual-axle pumper-tankers of this type are common in the northwestern states.

The Chicago Fire Department continued to purchase relatively small special-purpose fire equipment, like the compact high pressure fog unit shown here. Built by the John Bean Division of FMC Corp., it is on a 1964 International 1700 four-wheel-drive chassis, and carries 250 gallons of water. The front bumper extension carries a power winch.

Pierre Thibault Ltd., of Pierreville, Quebec, Canada delivered this 840 Imperial gallon-per-minute (1,050 U. S. gallons) to New Westminster, British Columbia. The Thibault Custom chassis utilizes some Budd cab components, notably the doors and cab front, of the type supplied to Ford. Note the overhead cantilever ladder rack and the radio speaker built right into the pump operator's panel.

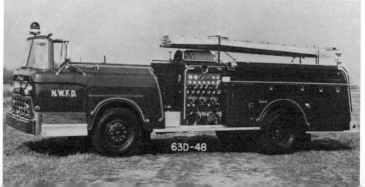

Mack Trucks, Inc. delivered the world's most powerful land-based mobile firefighting system to New York this year. The fantastic Super Pumper System was designed to replace 10 conventional pumpers at the scene of a major fire, and can deliver 10,000 gallons of water per minute through five oversized hose lines that constitute a portable pipeline. The Mack Super Pumper System actually consists of five vehicles: the huge Super Pumper itself, an equally massive Super Pumper Tender, and three Satellite Tenders. The Super Pumper System took several years to design and build.

The Super Pumper is a tractor-drawn combination pulled by a Mack Diesel tractor of the type normally used for long-distance highway hauling. It is equipped with an Allison automatic transmission. The Super Pumper's trailer is actually a pumping station on wheels. The pump is a Napier-Deltic 18-cylinder engine linked to a DeLaval 6-stage centrifugal pump which delivers 4,400 GPM at 700 pounds per square inch, or 8,800 GPM at 350 PSI. The Napier pump engine is also a Diesel. The Super Pumper can draw its water supply from eight hydrants, and is equipped with a rear winch to lower its oversized suction hose into a river or harbor. The Super Tender has the same type of tractor as the Super Pumper, but a 10,000 GPM water cannon is mounted behind the cab. A set of hydraulic outriggers stabilizes the truck when the water cannon is in use. The Super Tender's trailer is packed with 2,000 feet of 4½-inch hose. Each of the three Mack Model C cab-forward Satellite Tenders is equipped with a 2,000 GPM Stang deck turret. These units are strategically located around the city to respond with the Super Pumper and Super Tender on major alarms. The Super Pumper System was designed by Gibbs & Cox, a marine and naval architectural firm.

During the same year, Mack Trucks delivered a Diesel-powered 1,000 GPM pumper to New York. This C-Model cab-forward pumper was assigned to busy Engine Co. No. 5 in Manhattan.

American LaFrance in 1965 offered Diesel power in its custom 900 Series fire apparatus for the first time. The Diesel engine was now seriously rivalling gasoline engines, and was proving far superior in areas of economy of operation and maintenance. Within a few years, Diesel

engines would become standard in all custom-built fire apparatus.

The Seagrave Fire Apparatus Division of FWD Corp. had completed the move from Ohio to the Wisconsin dairyland. The FWD Corp. was now building two distinct lines of apparatus in a single plant. The FWD Tractioneer line of cab-forward pumpers was still being marketed, along with the Seagrave cab-forward and conventional models, and the FWD cab-forward chassis was the basis for most of the 75 and 85-foot elevating platforms being sold by

New York's gigantic Super Pumper is more than just a mind-boggling fire engine; it is a veritable pumping station on wheels. The tractor is a Mack cab-over of the over-the-road type, powered by a Mack END-864 diesel engine, coupled to an Allison automatic transmission. A second engine mounted in the trailer drives a DeLaval 6-stage pump. This engine is an 18-cylinder Napier-Deltic of 2,400 horsepower. In operation on the fireground, the Super Pumper can hurl an incredible 8,800 gallons of water per minute at 350 PSI in parallel, or 4,400 GPM at 700 PSI in series. This King Kong of land-based pumping engines can draw its water from as many as eight hydrants, or it can lift its fire-killing requirements directly from a river. A boom and winch are provided at the rear of the Super Pumper for this purpose.

Accompanying the Super Pumper to fires as a super hose wagon of the same staggering proportions. The Super Tender is also a tractor-trailer combination. The tractor is the same cab-over Diesel type used under the Super Pumper, but the Tender is equipped with a 10,000 GPM water cannon that is fed by four 4½-inch hose lines. That is "big water". A pair of hydraulic outriggers steady the Super Tender against the water cannon's reaction. The Super Tender carries 2,000 feet of 4½-inch line. Four manifolds are provided under the hose bed to supply four 2½-inch hose lines.

This was a big year for Mack, which began deliveries of standard Diesel-powered fire engines and placed the world's most powerful land fire engine, the Super Pumper System, in service in New York City. Aptos, Calif. received this Mack C-95F Diesel 1,000 GPM pumper with 500-gallon booster tank. Note the deep transverse hose bed for 1½-inch line over the pump panel, and the two overhead ladder racks which almost qualify this rig as a quadruple combination.

One of the more unique aerial platforms built by Seagrave was this job for Ottawa, Kan. It was built by Seagrave on the cab-forward International CO-8190 fire apparatus chassis with open semi-cab, and carries a 75-foot Daybrook-Ottawa elevating platform. This well-equipped one-truck fire department is also equipped with a 750 GPM pump and booster equipment. A tandem rear axle helps distribute the considerable weight of this unit. Note the covered hose bed above the enclosed ground ladder compartment.

Snorkel Fire Equipment. The Pierce Mfg. Co. of Appleto Wis., was building the rear bodies for the popular FWI Pitman aerial platforms.

Ward LaFrance had introduced a mid-range custo cab-forward pumper that used the increasingly popul Cincinnati cab.

Among the more interesting 1965 deliveries was towering Seagrave rescue squad truck with a Gerstenslag body and a huge, front-mounted A-frame winch built fo Syracuse, N. Y., and a Ward LaFrance Hi-Ranger quir delivered to Houghton, N. Y. Ward LaFrance had recentl introduced its own line of heavy-duty airport crash truck One of these big crash and rescue units, powered by tw Ford V-8 engines, carrying two 1,000 GPM pumps an 2,500 gallons of water and 500 gallons of foam, wa placed in service at Chicago's O'Hare International Airpor

A new name in the business was Fire Trucks Incorporate of Mount Clemens, Mich. This company succeeded th Fire Master Corp. and offered a complete range o pumpers, tankers and special apparatus on all makes o commercial truck chassis. The FTI plant is still i operation today.

Twenty-nine years after it pioneered the safety-sedan Seagrave van-type pumper, the City of Detroit in 1965 accepted delivery of the last three Seagrave sedan pumpers built. These 1,000 GPM sedans were powered by Waukesha engines and were built in Clintonville, Wis. instead of Columbus, Ohio. Engine Co. No. 53's brand new 1965 Seagrave Sedan is seen here the day it entered service. It is interesting to note that at the time other U. S. cities were turning to enclosed pumpers, Detroit—which had perfected the idea—switched back to conventional types which put the crew back out on the open on the rear running board.

This huge, white Seagrave rescue squad truck was designed and built to the specifications of the Syracuse, N. Y. Fire Department. The very high rig is built on a 1965 Seagrave conventional chassis, but the custom rear body was fabricated by the Marion Body Works of Marion, Wis. Note the heavy A-frame which was permanently attached to the front of the apparatus, and the speaker-warning light combination on the platform above the cab. The crew could comfortably stand up in the rear of this huge rescue truck on the way to an alarm.

Chattanooga, Tenn. took delivery of this 1965 Seagrave 1,000 GPM canopy-cab triple combination pumper. Note the full-length tool compartment above the rear fender. Chattanooga's Engine No. 3 also has a rear cab handrail. Fewer and fewer of these conventional-style Seagraves were now being delivered: customer preference was clearly for the cab-forward design.

The Seagrave Fire Apparatus Division of the FWD Corp. built two types of 100-foot aerial ladder trailers. The most popular had a 4-section ladder and fixed tillerman's seat, but the older style 3-section 100-foot ladder with swingover tiller was still available. Sacramento, Calif. purchased this 1963 Seagrave cab-forward tractor aerial with the 3-section ladder.

1965

New Orleans in 1965 placed this unusual custom-built tractor-drawn aerial ladder truck in service. It is drawn by a Ward-LaFrance tractor with open semi-cab, but has an enclosed trailer with a Canadian-built Pierre Thibault 100-foot metal aerial ladder. The trailer has four manually-operated outrigger jacks. The Thibault aerial had acquired a reputation as one of the strongest ladders on the market. Note the fixed tillerman's seat.

The Lake Erie port city of Cleveland, Ohio placed two of these 75-foot elevating platforms into service in 1965. Built on the Ward LaFrance custom chassis, they have special low-profile canopy cabs to reduce the traveling height of the Hi-Ranger 75-foot articulating boom. The tower shown here is assigned as Ladder 18.

The Ward LaFrance Truck Corp. built a number of pumpers in the mid-sixties that used the Cincinnati cab on the Ward LaFrance custom cab-forward chassis. This one was delivered to Memphis, Tenn. It has a 1,000 gallon-per-minute pump. Note the short attic ladder carried above the hard suction hose, and the fixed turret nozzle. The Ward LaFrance emblem was the French fleur-de-lis enclosed in a circle.

American LaFrance sold quite a few of these big Aero-Chief 900 Series quintuple combinations. The tandem-axle Aero Chief 80 quint shown here was built for South Holland, Ill. It has a 1,000-GPM pump and an 80-foot elevating platform. The American LaFrance Aero-Chief was also available on single or tandem rear-axle chassis without a pump, and could be ordered with an open cab.

This extra footage of ground ladders stored overhead almost qualifies this American LaFrance 900 Series pumper as a quad, or quadruple combination. Muskegon, Michigan's firemen must also stretch a bit to remove the length of hard suction hose. The Elmira, N. Y. manufacturer began to identify its products with the large block letter nameplates visible above the chrome strip over the towing eyes.

The Northern Ohio town of Clyde is protected by this white-painted American LaFrance 900 Series triple combination pumper. The basket on the extended front bumper pan holds a length of soft suction hose. The overhead rack contains a 50-foot extension ladder. An electronic siren is perched on the chrome-plated bracket just ahead of the windshield.

1965

Dearborn, Mich. retrofitted this 1965 Pirsch-Ford canopy cab pumper with a 50-foot "Squirt" boom, a basketless articulated arm fitted with a master stream nozzle only. The Snorkel Fire Equipment Co., which the Pitman Mfg. Co. formed to market its specialized firefighting devices, introduced the Squirt three years later. This canopy-cab Pirsch-Ford has a 1,000 GPM pump.

Here is something a little bit different. Peter Pirsch & Sons built this 1,000 GPM commercial chassis pumper for Akron, Ohio. Pirsch mounted a close-coupled canopy cab on a 1965 GMC Model 7000 chassis. The GMC-Pirsch pumper is a V-12 GMC engine. Note the dual flashers on the roof and the portable monitor nozzle on the hose body. The barrel has been removed but can be quickly attached for use.

As humorous as it may seem to many of us back on the mainland, standard equipment on Honolulu, Hawaii rescue squad trucks includes a couple of surfboards, for rescue operations along the city's famed beaches. Honolulu's Rescue 1 is a 1965 Crown Firecoach with custom built body. The front of the rig is equipped with a winch, and Rescue 1 is frequently called upon to tow a rescue boat trailer. A canvas canopy has been provided over the cab to keep the sun off the crew.

Just as Dearborn, Mich. has an understandable loyalty to Ford, Hamtramck, Mich. buys Dodges. Completely surrounded by the city of Detroit, Hamtramck is the home of Chrysler Corporation's huge Dodge Main plant. The Hamtramck Fire Dept. has several Dodge-chassised rigs. Engine No. 3 is a canopy-cab 1,000 GPM pumper built by a new firm with the name of Fire Trucks Inc. of Mount Clemens, Mich.

Carmichael, Calif. received this huge combination pumper-tanker. Built by Crown Coach Corp. of Los Angeles, it is equipped with a 1,250 GPM pump. Tandem axles are required to carry the weight of the 2,500 gallons of water in its booster tank. The top of the rear body is almost level with the cab roof.

Another product of Fire Trucks Inc. is this big quadruple combination, delivered to St. Clair Shores, Mich. Built on a Duplex chassis, it has a 1,000 GPM pump and full canopy cab. Note the high, enclosed ladder bed and the generous compartment space.

1965

Indiana has always been fertile territory for the Maxim Motor Co.'s sales force. The City of East Chicago, Ind. received this Maxim Model F cab-forward triple combination pumping engine, which is lettered for Engine Co. No. 7

Detroit's first elevating platform was this 85-foot Pitman Snorkel on a 1965 FWD cab-forward chassis with Pierce bodywork. This unit had a full complement of ground ladders and entered service as Ladder-Snorkel No. 1. Two years later it was stripped of its ground ladders and reassigned as a special purpose unit. The Snorkel responds to all multiple alarms and can be special-called. It also responds on some boxes in the downtown high value area. It is quartered with Engine 9.

The W. S. Darley Co., formerly of Chicago and now located in the Chicago suburb of Melrose Park, is best known for its standard-type commercial chassis pumpers. But Darley has turned out some pretty special rigs—and some big ones—as this photo attests. Butterfield, Ill. ordered this heavy quintuple combination built by Darley on a 1965 GMC V-12 chassis. The quint has a 1,250 GPM pump, and is equipped with an 85-foot Pitman Snorkel. It also carries booster hose and a complement of ground ladders.

During the 1960's, this type of heavy crash-rescue truck became the standard for many airport fire departments. This monster is built by the Yankee-Walter Corporation of Los Angeles, a firm specializing in airport crash trucks. This one was delivered to Chicago's O'Hare International Airport, which is protected by special units of the Chicago Fire Dept. This type of Yankee-Walter is powered by two big Ford V-8 engines. The flotation-type tires permit it to traverse unpaved off-runway areas. The large turret on the roof can be operated by remote control from inside the rig, and can hurl a large volume of fire-smothering foam within seconds. This type of apparatus is completely self-contained.

The Central Fire Truck Corp. of Manchester, Mo. delivered four of these 750 gallon-per-minute Central-St. Louis triple combinations to Philadelphia in 1965. All were built on International VCO cab-forward chassis with extended canopy cabs. The long pole over the rear body is for a protective tarpaulin.

The Hesse Body Co. of Kansas City, Mo. built this special chemical unit for Philadelphia. Three of these Internationals were delivered in this order. Chemical Unit 1's rig is seen outside of its quarters. Note the siren mounted above the cab.

In another corporate realignment, American LaFrance in 1966 became part of A-T-O Corp., formerly Automatic Sprinkler. A new product developed by the company this year was a special 900 Series combination foam pumper. The first American LaFrance pumper of this type delivered to a municipal fire department went to Bristol, Conn. To this day, American LaFrance refers to models of this type as Bristol foam pumpers. The Bristol pumper was equipped with a 1,000 GPM pump, but carried a 125 GPM foam turret on its cab roof.

American LaFrance's new Pioneer low-priced custom cab forward pumpers, introduced two years earlier, had been well received. By 1966, the Elmira, N.Y. manufacturer was delivering an improved model of its budget-priced model called the Pioneer I. The flat-faced Pioneer pumpers were built in sizes ranging all the way from 500 to 1,250 gallons per minute. Engine choices included a 257-horsepower Chrysler V-8; the Ford 534 cubic inch V-8; and 501 and 549 CID International Harvester gasoline engines. The plain, simply constructed Pioneer cab gave the driver what American LaFrance called control tower vision. Optional diesel power rounded out the Pioneer pumper power choices.

Mack Trucks found plenty of fire department enthusiasm for its new Diesel-powered fire apparatus. Mack's sales people had little convincing to do when they pointed out that Mack's Diesel pumpers possessed almost double the pumping capacity of gasoline-powered pumpers using about the same amount of fuel. This is a C-95 Diesel with 1,000 GPM pump. It is not certain whether this pumper went to Mount Vernon, N.Y., or the community of the same name in Pennsylvania.

Another style of Mack chassis began to appear on fire apparatus. The flat-faced Mack Type MB chassis boasted minimal bumper to back of cab length. The Chicago Fire Dept. modernized one of its older model Pirsch aerials by replacing the original 1946 Pirsch tractor with a new 1966 Mack MB-600 tractor. The C.F.D. eventually acquired four tractors of this type. The trailer retained its 85-foot stick.

Sutphen Fire Equipment of Columbus, Ohio, had placed its Sutphen Aerial Tower into production. The standard production model had an 85-foot tower. Oak Brook, Ill. received an 85-foot Sutphen Aerial Tower built on an International CO-8190 cab forward chassis, equipped with a 1,000 GPM Barton Pump, a 300-gallon booster tank and with hose beds packed with 1,600 feet of hose. The hard-hitting Sutphen Aerial Tower boasted 2-gun fire fighting power; a monitor nozzle was mounted on each side of the roomy basket.

Mack's 75-foot Aerialscope elevating platform was now in full production. In 1966, Mack delivered one of the few Aerialscopes with an open C-85 cab. This one was built for St. Louis, Mo. Late in 1966, Mack Trucks ended production of its familiar B Model engine-ahead-of-cab pumpers. The B Model had been in production for over 12 years, and fire chiefs had shown a marked preference for cab-forward fire engines. But Mack had a new conventional cab series on the drawing board for those who still preferred a hood out there in front. The new model would not appear until the following year.

The Seagrave Fire Apparatus Division of FWD Corp. was building cab-forward and conventional series pumpers, aerials and special purpose fire apparatus in its new home at Clintonville, Wis. In 1966, Seagrave delivered a 90-foot, 3-boom Eagle elevating platform on the Seagrave Custom cab-forward chassis to Melrose Park, Ill. During the same year, the company built a 1,250 GPM cab-forward pumper with a 4-door sedan cab for Los Angeles County, and a conventional series 100-foot. 1,000 GPM quint for Riverside, Ill. Like other manufacturers, Seagrave had noticed a sharp decline in orders for its engine-ahead-of-cab conventional series apparatus. The 70th Anniversary style Seagrave had now been in production for 15 years.

Chicago in 1966 took delivery of several 100-foot service aerials built on the Mack cab-forward C Series chassis, but with bodywork by Pirsch and with Pirsch 3-section aerial ladders. These Mack/Pirsch aerials had an exceptionally long rear overhang.

The Crown Coach Corp. of Los Angeles had added service and tractor-drawn aerial ladder trucks to its product line. The aerial ladder units were purchased from the Maxim Motor Co. Crown aerials continue to use Maxim ladders.

Chicago began a gradual transition from gasoline to Diesel power for its firefighting fleet. The CFD placed four of these Mack Type C-95D Diesel pumpers into service in 1966. These pumpers were powered by Mack 6-cylinder Thermodyne Diesel engines and had 1,000 GPM Waterous pumps. They also carried 500 gallons of water in their booster tanks. This one was assigned to Engine Co. No. 18.

East Orange, N. J. received this well-equipped American LaFrance 900 Series pumper. It has a 1,250 gallon-per-minute pump, and preconnected 1½-inch hose carried in a Mattydale transverse bed above the pump panel. Note the high rear body and lack of hard suctions. Several hose bundles are also carried atop the rear fender.

The type of rear fenders on this American LaFrance aerial ladder truck indicate that it may be a factory rebuild of an older model ALF 700. If so, the Cleveland, Tenn. ladder truck has been updated to 900 Series standard. American LaFrance sometimes did this for communities that may have had a truck badly damaged at a fire or in an accident. The truck shown has a 75-foot aerial ladder and two booster reels.

American LaFrance built very few 900 Series quadruple combinations. Fire departments by this time appeared to be willing to go one further, and specify a "quint" equipped with either a conventional aerial ladder or an elevating platform. This is a 900 Series quint with a 100-foot, 4-section aerial, a 1,000 GPM pump, two booster hose reels and a full load of hose and ground ladders. It has an open semi-cab and manual stabilizer jacks.

American LaFrance delivered this interesting 900 Series triple combination pumper to Berkeley, Calif. in 1966. It has a 1,250 gallon-per-minute pump and carries 300 gallons of water. The ground ladders are carried high above the rear body on a hydraulically-operated "ladder robot" that swings them down to lifting level at the touch of a button. Note the unique double front bumper. The lower one has been cut out to accommodate a preconnected soft suction hose.

The Baltimore City, Md. Fire Department placed four of these American LaFrance 900 Series Rescue 100-foot tractor-drawn aerial ladder trucks into service in the latter part of 1966. These aerials were painted the traditional Baltimore white-and-red, and carried wood ground ladders. The aerial shown in this delivery photo was assigned to the BFD's Truck Co. 29.

Here is an interesting combination. The trailer of this Little Rock, Ark. 85-foot aerial ladder truck is American LaFrance but the tractor is a bit of a mystery. The cab is an International CO-8190, but the rear sheet metal, including cut-down fenders, is ALF. This is either a new cab plunked down on a 700 Series ALF tractor, or a one-off replacement tractor built at Elmira.

Among the more unique hybrids built during the 1960s was this 1966 Coast-Howe triple combination pumper delivered to Brisbane, Cal. The custom chassis was built by Coast Apparatus of Martinez, Calif., but the rest of the pumper was supplied by the Howe Fire Apparatus Co. of Anderson, Indiana. This big pumper has a 1,250 GPM pump and totes 500 gallons of water in its tanks.

1966

The Manhasset-Lakeville Fire Dept., on Long Island, N. Y. decided to modernize a 1940's-vintage 85-foot aerial ladder truck by repowering it with a new tractor. The conversion was done by the Young Fire Equipment Corp. of Buffalo, N. Y. Young built a canopy cab tractor on a V-12 GMC chassis and adapted it to fit Manhasset-Lakeville's Seagrave trailer.

Fire departments in Southern California's balmy, but smoggy climes had traditionally used nothing but open-cab fire apparatus since the days of the horses. But more and more departments were turning to enclosed-cab apparatus to provide extra comfort for their men. Los Angeles County received this 1966 Seagrave 1,250-GPM pumper with 400-gallon booster tank. Engine Co. 66's rig has a 4-door sedan cab mounted on a Seagrave cab-forward chassis. The rear roof can be removed should it be necessary to take out the engine.

The elevating platform, or snorkel, by now had become a familiar piece of firefighting equipment on departments all over the country. Schiller Park, Ill. received this 1966 FWD-Pitman 85-foot Snorkel. It is built on an FWD 4 x 4 chassis and carries a 1,250 GPM pump as well as a full complement of ground ladders. Like most FWD-Pitmans, this snorkel has Pierce bodywork.

Fewer and fewer of the engine-ahead-of-cab conventional models were coming off the assembly floor at the FWD-Seagrave plant in Clintonville, Wis. But Louisville, Ky. ordered this 1966 Seagrave 100-foot tractor-drawn aerial ladder and fixed tiller seat, an uncommon arrangement for this model. Louisville's Aerial No. 3 has large, enclosed equipment compartments above the trailer running boards and a speaker mounted on the rear cab roof.

Melrose Park, Ill. ordered this 1966 Seagrave Eagle elevating platform. This very large piece of apparatus has a 90-foot, 3-boom aerial platform and a 1,000 GPM pump. It is mounted on a Seagrave cab-forward chassis with optional tandem rear axle. Melrose Park's platform responds as Eagle 1.

1966

Hershey, Pa., home of the world's biggest antique auto show and flea market, is protected by this trim-looking Snorkel-Quint. The chassis is reportedly a Mack, but it wears Pierce bodywork, and the cab is an International CO-8190. The windshield has been cut out to lower the travelling overall height of the 75-foot Pitman boom. Hershey's Snorkel also packs a 750 GPM pump.

The small grille between the towing eyes above the front bumper identify this chassis as an International CO-8190. This 75-foot snorkel was delivered to the Chicago Fire Dept. The boom is a Pitman, and the rear bodywork is by Pierce Manufacturing of Appleton, Wis. Unlike earlier Chicago snorkels, this one carries a full supply of ground ladders. It was assigned to Snorkel 4.

Jim Burner, Jr. found this unique pumper-tanker in North Haledon, N. J. The fire apparatus body is by Pierce Manufacturing, on a Ford C Series 4 x 6 chassis. This rig is powered by a Ford 534 cubic inch V-8, has a 1,000 GPM pump and carries 1,200 gallons of water. Ground ladders are carried on top.

Western States Fire Apparatus, Inc. of Cornelius, Ore. built this 750 GPM pumper with white paint job for the Taft-Nelscott-DeLake Rural Fire Protection District in Oregon. The chassis is a Dodge C-800. The pump is by American Fire Apparatus. Note the dual plated booster hose reels and the portable deck nozzle with barrel removed.

This unit is a good example of the highly specialized type of equipment required by fire departments that have been assigned special responsibilities. Protection of Chicago's O'Hare Field, the busiest airport in the world in terms of takeoffs and landings annually, falls to the Chicago Fire Department. For emergency evacuation of jetliners on or off the runways, the Chicago Fire Dept. uses this mobile stairway unit. The chassis is a Ford F-350 with four-wheel-drive. The hydraulically-operated stairs are by Wollard. This rig also carries two 150-pound Ansul chemical tanks.

Hamtramck, Mich., home of Chrysler Corporation's main Dodge plant, ordered this big Dodge quad. It was built by Fire Trucks Inc. of Mount Clemens, Mich., and is similar in appearance to an FTI-Dodge pumper delivered earlier to the same city. Hamtramck's quad No. 1 has a 1,000 GPM pump. Note the enclosed ladder bed and dual reels behind the extended canopy cab.

Peter Pirsch & Sons Co. built a small number of commercial-chassis-based tractor-drawn aerial ladder trucks, which cost several thousand dollars less than a full-custom job. This 100-foot tractor drawn aerial with a Ford canopy cab tractor was delivered by Pirsch to Atlanta, Ga., one of Pirsch's better customers in the south. A life net is carried in the large compartment behind the turntable.

This aerial view shows the functional, clean design of a Pirsch quintuple combination aerial ladder truck. The bed above the double-bank ladder racks contains a 300-gallon booster tank and space for hose. This compact quint has a 4-section 85-foot Pirsch aerial ladder.

The Boston suburb of Chelsea, Mass. owns the 1966 Peter Pirsch and Sons Co. 100-foot tractor-drawn Senior aerial truck shown here. Chelsea's Ladder 1 has a 4-section ladder with fixed tiller. This aerial, and every other piece of apparatus for miles around, saw action during the Chelsea Conflagration that levelled one-fifth of the city in October, 1973.

Chicago in 1966 also received this rather unusual combination. It is a 100-foot Pirsch metal aerial mounted on a Mack C-95 chassis. This aerial was built by Peter Pirsch & Sons. Note the Aurora Borealis Mars light on the roof and the booster hose reel above the rear fender. These aerials had a very long rear overhang.

Levittown, N. Y. received this Maxim 75-foot Service Aerial Ladder Truck. It is built on Maxim's own custom fire apparatus chassis with open semi-cab. Note the generous compartment space, and the air horn above the windshield. The speaker on the turntable permits the ladder operator to keep in touch with the fireman on top of the ladder, who is often lost from view in swirling smoke.

1967

Mack again dominated the new product picture with the introduction of two completely new fire apparatus chassis. The familiar C Series cab-forward design, which was derived from the original Ahrens-Fox/ C.D. Beck design designated the Mack Model CF. This handsome new cab was much wider than former C-85 and C-95 models, and featured flatter, more angular surfaces. The standard model was designated the CF-600, and was designed for diesel power.

The engine-ahead-of-cab B Model Mack fire apparatus chassis had been taken out of production in 1966. The Mack Conventional was replaced in 1967 with a new short-hood design called the Mack R Model. This chassis had a 3-man closed cab and a molded fiberglas front end that was hinged at the front for convenient servicing of the engine.

Mack Trucks had also introduced a high, flat-fronted commercial truck chassis designated the Mack Model MB and some of these were used as fire apparatus chassis. Chicago had purchased four of these for use as aerial ladder truck tractors in 1966, and in 1967 placed a special MB chassis equipped with a 50-foot snorkel and modular type rear cab into service as Snorkel Squad 1.

Seagrave had constructed a prototype of its new, cab-forward Rear Admiral rear-mounted aerial ladder truck. This compact, highly maneuverable 100-foot service type aerial had both 4-wheel drive and 4-wheel steering. The 4-section main ladder was mounted at the rear of the apparatus, and had minimal front overhang. The Seagrave Rear Admiral was widely demonstrated, and Chicago placed one in service along with two conventional Seagrave 100-foot midship-mounted service aerials.

The Snorkel Fire Equipment Co., which had relocated from Grandview, Mo., to a new plant at St. Joseph, Mo., reported that of the more than 400 elevating platforms now in service in the U.S., more than 300 were of the Pitman make.

American LaFrance had sold a number of Aero-Chief Quintuple Combination 900 Series elevating platforms. Typically, these were equipped with 90-foot booms, a 1,000 or 1,250 GPM midship-mounted pump, a full complement of ground ladders, hose and other standard fire department equipment. Because of the added weight, most of these were equipped with tandem rear axles.

One of the most innovative and visually striking cab-forward fire apparatus designs was being marketed by the Young Fire Equipment Corp. of Lancaster, N. Y. Called the Young Crusader, this was a 5-man canopy cab-forward chassis. The futuristic, low-profile Young Crusader chassis had a huge 1-piece windshield, built-in dual periscopic rear view mirrors, flashers integrated into the front corners of the roof and a roof of diamond tread plate, so the top of the apparatus could be used as a command post and observation platform on the fireground. The boldly styled Crusader was available as a pumper, or as a chassis for the Pitman Snorkel elevating platform.

The T. R. Grove Mfg. Co. of Shady Grove, Pa. now offered a complete range of hydraulic aerial ladders of up to 100 feet in length. Ward LaFrance was delivering custom chassis service aerials and quints using the Grove ladder.

Howe Fire Apparatus in 1967 announced a new concept in pumper design. This company introduced a cab-forward canopy cab pumper with an elevated pump control panel mounted transversely just behind the rear cab walkway. This top-control design gave the pump operator a 360-degree view of the fireground. Previously, the pump operator was often out of sight of firefighting operations as he manned the pump panel.

American LaFrance built this big Aero-Chief quintuple combination for the LaGrange, Ill. Fire Department in 1967. It has a 1,250 gallon-per-minute pump, and a 90-foot elevating platform. Note the dual hydraulic stabilizers behind the tandem rear axles. The Aero Chief was built in 70, 80 and 90-foot sizes. A short aluminum ladder is carried on top of the upper boom for use from the basket. The ground ladders are carried flat on the left hand side of the rig, and upright on the other.

Youngstown, Ohio added this American LaFrance elevating platform to its fire-fighting fleet in 1967. The apparatus is a Series 900 Aero-Chief with a 90-foot boom. Virtually all of the Aero-Chiefs being delivered by this time had tandem rear axles, and almost all were Diesel-powered.

Camden, N. J. received this American LaFrance 900 Series Rescue Model 100-foot tractor-drawn aerial ladder truck. The reel on the turntable feeds the cable for a remote-control ladder pipe, which can be operated from the control pedestal on the turntable. This electronically-controlled feature eliminates the need for a man on the ladder tip. Camden's Truck 1 has four manually-operated outriggers.

One of the first Seagrave customers to place a Rear Admiral aerial into service was Chicago. This 100-foot rear-mounted aerial was built on a 1967 FWD four-wheel-drive chassis, and had the four-wheel-steering option. Although this configuration permitted a much more compact ladder truck compared with conventional service and tractor-drawn aerials, the crew had quite a climb up to the turntable. The ground ladders are carried in two side-by-side beds under the turntable.

1967

The Seagrave Fire Apparatus Division of the FWD Corp. built this demonstrator model rear-mount 100-foot aerial ladder truck, which was shown to many fire departments in 1967. Seagrave designated its new rear-mounted aerial the Rear Admiral. This prototype has unique 4-wheel steering, which gives the compact unit incredible maneuverability in any situation. Note the depression in the center of the cab roof, which lowers the overall height. This style of aerial was not much longer than a conventional pumper.

The Wisconsin town of Brown Deer received this 1967 Seagrave cab-forward quintuple combination aerial. This unit has an 85-foot 4-section aerial ladder, a 1,250 GPM pump and a 200-gallon booster tank. It also is fitted with a front suction intake, and carries a portable deluge gun on the platform above the pump compartment. Stability when the main ladder is raised is provided by a single set of A-frame hydraulic outrigger jacks.

Chicago's Engine Co. No. 29 was assigned this new 1967 FWD-Seagrave 1,000 GPM pumper. Built on FWD's four-wheel-drive "Tractioneer" chassis, it carries 500 gallons of water and is powered by a Waukesha 6-cylinder gasoline engine. An identical 1967 FWD-Seagrave, but with conventional two-wheel-drive, also joined the Chicago Fire Dept. this year. The pumps in these engines were built by Seagrave.

The Chicago Fire Department placed two of these Seagrave 100-foot Service Aerial Ladder Trucks into service in 1967. Both were powered by Waukesha 6-cylinder engines. This one has two manually-operated ground jacks. Note the long rear overhang of the 4-section aerial ladder.

The Seagrave Corp. delivered this brand new 100-foot tractor-drawn aerial ladder truck to Buffalo, N. Y. It is lettered Truck 3. This model has the 4-section aerial ladder and fixed tillerman's seat. The dealer plate dangling from one of the ground ladders indicates that the truck was all checked out and ready to begin its delivery trip.

1967

Peter Pirsch & Sons Co. of Kenosha, Wis. delivered this 100-foot Senior tractor-drawn aerial ladder truck to Jackson, Tenn. It is painted white. This model utilizes Pirsch's own chassis. The cutaway rear cab roof with encircling handrail, and the type of rear tractor fenders on this aerial are Pirsch features. The tillerman's seat and windshield swing out of the way when the main ladder is to be raised.

The Detroit suburb of Warren, Mich. ordered this 1967 Pirsch-Mack 100-foot Senior tractor-drawn aerial ladder truck. Similar in design to apparatus built by Peter Pirsch & Sons for Milwaukee, this aerial is drawn by a Mack Type C-85 Diesel tractor. The aerial is a 3-section Pirsch aluminum-alloy ladder. The rear tractor bodywork is by Pirsch. The Pirsch-Mack aerial was assigned to Warren's Ladder Co. No. 2.

In one of the more complex corporate enterprises, the distinguished name of Boyer lived on, but as the Universal Fire Apparatus Corp. of Logansport, Ind. Midwest Fire & Safety Equipment of Indianapolis also continued to supply fire equipment. This 1,000 GPM pumper on an International CO-8190 cab-forward chassis, carries Midwest identification but is shown as a Universal. It was delivered to Bloomington, Ind.

DeKalb County, Georgia specified this interesting Pirsch elevating platform. DeKalb's Snorkel No. 1 was built by Peter Pirsch & Sons on an International CO-8190 chassis with an open semi-cab. The boom is a 75-foot Pitman. The apparatus shown carries full truck company equipment.

The Hahn Motor Co. of Hamburg, Pa. was beginning to turn out some big fire engines. This Hahn 100-foot tractor-drawn aerial ladder truck was built for Silver Springs, Md. It has a Cincinnati cab. The 4-section metal aerial ladder was supplied by Pierre Thibault Ltd., of Pierreville, Que., Canada. This tractor-drawn aerial is similar in configuration to an American LaFrance. It is finished in striking red-and-white, with gold leaf striping and trim.

Howe Fire Apparatus of Anderson, Ind. built this handsome 1,000 GPM triple combination pumping engine for the Roselle, Ill. Fire Protection District. It is built on a Ford C-Series tilt cab chassis and is powered by a Ford 534 cubic inch V-8 engine. Note the bell and Federal Q siren mounted on the cab corners, and the cleanly-styled extended canopy cab. This pumper has a large booster tank for rural service.

Ward LaFrance delivered four triple combination pumping engines to the Chicago Fire Dept. in 1967. Only one of these was a 1,000 GPM model. Engine Co. No. 42's rig is powered by a Cummins Diesel and carries 500 gallons of water. The other three were 1,250 GPM Wards, also powered by Cummins Diesels, but with 350 gallon tanks. Note the dual booster reels and two floodlights above the pump compartment on Eng. 42's Ward LaFrance.

1967

Knoxville, Tennessee's Engine 9 is hooked up to a hydrant and ready to play away. The engine is a 1967 Ward LaFrance 1,000 GPM pumper. The Elmira Heights, N. Y. firm delivered a fairly small number of pumpers of this type, utilizing the familiar Cincinnati cab, from the middle to late 1960s. Note the use of two large flashers on the roof.

Engine 3 on the Massport Fire Department at Boston's Logan International Airport is this 1967 Ward LaFrance crash truck. This powerful crash-rescue apparatus carries 3,000 gallons of water and 500 gallons of foam, and can discharge 1,000 gallons of foam mixture from its roof turret per minute. Hand lines are carried on reels in the lower body. The large dial visible just behind the front cab door tells the crew at a glance precisely how much water is left in the main trunk. The large flotation tires enable this rig to travel safely over soft ground at high speeds.

Philadelphia placed 10 of these Ward LaFrance-International 1,000 GPM pumpers into service in 1967. All were mounted on International VCO-196 tilt-cab chassis with extended canopy cabs, and had 1,000 GPM pumps. Note the dual booster reels and the Stang monitor. The long pole carried above the rear of the apparatus is for a protective canopy.

The Maxim Motor Company of Middleboro, Mass. delivered this tandem-axle elevating platform to Jeffersonville, Ind. in 1967. Jeffersonville's Snorkel No. 1 is built on a Maxim Custom 6 x 4 chassis, and carries a 1,000 GPM pump as well as a 75-foot Pitman Snorkel, making it a snorkel quint. This 75-footer has almost no front overhang.

Huntington, Ind. received this 100-foot Maxim aerial in 1967. Maxim built it on an International CO-8190 chassis. A quintuple combination, it has a 1,000 gallon-per-minute pump. Note the overhang of the 4-section aerial ladder, and the manually-operated ground jacks. A ladder pipe is permanently attached to the underside of the bed section of the aerial ladder for use as a water tower.

In the latter part of 1967, Mack replaced its famed B Series conventional fire engines with an entirely new series called the Mack Model R. This new series featured a one-piece, unitized front end that incorporated the hood and front fenders. The new R Type Mack was available with either gasoline or Diesel engines, and with pump capacities ranging from 750 to 1,250 gallons-per-minute. The roomy new cab offered much improved visibility and many other engineering improvements. This is one of the first Type R 1,000 GPM triple combination pumpers built.

1967

The Detroit Fire Department placed four of these 1,000 gallon-per-minute Mack Type C-85D Diesel-powered pumping engines into service in 1967. Two years later, two of these pumpers, assigned to Engines 36 and 37, were retrofitted with 50-foot Squrt articulated master stream booms. Engine 37's rig is seen outside D.F.D. Headquarters before it was placed back into service following this conversion. These are the only two Squrts on the Detroit Fire Dept.

The Chicago Fire Dept. replaced Snorkel Squad 1's former rig with this new Mack Type MB-600 in 1967. Snorkel squad 1's new rig had a 50-foot Pitman Snorkel and a modular-type rear cab for the crew. This versatile piece of apparatus is one of the busiest in the city and sees a great deal of action. Despite its relatively short overall length, Snorkel Squad 1 carries a large variety of heavy rescue gear. Its compact configuration permits it to squeeze into spaces that a conventional snorkel or an aerial ladder truck can't.

Philadelphia purchased two of these International–Hi Ranger 85-foot snorkels in 1967. Built on International Harvester VCO-196 chassis with canopy-type extended cabs, they were assigned to Ladders 2 and 5. Here, Ladder 5's rig rolls on an alarm from its quarters which it shares with Engine 1. The Philly snorkels are unique in that they have red-painted booms, rather than the standard white. These units carry full truck equipment and have tandem rear axles.

Mack's Fire Apparatus Division found an enthusiastic market for its Aerialscope elevating platform. Mack's platforms differed from the more popular articulating boom-type, in that the Aerialscope employed a 4-section telescopic boom that had a built-in ladder to the basket on the end. To this day, New York City will purchase no other kind. Mack Aerialscopes are built in only one size—75-foot. This 1967 model, on C Series chassis, was built for Missoula, Mont.

Watsonville, Cal. received this 1967 Crown 100-foot Service Aerial Ladder Truck. Like all Crown aerials, it has a Maxim aerial ladder. Watsonville's aerial is powered by a diesel engine. Note the over-and-under stacked headlights, a standard Crown Firecoach feature.

The 95th Annual Conference of the International Assn. of Fire Chiefs, held in Louisville, Ky., featured an unusual number of new products and innovations exhibited by fire apparatus manufacturers.

Twenty-four years after it had constructed a mock-up model of one based on its then-new 700 Series chassis, American LaFrance in 1968 introduced its first rear-mounted aerial ladder truck. Called the American La-France Ladder-Chief, the new 900 Series model was previewed at the Louisville convention. The unit shown was a closed, canopy cab model finished in white that was built for Gary, Ind. The Ladder-Chief had a 4-section, 100-foot aerial ladder mounted at the rear, and carried a full complement of ladders and other equipment. Two sets of A-frame hydraulic outriggers were mounted behind the single rear axle. At the same IAFC Convention,

American LaFrance exhibited its new 900 Series Chieftain high-capacity pumper. Powered by a V-8 Detroit Diesel engine, this pumper was rated at 2,000 gallons per minute.

The Snorkel Fire Equipment used the IAFC Convention to exhibit and demonstrate its latest idea in articulated boom firefighting devices. Called the Squrt, this was a miniature Snorkel boom of 50-foot height which carried a remote-controlled master stream nozzle at its tip instead of a basket. The versatile Squrt was designed for mounting on conventional pumpers and hose wagons. The one shown was mounted on a short-wheelbase Ford C tilt-cab chassis of the Indianapolis, Ind. Fire Dept. The new Squrt boom complemented the company's line of 50, 65, 75 and 85-foot elevating platforms.

The Maxim Motor Co. in 1968 introduced an improved conventional Model S chassis with a new, wider cab. The company also came out with a unique Top-Trol device which gave the man at the top of the ladder full control of aerial ladder operation. The ladder could also be operated by the man at the console on the aerial turntable.

The Ward LaFrance Truck Corp. unveiled its new Command Tower at the Louisville convention. Mounted on a 1,000 GPM Ward LaFrance/Ford C tilt-cab pumper chassis, the CT-22 Command Tower featured a roomy platform that rose vertically 22 feet at the touch of a button. The Command Tower platform was equipped with a 1,100 GPM monitor nozzle.

Seagrave's exhibit at the 1968 IAFC Conference included the company's 4-wheel drive and steer Rear Admiral rearmount aerial.

During 1968, Peter Pirsch and Sons Co. delivered two rear-mounted 100-foot aerials to the Chicago Fire Dept. These compact aerials were built on the new Mack Model CF cab-forward chassis and had 4-section main ladders of the patented Pirsch aluminum alloy lattice design.

Boston, Mass. in 1968 placed in service several American LaFrance 100-foot tractor-drawn aerials with special enclosed tiller compartments. The side windows of the tillerman's cab were fitted with plastic blisters which gave the tillerman full visibility, but protected him from thrown objects. Unfortunately, following the civil disturbances and riots that had seared most major U. S. cities in the past few years, the protection of fire fighters en route to and returning from fires had become an important consideration in fire apparatus design. Many

Charging up a dirt road is one of the Los Angeles County Fire Dept.'s big Crown Firecoach pumper-tankers. With many miles of highly volatile brush acreage to cover, the L. A. County F. D. must carry much of its own water to the fire. Like the neighboring Los Angeles City Fire Dept., the L. A. County Fire Dept. operates a sizable fleet of Crown pumpers. Engine 82's siren is mounted behind the screen in the front of the canopy cab.

Los Angeles owns what is certainly one of the most distinctive tow trucks around. Designated Heavy Utility Unit No. 6, this monstrous rig was built by Crown Firecoach on a tandem-axle chassis for the Los Angeles City Fire Dept. It is painted bright yellow for maximum visibility, and carries two 20-ton Holmes lifting booms, in addition to other heavy rescue gear. Note the double front bumpers that house a heavy winch. This special purpose apparatus is used for heavy rescue work, and also for towing disabled apparatus to the LAFD shops.

Crown Firecoach delivered this big 100-foot tractor-drawn aerial ladder truck to Berkeley, Cal. The 4-section ladder is by Maxim, and the apparatus is Diesel-powered. Note the large compartment behind the canopy cab, and on the trailer. This rig has manual ground jacks and wood ground ladders.

1968

ities had enclosed the rear steps and tiller seats of their
apparatus with protective shields, and many open-cab rigs
were retrofitted with shop-built cabs to protect the crew.

Interesting 1968 deliveries included a 1,500 GPM Crown
Firecoach pumper with a 50-foot Snorkel to the Los
Angeles City Fire Dept.; a Young Crusader Snorkel-Quint
for Henrietta, N. Y., and a cab-forward pumper with
front-mounted 750 GPM pump built by the Melray Mfg.
Co. of Hortonville, Wis. This unique pumper was delivered
to Fall River, Wis.

Paterson, N. J. erected a steel-and-plywood canopy over
each side of the semi open cab of its 1968 American
LaFrance 90-foot Aero-Chief elevating platform, to protect
the crew from objects thrown from above. Paterson's Snorkel
has a single rear axle, and when this photo was taken it
responded as Truck No. 3. The end of the boom has been
painted day-glo red for added safety in traffic.

Many fire apparatus, including some of the largest manufacturers in the country, were now using this type of cab
supplied by both Duplex and Cincinnati, making it difficult
sometimes to identify the builder. The Oren-Roanoke Corp.
built this Guardian Series Custom 1,000 GPM pumper for
Hawthorne, N. Y. It is powered by a Waukesha engine, and
has a Waterous CMB pump, and a 500-gallon booster tank.
The dual hose reels have electric rewinds.

Plainville, Conn. received this American LaFrance 900 Series
Aero-Chief 80 quintuple combination. This open cab unit
carries a 1,000 GPM pump and an 80-foot aerial platform.
Unlike most American LaFrance elevating platforms, which
were designated Aero-Chiefs, this one is lettered Snorkel 1
on the cab sides and the boom water piping.

Oren-Roanoke Corp., formerly of Roanoke, Va., but now
located in Vinton, Va., built this deluxe model commercial
chassis pumper for the City of Roanoke. The unique cab
used on this Ford C Series chassis is of the canopy style,
with a walkaway from the rear. This Oren-Ford is powered
by a Ford 534 cubic inch V-8 engine, and has a Waterous
750 GPM pump. Few canopy cab fire engines of this
design were built by any manufacturer.

Because of the escalating cost of custom-chassis apparatus,
and the availability of suitable heavy-duty commercial truck
chassis, fewer and fewer full customs were being built in
Canada. LaFrance Fire Engine & Foamite of Toronto,
ALF's Canadian subsidiary, delivered three of these 1968
LaFrance-Ford 100-foot service aerials to the Toronto Fire
Dept. All were powered by Ford 534 cubic inch V-8 engines.
Note the enclosed ladder beds and 6-man canopy cab. The
truck shown was still responding as Aerial No. 1 in 1975.

Buffalo, N. Y. placed this American LaFrance 900 Series
100-foot tractor-drawn aerial ladder truck in service with
Ladder Co. 3. It carries a complement of wood ground
ladders and has manually-operated stabilizer jacks. Note the
enclosed tillerman's seat with blister windows in the door.

1968

Elevating platforms were no means limited to the big cities. Many smaller communities found them just as useful. When the small city of Medina, Ohio went shopping for a snorkel in 1968, the town fathers chose an 85-foot Pitman on an FWD chassis. The tandem-axle rig proved too big for the firehouse when it was delivered, however, and had to be stored in a temporary building on the edge of town until a new fire station could be completed.

The old, reliable tractor-drawn aerial continued to hold its own, despite the growing popularity of elevating platforms and the new rear-mounted aerials. Seagrave delivered this 100-foot tractor-drawn aerial to the Baltimore County, Md. Fire Bureau. The Seagrave cab-forward tractor carries a booster reel, and the tiller seat does not have to be moved to raise the main ladder. The long box above the ladder bed is for storage of the 3-inch ladder line.

Crystal Lake, Ill. took delivery of this snorkel quint. It is built on an FWD 3 x 4 chassis with special low-profile cab, which permits a relatively low over-all height with the boom in the travelling position. This apparatus has a 1,000 GPM pump and a 75-foot Pitman Snorkel and sports a Chicago black-over-red paint job. The water pipe for the basket nozzle is visible alongside each of the two articulating arms.

Here is an interesting marriage of the old with the new. The Augusta, Ga. Fire Dept. shops built this city service ladder truck by taking the double bank ladder bed from an old American LaFrance ladder truck, and remounting it on a new International Cargostar C-1910 chassis. The result was a new ladder truck at a fraction of the cost of a factory-built one.

The Seagrave Fire Apparatus Division of FWD Corp. built this beautiful white-painted 1,250 gallon-per-minute triple combination pumper for the West Overland Fire Protection District. This type of body style, with enclosed cabinets in the area formerly reserved for the hard suction hose, was becoming popular in some areas where limited water sources made hard suctions useless. Note the twin electronic sirens mounted on the bumper and the air horns on the roof. The beacon flasher is mounted on a protruding bracket to reduce over-all height.

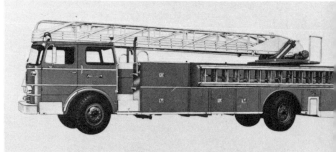

Seagrave's compact Rear Admiral rear-mount aerial ladder truck was drawing wide interest. This is a 100-footer with 4-wheel steering. The Rear Admiral was available with a 65, 75, 85 or 100-foot ladder and with two or four-wheel drive. American LaFrance introduced its own custom rear-mount aerial under the name of Ladder Chief in mid-1968.

Exactly 10 years after this revolutionary piece of equipment was introduced to the fire service by the Chicago Fire Dept., the elevating platform, or snorkel, had come into its own and was an important piece of equipment on hundreds of fire departments, large and small, across the U.S. and around the world. Milwaukee, Wis. got this 85-footer in 1968. It was built by Peter Pirsch & Sons on a Mack CF chassis, and utilized a Pitman boom. Mack's wide, new CF chassis had just been introduced as the successor to the Ahrens-Fox inspired C Series chassis which Mack had used since 1957.

1968

Peter Pirsch and Sons Co. also got into the rear-mount aerial ladder truck market in 1968. The Kenosha, Wis. manufacturer delivered this 100-foot rearmount aerial, on Mack's brand new CF fire apparatus chassis, to the Chicago Fire Dept. Ground ladders fit into the space under the turntable. Note the booster equipment, and the floodlights carried on the cab roof. This Pirsch-Mack was assigned to Hook & Ladder Co. No. 22.

Pirsch built this compact quintuple combination fire apparatus on a GMC tilt-cab chassis with canopy extension. It has a 750 GPM pump, a 75-foot Pirsch aerial ladder and booster equipment. The booster tank filler can be seen above the hard suction hoses.

Commissioner Paxton Mendelssohn presented this $65,000 mobile hospital to the Detroit Fire Department as a gift. The D.F.D.'s Medical Unit was custom-built by the Gerstenslager Corp. on a GMC chassis. This huge apparatus carries every piece of emergency medical equipment imaginable. Its interior is completely finished in stainless steel, and department doctors can actually operate on patients en route to the hospital. The Medical Unit automatically responds on all multiple alarms. This was the last of three ambulances presented to the D.F.D. by Commissioner Mendelssohn, in 1927, 1937 and 1968. The Commissioner underwrote the cost of rebuilding the 1937 model in 1951.

Salt Lake City, Utah prolonged the service life of a 30-year-old ladder truck by equipping it with a new tractor. A 1968 Ford C-1000 tractor complete with sleeper compartment behind the crew seat, was placed under the department's 1938 American LaFrance 100-foot aerial trailer. It isn't known if the bunker cab ever saw service at a fire. This appears to be a shop conversion.

Grant's Pass, Ore. ordered this custom chassised pumper from Western States Fire Apparatus, Cornelius, Ore. It has a 5-man canopy cab (Cincinnati), and a Mattydale transverse hose bed for preconnected 1½-inch attack lines above the pump compartment. The red-and-white pumper is lettered for Engine No. 3.

Logansport, Ind. bought locally when the city fathers went shopping for an aerial ladder truck. Universal Fire Apparatus Corp. of Logansport, successor to the old, established Boyer firm of the same city, built this 75-foot service aerial on a 1968 International CO-8190 chassis. The aerial ladder is a 3-section Grove. Note the ladder pipe affixed to the ladder tip for water tower use. Logansport's aerial has hydraulic A-frame stabilizer jacks.

1968

Hahn Fire Apparatus of Hamburg, Pa. built this good-looking service aerial ladder truck for the Wissahickon Fire Co. of Ambler, Pa. This apparatus, with open semi-cab, has a Canadian-built Thibault 100-foot, 4-section aerial ladder, and is powered by a Waukesha 325-horsepower engine. Note the clean appearance and the generous compartment space. This aerial bears a striking resemblance to a Mack Type C service aerial.

Cleveland, Ohio ordered several of these intriguing pumpers from the Sutphen Fire Equipment Co. Engine Co. No. 5's white-painted rig is mounted on a GMC tilt-cab chassis with extended canopy cab. It has a 750 GPM front-mounted pump with an integral turret pipe for close-in operations. This type of front-mount with a turret nozzle on top is quite common in northern Ohio.

The Yankee-Walter Corp. of Los Angeles, specializes in building big airport crash apparatus. This is a medium-sized unit, compared with Yankee-Walter's massive twin-engined standard airport crash rigs. Note the use of Ford C Series front-end sheet metal and cab doors. This crash truck has a swing-out hose reel and a single turret. The foam turret can be operated either from atop the cab or by remote control from inside.

Some five years earlier, the Sutphen Fire Equipment Co. had built and demonstrated its new Sutphen aerial tower. This new type of elevating platform utilized a 4-section telescoping boom of open lattice construction, instead of articulating booms. The end of the Sutphen boom was equipped with a roomy basket with one or two turret nozzles. The sturdy, versatile Sutphen quickly won wide acceptance by the fire service. This 85-foot Sutphen aerial tower with 1,000 GPM pump was built for the Cleveland suburb of Cuyahoga Heights, Ohio. Note the Cincinnati cab and the tandem-axle chassis.

Boston modernized four of its older tractor-drawn aerial ladder trucks by slipping new Diamond Reo tractors under the still serviceable ladder trailers. Ladder Co. No. 18 received this 1968 Diamond Reo, which is pulling a 1944 American LaFrance 100-foot aerial trailer. The massive Diamond Reo tractor gives this rig a truly awesome appearance.

This pumper is very similar in appearance to the International-chassised jobs delivered to Philadelphia the previous year. But the pumper shown here was built by Fire Trucks Inc. of Mount Clemens, Mich., not Ward LaFrance. The FTI firm delivered 15 of these 1,000 GPM pumpers on International VCO-196 chassis to the Philadelphia Fire Dept. in 1968. The wood frame over the rear body is for a protective cover. Engine 50's rig is seen here rolling out of its quarters on a run.

Pierre Thibault Ltd. of Pierreville, Que., which had previously built fire apparatus only for Canadian departments, began to export some of its products to the neighboring United States. Derby, Conn., received this 1968 Thibault Custom triple combination pumper. This model is powered by a Waukesha 6-cylinder engine and has a Thibault 1,000 GPM (U. S. gallons) centrifugal pump and a 500-gallon booster tank. Note the length of hard suction hose carried above the rear fender compartments.

One of the very few Maxims ever delivered in Illinois is this 1,000 gallon-per-minute Maxim Model S pumper, sold to the Chicago suburb of Westchester. Note the gothic-style lettering and the closed, 3-man cab. A soft suction hose is preconnected to the suction intake for quick hydrant hookup.

For many years a body builder for other fire engine manufacturers, Pierce Manufacturing Co. of Appleton, Wis. began to build its own complete line of motor fire apparatus. Menasha, Wis. received this low-slung Pierce 1,250 GPM pumper, which is built on an Oshkosh custom cab-forward chassis. Note the portable turret pipe on the rear cab roof and the enclosed booster hose reels.

This full-custom Howe pumper was built for Antioch, Cal. by Howe Fire Apparatus of Anderson, Ind. The open Duplex-style cab is unusual. This 1,250 gallon-per-minute pumper is powered by a Detroit Diesel engine and has a 350-gallon booster tank. This pumper carries both conventional booster hose and preconnected 1½-inch attack lines. Note the fully compartmented rear fenders.

Pierce Manufacturing has delivered many fire trucks mounted on popular commercial chassis. This is a Pierce-Ford 1,000 GPM pumper with extended canopy cab. Note the two white flashers on each side of the cab below the windshield and the Aurora Borealis light on the cab roof. The transverse hose beds above the ground ladders are for two preconnected inch-and-a-half hose lines.

The most important new product announcement of the year came from a West Coast firm. The Calavar Corp. of Santa Fe Springs, near Los Angeles, introduced the world's largest elevating platform. Calavar's remarkable Firebird had a 125-foot boom. The prototype was mounted on a special Seagrave cab-forward chassis, and was sold to Philadelphia, Pa. The high and far-ranging Calavar Firebird featured a 4-section, telescopic articulated boom. Four huge outriggers and a nose jack hoisted the monstrous tandem-axle apparatus nearly two feet off the ground when the boom was to be raised. Ground ladders were carried in enclosed compartments, which were hydraulically lowered to permit the turntable to rotate. Calavar had been building outsized aerial platforms for years, but principally for servicing large aircraft and special aerospace applications. The Firebird marked the company's entry into the fire apparatus field. At 125 feet, the towering Firebird could reach 25 feet higher than any aerial platform then being sold.

Five years had passed since The Seagrave Corp. had been acquired by FWD Corp., but the Seagrave name remained part of the Columbus, Ohio industrial scene. A Timpco-Seagrave Division had been formed by the Timmons Metal Products Co. of Columbus, and this firm manufactured a line of Seagrave commercial chassis pumpers and aerial ladder trucks that carried the Seagrave Commercial-By Timpco name. In 1968, Seagrave-Timpco delivered a rebuilt 85-foot tractor-drawn Seagrave aerial with a GMC tilt-cab canopy tractor to the Columbus Fire Dept. Two Timpco-Seagrave 100-foot tractor-drawn aerials with conventional style GMC tractors with extended canopy cabs were delivered in 1969. Timpco also built a Colt mini-pumper, mounted on a standard pickup truck chassis. Seagrave-Timpco delivered a number of canopy cab commercial chassis pumpers to area fire departments.

The Maxim Motor Co. had been delivering elevating platforms mounted on the company's standard cab-forward custom chassis. The Maxim Snorkels used Pitman elevating platforms, and larger models were equipped with tandem rear axles. A typical delivery was to South Euclid, Ohio. This Maxim elevating platform was equipped with a 1,250 GPM pump and an 85-foot Pitman Snorkel, and was diesel-powered. The bodywork rear of the cab was done by Pierce.

Pierce Manufacturing, which had built custom fire apparatus bodies for various manufacturers for many years, was now in the fire apparatus field itself. The Appleton, Wis. firm introduced its own complete line of commercial chassis pumpers, which it sold as Pierce Suburbans. The most popular model in this series was the Pierce Suburban-C, a 1,000 GPM pumper with 750 gallon booster tank, built on the Ford C Series tilt cab chassis, with an extended canopy style cab. A black, vinyl-faced pump operator's panel became a Pierce trademark. Pierce continued to build special fire apparatus bodies for other manufacturers.

The respected old name of Sanford was back in the fire apparatus business. The Sanford Fire Apparatus Corp. of East Syracuse, N. Y. offered a full range of large and small pumpers and specialized fire equipment. In 1969, the company delivered a big 1,500 GPM Diesel pumper with Cincinnati cab to the Syracuse Fire Dept.

A Canadian manufacturer, Go-Tract, of Bellevue, Quebec, introduced a series of enclosed, track-mounted crash fire trucks designed for high speed operation over snow-covered ground. These go-anywhere fire fighters were designed for airport crash rescue work.

The Snorkel Fire Equipment had greatly diversified its product line. In 1969 the company built a 1,000 GPM pumper on a Mack CF-600 chassis for Garland, Tex. This pumper, of course, was equipped with a Squrt boom.

Northlake, Ill. received this 1969 Snorkel quintuipl combination. Finished in high visibility yellow, it is built on an Oshkosh low-profile chassis and has a 75-foot Pitman Snorkel and 1,000 GPM pump. Note the spacing of the stabilizer jacks for maximum stability when the elevating platform is being used. Bodywork appears by Pierce. Three men can be safely carried in the basket.

Now and then, a proud old name re-emerges. The Sanford Fire Apparatus Corp. of East Syracuse, N. Y., built a highly-respected line of motor fire apparatus on its own chassis in the late 1920s. In 1969, the Syracuse, N. Y. Fire Dept. purchased this big Sanford Custom 1,500 gallon-per-minute diesel-powered pumper and assigned it to Engine Co. 6. This fine-looking pumper was painted Syracuse's traditional white, sports a small Stang monitor, booster equipment and a Cincinnati cab. Note the length of the air horn on the rear cab roof.

As a result of the tragic riots which left much of the inner city in ashes two years earlier, the City of Detroit obtained Federal funds for a large purchase of new fire apparatus. This order included 15 new Mack CF-600 pumpers and seven new American LaFrance 100-foot aerials. Engine Co. No. 50 received one of the new 1,000 GPM Mack diesel pumpers. All of these pumpers carry portable deluge pipes and are equipped with front suction intakes.

Ten years after it first appeared, this cab-forward pumper was still Seagrave's standard model. The 1,250 gallon-per-minute pumper built for Paterson, N. J. carries a portable turret gun above its hose bed. Two-and-a-half inch lines are preconnected to the right-hand side pump panel for quick deployment. Curved elbows are used to minimize kinking at the pump panel connection.

Here is a pair of matched 1969 Seagraves placed in service in Chicago. The rig on the left is a 1969 Seagrave 100-foot Rear Admiral aerial assigned to Hook & Ladder 3. Its mate is a 1969 Seagrave 1,250 GPM pumper with 500-gallon tank assigned to Engine Co. 42. Note the difference in cab heights in this front view. The special low-profile cab reduces overall height of the rear-mounted aerial ladder. Chicago had switched to the large, reflectorized numbers for quick company recognition on the fireground.

Seagrave's engine-ahead-of-cab conventional series fire apparatus was still available, but very few were now being ordered. Demand had swung almost entirely to the cab-forward design with its better visibility. The City of Paterson, N. J. ordered this 1969 Seagrave 100-foot tractor-drawn aerial. A shop-built enclosure has been added over the tiller-man's seat for his protection.

Cudahy, Wis. received this very clean-looking 1969 Seagrave 100-foot rear-mount aerial ladder truck. The aerial ladder has four sections, and a ladder pipe is permanently attached to the underside of the bed ladder. Note the large equipment compartments. Ground ladders are carried on each side of the apparatus and in two banks under the aerial ladder turntable. The 100-foot aerial is stabilized by a single set of A-frame outriggers.

The Chicago Fire Department purchased a wide variety of new pumpers in 1969, from Seagrave, Ward LaFrance and Pierce. Five Seagrave pumpers were placed in service, including three of these 1,000 GPM models, a 1,250 GPM model and a 1,500 GPM model. Two of the 1,000 GPM jobs, including Engine Co. No. 120's rig, are powered by Waukesha 6-cylinder engines. The third is a diesel.

Columbus, Ohio—the former home of the Seagrave Corp.—modernized one of its older model Seagrave tractor-drawn aerials in 1969. A new GMC tractor with 6-man canopy cab replaced a 1951 Seagrave V-12 tractor, and the trailer was rebuilt. This refurbished aerial is assigned to the Columbus Fire Dept.'s Ladder 23. Note the lack of rear windows in the tractor cab. The following year, Peter Pirsch & Sons delivered a new aerial to Columbus which is similar in appearance to this rebuild.

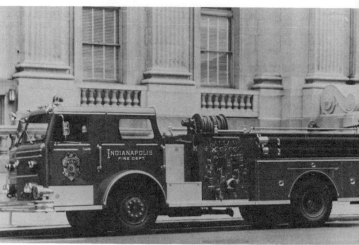

Boston, Mass. purchased two of these compact Squrts, which it operates as hose wagons. The Squrts are assigned to Engines 17 and 26. These interesting units were built by the Maxim Motor Co. on Ford C Series tilt-cab chassis, but have Pierce bodies, making them Maxim-Pierce-Fords. The 50-foot articulating boom, the tip of which is fitted with a high-capacity remote controlled master stream nozzle, was built by Snorkel Fire Equipment, a division of the Pitman Mfg. Co. The compact apparatus shown here is Engine 17's wagon.

A loyal Maxim customer for many years, Indianapolis continued to place orders with the Middleboro, Mass. manufacturer. This 1969 Maxim 1,500 gallon-per-minute canopy cab-forward triple combination pumper was assigned to Indy's Engine Co. 8. It carries a single booster reel with electric rewind, and has a 500-gallon booster tank. Indianapolis is by far Maxim's biggest customer outside of New England.

A new dimension in elevating platforms was introduced to the fire service this year, when the Philadelphia Fire Dept. placed the first Calavar Firebird into service. With a 125-foot boom with articulating arms and a telescopic upper boom, this was the highest aerial platform offered by any manufacturer. It was built by the Calavar Corp. of Santa Fe Springs, Calif., near Los Angeles and mounted on an FWD 6 x 4 chassis. The four stabilizer jacks swing out into the street, and ground ladders are carried in the chrome streamer-ornamented boxes, which are hydraulically lowered for use. Note the large single front jack visible below the bumper. Calavar offered 100, 125 and 150-foot Firebirds. A 90-footer was added to the line several years later.

Pierre Thibault Ltd. of Pierreville, Que., was appointed Canada's exclusive distributor for Mack fire apparatus chassis. Thibault continued to export pumpers and aerials to American fire departments. Warren, R. I. received this Thibault-Mack 1,000 Model pumper, built on the new Mack Model R conventional hood chassis.

Eight of these Ward LaFrance Ford 1,000 GPM joined the Chicago Fire Dept. roster in 1969. All have extended canopy cabs and are powered by Caterpillar Diesel engines. The pumps were supplied by Hale. These triple combinations have 500-gallon booster tanks and twin booster reels. Note the Aurora Borealis warning light.

Due largely to the changing nature of American cities during the 1960s, open-cab fire apparatus had declined greatly in popularity by the end of the decade. Cranston, R. I., took delivery of this Ward LaFrance Ambassador 1,000 GPM pumper with an open semi-cab. The bags visible at the rear cab entrance cover breathing apparatus, which can be quickly donned by the men riding in the cab rear upon arrival at a working fire.

The Memphis Fire Department apparatus division built this nice-looking salvage truck, utilizing an International CO-8190 cab-forward fire apparatus chassis. The completed rig was assigned to Salvage Corps No. 1. It carries a fixed Stang deck pipe. This is a good example of the very professional workmanship done by some municipal fire department workshop staffs.

The Fire Department of Memphis, Tenn. was for many years one of Peter Pirsch & Son's best customers. So, when Memphis went shopping for a new elevating platform, it was no surprise when the Kenosha, Wis. fire apparatus manufacturer got the order. Memphis' new 85-footer was built on a 1969 Pirsch Custom cab-forward chassis with tandem rear axles. It carries a full complement of ground ladders, an 85-foot Pitman Snorkel and responds as Snorkel Truck Co. No. 1. Memphis rigs are painted the traditional red, but have distinctive dark green running boards.

Winnipeg, Manitoba built two of these compact suburban-model aerial ladder trucks in its own fire department shops. Electric Aerial Ladder No. 7 has a 55-foot, electrically-raised 3-section Memco 55-foot aerial ladder mounted on an International tilt-cab chassis. These small aerials are used in residential and light industrial neighborhoods.

Evanston, Ill. received this 1969 Peter Pirsch & Sons Co. 100-foot Senior tractor-drawn aerial ladder truck, with Pirsch Custom canopy cab tractor. This aerial has the three-section aerial ladder and movable tiller. Note the road sanders just forward of the rear tractor wheels. Evanston purchased a considerable amount of Pirsch fire apparatus during the 1950s. This city was also a good Seagrave customer in the 1930s.

Chicago placed only one of these Pierce-Oshkosh Diesel 1,250 GPM pumpers into service in 1969. This handsome rig was assigned to Engine Co. No. 98. It was built on an Oshkosh chassis powered by a Detroit Diesel engine, and carries a Waterous pump. The cab is the special low-profile Oshkosh Custom. Note the dual booster reels, soft suction hose carried over the rear fender compartments and the bright metal trim used around the front of the cab.

Pierce Manufacturing of Appleton, Wis. now offered a complete line of custom and commercial-chassis fire apparatus of its own, as well as supplying high-quality Pierce fire apparatus bodies to several other manufacturers. This is a Pierce Suburban Model triple combination pumper built on a GMC chassis with extended canopy cab. Note the fillets used in the upper cab wheel opening.

American LaFrance built this heavy-looking commercial chassis pumper for Salinas, Cal. Mounted on a 1969 GMC 9500 diesel chassis, it has a 1,250 GPM pump and carries 750 gallons of water. Equipment carried includes a portable turret nozzle, two booster reels, two 1½-inch preconnected attack lines and a front suction intake. Suction hoses are carried above the compartments on each side.

The smooth-faced American LaFrance 900 Series fire engines by now were as familiar as their Series 700 and 800 predecessors. The 900 had now been in production at Elmira for 11 years. Parma, Ohio owns this 2-toned 1969 American LaFrance 900 Series 1,250 gallon-per-minute pumper. Note the dual dome lights and the Federal Q siren mounted in the nose. The barrel for the portable deck pipe is carried vertically in front of the booster tank.

The familiar 900 Series American LaFrance by now had been in production at American LaFrance even longer than its famed predecessor, the 700 and 800 Series. Few exterior changes, mainly in the type of nameplates used, had been made since the 900 first appeared in mid-1958. This 1,250 gallon-per-minute 900 Series pumper, delivered to Muskegon, Mich., carries both booster lines and preconnected Mattydale 1½-inch attack lines. An extra length of hard suction hose is carried on the right hand side of this truck.

The City of Detroit, for decades a user of Seagrave aerials exclusively, in 1969 purchased its first American LaFrance ladder trucks since the horse-drawn era. A total of seven American LaFrance 900 Series aerials were delivered to the Motor City, including four of these 100-foot tractor-drawn diesels, and three 100-foot service aerials, also diesel-powered. Two of the tractor-drawn models carry booster equipment. Detroit Fire Dept. photographer Capt. J. A. Mancinelli took this photo of Ladder 23's new American LaFrance the day it entered service.

Interestingly enough, the Canadian distributor for the Hi-Ranger elevating platform is a large lawn equipment firm. The Aerial Towers Division of Duke Lawn Equipment Ltd., of Burlington, Ontario built this 85-foot Hi-Ranger for the Toronto Fire Dept. It is mounted on a Ford C Series chassis. with 534 cubic inch V-8 gasoline engine and has an extended canopy cab. Toronto's Aerial Towers No. 2 protects the downtown area and responds as a ladder truck. Duke built a similar 85-foot model for Windsor, Ontario the following year.

American LaFrance entered the 1970s with the introduction of a new premium series of pumpers, aerials and elevating platforms built on the company's 900 Series custom cab-forward chassis.

The new top-line series was designated the 1000 Series, and could be distinguished from the standard production 900 models by a special American LaFrance Eagle emblem on the cab front and sides, and a band of bright metal trim used on the lower cab front. The new 1000 Series apparatus included Detroit Diesel power as standard equipment, and included many popular items that were previously available only as options. The new 1000 line complemented the 900 Series, which continued in production for its 12th straight year.

The Seagrave Fire Apparatus Division of the FWD Corp. quietly delivered its last conventional engine-ahead-of-cab pumper in 1970. The last of the 70th Anniversary line, which had been introduced 19 years earlier in 1951, was delivered to Jackson, Mich. Orders for the long-hood style of Seagrave had plummeted in recent years. In 1969, Jackson had received an 85-foot service aerial of this earlier style, one of the last of this type ever built.

The Ward LaFrance Truck Corp. received a substantial order for new pumpers and aerial ladder trucks from Chicago. This order included six big 2,000 GPM Ward LaFrance custom cab-forward pumpers, and five Ward LaFrance custom rear-mount aerials with 100-foot Grove aerial ladders.

Chicago at this time commissioned three of the most unusual fire fighting trucks ever used by an American fire department. These special master stream devices, as bizarre as they were in appearance, were highly effective when thrown into action at major fires.

The largest of these special service units was the John F. Plant, better known simply as the Big John. Bristling with rear hose inlets, the Big John was built up on an ex-U.S. Army 1952 International 6 x 6 truck chassis. Its armament includes two gigantic hydraulically raised water cannons, and two smaller turret nozzles mounted on its front bumper. The slightly smaller Big Mo was built on a 1953 International 6 x 6, but sports a single water cannon. The baby of the big-water bunch is the Little John, which is mounted on a 1961 Willys Jeep compact chassis. The

Little John can be driven right into a burning building.

The Pierce Manufacturing Co. of Appleton, Wis. introduced its own line of high capacity, custom chassis pumping engines. The Pierce Power Chief custom cab-forward pumpers used a special chassis supplied by the Oshkosh Truck Corp., of Oshkosh, Wis. Pierce's new models were offered in 1,250 and 1,500 GPM sizes, with Waterous pumps and a choice of Diesel or gasoline power.

Another firm that was building custom and commercial chassis fire engines for departments in the north central part of the U. S. was the General Safety Equipment Corp., of North Branch, Minn. In 1970, this company built a 1,250 GPM Diesel pumper for Moorhead, Minn. on a cab-forward Seagrave chassis.

The Sutphen Fire Equipment Co. of Columbus, Ohio was doing very well with its big Sutphen Aerial Tower. Built on a 3-axle custom cab-forward chassis with Cincinnati cab, the standard Sutphen Aerial Tower was diesel powered and had a 4-section, telescopic 85-foot boom. Two turret nozzles were mounted in its roomy basket, and the Sutphen Aerial Tower also carried a full complement of ground ladders and other equipment. Some fire departments equipped their Sutphen Towers with a 1,000 GPM midship-mounted Barton pump. Sutphen Fire Equipment delivered a small number of these towers on commercial chassis, and built a complete range of pumpers.

Mack's big Model CF cab-forward fire apparatus could now be found in fire stations from coast to coast. The exceptionally roomy CF cab has a very large glass area affording excellent visibility for the driver. This is a Mack Model CF-600 pumper of 1,000 gallon-per-minute capacity, with a 750-gallon booster tank. Note the 5-inch front suction intake, and the split Mattydale transverse 1½-inch hose compartment above the pump panel.

This huge piece of equipment packs a lot of fire apparatus onto a single chassis. Built for Hudson, Ohio, it is a quintuple combination on a 1970 Mack CF-600 chassis. The rear body was built by Pierce Mfg. This versatile fire fighter has a 70-foot Pitman Snorkel, as well as a 1,000 GPM pump. Two hard suctions are carried side by side above the ground ladders.

With American patriotism hitting a new high, Mack widely used this star-spangled red, white and blue Model CF-600 pumper in its advertising. Several fire companies around the country liked the idea and painted the cabs of their rigs this mind-boggling color. It isn't known if this patriotic paint job was any more effective than the new lime-greens and yellows that were gaining favor, but it sure looked great in parades.

Many large fire departments, including Boston, Washington, D. C. and Detroit, added Sutphen Aerial Towers to their firefighting fleets. Detroit's Ladder 6 was assigned this Sutphen Co. 85-foot Aerial Tower. Powered by a Detroit Diesel engine, it was retrofitted with a 1,000 GPM pump two years later. The Sutphen Aerial Tower has a basket with two turret nozzles. The tandem-axle chassis has a Cincinnati cab. This is one of Detroit's busiest ladder companies.

Boston began a major fire apparatus modernization program this year. The Boston Fire Department placed 14 of these Hahn 1,250 GPM diesel triple combination pumpers in service in 1970. These engines have Cincinnati cabs, extended front bumpers and preconnected soft suction hose. Boston Engine 3's Hahn is seen here at work at a multiple alarm fire in July, 1974. Note the portable monitor and the transverse beds for two 1½-inch preconnected attack lines.

Relatively few rigs with open semi-cabs were now being built. This is an American LaFrance 1,000 GPM 1000 Series pumper delivered to Pittsfield, Mass. It has twin electronic sirens mounted at each end of the bumper, an integrally-piped, fixed turret pipe and booster equipment. Diesel power was made standard equipment on the new 1000 Series American LaFrance fire apparatus.

American LaFrance had expanded its custom fire apparatus line with the addition of a new premium 1000 Series. The 900 Series was still offered, but the new 1000 Models included as standard equipment most of the features and options most frequently specified by Elmira's customers. To tell a 1000 Model from a 900, look for the bright metal dress-up panel above the front bumper. Kalamazoo, Mich. received this 1970 American LaFrance 1000 Series pumper with 1,500 GPM pump. This diesel-powered apparatus is built on a special long-wheelbase chassis.

Not all of the big fire engines built are delivered to big cities. Some of our smaller cities and towns can afford the best equipment available. The Detroit suburb of Plymouth Township, Mich. ordered this 1970 American LaFrance 900 Series Aero-Chief quintuple combination. This heavy quint mounts a 1,250 gallon-per-minute pump, a 90-foot ALF Aero-Chief elevating platform, a full complement of metal ground ladders and other firefighting equipment. Note the tandem-axle chassis and the preconnected front soft suction hose. Delivery time for a major piece of equipment like this was now nearly two years.

American LaFrance's new 1000 Series also included 4-wheel service and tractor-drawn Rescue Model aerial ladder trucks. The Minneapolis Fire Dept. received this 1970 American LaFrance 1000 Series tractor-trailer aerial ladder truck, which was assigned to busy Ladder No. 5. This diesel-powered aerial has the closed 5-man cab and four manually-operated stabilizer jacks. Larry Phillips caught Ladder 5's new rig on the engine house ramp. Note the large equipment compartment behind the rear cab entrance.

Baltimore Truck Co. No. 27 was assigned this Seagrave 100-foot tractor-drawn aerial ladder truck. This aerial has a 4-section metal aerial ladder, and a permanent enclosure for the tillerman with sliding doors. The covered box beside the aerial ladder contains the 3-inch line for the ladder pipe. Baltimore City F. D. was still painting its apparatus a distinctive white and red.

1970

Seagrave's popular Rear Admiral rearmount aerials were outselling the company's midship-mounted service aerials and even the tractor-drawn types. Grafton, Wis. purchased this standard 1970 Seagrave 100-foot rearmount aerial, built on the Seagrave Custom fire apparatus chassis with 4 x 4 drive. Note the two dry chemical fire extinguishers carried on each end of the extended front bumper pan. Grafton's aerial carries booster equipment and a full load of metal ground ladders.

The last vestige of the old Seagrave Corp. left in Seagrave's former home city of Columbus, Ohio was the Timpco-Seagrave Division of the Timmons Metal Products Co. Using some Seagrave components, Timpco-Seagrave built some fire engines, mostly lighter models mounted on commercial chassis. One of Timpco-Seagrave's most popular products was a small attack pumper. But Timpco-Seagrave built some big ones, too—like this 100-foot tractor-drawn aerial for the Columbus Fire Dept. This aerial is pulled by a 1970 GMC tractor. The trailer has hydraulic A-frame outriggers. Note the tiller enclosure.

After a production run of an incredible 19 years, Seagrave's engine-ahead-of-cab Conventional Series fire apparatus came to the end of the line. Virtually assembled from the parts bin, the last one was delivered to Jackson, Mich. in 1970. Despite running changes that included new fenders, more glass and revised front nameplate panel, the last of the "70th Anniversary" models, which had been introduced away back in 1951, looked surprisingly similar to the first. Jackson's red-and-white Engine 1 has a 1,250 GPM pump, and has enclosed equipment compartments instead of hard suction hose. Jackson specified Seagrave fire apparatus for many, many years.

Moorhead, Minn. received this interesting 1970 General-Seagrave. The chassis and cab were built by FWD's Seagrave Fire Apparatus Division, but the rest of the apparatus was designed and built by the General Safety Equipment Co. of North Branch, Minn. This clean-lined pumper has a pumping capacity of 1,250 gallons per minute and is diesel-powered. Larry Phillips had Moorhead's Engine 904 pulled out onto the ramp for this photo.

This is typical of the monstrous rescue squad trucks popular around Maryland and other areas along the eastern seaboard. This brute belongs to a volunteer department. The chassis is a heavy duty Brockway powered by a Cummins Diesel. The rear body, which looks big enough to accommodate a small convention, was built by the Providence Body Co. in Rhode Island. Note the saddle-type fuel tanks and the front-mounted winch.

Ward LaFrance delivered this 70-foot elevating platform to Greenville, N. C. Like most Ward LaFrance snorkels, it has a Hi-Ranger articulating boom and a special low-profile cab to reduce travelling height. Greenville's unit is also equipped with a 1,000 GPM pump. Notice the spacing of the outrigger jacks for maximum stability when the tower is in action.

1970

The District of Columbia Fire Dept., which protects the nation's capitol, has purchased many pumping engines of this design from both Ward LaFrance and American LaFrance. Engine Co. No. 8's 1970 Ford C-900 was built by Ward LaFrance A modular type rear crew compartment has been combined with the standard 3-man tilt-cab. The wide white paint band around the middle of the apparatus is for improved after-dark visibility. This is a 750 GPM pumper.

Ward LaFrance Truck Corp. delivered this versatile quintuple combination aerial ladder truck to the Plain Township Fire Dept., in Avondale, Ohio. This Ward LaFrance quint, built on the WLF Custom chassis, has a 1,000 GPM pump, and a 3-section, 65-foot Grove aerial ladder. Note how the bell is recessed into the front cab sheet-metal. A single set of hydraulic A-frame jacks stabilizes the truck when the aerial ladder is being used.

Chicago also placed five of these interesting aerial ladder trucks in service in 1970. They were built by Ward LaFrance on the company's custom cab-forward chassis, and have 4-section Grove 100-foot rear-mounted aerial ladders. These bulky-looking ladder trucks are actually quite compact in size considering the amount of equipment they carry. Note the booster reel above the ground ladders, and the Mars floodlight on the rear cab roof.

Ward LaFrance delivered seven of these special Model 80 pumpers, the largest pumpers ever built by the Elmira Heights, N. Y. firm, to the Chicago Fire Dept. Each is equipped with a 2,000 gallon-per-minute Hale pump. Cummins Diesel power is used, and these Super Pumpers have 500-gallon booster tanks. They are also equipped with automatic transmissions. One of these 2,000 GPM pumpers is assigned to each of Chicago's seven principal fire districts. Note the bright-faced pump panel on Eng. Co. No. 113's rig.

One of the most incredible fire fighting weapons ever conceived in the United States is Chicago's famed "Big John" turret wagon. This special purpose apparatus was built up on an ex-U. S. Army International 6 x 6 chassis. It carries two huge turret nozzles mounted on a hydraulically-raised boom. These turrets are fed by dozens of 2½-and-larger inlets Y-ed off at the rear. Two smaller turret pipes are mounted on the front fender. The heaviest artillery in Chicago's fire fighting arsenal, Big John is called out only to major fires where maximum punch is required. A smaller, somewhat similar unit called "Big Moe", and a small turret wagon named "Little John" are also on the Chicago Fire Dept.'s special equipment roster.

1970

One of the biggest fire apparatus manufacturers in the Southern United States is the Jack Cocke & Co. of Mobile, Ala. This company's products, built mostly on standard commercial truck chassis, are sold under the JACO name. The JACO 1,000 GPM pumper shown here is built on a Ford C chassis and is powered by a 225-horsepower Caterpillar diesel engine. The pump is a Waterous two-stage. Two shut-off nozzles are carried on the front bumper extension.

Memphis, Tenn. was still placing substantial orders with Peter Pirsch & Sons. The Memphis Fire Dept. placed this Pirsch 100-foot Senior tractor-drawn aerial truck into service in 1970. Truck Co. No. 4's rig has the 3-section ladder, and is powered by a Hall-Scott engine.

Although Peter Pirsch & Sons still offered a conventional engine-ahead-of-cab chassis, very few of these were now being delivered. This style, except for minor variations like boxed-in front fenders, had changed little in appearance in nearly 30 years. The Cincinnati suburb of Evendale, Ohio received this 1970 Pirsch 1,250 GPM pumper with canopy cab. Note the blanked in cab upper quarter panels and the number of warning lights. This pumper also has a front suction intake.

Tom Sutphen's busy factory has turned out a sizable number of these big Sutphen Custom pumpers, most of which have been built for fire departments in Ohio. Port Clinton, Ohio, near Sandusky, received this 1970 Sutphen 1,000 GPM pumper, which sports no less than three flashers on the roof of its Cincinnati cab.

Peter Pirsch & Sons Co. built this 100-foot Senior tractor-drawn aerial ladder truck for Milwaukee, Wis. Milwaukee had purchased several aerials of this type earlier, with the narrower Mack C series cab tractor. Ladder Co. No. 2's aerial is drawn by a 1970 Mack Model CF tractor, with Pirsch trailer and tractor bodywork. This aerial has a 4-section main ladder and fixed tiller seat.

While the bulk of its customers clearly perferred the cab-forward model, Peter Pirsch & Sons Co. was still building the odd engine-ahead-of-cab conventional for departments that specified this style of apparatus. The 1970 Pirsch 1,000 GPM pumper shown here with a side entrance canopy cab, was built for the city of Reading, Ohio.

Howe Fire Apparatus of Anderson, Ind. built this custom-chassis Howe Defender quintuple combination. This rig has a semi-open Cincinnati cab, a 1,000 GPM pump and a Grove 4-section 85-foot aerial ladder. Huntington's quint also carries booster equipment and ground ladders. Note the safety guard rail around the operator's pedestal on the turntable.

The American Fire Apparatus Corp. of Battle Creek, Mich., built this well-equipped pumper for the Nottingham Fire Co., of Bensalem Township, Pa. The chassis is a standard Ford C Series tilt. This pumper is equipped with a 750 GPM Barton-American pump and carries a Squrt articulating master stream boom. Nottingham's rig also carries both booster lines and 1½-inch preconnects.

Pierce Manufacturing of Appleton, Wis. designated its top-line, custom-built fire apparatus the Pierce Fire Marshall series. Pierce built this big 1970 Fire Marshall diesel pumper for Bridgeview, Ill. Bridgeview's Engine 15 has a 1,500 gallon-per-minute pump and is built on an Oshkosh 4 x 4 chassis. A preconnected soft suction hose is carried on the extended front bumper. Note the large equipment compartments, and the four Mars floodlight units atop the rear body. Pierce Fire Marshalls have distinctive black-faced pump panels.

The Pierce plant in Appleton, Wis. each year builds a substantial number of special purpose fire engines for fire departments large and small. A good example is this yellow-painted Pierce-Ford combination rescue squad and floodlight truck, built for McCook, Ill. Built on a Ford C Series tilt-cab chassis, it has a front-mounted switch and four triple-beam Mars floodlights. It also carries a portable Stang monitor. Note the Visibar warning lights on the cab roof.

Some interesting combinations can be found in firehouses in mid-America. Pierce Manufacturing built this 65-foot elevating platform on a Peter Pirsch & Sons Co. custom fire apparatus chassis for Wisconsin Rapids, Wis. in 1970. The pump is a 1,000 GPM Hale. This apparatus bears Pierce serial number 7088-C. It is powered by a Waukesha engine and carries 500 gallons of water. The boom is by Snorkel Fire Equipment.

For some time before it got into the manufacture of its own line of custom fire apparatus, Pierce Manufacturing was noted for its high-quality rescue squad and emergency truck bodies. Pierce continues to build specialized rescue units designed to order for the customer. This big Pierce rescue truck, on a GMC tilt-cab chassis, was built for the Dumfries Triangle, Va. Volunteer Fire Department.

Two fire apparatus manufacturers had transferred their production lines to new, larger plants. The Howe Fire Apparatus Co. had moved into a new and larger plant in Anderson, Ind., and the John Bean Division of the FMC Corp. had moved from Lansing, Mich. to a new plant located at Tipton, Ind.

American LaFrance upgraded and improved its low-cost Pioneer pumper, which had been introduced as a budget-priced custom pumper series seven years earlier. The improved model was named the American LaFrance Pioneer II. Besides a higher level of appearance and trim, the Pioneer II offered a much broader range of engine and pump options. The standard model Pioneer II was equipped with a 285-horsepower International Harvester V-8 gasoline engine and a 750 GPM American LaFrance Twinflow centrifugal pump. Detroit Diesel engines of 216 and 265 horsepower were optionally available now, along with 1,000, 1,250 and 1,500 GPM pumps. The Pioneer II retained the same boxy but practical cab introduced on the original Pioneer, and dual headlight units soon became standard.

In addition to the improved Pioneer II, the American LaFrance product line included 900 and 1,000 Series pumpers, tractor, service and rear-mounted aerials, quintuple combinations, elevating platforms and specialized crash fire trucks.

The largest fire apparatus builder in the U. S., American LaFrance had endeared itself to fire apparatus buffs everywhere the previous year when it formed the American LaFrance Classic Coterie, an informal organization for owners of vintage American LaFrance fire engines, whether fire companies or individuals. To date, Classic Coterie roster has nearly 400 names and is still growing. The American LaFrance factory keeps a register of all owners of old American LaFrance rigs, and has provided assistance in the form of delivery information, specifications and even reprints of old operator's manuals.

The American Fire Apparatus Co. of Battle Creek, Mich., introduced its own elevated master stream device this year. Called the American Aqua-Jet, it was a telescopic boom equipped with a high-capacity nozzle at its tip which was operated by remote control. The Aqua-Jet could be specified as original equipment on any new American Fire Apparatus pumper, or could be installed on an older pumper.

The Snorkel Fire Equipment Co. added yet another piece of specialized aerial equipment to its product line, which already included the Snorkel elevating platform and

the Squrt articulated master stream boom. The company's new product was the Tele-Squrt, a combination aerial ladder and water tower of telescopic design. The 55-foot Tele-Squrt could be installed on any pumper, new or old, greatly increasing the rig's usefulness. The water tower piping ran down the underside of the ladder.

The Calavar Corp. delivered a 125-foot Calavar Firebird elevating platform to Chattanooga, Tenn. The Firebird 125 was built on the special Seagrave chassis.

Peter Pirsch and Sons Co. built an 85-foot Snorkel for Milwaukee. This elevating platform was built on the Mack CF chassis, and had a Pitman boom. Maxim designed and built a special combination pumper and foam engine for the Massport Fire Dept. at Boston's Logan International Airport. This special pumper was designed for fighting both structural and aircraft fires. It complemented several much larger crash units at the airport fire station.

A new name in the business this year was Imperial Fire Apparatus, of Rancocas, N. J. The company built custom-chassis pumpers using the Cincinnati cab, as well as a complete line of smaller commercial chassis pumpers.

With an order for 40 more CF pumpers, Mack Trucks advertised that it had sold no less than 180 Mack fire engines to New York City in the past three years.

The Hahn Motor Co. of Hamburg, Pa. has delivered many of these custom-built pumpers to large and small fire departments, mostly in the eastern U. S. Paterson, N. J. ordered this 1971 Hahn 1,250 GPM triple combination, which carries a turret pipe just behind the engine compartment. Boston also purchased a large fleet of Hahn pumpers of this style.

The American LaFrances, the Macks, the Seagraves and Maxims, the Pierces and Pirsches are the glamour queens of the fire service. But the real backbone of America's fire defenses is the type of smaller commercial chassis pumper shown here. For every custom fire engine in service, there are dozens of these smaller pumpers in fire stations across the nation. This is a Boyer 1,000 GPM pumper built on a 1971 International chassis for the Sullivan Township, Ohio, Fire Dept. Note the post-mounted beacon light and the triple-sectioned transverse hose bed for 1½-inch attack lines above the pump compartment. Boyer fire apparatus has been built in Logansport, Ind. for many years.

The top of the Howe Fire Apparatus line is the Howe Custom Defender. Tullahoma, Tenn. ordered this 1971 Howe Defender with a 5-man canopy cab and 1,000 GPM pump. Tullahoma's Engine 6 carries an assortment of nozzles and tips on its front bumper pan. Note how the 2½-inch supply line on the pump panel is stuffed into the hard suctions.

The first American LaFrance Ladder Chief rear-mounted aerial was delivered to Gary, Ind. Introduced in 1968, this series was becoming very popular. Gary purchased a second 100-foot American LaFrance Ladder Chief in 1971. Although the 1968 model was painted white, the second was finished in American LaFrance Red. Here, Gary's Ladder 1 backs into quarters on its return from a run. It is a 900 Series model.

1971

While the rear-mounted aerial ladder truck and various types of elevating platforms were replacing older model conventional type aerials all across the country, some fire departments still preferred the handling and versatility of the old, reliable tractor-drawn aerial ladder truck. American LaFrance continued to build its Rescue Model tractor-trailer aerial in 85 and 100-foot versions in both the 900 and new 1000 Series. This is a 1000 Series 100-foot tractor-drawn aerial with four hydraulic outriggers. It is not known if this rig went to Hollywood, Fla. or the home of the movie stars in California.

Shreveport, La. took delivery of this American LaFrance 100-foot Ladder Chief rear-mount aerial ladder truck. This is a Series 1000 model. Note the clearance lights mounted on the topmost gusset of the bed ladder. The Ladder Chief rear-mounted aerial was rapidly eclipsing the conventional 4-wheel service aerial in popularity.

Along with the price of everything else, fire apparatus prices were skyrocketing. Only a few decades earlier, the most expensive aerial ladder truck cost about $50,000. But sophisticated new fire engines, like this 90-foot, 1,250 GPM American LaFrance Aero Chief quintuple combination, were coming in at well over $100,000. The white-painted apparatus shown here is a 1971 American LaFrance 900 Series Aero Chief built for Strongsville, Ohio. The generator over the pump panel is part of the backup hydraulic system.

Fire apparatus photographer Larry Phillips took this excellent shot of St. Cloud, Minnesota's Engine No. 4, a 1971 American LaFrance 1,000 Series triple combination pumper. This 1,250 GPM pumper has a front suction intake with preconnected soft suction hose, a fixed, integrally-piped turret nozzle and full compartmentation instead of the usual hard suction hose. Note the wrap-around handrail over the rear of the canopy cab. All 1000 Series American LaFrance apparatus included diesel power as standard equipment.

American LaFrance also offered a deluxe 1000 Series version of its lower-priced Pioneer fire apparatus. The improved Pioneer is known as the Pioneer II. The Cleveland suburb of Medina, Ohio purchased this 1971 American LaFrance Pioneer 1,250 gallon-per-minute pumper, powered by a Detroit Diesel 8-cylinder engine. It has an extended front bumper with soft suction hose tray, a portable turret nozzle and twin booster reels.

Lyons, Ill. received this 1971 Pierce-Oshkosh 1,250 gallon-per-minute pumper. This apparatus uses the low-profile Cincinnati cab mounted on the Oshkosh custom cab-forward fire apparatus chassis. The right-hand pump panel is somewhat unique. Note the extended front bumper. Pierce designates its custom fire apparatus the Fire Marshall Series.

Here's another reason why the State of Maryland is such a happy hunting ground for fire apparatus buffs. The Lutherville, Md. Volunteer Fire Co. purchased this imposing rescue squad truck, built on a Ford C Series chassis with canopy cab extension. The rear body was built by Pierce, and Lutherville's big squad carries a 7½-ton crane for emergency work.

This is the modern-day successor to the old conventional-style Seagrave sedan pumper. Baltimore received five of these 1,000 gallon-per-minute Seagrave pumping engines in 1971. The Diesel-powered engines have roomy 4-door sedan cabs. The roof is removable in the event major engine work is required. Baltimore's Engine Co. 25 got one of these good-looking rigs, which were designed to get the crew off the rear step and inside, out of the weather.

Some of the most glamorous fire engines in service anywhere can be found in the northeastern U.S., and particularly in Maryland. The Boulevard Heights Volunteer Fire Dept., in Maryland's Prince George's County, received this 1971 Seagrave 100-foot tractor-trailer aerial ladder truck with open semi-cab. The ladder compartment on the trailer is completely enclosed, and a wide, white band encircles the apparatus for optimum visibility while moving through traffic. This truck has hydraulic outriggers, a 4-section main ladder and fixed tiller seat.

The largest pumpers ever built in the Dominion of Canada were delivered to Vancouver, British Columbia in 1971. King-Seagrave Ltd., of Woodstock, Ontario built four of these special "Super Pumpers" for this Pacific Coast city, to protect the downtown high value area. All four are powered by diesel engines and have 3,000 GPM Stang monitors. They are built on Ford C Series chassis, and have 1,500 Imperial gallon-per-minute pumps (2,000 GPM U.S.) by Hale. Painted white-and-red, they carry three sizes of hose as well as booster equipment. The four "Super Pumps" were designed to replace a fireboat and the former high pressure system.

The Seagrave Fire Apparatus Division of FWD Corp. built five of these 1,250 gallon-per-minute triple combination Custom Series pumpers for the City of Livonia, Mich. These deluxe jobs have extended front bumpers and front suction intakes, dual booster hose reels and large equipment compartments above the rear fender. This pumper has a Federal Q siren mounted above the front suction intake, as well as an electronic siren-speaker mounted on the cab roof.

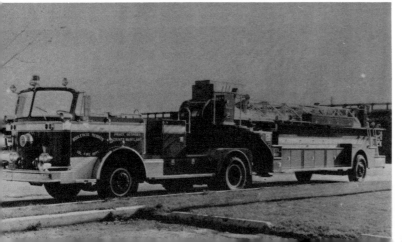

The largest city in the United States—New York—does not own, and has never owned, a single articulating-type snorkel. But the F.D.N.Y. has a huge fleet of Mack Aerialscopes, which it has ordered regularly since 1964. The F.D.N.Y. refers to its elevating platforms as "Tower Ladders". This 1971 Model CF Mack Aerialscope is assigned as Tower Ladder 107. New York Aerialscope orders have kept the Mack fire apparatus line at Allentown, Pa. humming for years. This plant has also turned out hundreds of pumpers for the New York City Fire Dept.

1971

Mack Trucks offered its fire apparatus customers a lower priced series of fire engines built on the flat-faced Mack Model MB chassis. These are available with standard three-man cab, or with a five-man canopy type cab. The Ogontz Fire Co. of Pennsylvania received this big Mack MB rescue squad truck with a Swab body. Baltimore and Chicago also purchased heavy squad rigs built on the MB chassis.

Mack introduced its Aerialscope elevating platform in 1964. This aerial platform was built in only one size—a telescoping 75-foot length. Cheltenham, Pa. received this all-white Mack CF-600 Aerialscope. This view shows effectively the elaborate stabilizing system used on this heavy piece of fire equipment. In addition to the main A-frame outriggers mounted amidships, additional stability is provided by a set of stabilizers mounted outboard of the front bumpers, and another pair at the rear of the apparatus.

Sutphen Fire Equipment Co. mounted many of its rugged Aerial Towers on heavy-duty commercial truck chassis. This big Sutphen Aerial Tower was built for Westland, Mich. on a GMC tandem-axle chassis. Note the ground ladders carried over the rear wheels, and the dual electronic sirens on the roof. Relatively few of these Sutphens, on conventional engine-ahead-of-cab chassis, have been built. Most are built on cab-forward chassis.

Mack Trucks' Fire Apparatus Division built this big combination foam pumper for the Selkirk Fire Co. No. 2 of Glenmont, N. Y. This CF-600 pumper is essentially two types of pumpers on a single chassis. For routine structural fires, it carries a standard 1,000 GPM pump and a fixed turret pipe above the hose body. But it also is equipped with a built-in foam system and has a remotely-controlled foam turret over the cab. This foam turret can be operated from inside the cab, and is backed up by another nozzle mounted under the bumper.

Cleveland, Ohio also received some pumping engines of this style from the Sutphen Fire Equipment Co. Engine Co. 17's pumper is mounted on a Ford L-900 Louisville chassis with canopy cab extension. It is equipped with a 1,000 GPM pump and carries 500 gallons of water in its booster tank.

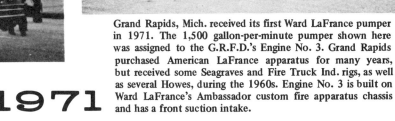

In 1968, Ward LaFrance introduced its unique Command Tower option for its custom and commercial chassis pumpers. Consisting of a fullwidth platform with integral turret pipe, this platform elevates to a maximum height of 22 feet for water tower or command post observation use. Houston, Tex. received this 1971 Ward LaFrance 1,000 GPM pumper with extra-long chassis and tandem rear axles. Note the booster hose reel carried in the open compartment ahead of the rear wheels, and the lime-yellow paint job, a color scheme aggressively promoted as a safety feature by Ward LaFrance.

1971

Grand Rapids, Mich. received its first Ward LaFrance pumper in 1971. The 1,500 gallon-per-minute pumper shown here was assigned to the G.R.F.D.'s Engine No. 3. Grand Rapids purchased American LaFrance apparatus for many years, but received some Seagraves and Fire Truck Ind. rigs, as well as several Howes, during the 1960s. Engine No. 3 is built on Ward LaFrance's Ambassador custom fire apparatus chassis and has a front suction intake.

A new type of pumper was beginning to find favor with urban fire departments. The small "Attack Pumper" could thread its way through congested streets and extinguish small fires, saving wear and tear on heavier, more specialized apparatus. Philadelphia operates this little "Tactical Unit" pumper, built by Ward LaFrance on a 1971 International 4 x 4 chassis. Note the two nozzles mounted under the front bumper and the dual booster hose reels.

Ward LaFrance constructed this special Foam Unit for the Philadelphia Fire Department. Foam Unit No. 2 has a 1,000 gallon-per-minute foam pump and a 1,000-gallon water tank. It is built on an International truck chassis. Note the roof turret and the booster reel above the hose body. This type of apparatus is used for the protection of airports, fuel depots and for major tank truck fires.

Oak Ridge, Tenn. took delivery of this 1971 Ward LaFrance Custom Ambassador 1,000 GPM triple combination. Equipment includes a Stang monitor and fully compartmented sides. A special reel just visible above the pump control panel carries 2½-inch hose.

With its angled lower windshield, Ward LaFrance Corp.'s standard Ambassador model fire apparatus boasts exceptionally good forward visibility. A good driver can literally dive into his hydrant for a quick hookup. The 1971 Ward LaFrance 1,250 GPM pumper shown here was built for Muskegon Township, Mich. It is powered by a Continental Diesel, and has a Federal Visibar lighting unit on the roof.

Among the larger cities that made the switch to rearmounted aerials is Cleveland, Ohio. The Cleveland Fire Dept. got this 1971 Pirsch 100-foot rearmount, built on a Ford C-9000 chassis with extended canopy cab. The ladder has four sections. Like most Cleveland rigs, this aerial is painted white. Cleveland still has some red apparatus, and recently began experimenting with yellow rigs.

1971

Peter Pirsch & Sons built this eye-catching 100-foot rear mount aerial ladder truck for College Park, Md. The windshield is extra low for minimum over-all height. Very few open cabs were now being built by any manufacturer, even for western states. College Park's Truck Co. No. 12 is painted red with white upper body.

The Maxim Motor Company delivered this 75-foot F Model service aerial ladder truck to Jamestown, R. I. in 1971. The bottom of the outrigger jacks can be seen under the running board. Jamestown's Maxim has the 5-man closed canopy cab.

Riverdale, Md. has always been noted for its stunningly appointed fire apparatus. This department's reputation was secure when the company's new aerial ladder truck arrived in 1971. Finished in white and black with plenty of gold leaf striping and trim, Truck Co. 7's rig is a Mack CF with open semi-cab (a rarity for this series) and a 4-section Maxim 100-foot ladder. Note the two electronic sirens and the big Federal Q siren mounted on the front bumper pan, and the air horns above the windshield. This rig is a favorite with parade fans wherever it goes.

Columbus, Ohio received this commercial chassised Pirsch 100-foot aerial ladder truck. The tractor is a GMC with extended canopy cab. The Peter Pirsch & Sons trailer has a 4-section aerial ladder and fixed tiller seat. Columbus has several other aerials of this type, all drawn by GMC tractors.

The Massachusetts Port Authority's Massport Fire Department is charged with the great responsibility of protecting Boston Logan International Airport, one of the nation's busiest. One of the most versatile units in the Massport Fire Dept. main station is this 1971 Maxim "all purpose" Model FFC-7510 pumper. Equipped with a 1,000 GPM Hale pump, it carries 1,000 gallons of water, 220 gallons of foam and 1,000 pounds of dry chemical. This pumper is powered by a Cummins Diesel engine, and can fight a fire while rolling along at a maximum speed of 25 miles an hour. It is painted high visibility yellow.

A major attraction at the 1972 IAFC Conference, held in Cleveland, was an experimental turbine-powered pumper that was exhibited and demonstrated by American La-France. The yellow-painted pumper was powered by a Detroit Diesel-Allison 325 horsepower Model GT-404 turbine engine supplied to American LaFrance by General Motors. This turbine was coupled to an Allison 4-speed automatic transmission. The American LaFrance Turbo-Chief was also equipped with a 1,750 GPM pump. During the convention, hundreds of visiting fire chiefs were taken for demonstration rides on the amazingly quiet jet-powered pumper. American LaFrance's re-entry into the field of turbine-powered fire engines was experimental and cautious, following the unsuccessful experience the Elmira, N. Y. firm had 12 years earlier. American LaFrance announced that it would not sell a turbine-powered fire engine for at least several years. The company was also installing a Ford 450 horsepower turbine engine in one of its pumper chassis for experimental purposes. Following the Cleveland convention, the Turbo-Chief pumper set out on an extended demonstration road tour to the West Coast.

At the Cleveland convention, American LaFrance un-veiled a completely new line of medium-priced fire apparatus. Called the American LaFrance Pacemaker, this series was positioned between the lowest-priced Pioneer II custom cab-forward pumpers, and the standard 900 and 1,000 Series apparatus. The cab-forward Pacemaker utilized the Cincinnati cab, and could also be ordered as an aerial truck. The standard model Pacemaker had a 750 GPM pump and was powered by a Detroit Diesel engine.

Seagrave introduced its new standard model PB-24098 Diesel-powered custom cab-forward 1,250 GPM pumper at the large Cleveland apparatus exhibit.

The main attraction at the Ward LaFrance exhibit this year was a futuristic experimental pumper called the Vantage. The modular type pumper had been developed by Ward LaFrance in conjunction with the United States Steel Corp. The advanced concept Vantage was built on a Ford C-900 chassis powered by a 534 cubic inch Ford V-8 gasoline engine.

Another new type of apparatus displayed at Cleveland was Grove's new tower ladder. The new Grove tower ladder combined the best features of a conventional aerial ladder with the advantages of an elevating platform. When in the travelling position, the basket of the Grove tower ladder rode out in front of the truck, rather than at the rear. The American Fire Apparatus Corp. exhibited an 85-foot Grove tower ladder mounted on a special Oshkosh

low-profile cab-forward chassis. Delivered to Pine Castle, Fla., this apparatus was also equipped with a 1,000 GPM Barton pump. American Fire Apparatus in 1972 also introduced a new Intra-Cab series of cab-forward pumpers, which incorporated a front-mount pump built into the cab front sheetmetal. This arrangement provided extra rear body space for a large water tank.

The Howe Fire Apparatus Co. marked its 100th year in the fire equipment field this year. The Calavar Corp. delivered its first 150-foot Firebird elevating platform to Tucson, Ariz. Pierce Mfg. came out with a small, 35-foot aerial designed for village use called the Pierce Aerial-Ett, and a complete line of Pierce Mustang minipumpers of from 500 to 750 GPM capacity. Also in 1972, International introduced a completely new custom cab-forward fire apparatus chassis. Built for International Harvester by the Hendrickson Mfg. Co., the angular new Hendrickson chassis succeeded the International CO-8190 which had been in production for nearly a decade. The low-profile Hendrickson chassis was available with a wide choice of gasoline or Diesel engines, and is widely used by fire apparatus builders today.

The Lockheed Aircraft Service Co., a division of Lockheed Aircraft Corp., developed and marketed the Lockheed Fire-Star, a modular firefighting outfit designed to be quickly mounted on a military or commercial truck. The completely self-contained FireStar carries 1,000 gallons of water, its own pump, fuel supply and electrical power. The FireStar was designed for fighting grass and brush fires in areas inaccessible to conventional fire apparatus. This is the prototype Lockheed FireStar mounted on a standard M-35 military 6 x 6 truck chassis.

The Hendrickson Manufacturing Co. of Lyons, Ill. in 1972 came out with this new style of custom fire apparatus cab, mounted on an International truck chassis. The pumper shown was built by Howe Fire Apparatus, and features a top-mounted pump control panel. The extended front bumper carries the bell and siren. Hendrickson had been a major supplier to International Harvester for many years. Note the plated front trim, which incorporates the towing eyes.

Old Town, Maine received this 1972 Custom Howe Defender from the Howe Fire Apparatus Co. of Anderson, Ind. It is equipped with a 1,250 gallon-per-minute pump with top control panel. This apparatus also carries 1,000 gallons of water. Note the baffled trough above the hard suction hoses, for preconnected 1½-inch attack lines. The screened opening just behind the cab door is for extra engine ventilation. This pumper has a Cincinnati cab.

The Chicago Fire Department in 1972 received the first American LaFrance pumpers it had purchased in more than 30 years. Five of these special 2,000 gallon-per-minute "Chieftain" diesel-powered American LaFrance pumpers were delivered to engine companies in Chicago's high value areas. These 1000 Series pumpers carry four lengths of corrugated-type hard suction hose, and have dual suction ports on each side of their pump panels. Note the recess cut into the right front of the cab sheet metal for the soft suction hose, and the Aurora Borealis roof lights. These massive-looking engines also carry dual booster hose reels. An oscillating white light is built into the front of the cab. Paint scheme is Chicago's standard black-over-red.

After an absence of 12 years, American LaFrance cautiously resumed experimentation with turbine-powered fire apparatus in 1972. But the Elmira, N. Y. fire apparatus builder stated that it would sell no turbine-powered apparatus until all problems had been overcome, and only after several years of development and testing. Despite the experimental status this American LaFrance Turbo-Chief pumper was a hit with delegates to the 1972 International Association of Fire Chiefs convention held in Cleveland, Ohio. The 1,750 gallon-per-minute pumper, finished in bright yellow, was powered by a General Motors-built Detroit Diesel-Allison GT-404 turbine engine rated at 325 horsepower. This engine was coupled to an Allison automatic transmission. More than 1,000 IAFC delegates took rides on the turbo-pumper, which also made an extensive proving tour across the country that year. Two exhaust stacks jut out of the engine compartment behind the cab.

The American LaFrance Ladder Chief rear-mounted aerial ladder truck could also be ordered as a quintuple combination. This is a Series 1000 Ladder Chief quint, with 1,000 gallon-per-minute pump and 4-section 100-foot aerial ladder. Note the four outrigger jacks and the tandem rear axle configuration. This well-equipped apparatus has zero front overhang.

American LaFrance introduced its new premium 1000 Series apparatus in 1970. Basically a package featuring Diesel power and the company's most popular options. the new series proved to be quite popular. Franklin, Tenn. received this 1972 American LaFrance 1,000 GPM 1000 Series pumper. This series can be instantly identified by the lower cab front bright trim, and the Eagle emblem used in conjunction with the ALF nameplate.

In addition to its premium model Crusader, Young Fire Equipment Co. built another top-line custom model known as the Bison. One of these was delivered to Allentown Rd., Md., and is one of the more visually striking rigs to be found anywhere. Engine Co. 32's 1972 Young Bison has a low profile, cut down open semi-cab and a 1,000 GPM pump. The large, hand-painted American flag on the front of this engine and the distinctive emblems on the cab doors make it an apparatus slide collector's delight. And its performance on the fireground reportedly matches its parade appearance.

The Young Fire Equipment Corp., of Lancaster, N. Y., came out with a limited production, premium model called the Young Crusader. This model employed a special low-profile cab with a huge expanse of glass and warning flashers built into the roof. Lakewood, Ohio ordered this 1972 Young Crusader Snorkel, with an 85-foot boom. The cab appears to be a modified Oshkosh, and the rear bodywork by Pierce. Note the hubcaps on the tandem rear wheels.

1972

Cincinnati received this 1972 Seagavre completely enclosed 100-foot tractor-drawn diesel aerial ladder truck. Truck 16's rig has a 4-door sedan cab, a fully-enclosed tillerman's compartment and two electronic siren-speakers on the cab roof. Even the ladder beds are completely enclosed. Civil disobedience and frequent attacks on police officers and fire fighters made this type of protection imperative.

In a truly depressing commentary on the times in which we live, Metropolitan American fire departments began to specify, out of necessity and for the protection of their fire fighters, enclosed, "riotproof" fire engines. Cincinnati purchased four of these special 1972 Seagrave 1,000 GPM diesel pumpers with 4-door sedan cabs and fully covered and enclosed rear bodies. A hatch is provided in the rear cab for operating a Stang monitor. Each cost $40,000. Engine 9's rig is seen in the C.F.D. shop yard before outfitting.

Seagrave Fire Apparatus of Clintonville, Wis. introduced a new standard diesel-powered triple combination pumping engine. This 1972 Seagrave has a white-painted upper cab and two booster hose reels. This standard model diesel pumper could be delivered in less time than a full custom-built and equipped job, and was competitive with American LaFrance's Series 1000 apparatus.

Seagrave Fire Apparatus sold some of its custom fire engine chassis to other manufacturers. Pierce Manufacturing, for instance, built this special rescue squad truck on a 1972 Seagrave chassis for Cottage City, Mo. It utilizes the Seagrave 4-door sedan cab. Note the paddle type door handles. This apparatus carries Pierce rather than Seagrave nameplates.

Tucson, Arizona had the distinction of receiving the first 150-foot Calavar Firebird elevating platform built. When it went into service, this was the tallest aerial unit in use by any fire department in the U.S. Built on a special Seagrave chassis, it differed from the standard 100 and 125-foot Calavar Firebirds, in that both the upper and lower booms were telescopic instead of just the upper one. With its four massive outriggers extended, all 10 tires of this huge piece of equipment are lifted completely clear of the ground. It's a diesel, of course.

FWD Corp.'s Seagrave Fire Apparatus Division had been out of the elevating platform market since the mid-1960s. But in 1972, Seagrave announced a new series of aerial platforms called the Seagrave Astro-Tower. This apparatus utilized the same basic chassis used for this company's popular rearmounted aerial ladder trucks. This is an 85-foot Seagrave Astro-Tower. This model used Seagrave's special low-profile custom cab for minimum over-all height.

Quincy, Mass. ordered this 1972 Ward LaFrance Custom Ambassador 1,000 gallon-per-minute diesel triple combination pumper. Instead of numbering this rig, the Quincy Fire Dept. used an alphabet designation, and it appears on this city's apparatus roster as "Engine B". This pumper carries a portable deluge nozzle and has two booster reels in addition to two 1½-inch preconnected attack lines.

Ward LaFrance Truck Corp. teamed up with United States Steel to design and build its radical new "Vantage" pumper. The 7-man, 4-door sedan cab was constructed using USS's "Galva" system, a welded safety cage cab frame. Officially designated the Series 72, the Vantage prototype was powered by a Ford 534 cubic inch V-8 gasoline engine and equipped with a 1,000 GPM two-stage pump. The pump operator's panel is concealed behind a roll-up door. The Vantage has a 750-gallon booster tank, and is finished in lime-yellow. The entire cab tilts up for access to the engine.

Ward LaFrance had become a major supplier of big, custom-built airport crash fire trucks. This Ward LaFrance Statesman 3500 aircraft fire and rescue truck was built for the Syracuse, N. Y. Airport. It is powered by two 276-horsepower V-8 engines and has two 1,000 GPM pumps. This model carries 3,000 gallons of water and has two 250-gallon foam tanks. The Ward LaFrance Statesman can discharge its 3,500 gallons of water and fire-killing foam in less than two minutes. Despite its size, this crash rig can hit a top speed of 62 miles an hour and can do zero to 50 miles an hour in a respectable 60 seconds. Cab, body and water tanks are assembled as separate modules.

The Ward LaFrance Truck Corp. displayed this lime-green Command Tower pumper at its exhibit at the 1972 International Association of Fire Chiefs Conference and Exhibition in Cleveland, Ohio. The ladder just to the rear of the rear cab entrance extends and retracts with the turret-equipped tower. A Visibar light unit is mounted on the cab roof.

St. Mary's, Ohio received this standard model Ward LaFrance 1,000 GPM triple combination pumping emblem. The Fleur-de-lis of France has been a Ward LaFrance Truck Corp. emblem for many years. Note the wrap-around handrail behind the canopy cab, and the Federal Q siren mounted in the center of the cab front.

Ward LaFrance used the 1972 IAFC Conference in Cleveland to introduce its new Teleboom telescopic aerial platform. The unit displayed at the WLF exhibit was mounted on a Ford CT-900 chassis with standard 3-man cab. This 75-foot Teleboom is also equipped with a 1,000 GPM pump.

Sunnyvale, Cal. received this 1972 Mack 1,000 gallon-per-minute pumper, mounted on Mack's Model R conventional style chassis. This yellow-painted pumper has a 500-gallon booster tank. It also carries a small Stang monitor, dual booster reels and has many enclosed equipment compartments.

1972

New York City continued to place massive orders for new fire apparatus with Mack Trucks. Well over 200 new Mack pumping engines had been delivered to the F.D.N.Y. in the previous decade. New York City has the largest diesel-powered firefighting fleet in the world. Here, one of our new Mack Model CF 1,000 gallon-per-minute pumpers undergoes its acceptance test of the New York waterfront. This pumper has a Stang monitor, transversely-mounted booster reel and front suction intake. Note the roof-mounted bell. The bows over the rear compartment are for a protective cover, and the rear of the canopy cab has doors for added crew safety.

Here is another interesting marriage of a chassis and body. Lewes, Del. specified this special rescue unit, which combines a Swab squad body with a Mack CF-600 chassis. The type of striping used on this rig is unusual for a Mack. This heavy duty model is assigned to Lewes' Rescue Squadron 82-6.

Tom Sutphen's busy plant near Columbus, Ohio turns out many commercial chassis fire engines each year, in addition to the famed Sutphen Aerial Tower. This type of front-mount pumper has become quite common in Ohio. The unit shown here was built by Sutphen Fire Equipment on a Ford L-Series truck chassis. It sports a 750 gallon-per-minute front-mount pump with a built-in turret nozzle on top. Mounting the pump at the front of the apparatus permits the use of an extra-large booster tank. This yellow-painted Sutphen-Ford was built for New London, Ohio.

The Sutphen Fire Equipment Co., in the Columbus, Ohio suburb of Amlin, built this turbine-powered 2,000 gallon-per-minute pumper in 1972, and demonstrated it at a number of fire chief's conventions in the midwest. It was powered by a Ford 3600 Series gas turbine engine built by Ford's Industrial Engine and Turbine Division in Dearborn, Mich. This powerplant was rated at 395 horsepower. Sutphen's first turbine-powered pumper was delivered to Boardman, Ohio, near Youngstown, in 1972. Here, the Sutphen Turbine Pumper goes through its paces in a test.

The increasingly popular Sutphen Aerial Tower is available on either the Sutphen custom fire apparatus chassis, or on any heavy duty commercial chassis favored by the purchaser. This is an 85-foot Sutphen tower mounted on a Ford CT-900 chassis, which has a canopy cab extension with blanked in rear quarters. The roomy Sutphen basket is normally equipped with a pair of turret guns.

The Snorkel Fire Equipment Co. had added the Tele-Squrt to its line of specialized master stream devices. Initially offered only in a 55-foot size, a second Tele-Squrt of 75-foot height was later added to the line. The Tele-Squrt consists of a telescopic water tower and aerial ladder. This 75-foot Tele-Squrt was shown at the 1972 IAFC Convention in Cleveland. The chassis is an Oshkosh. The body was fabricated by Pierce Manufacturing of Appleton, Wis. This one-truck fire department is also equipped with a 1,000 GPM pump.

1972

Also shown at the 1972 IAFC Conference in Cleveland was this very well appointed pump which was built for Kenner, La. This quadruple combination, on a Mack CF-600 diesel chassis, has a 1,000 GPM pump and a 55-foot Pitman Snorkel. The rear body was constructed by Pierce Manufacturing. The A-frame stabilizer jacks are visible beneath the running board. Note the oval Pierce emblem to the right of the dual, stacked electronic sirens.

Also exhibited at the Cleveland convention was American Fire Apparatus Corp.'s new Aqua-Jet telescopic combination water tower and aerial ladder. Mounted on an Oshkosh chassis with 1,000 GPM Barton pump, this apparatus was built for Pine Hills, Fla. The Aqua-Jet is identical in appearance to Snorkel's popular Tele-Squrt.

The Oshkosh Truck Corp. of Oshkosh, Wis. supplies the Pierce Manufacturing Co. with this special low-profile custom fire apparatus chassis for Pierce's Fire Marshall models. This Pierce Fire Marshall has a 1,000 gallon-per-minute pump and is diesel-powered. Note the extended and contoured housing for the headlights. The rear of the 5-man canopy cab has a wrap-around handrail.

Among the most advanced fire apparatus ever used in the United States is this wedge-shaped Pathfinder crash truck built for the Massachusetts Port Authority for the protection of Boston's busy Logan International Airport. Built by Chubb in England, this unique crash rig is powered by a V-16 Diesel engine and can be operated by a crew of only two. The Pathfinder carries 3,600 gallons of water and 432 gallons of foam. The huge roof turret can hurl 1,800 gallons per minute. A second Pathfinder was delivered to Massport in 1974 at a cost of more than $200,000.

Cleveland, Ohio received this 1972 Peter Pirsch and Sons Co. 100-foot Senior aerial ladder truck. The tractor is a GMC which has been given a canopy cab extension. The tillerman's seat and windshield must be swung aside when the 3-section aerial ladder is to be raised. This truck, unassigned when this photo was taken, is painted Cleveland's standard white.

Detroit joined the swing away from the traditional red to lime-green fire apparatus for improved night visibility. The Motor City went one step further and painted the upper cab area white. The first green-and-white rig on the Detroit Fire Dept. was Boat Tender No. 1. The rear body of former High Pressure Co. No. 1, a General-Detroit body that had been built on a 1950 GMC chassis, was transferred to a new Chevrolet chassis by the D.F.D. shops. The rebuilt fireboat tender was painted the controversial new color and was placed back in service in January, 1973. This high pressure hose rig carries 5-inch hose and two big turret pipes, and responds on all extra alarms in the city.

1972

Worcester, Mass. took delivery of this 1972 Maxim Model S 1,000 gallon-per-minute triple combination pumper. Built by the Maxim Motor Co. of Middleboro, Mass., it has a 7-man canopy cab and is finished in yellow. Maxim still found sufficient demand for engine-ahead-of-cab conventional chassis fire apparatus to keep the angular-lined S series in production.

One of Canada's largest fire apparatus manufacturers, Pierre Thibault (1972) Ltd., received a substantial order for new tractor-trailer aerial ladder trucks from the Los Angeles City Fire Dept. The first of these were delivered in 1972. These Thibault Customs, powered by Cummins Diesel engines, have Cincinnati cabs and four-section, 100-foot aerial ladders. The aerial shown was assigned to the L.A.F.D.'s Truck Co. 33

Boston's Rescue Co. No. 2 received this heavy rescue squad truck in 1972. It was built by the Gerstenslager Corp. on an International chassis. Note the American flag fluttering from the left side of the cab. Boston's rescue squads have white-painted roofs. A heavy duty tripod-type winch can be attached to the rear of Rescue 2 for removal of debris or other emergency duties.

One of the first pieces of fire apparatus built with Grove's new aerial tower with front-mounted basket was this impressive rig shown by American Fire Apparatus at the 1972 IAFC Conference in Cleveland. Built on an Oshkosh chassis with a 1,000 GPM Barton pump and 85-foot Grove ladder tower, it was delivered to Pine Castle, Fla., following the convention. The Grove tower ladder unit, with its front-mounted basket, is now built by Ladder Towers Inc., and combines the versatility of a conventional aerial ladder with an elevating platform.

The star of the American Fire Apparatus Corp.'s exhibit at the 1972 IAFC Conference was this impressive quintuple combination. The custom chassis unit has a 750 GPM pump built into the front of the cab, and a 100-foot Grove aerial ladder. It was built for North Aurora, Ill. Note the cut in the front bumper for the suction intake, and the Aurora Borealis warning lights on the cab roof.

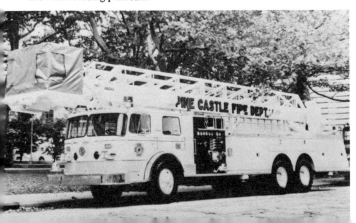

1973

The International Assn. of Fire Chiefs observed its 100th Anniversary at the 1973 IAFC Conference held in Baltimore. To mark the event, a huge parade of antique and modern fire apparatus was held as the highlight of the week.

American LaFrance in 1973 announced an extensively redesigned series of custom fire apparatus. The new series would be known as the American LaFrance Century Series. The pilot model Century Series pumper shown around the country had a much-revised cab with a widened rear section which used curved side window glass. The restyled cab also had a larger windshield for improved visibility, and wider cab doors. The pump panel was redesigned for easier operation and simplified maintenance, and stainless steel use was extended to the booster tank. Standard power would be Detroit Diesel. The new Century Series pumper came equipped with an even higher level of standard equipment and features than the 1000 Series American LaFrance. The standard 900 Series and 1000 Series apparatus remained in production at Elmira. American LaFrance had also developed a new type of fixed, integral water tower piping for its standard aerial ladders. The lower-priced Pioneer II model range had been extended to include, besides pumpers, service type and tractor-drawn aerials, a Pioneer Ladder-Chief rear-mounted aerial, and even a Bristol-type foam pumper.

American LaFrance had discontinued the manufacture of its Aero-Chief elevating platform. The company had purchased Snorkel Fire Equipment, and the Pitman Snorkel became standard equipment on all American LaFrance elevating platforms, on both the custom and commercial chassis. With the acquisition of Snorkel Fire Equipment, American LaFrance could offer several new models in its Pioneer 900 and 1000 Series. Equipped with a Squrt boom, an American LaFrance pumper became an Aqua-Chief; with a Tele-Squrt, a Duo-Chief, and with a 50-foot Snorkel, a Super Chief Jr.

Snorkel Fire Equipment had earlier added a 75-foot Tele-Squrt aerial ladder-water tower combination to the 55-footer already in production.

Ward LaFrance in 1973 announced a complete range of new aerial equipment. These included the Teleboom, a telescopic aerial platform and water tower in 65, 75 and 85-foot working heights; the Teleflow telescopic aerial ladder and water tower combination; a Telelift articulated elevating platform of 65, 75 and 85-foot heights, and the Telerise, a 54-foot articulated master stream boom.

The Radnor Fire Company of Wayne, Pa., which had placed the first motor-driven fire engine in the United States into service in 1906, took delivery of a new Imperial cab-forward pumper.

Other interesting deliveries included three 100-foot tractor-drawn, closed cab forward aerial ladder trucks built for the Los Angeles City Fire Dept. by Pierre Thibault (1972) Ltd., of Pierreville, Quebec. These aerials joined three similar models with open cabs which had been delivered by Thibault the previous year. The Thibault aerials were all equipped with Cincinnati cabs and diesel power. Rochester, N. Y. received a Pirsch 100-foot tractor-drawn aerial with a special 4-door sedan cab forward tractor enclosed tiller compartment.

John Bean came out with a modernistic cab-forward chassis of its own design, and the Duplex Division of Warner/Swasey introduced a special cab-forward fire apparatus chassis. The new Duplex chassis resembled the American LaFrance Pioneer, except for its rearward sloping single piece windshield. Oshkosh was now producing a popular cab-forward fire apparatus in standard and low-profile variations. This chassis was used by various builders, including Pierce.

This type of pumper is now fairly common in the north-central part of the country. The pumper shown was built on a Ford L Series chassis by the General Safety Equipment Corp. for Maplewood, Minn. It has an extended canopy cab, and a dark red paint job topped by a stylish black vinyl roof.

The first Calavar Firebird elevating platform sold in Canada was this 125-footer that was delivered to Vancouver, British Columbia early in 1973. This huge tower is built on an International-Hendrickson chassis and is diesel-powered. The upper boom is telescopic. Ground ladders are carried in two hydraulically-lowered side compartments. It cost $165,000 and has a horizontal reach of 66 feet.

Hendrickson's new custom fire apparatus chassis has proved highly popular with fire chiefs and fire apparatus builders alike. This good-looking Pierce-Hendrickson triple combination pumper was delivered to St. Louis Park, Minn., a Minneapolis suburb, in 1973. It is equipped with a 1,250 GPM pump. Note the absence of hard suction hose.

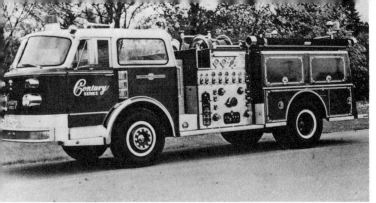

American LaFrance used the 100th Annual Convention of the International Assn. of Fire Chiefs, held in Baltimore, for the introduction of its new Century Series custom fire apparatus. The new Century Series models have redesigned cabs with swelled sides behind the cab doors, permitting wider rear crew seats. The rear window glass is curved to accommodate the wider rear cab. Other features include a stainless steel pump panel and water tank. The prototype Century Series pumper was displayed on a turntable in the Baltimore Civic Center. Diesel power is standard in the new series, latest in a line that began with the introduction of the American LaFrance 900 Series fire apparatus in 1958.

1973

No, Crestline Publishing does not have its own fire department. But the Ohio town of Crestline is the proud owner of this 1973 American LaFrance 1,250 gallon-per-minute Pioneer II Diesel pumper. Note the nozzles and fittings carried above the rear fender. This white-painted pumper has a portable deluge nozzle and two booster reels. We just couldn't resist throwing this one in!

Although it was marketed as a lower-priced custom series, the American LaFrance Pioneer II chassis was used for some pretty fancy fire apparatus. This is a 1,000 gallon-per-minute Super Chief Junior equipped with a 50-foot Snorkel elevating platform. When euqipped with a Squrt, American LaFrance Custom Series pumpers were called Aqua Chiefs and when fitted with Tele-Squrt combination water tower-aerial ladders, they are designated Duo Chiefs. This well-equipped Pioneer II was delivered to Goshen, Ind.

American LaFrance bridged the gap between its full custom 900 and 1000 Series apparatus and the budget-priced Pioneer Custom line with a new medium-priced series called the American LaFrance Pacemaker. This series uses the American LaFrance cab-forward chassis and a Cincinnati cab. This is an American LaFrance Pacemaker Ladder Chief 100-foot rearmount aerial built for Oklahoma City.

A-T-O Corp., American LaFrance's parent corporation, acquired the Snorkel Fire Equipment Co. of St. Joseph, Mo. American LaFrance halted the production of its own Aero-Chief articulating aerial platform, which had been introduced in 1962, and began mounting Pitman Snorkels on both custom and commercial chassis. This is an 85-foot American LaFrance 1000 Series Custom elevating platform delivered to Salinas, Cal.

This American LaFrance Pioneer II tractor-drawn aerial ladder truck is a rare bird. Pittsburgh's Truck Co. 47 received it in 1973. In 1975, the Tulsa, Okla. Fire Dept. also received a couple of these rigs. Note the protective "bubble" window in the enclosed tillerman's cab. This is a 100-footer.

Boston, Mass. placed five of these big Maxim 1,500 gallon-per-minute diesel triple combination pumping engines in service in 1973. All have single-stage pumps. Note the extra-long length of hard suction hose carried over the rear of the hose body, and the transverse beds for preconnected 1½-inch hose. Engine 14's new Maxim has a front suction intake and beautiful hand-painted emblems below the company number on the door. All Boston engine companies carry portable turret pipes.

Somerville, Mass. received this light yellow 1973 Maxim Model S conventional style pumper with 3-man closed cab. Note the preconnected front-mounted soft suction hose. The posts at each end of the front bumper extension permit the driver to carefully spot his rig at the hydrant.

1973

Apparatus photographer Shaun Ryan posed Clinton, Maryland's new Maxim Model S pumper in front of the company's quarters for this portrait. Open-cab apparatus is rare now. Note the two-tone paint job and the windshield for the crew on the rear step. A portable turret pipe is carried above the pump.

In addition to its Model S conventionals and custom cab-forward fire apparatus, the Maxim Motor Co. also offers a complete line of equipment built on commercial truck chassis. Reading, Mass. ordered this 1973 Maxim-Ford built on a Ford C Series chassis with full canopy cab and 1,000 gallon-per-minute pump. Reading's Engine No. 1 is painted yellow. Note the unusual placement of the bell, ahead of the front bumper.

The Maxim Motor Co. of Middleboro, Mass. delivered three of these handsome 100-foot custom tractor-drawn aerial ladder trucks to the Boston Fire Department in 1973. All are diesel-powered, and have enclosed tiller compartments. Truck Co. 15's new rig, photographed by the author at the Boston Fire Dept.'s Moon Island Training Center, has a 3-way turret pipe mounted on the right-hand side of the trailer. Boston's Ladder 6 received a similar rig in 1972.

The Detroit Fire Department ordered five of these special Tactical Mobile Squads. They are built on four-wheel-drive GMC chassis and are powered by V-8 gasoline engines. The TMS units carry booster equipment and 300 gallons of water. The FWD configuration and large, flotation tires were designed to enable these units to climb expressway embankments. The TMS units are painted lime-green and white, and have crew benches behind the cab. The bodies were built by Joyce equipment, a local firm. This is TMS-7, the first of these units to enter service.

1973

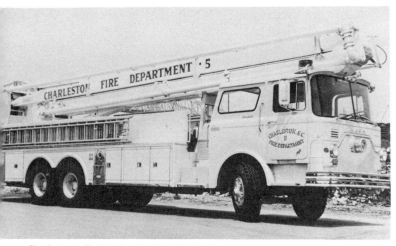

Atlanta, Ga. placed two of these Mack 75-foot Aerialscopes in service in 1973. One was stationed at the Atlanta Fire Department's No. 24 Fire Station, while the other was assigned to the city's airport fire station. The airport rig is painted bright yellow. Note the front stabilizer jacks on this Model CF Aerialscope. No. 24's elevating platform is painted red.

Charleston, S. C. placed this big Mack elevating platform into service in 1973 as Ladder 5. The Mack CF-600 chassis is equipped with a body by Pierce Manufacturing, Inc., and a 75-foot Pitman Snorkel. The white-painted rig presents a handsome and imposing appearance in this fine Richard Adelman portrait.

Baltimore, Md., which for many years used distinctive red and white fire apparatus, began to switch to a new orange-and-white paint scheme for its rigs. In 1973, the Baltimore Fire Department placed this new heavy rescue truck in service as Rescue 1. This huge rescue truck was built on a Mack Type MB chassis. The body was designed and built by Swab Wagon Co. of Elizabethville, Pa., a firm specializing in rescue and emergency squad and ambulance bodies.

The very old Swab Wagon Co. in Elizabethville, Pa. has specialized in designing and building custom rescue squad bodies for many years. Swab constructed this heavy duty rescue squad truck for the Mount Airy Volunteer Fire Dept. of Carroll County, Md. It is mounted on a 1973 Mack R Model chassis.

The American Fire Apparatus Co. of Battle Creek, Mich. introduced a new full custom line of apparatus built on a special Oshkosh cab-forward chassis. This beautiful yellow-and-black rig was the prototype for this new series. It has a 1,000 gallon-per-minute pump and a windshield for the men on the rear step.

American Fire Apparatus Corp. of Battle Creek, Mich. built this versatile combination pumper and snorkel for Muskegon Heights, Mich. Built on the ubiquitous Ford C Series tilt-cab chassis, it has a 1,000 GPM Barton pump, and a 55-foot Pitman Snorkel. This compact piece of major equipment also carries booster equipment.

DeKalb County, Ga. is another good Pirsch customer. The Kenosha, Wis. plant built this 1,500 gallon-per-minute for the DeKalb County Fire Dept. Notice how high the hard suction hoses are mounted above each side of the rear body. Evidently, the ground ladders get a lot more use than the suctions.

Memphis, Tenn. took delivery of yet another batch of new Pirsch fire engines this year. Engine Co. No. 11 was assigned one of these. This is a diesel-powered 1,000 gallon-per-minute pumper with a 500-gallon booster tank and a fixed turret pipe. These Pirsch pumpers came with a new type of highly flexible hard suction hose.

Here is something a little different from the Kenosha, Wis. plant of Peter Pirsch & Sons. Atlanta, Ga. received this 1973 Pirsch 1,000 gallon-per-minute pumper built on a Hendrickson-International chassis. Equipment includes a 55-foot Tele-Squrt combination aerial ladder and water tower. Atlanta's Engine 5 is powered by a Cummins diesel engine and has an Allison automatic transmission.

The Sanford Fire Apparatus Corp. built this 1,500 gallon-per-minute triple combination pumper for DeWitt, N. Y. It is mounted on a 1973 Warner/Swasey Duplex chassis with Cincinnati cab, and is powered by a Waukesha engine connected to a Hale pump. It has a 750-gallon booster tank. Mike Waters took this nice profile shot shortly after the Sanford went into service.

Truck Co. No. 11 in Memphis, Tenn. received a new aerial truck in 1973. The rig was this compact Pirsch 75-foot service aerial, which has almost no rear overhang. The cutout in the rear roof canopy permits crew members to stand up. A full width handrail is provided for their safety.

Long a loyal Pirsch customer, the Memphis, Tenn. Fire Dept. added this Ward LaFrance Ambassador model pumper to the fleet in 1973. The 1,000 GPM pumper has a fixed turret nozzle and a single booster hose reel. Like the Pirsches purchased the same year, this one is also diesel-powered.

A new name entered the aerial platform business this year. Ladder Towers Incorporated had acquired the former Grove Manufacturing Co. of Shady Grove, Pa. The new company, LTI, took over the manufacture of Grove's aerial tower and aerial ladders in a new plant at Lancaster, Pa. The new company's principal products included the 3-section, 85-foot ladder tower, and conventional type aerial ladders of 65, 75, 85 and 100-foot sizes in 3 and 4-section models. Grove front-mounted basket aerial towers had been delivered in the meantime to Eau Claire, Wis., Elkins Park, Pa., and Wayne Township, Ind.

Mack Trucks had the honor of delivering the 1,000th motor pumper purchased by New York City. The 1,000th pumper purchased by the FDNY since the first was delivered away back in 1911 was a 1,000 GPM CF diesel that was assigned to Engine Co. 234. Every front-line pumper in service in the largest city in the United States was now a Mack. The Allentown, Pa. Mack plant had also received an order for 20 more Mack Aerialscopes for New York. In 1974, Mack delivered its first Aerialscope equipped with a pump to West Trenton, N. J. This big tandem-axle apparatus, white in color, carried a 1,500 GPM pump in addition to the 75-foot aerial tower.

American LaFrance had constructed a prototype Century Series 100-foot rear-mount aerial ladder truck, and was tooling up to produce its newest series. Following its debut at the 1973 IAFC Conference in Baltimore, the pilot model Century Series pumper had been returned to the Elmira, N. Y. plant for further testing and tooling tryout.

Chicago had placed in service a monstrous Hendrickson Diesel-powered straight frame aerial ladder truck equipped with a Japanese-built Morita 136-foot aerial ladder, with a 2-man elevator. This very unusual aerial had a 3-man cab and a rear-mounted aerial ladder.

The mini-pumper concept had taken hold, and several manufacturers were building small, lightweight pumpers on standard light duty truck chassis. These mini-pumpers could handle a high percentage of routine fire calls, saving much wear and tear on heavy, expensive specialized equipment. Pierce offered its Mustang and PDQ mini-pumpers, and Fire Trucks Incorporated had come out with a compact FFR mini, for Field Fire Rescue. FMC-Bean also offered a series of compact, lightweight attack pumpers.

As unlikely as such a thing might have seemed only a few years ago, the color of fire apparatus had become a

point of controversy all over the country. Several years earlier, Ward LaFrance had conducted a study of fire apparatus colors, and discovered that the traditional fire department red was among the most difficult to see at night. A lime-green "safety yellow" color was determined to be the most visible under all conditions, so Ward LaFrance began to market its fire equipment painted this color. Many fire departments subsequently made the switch to the controversial new color, but many others decided to stick with the traditional fire engine red no matter what. Other departments selected other colors, including yellows, oranges and combinations of these. Some departments preferred greens and yellows with a white upper cab. One thing is for certain: no issue has raised such emotions within the fire service in this country since the motor truck replaced Old Dobbin.

Two well-known fire apparatus builders—the Oren-Roanoke Corp., of Vinton, Va., and the Coast Apparatus Co., based in Martinez, Calif., had become subsidiaries of Howe Fire Apparatus Co. Howe was now in its second century in the fire equipment industry.

Stoughton, Mass. received this interesting new piece of apparatus. The 1,250 gallon-per-minute pumper was built by the Farrar Co. of Woodville, Mass. on a Warner/Swasey Duplex Diesel chassis. The pump, with its top-mounted control panel, is a Barton. This engine has a front suction intake, a portable deluge set and transverse hose beds for preconnected inch-and-a-half attack lines.

The General Safety Equipment Corp. of North Branch, Minn., built this very impressive quintuple combination for the fire department of Cloquet, Minn. This is said to be to be the first piece of fire equipment built on a Peterbilt chassis of this type. It also boasts a 75-foot Tele-Squrt combination water tower and aerial ladder. Make no mistake about it – this is a big piece of equipment, and a rare one.

One of the most remarkable pieces of apparatus placed into service anywhere in the U.S. in 1974 was this very unusual rig. It is on a Hendrickson Diesel chassis with 3-man cab. The ladder is a Japanese-made 136-foot Morita-lift, which has a 2-man elevator that runs up the center of the extended 6-section aerial ladder. Although originally intended for assignment to Hook and Ladder Co. 2, for which it is lettered in this Dan Martin photo, the huge apparatus proved too big for the company's quarters, and it was subsequently placed in service as Hook and Ladder No. 1. Notice how the ground ladders are stacked under the aerial ladder. This is a strange looking one, even for Chicago.

Despite the continuing trend toward enclosed fire apparatus, some departments still prefer the extra visibility afforded by the open semi-cab. Ward LaFrance built this open-cab Ambassador 1,500 gallon-per-minute pumper for Tiburon, Cal. This pumper has a 600-gallon water tank, Mattydale preconnect 1½-inch hose tray and a Stang monitor. Note the dual beacon lights.

The Detroit Fire Department in 1974 also got three new Ward LaFrance pumpers. These Ambassador Model diesels have 1,000 gallon-per-minute pumps and portable deluge nozzles. They are painted lime-green and white. The engine shown here is assigned to busy Engine Co. No. 29 on the city's West Side.

Eau Claire, Wis. in 1974 accepted delivery of this first Seagrave aerial equipped with a Grove 85-foot ladder with basket. This Aerial Tower is painted lime-yellow and is powered by a Detroit Diesel engine attached to an automatic transmission. The basket is equipped with a 1,000 GPM nozzle. A center hose bed contains 5-inch hose which is Y-ed off into three 2½-inch sections for connection to a pumper.

Belmont, Cal. ordered this high-capacity 1974 Seagrave pumper. The 1,500 gallon-per-minute pumper also has a 600-gallon booster tank and front suction intake. It carries no hard suction hose and is fully compartmented.

The Seminole Volunteer Fire Dept., down in Seminole, Fla. took delivery of this beautiful new Maxim triple combination pumper in 1974. The 1,250 GPM pumper is powered by a Cummins Diesel engine, and it has a front suction intake. The basket slung under the running board holds a 2½-inch hydrant line. Elliott Kahn, a Clearwater Beach truck fancier, took this shot shortly after the new Maxim went into service.

This one just has to be called "when east meets west"—the Maxim Motor Co. of Middleboro, Mass. in the heart of New England, built this highly unusual pumper on a Seattle-built Kenworth chassis for the fire department of Chillum-Adelphi, Maryland. The Kenworth-Maxim has a 750 GPM pump and carries 750 gallons of water in its tank. Note the preconnected 1½-inch hose drooping over the edge of the Mattydale transverse hose bed.

Albert Lea, Minn. owns this interesting 1974 American LaFrance Pacemaker pumper. The 1,500 GPM pumper has a Cincinnati 4-door sedan cab and a 55-foot Squrt boom. Powered by a Detroit Diesel engine, it is equipped with road sanders. The moderately-priced Pacemaker fills the gap between the economy model American LaFrance Pioneer and the company's full-custom 1,000 and Century Series apparatus.

1974

The small city of Findlay, Ohio received this new American LaFrance Snorkel-Quint in mid-1974. The 1000 Series American LaFrance has a 1,250 gallon-per-minute pump, carries a full complement of ground ladders and is equipped with an 85-foot Pitman elevating platform. Findlay's Unit No. 23 is diesel-powered and has a dual rear axle.

When it was introduced 10 years earlier, American La-France's low-cost custom Pioneer was designed as a smaller series pumper with a standard 750 GPM pump. But with the introduction of the improved Pioneer II series in 1971, this model was available with pump capacities of up to 1,500 GPM. Jamestown, N. D. placed this 1974 Pioneer II 1,500 GPM diesel-powered pumper in service in April, 1974. It carries 500 gallons of water. A twin Mattydale cross lays behind the engine compartment.

Minneapolis placed five of these General-Ford in service in 1974. They were built on Ford LS chassis with set-back front axle by the General Safety Equipment Corp. of North Branch, Minn. Each carries a 1,250 GPM Waterous pump and is powered by a Detroit Diesel engine. The 4-door sedan cabs were fabricated by Kolstadt of Minneapolis, All of these pumpers respond from heavy response stations. Walt Schryver photographed Engine 8's rig.

American LaFrance began production of its new Century Series fire apparatus in 1974. Volume deliveries, however, did not begin until the following year. One of the first Century Series pumpers delivered was this 1974 model 1,500 GPM pumper with 500 gallon booster tank, for Inglewood, Calif. This pumper closely resembles the ALF Century Series prototype.

Chicago, the city that placed the first firefighting Snorkel into service in 1958, received three new Snorkel-Quints in 1974. These were assigned to Snorkel Companies No. 3, 4 and 5. Built on Oshkosh 4 x 2 chassis with low-profile Cincinnati cabs, the Snorkel-Quints are equipped with 1,000 gallon-per-minute pumps, two booster hose reels and 75-foot Pitman elevating platforms. Bodywork is by Pierce. This is Snorkel Co. No. 5's new rig shortly before it entered service.

During the first three-quarters of this century, fire apparatus building in the United States progressed from horse and hand-power, to the efficiency of the diesel. Development spanned all the way from the steamer to the superpumper, and from soda-and-acid to rapid water and Purple-K powder. The wood, muscle-raised aerial ladder and the old water tower had given way to aerial platforms up to 150 feet in height. The helicopter had become an accepted, proven firefighting weapon. Radio had made instantaneous communication possible, and specialized firefighting devices had been perfected which could be operated entirely by remote control.

The internal combustion engine had spluttered noisily and uncertainly into the firehouse 69 years earlier, and while the regenerative gas turbine continues to hold considerable potential, it is likely that improved forms of diesel and conventional type reciprocating piston engines will opwer fire apparatus into the next century. Fire suppression has come a long way since 1900, but man's oldest enemy—fire—remains a serious threat to life and property today.

Certainly the most intriguing new piece of fire equipment introduced in 1975 was the gigantic Astrotower developed and built by Ladder Towers Incorporated. This huge aerial tower consists of a massive trailer equipped with a telescopic tower and boom that can reach the top of a 24-story building. The 4-section main mast is raised to an upright position and extends vertically. An upper boom equipped with a platform extends from the top of the tower. A small cable-operated elevator whisks men from the ground to a work platform 140 feet above the ground. The 240-foot model is equipped with a 100-foot aerial platform. A 225-foot model has an 85-foot platform. The Astrotower can be set up in 20 minutes. It is the largest and tallest aerial rescue and fire-fighting device in the world today.

Ladder Towers Inc. in 1975 also introduced its new Streamliner aerial tower. Built on a special chassis designed by LTI in conjunction with the Oshkosh Truck Corp., the Streamliner has a low, futuristic profile. Overall height is only nine feet, seven inches. The 3-man forward cab seats three men and two more can ride in an optional canopy cab extension. Aerial equipment choices include the LTI tower ladder with front overhanging basket, or

any of the company's aerial ladders.

Early in 1975, American LaFrance commenced deliveries of its new Century Series apparatus. Production had begun in mid-1974. Early deliveries included a big pumper-tanker for Ellington, Conn.; a pumper with Squrt boom and another with deck turret for Lynn, Mass.; a 100-foot Ladder-Chief Rearmount Aerial for Poquonock Bridge, Conn., and another rearmount for Bartlesville, Okla. The Elmira plant also produced Century Series 4-wheel service and tractor-drawn aerials and elevating platforms equipped with the Pitman Snorkel. During 1975 American LaFrance also introduced its first production mini-pumper, known as the American LaFrance Stinger attack pumper, and came out with an improved budget model custom series pumper designated Pioneer III. The company was also delivering aerials with its new Water-Chief integrally-piped water tower equipment.

Ward LaFarnce now offered in addition to its standard models a tractor-drawn aerial with its Ambassador custom cab, a 4-section 85 or 100-foot aerial ladder and a completely enclosed tillerman's cab.

The mini-pumper continued to gain in popularity. Standard production models included the ALF Stinger, the Pierce Mustang, FTI's "FFR", City Fire Equipment's little Scat, and the new Quick-Attack Rescue Pumper offered by a new manufacturer, Emergency One, Inc., of Ocala, Fla.

Howe Fire Apparatus introduced a compact, four-way combination fire engine called the Attack Four. This short-wheelbase combination was built on a Ford C Series tilt-cab chassis, carried a 1,000 GPM Waterous pump, 300 gallons of water and a rear-mounted 65-foot LTI aerial ladder. Powered by a Caterpillar Diesel, the first was delivered by Bay City, Texas.

Fire Trucks Incorporated, of Mount Clemens, Mich., offered a standard custom-chassis pumper using the new cab-forward fire apparatus chassis introduced by Duplex two years earlier. Peter Pirsch and Sons Co. for the first time bridged the gap between its commercial chassis and custom fire apparatus with a new moderately priced custom model utilizing the Cincinnati cab.

At the current pace of American technology, it is entirely likely that fire apparatus development in the final quarter of this century will eclipse all that has been accomplished so far. What the firefighter will be using to combat his old foe in the year 2000 is anybody's guess.

The first apparatus of this type delivered in Canada, and one of the first of its kind produced, this is the versatile Fire Commander, a highly automated quintuple combination built by Young Fire Equipment of Lancaster, N. Y. Interestingly enough, the 65-foot Ladder Towers Inc. tele-scopic water-tower ladder unit was built by LTI in Lancaster, Pa. The 1,250 GPM Fire Commander on Ford C chassis was built to order for the city of Cambridge, Ontario. The diesel-powered aerial quint carries 200 gallons of water.

A major Canadian fire apparatus builder, Pierre Thibault Ltd. of Pierreville, Que., has delivered many of its aerial ladder trucks to American fire departments. This eye-catching Thibault-Ford rearmount 100-foot aerial was delivered to St. Paul, Minn., in mid-1975. The chassis is a Ford L Series diesel. Note the modular type rear cab and the single rear axle. The Los Angeles City Fire Dept. had six Thibault 100-foot tractor-type aerials delivered in 1972 and 1973.

Lynn, Mass. took delivery of this 1975 American LaFrance Century Series 1,000 GPM diesel pumper. The chrome-yellow rig, assigned to Engine 1, has a deck turret which is piped directly into the pump. Note the optional recessed suction intake and the new, larger bezels above the head-lights containing flashers and turn signals. Lynn also received a 1975 ALF Century Series pumper with a Squrt boom.

1975

Although the new wide-cab Century Series apparatus was now in volume production, American LaFrance continued to build the 1000 Series models which use the older, narrower canopy cab. The Cleveland, Ohio suburb of Shaker Heights took delivery of this American LaFrance 1000 Series pumper early in 1975. It has a 1,500 gallon-per-minute pump and Detroit Diesel power. The Gothic-style lettering visible on the side of the cab appears on all Shaker Heights rigs – almost all by American LaFrance.

Delivered to Minot, N. D. in June, 1975, this American LaFrance Pioneer II diesel pumper is finished in high visibility yellow. It has an enclosed, heated booster reel compartment and full Campbell compartmentation. In mid-1975, American LaFrance announced yet another improved version of this model designated the Pioneer III. Exterior appearance remained basically unchanged, but the Pioneer III incorporates upgraded equipment and trim.

Posed on the ramp in front of an Elmira, N. Y. fire station is a 1975 American LaFrance Century Series elevating platform. Note the swelled rear cab sheetmetal and curved window glass. The boom is an 85-footer by Snorkel Fire Equipment. Cedar Hammock's handsome new snorkel responds as a straight ladder truck.

The first piece of apparatus of this type delivered in the state, this 1975 American Fire Apparatus Corp. aerial quint was delivered to Grand Forks, N. D. Mounted on the Oshkosh custom low-profile fire apparatus chassis, it is equipped with a 1,250 GPM Barton pump and carries an 85-foot Ladder Towers Inc. aerial tower. The eye-catching paint job is lime-green with a white upper cab.

The famed children's home operated by the Moose Lodge at Mooseheart, Ill., near Chicago, is protected by this FMC/Bean 750 GPM pumper delivered early in 1975. Built on a GMC chassis, it carries 750 gallons of water. The enclosed booster reels are something of a Bean trademark. Bearing the bicentennial Spirit of '76, it is red and white in color.

One of Seagrave's most popular models continues to be the company's standard rear-mounted 100-foot aerial. This 1975 Seagrave Rear Admiral was built fo the Niagara Fire Co. of Merchantville, N. J. It has a permanently mounted ladder pipe under the bed section of the aerial ladder and carries 203 feet of ground ladders.

1975

Sacramento, Calif. in 1975 placed this new Seagrave 1,500 gallon-per-minute pumper into service. Built by Seagrave Fire Apparatus of Clintonville, Wis., employing the same basic sheetmetal introduced in 1959, it is Detroit Diesel powered and carries 500 gallons of water.

At first glance, this apparatus appears to be a Seagrave rescue squad truck. But a look behind all those compartment doors reveals that it is actually a triple combination pumper. The fully-enclosed pumper was built on a Seagrave chassis for Grand Forks, N. D. by the General Safety Equipment Corp. of North Branch, Minn. Delivered in March, 1975, it has a 4-door sedan cab. It is painted lime-yellow with white upper cab.

Defender Fire Co. No. 1 of Audubon, N. J. received this good-looking Imperial Service Aerial in 1975. The Diesel-powered aerial, with Cincinnati cab, sports a 4-section, 100-foot Ladder Towers Inc. aerial. It carries 233 feet of ground ladders, 600 feet of 2½-inch hose and 200 feet of 3-inch line. Note the fully enclosed rear body.

Along with a custom-chassised Seagrave pumper, Seagrave Fire Apparatus delivered this commercial-chassised pumper to Sacramento, Cal. The Ford C Series chassis with extended canopy cab mounts a 1,250 GPM pump and carries 500 gallons of water. It is powered by a Caterpillar diesel engine.

In July, 1975, the Detroit Fire Dept. placed two new Hahn diesel pumpers into service, the first pumpers of this make delivered in the area. One of the new Hahns was assigned to Engine Co. No. 5 to replace this company's 1964 Seagrave cab-forward pumper which had been wrecked in an accident three years earlier. The other went to Engine 42. The 1,000 GPM Hahns are painted lime-green with white upper cabs.

Mack's highly regarded Aerialscope elevating platforms have a habit of all looking very much alike. But here is something a little different. This is believed to be the first Mack Aerialscope delivered with a pump. The monstrous apparatus was built for the West Trenton, N. J. Volunteer Fire Dept. It is equipped with a 1,500 GPM pump. Because of the tandem rear axle, there is no rear overhang of the basket at the end of the 75-foot boom.

Here is an interesting hybrid. The chassis is Mack's flat-faced MB-600, but the body and equipment is by Howe Fire Apparatus. The 1975 Howe-Mack 1,000 GPM canopy cab pumper was delivered to Harvey, Ill., which has discontinued its Chicago-style red-and-black livery in favor of Safety Yellow.

Columbus, Ohio has four of these unusual Mack-Thibault tractor-drawn aerial ladder trucks in service. The tractor is a Mack CF-600 diesel, but the bodywork, trailer and aerial ladder were done by Pierre Thibault (1972) Ltd., of Pierreville, Que., Canada. Two of these 100-foot aerials were placed in service by the CFD in 1974, and two more were delivered in 1975. Note the bottle-body type side compartments on Ladder 13's rig as it pulls into quarters.

Sacramento, Cal. in 1975 joined the elite group of fire departments that owned 150-foot Calavar Firebird elevating platforms. Sacramento's monstrous Firebird is on the Hendrickson custom fire apparatus chassis. Willard Sorensen caught the California capital's big Bird out in the drill yard.

The Ashland Fire Co. of Voorhees Twp., N. J. received this 1975 Mack Aerialscope. The standard model is red with a white upper body paint treatment. The 75-foot tower ladder is supported when in use by a pair of midship-mounted outriggers, plus two more at the front and another pair at the rear of the apparatus. The Mack Aerialscope continues to be built in only one size.

Marblehead, Mass. placed this new Maxim custom chassis pumper into service in September, 1975. Engine 3's new pumper, with a 1,250 GPM pump, sports two flashers on its roof and carries twin booster reels. Maxim now offered its customers a wide selection of in-stock pumpers and aerials which could be equipped to the buyer's specifications and delivered in a short time. Lead times for a new custom rig were now as long as 2½ years for a ladder truck.

Peter Pirsch & Sons Co. in 1975 came out with a new medium-priced fire apparatus line which utilized the familiar Cincinnati cab for the first time. The 1,000 GPM Pirsch pumper shown here, en route from the Kenosha, Wis. plant to the Memphis suburb of Bartlett, Tenn., was photographed in Naperville, Ill. The gentleman at the rear of the rig is Capt. Dick Adelman of the Memphis Fire Dept. who went along for the delivery trip.

1975

Here is another interesting mixture. Similar in design to several aerials delivered on the earlier C Model Mack chassis in the mid-1960s, this is a Pirsch 100-foot service aerial mounted on the Mack CF-600 chassis. Delivered to LaCrosse, Wis., it replaced an American LaFrance aerial which had seen more than a quarter of a century of service.

Jackson Township, Ohio placed this heavy-duty rescue squad apparatus into service in 1975. The Swab Wagon Co., an old Pennsylvania body builder specializing in heavy rescue bodies, designed this body for mounting on a big Peterbilt cabover chassis. Jackson Twp. is a Columbus suburb.

Some small communities boast some big-city fire engines. In June, 1975, Huron Township, Ohio took delivery of this standard model Sutphen Aerial Tower. Carrying a $133,000 price tag, it is an 85-foot model with Cincinnati cab and a 1,000 GPM pump. In mid-1975 Sutphen began the manufacture of a 90-foot platform. Huron Township's pride and joy is lime-green with a white upper cab.

A new company, Ladder Towers, Inc., took over the Grove Mfg. Co. plant at Lancaster, Pa. A small number of front-basket tower ladder trucks of this type, on varous chassis but bearing the Grove nameplate on the ladder-tower unit, had been delivered beginning in 1973. But by late 1974, the new LTI firm was marketing aerial ladders and towers under its own name. Shown here is an LTI 85-foot ladder tower mounted on a 1975 Hendrickson chassis. This impressive piece of apparatus was built by Nordic International, of Port Credit, Ont., Canada. The first of its type delivered in Canada, it was built for New Westminster, B. C. The apple-green rig is powered by a Detroit Diesel engine, has a 1,050 Imp. GPM Barton-American pump and carries 150 gallons of water in its tank.

The Sutphen Fire Equipment Co. of Columbus, Ohio, delivered three of these clean-lined, fully enclosed 1,000 GPM diesel pumpers to the Columbus Fire Dept. These dark red pumpers have 4-door sedan-type Cincinnati cabs, completely enclosed rear bodies and Barton pumps. For maintenance, the engine can be removed through a large panel in the cab roof.

By 1975, the Ward LaFrance Ambassador Series apparatus was almost as familiar as the American LaFrance 700. This 1975 Ward LaFrance Model DD-5 pumper was delivered to New Haven, Conn., which continues to use white-painted apparatus. Powered by a Detroit Diesel engine, it has a 1,000 GPM Hale pump, carries 500 gallons of water and is equipped with a 3,500-watt Onan generator.

1975

History repeats itself. In 1965, Ward LaFrance Truck Corp. delivered a number of pumpers of this style, with the Cincinnati cab. Exactly a decade later, the Elmira Heights, N. Y. firm again offered a custom series pumper of this type. The 1,000 GPM Ward LaFrance pumper shown here, fitted with a 1,000 gallon booster tank, was delivered to Weedsport, N. Y. Note the high rear body, Mattydale preconnects and businesslike deck pipe.

The General Safety Equipment Co. of North Branch, Minn. now produces a complete range of fire apparatus, ranging from small commercial pumpers to full custom elevating platforms. General delivered this 85-foot snorkel to Red Wing, Minn. The boom is by Snorkel Fire Equipment. Red Wing's platform is equipped with a 1,250 GPM Waterous pump and is Detroit diesel-powered.

What's this, a Crown pumper in service in New Jersey? Few of this species can be found east of the Rockies. But Montvale, N. J.'s fire department knows what it wants. This department purchased a Crown in 1966, and added this 1,500 GPM beauty in 1975. Powered by a Cummins deisel, it carries Crown Firecoach Serial No. F-1735 and has a 500 gallon tank.

As unattractive as this style of apparatus may be to the custom fire apparatus buff, this type of rig is the backbone of thousands of smaller fire departments across the country. What makes this 750 GPM pumper on Ford C chassis by Alexis Fire Equipment Co. interesting is the plain, non-compartmented rear fenders. This pumper was sold to Mount Carroll, Il.

While most of the Tele-Squrt combination aerial ladder-water towers produced by Snorkel Fire Equipment are of the 55-foot size, the company also builds a 3-section, 75-foot Tele-Squrt. Inglewood, Cal. received this 1975 Crown Fire-coach quint on tandem axle chassis with a 75-foot Tele-Squrt and 1,500 GPM Waterous pump. Inglewood's bog Crown also carries 200 gallons of water.

INDEX OF MOTOR FIRE APPARATUS MANUFACTURERS

The following index lists principal builders of motor fire apparatus in the United States and Canada. Also included are major component suppliers. Inasmuch as fire equipment has been mounted on virtually every make of truck produced, it is impossible to list all of these here. This index does not include very small one-off builders or ambulance manufacturers.

Ahrens-Fox Fire Engine Co., Cincinnati, O.
Ajax Fire Engine Works, Brooklyn, N. Y.
Alexis Fire Equipment Co., Alexis, Ill.
*Allegheny Fire Equipment Co., Huntington, W. Va.
American & British Mfg. Co., Providence, R. I.
*American Fire Apparatus Corp., Battle Creek, Mich.
    (Barton-American pumps)
*American LaFrance, Elmira, N. Y. (Division of A-T-O, Inc.)
American Magirus Fire Appliance Corp., Indianapolis, Ind.
American Marsh Pumps (Canada) Ltd., Stratford, Ont., Canada
Anderson Coupling and Fire Supply Co., Kansas City, Kans.
Anderson Fire Control Co., Sioux City, Ia.
Ansul Co., Marinette, Wis.
Approved Fire Equipment Co., Rockville Center, N. Y.
Army's Fire Service, Old Forge, N. Y. (Little Mo)
Atlantic Fire Apparatus Div., Park Machinery Co., Fort Lauderdale, Fla.
Auto Car Co., Buffalo, N. Y.

Barkow Body Co., Milwaukee, Wis.
Baker Equipment & Engineering Co., Charlotte, N. C.
Baugham Manufacturing Co., Jerseyville, Ill.
Beal Apparatus Co., Boise, Id.
Bean (see John Bean)
Beck, C. D. Co., Sidney, O. (successor to Ahrens-Fox)
Bickle Fire Engines Ltd., Woodstock, Ont., Canada
Bickle-Seagrave Ltd., Woodstock, Ont., Canada
Black, Adam Co., Trenton, N. J.
Blitz Buggy Co., Old Forge, N. Y.
*Boardman Co., Oklahoma City, Okla.
Boyd, James & Bro., Inc., Philadelphia, Pa.
Boyer Fire Apparatus Co., Logansport, Ind.
    (Obenchain-Boyer Co. successor)
Boyertown Body Co., Boyertown, Pa.
Brockway Motor Truck Co., Cortland, N. Y.
*Brumbaugh Body Co., Altoona, Pa. (Bruco)
Brush, Buggie, Inc. LaPorte, Ind.
Buffalo Fire Appliance Corp., Buffalo, N. Y.

*Calavar Corp., Santa Fe Springs, Calif. (Calavar Firebird)
Cardox Division, Chemetron Corp., Chicago, Ill.
*Car-Mar, Inc., Berwick, Pa.
Cayasler Mfg. Corp., Buffalo, N. Y.
Central Fire Truck Corp., St. Louis, Manchester, Mo. (Central-St. Louis)
Challenger Corp., Memphis, Tenn.
Childs, O. J. Co., Utica, N. Y.
Christopher Corp., New York, N. Y.
Christie (see Front Drive Motor Co.)
City Fire Equipment Co., Perrysburg, O. (Scat)
Coast Apparatus, Inc., Martinez, Calif.
Cocke, John & Co., Mobile, Ala. (JACO)
Combination Ladder Co., Providence, R. I.
Commercial Truck Co. of America, Philadelphia, Pa.
Couple Gear Freight Wheel Co., Grand Rapids, Mich.
Cross, C. J., Front-Drive Tractor Co., Newark, N. J.
Crown Coach Corporation, Los Angeles, Calif. (Crown Firecoach)
Curtis, L. N. & Sons, Oakland, Calif.
Capital Fire Equipment Co., Sacramento, Calif.

Dakota Fire Apparatus Co., Brookings, S. D.
*Darley, W. S. & Co., Chicago and Melrose Park, Ill.
Dixon Cascade Pump Co., Newark, N. J.
*Duplex Division, Warner/Swasey Co., Lansing, Mich.
    (successor to Duplex Trucks)

Edgar Road Tank Works, Linden, N. J.
Eustice Equipment Co., –

F.A.B. Mfg. Co., Oakland, Calif. (Fabco)
*Farrar Co., Woodville, Mass.
Farrell Mfg. Co., Lockport, N. Y.
Fire Champ, Mount Pleasant, Ia.
Fire Control Engineering Co., Fort Worth, Tex.
Fire Fighter Truck Co., Rock Island, Ill.
Fire Fox Corp., Houston, Tex.
*Fire Trucks Incorporated, Mount Clemens, Mich. (FTI)
Fire Master Corp., Mount Clemens, Mich.
Fire Wagon Co., Inc., Mount Kisco, N. Y.
Filleul, James B, & Sons Co., Manchester, N. H.
Foamite-Childs Corp., Utica, N. Y. (successor to O. J. Childs)
Flour City Body Co., Minneapolis, Minn.
*Four Wheel Drive Auto Co., Clintonville, Wis. (now FWD Corp.)
*Forstner Bros., Medalia, Minn.
Front Drive Motor Co., Hoboken, N. J. (Christie Front Drive Tractors)

General Body Co., Chicago, Ill.
General Fire Truck Corp., Detroit, Mich. (General-Detroit)
General Pacific Corp., Los Angeles (subsidiary of General-Detroit)
General Mfg. Co., St. Louis, Mo. (General Monarch, General-St. Louis)
*General Safety Equipment Corp., North Branch, Minn.
*Gerstenslager Corp., Wooster, O.
Gray Fire Apparatus Co., Lewiston, Id.
Great Eastern (used on apparatus sold by Ernie Day, Dunellen, N. J.)
Grove, T. R. Mfg. Co., Shady Grove, Pa. (Grove aerial ladders)

*Hahn Motors, Inc., Hamburg, Pa.
Hale Fire Pump Co., Conshohocken, Pa. (George C. Hale, Kansas City, Mo.)
Hanley Fire Apparatus Co., Prospect, O.
Harder Auto Truck Co., Chicago, Ill. (also known as Harder Storage & Van Co.)
Harless, L. P. Co., Birmingham, Ala.
Harwood-Barley Mfg. Co., Marion, Ind. (builders of Indiana fire trucks)
Halstead Fire Apparatus Div., Novelty Carriage Works, Spokane, Wash.
Hardwick Mfg. Co., West Point, Pa.
H & H Truck Tank Co., Jersey City, N. J.
Hedberg, J. N. Co., San Jose, Calif.
Hesse Body Co., Kansas City, Mo.
Hendrickson Mfg. Co., Lyons, Ill. (International Harvester subsidiary)
Hi Pressure Fog Equipment Co., Old Forge, N. Y.
Holden Engineering Division, Newington, N. H.
Hortonville Body Co., Hortonville, Wis.
Houston Fire & Safety Equipment Co., Houston, Tex.
Howard-Cooper Corp., Portland, Ore.
*Howe Fire Apparatus Co., Anderson, Ind.
Hub Fire Engines Ltd., Abbotsford, B. C., Canada
Hurst, O. N. Co., –Calif. (Challenger)
Hunter Apparatus Co. –

*Imperial Fire Apparatus Co., Rancocas, N. J. (Pem-Fab Corp.,)
Indian Motorcycle Co., Springfield, Mass.
*International Harvester Co., Chicago, Ill.
Interstate Fire Equipment Co., Fargo, N. D.

Jackson Body Co., Jackson, Wis.
Jacob Press Sons, Chicago, Ill.
*John Bean Division, FMC Corp., Lansing, Mich. and Tipton, Ind.
*Joyce Fire Apparatus Co., Romulus, Mich.

Kelly Motor Truck Co., Springfield, O.
Kenworth Motor Truck Co., Seattle, Wash.
Kidde, Walter & Co., Belleville, N. J.
*King-Seagrave Ltd., Woodstock, Ont., Canada
Kissel Motor Car Co., Hartford, Wis.
Kinney Apparatus Co. –
Klein Products, Inc., Ontario, Calif.
Knox Automobile Co., Springfield, Mass. (also Knox-Martin tractors)
Kress, O. F. & Sons Co., Lawrence, Mass.

Lacey Body Co., Boston, Mass.
*Ladder Towers Incorporated, Lancaster, Pa. (successor to Grove)
LaFrance Fire Engine & Foamite Ltd., Toronto, Ont. Canada (ALF subsidiary)
Luitweiler Co., Rochester, N. Y.
Luverne Fire Apparatus Co., Luverne, Minn.

*Mack Trucks, Inc., Allentown, Pa. (formerly International Motor Co., N. Y.)
Maday Body & Equipment Co., Buffalo, N. Y.
Marion Body Works, Inc., Marion, Wis.
Martin Carriage Works, York, Pa.
*Maxim Motor Co., Middleboro, Mass. (Seagrave subsidiary)
Maynard Fire Apparatus Co., Marshfield, Mass.
McAllister Co., Dallas, Tex.
McCann's, D. E. Sons, Portland, Me.
Melray Mfg. Co., Hortonville, Wis.
Memco Aerial Ladder Co., Oklahoma City, Okla.
Middlesex Fire Equipment Co., Montpelier, Vt.
Midwest Fire and Safety Equipment Co., Indianapolis, Ind.
Minnesota Fire Apparatus Co., North Branch, Minn.
Minnesota Fire Equipment Co., Lindstrom, Minn.
*Mobile Aerial Towers, Inc., Fort Wayne, Ind. (Hi-Ranger platforms)
Moreland Truck Co., Burbank, Calif.

National Fire Apparatus Co., Galesburg, Ill.
National Foam Systems, Inc., West Chester, Pa.
Neep Co., Portland, Ore.
New England Truck Co., Fitchburg, Mass. (Netco)
Newberry Tank & Equipment Co., West Memphis, Ark.
New Stutz Fire Engine Co., Hartford City, Ind.
*Nordic International Ltd., Port Credit, Ont., Canada
Northern Fire Apparatus Co., Minneapolis, Minn.
Nott, W. S. Co., Minneapolis, Minn. (Nott Universal & Nott Fire Engine Co.)

Obenchain-Boyer Co., Logansport, Ind.
Olsen Mfg. Co., Minneapolis, Minn.
One-Wheel Tractor Co., St. Louis, Mo. (Coach Wheel Co.)
Oren-Roanoke Corp., Roanoke and Vinton, Va.
Oshkosh Truck Corporation, Oshkosh, Wis.

Pacific Pumpers, Inc., Seattle, Wash.
Parrett Tractor Co., Chicago Heights, Ill. (successor to South Bend)
*Pirsch, Peter & Sons Co., Kenosha, Wis.
*Pierce Mfg. Co., Appleton, Wis.
*Pierre Thibault (1972) Ltd., Pierreville, Que., Canada
*Pierreville Fire Trucks Ltd., Pierreville, Que., Canada
Pitman Mfg. Co., Grandview, Mo. (became Snorkel Fire Equipment Co.)
Pope-Hartford, Pope Mfg. Co., Hartford, Conn.
Proctor-Keefe Body Co., Detroit, Mich.
Prospect Fire Engine Co., Prospect, O. (Prospect-Biederman Master Fire Fighter)
*Providence Body Co., Providence, R. I.
Progress Mfg. Co., Arthur, Ill.
Phillips Engineering Co., Clayton, N. J.

Regal Fire Apparatus Div., Florida Truck Equip. Co., Gaton Park, Fla.
Reading Body Works, Reading, Pa.
Republic Motor Truck Co., Alma, Mich.
Robinson, A. F. Co., Cambridge, Mass.
Robinson Fire Apparatus Mfg. Co., St. Louis, Mo. (Monarch, Jumbo)
Rochester Fire Pump Co., Rochester, N. Y.
Rowland Co., Sand Springs, Okla. (Roco)
Ribley & Harbinger Co. — N. Y.

*Sanford Fire Apparatus Corp., East Syracuse, N. Y.
*Saskatoon Fire Engine Co., Calgarty, Alta., Canada
Saulsbury Fire Equipment Co., Tully, N. Y.
Schnerr, J. J. Co., —Calif.

Seagrave Corporation, The, Columbus, O.
*Seagrave Fire Apparatus Division, FWD Corp., Clintonville, Wis.
Seagrave Fire Engines Ltd., St. Catharines, Ont., Canada
Seagrave, W. E. Fire Apparatus Co., Walkerville, Ont., Canada
Sealand Corp., Southport, Conn.
Security Fire Equipment Co., Trenton, N. J.
Selden Truck Corp., Rochester, N. Y.
Sharpsville Steel Fabricators, Sharpsville, Pa.
Simms Fire Equipment Co., San Antonio, Tex.
Slagle Fire Apparatus Co., South Boston, Va.
Smeal, Donald L. Mfg. Co., Snyder, Neb.
Smith, L. B. Inc., Camp Hill, Pa.
*Snorkel Fire Equipment Co., St. Joseph, Mo. (Pitman Snorkel)
South Bend Motor Car Works, South Bend, Ind.
Southern Fire Apparatus Co., Dallas, Tex.

Southworth Machine Co., Chelsea, Mass.
Stoughton Wagon Co., Stoughton, Wis.
Spangler, D. H. Engrg. Co., Hamburg, Pa. (Spangler Dual)
Sponco Aerial Ladder Co., Oklahoma City, Okla.
Stutz Fire Engine Co., Indianapolis, Ind.
Superior Fire Apparatus Co., Helena, Mont.
*Superior Emergency Equipment Ltd., Red Deer, Alta., Canada
*Sutphen Fire Equipment Co., Columbus, O. (Sutphen Aerial Tower)
*Swab Wagon Co., Elizabethville, Pa.

Task Master Equipment Co., Dundee, Ill.
Tea Tray Mfg. Co., Newark, N. J.
Thiele & Sons Co., Inc., Johnstown, Pa. (Thiele Fog-Kar)
*Timpco-Seagrave Div., Timmons Metal Products Co., Columbus, O.
Thomas, E. R. Co., Buffalo, N. Y.
Thomas Automatic Fire Engine Co., Columbus, O.
*Towers Fire Apparatus Co Inc., Freeburg, Ill.
Trautwein's, Inc., Woodbridge, N. J. (TASC)
Tower Iron Works, Greenville, Mich.
*Truck Cab Manufacturers, Inc., Cincinnati, O. (Cincinnati cabs)
Trump Ltd., Oliver, B. C., Canada (Trump Snorkel)
Turner Machine & Supply Co., Fort Pierce, Fla.

*United Fire Apparatus Co., Cridersville, O.
Universal Fire Apparatus Corp., Logansport, Ind. (Boyer successor)
U.S.A. — U.S. Army Ordnance Plant, Camp Holabird, Md.
U.S. Fire Apparatus Co., Wilmington, Del.

Valley Fire Truck Co., Bay City, Mich.
*Van Pelt, P. E. Inc., Oakdale, Calif.

Walter Motor Truck Co., Long Island City, N. Y.
*Ward LaFrance Truck Corp., Elmira Heights, N. Y.
Waterous Engine Works, Brantford, Ont., Canada and St. Paul, Minn.
Webb Motor Fire Apparatus Co., Vincennes, Ind.; St. Louis, Mo.; Allentown, Pa.
Wendell Auto Body Co. —
*Western States Fire Apparatus, Inc., Cornelius, Ore.
Welch Fire Equipment Co., Marion, Wis.
White Motor Co., Cleveland, O.
Winther Motor Truck Co., Kenosha, Wis.
Woods Engineering Service, Topsfield, Mass.
Wesco Fire Engine Div., Industrial Steel Tank & Body Works, Los Angeles, Calif.

Yankee Body Co., Los Angeles, Calif.
*Yankee-Walter Corporation, Los Angeles, Calif. (Y-W crash trucks)
*Young Fire Equipment Corp., Lancaster, N. Y.

Zabek Fire Apparatus Inc., Palmer, Mass.

*Denotes firms still in fire apparatus business in 1975

About the author

Like most fire apparatus buffs, Walter P. McCall can pinpoint his addiction to firefighting equipment almost to the hour. It was in Toronto, Ont., on a spring evening in 1951. The author was walking past Fire Station No. 22 when he paused to gaze at the gleaming red-and-chrome rigs inside. An understanding fireman beckoned him inside, and, in his own words, Walt has been "hopelessly hooked-and-laddered ever since."

Born in Simcoe, Ontario, Canada, he moved to Toronto with his family in 1947 at the time, he points out, when H & L No. 22 was still running with a beautiful 1923 American LaFrance Type 33 tillered city service ladder truck. Five years later he moved to Windsor. Upon graduation from high school. Walt went into journalism. He was a reporter-photographer for The St. Thomas, Ont., Times-Journal for 2½ years before joining the editorial staff of The Windsor Star. Following several years of general assignment duty, including of course the fire and police beats, he became the only full-time automotive writer on a Canadian newspaper. His twice-weekly column appeared for nine years. In 1972 he joined the public relations department of Chrysler Canada Ltd., where he is Manager — News & Community Relations. In 1960 he was awarded Canada's highest journalism award for his coverage of a department store explosion and fire in downtown Windsor.

Walt McCall is a trustee of the Ontario Fire Buffs Assn. He is only one of two people ever to hold active membership in all three of Detroit's fire buff clubs: the Detroit Fire Buffs Assn., Box 12 Association and Box 42 Associates. He is a member of the Society for the Preservation and Appreciation of Antique Motor Fire Apparatus in America, Inc. (SPAAMFAA) and Associate Editor of the organization's quarterly magazine, *"Enjine, Enjine!".*

He is also Charter President of the Greenfield Village International Antique Fire Apparatus Assn., Great Lakes Chapter, SPAAMFAA, Inc. and Editor of this club's newsletter. He also edits the "Third Alarm", the Ontario Fire Buffs Assn.'s newsletter, is editor of the Detroit Fire Buffs Assn. newsletter and correspondent for "Turn Out", the official publication of the International Fire Buff Associates. He is also a regular contributor to fire service trade journals, including *"Fire Engineering"* and *"Fire Fighting in Canada".* But Walt is probably best known, however, as Editor of *"The Visiting Fireman",* an annual fire buff's directory that is considered the "Bible" of the hobby. He is also a fire apparatus modeller.

Among other things, Walt is a member of the Windsor Branch of the Historic Vehicle Society of Ontario and custodian of the club's 1925 American LaFrance Type 12 pumper. Walt's other hobby is, of all things, hearses. He is an avid collector of funeral car photos, literature and ads and owns two vintage funeral coaches, a 1936 Henney-Packard and a 1959 Superior-Cadillac. Walt, his wife Denise, son Walter Jr. and daughter Perri reside in Windsor, Ont.